Housing
Urban America

Social Research and Public Policy
A series edited by Lee Rainwater, Harvard University

Housing Urban America

Edited by
Jon Pynoos, *Harvard University*
Robert Schafer, *Harvard University*
Chester W. Hartman, *University of California, Berkeley*

ALDINE PUBLISHING COMPANY / CHICAGO

ABOUT THE EDITORS

Jon Pynoos is a Ford Foundation Fellow in Urban Studies, Harvard University, and Fellow of the Joint Center for Urban Studies of Harvard and M.I.T. He received his M.C.P. in city planning from Harvard and has written articles for *Politics and Society*, the *Journal of Urban Law*, and the House Committee on Banking and Currency.

Robert Schafer is an Assistant Professor of City Planning at Harvard University. He received his J.D. from Harvard Law School and his Ph.D. in city and regional planning, also from Harvard. He has contributed articles to several journals, including the *Journal of Urban Law*, *Public Policy*, *Land Economics*, and the *Journal of the American Institute of Planners*.

Chester W. Hartman is a member of the Institute of Urban and Regional Development and the National Housing and Economic Development Law Project at the University of California, Berkeley. He received his Ph.D. in city and regional planning from Harvard University and is the author of *Housing and Social Policy* (forthcoming), and many articles.

First published 1973 by
Aldine Publishing Company
529 South Wabash Avenue
Chicago, Illinois 60605

ISBN 0-202-32006-5
Library of Congress Catalog Number 74-182911

Printed in the United States of America

Contents

Preface ix

Introduction 1

I   POLITICS   15

1. Social Class and Housing Reform
   Lawrence M. Friedman 25

2. The Homebuilders' Lobby
   William Lilley III 30

3. The Rise of Tenant Organizations
   Peter Marcuse 49

4. Boardwalk and Park Place: Property Ownership, Political
   Structure, and Housing Policy at the Local Level
   John Mollenkopf and *Jon Pynoos* 55

5. Redesigning Landlord-Tenant Law for an Urban Society
   Paul G. Garrity 75

6. Alternative Strategies for the Urban Ghetto
   National Advisory Commission on Civil Disorders 87

7. The Case Against Urban Desegregation
   Frances Fox Piven and *Richard A. Cloward* 97

8. Public Housing and Urban Policy:
   Gautreaux v. *Chicago Housing Authority*
   Yale Law Journal 108

v

9. Public Housing: The Contexts of Failure
   Jewel Bellush and *Murray Hausknecht* 114
10. The Politics of Housing
   Chester W. Hartman 119

II SOCIAL ASPECTS 131
11. The Balanced Community: Homogeneity or Heterogeneity
   in Residential Areas?
   Herbert J. Gans 135
12. Equal Status, Housing Integration, and Racial Prejudice
   George E. Simpson and *J. Milton Yinger* 147
13. The Effects of Poor Housing
   Nathan Glazer 158
14. An Alternative to a Density Function Definition
   of Overcrowding
   R. J. Greenfield and *J. F. Lewis* 166
15. Determinism by the Urban Environment
   William Michelson 171
16. Fear and the House-as-Haven in the Lower Class
   Lee Rainwater 181
17. Environmental Preferences of Future Housing Consumers
   Mark L. Hinshaw and *Kathryn J. Allott* 191

III ECONOMICS 203
18. The Journey-to-Work as a Determinant of Residential Location
   John F. Kain 211
19. A Competitive Theory of the Housing Market
   Edgar O. Olsen 228
20. The Determinants of Dwelling-Unit Condition
   Richard F. Muth 239
21. Effect of Housing Market Segregation on Urban Development
   John F. Kain 251
22. An Economic Analysis of *Property Values and Race* (Laurenti)
   Anthony Downs 267
23. The Ghetto Makers
   Jack Rothman 274
24. Restrictive Zoning
   National Commission on Urban Problems 279
25. Price Discrimination against Negroes in the Rental Housing Market
   Chester Rapkin 290

IV PRODUCTION 299
26. Mortgage Market Developments in the Postwar Period
   Commission on Mortgage Interest Rates 307
27. Fiscal and Monetary Policy
   Commission on Mortgage Interest Rates 316
28. Bureaucratic and Craft Administration of Production
   Arthur L. Stinchcombe 321
29. Efficiency in the Construction Industry
   Christopher A. Sims 329

30. Building Codes
    National Commission on Urban Problems 343
31. Restrictive Union Practices
    National Commission on Urban Problems 359
32. Reducing the Cost of New Construction
    Michael A. Stegman 372
33. Trade Union Discrimination in the Pittsburgh
    Construction Industry
    Irwin Dubinsky 376
34. Federal Income Taxation and Urban Housing
    National Commission on Urban Problems 392

V   POLICIES AND PROGRAMS   403
35. The Bias of American Housing Policy
    Nathan Glazer 405
36. Federal Housing Policy: A Political-Economic Analysis
    Michael E. Stone 423
37. The Social Utility of Rent Control
    Emily Paradise Achtenberg 434
38. Public Housing and the Poor
    Lawrence M. Friedman 448
39. Section 235 of the National Housing Act: Homeownership
    for Low-income Families?
    Robert Schafer and *Charles G. Field* 460
40. The Boston Rehabilitation Program
    Langley C. Keyes, Jr. 472
41. An Evaluation of the Boston Rehabilitation Program
    Urban Planning Aid, Inc. 484
42. BURP and Make Money
    Eli Goldston 493
43. Housing Codes
    National Commission on Urban Problems 497
44. Effects of the Property Tax in Urban Areas
    Dick Netzer 510
45. New Communities
    Edward Eichler and *Marshall Kaplan* 523
46. Private Participation in Low-income Housing
    Michael A. Stegman 532
47. The Private Sector and Community Development:
    A Cautious Proposal
    Chester W. Hartman 536
48. Toward a New Federal Housing Policy
    Irving H. Welfeld 543
49. The Lessons of Pruitt-Igoe
    Lee Rainwater 548
50. Income Strategy and Housing Supply
    Dick Netzer 556
51. Housing and Public Policy Analysis
    Arthur P. Solomon 558
    Bibliography 579
    Index 595

Housing
Urban America

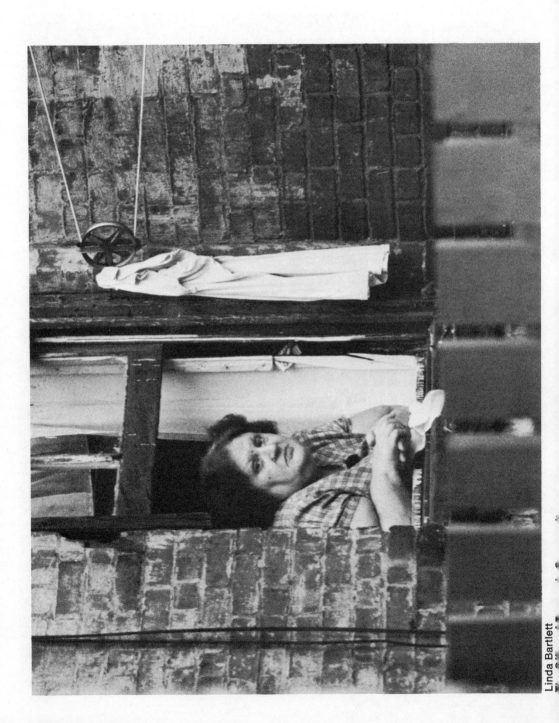

Harvey Hacker and Neal Mitchell Associates

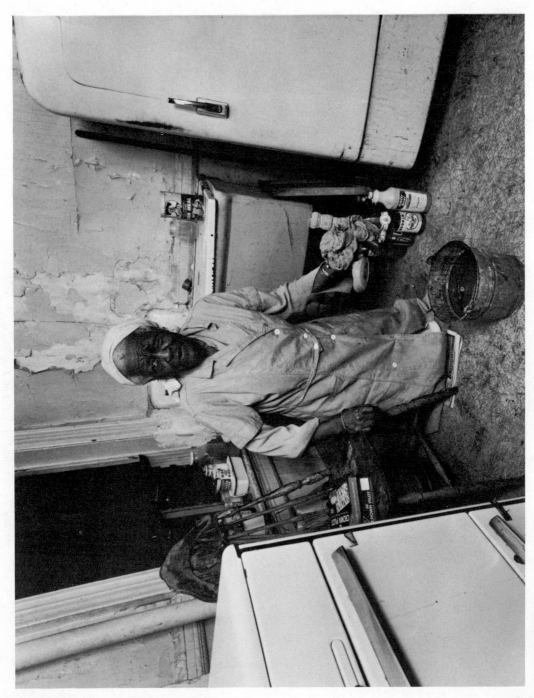

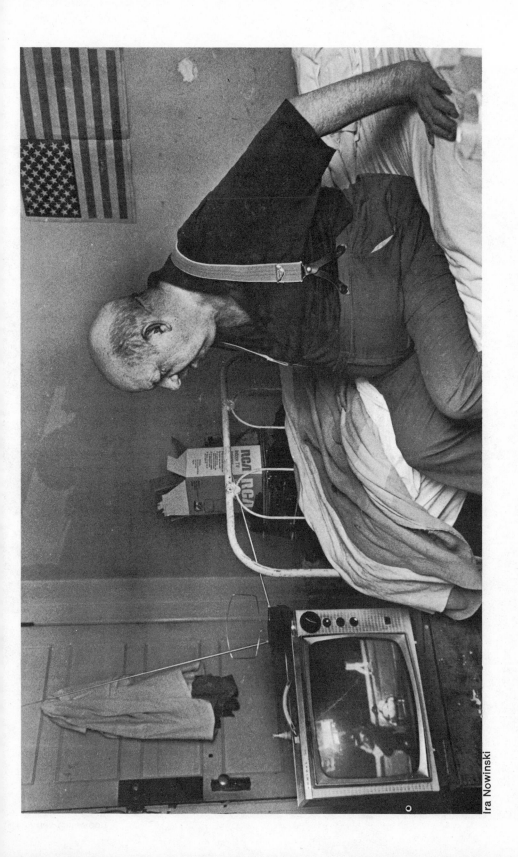

Ira Nowinski

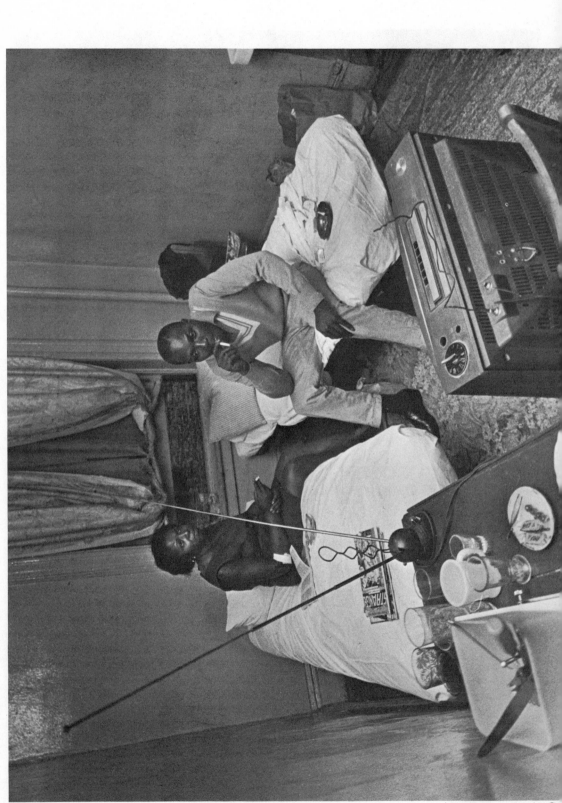

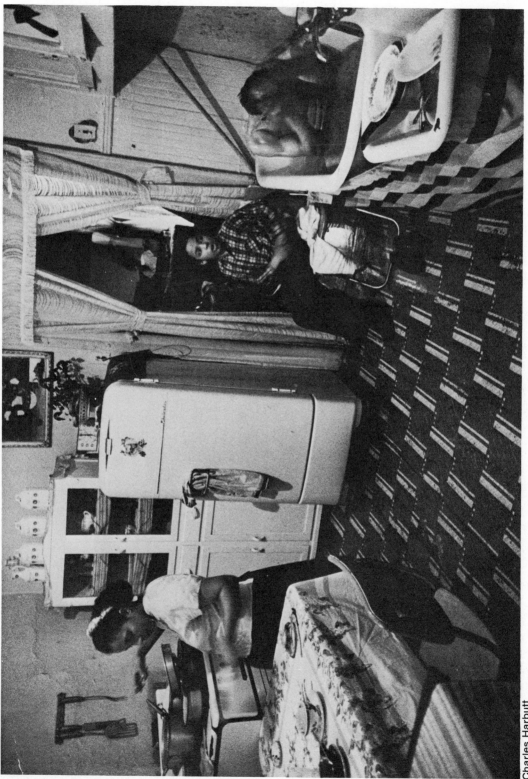

UPI

Harvey Hacker and Neal Mitchell Associates

Harvey Hacker and Neal Mitchell Associates

©Charles Gatewood

John Mount

© Charles Gatewood

Harvey Hacker and Neal Mitchell Associates

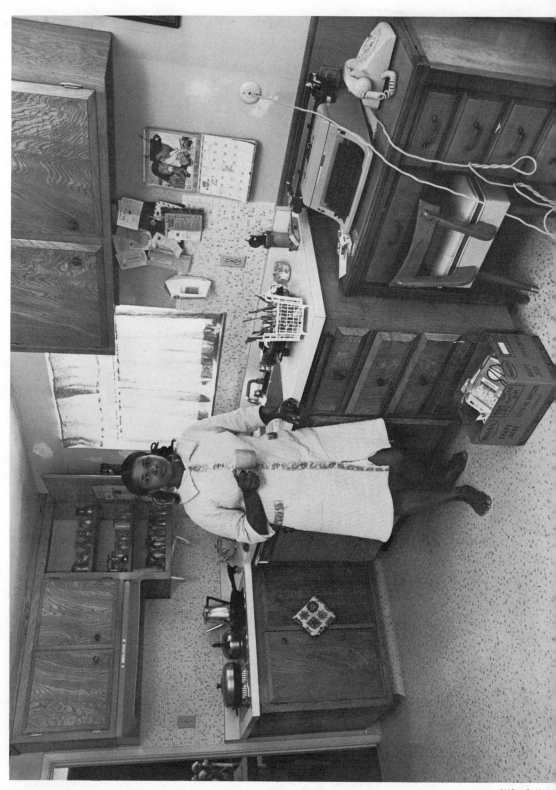

Preface

Housing plays a major part in all our lives. For most households it is the largest single investment, and it accounts for the largest proportion of consumer expenditures. Its quality and location affect the security, happiness, and stability of families, and have serious implications for the economic and social well-being of our urban and rural areas. Planners, architects, government officials at all levels, realtors and developers, lawyers, labor leaders, and other professionals need to understand housing markets, the production of housing, and the distribution of its services over the population. At the same time, the area of housing has become a basic part of city planning and urban studies curricula at colleges and universities. This book contains a comprehensive collection of readings aimed at serving the needs of professionals and students in this area. We believe that the articles collected here are significant contributions to housing analysis, providing a balance between theory, empirical verification, and policy.

The focus of the book is on the housing problems of the poor and members of minority groups who live in urban areas of the United States, although much of what is said in the urban context is also applicable to rural housing. The collection contains articles drawn from a wide variety of sources—academic and professional journals, books, government reports, and more popular magazines—and includes four articles written especially for it (the articles by Mollenkopf-Pynoos, Stone, Achtenberg, and Solomon). The book is divided into five sections: Politics, Social Aspects,

Economics, Production, and Policies and Programs. Dividing lines between the sections are not precise, but this, of course, reflects the overlapping nature of the housing issue. The Bibliography contains a selective list of post-1960 articles and books plus important earlier works.

All of the editors helped to select and edit the articles in this book; the primary responsibility for drafting the introductions is as follows: Introduction—Schafer, Pynoos, and Hartman; Politics—Pynoos and Schafer; Social Aspects—Pynoos and Hartman; Economics—Schafer; Production—Schafer; Policies and Programs—Hartman.

Although it is not possible to list all the persons who have assisted us in the preparation of this book, we are especially indebted to Clinton Bourdon, Richard Coleman, Alan Dolmatch, Nathan Glazer, Gail Hall, Elizabeth Hanna, Ralph Jones, John Kain, Robert Komives, Peter Marcuse, John Mollenkopf, Lee Rainwater, and Carl Sussman. A special note of thanks is owed to Penelope H. Schafer for reading the manuscript and assisting in preparation of the Bibliography. We want also to thank Denise L. Aronson, Judith W. Augusta, Karla N. O'Brien, N. Teresa Rea and Sara W. Stewart for their technical assistance in preparation of the manuscript. In addition, we acknowledge the support of the M.I.T.-Harvard Joint Center for Urban Studies, the Ford Foundation's Urban Studies Grant to Harvard University, and the Institute of Urban and Regional Development at the University of California, Berkeley.

The order in which the editors are listed was determined by drawing names from a Stetson hat. We would like to thank Sarah Rubin for gracefully performing this task.

Introduction

The 51 articles gathered in this book represent an approach to housing considerably broader than the traditional concerns with overcrowding, physical deficiencies, and inadequate facilities. When households consume "housing," they purchase or rent more than the dwelling unit and its characteristics; they are also concerned about such factors as health, security, privacy, neighborhood and social relations, status, community facilities and services, access to jobs, and control over environment. Being ill-housed can mean deprivation along any of these dimensions, and relative deprivation can lead to widespread discontent and suffering. Since housing is so all-encompassing and is the largest household budget item for most families, it is no surprise that, according to the official report on the Newark rebellion (Governor's Select Commission, 1968), ". . . Negroes cited bad housing conditions most often when they were asked to choose among fifteen possible underlying causes of the 1967 disorders." Our concern in this book is the economic, social, and political factors that account for poor housing, and some of the policies and strategies that may be brought to bear to improve conditions in these areas.

THE HOUSING BUNDLE

Dwelling units is the term most widely used to describe housing, but it fails to capture housing's complexity and heterogeneity. It is more accurate to describe housing as a bundle of attributes, such as lot size, floor area, plumbing and kitchen facilities, number of bathrooms, heating systems, structure type, intensity of use, tenure, neighborhood status, neighborhood characteristics (physical and sociopsychological), neighbors, location, and quality of public and quasi-public services (schools, garbage collection, etc.). It is this bundle of attributes that members of a household consider when they choose a residence or when they express dissatisfaction with their living arrangements. For example, in a recent study of the St. Louis housing market, John Kain and John Quigley used 39 measures merely to describe the physical or visual quality of dwelling units, adjacent properties, and the block face (Table 1).[1]

Analysis of the multidimensional aspects of housing has been and continues to be hindered by the limited amount of collected information. Data limitations have also restricted efforts to investigate the dynamics of the housing market and the various effects that deficiencies in one or more of these dimensions have on occupants and on society. As a result, attention has focused on those aspects of housing for which data are available. In general these fall into one of three categories recorded in the decennial housing census: (1) structural condition, (2) density of occupancy, and (3) price.

Housing Condition

The 1960 census used three categories to describe housing condition: *sound, deteriorating,* and *dilapidated. Sound* housing was defined as having no defects or only slight defects that were normally corrected during the course of regular maintenance. *Deteriorating* housing needed more repair than would be provided in the course of regular maintenance. *Dilapidated* housing did not provide safe and adequate shelter and was characterized by one or more critical defects, such as holes over large areas of the foundation, walls, roofs, or chimney, and inadequate original construction. The absence of a private bath or shower and hot running water was reported separately. *Standard* denoted all housing units that were in sound or deteriorating condition if they had adequate plumbing facilities; the term *substandard* was used to denote housing units in dilapidated condition (regardless of plumbing facilities) and housing units no matter what structural condition if they lacked one or more of the following plumbing facilities: hot running water in the structure, flush toilet for private use, bathtub or shower for private use.

According to the 1960 Census of Housing, 8.5 million American families (including one-person households) were living in substandard housing. This statistic, however, may be regarded as a minimal statement of the inadequacy of housing conditions. The poor quality of census data on housing conditions is widely recognized. A special Census Bureau study and review of the 1960 census revealed, first, that only about one-third of the dwelling units rated as dilapidated or deteriorating would have been

1. J. F. Kain and J. M. Quigley, "Measuring the Value of Housing Quality," *Journal of the American Statistical Association* 65 (June 1970): 532-48. This study also included information about the occupants; objective characteristics of the dwelling unit (e.g., number of rooms, number of bathrooms, structure age, structure type, central heating, and the presence of hot water), parcel area, length of occupancy, owner's presence in building, and rent or value of the unit. Supplementary information covered neighborhood schools, crime rates, location, and characteristics of the census tract (e.g., racial composition). See also J. F. Kain and J. M. Quigley, "Evaluating the Quality of the Residential Environment," *Environment and Planning* 2 (1970): 23-32; St. Louis Planning Commission, with Alan M. Vorhees and Associates, Inc., *Technical Report: Residential Blight Analysis* (McLean, Virginia, 1969). Some studies in addition to the Kain and Quigley work are: R. G. Ridker and J. A. Henning, "The Determinants of Residential Property Value with Special Reference to Air Pollution," *The Review of Economics and Statistics* 49 (1967): 246-57; R. F. Muth, *Cities and Housing* (Chicago: University of Chicago Press, 1969); H. O. Nourse, "The Effects of Air Pollution on Property Values," *Land Economics* 43 (1967): 181-89.

TABLE 1. *Some Physical and Visual Attributes of the Housing Bundle*

Dwelling Unit

Overall structural condition
General housekeeping
Condition of ceilings
Condition of walls
Condition of floors
Condition of lighting
Condition of windows

Structure and Parcel

Condition of structure exterior
Overall parcel condition
Quality of exterior
Parcel landscaping
Trash on parcel
Nuisances affecting parcel
Condition of drives and walks

Adjacent Structures and Parcels

Condition of structures
Condition of parcels
Structural quality of poorer adjacent structures
Structural quality of better adjacent structures
Parcel quality of poorer adjacent parcels
Parcel quality of better adjacent parcels
Nuisances affecting adjacent properties
Sample property relative to adjacent properties

Block Face

Neighborhood problems
Percent residential
Percent commercial and residential
Percent vacant
Percent in poor condition
Percent in fair condition
Percent in good condition
Block landscaping
Trash on block
Condition of sidewalk
Condition of street
Condition of curbs
Amount of commercial traffic
Nuisances affecting block
Condition of alleyways
Cleanliness of alleyways
Overall block condition

SOURCE: John Kain and John Quigley, "Measuring the Value of Housing Quality," *Journal of the American Statistical Association* 65 (June 1970): 535.

rated the same by two different groups of enumerators and, second, that there was substantial undercounting of dilapidated dwelling units (U.S. Bureau of the Census, 1967). In other words, the 1960 effort to evaluate structural quality was both unreliable and inaccurate. Doubts about the reliability and validity of previous housing census data have led, in the 1970 census, to virtual abandonment of attempts to obtain national data on the structural quality of dwelling units. (The latest census includes no rating of the structural condition of dwelling units.) The 1970 census did, however, record that dwelling units "lacking some or all plumbing" numbered 4.7 million,[2] which is below the 1960 level of 7.7 million. While the 1970 census provides less information on structural quality than did previous censuses, the information in it is reported in much greater detail than at any time in the past. For example, samples of metropolitan area populations containing housing and population characteristics for one in every hundred households will be available.

State and local housing codes, which set legal minimum standards for residential occupancy, contain a more detailed and comprehensive cataloging of standards and critical defects. It is widely acknowledged that:

> even the most conscientious user of Census data who added "Total dilapidated" plus "Total deteriorating" plus "sound lacking some or all (plumbing) facilities" would arrive at a total "substandard" housing figure which grossly underestimated the number of dwelling units having serious code violations. To use a total thus arrived at as a figure for substandard housing is grossly inaccurate and misleading, because it flies in the face of extensive considerations given by health experts, building officials, model code drafting organizations, and the local, state and federal court system to what have become over a period of many years, the socially, politically and legally accepted minimum standard for housing of human beings in the United States. . . .
> Even if public and private efforts eliminate all housing which is substandard under most current federal definitions, there will still be millions of dwelling units below code standards [Sutermeister, 1969].

Density

Some housing experts now believe that overcrowding can cause more physical and psychological damage than does poor structural condition of the dwelling itself (Schorr, 1966). Overcrowding may lead to increased stress, poor development of a sense of individuality, sexual conflict, lack of adequate sleep leading to poor work and school performance, and intrafamilial tensions. The census classifies a household as living in overcrowded conditions if the ratio of persons in the household to the number of rooms occupied by the household exceeds 1.0. The 1960 census reported that 6.1 million households were living at density ratios higher than 1.0 persons per room; of these, 1.9 million households were living at density ratios of 1.5 or more persons per room. In 1970 the census reported 5.2 million households living at density ratios higher than 1.0 persons per room; of these, 1.4 million were living at densities of 1.5 or more persons per room. A recent study, which compared the census definition of overcrowding with a more sophisticated standard that takes into account the age, sex, and relationship of household members, found that the amount of overcrowding

2. " 'Lacking some or all plumbing' means that the unit does not have all three specified plumbing facilities (hot and cold piped water, as well as flush toilet and bathtub or shower inside the structure), or that the toilet or bathing facilities are also for the use of the occupants of other housing units." U.S. Bureau of the Census, *1970 Census of Housing: General Housing Characteristics: United States Advance Report*, HC (VI)-1 (Washington, D.C., February 1971).

thus defined may be nine times that estimated by the Census Bureau (Greenfield and Lewis, Chap. 14).

Expenditures for Housing

The price and quality of housing are obviously related in that a person generally pays higher prices for better and more space and for convenience and quality of location. Expenses for housing consumption as they relate to ability to pay (family income) may be looked at as a distinct housing problem and one of particular importance to low income families and to households that are experiencing increases in housing costs while their incomes remain relatively fixed (for example, the elderly and other families that rely on pensions for income). Racial discrimination accentuates the problem, because members of minority groups pay higher prices for poor quality housing in deteriorating areas that may also have locational disadvantages. Among the 6.9 million renter families living in substandard housing in 1960, 2.2 million were paying more than 25 percent of their income for rent; 1.4 million, more than 35 percent. And of the 13 million renter families not living in substandard housing, 4 million were paying more than 25 percent of their income for rent; 2.3 million, more than 35 percent.

The 1970 distribution of rent-income ratios by income class of families living in metropolitan areas is shown in Table 2. Within each income class there is a significant concentration about some range of rent-income ratios; households in the lowest income category have the highest rent-income ratios. At the same time, the amount spent on rent varies within each income class. These variations are the result of several factors: family size, household assets, lags between income changes and effects on expenditure patterns, structural quality, and the location of dwelling units within metropolitan areas (Rapkin, 1957; Newman, 1971).

One objective of housing programs intended to benefit the poor would, of course, be the reduction of housing expenditures. Such a reduction would permit families to spend adequate amounts on food, clothing, medical care, and other necessities, and would also maximize opportunities for families to improve their life situations by devoting some income to vocational training, the search for jobs, and other possibilities for advancement. (At present, families that receive assistance from government housing subsidy programs do pay a fixed rent-income ratio, although these ratios are not uniform across the various programs.)

HOUSING NEEDS AND GOALS

Use of the term *housing* creates certain empirical problems in attempting to define and quantify needs and to establish housing goals. As defined by the individual, for example, housing needs must be distinguished from housing demands. A household's demand for housing is the amount of housing services (the attributes of the bundle) it wants to consume, given the prices of housing and other goods, and its income and assets. The overall demand for housing is the aggregation or sum of each household's demand. Needs, though, refer to differences between a household's consumption and that household's concept of minimally acceptable living conditions. Housing demand can be less than housing need for such reasons as inadequate family incomes and racial discrimination. When the society establishes a minimum acceptable standard for human habitation, housing needs may be regarded as the society's goals, and the thrust of housing policy is to achieve these goals.

Measured along one dimension, such as soundness of structure or presence of

TABLE 2. *Percent of Primary Families and Individuals in Each Income Class Having The Designated Ratio of Gross Rent to Income: Renter-occupied Dwelling Units Inside Standard Metropolitan Statistical Areas, for The United States: 1970*

Gross Rent as a Percentage of Income	Annual Income in 1969									
	less than $2,000	$2,000-2,999	$3,000-3,999	$4,000-4,999	$5,000-5,999	$6,000-6,999	$7,000-9,999	$10,000-14,999	$15,000-24,999	$25,000 or more
Less than 15 %	0*	1	3	5	10	16	30	54	77	88
15-19 %	0*	3	6	13	20	26	30	29	14	6
20-24 %	1	5	12	19	23	23	21	10	4	1
25-34 %	4	17	29	33	29	25	12	4	1	1
35 % or more	75	70	47	27	14	7	2	1	0*	0*
Not computed	19	4	4	4	4	4	4	3	3	3
Total†	100	100	100	100	100	100	100	100	100	100

* less than 0.5 percent.
† May not add to 100 percent because of rounding.
SOURCE: Calculated from U.S. Bureau of the Census, *U.S. Census of Housing: 1970; Metropolitan Housing Characteristics, Final Report HC (2)-1,* "United States and Regions" (Washington, D.C.: U.S. Government Printing Office, 1972), Table B-3, p. 1-22.

adequate plumbing facilities, housing conditions in the United States have clearly been improving over recent decades. (Recognition of this fact should not lead us to overlook the severe fire dangers, the high rate of home accidents, rat bites, lead poisoning, and other hazards to health and safety that are still all too common in certain areas, given the country's affluence and prevailing housing standards.) However, along other dimensions, such as the percentage of income the family must spend on housing or general neighborhood and environmental conditions, the situation of large segments of the population, especially low income families, may not be improving. Thus it is almost impossible to state with any certainty the magnitude of the country's housing needs. If we take as the definition of needs the sum of those living in substandard quarters (as measured by comprehensive local code standards), those living in overcrowded conditions (as measured by criteria more sophisticated than those used in the housing census), those living in substandard neighborhoods regardless of individual housing conditions (measures for which presently do not exist), and those paying excessive amounts of their budget for housing (decent or not), then the number of inadequately housed households would be several times the figure generally acknowledged by government sources and other observers.

More than 20 years ago Congress declared a national housing goal of "a decent home and a suitable living environment for every American family." No definition was given to the concepts of "a decent home" and "a suitable living environment," however, and no effort was made to determine the resources necessary to achieve the stated goals. Nor did Congress pass legislation to provide appropriations sufficient to achieve the goals, nor was mention made of the special problems confronting America's minority households. In the Housing Act of 1968 Congress explicitly reaffirmed the 1949 goal while acknowledging that it had not been fully realized. (Historically, of course, declarations have always outstripped the commitment of resources needed to meet stated goals.)

More specifically, the 1968 act declared that nearly every American could be provided a decent home and a suitable living environment "within the next decade by the construction or rehabilitation of twenty-six million housing units, six million of these for low and moderate income families." These figures represented a rough average of the estimates of need derived by the Department of Housing and Urban Development, the President's Committee on Urban Housing, the National Commission on Urban Problems, and the National Advisory Commission on Civil Disorders. Almost no knowledgeable analyst believes we will actually meet these goals. As Anthony Downs (1968) notes:

> These rhetorical claims appear patently false to anyone who knows much about the problems concerned. Moreover, they have a devastating long-run impact upon the citizenry's confidence in government programs—and even authority in general. For such claims at first tend to generate great expectations among the relatively poorly informed persons suffering from the ills concerned. But repeated disillusionment eventually induces a deep cynicism toward all government programs. . . .

It must be recognized that as elusive as the 1968 goal may be, it falls short of the upper bound description of need. In arriving at the estimated need of 26 million housing units, those units in the census category "deteriorating, with all plumbing facilities" were not deemed substandard, elimination of overcrowding was not included, and neither environmental features nor local code standards were taken into account. Moreover, the public costs would be even higher had subsidies for families paying too high a proportion of their income for housing been included in the definition of housing needs.

It is not clear how much progress we have made over the last decade toward attainment of the national housing goal. While there has been a reduction in overcrowding from 6.1 million to 5.2 million households, local surveys indicate that conditions have actually deteriorated in some areas. For example, a special Census Bureau survey of two areas of Los Angeles, taken after the Watts "riots" showed that over the 1960-65 period in East Los Angeles the proportion of dwelling units that were either dilapidated or deteriorating rose from 25 to 35 percent while the median gross monthly rent was rising from $63 to $75; in South Los Angeles the proportion of dilapidated and deteriorating housing rose from 18 to 33 percent at the same time that median monthly rent was rising from $69 to $78 (U.S. Bureau of the Census, 1966). A study of the Boston area showed that in the 1960s rents rose 66 percent, from a monthly median of $78 in 1960 to $130 in 1970, while during the same period the general cost of living index rose 27 percent, and family incomes rose only 33 percent.[3] Another Boston study showed that during the 1960-65 period the proportion of dilapidated and deteriorating housing in the city rose from 21 to 26 percent.[4] According to the Bureau of the Census (1971b), median monthly contract rent for the United States rose from $58 in 1960 to $90 in 1970, a 55 percent increase, while the consumer price index increased from 88.7 in 1960 to 116.3 in 1970, a 31 percent increase (U.S. Bureau of the Census, 1971c).

Although sufficiently comprehensive and accurate data are not available to permit reliable statements about recent trends, it is likely that in certain areas of the country (notably large central cities and possibly rural areas as well) and for certain groups within the population (the poor, racial minorities, and the aged) housing conditions may not be improving at all or may be declining. That we do not collect the data necessary to make such assessments in itself says much about housing's low priority.

An even larger issue in housing goals is whether they should relate to absolute standards that establish some universally applied minimum or should, instead, refer to some standard that reflects where one's total housing bundle is relative to the rest of society. In this respect it should be noted that improvement in absolute quality of housing occupied by nonwhites during the period 1950-60 failed to narrow the differential between white and nonwhite housing conditions (Frieden, 1970). In a fashion similar to Lee Rainwater's definition of income need (Rainwater, 1969), one might define housing need not in terms of an absolute amount but as relative to the housing package of other consumers as measured by a national median.

HOUSING ASSISTANCE PROGRAMS

The federal government has been active in the housing market since the Great Depression. Some of its programs only provide federal insurance of market interest rate mortgages and have little effect on the price of housing. The following programs,

3. See report of *Boston Area Study*, undertaken by the MIT-Harvard Joint Center for Urban Studies. The report also notes that 1 out of 3 Boston area families, and 9 out of 10 families earning less than $3,000 per year, now pay more than 30 percent of their income for housing.

4. See Boston Redevelopment Authority, Planning Department, *A Study of Factors Bearing on Residential Rents in the City of Boston* (January 1969). Other local indications of increased housing costs and deteriorating housing conditions may be found in the *Report of Housing and Urban Renewal Task Force to Mayor John V. Lindsay* (Charles Abrams, Chairman) (New York, January 10, 1966). See also the minimum budgets prepared periodically for different areas of the country by the Bureau of Labor Statistics, Department of Labor; "Economics of Aging," report of the Special Senate Committee on Aging (January 1971); and *Pieces and Scraps: Farm Labor Housing in the United States* (Washington, D.C.: Rural Housing Alliance, September 1970).

however, are expressly concerned with reducing the housing prices that consumers face: low-rent public housing, rent supplements, below market interest rate loans (sections 221 [d] [3], 221h, 235, and 236), rehabilitation grants (section 115), and rehabilitation loans (section 312). The record of these programs is summarized in Table 3. The average annual need for subsidized dwelling units projected in the 1968 Housing Act was 600,000, but though the 1970 level of subsidized housing production (384,041 dwelling units) is by far the best in recent times, it is less than two-thirds of the projected need figure—and as discussed in the introduction to Section IV (Production), this higher level of subsidized starts may be temporary. An equally important question is: Whom do the subsidy programs listed in Table 3 serve? That is, most of these programs provide households with an inadequate amount of financial assistance. As a result, many low income families cannot afford to live in units financed under the programs.

The median annual income of beneficiaries of the subsidy programs is as follows.[5]

Section 235, New Construction	$6,100
Section 235, Rehabilitation	5,816
Section 236	5,303
Public housing (nonelderly families)	3,636
Public housing (elderly families)	1,797
Rent Supplements	2,414
Section 115	less than 3,000
Section 312	60 percent have incomes greater than 6,000

In 1970, by comparison, 10 million households (families and unrelated individuals) had incomes below the poverty cutoff. (The cutoff figure, or poverty index, is adjusted for such factors as family size, sex of family head, number of children under 18 years of age, and farm/nonfarm residence. U.S. Bureau of the Census, 1971a.) Since the average value of this index for a nonfarm family of 4 is $3,968, it is clear that sections 235, 236, and 312 subsidy programs, which together amounted to 57 percent of the total 1970 figure of 384,041, do not serve the poor.

It is often contended that subsidizing higher income households will eventually lead to better housing for the poor. The limitations of this filter-down argument are discussed in the introduction to Section III (Economics). Even the total of all currently existing subsidized housing units for moderate and low income families —1.579 million units—is only a small fraction of the minimal statement of need indicated by the poverty index.

Federal and state public assistance, or welfare, generally is not regarded as a housing program, but as of August 1968 the 8.5 million persons receiving assistance under federally aided programs were annually spending $1.1 billion in public moneys on housing. A recent study by the Department of Health, Education and Welfare (1969) "estimated that at least one-half of all assistance recipients live in housing which is

5. The figures for sections 235, 236, and public housing are for 1970. U.S. Department of Housing and Urban Development, *1970 HUD Statistical Yearbook* (Washington, D.C.: Government Printing Office, 1971), tables 112, 236, 239, 240. U.S. Congress, Senate, Subcommittee on Housing and Urban Affairs, Committee on Banking and Currency, *Hearings on the Housing and Urban Development Legislation of 1970, 91st Cong., 2d sess., pt. 1, p. 718.* The figure for rent supplements is based on a 1969 survey. Id., p. 721. The section 115 legislation requires that recipients have annual incomes less than $3,000. The section 312 figure is for 1969. R. Taggart, III, *Low-Income Housing: A Critique of Federal Aid* (Baltimore: Johns Hopkins Press, 1970), p. 88.

TABLE 3. *Subsidized Housing Starts*

Year	FHA Multifamily 221(d)(3) BMIR New	Rehab	236 New	Rehab	Rent Supplements* New	Rehab	FHA Homes 235 New	Rehab	221h Rehab	Low-Rent Public Housing† New & Rehab	Rehabilitation Grant Program Section 115‡	Residential Rehabilitation Loan Program Section 312‡	All Subsidized Programs
1960										29,209			29,209
1961	320									30,493			30,813
1962	3,182	685								22,402			26,269
1963	6,889	1,807								24,030			32,726
1964	13,906	601								25,591			40,098
1965	11,098	886								33,298	9	13	45,629
1966	12,766	142								31,999	1,990	636	47,858
1967	23,644	1,771								34,015	2,515	2,017	76,268
1968	43,645	6,077					4	35	369	71,606	4,103	3,897	142,042
1969	32,762	4,552	11,536	263	} 35,943	} 1,628	11,083	14,647	920	64,231	6,053	4,473	162,826
1970	17,683	1,462	104,413	7,819	22,847	1,862	78,412	27,212	529	104,410	10,839	6,553	384,041
1935-70 Total	165,895	17,983	115,949	8,082	58,790	3,490	89,499	41,894	1,818	1,032,471	25,509	17,589	1,579,057

*The rent supplement program operates under both the market interest rate and below market interest rate mortgage insurance programs of sections 221(d)(3) and 236. In order to prevent double counting, the figures in this column include only rent supplements on dwelling units that bear market interest rate mortgage insurance. The others are counted as either 221(d)(3) BMIR or 236 starts.

† The yearly figures include the number of units constructed, rehabilitated, and leased.

‡ A grant under section 115 or a loan under section 312 is treated as a dwelling unit that receives assistance.

SOURCE: U.S. Department of Housing and Urban Development, *1970 HUD Statistical Yearbook* (Washington, D.C.: U.S. Government Printing Office, 1971), Tables 33, 34, 146, 147, 162, 164

deteriorating or dilapidated, unsafe, insanitary or overcrowded." The responsibility for determining the adequacy of financial assistance rests with the states, and most state allowances for housing are too low to permit recipients to secure standard housing. Whereas cost standards for food and clothing are based on definitions of minimum adequate requirements, allowances for rent and home maintenance are not. "For more than 3 million recipient households, the average allowance for housing is less than $400 per year. This amount is grossly inadequate for either rental housing or home ownership" (HEW, 1969).

SUMMARY

Whether one considers the housing goals projected in the 1968 Housing Act, the goals implicit in critiques of census standards, or the greatly expanded goals implicit in a standard related to the nation's median, a redistribution of income (direct or indirect) as well as greater planning and public control over the factors and conditions related to the provision of housing will be necessary to achieve a better housing environment for the poor. The two major problems to be solved are: (1) how to increase the effective purchasing power of households that cannot afford decent housing without a subsidy, and (2) how to eliminate discrimination in the housing market against nonwhites and other groups (such as large families and families dependent on welfare payments).

Solution of these problems will require facing such questions as: the efficiency of the residential construction industry; the responsiveness of the supply side of the housing market to changes in demand; the choice of an appropriate subsidy mechanism (supply side versus demand side and direct versus indirect mechanisms); the costs and benefits of various institutional reforms (the property tax, building codes, and trade union practices); the formulation of adequate delivery mechanisms and administrative vehicles at national, regional, and local levels; the role of rehabilitation; the location of subsidized units within metropolitan areas; the role of homeownership; and the creation of greater control over the residential environment by occupants and local communities. And it should not be overlooked that the housing issue must be approached within the broader context of the nation's economy and political institutions. How should an adequate housing program be financed? How can our housing goals be reached without dislocation of the economy? How are we to decide priorities among many different social welfare programs and approaches to ending poverty, such as welfare, job training and creation, compensatory education, and general income maintenance?

The articles in Section I of this book discuss the political constraints on U.S. housing policy, the past performance of some of the principal institutions, and alternative strategies that could be adopted. Section II deals with urban social structure, the ill effects of bad housing, and housing preferences. Section III examines residential location decisions, "filtering," the causes of substandard housing, and racial discrimination in the housing market. Section IV analyses inefficiencies in the production of housing (building codes, unions, the organization of the industry, and federal income tax laws). Finally, Section V presents an evaluation of past, present, and proposed housing programs.

The housing issue emerges as a major test of our society and our economic system. The question remains: Are we willing and able to pay the costs—monetary, social, and institutional—required to provide all of our people with a decent home and suitable living environment?

REFERENCES

Downs, Anthony. "Moving Towards Realistic Housing Goals." *Agenda for the Nation*, ed. Kermit Gordon. Garden City, New York: Doubleday, 1968: p. 177.

Frieden, Bernard. "Housing and National Urban Goals." *The Metropolitan Enigma*, ed. James Q. Wilson. Garden City, New York: Doubleday, 1970: p. 185.

Governor's Select Commission on Civil Disorder, State of New Jersey. *Report for Action*. February 1968, p. 55.

Newman, Dorothy K. "Housing the Poor and the Shelter to Income Ratio." *Papers Submitted to the Subcommittee on Housing Panels*. U.S. Congress, House, Committee on Banking and Currency, 92d Cong., 1st sess., 1971: pp. 555-78.

Rainwater, Lee. "The Problem of Lower-Class Culture and Poverty-War Strategy." *On Understanding Poverty*, ed. Daniel P. Moynihan. New York: Basic Books, 1969: 229-59.

Rapkin, Chester. "Rent-Income Ratio." *Journal of Housing*. January 1957: 8-12.

Schorr, A. L. *Slums and Social Insecurity*. Washington, D.C.: U.S. Government Printing Office, 1966.

Sutermeister, Oscar. "Inadequacies and Inconsistencies in the Definition of Substandard Housing." *Housing Code Standards: Three Critical Studies*. Research Report No. 19. National Commission on Urban Problems. Washington, D.C., 1969: pp. 83, 102.

U.S. Bureau of the Census. *Current Population Reports: Consumer Income*. Series P-60, No. 81, "Characteristics of the Low-Income Population 1970." Washington, D.C.: U.S. Government Printing Office, 1971a: p. 20, Table N and p. 63, Table 11.

U.S. Bureau of the Census. *Measuring the Quality of Housing, An Appraisal of Census Statistics and Methods*. Working Paper, No. 25, Washington, D.C., 1967.

U.S. Bureau of the Census. *1970 Census of Housing: General Housing Characteristics: United States Advance Report*. HC (VI)-1. Washington, D.C., February 1971b.

U.S. Bureau of the Census. *Special Census Survey of the South and East Los Angeles Areas, November 1965*. Series P-23, No. 18, June 28, 1966, Tables 3 and 9.

U.S. Bureau of the Census. *Statistical Abstract of the United States: 1971*. Washington, D.C., 1971c.

U.S. Department of Health, Education and Welfare. *The Role of Public Welfare in Housing: A Report to the House Committee on Ways and Means and the Senate Committee on Finance* (January 1969): pp. 8, 11.

TENANTS!
WHAT HAPPENS WHEN WE STAND UP?

I

Politics

The political struggles associated with housing emanate largely from the inequality in the present distribution of housing services as reflected in the substandard physical conditions and the restricted locations of housing that minorities and the poor occupy. To secure better housing services these groups and their supporters have pressured the government to intervene on their behalf and to pass tenement laws, sanitary codes, and programs such as public housing and rent supplements. But because income distribution has remained fairly constant over a long period of time, these efforts have scarcely improved the housing situation of the poor and minorities relative to other groups in society.[1] In addition, government housing programs for the poor have received only limited funding, and millions of families continue to live in inadequate housing.

Overall, government housing policy, including the income tax laws, has aided the middle and upper income groups more than poor and minority groups. One analyst has found that while in 1962 the government spent approximately $820 million to subsidize housing for poor people (including public housing, public assistance, and savings because of homeowners' income tax deductions), it spent approximately $2.9 billion to subsidize housing for those with middle incomes and above (including only

---

1. For example, in 1970 the 20 percent of total families who had the lowest incomes received only 5.5 percent of total money income (including transfer payments such as public assistance but before income taxes), while the 20 percent with the highest incomes received 41.6 percent. U.S. Bureau of the Census, "Income in 1970 of Families and Persons in the United States," *Current Population Reports: Consumer Income*, Series P-60, no. 80 (October 4, 1971). This situation differs only marginally from the 1947 income distribution, and taking income taxes into account does not significantly alter the picture. It has been estimated that the lowest fifth's share of 1962 family personal income was 4.6 percent before taxes and 4.9 percent after taxes, while the highest fifth's was 45.5 percent before taxes and 43.7 percent after taxes. E. C. Budd, *Inequality and Poverty* (New York: W. W. Norton, 1967), pp. xiii, xvi. Further, consumer units that had more than $200,000 in wealth (homes, automobiles, businesses, farms, investments, and liquid assets) owned 35 percent of the total wealth in 1962. D. S. Projector and G. S. Weiss, *Survey of Financial Characteristics of Consumers* (Washington, D.C.: Board of Governors of the Federal Reserve System, 1966), p. 136. For a good summary of these data, see Letitia Upton and Nancy Lyons, *Basic Facts: Distribution of Personal Income and Wealth in the United States* (Cambridge, Mass.: Cambridge Institute, 1972).

savings from homeowners' income tax deductions).[2] Apparently, as much as one-fifth to one-half of federal housing aid to low and moderate income families has been diverted to such intermediaries as private housing sponsors and public bureaucracies (Frieden, 1971). Moreover, programs such as urban renewal and highway construction have destroyed some 2 million dwelling units of low and moderate income residents. In addition, zoning and building codes have often been used to exclude low income families from communities by making housing prohibitively expensive and by excluding multiple dwelling units. In this way many federal, state, and local policies and programs have neglected or harmed the poor.

An understanding of this phenomenon is possible only through comprehension of the economic, social, and political institutions that underlie housing policy and its implementation. Therefore, it is important to know how, by whom, and for what reasons housing policy has been made. While the selected articles cover a broad range of material, the focal point of this introduction will be the political conflict associated with public housing, because it is the principal housing program for the poor and because it has been given the most careful analysis.

At the national level several biases have hindered the public housing program (Bellush & Hausknecht, Chap. 9; Hartman, Chap. 10; Miller, 1968; Freedman, 1969; Friedman, 1968). First, the program's reliance on public development, ownership, and management has clashed with American partiality toward private ownership. Second, the program has been selective (serving only the poor) rather than universalistic (serving many classes). Third, tenants in the early days of public housing (the late 1930s) were predominantly working-class whites, who were viewed as the deserving poor caught in the throes of the Depression. In the era of postwar prosperity, tenants—increasingly welfare recipients and blacks—have come to be viewed as undeserving and undesirable as neighbors. Fourth, the initial proponents of the program had operated on the assumption that changing the physical housing conditions of the poor would have a major impact on tenants' behavior. It has become increasingly difficult to demonstrate the program's effectiveness in these terms. Finally, the product has often been of inferior quality because of lack of maintenance and an unwillingness to provide more than a minimal level of amenities to the poor.

Within the last decade several modifications have been made in the public housing program to overcome one or more of these obstacles. For example, privately owned units that meet code specifications now can be leased by local housing authorities on behalf of eligible tenants; then the tenant pays between 20 and 25 percent of his income for rent, and the housing authority pays the landlord the difference between this amount and the prevailing market rent. Another modification that offers private groups greater business opportunity has been the "turnkey" provision, under which housing authorities contract with private developers to build public housing units, which are then sold to the authorities. The program has also been reoriented toward a different group of tenants. By 1966 nearly half of the public housing units constructed annually were exclusively designed for the elderly, a group that almost everyone

2. Alvin Schorr, *Explorations in Social Policy* (New York: Basic Books, 1968), pp. 272-87. Treasury Department data show that in calendar year 1971 housing received a $5.8 billion break in tax deductions (mortgage interest, property tax, and depreciation). These deductions were distributed across adjusted gross income classes as follows: $3-5,000—$72 million; $5-7,000—$172 million; $7-10,000—$554 million; $10-15,000—$1,385 million; $15-20,000—$1,064 million; $20-50,000—$1,474 million; $50-100,000—$379 million; $100,000 and over—$215 million. *Housing Affairs Letter*, July 28, 1972, p. 5.

has considered deserving (and, in contrast to public housing families, has been primarily white).

Another factor that affects the outcome of housing programs is how well poor and minority groups are represented in the decision-making process, how open the process is, and the extent and effectiveness of the resources they have to influence policy. (Friedman, Chap. 1). Studies of the controversy surrounding passage of the 1949 Housing Act have indicated that interest groups such as materials producers, builders, financiers, housing officials, and labor unions dominated the lobbying efforts. These groups generally supported the urban redevelopment provisions of the act but split on the public housing section of the bill (Foard and Fefferman, 1960) with opposition coming from organizations that represent businesses engaged in the building, selling, or financing of housing (Freedman, 1969; Meyerson, Terrett, and Wheaton, 1962). The National Association of Real Estate Boards (NAREB), the National Association of Home Builders (NAHB), and the United States Savings and Loan League (USSLL) formed the nucleus of the opposition.

In efforts to obtain a public housing program the poor played virtually no direct role because they lacked money, legal skills, and organization. Instead, other groups represented their interests, the major proponent being the National Association of Housing Officials (now known as the National Association of Housing and Redevelopment Officials—NAHRO), which represented persons who work for local housing authorities. It was joined by the National League of Cities, the United States Conference of Mayors, and labor, social work, church, women's, Negro, and veterans' groups. After four years of debate, Congress approved legislation authorizing the construction of 810,000 units of public housing over the succeeding 6 years, but opponents crippled the program after passage by successfully lobbying for restrictions on appropriations and through actions at the local level. Between 1949 and 1955 barely 200,000 units had been completed. In one year, 1954, the appropriations bill included no new starts. Finally by 1970, over 20 years after passage, the original goal of 810,000 units was met.

Interests opposed to redistributive housing programs have operated more effectively at the national and local levels than have supporters of such programs. During the 1950s the relationships that existed between local and national groups facilitated the exchange of successful tactics and the distribution of packages of propaganda material used in antipublic-housing campaigns (Freedman, 1969). While private housing groups opposed to public housing (NAREB, NAHB, and USSLL) were relatively homogeneous, well funded, and primarily concerned with housing, proponents were more diverse and their concerns more fragmented. Only NAHRO was primarily concerned with housing; for the others it was one of many concerns. These differences are in part attributable to the economic requirement that businesses be organized along relatively narrow lines while there is little incentive for consumer organization.

Opportunities for local resistance to the public housing program have been many. For example, the Housing Act of 1937 as amended requires local communities to establish quasi-autonomous authorities in order to build and operate public housing. In many areas the poor and their supporters have been so underrepresented or powerless that it has been impossible to set up such authorities,[3] but even where public housing authorities have been formed, the program has run into roadblocks.

3. In 1968 approximately 56·percent of the population lived in areas not served by local housing authorities. See Chester Hartman and Gregg Carr, "Rejoinder," *Journal of the American Institute of Planners* 35 (November 1969): 435.

In many communities the issue of whether or not to have public housing has been put to the test of a referendum, and often it has been defeated. Ostensibly the referendum was to be a means of keeping policy decisions in the hands of the general populace, but, as Leonard Freedman (1969) has illustrated, lobby groups have often dominated local public housing controversies through expenditures on extensive mass-media campaigns.

Public housing site selection has also been controversial. In some central cities, such as Chicago, sites for conventional public housing have been largely restricted to black neighborhoods, in part because of opposition in white working-class neighborhoods plus the high cost of land in middle-class neighborhoods. In Chicago city council aldermen often have played a key role by vetoing proposed projects in individual aldermanic wards (*Yale Law Journal*, Chap. 8; Meyerson and Banfield, 1955).

While many studies of housing issues have been made, few have placed these issues within the broader framework of local decision-making structures. Robert Dahl (1961), in a study of New Haven, contends that overall no one group dominates the decision-making process but that different groups or individuals are influential in different sectors of public activity. With respect to urban renewal, the only housing-related issue studied, Dahl found that the mayor and his redevelopment team were the most important direct influence because organized interest groups were too weak and divided to initiate or coordinate development. Although their vigorous opposition might have blocked a proposed redevelopment project, a situation to test this capability never occurred. To the extent that business interests, banks, and Yale University were influential in New Haven's redevelopment program, their efforts were largely in the area of nondecisions (Bachrach and Baratz, 1970); that is, the mayor and his associates were careful to frame proposals they perceived to be within the realm of acceptability.

However, a recent study of Cambridge, Massachusetts, by John Mollenkopf and Jon Pynoos (Chap. 4) contends that virtually every local decision that bears on housing policy is dominated either directly or indirectly by large property and financial interests that succeed in achieving outcomes favorable to their private financial interests. Mollenkopf and Pynoos attribute these outcomes to the concentration of property ownership, the interlocking institutional networks that exist among owners, bankers, and politicians, and more generally to the private property system. They suggest it is this structure rather than simply their lack of political resources that thwarts efforts of poor and minority groups to affect the housing market and to implement government programs that might make less expensive and more adequate housing available. Further, they assert that any new housing programs to benefit the poor (including those that community groups control) that do not break down these structural relationships will only perpetuate the inequities in the present system.

Another major area of political controversy has been the administration of housing programs. Under the public housing program local authorities determine the number, location, and type of units to be built or leased. In addition, within the boundaries of federal requirements they have wide discretion in selecting applicants, assigning tenants to projects, determining rent levels, and evicting tenants. Policy usually is set by a five-member board of commissioners, in whom virtually all legal powers reside. A 1968 survey by Chester Hartman and Gregg Carr found a predominance of conservative interests among housing authority members—business executives and persons associated with banking and finance, insurance, and real estate (Hartman and Carr, 1969). The commissioners in no sense represented the interests of tenants or the low income population. For example, over 55 percent of all households in public housing were nonwhite, yet only 6 percent of the commissioners were nonwhite. The median income in public housing nationally was $3,132 for nonelderly housing and $1,468 for elderly housing, compared with $11,700 for commissioners. The survey found that to a great extent the commissioners were not advocates of increased public housing, even in its newer forms, such as leased and scattered-site housing. In direct contradiction to the tenants' desires for the removal of arbitrary and harmful rules, most commissioners felt that stricter regulations and enforcement mechanisms were needed. In addition, many of the commissioners displayed antagonistic attitudes toward the tenants themselves.

Because the poor and minority groups usually have lacked the numbers, money, skills, and status to be effective in lobbying efforts, they have often attempted to improve their housing conditions through the legal system. The last decade has seen increasing numbers of legal aid organizations and of class action suits brought on behalf of groups of poor and minority citizens in order to parlay a small amount of resources into a court decision that will affect a large number of people. Legal suits have covered such issues as exclusionary zoning, open housing, displacement by highways and urban renewal, entry into the construction trades, tenants' rights, and discrimination in housing admissions and site selection. For example, a suit brought against the Chicago Housing Authority on behalf of a group of tenants charged that the authority's site and tenant selection procedures were designed to perpetuate racial segregation of the housing market. A federal court ordered the authority to build small housing developments on scattered sites, primarily in white areas (*Yale Law Journal*, Chap. 8). However, for more than three years the City of Chicago has managed to evade the decree, and no new public housing has been constructed as a result of the court's action.

In some instances, frustrated by the slowness and ineffectiveness of more conventional political approaches, poor and minority groups have used organized group protest to focus the public's concern on their housing conditions and to increase their bargaining power. The targets of these protests often have been the program administration and housing management of both private and public landlords, and a major issue has been bias in the law itself. Landlord-tenant law has historically operated in favor of landlords and has not adequately recognized or sufficiently protected a tenant's status or interest in the apartment he rents (Garrity, Chap. 5). Existing legal remedies available to tenants have not been very effective because they usually have been invoked just prior to eviction or subsequent to departure from substandard premises.

In the 1960s tenant groups began organized protest activities aimed at changing landlord-tenant relations and improving their housing conditions. In New York City during 1963-64 this protest took the form of rent strikes, but these strikes did not bring substantial changes in the housing conditions of the poor, and the incremental improvements that did occur were not commensurate with the organizing effort (Marcuse, Chap. 3; Lipsky, 1970). This apparent failure has been attributed to the choice of targets (slum landlords) and tactics (long-term organizing) (Piven and Cloward, 1967). While some large absentee slumlords have profited greatly and may have the resources to renovate their buildings, small neighborhood landlords with limited capital who can take little advantage of the tax laws usually cannot make the necessary repairs without raising rents (Sternlieb, 1966). Moreover, the focus on individual landlords, who generally own only a few buildings, may limit the number of beneficiaries of any organizing effort. Rent withholding and rent receivership are quite complicated, require detailed knowledge of the law, and also force the tenants to go through lengthy bureaucratic procedures to avoid eviction. Against the powerful groups they oppose, tenants are at a severe disadvantage in terms of the skills and resources necessary to sustain this type of an effort.

The rent strikes that have reappeared recently in tenant efforts to improve living conditions in public housing have resulted in part from inadequate maintenance and deteriorating conditions, which in turn are attributable to the near-bankruptcy of large-city housing authorities (de Leeuw, 1970). This financial plight exists mainly because the original programs were designed to support the capital costs of constructing the physical plant but not the ongoing provision of housing services associated with safety, security, and comfort (Isler, 1971), such as adequate trash collection, police protection, lighting, landscaping, and recreation facilities. Until 1969 the federal government paid only the capital costs of public housing, but tenant incomes (and hence rents, which in public housing are based on ability to pay) have lagged behind rising maintenance costs. Recent changes in housing legislation prevent local authorities from charging rents of more than 25 percent of tenant income and provide for additional federal subsidy of operating costs; however, only limited funds have been appropriated to implement these changes (Nenno, 1970, 1971; Genung, 1970; Brooke, 1972).

The situation in public housing has resulted in rent strikes even larger than those that have occurred in private housing (Marcuse, Chap. 3).[4] In St. Louis over a thousand families staged an eight-month rent strike that ended in the appointment of a new Housing Authority Board consisting of two tenants and three nontenants selected by tenants and a group of civic associations. In addition, the residents elected a Tenants Affairs Board to arbitrate disputes between the authority and themselves.

Several factors contributed to the tenants' initial success in St. Louis. First, the financial plight of the Authority has made it very vulnerable to pressure for change. Second, the tenants were concentrated in a relatively small number of buildings operated by one landlord, a federally financed municipal agency, which suggests that the government as landlord may be more responsive to these tactics than are private landlords. Third, the tenants received political support and technical assistance from the St. Louis Civic Association, which included representatives from organized labor (notably the Teamsters).

Although the tenants do not control public housing in St. Louis, they have expanded their influence and share control with politically powerful allies. The advantages of this new role, particularly when it has resulted from the tenants' own political struggle, may be several. Participation may allow the administration of public housing to conform more closely to tenant preferences; involvement of those the program serves may result in a more positive attitude toward the care and upkeep of their housing; and increased participation may cause the local housing authority to employ a greater number of tenants. Finally, control of housing may increase tenants' capacity to bargain effectively for equitable shares of other public goods and services (Lipsky, Dickson, Mollenkopf, and Pynoos, 1971). Unfortunately, tenant control of public housing may lead only to the filing of bankruptcy papers on a public enterprise destined to fail. Local housing authorities have little power to obtain the funds needed significantly to improve the quality of life in public housing.

4. Michael Padnos, "The Tenant Movement," in Committee on Banking and Currency, U.S. House of Representatives, 92d Cong., 1st sess., *Papers Submitted to Subcommittee on Housing Panels* (Washington, D.C.: U.S. Government Printing Office, 1971), pt. 2, pp. 651-73. See also Al Hirshen and Vivian N. Brown, "Too Poor for Public Housing: Roger Starr's Poverty Preferences," *Social Policy* 3 (May-June 1972): 28-32. But see Roger Starr, "Which of the Poor Shall Live in Public Housing?" *The Public Interest*, no. 23 (Spring 1971): 116-24.

Tenant organizations have arisen in many cities, and a coalition of these groups, the National Tenants Organization (NTO), has been formed. Tenant organizations advocating their own interests in the political arena are an encouraging sign, although to see their influence in perspective one must compare them with other lobbying groups, such as the National Association of Home Builders with its large, well-paid staff and close political connections (Lilley, Chap. 2). NTO's most visible impact thus far has been HUD's acceptance of it as the legitimate spokesman for public housing tenants. NTO has worked with HUD and NAHRO on the development of a model lease and grievance procedure to safeguard the rights of tenants and to provide them with fair hearings, but perhaps its most significant contribution will be to increase tenant awareness of more basic issues, such as program control and income redistribution.

Resolution of specific housing conflicts can take place only within the context of a more general urban policy, particularly with respect to race and residence. Few issues are closer to the raw nerves of this country than racial integration, particularly residential integration, where housing policy and programs meet their most severe test. In April 1970 over 14.3 million nonwhites, 13.1 million of whom were blacks, lived in central cities (U.S. Bureau of the Census, 1971), highly segregated residentially from the rest of the population (Taeuber and Taeuber, 1965). Recent tabulations of 1970 census data for the city of Boston show that a single large ghetto contains over 90 percent of the city's nonwhite population, which includes a range of income groups (Boston Redevelopment Authority, 1971), and 1970 data also indicated that 15 central cities had populations that were more than 40 percent nonwhite (U.S. Bureau of the Census, 1971). If current policies continue, segregation will remain along with the concentrations of poverty. Faced with this problem and recognizing the growth of black militancy, urban policy analysts have advocated either integration or ghetto enrichment as alternative strategies to improve the situation of blacks and other racial minorities.

Advocates of the ghetto enrichment approach reject integration as a realistic goal at present and point to the ineffectiveness of liberal coalitions in attaining this objective through legislation, investigative agencies, fair housing committees, public subsidies, the courts, and employment plans (Piven and Cloward, Chap. 7). Further, in the relatively few situations where integration has been tried ghetto enrichment supporters claim that the limited successes have cost too much in terms of hostility against blacks. In addition, the political feasibility of a truly integrative approach is questioned because of the large number of blacks and whites who would have to move in order to bring about racially heterogeneous communities.

Black power exponents conclude that integration can occur only after blacks have gained sufficient self-respect and political and economic power to force the white majority to make concessions (Piven and Cloward, Chap. 7; Carmichael and Hamilton, 1967).[5] They suggest that the most practical way to begin to acquire such self-respect and power within the existing political framework is through black-controlled communities and institutions. Such control requires the existence of political jurisdictions in which blacks comprise a majority of the population and, hence, can elect a majority of black representatives. Proposals for metropolitanization, which threaten to dilute central city power, are therefore viewed with suspicion (Piven and Cloward, 1967). The actions of black-controlled local governments would favor blacks and allow them

5. See also Alan Altshuler, *Community Control* (New York: Western Publishing Co., 1970); and Martin Duberman, "Black Power in America," *Partisan Review* 35 (Winter 1968): 34-68.

to gain an economic foothold through jobs in public agencies, city contracts, the development of minority businesses, and the growth of community development corporations (Edel, 1970). One key element of such an approach would be the improvement of conditions in the ghetto itself through the creation of community institutions to plan, build, renovate, own, and manage housing.

Analysts who support the integrationist strategy, though, argue that several political and economic factors limit the ghetto enrichment strategy. Although protest activity and bloc voting have recently proved to be effective tactics for blacks, integrationists believe that continued efforts along these lines may threaten the coalition of groups whose support is necessary to obtain additional federal funds for such programs as housing, education, and income maintenance. Some analysts feel that escalation of militant activity could set the stage for racial confrontation between communities of blacks and whites (National Advisory Commission on Civil Disorders, Chap. 6; Downs, 1970), and that the political and economic power obtainable through an enrichment strategy is somewhat illusory because of the depleted resources of core cities, the continuing exodus of businesses, and the dependence of communities on white-owned corporations that dominate the urban economy. Integration is also viewed as a prerequisite to equality in jobs, schools, and housing. For example, the increasing suburbanization of jobs places a geographical constraint on the employment of blacks who live in centrally located ghettos (Kain, 1968); school desegregation will ultimately require residential integration or a vastly different organization of the educational system; and a policy of enriching only the ghetto would provide better housing for its residents but not the range and variety of housing services available in white suburbs.

It may be possible to devise a strategy that combines the elements of both approaches. For minority members who want suburban living, justice requires some kind of dispersal program, and dispersal is necessary to avoid perpetuation of two separate and markedly unequal societies. Dispersal could be of the segregated or integrated variety, the first represented by the growth of separate white and black suburban areas, the second involving racial integration throughout the metropolitan area. However, given the time necessary to implement a dispersal strategy, the belief of many that black power is a precondition to integration, and the central city ties that many blacks have, an enrichment program also will be necessary. It must be emphasized that contrary to present policies both strategies will require strong government action because of prevailing racial discrimination and existing inequalities among black and white communities.

REFERENCES

Altshuler, Alan. *Community Control*. New York: Western Publishing Co., 1970.
Bachrach, Peter, and Baratz, Morton. *Power and Poverty: Theory and Practice*. New York: Oxford University Press, 1970.
Boston Redevelopment Authority. *Analysis of Census Information: Population by Race 1950-1970*. July 1971.
Brooke, Edward. "How New Public Housing Rent Reductions and Operating Subsidies Will be Funded by HUD." *Journal of Housing* 29 (March, 1972): 69-71.
Carmichael, S., and Hamilton, C. V. *Black Power: The Politics of Liberation*. New York: Vintage, 1967.
Dahl, Robert. *Who Governs?* New Haven, Conn.: Yale University Press, 1961.
deLeeuw, Frank. *Operating Costs in Public Housing: A Financial Crisis*. Washington, D.C.: Urban Institute, 1970.
Downs, Anthony. "Alternative Futures for the American Ghetto." *Urban Problems and Prospects*. Chicago: Markham, 1970.

Duberman, Martin. "Black Power in America." *Partisan Review*, 35 (Winter, 1968); 34-68.

Edel, Matthew. "Development vs. Dispersal: Approaches to Ghetto Poverty." *Readings in Urban Economics*, ed. Matthew Edel and Jerome Rothenberg. New York: Macmillan, 1970: 307-24.

Foard, Ashley A., and Fefferman, Hilbert. "Federal Urban Renewal Legislation." *Law and Contemporary Problems* 25 (Autumn, 1960): 635-84.

Freedman, Leonard. *Public Housing: The Politics of Poverty*. New York: Holt, Rinehart and Winston, 1969.

Frieden, Bernard J. "Improving Federal Housing Subsidies: Summary Report." Committee on Banking and Currency, U.S. House of Representatives, 92d Cong., 1st sess., *Papers Submitted to Subcommittee on Housing Panels*. Washington, D.C.: U.S. Government Printing Office, 1971: Pt. 2, 473-88.

Friedman, Lawrence. *Government and Slum Housing*. Chicago: Rand McNally, 1968.

Genung, George R., Jr. "Where Have We Come with the Brooke Amendment?" *Journal of Housing* 27 (June 1970): 232-35.

Hartman, Chester and Carr, Gregg. "Housing Authorities Reconsidered." *Journal of the American Institute of Planners* 35 (January 1969): 10-21.

Isler, Morton. "The Goals of Housing Subsidy Programs." Committee on Banking and Currency. U.S. House of Representatives, 92d Cong., 1st sess., *Papers Submitted to Subcommittee on Housing Panels*. Washington, D.C.: U.S. Government Printing Office, 1971: Pt. 2, 415-24.

Kain, John F. "Housing Segregation, Negro Employment, and Metropolitan Decentralization." *Quarterly Journal of Economics* 82 (May 1968): 175-97.

Lipsky, Michael. *Protest in City Politics*. Chicago: Rand McNally, 1970.

Lipsky, Michael; Dickson, Donald; Mollenkopf, John; and Pynoos, Jon. "Citizen Participation in Federal Housing Policies." Committee on Banking and Currency, U.S. House of Representatives, 92d Cong., 1st sess., *Papers Submitted to Subcommittee on Housing Panels*. Washington, D.C.: U.S. Government Printing Office, 1971: Pt. 2, 895-926.

Meyerson, Martin, and Banfield, Edward C. *Politics, Planning, and the Public Interest*. New York: The Free Press, 1955.

Meyerson, Martin; Terrett, Barbara; and Wheaton, William L. C. *Housing, People, and Cities*. New York: McGraw-Hill, 1962: 269-87.

Miller, S. M. "Criteria for Anti-Poverty-Policies: A Paradigm for Choice." *Poverty and Human Resources Abstracts*, 3 (September-October 1968): 3-11.

Nenno, Mary. "Housing and Urban Development Act of 1969." *Journal of Housing* 27 (January 1970): 14-17.

Nenno, Mary. "Housing and Urban Development Legislation of 1970." *Journal of Housing* 28 (January 1971): 17-18.

Piven, Frances, and Cloward, Richard. "Black Control of Cities: Heading It Off by Metropolitan Government." *The New Republic*. 157 (September 30, 1967), 19-21 and *The New Republic* (October 7, 1967), 15-19.

Piven, Frances, and Cloward, Richard. "Rent Strike: Disrupting the Slum System." *The New Republic* (December 2, 1967).

Sternlieb, George. *The Tenement Landlord*. New Brunswick, N. J.: Rutgers, 1966.

Taeuber, Karl E., and Taeuber, Alma F. *Negroes in Cities: Residential Segregation and Neighborhood Change*. Chicago: Aldine, 1965.

U.S. Bureau of the Census. *Census of Population and Housing: 1970. General Demographic Trends for Metropolitan Areas, 1960 to 1970*. Final report PHC (2)-1. *United States*. Washington, D. C.: Government Printing Office, 1971: Tables 1, 10.

1. Social Class and Housing Reform

LAWRENCE M. FRIEDMAN

. . . [T]he welfare approach[1] [to analyzing the slum] has been a useful catalyst, a goad to the national conscience. By itself, it has rarely succeeded in passing a law; it needs allies. Nor does zeal alone ensure that a program will remain vital, actively enforced, and responsive to new needs. Passion is transient; interest remains. By and large, in the history of government and housing, welfare-oriented legislation has not had staying power, unless it could enlist in its aid some coalition of groups with a strong nonwelfare stake or a bureaucracy with a vested stake in keeping the program alive.

The urban poor, by and large, are not such a powerful interest group. They are a numerous tribe, and they vote; they have, therefore, some political power. But the history of housing legislation strongly suggests that little action so far can be traced directly to the political strength of the urban masses. The poor may be underrepresented in legislatures; their political representatives may be corrupt or corruptible. Even aside from these considerations, the urban poor (those who would benefit from programs to remedy slum housing conditions) have been too few and too weak to have their way against the opposition of the middle class.[2] Significantly, the first, major federal housing program was enacted during the New Deal period (1933-1937) when, alas, tremendous numbers of new and unwilling recruits joined the ranks of the unemployed, the underemployed, and the marginally employed. Millions of the new poor were culturally members of the middle class who had fallen from economic grace after 1929. Many of these were articulate, educated people; they were used to a better way of life. As a whole, these people were better equipped to demand measures of alleviation than the lowest group of the urban poor before or since. The later career of public housing also attests, in a negative way, the power of influence and numbers. The war, of course, interrupted housing construction. Afterward, the housing energies of government were diverted to the quite distinct task of providing "veterans' housing"—housing for the benefit of a large, powerful, articulate, and by no means poverty-stricken group. In the period of postwar prosperity, public housing lost most of its middleclass clientele. With the decline of veterans' housing, the program suffered from failure of momentum; it survived in an arrested form, while the urban renewal program—middle-class and social-cost oriented[3]—took the

Reprinted from Lawrence M. Friedman, *Government and Slum Housing* (Chicago: Rand McNally, 1968), pp. 14-16, 180-82, 191-94 (edited), by permission of the publisher and author. Lawrence M. Friedman is a professor of law at Stanford University.

1. Editors' note: This approach defines the slum in terms of the costs the slum imposes on the people who live in it. L. M. Friedman, *Government and Slum Housing* (Chicago: Rand McNally, 1968) p. 4.

2. Majority rule, of course, is much more than a matter of a headcount. Other factors, such as the intensity of positions taken by those with a voice in the question, are equally important. For the purposes of this general discussion, however, these other factors will be ignored.

3. Editors' note: Social cost refers to a definition of slums in terms of the costs the slums imposes on society at large. L. M. Friedman, *Government and Slum Housing* (Chicago: Rand McNally, 1968) p. 4.

center of the stage. Public housing has begun to show signs of life again under the auspices of the war against poverty or at least as a by-product of the recent, fresh infusion of welfare passion. . . .

[After reviewing recent efforts aimed at improving housing conditions, Professor Friedman continues with an analysis of what these efforts imply for the future.]

. . . [T]he very fact of an outpouring of plans, proposals, demonstration projects, pilot projects, bills, laws, rules, schemes, devices, and propositions is an important *new* fact. Some proposed techniques will turn out to be better than others. None of the techniques in themselves are likely to be true solutions to the housing problem. The cumulation of them all is no solution either, but is a symptom of a *will* to succeed, which is tremendously important, and perhaps also of an inclination to devote the necessary resources, which is the *sine qua non* of success. The housing problem is not going to be solved by gimmicks, but by spending enough money on very simple things. The curse of American housing movements has been inadequate cash. Even anti-slumlord campaigns . . . can be analyzed as symptoms of public miserliness. It is an infinitely cheaper response to a concrete problem to pass a law and blame somebody else. If rats are a slum problem, it is cheaper to make rats a crime and landlords criminals than to take positive public action against rats. Moreover, if the rats are not eliminated, the "criminals" can be blamed and the public absolved. Public housing, in the broad sense, is the only program which might perhaps *actually* provide a significant supply of decent homes for people below the poverty level. Other programs, such as code enforcement, are not inherently incapable of making a major contribution. But they are less likely to do this because they are so strongly imbued with notions of fault and attempt to place the moral and financial burden on private shoulders.

The *scale* of housing reform is a critical factor, too, in that it indicates a shift in the alignment of political forces in regard to housing. One major point made in this study is that the problem of slum housing can be in part reduced to a problem of political leverage. The dependent poor and the Negroes have never had much social and economic power. Laws have sometimes been passed *for* them, to be sure, but usually much compromised and weakened in passage or in administration. In the age of the war against poverty, government claims to be willing to spend time, energy, and money to eliminate poverty. Logically, much of this time, energy, and money ought to go toward solving the problem of the slums. The cynic will remind us, however, of many past wars against poverty. The history of housing reform is a history of such wars. They have usually ended in stalemate. This war may be no different. Misdirection and indirection are frequent in the history of so-called welfare laws.

Despite all the setbacks of the past, there are reasons for guarded optimism in the 1960s. The first of these is the militancy of the poor, particularly of the Negro poor. The militancy arose and remains strongest in the civil rights movement; but it has spilled over into other areas. The rent strikes are an example. Militancy, of course, may be and often is maddening, misguided, and ultimately self-defeating. The poor may use new-gained power only to create a whole new set of problems. The poor may turn out to foolishly misconceive their long-term self-interest and perhaps even their short-term self-interest. Yet through militant action the poor gain a chance to state forcefully their views and their wishes. And militancy may succeed by persuading the white, middle class majority that its own self-interest requires concessions in order to avoid continued riots and confusions—a cruel but necessary calculus. In any given case, success depends upon the precise demands that are made, upon the skill of the leadership, upon the social and economic costs that the whites are asked to incur, and upon how these costs compare with the costs of resistance.

In addition, reform forces committed to the war against poverty were never stronger. Reformers have made many errors in the past; but they have played an indispensable role. Reform is difficult, and perhaps impossible, on welfare grounds alone; yet reform is unthinkable without reformers. There are plenty of them today, and they are supported by powerful interests within government and in foundations, universities, and church organizations. The academic community, the philanthropic community, the enlightened bureaucratic community—each seems more powerful today than in the past. Churches, too, have awakened to preach the social gospel again. The official war against poverty, for all its blunders and hypocrisies, is a hopeful symptom. The new Department of Housing and Urban Development symbolizes increased governmental sensitivity to housing problems. . . .

SOCIAL CLASS AND SOCIAL WELFARE

Laws *for* the poor, we have suggested, are unlikely to be generated unless (*a*) the poor are a majority and have fair and adequate political representatives, or (*b*) on balance, proposed legislation serves the interests of some class larger and broader than the poor. The history of American housing law suggests that the second condition has been much more important in the genesis of housing policy than the first. The early tenement house laws were buttressed by social cost arguments. Public-housing laws first appeared in a few states in the 1920's as laws to stimulate the establishment of "homesteads" among sturdy yeomen of the lower middle class. The federal housing program of the 1930's made jobs for workers and contracts for manufacturers with idle plants; in addition, the Depression added millions of new, if unwilling, recruits to the lower orders of society. When increased prosperity removed the conditions for passage of the original program, political support for public housing melted like butter in the sun. The shift in emphasis to veterans' housing and then to housing for the elderly finds at least a plausible, partial explanation in considerations of the social and economic interests of groups other than the dependent urban poor. The urban renewal program uses the plight of the poor for propaganda purposes; but the size and character of urban renewal is determined by other interests—e.g., downtown merchants, university presidents, city officials—united only by a common desire to use federal money for their own ends. Model tenement house programs turn out to be lower-middle-class programs. Even in the midst of the "war against poverty," the Johnson Administration introduced a supposedly radical, new, rent-supplement bill—designed for the lower middle class. (Congress removed this feature.)

There should be no cause for surprise in these facts. The United States is a middle-class nation and will remain so. However one defines poverty, the poor are a minority of the nation. The middle class is so numerous that the "general good" is apt to be identified with middle-class interests. Mobility into the middle class has always been high enough to make this equation tolerable to the potential middle class. The concept of class, indeed, is repugnant to Americans both on ideological and pragmatic grounds. The idea that America is classless is at least halfway plausible by virtue of the sheer weight of numbers of those with some stake in the economy. The interests of the urban dependent poor are minority interests.

Moreover, the middle class is white, and the lower class is disproportionately Negro. What bargain, realistically, can the poor, urban Negro strike? He can hardly achieve goals which conflict with the strong material interests of major economic forces in this society and especially with the vital interests of his reluctant white neighbors of the lower middle class. These neighbors deeply cherish the value of their homes and the stability of their neighborhoods. Whether or not the presence of poor people or Negroes around the corner impairs or ought to impair these values,[4] clearly people *think* that they do. Moreover, largely for ignoble reasons, millions of whites are uncomfortable or worse in the presence of Negroes. They are also uncomfortable in the neighborhood presence of "inferiors" in culture or cash. Income and race segregation have been powerful villains in housing history. Public housing has suffered terribly from their effects. Majority interests have denied public housing its best sites and boxed it into urban ghettos, effecting unfortunate results for the poor and for the public housing program. Those safely outside the ghetto walls have, in the past, been willing to tolerate the existence of a ghetto. Urban renewal capitalizes on the harm and disgust that the ghetto evokes; but it is not a response derived from or conducive to social justice.

Are the slums then incurable, short of revolutionary change? The answer is not necessarily "No." Social change has not been impossible in this country; quite to the contrary, social change has been rapid and unceasing. Indeed, one chronic source of the current problem of the slums lies in the constant upgrading of the working class to the point where the really poor are a national minority. One reason the poor lack political leverage is because so much political and economic power is in the hands of the masses who are *not* poor and, indeed, are rather hostile to the poor. The working class has achieved striking gains at the bargaining table, in the market, and in the legislative forum. In the late nineteenth and early twentieth centuries, the working classes used industrial unrest as a tool of bargaining—they raised the price of social order. A strike is a cost to business just as it is to labor. Over the course of years, various groups and interests have asserted claims to legislative attention, claims that sharply conflicted with each other. In time, elaborate compromises have been worked out in the form of programs emanating from farm bills, labor bills, bills for and against business, bills appealing to or unattractive to doctors, lawyers, barbers, bakers, and countless other groups. Each articulate interest has staked a claim and, quite frequently, succeeded in winning a share of legal protection or subsidy. The legal system is largely built up of a constant, shifting succession of compromises between demands of interest groups, taking the form of legislative programs. In this series of compromises, the lowest class—i.e., the very poor—has been conspicuously underrepresented. The poor have had neither the power nor the numbers to assert their claims with success. Consequently much "welfare" legislation is really for unionized workers, for the submerged middle class, for the half-poor or the pseudo-poor, or is so riddled with measures aimed at quarantining the larger society from by-products of poverty that the *true* interests of the poor, whatever they are, are entirely left out of calculation.

As we have mentioned, the way is open to the poor to achieve some goals by raising the price of good behavior. The poor have the power to harass, to annoy, to riot, and to picket. They may make plenary use of their power to disrupt, of their vote, of their small but definite economic power, and of the impact of domestic problems on foreign affairs. Not least of all, they may appeal to the conscience and invoke classic American values. An uneasy conscience is unpleasant and therefore a burden to its owner; he may be willing to take some action to put an end to the pangs of the heart. Some people—those only slightly opposed to a given reform—can sometimes be called upon to change their minds in the name of conscience.

Many reformers are at work today to enlist the neutrals on the side of the poor.

---

4. See, on this question, Luigi Laurenti, *Property Values and Race* (Berkeley: University of California Press, 1960).

Some nonreform interests are tending in the same direction, e.g., status-group interests and even the desire of political leaders, such as the President, to make a name in history by solving major social problems. Ranged on the opposite side are groups with interests in the status quo. It is by no means clear that the tactics of the poor, on or off the streets, are proper and effective ones. A riot may provoke appeasement if the majority is convinced that the price of civil order has been effectively raised and that the minority must be bought off with reforms. It provokes suppression if the majority feels the price is too high, that is, that the only reforms which would end unrest impinge too dearly or directly on the interests of the majority. Or, by enraging the good neutral citizens, a riot may destroy the necessary reform coalition and encourage formation of a coalition of suppression. Genuine reform through legislation is politically possible; the housing problems of the poor can be solved even though the poor are a minority; but a solution will not *necessarily* come around.

2. *The Homebuilders' Lobby*

WILLIAM LILLEY III

For 50 dollars a year, the small homebuilder—the generic American builder-speculator-developer who constructs fewer than 25 units per year—gets one of the best lobbying bargains in Washington: membership in the National Association of Home Builders.

NAHB is at a membership peak of 51,602. It commands broad expertise and influence. Government officials and lobbyists close to the housing field regard NAHB as the most effective pressure group concerned with housing and urban development, and one of the most effective in all Washington.

Nathaniel H. Rogg, top Washington staff official for NAHB, has said that the lobby's mandate is "to reflect the views of thousands of small homebuilders regarding public policy."

Declining to be identified by name, a top staff member for the House Banking and Currency Committee, which handles much of the authorization legislation for housing matters, recognized the NAHB's effectiveness.

"I don't like them," he said, "but I'd still have to say that they're damn competent. They're at the very top when it comes to lobbying clout in Washington, especially because they're strong on both sides of the aisle and not confined mostly to Democrats, like organized labor."

A southern Republican in Congress who does not support many of NAHB's favorite programs and resents the lobby's aggressive armtwisting still gave the homebuilders high marks.

"When they get cranked up for something, they're really effective— telegrams, phone calls and constituent contacts from someone you know. You just can't shrug something like that off," said the member, who asked not to be identified.

Credit and Subsidies

Rep. Robert N. Giaimo, D-Conn., described NAHB as "basically single-family-housing guys who want more and cheaper mortgage money and more FHA subsidies. They do a good job of getting both. In fact, we have been full funding their programs."

A seven-term representative, Giaimo is a member of the body which controls housing program subsidies—the House Appropriations Subcommittee for HUD-Space-Science.

Rep. Thomas L. Ashley, D-Ohio, a nine-term member of the House Banking and Currency Subcommittee on Housing, described NAHB as "a bunch of guys with a heterogeneous membership—a strange breed made up mostly of small builders, a few big builders, some realtors, some land speculators, some mortgage bankers, almost anyone associated with residential housing."

"Historically, they have worked to soften the government up so it's a patsy for tight money bail-outs," Ashley said. "Recently, they have gotten religion about govern-

Reprinted by permission from William Lilley III, "Washington Pressures/Home Builders' Lobbying Skills Result in Successes, 'Good-guy' Image," *National Journal*, February 27, 1971, pp. 431-45 (edited). The *National Journal* is a nonpartisan weekly publication that reports on principals and pressures creating federal policy changes.

ment subsidies. Before, they used to be opposed to government intervention for all kinds of ideological reasons. Now, they've flopped over and are making a good thing of it. They really hustle the Southerners in Congress for the subsidies and the cheap mortgage credit. Thus, guys like Sparkman, Tower, Al Rains and Bob Stephens become their champions."

(Sen. John Sparkman, D-Ala., is chairman of the Senate Banking, Housing and Urban Affairs Committee; and Sen. John G. Tower, R-Tex., is the committee's ranking minority member; former Rep. [1945-65] Albert M. Rains, D-Ala., was the influential chairman of the Housing Subcommittee from 1955 to 1965; and Rep. Robert G. Stephens, D-Ga., is a six-term member of the Housing Subcommittee.)

Further Effectiveness

The homebuilding lobby has earned its high marks principally for success in two areas: pressuring the federal government to adopt monetary policies which give preferential treatment to mortgage credit; getting federal subsidies for the production of new housing.

But NAHB has had success in other undertakings as well: negotiating with the federal bureaucracy over regulations affecting the housing industry; maintaining the image—and influence—of an industry-wide spokesman, despite the increasing number of associations in the housing field; reporting frequently and diversely to its specialized builder membership and to the Washington political community on federal activities affecting the housing industry.

Joseph B. McGrath, top lobbyist for NAHB, said: "In spite of the increasing range and complexity of federal actions affecting housing in the last decade, and in spite of the formation of spinoff associations in the housing field—such as the Home Manufacturers Association, the Council of Housing Producers and the Mobile Home Manufacturers Association—the NAHB has continued to speak as the homebuilders' voice in Washington. Even with the formation of these new trade associations, NAHB has such a momentum and weight to it that it remains the principal voice of the industry. All the guys in the spinoff operations remain active members of NAHB. Their organizations act in a supportive way with us rather than in a competitive way."

NAHB's claim to top rating among Washington lobbies is a recent development. Not until the late 1960s was NAHB's muscle evident, after the lobby had shifted ideologically from opposition to support of federal subsidies for housing production.

Ideological Shift

At the 1961 annual convention, for the first time since NAHB's inception in 1942, the homebuilders dropped from the yearly "NAHB policy statement" their traditional attack on the public housing program.

By the mid-1960s, the homebuilders had moved from neutrality to active collaboration with big city mayors and with the Johnson Administration in pushing for enactment of Great Society programs.

Led by Fort Worth, Tex., builder Larry Blackmon (a close friend of Mr. Johnson, who was elected NAHB president in 1966), NAHB provided important support in the House for model cities and rent supplements, two of Mr. Johnson's major Great Society programs.

"NAHB got a new breed of builder-president beginning in 1966—one more hospitable to the public sector," said a staff member for the Housing Subcommittee. "At the same time Rogg, also a political activist, took over the Washington staff."

Administration Response

The Nixon Administration has favored the home builders with two major actions to encourage home construction: It committed $13 billion through the Federal National Mortgage Association and the Government National Mortgage Association during a period of tight money in 1970 to increase the supply of mortgage credit. It committed in the fiscal 1972 budget $450 million in subsidies for the homeownership and rental assistance programs. Enacted in 1968 as Sections 235 and 236 of the National Housing Act (12 USC 1715z, 1715z-1), the two programs have become staples of the NAHB's membership during tight money periods.

The President's role. Charles W. Colson, special counsel to the President, said, "Mr. Nixon called in their top people in January 1970—they flew up from their convention in Houston to meet with him—when things were looking bad for housing. During the meeting the President ordered that housing be given top priority. He said he wanted priority support for the mortgage market, full funding for the subsidy programs, and top Administration backing for the Emergency Home Finance bill. He also instructed Romney and other agency heads to cooperate with certain home-builder procedural requests."

Rogg said that he and former NAHB president (1970) Louis R. Barba, a Chatham, N. J., builder with close Republican connections, "flew up by Lear jet, got a lengthy Presidential audience, and then a Presidential commitment to make housing a top national priority. Administration actions followed in 1970 so that housing did not become the casualty it had in the past when anti-inflationary policies were being imposed."

NAHB and HUD. An aide to HUD Secretary George W. Romney said, "We have no problems taking care of the home builders. Both HUD and the home builders are moving in the same direction.

"Romney himself, with his own production orientation, has a classic home builders outlook. Nor would I be surprised to see Gene Gulledge go back to the home builders after he leaves his HUD job. He wouldn't have to change his outlook one bit, if he was to move from FHA back to NAHB tomorrow."

(Eugene A. Gulledge, assistant secretary for housing production and mortgage credit, and FHA commissioner, was president of NAHB when President Nixon appointed him in October 1969 to his assistant secretaryship. Long active in local, regional and national home builder politics, Gulledge was a successful homebuilder in Greensboro, N.C.)

Modus Operandi

John C. Williamson, the chief lobbyist for the National Association of Real Estate Boards (NAREB)—the most frequent opponent of NAHB in struggles with Congress and the bureaucracy—said that "the home builders are successful because they are wedded to the subsidy concept and to the increased involvement of the government in their business. Whereas the realtors care philosophically about the percent of government involvement, the home builders don't."

No enemies. "For example, we entered the open housing battle and were the only ones to really fight it," Williamson said. "They stayed out of it. That way we made the enemies and they didn't. Instances like that occur repeatedly. Because they support the principle of an expanding government, they start out with HUD behind them.

And because they generally go along with more and more liberal programs, and more and more government subsidies, they always start out with a lot of friends in this town."

Emphasis on committees. "They make their greatest achievements in committees," said Williamson, "and they do everything they can to avoid a floor fight. A real mark of their skill is their ability to have decisions made which are favorable to them in authorization committee, appropriations committee, or in conference committee.

"This is where their influence is strongest and where they can make the most of Sparkman and Tower, who are their big housing-production allies. Let's face it, they have set themselves up to do this. Their No. 2 lobbyist—Carl Coan Jr.—is the son of Carl Coan Sr., who is staff director for the Senate Housing and Urban Affairs Subcommittee. I'm envious; I'd like to have someone like that working for me."

A top staff member of the House Banking and Currency Committee said that NAHB's influence is no less pervasive on the House side: "Whenever something is proposed during executive session, all the members ask right away, 'What do the Home Builders think of it?' "

Richard K. Cook, who handles White House legislative liaison with the House of Representatives, said, "The home builders are really in close with their Banking and Currency Committees and their appropriations subcommittees. And they have a high degree of success with them. They're one of the classic examples of an expert lobby that takes the long view and therefore one good reason why so little changes in this town from year to year.

"Presidents come and go in the eyes of the really professional lobbies. They know where their bread is buttered, and they won't sidle up to a President unless he is really running the Congress. Instead, they always go to where they will be doing business six or seven years from now.

"Lobbies like the home builders have their own pet committees and their own GS-17s, and they all know each other. That's why something like the President's reorganization reforms—which would scramble those relationships—will require a real fight."

Muffled oars. A great measure of the lobby's success can be attributed to its technique of rowing with muffled oars. NAHB makes its big gains in the quiet arena of·committees or lobby coalitions.

"I am a great believer in not exhausting our credits," said Rogg. "I consider myself a personal friend of every HUD Secretary, every chairman of the Federal Reserve System, and every chairman of the Council of Economic Advisers. They remain as my friends because we don't pester them on every issue.

"We let them know that we are trying to understand their problems, and that's why we hold our fire whenever we see something in the press which could be interpreted as hostile to us. We always check it out with their people. And because we store up our credits, they know that when we do want to see them about something, then there is an issue of real substance involved."

Selectivity. According to several committee staff members, NAHB always gets a little extra attention because it limits its demands.

An aide to Sen. Sparkman said: "When the time comes to work on the annual omnibus bill, all the interested groups submit laundry lists of what they want. Most of them, like the National Housing Conference's list, are just too long and therefore self-defeating. The smarter lobbies like the home builders and the U.S. Savings and Loan League keep their lists limited. That way they get more attention and they end up with a higher batting average."

LEGISLATIVE BRANCH LOBBYING

Rogg said that in lobbying the legislative branch, NAHB stresses only those issues where the small individual entrepreneurs in homebuilding can combine to speak with some degree of authority.

NAHB officials rationalize the lobby's demands upon Congress as tending to increase housing production and, thereby, the nation's housing supply.

Natural Allies

By knitting all NAHB demands to the congressionally mandated national goal of stepped-up housing production, "we keep ourselves always on the side of the angels as far as issues are concerned," said Burton C. Wood, a lobbyist for NAHB. "Almost no one wants ever to tangle with us because then they'll end up looking like they're against housing."

Making housing into a "motherhood" issue has paid off handsomely with Congress, especially with members from southern and small-town backgrounds. These congressmen are what an aide to Sen. Vance Hartke, D-Ind., called, "the ideological friends of homebuilding."

Small-towner sympathies. "Hartke himself is a small-town guy who believes that everyone who really wants to should own his home and that the government should do everything within reason to help him," the aide said. "That's why he uses his leverage on the Senate Finance Committee to push for lower interest rates and other cheap credit mechanisms. As a result, Hartke and Indiana homebuilder groups have become good friends, even though the state and local builder organizations used to be Republican-oriented. Twice a year now, delegations of Indiana home builders come here and meet with Hartke in his office."

Southern support. "In the South the home builders are more a part of the political-economic power structure than they are in other, more developed areas of the country," said a staff member of Sparkman's Senate Banking, Housing and Urban Affairs Committee.

Of the 484 local homebuilder associations in the nation, 172, or 36 percent, are in the 11 southern states of the Old Confederacy.

"That's why Chairman Sparkman has always been a housing man. Construction, FHA, the building industry—that's his great love; he knows the programs well and he knows the homebuilders well. Compared to his interest in housing, Sparkman is much less interested in urban development programs, and he knows the mayors hardly at all compared to his relationships with the homebuilders," the Sparkman aide said.

Friendships and affinities. A staff member of the House Banking and Currency Committee said: "One reason why the home builders have clout is because every Congressman probably has at least one local home builder who is a good friend and who can really talk to him. This becomes magnified with Congressmen from the South, the Southwest and Southern California—the growing parts of the country—because the home builders are disproportionately strong there compared with their membership from areas like the New England states. Thus, they have become strong with Sparkman and Tower on the Senate side and guys like Rains, Stephens and Hanna on the House side."

(Rep. Richard T. Hanna, D-Calif., a five-term Democrat from Orange County, has received strong local backing from Southern California homebuilder organizations in several close contests for reelection, according to House committee staff members and NAHB lobbyists.)

Picking Up Friends

While working southern and small-town congressmen for subsidies and liberal mortgage credit on the basis of their ideological friendship to housing production, the NAHB has been careful since 1965 to cultivate a "good guy" image with urban congressmen and the Washington press.

McGrath said that the lobby has deliberately cultivated an "aggressively constructive" image during Rogg's tenure.

In a speech in August 1967, which was handsomely reprinted and widely circulated by the Washington office, Rogg related instances of high-ranking federal officials —President Johnson among them—speaking of NAHB as one of Washington's most "constructive" and public-spirited trade associations. "Our organization has developed an image and a credibility with these officials and with the press of which all of us can indeed be proud," Rogg said.

Giving assistance. Not only is NAHB promoting its goal of housing production as being in urban America's interest; it also makes a point of assisting public interest lobbies, such as the National League of Cities-U.S. Conference of Mayors, on urban development programs in which the homebuilders' interest is an indirect one.

"We used to disagree strongly with them on many issues and particularly on public housing," said John J. Gunther, executive director of the U.S. Conference of Mayors, "but now we work hand-in-glove with them, probably closer with them than any other business group. They've had considerable success in approaching issues so that what is good for the home builders can be defended persuasively as being good for the public interest. Nowadays the mayors and the homebuilders have the same goal—more housing."

Back scratching. Since much of the federal government's housing legislation is consolidated in the annual omnibus housing and urban development bill, the homebuilders help the city lobbies on urban development issues, and the mayors help the builders on housing issues.

Meetings. To keep that relationship in fighting trim, Rogg said, he and Patrick Healy, executive vice president of the National League of Cities, chair monthly meetings of the "housing information group," which keeps the allies up to date on political events in the housing and urban development field. Member organizations are NAHB, the National League of Cities-U.S. Conference of Mayors, the National Association of Counties, the Council of State Governments, the National Association of Real Estate Boards, the American Bankers Association, the U.S. Savings and Loan League and the National Forest Products Association. The meetings are held at NAHB headquarters.

A comparable meeting of the "big five" lobbies interested in mortgage credit legislation also convenes on a bimonthly basis at NAHB headquarters. Members of that group are NAHB, NAREB, the U.S. Savings and Loan League, the Mortgage Bankers Association and the National Association of Mutual Savings Banks. Rogg said the American Bankers Association and the National Forest Products Association occasionally send representatives.

LEGISLATIVE RECORD

Starting slowly in 1965 and gaining influence steadily through 1970, NAHB has been able to compile an impressive list of lobbying triumphs.

Rent Supplements

In 1965, NAHB was instrumental in the enactment of rent supplements legislation (12 USC 1701s). This was NAHB's first active lobbying effort in support of subsidized housing programs and testified to the influence of Larry Blackmon, a large-volume builder of low and moderate income housing who was then vice president of NAHB. Blackmon used his chairmanship of NAHB's legislative committee in 1965 "to move the organization in a much more politically liberal direction," a House Banking and Currency Committee staff member said.

Rent supplements passed the House by six votes, and "we just couldn't have done it without the homebuilders," said a member of the staff of Banking and Currency Committee Chairman Wright Patman, D-Tex.

John E. Barriere, the Housing Subcommittee's staff director in 1965, drew up a list of about 60 members who might be susceptible to NAHB influence on rent supplements, according to another staff member.

NAHB lobbyists used the list, made up largely of members from southern Democratic and suburban Republican districts, to focus their efforts on behalf of rent supplements.

Model Cities

In 1966, with Blackmon serving as the association's president, NAHB strongly supported two major Great Society programs—model cities (42 USC 3301) and the initial funding of rent supplements. Both carried narrowly, and committee staff members credit NAHB with swinging southern Democratic votes in the House that were originally counted as lost.

FNMA Assistance

Also included in the 1966 omnibus housing bill was $1 billion in special assistance money for the Federal National Mortgage Association. The homebuilders worked with Sen. Sparkman to push the $1 billion through the Senate and then to have it retained in conference committee.

Collaborating with NAHB on the FNMA amendment were the homebuilders' traditional allies on mortgage credit issues: the U.S. Savings and Loan League; the National Association of Mutual Savings Banks; the Mortgage Bankers Association; and the Realtors.

Regulation Q

Also in 1966, the same mortgage credit allies pushed through "Regulation Q" (80 Stat 823), under which the Federal Reserve System requires commercial banks to pay 0.25 percent less interest on savings than savings institutions. The same allies have successfully lobbied to have Regulation Q continued every year since 1966 and expect it will be renewed on or before its March 21, 1971, expiration date.

HUD Act of 1968

But it was not until 1968 that NAHB really hit the jackpot. In the Housing and Urban Development Act of 1968 (82 Stat 476), the homebuilders extracted important economic concessions for their industry from the Johnson Administration and Congress.

Goals. The homebuilders' most significant accomplishment was the establishment of national housing goals, including numerical targets for each year and a requirement that the President make annual reports on federal performance in meeting the goals.

Carl Coan Jr. said that when NAHB tried to get the national goals included in the 1968 act, "we got a lot of opposition from HUD and from the Budget Bureau. They knew that NAHB would use it as a yardstick for performance and as a political whip to hold the Administration to account. They wanted generalized goals, but we worked with Proxmire to get the numbers locked into statute."

Philip N. Brownstein, former FHA Commissioner (1963-1969), said that establishing the housing goals was one area "where I think of NAHB as really taking the political lead. The goals, broken down as they are into numerical targets, serve to make the government take a hard position on the need for an exact amount of housing. For the homebuilders the goals serve as a great bargaining lever for forcing higher funding levels."

Niblack (senior staff vice-president of NAHB), who did much of the staff work on the goals, said, "Larry Blackmon got the idea in the spring of 1966. He had the economics department develop a pamphlet with philosophical assumptions and numerical targets. Then, in 1967, President Leon Weiner held two housing goals conferences, which I put together. We got together all the trade associations interested in mortgage credit, plus the National League of Cities-U.S. Conference of Mayors, the National Association of Housing and Redevelopment Officials, the National Association of County Officials, the Chamber of Commerce and the AFL-CIO. We succeeded in getting broad consensus on the idea of goals, on numerical targets, and on some mechanism for annual reassessment by the government of progress in reaching the goals."

New subsidies. The 1968 act also authorized the two subsidy programs for home ownership and rental assistance—sections 235 and 236 of the National Housing Act—which have quickly developed into main supports of homebuilder activity.

In both programs, the federal government can subsidize mortgage interest rates down to a minimum of 1 percent, making the programs especially attractive to builders during periods of tight money and high interest rates.

Staff members for the two Banking Committees said that programs were drafted so as to be acceptable to NAHB.

Designing the programs. The homeownership program was studied by the Senate committee during 1967 and then reworked by the HUD general counsel's office. The rental program was put together by a special Presidential task force in 1968. NAHB provided major inputs to both efforts, said homebuilder lobbyists and committee staffers. "That's why they are builder programs," said a House Banking Committee staff member. "They are oriented toward housing production—units, starts and property—with people being secondary considerations."

The two programs have been a bonanza for NAHB's builder membership. During 1970, when money was scarce and builders were struggling to keep their crews together, the motto of the Tennessee Home Builders Association became: "Stay alive with 235."

Housing starts. Boosted by the heavy use of the new programs, the share of total housing starts represented by government subsidized programs jumped from 12 percent in 1969 to 25 percent in 1970, the first year in which 235 and 236 had any real impact. In 1970, with approximately 60,000 starts under 235 and approximately 100,000 under 236, those two programs alone accounted for about 12 percent of all housing starts.

Projections. For 1971, HUD Secretary Romney has projected 162,000 starts under 235 and 170,000 starts under 236. The targets for 1972 are 207,900 and 177,300, respectively, for the two programs. At that rate, sections 235 and 236 will become a way of life—a subsidized one—for many homebuilders whose previous involvement in government housing programs had been confined to standard FHA insurance.

1969

Pausing in 1969 to digest their gains of 1968, the homebuilders concentrated successfully on the extension of Regulation Q; enactment of $1.5 billion in special assistance for the Government National Mortgage Association, an increase from $1 billion to $4 billion in the Federal Home Loan Bank System's borrowing authority from the Treasury, and extensive collaboration with Sens. Sparkman and Tower over provisions in the Tax Reform Act of 1969 (83 Stat 487) aimed at preserving some tax incentive through accelerated depreciation for multifamily housing builders.

1970

Making political capital out of the sharp drop in housing starts in January 1970, NAHB was able to press Congress into creating a secondary market for conventional mortgages, a top NAHB goal since 1954.

Under the provisions of the Emergency Home Finance Act of 1970 (84 Stat 450), which NAHB helped to draft, FNMA and the Federal Home Loan Bank Board were authorized to provide a secondary market for conventional (non-FHA, non-VA) mortgages.

"This central mortgage facility has implications so wide we can't even see them yet," said NAHB's Coan.

"It's always been extraordinarily difficult to get Congress and the Administration to give attention to something like this when the times are fat; it was always one of those cases where nobody wanted to fix the roof when it wasn't raining. Our thrust for the central facility would always get hung up over arguments about who should run it—FHLBB or FNMA—and arguments about whether or not the federal government should give assistance to conventional mortgages, a step which gives further priority assistance to mortgage financing.

"We worked in the last few years with Sparkman, Tower and Widnall on this and just built up the momentum. A key factor was that we brought all mortgage credit interest groups together, and got them to give up their pet projects in order to pass a common bill in the space of a few months when the emergency conditions were still in effect. We were the real initiative force, but we wouldn't have gotten anywhere without all the others."

(Rep. William B. Widnall, R-N.J., is the ranking minority member on the House Banking and Currency Committee and on its Housing Subcommittee.)

Bigger subsidy. Also enacted in the emergency home finance bill was a program (section 243 of the National Housing Act) in which the federal government may subsidize mortgage interest rates for middle income families when rates rise above 7 percent.

Sen. William Proxmire, D-Wis., who authored the bill, and NAHB collaborated on its drafting and passage.

Though it has not been funded by the Nixon Administration because interest rates have dropped to 7 percent, NAHB still regards section 243 as an important backup tool in its growing arsenal of housing subsidies.

Full funding. Also in 1970, the homebuilders were able to achieve full funding of both sections 235 and 236. Amounts provided for each program, $130 million and $135 million respectively, brought the total for each program through fiscal 1971 to $325 million, the full amount authorized for both.

The Lineup

NAHB's lobbyists said that they worked with Reps. Joe L. Evins, D-Tenn., and Charles Raper Jonas, R-N.C., the chairman and ranking minority member of the House Appropriations Subcommittee on Independent Offices and HUD, and also with G. Homer Skarin, the chief staff member for the subcommittee. McGrath and Wood do the contact work with Evins, Jonas, and Skarin; Coan works with Rep. David Pryor, D-Ark., a junior member of the subcommittee. (Since the beginning of the 92nd Congress, Evins has moved to the chairmanship of the Public Works Subcommittee, and Rep. Edward P. Boland, D-Mass., has taken over the HUD subcommittee, now called the Subcommittee on HUD-Space-Science.)

In keeping with Rogg's "don't pester" edict, NAHB's lobbyists do not pressure the northern members of the subcommittee, such as Boland and Giaimo.

"They know they have my vote on housing programs, so why should they lobby me?" said Boland.

Negative Power

NAHB flexed its muscles in 1970 to kill legislation also. In an all-out effort, NAHB succeeded in defeating a NAREB-inspired amendment to divert section 235 moneys from new production and into existing housing.

NAHB also worked hard to kill an Administration-sponsored "bare bones" substitute bill to the Housing Subcommittee's own larger version of the omnibus 1970 housing bill.

The Administration version, sponsored by Rep. Garry Brown, R-Mich., was a $695-million alternative to a compromise bill by Widnall and Stephens calling for $2.8 billion. Staff members for the Housing Subcommittee said that NAHB opposition was very important in defeating the Brown substitute (94-101).

"As soon as we were able to lay out the alternatives between the Brown and Stephens bills," one staff member said, "we called them and told them what was coming. In turn, they mobilized the troops and got the telegrams flying—they responded very fast. And after the Stephens-Widnall version passed, and the President was delaying signing the bill because the price tag was too big, they let the White House know how badly they wanted it signed."

Reflecting on NAHB's growing string of triumphs in the 1960s and early 1970s, one staff member for the Housing Subcommittee said, "It is very hard, if not impossible, to get any piece of legislation through that the home- builders are against."

EXECUTIVE BRANCH LOBBYING

The McGrath-Coan-Wood legislative lobbying operation concentrates on the two issues that unify NAHB's membership—easier mortgage credit and expanded subsidies.

Executive Branch Lobbyists

Richard J. Canavan and Milton W. Smithman direct NAHB's lobbying with the executive agencies. Their objective is to serve quietly the diverse needs of the membership. Both Canavan and Smithman combine long years with NAHB and with the technical bureaucracy of the federal government.

An architectural engineer, Canavan, 48, was FHA's assistant commissioner for technical standards from 1961 to 1965 and, thus, once controlled the bureaucracy with which NAHB deals most frequently.

Also an expert on standards, with a degree in civil engineering, Smithman, 52, has been with the homebuilders for 16 years. From 1952 to 1957, he was assistant chief appraiser for the VA's Midwest regional office.

Staff. Canavan's operation is by far the largest in NAHB, with 29 professional staff members divided into 12 functional areas: apartment construction and management; business management; commercial and institutional management; environmental design; labor relations; land use and engineering; manpower development; manpower training (a Labor Department funded program); marketing; mortgage finance and specialized housing; seminars and workshops; and technical services.

Negotiators. The great bulk of the Canavan operation consists in negotiating technical revisions in proposed or existing government rules and regulations.

"Our jurisdiction is anything in the federal government that affects housing," Canavan said. "We're the watchdog that tries to keep the costs from going up in housing. We do this by going into great detail on regulations and guidelines, and on proposed legislation. In that area, we provide technical backup for McGrath. And right now we're really starting to get into this whole environmental regulation business, like water pollution control."

Ruefully, Canavan said: "Nobody pays any attention to us until we miss one, but then all hell breaks loose."

FHA Beat

Canavan said that "FHA is our major point of contact with the federal bureaucracy; we deal on a weekly basis with some officials in Gulledge's operation. We'd like to believe that our relations with them are very professional. For example, we will not personally intercede and negotiate for some builder whose arguments we do not agree with. Our most frequent negotiations—in fact they are continuing negotiations —concern FHA's minimum property designs. These are like a building code and are continually being revised. We try to negotiate changes that benefit the builder."

Watchdog on costs. Smithman said, "FHA is continually being pushed by the materials producers to include new improvements in their standards. In turn, we watch the cost to the builder of those improvements. A classic case would be the amount of cement required for concrete: Where do you draw the line on cost versus what is needed to do the job?

"FHA will negotiate with the Portland Cement Association, which is pressing them to increase the amount of cement, and then with us, who are looking out for the builder on the cost side. If we didn't participate, then the builder would get screwed, and subsequently the consumer of the housing."

Dockser. William B. Dockser, assistant FHA commissioner for subsidized housing, said, "We meet with them almost weekly on processing and technical questions. They'll bring in builders from the different regions of the country—for example, single-family builders if it is a 235 problem and multifamily builders if it is something to do with 236. They do an excellent job as a technical staff in representing the many diverse sides of their membership, and in analyzing our circulars to make sure that what we want to say will be clearly understood."

Finger. Harold B. Finger, HUD's assistant secretary for research and technology, also praised the quality of NAHB's technical staff, especially its ability to serve diverse kinds of builders. "We have work on contract with their research foundation in Rockville," said Finger, "and we are cooperating on such new approaches to housing as the adoption of model building codes, something in which both of us are interested."

Broad Contact

"Besides our heavy contact with HUD on metropolitan development issues like water and sewer, as well as FHA, we have a very broad spectrum of contact with the entire federal bureaucracy," Smithman said. He listed several frequent points of NAHB-federal government negotiations: Agriculture Department, with the Farmers Home Administration, the Forest Service and the Forest Products Laboratory; Commerce Department, usually with the Bureau of Standards; Defense Department, on military housing; Federal National Mortgage Association and Federal Home Loan Bank Board, on all regulations affecting mortgage credit; Federal Reserve Board and the Federal Trade Commission, on truth-in-lending procedures and regulations; Internal Revenue Service, on tax policies and regulations affecting construction; Labor Department, with the Wage and Labor Standards Administration and with the Manpower Administration; Veterans Administration, in connection with the home loan guarantee program.

GOALS FOR THE 1970s

NAHB's staff has laid out an ambitious agenda for the 92nd Congress and beyond. Their list for the 1970s reflects the lobby's confidence in its political muscle developed in the late 1960s.

Easier Credit

"We're going to really work to straighten out this flow of mortgage funds problem—where it is either feast or famine," Coan said. "We know that Patman is going to come up with his development bank, and we know that both Proxmire and Patman are going to go after the Fed again and try to get some statutory priority for mortgage credit. We'll support any reasonable moves in that direction."

In separate interviews, NAHB's President Stastny, Rogg, McGrath and Wood corroborated Coan's statement—especially his remark that the Fed would no longer be immune from NAHB attack.

Full Funding

All NAHB officials said that the lobby wanted to continue getting full funding for housing production subsidies. Coan also said he planned a careful watch on the

President's budget office to see if the Administration tried to impound housing funds for anti-inflationary purposes.

Challenge to HUD

McGrath said that NAHB planned to challenge HUD on its right to "set aside" 235 and 236 moneys for use by other programs, such as urban renewal, model cities, Operation Breakthrough, and new communities.

"There are all kinds of deals going on among the HUD assistant secretaries to carve up housing appropriations and siphon them off to make sure that other programs work.

"Suppose a group of big corporations tried to corral a big set-aside, or some new and powerful state nonprofit corporation got a big set-aside. This would give them a preferred status over our membership. Believe me, we intend to straighten out that set-aside business before the next appropriations round, or you can be sure that HUD is going to have a real fight on its hands," said McGrath.

Timber Cutting

"We're going to work again for legislation to get more appropriate use of the national forests for housing purposes," said McGrath. "The environmentalists beat us last year on a bill which provided for increased cutting in the national forests. They used all kinds of deliberately deceptive practices which were phony but which scared a lot of Congressmen.

"We'll be coming back with a different bill, even though we know we'll run into these environmentalist guys again, because the truth of the matter is that lumber and wood products are going to be the essential ingredient in building housing for the rest of the century."

Labor Legislation

Stastny and McGrath both said NAHB will seek changes in the National Labor Relations Act to readjust the balance of power between management and labor, now too heavily weighted toward the unions, in their opinion.

Stastny is an enthusiastic member of the President's Commission on Collective Bargaining in the Construction Industry, and the commission's spokesman, John T. Dunlop—dean of the Harvard arts and sciences faculty and a labor economist—is a close personal friend of Rogg's.

Stastny hailed the President's suspension on February 23 of the Davis-Bacon Act (46 Stat 1494), under which the labor secretary establishes prevailing wage rates for all federally assisted construction. He said the suspension was an example of the kind of change in wage-rate patterns for which NAHB is pressing.

Tax Exemptions

McGrath and Coan said that work was well under way to get a congressional exemption on federal income taxes on interest up to $750 per year from a savings account. Rep. Donald E. Lukens, R-Ohio, introduced legislation to that effect in 1970; already in the 92nd Congress, Sen. Robert Taft Jr., R-Ohio, has introduced a bill (S 486) exempting the first $500 of interest.

Pension Funds

Wood said that NAHB planned campaigns on several fronts to get pension funds to invest more heavily in residential mortgages. "It's a large and relatively untapped credit source. We're working against the Treasury's wishes to get the National Service Life Insurance Fund, which is the GI insurance program, to invest in VA mortgages, and we're going to work with Patman to try to get legislation conditioning (pension fund) tax exemptions so as to encourage their effort in mortgages."

Equity Participation

Coan said that NAHB would collaborate with Patman on "the matter of equity participation, whereby lenders in rental construction projects get a piece of the action with no risk to themselves. It's a practice that grew up during tight money, and all it serves to do in the end is drive up the cost of housing to the consumer and drive builders out of the market. We're going to try to get it prohibited."

OUTLOOK

The homebuilders are at their peak of influence.

Political Committee

The symbol of their coming of age, in the opinion of realtor lobbyist Williamson, is the formation in 1970 of a Builders Political Action Committee (BPAC), led by the most politically savvy of all NAHB presidents, Larry Blackmon.

Williamson said the time was long past due when the homebuilders should have begun to centralize their political activity, especially contributions.

"Money in politics just has to be organized," he said. "A guy in a tough fight is going to really know when a national association gives $5,000, as opposed to scattered contributions by local builders."

The formation of a homebuilders' political action committee is a sign of strength. But even though the committee is completely independent of the trade organization, its activities are bound to increase the politicization of NAHB and call into question the good-guy image so carefully nurtured by subtle tactics and a cooperative posture.

Blackmon said he intends a nationwide organizing campaign in 1971 to clear the way for important political contributions in 1972. As Blackmon delivers on his pledge, BPAC will increase the homebuilders' weight with candidates. But the organization's aims also will come more clearly into public focus—and question.

Even more important for the future, NAHB is on a collision course with some of the toughest political foes it has yet faced.

Environmental Wars

For the first time in recent memory—at least since the very late 1950s, when NAHB strongly opposed public housing and thereby gained the reputation of being antipoor and antiurban—the lobby is being called an enemy of the public interest. Environmental groups attacked NAHB over timber-cutting policy in 1970.

The defense. "We really bombed on that timber bill," Coan said, "just about as bad as you can bomb."

"I was appalled by the tactics those guys used," said McGrath in lamenting the House's refusal on February 26, 1970, to bring to a vote the National Forest Timber Conservation and Management Act of 1969 (HR 12025). "I'm for conservation, and I don't know anyone in NAHB who's against it."

Accusers. Robert S. Waldrop, a Washington representative of the Sierra Club, the environmentalist lobby which led the fight against the timber cutting bill in 1970, said, "We're not against housing and don't like to give the homebuilders a hard time. We are very concerned about the housing shortage, too—and especially the state of housing in the nation's cities. Nevertheless, the homebuilders are going to face the same kind of rough opposition this year as they faced last year if they support a similar version of the timber bill.

"That kind of bill authorizes the mining of marginal lands for timber, and that's a frightening situation. The homebuilders were in with a group of private interests that wanted to overcut marginal timber lands. They represent part of a trend of private interests who are trying to make a profit out of exploiting the nation's natural resources.

"In this instance, they were after a short-run and selfish goal, and in the long run they would be cutting their own throat by destroying the resource."

Waldrop said the NAHB was going to have rough sledding in the 1970s with the environmentalist lobbies as long as NAHB "focuses on the housing production environment—an economic environment—rather than the total environment."

Rep. Ashley said, "I look at NAHB cross-eyed whenever I think of their attitude toward some kind of rational land-use controls. They're very anti-planning and anti-land banking; and they're very big, big defenders of the kind of suburban sprawl development we had in the 1950s and 1960s. It took them years to become neutral on new towns, and that's only because their staff rather than the membership is progressive."

Housing Production

Similarly, the central thrust of NAHB's activity in support of increased housing production is coming under attack on several fronts.

ZPG. Environmental groups espouse the goal of "zero population growth," which runs counter to the homebuilders' basic ideology. "We're in favor of an expansive population," McGrath said; "all this ZPG business seems like a lot of nonsense to me."

National housing goals. Lobbies which see their stake in churning the existing housing market—such as the realtors and the mortgage bankers—have opened verbal attacks on the NAHB's most prized political accomplishment, the national housing goals. Miles L. Colean, the prestigious economist for the Mortgage Bankers Association, has denounced the housing goals as "inflationary" and as "a fraud."

Subsidies. And on another front in the housing production campaign, the President's Office of Management and Budget has begun warning HUD and NAHB that it cannot continue to escalate the 235 and 236 subsidies indefinitely.

Each commitment is a 30-year, life-of-the-mortgage commitment, so that budget expenditures become cumulative. Only a few years old, each program is already eating up approximately half-a-billion dollars a year.

Moreover, an aide to Sen. Proxmire said that as 235 and 236 accelerate and become more visible in suburban and rural areas, the homebuilder demand for the production subsidies will generate substantial political opposition. This opposition will come "from the lower middle class homeowners, who are going to be writing their Congressmen about how they worked and saved to buy a house, and now some guy, with none of that blood and sweat, has gotten a subsidy for an even newer house. These subsidies are going to get resented, especially by the guy at the end of the line who is just a little bit too rich to qualify for the program.

"It didn't matter with public housing. That was invisibly sited in the ghetto and insignificant numerically. This stuff is visible and is big business, several hundred thousand in just two years, and a lot of it in the suburbs."

Labor

NAHB itself claims to be on a collision course with organized labor over wage rules and rates in the construction industry. An aide to Sen. Sparkman said that "labor and NAHB are two of the toughest and most influential lobbies. So far NAHB has avoided really tangling with them. If they ever did, and even though NAHB is one of the best, labor would probably beat them because their support runs deeper."

Administration

Although NAHB has long been critical of the Fed's tight money policies as they affect mortgage credit, the lobby has always shied away from supporting any legislative move to limit by statute the independence of the Fed. Aides to Proxmire and Patman, members of Congress keen on setting statutory priorities for Fed monetary policies, claim bitterly that Administration pressure always swings the incumbent builder-president away from a tough stance.

Stastny is talking tough, however. And permanent NAHB staff members are doing the same, all denying that the NAHB has been scared off in the past by White House pressure.

Political Savvy

Although NAHB will not have it so easy in the future—a development inevitable for any lobby which has made it to the very top—its political savvy should save it from any ruinous bloodletting with an established lobby (organized labor) or a rising newcomer (the environmentalist forces).

But this presumes the continued ability of the professional NAHB staff to function as effective leadership for an industry that seems to shift ideological positions for economic reasons.

As one high-ranking official at the National League of Cities-U.S. Conference of Mayors said: "The homebuilding industry is not the best climate to give professional leadership to. It's made up of building trades people—bricklayers, carpenters, plumbers—and lots of small-time land speculators who have all graduated to becoming businessmen.

"Thus, they have a tendency to swing erratically and sharply with the trends in homebuilding: When building drops, then they get radical; but when times get good and they get fat, then they go conservative. That's when they don't want to help us with things like urban renewal and public housing.

"This puts a real burden on their staff, and—to their credit and agility—they have moved the membership away from this."

White House lobbyist Cook said NAHB has conducted its business efficiently because it always plans seven years ahead. And chief lobbyist McGrath spoke proudly of how NAHB had kept as allies veteran Washington housing professionals, such as Philip N. Brownstein, now chief counsel for the Council of Housing Producers, and Milton P. Semer, former general counsel of HHFA (1961-1965) and now Washington counsel for National Homes Corporation.

Brownstein and Semer are special lobbyists for the big housing producers, the manufacturing corporations that are listed on the New York Stock Exchange, in contrast to the small homebuilder that NAHB traditionally has spoken for.

"We've had our fights with these guys," said McGrath, "but after 20 years of sorting out our relationships we still respect each other and still work with each other."

APPENDIX: THE NAHB WASHINGTON STAFF

The strength of the NAHB lies in its highly qualified and well-paid staff. The lobby's staff is so well regarded by rival lobbies and the federal government that they make frequent attempts to raid it. Top staff members:

Nathaniel H. Rogg, 57, executive vice president and staff director. Promoted to the top administrative position in 1966 after 13 years of service, "Nat" Rogg has participated in the lobby's change in outlook and the steady increase in its political influence.

Before coming to NAHB as its chief economist, Rogg was head economist and statistician in the Housing and Home Finance Agency (1947-54); before that, he was an economist with the Veterans Administration (1942-46) and with the Works Progress Administration (1934-41).

An institutional economist by training, with B.A., M.A. and Ph.D. degrees from New York University (where his doctoral thesis was a study of the insured mortgage certificate), Rogg is highly respected as an expert on housing economics.

One House Banking Committee staff member described Rogg as "the best practical economist on housing in the country." Another said that Rogg and NAHB's chief economist, Michael Sumichrast, "are annually the best witnesses to appear before this committee."

Rogg, who has written scholarly articles on housing economics in the *American Journal of Sociology* and the *American Statistical Journal*, said in an interview: "I'm kind of proud that our membership is proud to have a director who has his own professional reputation in the field."

Rogg's political credentials are as impressive as his academic ones. "I consider myself a good friend of William McChesney Martin," said Rogg, "and I used to play tennis with him on a pretty regular basis." (Martin was chairman of the board of governors of the Federal Reserve System from 1951 to 1970.)

The walls of Rogg's office are covered with autographed pictures of Rogg doing something with the famous or the powerful in the politics of housing. Among those on Rogg's wall: Presidents Johnson and Nixon; Sens. Edward W. Brooke, R-Mass., Charles H. Percy, R-Ill., and William Proxmire, D-Wis. (Brooke and Proxmire are members of the Senate Banking, Housing and Urban Affairs Committee; Percy is a former member); former HUD Secretary (1966-1968) Robert C. Weaver; Gov. Ronald Reagan, R-Calif.; David Rockefeller, chairman of the board of Chase Manhattan Bank.

Rogg said he divides his time so that 50 percent is devoted to public policy matters, 30 percent to the annual convention and 30 percent to internal management affairs.

M. Ray Niblack, 45, senior staff vice president and Rogg's deputy. Niblack is the NAHB executive officer in charge of day-to-day operations for the 200-man Washington staff and of ongoing relations with state and local homebuilder organizations. Niblack also participates with Rogg and the legislative staff in drafting all congressional testimony and preparing formal policy positions.

Like all the other top staff members, Niblack has significant political connections. From 1961 to 1966, Niblack worked at FHA, starting as director of public information (1961-62), moving to congressional relations (1963-64) and finishing there as deputy commissioner (1964-66). As deputy commissioner, Niblack had responsibility for congressional relations, budget, personnel, investigation, public information and general management.

Joseph B. McGrath, 48, chief legislative counsel, staff vice-president for governmental relations and chief lobbyist.

McGrath has responsibility for all association activities as they affect congressional legislation. While policies might be hammered out by any number of NAHB officials—by the 5 top builder officials, by the 28-man builder executive committee, or by Rogg, Niblack and other professionals in NAHB—it is McGrath and his people who deliver the program to the Hill and who do the work with the committee staffs and with the key members of Congress.

Formal in appearance and manner—he is usually attired in a banker-gray, three-piece suit—McGrath has run NAHB's governmental affairs operation for 18 years, from 1952 to 1965, and from 1967 to the present.

A graduate of Harvard College and Harvard Law School, and very active in Harvard alumni affairs, McGrath reflects the organization's successful attempt to identify itself in Washington as public spirited and progressive and not preoccupied with narrow self-interest.

From 1966 to 1967, McGrath was chief counsel for Newark's model cities program; from 1965 to 1966 he administered a Ford Foundation funded Urban America program aimed at stimulating private enterprise involvement in nonprofit housing corporations.

He is now a member of the board of directors of the National Housing Conference, a public interest lobby which promotes federal policies for low-income housing and urban slum redevelopment. And he is a member of the board of directors of the National Committee against Discrimination in Housing.

Rep. Thomas L. Ashley, D-Ohio, the House Banking and Currency Committee's leading expert on housing and urban development legislation, said: "McGrath does a terrific job; he and Rogg have been able to neutralize their membership's opposition to my new-towns bills over the last few years, even though the average homebuilder has no liking for land-use planning."

Richard Cook, who was a minority-side staff member for the committee before going to the White House, said, "McGrath is known as one of the most able lobbyists in Washington."

A staff member for the House Banking and Currency Subcommittee on Housing, who declined to be identified by name, said, "McGrath really knows housing legislation; his bi-weekly report on political activities affecting housing is a first-rate technical job; a lot of committees' staffers and members make use of it."

Carl A. S. Coan Jr., 37, McGrath's deputy. Coan was stolen from HUD by NAHB in 1969. Coan's employment by NAHB is regarded by rival lobbies and by congressional committee staffs as a great coup for the homebuilders and as evidence of NAHB's increasing ability to attract top people by virtue of lobbying professionalism and high salaries.

From 1958 to 1961, starting fresh from Georgetown University Law School, Coan worked on FHA's legal business for multifamily housing. From 1961 to 1967, he held a variety of legal and administrative positions in the Urban Renewal Administration, rising to become legislative opinions counsel for the URA.

From 1967 to 1969, he worked in the Office of General Counsel as assistant general counsel for legislative policy coordination; and, in 1968, he handled the drafting and political liaison for the department's massive Housing and Urban Development Act of 1968—legislation which President Johnson liked to call "the magna carta of housing." For his work in connection with the 1968 Act, which included drafting the 235 and 236 housing subsidy programs, Coan is widely known around Washington.

"The hiring of Coan is the ultimate proof of the old adage that lobbies should hire only those people who know their way around town," said the House Banking and Currency Committee staff member. "Carl Coan Jr. is one of those master technicians who can change three words or just a comma on a piece of legislation in order to help the homebuilders.

"Those guys at the homebuilders have their own underground railway operation. They don't have one top policy guy who didn't work for HUD at one time or another. And George Gross, top staff man for our Housing Subcommittee, was a lobbyist for NAHB in 1966. But their biggest asset of all is Carl Coan Jr., whose daddy is the top staff guy for the Senate Banking, Housing and Urban Affairs Subcommittee."

Burton C. Wood, 48, legislative relations. Wood brings to NAHB impeccable political credentials: four years on the Hill as administrative assistant (1953-56) to Rep. John Jarman, D-Okla.; seven years with NAHB as a lobbyist (1956-61); eight years in the federal bureaucracy, as director of congressional liaison for FHA (1961-69). Wood is a graduate of Harvard Law School.

"You can look at McGrath and Coan as the supertechnicians on housing," said a staff member of the House Subcommittee on Housing, who would not speak for attribution, "and you can look at Wood as the expert on political contacts. Wood has built up political ins all over the place on the Hill—first as an aide with a long-time Oklahoma congressman and then as JFK's and LBJ's man on the Hill for the FHA."

Staff and Salaries

There can be little doubt that NAHB's attractive salary scale is a big drawing card for lobbyists with the credentials and talent of a Rogg or a Coan.

National Journal could not confirm the exact amounts that top staff members were making, but several officials corroborated that Rogg earns about $50,000; Niblack, about $45,000; McGrath and the other six vice-presidents, about $40,000 (including Michael Sumichrast, economics and statistics; Oliver W. DeWolf, association activities; Richard J. Canavan and Milton W. Smithman, builder services; Ralph J. Johnson, the NAHB research foundation in Rockville, Md.; and Stanley Baitz, information and public relations). Assistants and deputy vice presidents, such as Coan, are earning approximately $30,000; and department heads and associate counsels, such as Wood, are earning about $25,000. Liberal pension and health insurance plans are additional attractions.

Rogg said, "We have to pay our top people at the level comparable to assistant secretary ($38,000), and the steady rise in top government salaries has been a real problem. But we have to keep up with it."

Staff Growth

Vice-president Niblack said, "We're in the ironical position of having to keep staffing up in order to respond to our own initiatives on federal legislation—particularly the several major new initiatives included in the 1968 Housing Act."

The staff has grown from 36 in 1952 to approximately 110 in 1964, approximately 170 in 1968 and 200 in 1971. The staff now includes 102 professionals and 98 clerical workers. The largest number of professionals—29—work in the various technical sections of the builder services division.

3. The Rise of Tenant Organizations

PETER MARCUSE

With the possible exception of the Boston Tea Party, consumer interests have been more the occasion for rhetoric than for direct action or organization. Supermarket picketing against high prices has never gotten far; Consumers Union is buyers' guide, not mass action, oriented; and Ralph Nader accomplishes more with publicity and lawsuits than with protest movements. Mainly middle and upper class families are the ones drawn to such causes, and to the somewhat related ecology crusades. Working-class families, the poor, or minority groups rarely get deeply involved, although these groups spend much more of their total earnings on consumer items than do wealthier families.

Only in one area, housing, is the picture different. Actually, housing is the largest single consumer expense for most families: generally about 20 percent of a family's budget, but going up to 30 percent and even 40 percent for many poor families. (In St. Louis one of the things that touched off the famous rent strike against the public housing authority there was the discovery that one poor family was being forced to pay 46 percent of its income in rent in the supposedly low-income Pruitt-Igoe project!) Not only is housing a major consumer item; it is purchased from visible, accessible people, landlords, on a continuing basis, by individuals who know one another as neighbors. Perhaps the surprising thing is not that a National Tenants Organization, formed in 1969 to represent the interests of tenant-consumers of housing, already has more than 700 local affiliates throughout the country, but rather that it did not happen sooner.

The source of the current impetus for tenant union organization was probably Harlem in the fall of 1963. Harlem undoubtedly displays more bad housing per square foot of ground than any other spot in the country. When to that is added an increasing frustration with official rhetoric about future improvement, the growing militancy of the black community, the liberal-civil rights receptivity to dramatic action, the appeal of the strike as a simple, direct, and immediately productive way of securing dollar-in-the-pocket benefits, and the leadership and public relations talents of Jesse Gray, things are bound to happen. In fact, at the height of the 1963 Harlem strikes more than 500 buildings were involved, and 15,000 tenants were not paying their rents to their landlords.

The long-range results of these early strikes still left much to be desired. Economic pressure undoubtedly forced many of the landlords directly affected to make repairs; a few judges, in the flare of concentrated publicity, rendered decisions favoring tenants that might not otherwise have been forthcoming; the tortuous, step-by-step improvement of New York's statutes and ordinances covering landlord-tenant relationships may have been accelerated a little; some administrative reforms in New York City's

Reprinted by permission from Peter Marcuse, "Goals and Limitations: The Rise of Tenant Organizations," *The Nation*, July 19, 1971, pp. 50-53. Peter Marcuse is an attorney, former member of the City Plan Commission and majority leader of the Board of Aldermen in Waterbury, Connecticut, and now teaches in the Urban Planning Program at UCLA.

Kafkaesque building and health inspection and enforcement procedures may have been achieved. But a few months later, according to Frances Fox Piven and Richard Cloward, few traces of the great Harlem rent strikes could be seen in New York.

The traces in other parts of the country were not so obscure. Rent strikes spread, their techniques became more sophisticated, their legal rationale more fully developed, their goals more clearly defined, their statutory support strengthened, their consequences better understood by landlords as well as tenants, alternative forms for their resolution evolved. Strikes have been documented in more than 67 cities, and trade publications and organizations in the real estate industry now feel it necessary to educate their members on how to deal with them.

But rent strikes are a one-shot affair; more is needed if housing conditions are to be basically altered. It is too easy for a landlord to promise repairs and changes to end a rent strike, wait till things simmer down a little, then slowly rid himself of the troublemakers and revert to his old ways. Taking a leaf out of labor's book, strike organizers in Chicago decided to try forming permanent tenant "unions" and getting signed "collective bargaining agreements" with landlords. The Harlem rent strikes of 1963 and the Chicago tenants' unions of 1966 were the direct progenitors of the National Tenants Organization (NTO).

"Outside" groups were as active as tenants in initiating the successful campaigns to organize around landlord-tenant issues in Chicago. In the summer of 1966, Students for a Democratic Society, through JOIN, succeeded in organizing three smallish buildings, more by publicity, picketing landlords' homes, etc., than by rent strikes. The agreements negotiated as a result did not last long, and one was voided in a subsequent court action. Much stronger forces were needed to pioneer more durable agreements.

The Southern Christian Leadership Conference, with Martin Luther King's personal involvement, had been active in Chicago slum areas since the Freedom Campaign of the summer of 1965. It had then formed an alliance with CCCO, the militant local coordinating group of civil rights and minority organizations that had almost succeeded in overthrowing Chicago's entrenched public school educational hierarchy. With the active financial support of the Community Union Center of the Industrial Union Department of the CIO, and with the skill and experience of Reuther's Auto Workers union behind them, tenant organizers moved into East Garfield and found a quick receptivity to the idea of strong tenant organization. Tony Henry, later to become the executive director of the NTO, was one of the key figures in the East Garfield drive. The largest landlord in East Garfield, a corporation owning or managing more than 45 buildings, was singled out; a start was made on organizing; and, when only 5 buildings were solid, a contract was demanded covering all 45. Rent strikes, publicity, political pressures, and behind-the-scenes activity by the national organizations involved brought results. In July 1966, a pioneering contract was signed calling for repairs, setting up a grievance machinery, preventing evictions except for cause, and spelling out the rights and obligations of the landlord to the tenant organization as well as to the individual tenants. The success at East Garfield was followed by other organizing activities, some spontaneous, some planned, which resulted in a few months in the formation of some 45 different unions with up to 2,000 members each, and then to the formation of the Chicago Tenants Union.

The movement spread to other cities in 1967 and 1968. Cleveland, under SCLC's leadership again; San Francisco, usually to be found among communities where there is militant action; Detroit, where UAW support and the organizing tradition were powerful; Boston, Philadelphia, Milwaukee, St. Louis, and Muskegon Heights, and probably 25 other major cities, all saw active organization, rent strikes, some successes, and some failures. The Muskegon and St. Louis experiences were significant in the light of subsequent events, for they were the first organizing activities and rent strikes in public housing.

In private housing, it has proved difficult to keep tenant organizations going after the first excitement of combat is over. New organization appealed only to the most advanced of the already organized tenants; landlord relationships usually settled down to a minimally acceptable pattern; resources for really basic changes were generally not present. Nor could the formation of citywide tenants' groups really help much in individual cases. Since most private landlords were small operators of limited resources, unorganized, unsophisticated, often absentee, and not susceptible to public pressures, organizing their tenants was frustrating.

But one landlord, the United States of America, has just the opposite characteristics. While technically the 2,800,000 tenants of public housing projects throughout the country pay their rents to more than 1,900 local autonomous housing authorities, their projects are built with federal funds, controlled by federal regulations, subsidized under federal formulas, and administered subject to federal standards. The resources, the political sensitivity, the number of tenants, the visibility, were all there.

First in Muskegon, then in St. Louis with the nationally publicized strike in the massive Pruitt-Igoe high-rise public housing project (the symbol for everything wrong with public housing), and then quickly in Philadelphia, New Orleans, Newark, and elsewhere, public housing tenants found they could get results—or at least attention—by militant action. Public housing held the hope for solid, permanent accomplishment for tenant organizers. A national review of strategy seemed called for.

On January 26, 1969, the meeting that launched the NTO took place. The Chicago Tenants Union was the host; co-sponsors included Jesse Gray's New York Tenants Union, the American Friends Service Committee, and several others. The Friends, long one of the most sensitive and courageous, as well as soft-spoken and self-effacing, of all the organizations in the civil rights field, agreed to hire Tony Henry as director of their program, and when NTO held its first official national convention in St. Louis in October 1969, it was already an organization with more than 60 affiliate groups, filling an obvious need and with an obvious role to play.

As NTO hit the national scene, it found the ground prepared for it by two natural allies: the civil rights-black liberation movement, and the antipoverty crusaders of the Kennedy and Johnson years. The riots of the late 1960s, with their deep involvement in public housing projects, and the multiple financial and social problems those projects were developing entirely by themselves, had given these allies something to sink their teeth into. With "minority representation" and "tenant participation" as their watch-words, they had already succeeded in shaking up the public housing establishment. Tenants began being elected or appointed to Housing Authorities, tenants' councils were organized and sponsored by OEO community action agencies, Congress was writing participation in planning into the modernization program, and the spirit of tenants' rights was being heard in the bleak, prisonlike walls of one project after another.

But before NTO arrived, these were just local happenings. NTO tried to pull them together into a force that would be felt nationally as well. NTO filled a vacuum; the legitimacy of its voice could not be denied. Congress was calling for tenant participation, and here was an organization knocking on HUD's doors and claiming to speak for its tenants. Locally, of course, housing authorities could and did challenge NTO's legitimacy. In New Orleans and Houston, rival organizations were organized and dealt with; in Chicago, when an NTO-affiliated group claimed to speak for tenants, the authority staged an election of its own and negotiated with its victors. But on a national level there was just no one else around against whom NTO could be played off. It had to be recognized, and recognized it was.

Uniform national protection for public housing tenants, written into equitable and binding leases, became NTO's first objective in discussions with HUD in Washington. Over a period of 9 months, after many more than 20 separate negotiating sessions, a new model lease was finally hammered out. It was followed by a detailed grievance procedure recommended by HUD to all local housing authorities.

Both the negotiating process and its result showed that the public housing establishment had to reckon with a major new force on the national scene from then on. The new lease differed from the traditional landlord-oriented lease used by most public housing authorities as night differed from day. The legal sophistication of the OEO-funded National Housing Law Project helped achieve the final agreement, but the political strength NTO and its constituents, and indeed the fact that even in public housing the simple justice of the idea that a lease should attempt to protect the tenant's interest as well as the landlord's, were what finally carried the day. The National Association of Housing and Redevelopment Officials (NAHRO), the respected organization of the local administrators of public housing, was invited to participate in the negotiations also. Like HUD, it found itself forced to recognize a new voice on the scene, and divided sharply within itself before finally giving, then withdrawing, then hedging, its approval of the new lease.

NTO's achievements in public housing are beyond dispute; its record in private housing is more questionable. This may not be NTO's fault; the problems of private housing for poor people may simply be insoluble within the framework of the private housing market.

The reasons are not hard to find. Slum buildings are in slum neighborhoods. The services that are needed to make them into decent housing include upgrading the neighborhood conditions. To try to supply the remedies at the building level is a tremendously expensive, and in the end probably a fruitless, task. The Garfield Tenants Union wanted to get the following from a private landlord in Chicago: closed circuit TV surveillance, intercom systems for entrances, guard service, snow removal, laundry rooms, full-time recreation and supervised play programs for children. These are either *public* services, or services required by the default of public services. To internalize these externalities may be feasible for the developer of 40,000 homes in walled-in suburban "new town" developments in California, but they cannot be provided privately at rents the average low income family can afford to pay.

The economics of slum housing and of slum income cannot be organized away. If Ford had given the River Rouge plant to the UAW in 1937, it would have been a stunning success for the union. But when a Detroit slumlord turns over 27 units to a tenants' union, the union finds itself inheriting insoluble problems, including lack of money to make repairs, the need to control and police the private conduct of its own members, the low level of public and private services in the area, blighting effect of other structures not owned by it, and so forth. Poor tenants have learned by costly experience that tenant ownership is no panacea. It may reduce rents only at the expense of even further deteriorating housing quality.

This is not to say that there is no future in tenant organization in private housing. First, a reduction in rents is by itself nothing to sneeze at. For some tenants at least a reduction in rents is more important than an improvement in housing. Second, in the apparent minority of slum buildings which show a cash flow profit, or in middle income buildings in relatively stable neighborhoods, tenant ownership may improve housing. Third, tenants may not be able to take over the existing liens and mortgages on a building, collect rents comparable to those in the neighborhood, and yet have enough left over to make necessary repairs and provide the necessary maintenance. So, say the economists, slum properties are not "economically viable," even where the owner gets nothing for his equity. It might be interesting to ask whether such properties would become viable again if all mortgages and liens on them were also wiped out, where the value of the property is in fact less than their amount. But that idea is too radical in its implications to be politically feasible at this point. Whether the various schemes now being discussed for subsidized tenant condominiums or cooperatives will work out remains to be seen; without subsidies for operating costs as well as for acquisition, they may only increase the burden on poor occupants. Their single advantage then will be that those in authority can wash their hands of the problem, blaming slum dwellers for the slums which they now "own" themselves.

If NTO shies away from tenant ownership, then, its reluctance is not so hard to understand. The same causes in the long run undermine some of the strategy of bargaining to extract concessions from private landlords as a means of improving housing. NTO is finding that rent strikes and collective bargaining can be undertaken effectively only in limited instances. No wonder that NTO and its affiliates are beginning to turn their attention more toward public action, seeking local and state legislation, as well as federal action, in support of tenants' rights.

The possibilities had always been apparent. One of the few tangible results of Jesse Gray's first rent strikes in New York was public recognition that the rat problem was still a major slum problem, and a concerted, if short-lived, city campaign against rats. Protective legislation was introduced in the New York State legislature largely because of those same strikes, and the legal balance between landlords' rights and tenants' rights has been somewhat redressed in most states in the recent past as a result of concerted tenant action. The Brooke amendment, prohibiting public housing authorities from charging more than 25 percent of a tenant's income as rent, was passed by Congress with significant political support from NTO's members. NTO has participated in lawsuits, testified on the invitation of state and national legislative committees, prepared position papers, participated in task forces, and submitted proposals to state legislative bodies, and its impact has been substantial.

In New York recently, organized tenants' groups were bitterly opposed to the Governor's Vacancy Decontrol Bill. Calling it a "direct official invitation to unscrupulous landlords to harass tenants into leaving," they have suggested that tenants might not only pay no increases, they might soon pay no rent at all. Senator Ohrenstein has proposed legislation specifically protecting organized tenants' unions, and providing in effect a Tenants Relations Act similar to the National Labor Relations Act to adjust the balance between two unequal contestants, who might then resolve their own problems privately. The bill is modeled on one drafted at the National Housing Law Project, based in part on NTO's experiences.

NTO's image is still not clear. Tony Henry, its executive director,[1] is committed to a thoroughly democratic, grassroots, completely participatory organization, as fully decentralized as possible, with a minimum national staff acting in a supporting, not a leadership, role. In local communities across the country, it is a militant organization

---

1. Jesse Gray became full-time director of NTO, after having been its chairman, when Tony Henry moved over to become director of the newly formed National Tenants Information Service, a tax-exempt group formed to provide information on technical assistance in the areas of concern to the tenants' movement.

of poor, overwhelmingly black tenants, modeling itself in tactics, organizing strategy and spirit on the CIO of the mid-thirties. In such communities its role is one of confrontation, its interests are opposed to the interests of landlords, and the issue is seen as one of bargaining and concessions, victory or defeat.

In its relationship with HUD, NTO has played, quite effectively on a national level, the role of spokesman for one constituent of HUD among many; a major one, indeed, but by no means the exclusive or only legitimate one. In conferences, state legislative battlefields, and internal discussions, NTO sometimes sees itself as the spokesman for the consumer of housing, not only vis-à-vis the federal government but generally vis-à-vis the housing market as a whole, i.e., as an interest group on a par with the National Association of Real Estate Boards, the National Association of Home Builders, etc. Finally, every now and then there are rumblings that tenant organization should be the basis for a deeper strategy of social change, one that would link the interests of tenants as housing consumers with the interests of welfare recipients, union employees, minority groups and others in a broad coalition for social change.

NTO's greatest success thus far, and the easiest strategy for it to follow, is as the official spokesman for the consumer of public housing; whether it will ultimately be content with that role, or will try to build on a broader and yet untried organizational base—the residential interests of the underprivileged of this country—remains to be seen.

4. Boardwalk and Park Place: Property Ownership, Political Structure, and Housing Policy at the Local Level

JOHN MOLLENKOPF
and JON PYNOOS

Public policies related to the housing market, no matter what the goals or intent of those who draft them, frequently run head-on into entrenched, powerful local interests. Analysis of the structure of these interests, the power that they wield, and how that power shapes the local housing market goes far toward accounting for the failure of public policy to provide adequate housing for all.

Such an analysis is advanced in this paper. We have examined the interplay of economic and political power in one city—Cambridge, Massachusetts—in terms of its effects on the housing of Cambridge residents. In this city large property owners (6 percent of the city's households own and control some 70 percent of Cambridge's housing units) are closely tied to city government. The result has been city policies, especially development policies, that favor large property interests at the expense of tenants, particularly among the working class and the elderly. The property-politics bloc has largely succeeded in thwarting attempts to provide low-to-moderate-income housing and has even managed to turn apparently tenant-oriented rent control to its own advantage.[1]

Our analysis deals with the relationship between property ownership, political structure, and housing policy as typified in one central city. Although development trends differ for Cambridge because its population is becoming more middle-class rather than less so, we believe that the relationships which control the overall process are similar in most cities, although they may be institutionalized differently. While Cambridge is almost unique because of its two universities, it is typical with respect to its decreasing manufacturing capability, concentrated property ownership, and the existence of a property-related political elite.

Our method of analysis may prove useful in gathering further information about this relationship in other cities. In brief, the method is as follows.

1. Examine recent trends in the city's development, such as migration of population and industry, and determine how the costs and benefits of this process are distributed.

1. As yet the comparative literature on community power structures is sparse and inadequate. This study, as an investigation of one case, can obviously do no more than to suggest one particular form that the interrelationships between ownership, politics, and public policy may take. It is *not* an argument that this area is always subject to graft (although it seems likely to generate graft), nor that graft or machine-like mechanisms are necessary for the meshing of the interests of dominant institutions with government policy. Neither are we advocating a conspiracy theory based on a clique of wayward but powerful men. We proceed from the different institutions, elaborate their interests, and examine the way they are tied to politicians and their output. The mechanism involved and the closeness of the ties clearly vary. We urge others to investigate this problem for other cases. See Appendix to this article.

2. Ascertain how property is held, who mans the institutions (such as savings banks) which determine investment in housing and urban development, and how these individuals are related to local government officials who make urban development policy.
3. Determine whether this set of relationships is stable and whether it exercises and consolidates control over development policies.
4. Examine how the benefits and costs of public and private policies are distributed.
5. Trace the successes or failures of opposition groups which seek to alter this distribution.

TRENDS IN CITY DEVELOPMENT

Cambridge is a mature industrial city of 100,000 adjacent to Boston. It contains a large but old manufacturing district, many ethnic blue-collar neighborhoods, and two large universities—M.I.T. and Harvard. The postwar boom set the scene for major alterations in Cambridge's economic structure.

Between 1960 and 1970, Cambridge's population declined from 107,000 to 100,000 while the housing stock increased from about 34,000 units to about 36,000 units. In the same period, the number of students associated with M.I.T. and Harvard increased by roughly 35 percent. As of 1968 more than 4,000 Harvard students and 1,800 faculty occupied about 4,000 units of Cambridge's privately owned housing. M.I.T. students and staff occupied about 2,000 units.[2] The universities together own, as of 1970, about 1,300 units of rental housing.

As the universities have waxed, the heavy industry which came to Cambridge in the 19th century has waned. Since 1960, Lever Brothers, the Daggett Company, Simplex Wire and Cable Company, the Riverside Press, and many other industrial employers have abandoned obsolete Cambridge plants to relocate elsewhere. In their place have risen highly technical, university-oriented firms, many of which are engaged in defense research, social science consulting, architecture, business consulting, and so forth.

These trends—university growth and the shift from manufacturing to research and development—have had severe effects on Cambridge's poor and working-class ethnic population. Students and young professionals have steadily invaded ethnic neighborhoods, causing rents and land values to skyrocket.[3] The poor and elderly, in turn, have been forced out.

According to one source, "The relocation department of the Cambridge Redevelopment Authority estimates that . . . some 500 persons and families are evicted every year in Cambridge by actions of private landlords in the process of assembling private development sites, raising rents, or converting structures into higher-income producing uses."[4] This figure is of the same magnitude as the annual net population decrease (700) for the city.

Are these trends simply the result of freely operating economic forces? The answer, of course, is that behind all such forces stand institutions whose needs and interests

2. Harvard University Graduate School of Design Faculty Statement, 15 April 1969, p. 4. In 10 years Harvard's enrollment has gone from about 11,000 to about 15,000. M.I.T.'s enrollment climbed from 5,000 to 7,000. For M.I.T.'s enrollment and dwelling unit occupation statistics, see Steven Kaiser, "Citizen University Negotiations on Community Housing: The Cambridge Experience," mimeographed (M.I.T., 1969).

3. See Cambridge Housing Convention, *Cambridge: Crisis in Housing* (Cambridge, 1969), for a study of the Harvard Housing Office's listings.

4. Massachusetts Housing Finance Agency, minutes of the board meeting, 25 March 1969.

create and shape them. For example, the 17 major defense contractors in Cambridge would hardly have located there were it not for M.I.T.'s presence.[5] To discover the nature of these interests we will examine the concentration of property ownership and the relationship between owners and the political system. Keeping these relationships in mind we will then turn to their consequences.

THE NEXUS BETWEEN PROPERTY AND POLITICS

Land tenure patterns, the obvious place to begin this analysis, are difficult to document. Since the federal government will not release individual tax returns and city governments do not require owners to divulge their aggregate property holdings (which owners often have reason to conceal), the evidence presented here is necessarily somewhat circumstantial.

One way of estimating inequality is by examining the makeup of the housing stock. In 1960, according to the U.S. Census, approximately 77.5 percent, or 26,500 of the city's housing units were tenant occupied. It is safe to assume that these tenants owned very few of the city's 34,000 units. Single-family and two-family owner-occupied structures contained a total of 5,600 units. Given the large number of university personnel, professionals, and other homeowners whose source of income is not the housing market, it is reasonable to estimate that the 5,600 households in these units owned at most 5,000 additional units. Thus 5,600 (or 16.5 percent) of the city's households owned roughly 10,600 units. The remaining 23,400 units (in large, nonowner-occupied structures) are owned by the remaining 6 percent of the city's households and an unknown but probably small number of outsiders.[6] Figure 4.1 graphically demonstrates the inequality of such a distribution.

Confirmation of this pattern comes from the Cambridge Property Owners' Association, a landlord's political action group. Although there are 14,000 tax billing accounts, according to the president of this organization, there are only 6,500 actual owners. He asserts that his organization has 700 members who collectively own 17,000 of the city's current rental housing units. Furthermore, he claims that the bulk of his members are only small property owners residing in Cambridge, while there are "12 to 15 really big land-owning members" who account for most of the units.[7] If 680 of the members each own 2 of Cambridge's typical 3 decker flats, then they logically account for about 3,400 (or 5 times 680, assuming they live in one of their own buildings) of the 17,000 rental units, while 20 landlords own 13,600 units, or roughly 40 percent, of Cambridge's rental housing. This figure may well underestimate inequality because several known large landowners (including the universities) do not belong to the association.

A third source of evidence on ownership concentration is provided by direct investigation of the holdings of large owners and developers. Although such research is hindered by the use of realty trusts, corporations, and "straw" owners,[8] the Cambridge Tenants

---

5. See Cambridge Redevelopment Authority, "Kendall Square Urban Renewal Area/'Triangle' Property Regional Location and Accessibility," 12 December 1969.

6. These figures come from the U.S. Bureau of the Census, *1960 Census of Housing*, vol. 1, States and Small Areas, pt. 4 (Iowa-Massachusetts), pp. 23-34, table 14.

7. Carl F. Barron, president of the Cambridge Property Owners' Association, interview, 14 July 1971.

8. Boston's largest landlord, Maurice Gordon, for example, uses over 60 different corporate fronts. See the Boston *Globe's* analysis of his activities, 3-6 May 1971, especially the issue of 5 May 1971, for a list of his corporations and reasons for having them.

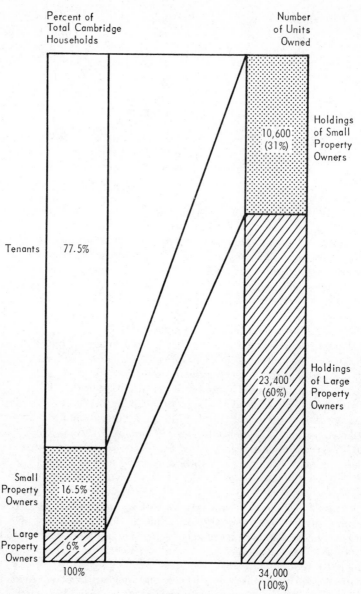

Percent of
Total Cambridge
Households

Number
of Units
Owned

Holdings
of Small
Property
Owners

10,600
(31%)

Tenants   77.5%

Holdings
of Large
Property
Owners

23,400
(60%)

Small
Property
Owners   16.5%

Large
Property
Owners   6%

100%

34,000
(100%)

FIGURE 4.1   *Estimates of Property Ownership Concentration, Cambridge, 1970*
SOURCE: Estimates based on *1960 Census of Housing*, vol. 1, pt. 4, pp. 23-34.

Organizing Committee has begun to investigate landlord holdings. While the work
is incomplete, it has so far discovered 20 landlords each holding between 600 and
1,200 units.

As imperfect as this information is, it is strong enough to show that a relatively
small number of landowners own a very large proportion of Cambridge's housing
stock. While this concentration does not correspond directly to the economist's concepts
of monopoly or oligopoly, tacit or explicit combinations among landowners, banks,
and politicians can give it the same extensive economic and political power. It is

by exploring these interlocking networks that we begin to see the enormous implications land tenure patterns have for housing market performance and urban development.

In Cambridge, as we shall demonstrate, concentrated property ownership is at the heart of a political nexus that wields power vastly out of proportion to the number of Cambridge citizens it represents. The extent of this nexus is indicated in Table 4.1 and in Figure 4.2. The 9 savings banks which finance more than 75 percent of Cambridge housing acquisitions[9] have a total of 237 directorships (including 19 direct and at least 25 indirect overlaps).[10]

TABLE 4.1   *Occupations of Savings Bank Directors, Cambridge, 1970*

Total number of directorships of 9 Cambridge Savings Banks	237
Number of direct interbank overlaps	19
Number of indirect overlaps (through common firm or family)	25
Number identifiable from biographical sources	119
Occupations of identified directors:	
University officials	6 (5%)
Industrial executives (including construction)	26 (22%)
Commercial executives (including finance)	25 (21%)
Government employees (including judges)	8 (7%)
Real estate and insurance (not large owners)	11 (9%)
Real estate (large owners)	30 (25%)
Partners of law firms	13 (11%)
Public officials or appointees serving as directors:	
City councilors	4 of 9
Cambridge Redevelopment Authority Board members	4 of 5
Planning Board members	3 of 6
Assessors Board members	2 of 3
Board of Zoning Appeals members	1 of 5
Cambridge Housing Authority Board members	2 of 5
Eastern Middlesex District Court judges	2 of 3

SOURCES: Quarterly or Semiannual *Statements of Condition* for banks, dated variously December 31, 1970, or January 1, 1971; Poor's *Cambridge Directory* (New Haven, 1965 and 1968).

These directors include: key officers of M.I.T. and Harvard; 4 of the 9 city councilors (several of whom sit on more than one board); 2 of the 3 district court judges (who have jurisdiction over landlord-tenant relations); 2 superior court judges; the county clerk of court; many board members of such agencies as the Cambridge Housing Authority (CHA), Cambridge Redevelopment Authority (CRA), and the Planning Board; the city's tax collector; 2 of 3 city assessors; and at least 30 of the city's large rental property owners and developers. In addition, the savings bank boards contain 50 lawyers, insurance brokers, realtors, and contractors who derive their primary income by serving the housing market. The remainder represent various commercial, industrial, and financial interests (see Table 4.1).

The government agencies involved in this nexus play crucial roles in shaping local policies bearing on the operation of the Cambridge housing market. The city council

9. This figure comes from a survey by the authors of Cambridge housing transactions 1960 to 1970 based on a file maintained by the Cambridge Corporation (a private, nonprofit community development corporation). Data were originally supplied by Appraiser's Weekly, Inc., and Banker and Tradesman, Inc., which monitor the Eastern Middlesex Registry of Deeds.

10. Lists of directors come from Quarterly Statements of Condition from the banks for end of calendar year 1970. According to our definition, an indirect overlap occurs when different banks have directors who either work for the same firm or come from the same family.

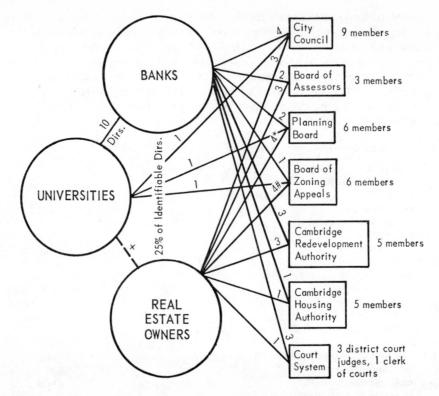

FIGURE 4.2   *Cambridge Real Estate, Banking, and Political Interlocks, 1970*

* Through three contractors and a lawyer.
+ Both universities are large landholders.
‡ Through four lawyers.

SOURCES: Price and Lee's *Cambridge City Directory* (New Haven, 1968); Quarterly Statements of Condition, various banks, 1970; Property Assessments Listing, City of Cambridge, 1970.

appoints the city manager, and together they set the tax rate. The manager, in turn, appoints the members of the governing boards of the other agencies and the city solicitor. Though the solicitor's rulings are only advisory, they generally buttress whatever position a council majority has taken, since he is the political creature of that majority. In recent years his rulings have been used to thwart various threats to landlords' interests.

The Board of Assessors (three men, all of whom are real estate owners and two of whom are bank directors) not only determines the value of real estate for property tax purposes but also has the power to grant tax abatements. It thus determines the relative incidence of taxation. The courts (including three bank directors and a real estate owner) act as a collection agency for landlords, determine whether city agencies are behaving lawfully, and secure landlord property rights when necessary. Thus, the institutions which oversee the housing market and determine the relative incidence of taxation are dominated by those with banking and property interests.

The control these interests have over urban development is also crucial. The Citizen's Advisory Committee (originally set up to fulfill the federal requirement for local participation in urban renewal), the CRA, and the city council are all dominated by men with property interests and bank directorships.[11] These agencies determine which areas will be picked for renewal, what sort of development will occur, who will undertake it, and who will be the new owners or tenants.

Aside from the powerful tool of urban renewal, the city has at its disposal tax incentives, zoning powers, and disposition of city-owned land with which to influence development. Since nearly every substantial project requires some authoritative action by city agencies, the city government can play a determining role in development.

The network illustrated in Figure 4.2 contains several types of powerful individuals. Some are banker-politicians. Often they are part of families which have built wide political followings on the basis of their ability to grant favors. One former mayor has a brother who is clerk of court (and thus exercises patronage control over courthouse jobs), is an assistant clerk of court himself, is a member of the city council, and is bank vice-president and board member. Another city councilor, a drugstore owner, is a bank board member and brother of a county commissioner who is also a large realtor and bank officer. Others in this network are landlord-bankers or developer-bankers. One bank director has used his connections to acquire financing for expansion of his holdings from 20 to nearly 1,000 units (including several luxury apartment buildings he developed).

Although such individuals are powerful in their own right, the overall *pattern* of relationships is much more significant than the connections of any one man. The tightness and the inclusiveness of the pattern mean that the banker-politician and the banker-landowner share similar interests, interact with one another, and, as we will attempt to show, coordinate their decisions. While personnel changes, the network goes on. It has been stable since the Second World War, thus lending credence to the notion of a local "ruling elite."[12]

This three-cornered set of relationships—between politicians, bankers, and property owners and developers—is based on a solid coincidence of interest. Bankers and politicians get along well because, for the banker, the politician attracts depositors, provides important contacts, and ensures that no policies which are likely to hurt land values are adopted. For the politician, the banker represents a source of inside deals on development, a way of influencing mortgage decisions and thus a way of influencing constituents, and a source of status. Hence there are many politicians on bank boards. Owners and bankers have an even closer identity of interest. Banks provide the crucial credit source for large-scale owners, and thus owners seek to become directors. For banks, large owners provide sound investments and additionally provide detailed information on land value trends. Finally, politicians and owners find mutual interest in the influence which owners can extend in behalf of candidates (money, votes of relatives, endorsements) and the favorable government decisions which politicians

11. For an analysis of residence and occupation of board members of all city boards, see David D. McNally and Howard Mantel, *Effective Government for Cambridge* (New York: Institute for Public Administration. 1970).

12. On the stability of the network, see the Appendix to Steve Shalom and Bob Shapiro, "Two, Three, Many Tech Squares" (Cambridge: Rosa Luxemburg SDS, 1969) and Susan Schildkraut's "The City Manager" (unpublished case study for a course taught by Professor Francis Duehay of the Harvard University Graduate School of Education, Fall 1970). The concept of ruling elite must include the institutional structure which supports power as well as the particular individuals who hold power. Perhaps "ruling structure" would be a better term. The pluralists' view on this question is presented in Robert Dahl's "Critique of the Ruling Elite Model," *American Political Science Review* 52 (June 1958): 953-70. See Isaac Balbus, "The Concept of Interest in Pluralist and Marxian Analysis," *Politics and Society* 1:2 (February 1971), and Paul Sweezy, "The American Ruling Class," in Maurice Zeitlin, ed., *American Society Inc.* (Chicago: Markham Publishing Co., 1970), pp. 356-72, for the Marxist formulation.

can render (both collective, such as against rent control, and individual, such as zoning changes and tax abatements).

In Cambridge such interests are meshed in a very old-fashioned way: personally, in key figures and the patronage-based machine government they have created. Although these same interests exist in other cities, they may not be integrated in the same fashion: bank boards, businessmen's committees, or even "good government" organizations based on a prodevelopment platform may serve this purpose instead.

It might be held that this is a desirable state of affairs—those most knowledgeable about real estate make city policy concerning it. Yet, as we shall see, the actions of this interlocking network have not been benign. One city councilor (who is a lawyer associated with a large developer, a director of two local banks, and who was for many years the city's mayor) defended his opposition to rent control by stating "the property owners are the city's backbone—we should be grateful to them."[13] This attitude has been echoed repeatedly by other councilors in debates on rent control, urban renewal, and other housing-related matters.

HOW POWER IS MAINTAINED AND CONSOLIDATED

Because of its legislative, tax-setting, and appointive powers, the city council is the obvious place to begin an analysis of local government housing policies. The Cambridge City Council elects the mayor and appoints the city manager. The manager, in turn, appoints the department heads and board members, and administers the city. He is theoretically a politically neutral figure, but Cambridge's history has been marked by struggles over his appointment and over control of the appointments he is empowered to make. Basically this struggle has involved competition among ethnic, property-based leaders for control of patronage.[14] So far these contending leaders have united on development questions. Five conservative councilors, three of whom hold five bank directorships and have considerable property interests, joined together in January 1970 to elect one of their number, commonly identified as a populist, mayor (he also is a property owner, although only a small one).

While the specific makeup of this coalition has changed slightly from time to time, each administration has had a consistent stance on basic property-related issues. Ethnic electoral organizations which have competed against each other for such offices as county sheriff, for example, joined together to vote against rent control in 1969 and joined once again in 1971 to prevent the removal of a rent control administrator who favored landlords. These property-oriented council elements also joined on impor-

---

13. Edward A. Crane, statement to Cambridge City Council meeting, 12 August 1969.

14. The bloc which has been dominant on housing and property issues includes Walter Sullivan, a property owner, brother of the county clerk of courts, former mayor, director and senior vice-president of the Charlesbank Trust; Edward Crane, a lawyer, former mayor, reported business associate of Cambridge's largest property-holder and developer Max Wasserman, and director of the Harvard Trust Co. and the Central Co-op Bank; Thomas L. Danehy, property owner, pharmacy owner, brother of a realtor who is a county commissioner, vice-president of the University Trust Co. and director of the North Cambridge Cooperative Bank; Daniel Clinton, now a political associate of Danehy who has a job at the county courthouse because of Sullivan and Danehy's patronage influence, and whose father has been appointed to a salaried Housing Authority board membership; and Alfred Velucci, who is mayor, a small property owner, and has a job with the State Department of Taxation which he acquired shortly after forming a political alliance with the state Democratic Committee chairman (which occurred the year he was first elected to council, 1952). Velucci is a long-time friend of Crane. On city manager appointments and patronage appointments, Sullivan is replaced by Thomas Coates, a black former insurance salesman now employed as a recruiter by the Hotel Corporation of America, which owns a hotel in Cambridge.

tant zoning decisions. The unity on these issues is so clear that such elements might be called the property-politics coalition.[15]

Aside from the council's indirect control over appointments, it has two main property-related functions: setting the tax rate and approving or vetoing federal projects such as urban renewal. In both areas the property-politics coalition has struck a deal between the interests of large rental property owners and those of homeowners. It has also relied heavily on retaining support in ethnic working-class neighborhoods by granting personal favors and attention.

There seem to be two reasons why voters support these politicians. First, in advancing the interests of developers and rental property owners, the city government has been constrained to give some concessions to small property owners and homeowners. In exchange for support, the government, according to one study,[16] employs assessment practices which give a tax break to owner-occupied residences. Thus tenants, a larger but politically less cohesive group than owners, bear the burden of the regressive property tax, which is passed on to them in the form of higher rents.[17]

Urban renewal is another example of the political tradeoff between the interests of large property owners and small ones. A proposed urban renewal plan in the Wellington-Harrington area, which would have displaced many homeowners, was defeated by the city council because of homeowner opposition. The council also vigorously opposed an innerbelt freeway loop, which would have destroyed hundreds of homes in this area, even though such a highway is favored by development interests.[18] On the other hand, the council has supported commercial development and luxury housing where tenants rather than homeowners are displaced. One mayor heralded this process as "blitzing the slums."[19] The NASA electronics laboratory, the Tech Square office complex adjacent to M.I.T., and Riverview luxury housing are among the more notable examples of this policy.

The second major source of support for property-related politicians lies in the fact that most of them control rewards and sanctions within their neighborhoods. Those who sit on bank boards influence who gets mortgages; others owning small businesses have neighbors as clients and have extended them credit, or have political associates who are in this position. Through their patronage control over bureaucracies, they may grant or threaten to withhold scarce resources such as public housing. They can and do give their friends city jobs. Residents, if they know and support a city councilor in the property-politics faction, may have a large hospital bill forgiven or gain a place in public housing without undue worry about the waiting list. Tales of such happenings abound in city hall gossip. More important, political associates are appointed to boards where they have an excellent chance to do favors for friends in return for monetary and campaign support. In other words, by constraining policies so as to minimize antagonism with small property owners, exercising considerable influence over their neighborhoods, and offering rewards where necessary, the dominant property-politics faction is able to manage the electorate. The Cambridge Election

15. The unity on property issues contrasts with the competition for control of patronage, which now is between the Sullivan family on one side and the Danehys and Veluccis on the other.

16. Cambridge Planning Board, "Study of Assessments" (unpublished, 1970).

17. See Dick Netzer, *Economics of the Property Tax* (Washington: Brookings Institution, 1966).

18. See the numerous reports on the Inner Belt, including (Massachusetts) Governor's Task Force on Transportation, "Report to Governor Sargent," mimeographed, (1970).

19. Edward A. Crane, quoted in Shalom and Shapiro, op. cit., p. 12

Commission's recent refusal to enfranchise 18- to 20-year-old college students is but another example of this policy.[20]

THE DISTRIBUTION OF ECONOMIC BENEFITS

Concentration has the potential for squeezing surplus from the consumer while providing a shoddy product. The average citizen relies for protection on government regulation of concentration and economic performance. Because of interlocking interests among owners, bankers, and politicians, however, the Cambridge city government has failed to protect the interests of the majority of its citizens (the tenants in this case). It has promoted development of commercial facilities and luxury apartments. It has failed to enforce housing codes, build low-rent housing, or regulate rent increases.

The redevelopment authority (CRA), dominated by commercial and residential property interests, has abetted the city council in supporting development. This important body conforms to urban renewal's national emphasis on commercial facilities and luxury apartments over low-to-moderate-income housing.[21] Even now (in the midst of an acknowledged housing crisis), the CRA is seeking "the development of prestige office buildings, retail stores, apartments, and hotels" for more than 13 acres of "excess" land taken for the NASA electronics laboratory.[22] Completed or active projects include luxury housing, Tech Square, and a revamped Wellington-Harrington project. While the CRA has planned low-to-moderate-rent housing (including some for the nearly decade-old Wellington-Harrington site), it has never managed to get developers to construct much of it.

These projects were supposedly planned to eliminate slum housing, reduce the property tax rate, and stimulate new housing production. However, the housing eliminated was inhabited by the poor, and the new housing built occupied by middle- and upper-middle-income residents. Moreover, it is unclear whether the new projects do reduce the tax rate (there are large losses in the first several years, and the services demanded by the new uses might outweigh any increased tax advantage). There can be no doubt, however, about the overall impact of these changes—to transform Cambridge from a mixed-income city to a middle-, upper-middle-income community.

The Cambridge Housing Authority, while having less direct representation of property interests, is similarly uncongenial to the poor.[23] Community groups struggled

20. Cambridge *Chronicle*, 5 August 1971.

21. In 1970 the CRA Board included Paul Corcoran, president and owner of one of Cambridge's largest department stores, a director of Harvard Trust, Columbian Co-op Bank, and the Cambridge Savings Bank, former president of the urban renewal citizen's advisory group, and former Chamber of Commerce president; J. A. Lunn, retired president of the Cabot Corp., life member of the M.I.T. Corporation, vice-president of the Kendall Co., director of the Bay State Corporation (a rental housing firm), director of the Chamber of Commerce, the North Avenue Savings Bank, and the Cambridge Savings Bank; Thomas Murphy, executive secretary of the Boston Finance Commission and director of the Cambridgeport Savings Bank; and John C. Smith, a black professional and Republican appointed by Governor Sargent. The fifth seat was vacant. In 1971 (after much of the original renewal had been completed), Lunn and Corcoran were replaced and the vacancy filled by political appointees friendly to the dominant council faction.

22. *Cambridge Annual Report 1968* (Cambridge *Chronicle*, 16 June 1969).

23. The CHA Board includes John Clinton, father of Councilor Daniel Clinton (Clinton was appointed due to tenant pressure for a tenant board member); Gerald Hovenanian, a Republican appointee who works for the First National Bank of Boston; Norman C. Watson, a black small businessman associated with Councilor Coates; Mary Castriotta, a homeowner and Velucci associate; and Walter Reed, owner of a funeral home and Crane associate. For a general discussion

a year simply to implement a leased-housing program.[24] The CHA has attempted to stymie tenant efforts to control the modernization program,[25] and has recently raised rents sharply in order to balance its books. According to black spokesmen, the CHA has also discriminated against minority groups.[26] These practices have recently prompted a rent strike and litigation designed to make the CHA more responsive. As for building new housing, the CHA has built only 155 units, all for the elderly, since 1948.

The Planning Board and the Zoning Appeals Board are dominated by real estate and developer interests, and have used their authority to stimulate high-rise development.[27] In instances where variances have been sought and there is little opposition from homeowning abutters, they have usually been granted (even though in some instances they grossly violate the zoning ordinances).[28] It seems likely that Cambridge's central artery, Massachusetts Avenue, now the scene of small shops and apartment houses, will be rezoned for the highest level of development, as has been advocated by the president of the Property Owners' Association.[29]

The benefits of public and private actions taken by the owner-banker-politician network seem rather clearly to accrue to the members of that network. The costs have been of several kinds and have been borne by housing consumers, especially by working-class and elderly tenants. These costs include direct monetary costs and uncompensated losses, such as loss of neighborhood. Concentration by itself probably leads to relatively higher prices and a relatively poorer housing stock, although we presently lack adequate time series and comparative data to demonstrate this relationship.[30]

When demand considerably outruns supply in a market, industry generally responds by increasing and upgrading the supply. The response of the housing market in Cambridge, however, has been in terms of increased rents rather than new construction;

---

of the attitudes of housing authority boards, see Chester Hartman and Gregg Carr, "Housing Authorities Reconsidered," *Journal of the American Institute of Planners* 25 (January 1969): 10-21.

24. Two years after 400 units had been authorized, only 100 had been leased. See Ad Hoc Housing Development Task Group, Progress Report No. 1, mimeographed (1969).

25. At this time the bulk of the modernization funds remain unspent. None has gone for management overhaul. Design has been controlled by the CHA, not by the tenants. On this point see Michael Lipsky, Donald Dickson, John Mollenkopf, and Jon Pynoos, "Citizen Participation in Federal Housing Policy," in U.S., House, Committee on Banking and Currency, *Papers Submitted to the Subcommittee on Housing, Panels on Housing Production, Housing Demand, and Developing a Suitable Living Environment*, 92d Cong., 1st Sess. pt. 1, 895-926 (1971).

26. Cambridge *Chronicle*, "Housing Authority: Discrimination Charges Reach Federal Level," 3 June 1971.

27. The planning board lost two members in 1971: George Najarian, a developer, and John Myers, an architect and bank director. It now has Paul Dietrich, another architect; Fred Cohn, a developer and past supporter of Councilor Crane; Lillian Denkewitz, wife of a roofing contractor, Democratic ward committee chairwoman, and Model Cities Board member; Arthur Parris, a black engineer and son of a Riverside property owner; Dominic Percoco, an electrical contractor related to a family of large landlords; Frank Berochi, a builder and Velucci ally, and John Woolsey, legal counsel for M.I.T. The Board of Zoning Appeals includes Theodore Anastos, Louise Counihan, whose brother-in-law is a lawyer who has represented developers before the board, Paul Gargano, a lawyer and real estate owner who has represented similar developers, Milton Reddick, and William Adario, a small businessman and Velucci associate.

28. See the Boston *Phoenix*, "The Ecology Action Bust," 3 August 1971.

29. Speech to Cambridge City Council by Carl F. Barron, 7 December 1970, as reproduced in Cambridge Property Owners' Association, "Public Notice" (nd).

30. Although it may have this effect, concentration of property ownership is hardly the sole cause of the rent and housing crisis.

units are more likely to be subdivided than rehabilitated. Because of the profitability of existing housing and the present owners' influence over the flow of mortgage money, only 1,900 new units of housing (all in luxury high-rise buildings) were built in the period 1960 to 1970; they displaced 700 units of low-cost housing. An additional 1,000 units of federally subsidized housing were built. Thus the overall change in supply was from about 34,000 units in 1960 to about 36,000 units in 1970.[31]

The demand for housing has led to a "filtering up" of housing from less well-off working-class tenants to more well-to-do professionals and students. The role of the universities, whether they consciously plan it or not, is crucial in attracting new tenants from outside Cambridge who will bid up housing prices. In addition to increasing profits for landlords, this situation diminishes any incentive to improve the housing stock.

Rent increases for Cambridge housing have been spectacular. They have also been disastrous for low-income residents. Median rents, according to census figures, rose from 63 dollars per month in 1960 to 119 dollars in 1970.[32] A survey of newspaper advertisements for rentals indicates median prices climbed from 65 dollars in 1960 to 145 dollars in 1968—an increase of 123 percent.[33] According to national cost-of-living indicators, the housing component of living cost rose more rapidly in metropolitan Boston than in any other major urban area, and another study showed Cambridge's rents to be the highest and most rapidly increasing within the area.[34] In a 1969 city survey it was found that 46 percent of those residing in apartments for more than a year had their rent increased, with the average increase over 15 percent.

Furthermore, these increases were concentrated among the poor and elderly—those least able to bear them. Not only have they incurred the largest percentage increases (a possible statistical artifact of moderate increases on a low rent as compared to moderate increases on a luxury rent), but poorer tenants are *(a)* more likely to have received increases at all and *(b)* have received on the average a higher dollar amount.[35]

One response to increased rents has been to move out of Cambridge. The resulting adverse psychological and physical effects have been particularly harsh on the elderly, who comprised about 11.5 percent of Cambridge's 1970 population.[36] The threat of forced removal is evidently quite real. The 1969 city survey indicated that about one in three residents expected to have to move out of Cambridge soon, but four out of five of these people said this relocation would be involuntary.

Another response to increased rents has been for tenants, especially low-income and elderly tenants, to pay an increased portion of their income for housing. While federal guidelines suggest a maximum of 25 percent, many Cambridge elderly pay more. A 1969 Cambridge Economic Opportunity Committee survey discovered 1,400 elderly paying over 60 percent of their gross income for housing.[37] Another survey,

31. See Cambridge Corporation, "Changes in the Cambridge Housing Stock since the 1960 Census" (June 1969).

32. Census figures for 1960 and 1970 as given in the Cambridge Planning and Development Department's "1970 Census Summary Statistics."

33. See Cambridge Economic Opportunity Committee, "Rent Control, An Analysis" (Cambridge, nd), p. 6.

34. Ibid.

35. Cambridge Community Development Office, Community Renewal Program, *1969 City Survey*.

36. Marc Fried, "Grieving for a Lost Home," in Leonard Duhl, ed., *The Urban Condition* (New York: Basic Books, 1963), pp. 151-71.

37. Cambridge Economic Opportunity Committee, *Survey of Cambridge Elderly Persons and Families*, July 1, 1968.

based on a random sample, indicated that 10 percent of Cambridge's population were elderly, earned less than 4,000 dollars per year, and paid more than 35 percent of their income for housing.[38] As a result, many elderly persons are deprived of other necessities of life, such as food, health care, and transportation.

A third response of low-income residents faced with rising rents is to overcrowd units. While the data are not comprehensive, it appears that the relative proportion of overcrowding is increasing. Between 1960 and 1970 the number of units in Cambridge increased slightly, the city's population decreased slightly, yet the number in overcrowded conditions remained about the same.[39] It is reasonable to assume that many of these overcrowded units are occupied by the poor, since low-rent housing has disappeared faster than low-income people over the last decade.

It might be argued that much of this increase would have occurred whether or not ownership is concentrated. Given a scarcity of land, the difficulty and price of new construction, and growing student demand, rents will inevitably skyrocket. Even if the city council so desired, this argument goes, it could do little one way or the other about the rent increases.

There are three problems with the claim that concentration is irrelevant, however. First, given a market-generated base, rates will vary additionally according to such factors as how effective well-organized owners are in pressing increases and how well-informed they are about the profitability of different uses and rent levels. Bigger owners tend to evaluate and act on these factors more effectively. Smaller landowners (particularly owner-occupants) are constrained by having relatives, friends, or long-term residents as tenants, and because housing investment is usually a long-term income supplement. Such tenants would greatly resent increases over and above rising costs.

Secondly, this argument ignores the way in which demand comes to pass. Large property owners are particularly sensitive to land value trends (exploiting them is their main source of income) and are in a unique credit position to capitalize on them. They thus push for policies and developments which will enhance values—something numerous small owners would not do.

Finally, this argument ignores the ability of a small number of large producers to "administer" the prices when they control the bulk of the supply. While consumer choice to consume less housing or to leave the area involves a small constraint, large owners still have great latitude in raising rents. Nor is this situation threatened by the entry of small, inefficient owners into the market. We must conclude, then, that the structure of ownership probably has a great deal to do with the way rents increase. Ownership structure has not only a direct impact but a very important indirect impact on rents through its influence on demand-generating public policy decisions.

Again, there has been little upgrading or expansion of the supply of housing. Because there is a relative shortage of vacant land in Cambridge, new housing is produced only when it is comparatively more profitable than existing housing. Land costs are a major factor in this calculation, as are financing costs (the latter being generally the major factor in new housing cost).[40] Because of the speculative and aggressive activities of the large owners, land costs have risen rapidly. This means that new housing, if it is to be built, must be either government-subsidized or else high density, high priced luxury housing. That so little of either kind has been built attests to

38. Cambridge Community Development Office, *1969 City Survey*, op. cit.

39. "1970 Census Summary Statistics," op. cit.

40. See Michael Stone, "Federal Housing Policy: A Political-Economic Analysis," Chap. 36 in this book.

the profitability of the existing market. The mortgage cost factor and the ties between large property owner-developers and the banks have guaranteed, however, that when such development occurs it will be owned by those who already dominate the market.[41]

The tie between large housing owners and Cambridge's lending institutions (which supply most of the mortgage money in Cambridge) is likely to foster added concentration of housing ownership. In a tight money market, inside connections and "established track records" are invaluable to landowners and developers in the competition for scarce funds. Since local banks are deeply committed to highly mortgaged local landlords, they are strongly interested in opposing any trend (such as tenant unions or rent control) which might impair projected profitability and thus land values.[42]

In turn, the control of city political machinery by landowning and banking interests becomes imperative. The influence of concentration and interlock on Cambridge's political structure is thus a crucial factor in the market's performance. When a threat to property interests arises, political means must be used to moderate it.

ATTEMPTS TO RECTIFY MALDISTRIBUTION OF BENEFITS

Working-class, poor, and student tenants have responded to city policies on three fronts: agitation for low-rent housing construction, rent control, and opposition to specific developments. Students are part of the problem because they are both displacers of working-class residents and sufferers from it because of the high rents they must pay. This produces the potential organizing problem of overcoming student versus working-class antagonism. At some points the tenant movement has two components, one student and one long-time resident. At other times this tension has been masked by common efforts. In each instance, however, the city government has tried to coopt, obstruct, or defeat tenant efforts.

In order to protect themselves from being forced to move from Cambridge, community groups have attempted to pressure the city and the universities into sponsoring federally assisted low-to-moderate-rent housing. Except for a small amount of housing for the elderly, homeowners have opposed low-rent housing in their neighborhoods. Besides arguing that low-income housing poses a threat to property values, some individuals have used implicitly racist appeals to mobilize their neighborhoods.[43] Second, because the poor lack technical resources, they must pressure other institutions to produce housing, and these institutions generally treat such pressure as an obnoxious distraction from their main goals. These institutions are the very same ones (banks, large landowners and developers, city officials, and the universities) which have exacerbated the housing crisis for their own benefit and whose long-term interests are best served by transforming Cambridge into a white professionals' community.

Prolonged negotiations over housing construction involving the elderly, community groups, Harvard, and M.I.T. have resulted in many promises, less than a thousand units on the drawing board, fewer than a hundred constructed, and considerable evasion. Harvard's refusal to use two large tracts (one within a poor neighborhood and the other a buffer between an affluent and a poor neighborhood) for low-rent

41. The new housing developments in Cambridge, whether federally aided or private, have been built either by existing large owners or by the Cambridge Corporation, a private, non profit developer sponsored by the universities.

42. Even Cambridge's rent control administrator sees this as an important part of his job. The Cambridge *Chronicle*, 12 August 1971, reports he is worried about bank investment, and quotes him as saying, "Banks invest on the basis of projected income and it's impossible to project the income from controlled buildings." He is administering the law in order to prevent disinvestment (i.e., lowered profits).

43. See Richard Cahill's leaflet, "Dear Neighbor. . . ." (Cambridge: February 1970).

housing led to demonstrations, including a takeover of Harvard's 1970 graduation exercises.[44] Similar attempts to pressure the CRA and CHA have also failed.

The inability of working-class Cambridge residents to get low-rent housing built has led them to seek redress through ad hoc and formal regulation. These piecemeal attempts have usually taken the form of rent-withholding actions (rent paid into escrow account) or rent strikes (rent not paid). Massachusetts law provides for the former where there are serious housing code violations. With the assistance of OEO lawyers, a small number of tenants (on the order of 200) have succeeded in forcing their landlords to make repairs. Deficiencies in administering the law have, however, made the tenants' experience with rent-withholding less than satisfying. When landlords indicate to the court that repairs are under way, judges frequently release escrow funds. Tenants thus find it difficult to retain their bargaining power. The biased laws and the property-oriented judges are key elements in weakening tenant attempts to enforce minimum housing standards.[45]

Extralegal rent strikes theoretically can be effective where legal ones are not because most large landlords are highly mortgaged. If solidarity can be maintained among enough tenants and the owner is unable to make a deal with his mortgagee, he may well be faced with losing his property. If this solidarity cannot be maintained, however, the risks of such a strike are high. As a result, extralegal rent strikes are usually organized among those tenants who have little to lose by eviction and who are judgment-proof. This rules out most working-class families.[46]

This type of strike has worked in the small number of cases where it has been tried in Cambridge, but only because a large number of people have been willing to risk arrest. Here, too, tenants are ultimately blocked by the way the legal system operates. Not only do court officials act as a collection and eviction agency, but many Middlesex County deputy sheriffs (whose income derives from fees) are themselves landlords, and in effect constitute a landlord's private police force.[47]

The failure of ad hoc efforts to resist rent increases and low-rent housing depletion has led to appeals for rent control. While the same cry has been raised in other cities, Cambridge is one of the few cities where rent control legislation has been recently passed. Its promulgation has been a superficial concession by the dominant property-politics coalition; its history demonstrates this coalition's resilience and strength.

In the fall of 1969, two groups (the Rent Control Referendum Committee[48] and the Cambridge Housing Convention[49]) began separate campaigns for rent control.

44. Harvard *Crimson*, summer registration issue, 30 June 1970.

45. Paul G. Garrity, "Redesigning Landlord-Tenant Law for an Urban Society," Chap. 4 in this book.

46. See Michael Lipsky, *Protest in City Politics: Rent Strikes, Housing, and the Power of the Poor* (Chicago: Rand McNally, 1970).

47. Cambridge Tenants Organizing Committee, *Tenants Newsletter* 2 July 1971, p. 6. "They're more like Justices of the Peace—freelancers whose whole income is based on fees from landlords and bill collectors. . . . For a constable to build a reputation he has to get tenants out of their homes as quickly and cheaply as possible."

48. The Rent Control Referendum Committee (RCRC) was a relatively small group composed mainly of ex-student, working members or friends of the Progressive Labor Party (PL). Outside of acquiring signatures this group built little community organization. It has been succeeded by the Cambridge Tenants Organizing Committee, a radical but nonsectarian group composed of non-PL RCRC people and the left wing of the Housing Convention. See note 49.

49. The Cambridge Housing Convention was created and supported by the Housing Assistance Program of the Cambridge Economic Opportunity Committee, the local Community Action

(continued on p. 70)

Although they disagreed on analysis and tactics (the former being radical and the latter being OEO-financed), their efforts were complementary. While the radicals gathered signatures on a referendum petition, the Housing Convention wrote an ordinance, called mass meetings in support of it, and sought endorsement from councilors and other influential groups. These two forms of publicity built wide community support for the concept of rent control.[50]

After considerable lobbying and several large meetings, the Housing Convention attempted to get the city council to pass its ordinance. Repeatedly, the dominant property-oriented faction defeated the measure. These defeats led the two groups to throw their efforts into the referendum, which had been specifically designed to bypass city officials. Although the petition was filed with more than enough signatures, rent control supporters were dismayed when the city solicitor (a lawyer appointed because of his friendship with the dominant faction, and who had, in the past, represented landlords) held that the electorate was not empowered, under the home rule provisions of the Massachusetts constitution, to vote on the matter. The election commission immediately voted to keep the measure off the ballot. The radicals, who originally thought they would elude the tentacles of the politicians, became thoroughly entangled in them by engaging in a complicated lawsuit which they lost.

Tenants regrouped and spent the next year convincing the state legislature to pass the enabling act that the solicitor and courts had deemed necessary. After last-minute attempts to defeat the measure, the legislature took the politically expedient alternative (in an election year) and passed an enabling statute basing controlled rents on an undefined "fair return."[51]

In Cambridge, municipal elections failed to provide the clean sweep sought by tenants. The Housing Convention was forbidden by the Hatch Act to engage in electoral politics, and the Referendum Campaign was disinclined to do so on a large scale. Politicians with property ties retained their strength, although some property-oriented newcomers to council endorsed "some form" of rent control. Because of immense public pressure the council ultimately enacted the local option in the fall of 1970.

Several factors underlie this result. Voters do not necessarily see themselves predominantly as tenants. They often choose a property-related candidate on other grounds —ethnicity, residence or influence in the neighborhood, age, etc. Also, as we have argued, pro-landlord politicians have extended many political favors and have created strong electoral organizations on that basis. Finally, homeowners and property owners, while numerically smaller than tenants, have a much higher voting rate.

This victory, however, proved to be illusory. The dominant faction, through their city manager, at first appointed the city solicitor temporary administrator, and then appointed a lawyer with landlord ties as permanent administrator of rent control. The solicitor unilaterally "exempted" many large landowners from the law, and the permanent administrator promulgated definitions of "fair return" which converted

---

Program. It was bitterly attacked by the RCRC as a "tool of the bosses" and by the landlords as "a bunch of outside agitators." It was, however, composed of many community elements. For a description of their campaigns see J. Mollenkopf "Rent Control: The Politics of Property," mimeographed (1969).

50. See J. Mollenkopf, "Rent Control," and Susan Schildkraut, "Rent Control in Cambridge" (a case study done for a course taught by Professor Duehay at the Harvard Graduate School of Education, Fall, 1970).

51. Massachusetts General Laws Chapter 842 (Acts of 1970). Section 7 (b) discusses return. For a general discussion of this issue see Emily Paradise Achteuberg "The Social Utility of Rent Control," Chap. 37 in this book.

the law into a device for rationalizing and in some cases *increasing* rates of return to landlords![52]

Aside from adopting a "fair net operating income" formula which guaranteed a rent increase to landlords in practically every instance where one was requested, the rent control administrator adopted many other discriminatory procedures. Hearings were held during the daytime; tenants were not allowed to examine the landlords' books; they had no access to the records of their hearings; "letters of intent to raise rents" were issued to landlords for use in dealing with banks or prospective property buyers; and whenever tenants contested increases, the sums in dispute were nevertheless deemed payable to the landlord rather than to an escrow account. These were just a few of the many administrative practices which outraged tenants.

By appointing an administrator who used the rent control law to rationalize and regularize profits, the dominant coalition both had their proverbial cake and ate it, too. Their actions were typical of the American pattern of liberal law-making and conservative policy output. Part of this process was their reliance on decentralized government—a decentralization which prevented their opponents from overturning their policy but which helped them advance it. This is nowhere more clear than in the fate of a "reform" coalition which was narrowly elected in November 1971, to a council majority in reaction to the property-dominated faction's policies.

Even though this group succeeded in gaining control in one unit of government, all the others remain in the hands of the property faction. There have been no new appointments to any of the boards discussed, only reappointments of old members, because the new faction has been unable to replace the city manager. It has failed to do so because of internal division among the reformers, at least one of whom, but for being black, comes from a background very similar to that of the property faction. They seem hardly likely to act decisively against development trends if and when they gain control over more of the city bureaucracy (which in itself will take years). The new mayor, a representative of this group, has repeatedly stressed "fair" policies which account for both landlords' and tenants' interests, without seeing that in many cases these interests are opposed. Thus the grip of interlocking property and political interests on Cambridge development patterns seems likely to remain strong.

The third area of popular attempts to influence the housing power structure concerns development trends. Property interests (including the universities) have directed this policy through their influence on bodies such as the CRA, Zoning Appeals Board, and city council, and through their own activities. Community efforts to influence development have as a result manifested themselves as more or less backward-looking attempts to halt official projects because of the difficulty of proposing a socially progressive alternative plan.

At present several major developments are being planned. M.I.T. is on the verge of developing high-rent housing, office space, and shopping facilities on the Simplex Wire site. Harvard has acquired an option on a book printing and binding facility near a poor black neighborhood, and is planning high-rent faculty housing on the last remaining riverfront site near that neighborhood. Harvard also owns several complete blocks near another neighborhood which may very well be used for expansion. The Kennedy Library will take over a large area now used for transit parking and

52. Rent Control Administration, "Determination of 'Fair Net Operating Income' " (3 February 1971) and CTOC's critique of it in "Economic Bulletin no. 2" (1971). This formula guarantees an increase in rents unless landlord costs are less than 50 percent of income—which they almost always are not.

repair. In North Cambridge an extension of the subway and an industrial park are being actively proposed. In East Cambridge, also near M.I.T., the Golden Triangle awaits commercial development. If these developments occur as planned, the changes in Cambridge over the next 10 years will be at least as dramatic as those of the past 10.

Community groups have pressured the universities to use these and other sites for low cost housing and have been told that the land "was too valuable to be used for that purpose."[53] They have also attempted to change the direction of urban renewal in order to use sites for low-rent housing and have in large part failed. Opposition by tenants to the demolition of housing to make way for high-rise offices and luxury housing has been ignored. But even if the Zoning Appeals Board were inclined to turn down the variance applications, it could not affect new developments which already conform to the ordinance. All these community efforts have gained at most several hundred units of low-to-moderate-rent housing where thousands would be necessary simply to preserve Cambridge's neighborhoods.

One of the few encouraging government responses has been the Model Cities program. It was conceived as a means of mutually adapting a neighborhood of working-class homeowners and the development process to each other.[54] Although it is too early to give a definitive report, the Model Cities program does not appear to be succeeding. While the Inner Belt Highway (which would have displaced 6,000 residents) appears to be stalled for good, and the Model Cities Agency has helped some home-owners to renovate and withstand short-term inroads by M.I.T. and speculators, it cannot guarantee adequate employment or income, nor can it provide sufficient low-rent housing to poor neighborhood residents. Employers continue to leave Cambridge, and young professionals continue to enter. Furthermore, the program is in the midst of a crisis which may end it. It has until now been the only truly resident-controlled program in the country. The city manager, with HUD's encouragement, has been trying to take control of the program in order to bring it in line with national policy. The resulting conflict may cause the program's demise.[55]

CONCLUSION

It is clear on the basis of this evidence that the city government has, at the behest of property interests, successfully opposed all political action aimed at altering power relationships within the housing market. The city government has failed to use its influence to construct low-rent housing. The legal machinery has been used to attack tenant unions and rent strikers. The city council has turned rent control inside out

53. This was Harvard's response to the Riverside Planning Team's plea to use the Treeland site for low-rent housing.

54. The Cambridge Model Cities Planning Year Document, "Comprehensive Demonstration Program" (20 December 1968) states on p. v, "Much of the attention which has been directed to the neighborhood's problems in recent years has been focused on reaction to external pressures. Control of these pressures is a difficult task, one which many communities confronting similar problems have not been able to accomplish. . . . If the Model Cities program succeeded in going no further than to preserve the community over the next five years, it would be a monumental feat." In fact, community efforts have resulted in only one development for the elderly. Harvard plans fewer than 300 units, and M.I.T. has promised to deliver fewer than 500 units for low to moderate income uses. In a city losing about 700 citizens a year in large part due to the unavailability of adequate housing this is a totally inadequate program.

55. Cambridge *Chronicle*, 29 April 1971, and Lipsky et al., "Citizen Participation," discuss the issue of city hall control of the Model Cities program.

so that tenants now feel compelled to attack the law. The bodies officially concerned with directing urban development have failed to take steps to assist Cambridge's working-class, poor, and student tenants who are by far its majority of citizens.

These actions have taken place during a period of rapid increase in land values, rents, and real estate profits. It has been a period of steady transformation. The city's government and universities have chosen to do little about the social costs of this transformation. Instead, they have responded to the loss of manufacturing plants by searching for alternative contributors to the tax base—such as office buildings, luxury housing, and highly technical light industry. A very small number of individuals have profited from these changes. As we have seen, the bulk of land ownership is in a few hands; these same people dominate the city's lending institutions and are closely associated with those who man planning-related agencies. Those who have paid the costs are the elderly pensioners, working-class families forced to locate elsewhere, and students paying exorbitant rents.

In this process local government and federal programs have played a crucial role. Local government actions can be explained by analyzing the network of shared interests among owners, bankers, and politicians, and matching these interests against the differential impact of official policies. Any program aimed at "community control" of housing or a "decent home and a suitable living environment" must address itself to these structural relationships. Unless these relationships are broken down, any new housing policies are destined to provide simply another means of entrenching and enriching those who are already in control.

APPENDIX: COMMUNITY POWER STRUCTURES

Groundwork for comparative studies has been laid by Robert Perucci and Marc Pilisuk, "Leaders and Ruling Elites: The Interorganizational Bases of Community Power," *American Sociological Review* 35 (December 1970): 1040-56; Charles Kadushin, "Power, Influence, and Social Circles: A New Methodology for Studying Opinion Makers," *American Sociological Review* 33 (October 1968): 685-99; and John Walton, "A Methodology for the Comparative Study of Powers: Some Conceptual and Procedural Applications," *Social Science Quarterly* 52 (June 1971): 36-61. Some of the initial, though inadequate, attempts at comparative research are conveniently collected in Charles Bonjean et al., eds., *Community Politics: A Behavioral Approach* (New York: Free Press, 1971); while most of the early criticisms of pluralism are gathered in Charles McCoy and John Playford, *Apolitical Politics* (New York: Thomas Y. Crowell, 1967).

The articles cited are the culmination of a long and confused debate over whether power in cities is "pluralist" or "elitist," an argument which questions whether or not power is centralized in a specifiable group of people. As many have pointed out, however, centralization and stratification of power are somewhat independent dimensions. Power need not be held by a clique of mill owners, for example, to exclude both given strata and given questions from decision-making.

The network approach advocated by this and the cited articles accepts that power may not be tightly centralized but may instead be coordinated over different issue areas. Such a method points out the nature of dominant institutions and their ties to one another without making an a priori assumption of their nature. It has the further advantage of pointing toward historical and comparative studies.

Practical guidance for this kind of study can be found in: W. Ron Jones, *Finding Community: A Guide to Community Research and Action* (Palo Alto, Calif.: James E. Freel and Assoc., 1971); Jill Hamburg, *Where it's At: A Research Guide for Community Organizing*

(Boston: New England Free Press); and Mike Stone, *People Before Property* (Cambridge: Urban Planning Aid). The following are key sources of information: quarterly bank statements listing directors, city directories giving residents' occupations, assessors' records giving property owners' holdings, registry of deeds' recording dates and prices of sales, and tax departments' records of tax abatements. Newspaper files occasionally produce membership lists, data on individuals, and other evidence of informal ties. These sources generate a great deal and should be exploited prior to interviewing. For example, by looking under a bank's name in the grantee index at the registry of deeds one finds a complete list of all mortgages held by that bank. With this data it is possible to have a much more exciting interview with bank officials. Interviewing knowledge is crucial in sorting out patterns of ties.

We would like to acknowledge the guidance and criticism of Chester Hartman, Robert Schafer, Emily Paradise Achtenberg, Michael Lipsky, Frank Ackerman, Matthew Edel, Charles Campbell, Theda Skocpol, and Cynthia Mollenkopf.

5. Redesigning Landlord-Tenant Law for an Urban Society

PAUL G. GARRITY

. . . In contrast with concern for and protection of consumers of other necessities of life, legislatures have reinforced the legal status of suppliers of rental housing and have underregulated their responsibilities.[1] Moreover, by refusing to overturn or condemn illogical precedents or unreasonable practices, courts have further entrenched landlords' prerogatives and have impeded needed improvements to much urban low income housing. There has been a conspicuous reluctance to revise legal theory to respond to the exigencies of the contemporary housing crisis. Courts also have not been especially imaginative and innovative when confronted with a particular demonstrated need for reform and change. This paper will explore and consider these issues and develop proposed revisions in current landlord-tenant law and practice impelled by the urgency to achieve solutions resolving this housing crisis.

ECONOMIC AND HISTORICAL IMPEDIMENTS TO CHANGE

It is debatable whether economics or history has determined the condition and the status of the modern urban tenant. The economic impotency of the ghetto resident is underscored by statistics which are readily available to indicate that a very large percentage of low-income urban residents are tenants rather than owners of their own homes. The quantity of suitable low-income housing alternatively available to these urban tenants is appallingly deficient. If food, clothing, or other necessities were in similarly short supply, government would be compelled to institute rationing or massively intervene with other appropriately severe controls. Urbanologists pathetically decry the disparate bargaining power between the urban landlord and his tenant as if this condition were a recent phenomenon. However, even assuming an ample supply of suitable low-income housing, it could be argued that the "take it or leave it" attitude of most urban landlords would continue unchanged unless current landlord-tenant law is revised.

Unfortunately, the few reported decisions restating or expanding the paucity of remedies available to urban low-income tenants fail to reflect the dynamics of the urban landlord-tenant relationship.[2] Courts occasionally reflect on the causes and

Reprinted from the *Journal of Urban Law* 46 (1969): 695-721 (edited), by permission of the publisher and author. Copyright © 1968 by the University of Detroit School of Law. Paul G. Garrity was an assistant professor of law at Boston College Law School and a fellow in urban legal studies at Harvard Law School, and is currently the judge of Boston's new Housing Court.

1. There has been no state which has completely revamped its law of landlord and tenant. Any legislative efforts at reform have been piecemeal and are bitterly resisted by lobbyists for landlords. Consider the see-saw battle in Massachusetts waged between landlord and tenant interests in limiting and extending the time allowed tenants to relocate after termination of a tenancy not by fault of the tenant under Mass. Gen. Laws Ch. 239, § 9 (1932). The original statute provided for a discretionary stay of execution of the landlord's judgment for possession for one month. In 1952 this was extended to 12 months, in 1956 it was restricted to 6 months, in 1957 the allowable stay was 9 months and in 1967 the time delay was established at 3 months.

2. In *Brown v. Southall Realty Company,* 237 A.2d 834 (D.C. Ct. App. 1968), *cert. denied* 89

(continued on p. 76)

conditions of urban slums and even less frequently do they display an appreciation of the significance and scope of the broader issues involved. Moreover, where courts react favorably to tenant requests for relief, inappropriate after-the-fact remedies are compelled by juridical inability to fashion solutions constructively. A court may excuse a tenant from paying rent for premises which were untenantable at the time of the letting, but this prevailing tenant most likely will relocate to or is already occupying premises only somewhat more suitable but still in violation of the local housing code.

The typical urban low-income tenant rarely appreciates or considers the unsuitability of the premises he occupies unless a crisis in habitability occurs or he is contacted by an organizer. Either he has been evicted from or he has abandoned a prior uninhabitable apartment, and he must house his family as quickly as possible. Once in possession of new premises, the low income tenant is subject to continued oppression by his landlord. Either the tenant has executed a standard lease both reinforcing protectionist legal principles favoring the landlord and waiving what few benefits that he may have, or he occupies his apartment at the will of the landlord for a mutually renewable or cancelable term. While the attitude of the landlord at the letting is "take it or leave it," his attitude now is "if you don't like it, move." If the tenant becomes militant or overly demanding in the landlord's judgment, he will be forced to vacate and to incur the expense and social dislocation of removing his family to a questionably improved or equally substandard apartment.

Numerous historical factors have combined to contribute to the unfortunate modern legal status of the urban tenant. The earliest tenants were either serfs or small farmers renting land for agricultural purposes with little thought given to housing which may have been included within the terms of the tenancy or negotiated separately. If a lease was executed between the parties, realty rather than housing was the basis of the transaction. The terms and conditions of these early tenancies were recognized and reinforced by the common law of conveyancing and were designed and structured for a rural society by landlord-oriented lawyers and courts. Typical premedieval and medieval tenants were without a lease and occupied premises, which between the parties were viewed as consisting of land for tillage, made available entirely at the will of the landlord. Remedies that developed, such as ejectment and actions for waste, focused on land, rather than dwellings, which constituted the basis of the landlord-tenant relationship.

As commerce and business developed, theories and practices were revised, and certain contract principles became intertwined with the conveyancing-based law of landlord and tenant in response to the demands of an increasingly mercantile society. The subject of negotiations between the landlord and the merchant-tenant was a business or commercial property or both. However, these parties also had to contend with the rigid rules and concepts that had been carried over from earlier periods, and provisions were developed concerning assignment, repairs, insurance, and the like, which, although intended for use solely in commercial transactions, in turn became inflexible and grafted onto the common law of landlord and tenant. Medieval conveyancing doctrines were not sufficiently modified, however, to incorporate into landlord-tenant theory such contract principles as mutuality of convenants and mitigation of damages.

Sup. Ct. 621 (1969) where the Court voided a lease entered into by a landlord who at the time had knowledge of existing code violations, Judge Quinn restricted his opinion to a discussion of purely technical issues and appeared to scrupulously avoid any consideration of policy problems.

As society became predominantly urban, the theory that a lease or tenancy was a conveyance and in some respects an express contract with certain implied convenants did not become further altered to adapt to the reality that the non commercial urban landlord-tenant relationship involved a hiring of premises suitable for dwelling purposes. The "take it or leave it" and "if you don't like it, move" responses imputed to the urban landlord have been fostered by almost a millennium of legal theory protective of his interests and are quite inappropriate when contrasted with contemporary needs and realities.

THE TREND OF THE LAW

Early Legislative Efforts at Reform

As slum conditions became intolerable, as pressures for change multiplied, and as most American courts reacted unfavorably to efforts to mitigate some of the harsher and most inappropriate landlord and tenant rules, local and state governments responded by assuming varying regulatory powers over housing. These early attempts at reform instigated by states and municipalities focused on unsuitable housing and were based on extensions of the police power to remedy unsafe and unsanitary conditions in the community. Housing codes were enacted which established residential dwelling standards, and procedures were developed to inspect and to ascertain noncompliance with these codes. However, administrative enforcement of housing codes has been studied and analyzed as haphazard and sporadic. Courts have been reluctant to impose realistic civil or criminal penalties for such revolting violations as failure to provide heat even when the severity of the fines provided approximated the gravity of the violations. Perhaps there is an implied judicial appreciation that excessively punitive sanctions will force the slumlord to abandon his properties which, as deficient as they are, provide a semblance of shelter to the very poor. This well-intentioned belief, however, fails to take into account the high rents levied by most slumlords, which quite often equal rentals for suitable housing outside the urban slum.

Conceptually, these early housing codes, which remain listed among the statutes of nearly every state, are also deficient. Most require tenant initiation which presupposes an aggressiveness that one rarely finds among unorganized tenants in a sellers' market. For each reported case involving a retaliatory eviction defense successfully maintained, scores of other unreported situations must exist when landlord intimidation or tenant apathy has resulted in tenant forbearance in reporting code violations. Also, without complementary remedies, there is the possibility that a rigorously enforced housing inspection program, with the ultimate sanction of condemnation and vacating of the premises indiscriminately applied, will in fact somewhat diminish the available supply of low income housing.

Early Litigation Aimed at Reform

Decisional law focusing on mitigating certain harsh aspects of landlord and tenant law developed some impetus at the time housing codes became widely adopted. The remedy of constructive eviction was fashioned to relieve a tenant of liability for rent for premises which deteriorated during the tenancy to an extent precluding use or occupancy, assuming the untenantable conditions were not caused by the act or omission of the tenant. This theory gained wide acceptance and was rationalized variously on contract principles. Most reported decisions, however, have involved commercially leased premises. Courts, moreover, manifested certain misgivings in departing from venerable precedent by emasculating or seriously restricting the scope of this remedy. In most jurisdictions, a precondition to its utilization has involved relinquishment of the premises by the tenant. Procedural technicalities and intricate problems of proof of facts have also militated against the use by low income tenants of this essentially negative remedy. Such tenants usually have unsuccessfully asserted a defense of constructive eviction, after abandoning substandard premises, in answer to a slumlord's claim for rent due for the unexpired remainder of a term.

Recent Litigation

Only during the last decade and especially within the past few years has any significant litigation been initiated which was directed at modifying traditional landlord-tenant concepts.[3] The thrust of most of the cases decided has revolved around problems of unsuitability for occupancy existing either at the original letting of the premises or arising during the course of occupancy. A plethora of imaginative theories based on current and emerging contract, tort, equity, and consumer doctrines have been advanced and argued with disappointing success.

At common law, there was no implied condition or convenant of suitability for occupancy at the commencement of the tenancy in the absence of statute. The rule then, as now, in most jurisdictions was simply *caveat emptor*. Additionally, landlords had no duty to repair premises deteriorating during the course of tenancy. These rules may have had an arguable rationale in an agrarian milieu where a tenant-farmer's expectations were limited to four walls and a roof or between the landlord and a merchant-tenant at least theoretically engaged in some negotiating process. However, these concepts are absurd when applied to immigrants or migrants arriving in the North during winter months to occupy barely livable and inadequately heated apartments. One jurisdiction has abrogated the common law and has determined that there is an implied warranty of habitability at the letting of premises.[4] This rule, however, has not been widely adopted, and the few cases which have followed this decision rely on an implied statutory mandate.[5]

In response to the inadequacies of constructive eviction as a remedy available to tenants of deteriorating premises, theorists have resurrected and some courts have adopted the contract theories of mutuality of remedy and illegal contract to relieve the urban tenant of liability of rent due for premises which become substandard during the course of occupancy. One commentator has proposed the creation of a separate tort category termed "slumlordism."[6] He argues that a tenant of premises not in compliance with a housing code should be allowed to recover in tort for inten-

---

3. E.g., in January 1969, the Supreme Court decided one and indirectly resolved two eviction cases involving low-income tenants and resolved each in favor of the tenants. 2 *Law in Action* no. 8 (January 1969). The three cases were *Thorpe* v. *Housing Authority of the City of Durham*, 393 U.S. 268 (1969), *Habib* v. *Edwards*, 397 F.2d 687 (D.C. Cir. 1968), *cert. denied* 89 S. Ct. 618 (1969), and *Brown* v. *Southall Realty Co.* 237 A.2d 834 (D.C. Ct. App. 1968), *cert. denied*, 89 S. Ct. 621 (1969).

4. *Pines* v. *Perssion*, 14 Wis. 2d 590, 111 N.W. 2d 409 (1961). . . .

5. See. e.g., *Brown* v. *Southall Realty Co.* 237 A.2d 834 (D.C. Mun. Ct. App. 1968) *cert. denied*, 89 S. Ct. 621 (1969), where the court ruled that a landlord cannot recover rent for premises let in violation of the District of Columbia Housing Regulations. [Editors' note: The District of Columbia Circuit Court of Appeals recently accepted the principle of an implied warrant of habitability, noting, "In our judgment the old no-repair rule cannot coexist with the obligations imposed on the landlord by a typical modern housing code, and must be abandoned in favor of an implied warrant of habitability." *Javins* v. *First National Realty Corporation*, 428 F.2d 1071 (D.C. Cir.), *cert. denied* 91 S. Ct. 186 (1970). See also Myron Moskovitz, "Rent Withholding and the Implied Warrant of Habitability—Some New Breakthroughs," *Clearinghouse Review* 4 (June 1970): 1ff.]

6. Sax, "Slumlordism as a Tort," 65 *Mich. L. Rev.* 869 (1967). But see Blum & Dunham, "Slumlordism as a Tort: A Dissenting View," 66 *Mich. L. Rev.* 451 (1968). Litigation was instituted

tional infliction of mental and physical suffering against the landlord who rents such housing being well aware of its substandard condition. Another suggests the fashioning of an affirmative equitable remedy which would incorporate the doctrine of receivership into the law of landlord and tenant to upgrade below-standard housing.[7] This solution has received very little support from courts absent a statutory scheme. The consumer defenses of adhesion and unconscionability, while conceptually valuable in mitigating especially oppressive clauses in standard form leases, are unlikely to have an appreciable impact as a low income tenant remedy.

These imaginative proposals to provide additional tenant remedies are essentially unresponsive to the needs of most urban low income tenants. Applying consumer principles is intriguing since the tenant is certainly a consumer of housing, but the tactic required in this instance is legislation and not litigation. The contract and consumer remedies convincingly argued are unfortunately defensive and come into play either just prior to or subsequent to eviction from or abandonment of the substandard premises. Tort actions for damages involve difficult problems of proof unless one adopts a *per se* approach, and even then the deterrent effect on other slumlords may not even approximate the impact of the hangings at Tyburn on the pickpockets in the crowd.

Recent Legislation

Evolutionary legislation attempting to render code enforcement more viable by the creation of affirmative tenant remedies has been widely adopted and has taken the form of rent withholding, rent escrow, and rent receivership. In addition to a recognition that housing codes standing alone are conceptually and practically inadequate, other rationales exist for this spate of legislation authorizing economic retaliation by tenants. Absent statutory approval, the individual rent strike to compel code compliance has often led to a judicially sanctioned eviction for nonpayment of rent. Moreover, while organized tenants acting in concert may lead to an equalization of bargaining power, the slumlord of marginally profitable housing may well decide to abandon the premises.

Under the usual rent withholding statute, the tenant withholds his rent if the premises are in violation of the local sanitary code, and he may subsequently assert this fact as a defense to eviction for nonpayment of rent. Such statutes variously require notification by the tenant of an intent to withhold, a prior certification of code violations, and perhaps payment of back rent when the complained of conditions are corrected. Rent escrow statutes require paying of rent due to a court or local administrative agency and may or may not allow use of the rent collected to correct the violations complained of. Under statutory rent receivership, courts are granted broad equitable powers to provide for the suspension of the incidents of ownership to a building to enable an appointed receiver to collect rent and to apply it to needed repairs. A revolving fund may be authorized and may possibly be appropriated to facilitate early and speedy rehabilitation. Unfortunately, all of these remedies are quite complicated, require initiation by well-counseled tenants, and often become a trap for

---

recently in California testing this theory. *Mendoza* v. *Gonzalez*, C.C.H. Pov. L. Rep. 9416 (Sup. Ct. Cal., January 31, 1969).

7. See Levi, "Focal Leverage Points in Problems Relating to Real Property," 66 *Colum. L. Rev.* 275, 280-83 (1966) where the author recommends the appointment of a receiver to perform required repairs where the landlord is unwilling to do so. But see *St. Louis* v. *Golden Gate Corporation*, 421 S.W. 2d 4 (1967) where the court refused to appoint a receiver in the absence of a statute despite the existence of numerous housing code violations. The court felt that statutory safeguards suffient to protect landlords and lienholders were required.

the unwary.[8] Moreover, they have seldom been availed of by low income residents absent time-consuming efforts by organizers attempting to unify and to infuse militancy into the life style of the urban poor.

Summary

Assuming an attainment of competitive parity between urban landlords and tenants in the renting of premises for dwelling purposes, the public interest demands that government ensure such premises be in conformance with housing codes. To achieve this end, litigation is too time-consuming and its impact is not sufficiently broad to upgrade low-income housing generally. Considering the magnitude of the problem, the case-by-case approach is almost irrelevant.[9] Most legislative proposals also develop after-the-fact remedies, *e.g.*, the unfortunate tenant or tenants' council is either attempting to have upgraded a particularly dilapidated apartment or is asserting a defense to an action for rent after being forced to vacate substandard and perhaps unsafe premises. The private counsel to poor clients and the legal services program attorney rarely have the opportunity to engage in preventive law practice as do their downtown colleagues and, aside from mostly ineffective community education projects, this dilemma is highlighted by the results obtained in representing ghetto tenants.

MODERNIZING THE LANDLORD-TENANT RELATIONSHIP

A thorough revamping of landlord-tenant legal concepts is imperative to respond to the peculiar problems created by the urbanization of modern America. The nature of existing landlord-tenant relationships is characterized by the law's failure to recognize adequately or to protect sufficiently a tenant's status and interest in the dwelling-property which he rents. Statutory schemes which have been created and precedents which have been established have been inappropriate to alleviate the chronic shortage of low-income housing and to secure safe and decent housing. Noninvolvement in regulating terms and conditions of occupancy by courts and legislatures has led to unconscionable and oppressive results. The indigent urban tenant's situation is exacerbated by virtue of his poverty. I have selected four areas which are especially demanding of reform in which to recommend proposals for the restructuring of landlord-tenant relationships. The ultimate and perhaps only appropriate solution is a complete revamping of landlord-tenant law and perhaps a Model Code or Uniform Act.[10]

8. Note, 78 *Harv. L. Rev.* 801, 828-30 (1965). In Boston, local community agencies have acted as escrow agents in collecting and holding rents for tenants under the Massachusetts rent-withholding legislation. Some of these agencies proceeded without advice of counsel during early stage of the proceedings, and the result was quite often dispossession of the tenants from their premises.

9. For an illustration of a proposed litigation strategy in the area of law and poverty see Albert, "Choosing the Test Case in Welfare Litigation. A Plea for Planning." 13 *Clearinghouse Review* 4 (November 1968).

10. There is no "Model Landlord-Tenant Code" or "Uniform Tenancy Act." The closest approximation to a restatement of the law of landlord and tenant is contained in I *American Law of Property*, Pt. 3 (1952). See also Schier, "Protecting the Interests of the Indigent Tenant: Two Approaches, in Ten Broek. *The Law of the Poor* 359 (1966). [Editors' note: *See also* Myron Moskovitz and Peter J. Honigsberger, "Tenant Union-Landlord Relations Act: A Proposal," 68 *Georgetown Law Journal* 1013-62 (1970). In 1972 the National Conference on Uniform State Laws adopted a Uniform Residential Landlord and Tenant Act. The Uniform Laws Commission is obligated to introduce this Act and press for its passage in each state legislature. While not very strong and not as advanced as the statutes in some states, the Uniform Act would provide a substantially better set of landlord-tenant laws than exist in many states. See *Law Project Bulletin*, Vol. II, Issue 7 (August 15, 1972; National Housing and Economic Development Law Project, University of California, Berkeley).]

The Anachronism of Discretionary Termination of Tenancies

One of the more repugnant aspects of landlord-tenant law, irrespective of the affluence of the tenant, is the long-established doctrine, statutorily authorized, of allowing the landlord to terminate a tenancy unilaterally and permitting him to institute process to expel his tenant without requiring an assignment of any reason for this action. The tenant who rents premises for a term without the dubious benefit of a lease, and alternatively described as a "periodic tenant" or a "tenant at will," occupies the premises by the grace of the landlord. The unchallenged rationale underpinning this rule is that the owner of property should be free to use it as he sees fit. In all jurisdictions requiring a legal process, a court merely rubber stamps and approves a landlord's application for eviction assuming notice provisions are complied with. In such cases, unless the tenant can prove that the termination and eviction are motivated by racial or other discrimination or in retaliation for informing public officials of housing code violations, or the tenant's attorney can ferret out a procedural flaw in the dispossess proceedings, the tenant must vacate.[11] Some jurisdictions allow the dispossessed tenant time to secure new dwelling premises. In most cases, this allowance of time for voluntary, unaided relocation rests with the discretion of the court, and, while such a remedy may be theoretically appropriate, it falsely assumes that alternative housing is readily available to the indigent tenant or to the tenant with a large family.[12] This rule authorizing a landlord unfettered discretion to evict operates with equal harshness on the tenant for years whose lease has expired at the end of the stated term. Such tenants are rarely allowed a grace period to secure alternative premises since it is again erroneously assumed that such housing is available and also that this tenant has made advance arrangements to occupy a mythical apartment. In some jurisdictions, the tenant with a lease can be summarily evicted by the terms of his lease without notice or court process.

The nonavailability of suitable, alternative low income housing requires the modification or suspension if not the abolition of the rule sanctioning untrammeled discretion in the landlord to terminate tenancies. Aside from intrafamily rentals, the urban landlord constantly stresses to his critics and proponents of government regulation that he is an entrepreneur engaged in the business of furnishing premises for occupancy at a profit. It logically follows that he should have no objection to allowing the continuation of occupancy by orderly and nondestructive tenants who pay their rent. A landlord should certainly have the right to control the use of his premises by evicting undesirable tenants. If a new rule creating a tenant vested-interest in continuing occupancy is adopted, the landlord should not be allowed to resort to subterfuge by dispossessing tenants through arbitrary and excessive rent increase.[13] The adoption of appropriate safeguards may require the imposition of a regulatory scheme controlling unreasonable spiraling of rentals for the duration of the low income housing crisis.

A less stringent proposal modifying the classical rule of absolute discretion to evict

11. If the tenant refuses to vacate once the landlord obtains a court order entitling him to repossession, a quasi-public peace office of some sort is usually retained to summarily eject the tenant from the premises. . . .

12. In the author's experience, which is confined to greater Boston, apartments for large families are simply not available or are not rented to such families. As far as public housing is concerned, large units are extremely scarce and are not being constructed nor are they available except in the inner city.

13. A favorite device employed by more unscrupulous Boston landlords involves requiring a tenant to sign a lease without a copy being delivered to the tenant. The landlord then can either hold the tenant to a definite term or increase the rental while denying the existence of a lease for a fixed term at an established rent.

might be to require landlords who terminate a tenancy without cause to assume the responsibility of finding alternative housing and to bear the expense of relocating the dispossessed tenant. This could be accomplished in partnership with the local urban renewal agency supposedly expert in such matters. Such a program should not be available to the tenant evicted for cause or who has voluntarily relinquished his premises, although many critics of urban renewal relocation efforts have pointed out that tenants fearing eviction often voluntarily move prior to becoming eligible for relocation assistance and benefits. This rule would in part suitably counterbalance the protectionist legal principles allowing landlords to accelerate term rentals when a tenant fails to pay rent on time or abandons the premises as well as the failure of most courts to adopt the contract rule of mitigation of damages in such cases. There can be no rebutting the fact that when the landlord unilaterally decided upon eviction, his intentional action results in monetary and social harm to the unfortunate tenant which should be compensated and redressed.

Adoption of Occupancy Codes or Licensing of Dwellings As To Habitability

Housing codes either alone or combined with tenant-initiated remedies have been inappropriate and inadequate to correct substandard housing conditions. Except for the isolated case, decisional law has been too bogged down with feudal concepts and considerations even to attack narrowly the problem. However, other aspects of property law, notably commercial conveyancing law and practice, have experienced some promising developments. In certain localities, it has been considered reasonable conveyancing practice for the purchaser of income-producing residential property or a home destined for personal use by the buyer to insist upon and to receive a certificate from the seller to the effect that the property to be purchased complies with local housing codes in addition to zoning ordinances. It would be quite unrealistic to expect a slum tenant to demand on his own initiative a "certificate of occupancy" from an urban landlord although a statutory provision exists mandating this requirement. I would recommend that a landlord be required to obtain a certificate of occupancy or to be granted a license to rent, which would state in effect that the premises comply with the local housing code. Such a certificate or license would be required prior to renting an apartment to a tenant and at periodic intervals thereafter.

The regulatory controls proposed to ensure safe and adequate low-income housing are certainly drastic, but such action is necessary in view of the scope of the problem. There may very well result a conclusion that adequate private low income housing is economically impossible to achieve. The answer may very well be increased rent subsidies and public housing. . . .

Landlords certainly should not be required to pay for untenantable conditions caused by tenants or for repairs occasioned by vandalism or destruction where one is unable to assign responsibility for such depredations or for excessively expensive insurance to protect against such costs. Government which should require and enforce compliance resulting in the incurring of such expenses should perhaps reimburse landlords for such damages.

Statutory Terms and Conditions of Occupancy

Among low-income tenants, the impetus to execute a lease usually comes from the landlord. Where local law is ambiguous or extends a tenant's common law rights as to significant terms and conditions of occupancy, it is clearly to the landlord's advantage to propose to the prospective tenant a lease favoring the landlord's interests and usually on a "take it or leave it" basis. It is conjectural whether in fact any bargaining takes place at the original execution of a lease for low income premises. Where statutes and decisional law reinforce the disparate status between landlord and tenant, the landlord may either propose a lease or let the premises under an oral tenancy depending on local practice and circumstances. In such cases, any lease that is entered into is for a relatively short term or contains an escalation of rent clause to enable the landlord to increase rentals at the expiration of the brief terms or at his option.[14]

Most noncommercial standard form lease agreements borrow heavily from landlord-oriented commercial leases. Very few, if any, practice formbooks contain leases favorable to tenants. The typical public housing lease is especially pernicious and has been the subject of much comment and controversy. Such leases are usually agreements for month-to-month tenancies containing recitals of landlord rights and tenant duties. However, as oppressive and one-sided as the typical public housing lease may seem, it usually does not contain the additionally onerous waivers of tenant rights included in private leases.[15]

The most repugnant features of such private landlord-tenant leases are the waiver and exculpatory clauses which they contain and which have been judicially upheld unless contrary public policy considerations prevail. Waivers have been incorporated into leases where the tenant has relinquished a statutory notice to vacate, a judicially supervised civil process of eviction, or the right to notify enforcement agencies of housing code violations. Exculpatory lease provisions have been drafted which relieve the landlord of his responsibility to repair untenantable premises, which do not hold him responsible for a failure to provide necessary utilities such as heat and water, and which absolve him of liability caused by his negligence or culpable nonfeasance.

Most objectionable lease provisions other than waiver or exculpatory clauses center around terms imposing on the tenant the duty to repair irrespective of fault, allowing the landlord unrestrained apartment inspection privileges, including automatic lease renewals providing for rental increases at the option of the landlord, and such procedural matters as acceleration of the term rent in event of nonpayment of a portion thereof and reimbursement by the tenant of court costs and attorney's fees. The dimensions of the problem are such that when tenants' councils have become sufficiently organized to achieve a semblance of bargaining power, the initial manifestation of their militancy is usually an insistence to commence negotiations for a lease treating equitably both the landlord and his tenants.

14. In Boston, located in what is generally known as "landlord" jurisdiction, most ghetto landlord-tenant relationships are of the oral variety. Middle income and student housing terracils usually involve leases.

15. Many private leases contain provisions absolving the landlord from liability for his own negligence. Such a clause is expressly forbidden by federal housing authorities. *Local Housing Authority Management Handbook*, Part IV *Leasing and Occupancy* § 1, Occupancy Policies. [Editors' note: In 1971 the Department of Housing and Urban Development (HUD) issued regulations requiring all housing authorities to adopt a lease form and grievance procedures that meet minimum HUD standards. Clauses abrogating tenants' legal rights are now prohibited; housing projects must conform to local housing code standards; tenants will be entitled to rent abatements if required to live in hazardous quarters; fines and other charges must be collected separately from rents; inspection of a tenant's dwelling unit now requires advance written notice; and leases are now perpetual and can be terminated only for good cause, in contrast to the previous month-to-month lease used by most authorities. In addition, a detailed grievance procedure is mandated, which includes hearings before an impartial body and adequate notice provisions. RHM 7465.8 (February 22, 1971); RHM 7465.9 (February 22, 1971). Renewal and Housing Management (RHM) circulars are the customary vehicle for HUD rulings and are kept in the various HUD-FHA offices throughout the country. See George Lefcoe, "HUD's Authority to Mandate Tenants' Rights in Public Housing," 80 *Yale Law Journal* 463-514 (January, 1971).]

Terms and conditions of occupancy based on local statutes and case law not incorporated in most form leases or underlying the creation and duration of oral tenancies are in some cases more repugnant than standard landlord leases. At common law as now in most jurisdictions the landlord has no duty to repair deteriorated or deteriorating premises absent an effective housing code or similar remedies. The landlord is usually under no duty to mitigate damages when a tenant abandons the premises, and there exist no realistic tenant remedies when he is summarily ejected from an apartment without notice or process.

Many commentators have applied contract and consumer law principles recommending theories of unconscionability and adhesion to relieve the low income tenant from onerous lease provisions. However, courts have been slow to react in this moribund area of landlord-tenant law. Moreover, such theories suffer from defects similar to the inherent drawbacks of the code inspection and rent withholding spectrum of remedies. These theories presuppose tenant initiation, they ignore preventive law considerations, and they are not applied to a class of landlords for truly effective results. Additionally, many equally unconscionable common law concepts of landlord and tenant, either standing alone, included in a lease, or incorporated in a statute, are not susceptible to change by application of these inadequate theories. What is needed is a broad legislative revision and recodification of the terms and conditions of occupancy affecting low income tenants with strict provision for nonwaiverability.

An alternative to this method of reform would be mandatory administrative approval required prior to signing by the parties of all noncommercial dwelling leases. Unfortunately, this approach has been unsuccessful in preventing the adoption of one-sided leases and would not affect those tenants occupying premises under oral tenancies. A third possible resolution of the problem also presupposes legislative intervention and would involve the enactment of a model lease, with negotiable minor provisions, to be executed by all landlords and tenants of dwelling premises. This solution borrows from retail installment sales acts which have been uniformly adopted and minutely regulate an area as subject to abuse as low income housing. The consumer analysis is most appropriate and effective when considered in this frame of reference.

Situations Especially Oppressive to Low-income Tenants

The three interrelated factors of a severe shortage of low-income housing, the deterioration of many innercity dwellings, and the inordinately disparate bargaining position between the urban landlord and his tenant fostered by protectionist legal principles compel governmental regulation and intervention in urban housing problems. The laissez-faire approach to such a basic commodity as housing must be abandoned when a crisis of contemporary proportions demands an institutional response.

Certain aspects of landlord-tenant legal theory and practice are especially repugnant to and oppressive of low income tenants. Many low-income tenants are recipients of inadequate public assistance and social security benefits or are underemployed. Their indigency is compounded by unregulated security deposit practices, by rental of premises where local law is unclear as to whether the landlord or tenant is obligated to provide for utilities and essential appliances, by summary evictions for late or nonpayment of rent where the tenant has not been responsible for the delinquency, and by the conditioning of appellate review in dispossessory proceedings on the filing of appeal bonds.

The security deposit of one or two months' rental payments or a fixed sum in advance theoretically is designed to reimburse the landlord for tenant-caused damages to the premises or to assure financial protection in the case of the tenant who cannot be traced after abandoning his apartment when the landlord is unable to relet it immediately. Where the required security deposit amounts to a few hundred dollars in this era of inflated rentals, the nonwelfare low-income tenant is often effectively precluded from occupancy.[16] Moreover, it may be somewhat unrealistic to expect the low income tenant to bring suit for an unreturned security deposit and then overcome the defense of unexplained injury to the premises when this tenant neglected to obtain a list of defects at the commencement of his tenancy. Landlords complaining of abandoning tenants who supposedly financially balance matters by unilaterally applying the security deposit to a final month's rent usually have no difficulty in locating these tenants and commencing suit for damages to the premises or for rent due in the amount of an unexpired term. Merchants of commodities in plentiful supply usually exact no deposit for goods sold and delivered even to low income consumers. However, utility companies, of a somewhat analogous situation to landlords of low income housing because of a comparable market situation, exact security deposits from customers and especially discriminate both in frequency and in amounts against low income residential areas. Because of these facts there has been increasing governmental interest in and regulation of deposits by utilities. Such an approach would not be uncalled-for in the area of low income housing, and one solution might require justification by landlords before such deposits are levied with the paying in of deposits to an escrow fund maintained by the municipal housing agency which would adjudicate conflicts as to its payment on the termination of a tenancy.

In the absence of a lease provision, there is usually some doubt under local law as to whether the landlord or the tenant is responsible for furnishing essential utilities such as electricity and natural gas. There is often some question as to who provides the heat and also the heating facility. Although some statutes and municipal ordinances require that such necessary appliances as a stove and a refrigerator be supplied by the landlord, the law is usually silent, and provision of these items depends on a landlord's practice which in turn hinges on the tenant's bargaining power which is clearly nonexistent for low income tenants. It would seem that in the case of low-income tenants that a tenantable apartment should include these utilities and appliances as integral to the premises. In middle-income and luxury-class buildings, such utilities and appliances are usually included with the rental.

An unchallenged tenet of landlord-tenant theory is the absolute right of a landlord to summarily evict with or perhaps without court process a tenant who is late in tendering or neglects to pay rent due. Again, the shortage of low-income housing generally results in intransigent landlord rejection of valid reasons for lateness or for nonpayment combined with promises and even offers of payment. A landlord should probably be permitted, however, to evict a tenant for nonpayment unless government intervenes to subsidize the defaulted rent. But what of the recipient of public assistance or social security benefits whose periodic allotment has been delayed, or of the underemployed parent who has been temporarily laid off or fired and who is unable to secure immediate reemployment, and whose welfare department is slow to begin assistance? Landlords, irrespective of the fault of the tenant, should not be allowed to dispossess summarily without some court proceeding. To permit a landlord to change locks and literally force the tenant to the sidewalk is unconscionable in terms of basic justice. In a summary dispossessory proceeding for nonpayment of rent, perhaps a valid defense would be nonpayment caused by some intervening

16. In the author's experience, most recipients of public assistance required to advance a security deposit are reimbursed for this expense by means of a special grant from their welfare worker.

factor precluding payment because of absence of funds. Continuation in occupancy conditioned on repayments of rent due by either the tenant himself or a welfare agency might be an appropriate result.

The practice of conditioning appellate review in eviction cases on posting appeal bonds is well documented as an especially onerous discrimination against the poor. There appears to be no rationale for such a practice other than a recognition of sorts that a landlord should be allowed to summarily evict a destructive tenant. Since no reason is assigned for most evictions other than for nonpayment of rent, a responsive solution might be speedy appellate hearing with continued occupancy conditioned on paying rent into court in turn to be forwarded to the landlord.

CONCLUSION

The national low-income housing crisis is by no means a recent phenomenon. The fact of the matter is that to subject a rather significant percentage of the population to inadequate and insufficient housing becomes intolerable as the remainder of society becomes more affluent. To speak of redressing inequality of bargaining power by tenants' councils or unions and by tenant-initiated remedies sanctioned by legislation or precedent seems really to beg the question in terms of realistic remedies for the overwhelming proportion of slum tenants unorganized or unorganizable and unwilling or unable to stand the strain of litigation. True bargaining equality results from economic power, and in this case such power presupposes available alternatives. These alternatives are either substitute housing which is not available and will not be for the foreseeable future, or additional income to expand one's access to other available housing.

The test case, although plaintiff may represent a class, is not broadly effective unless the entire class undertakes affirmative action under the usually narrow holding. The essential deficiency of a test case is that all landlords participating in the violation cannot be joined in the class as party defendants. The only effective and immediate alternative is governmental intervention to reform landlord-tenant concepts to conform to contemporary urban needs.

6. *Alternative Strategies for the Urban Ghetto*

NATIONAL ADVISORY COMMISSION ON CIVIL DISORDERS

The complexity of American society offers many choices for the future of relations between central cities and suburbs and patterns of white and Negro settlement in metropolitan areas. For practical purposes, however, we see two fundamental questions:

Should future Negro population growth be concentrated in central cities, as in the past 20 years, thereby forcing Negro and white populations to become even more residentially segregated?

Should society provide greatly increased special assistance to Negroes and other relatively disadvantaged population groups?

For purposes of analysis, the Commission has defined three basic choices for the future embodying specific answers to these questions.

The Present Policies Choice

Under this course, the nation would maintain approximately the share of resources now being allocated to programs of assistance for the poor, unemployed, and disadvantaged. These programs are likely to grow, given continuing economic growth and rising federal revenues, but they will not grow fast enough to stop, let alone reverse, the already deteriorating quality of life in central-city ghettos.

This choice carries the highest ultimate price, as we will point out.

The Enrichment Choice

Under this course, the nation would seek to offset the effects of continued Negro segregation and deprivation in large city ghettos. The enrichment choice would aim at creating dramatic improvements in the quality of life in disadvantaged central-city neighborhoods—both white and Negro. It would require marked increases in federal spending for education, housing, employment, job training, and social services.

The enrichment choice would seek to lift poor Negroes and whites above poverty status and thereby give them the capacity to enter the mainstream of American life. But it would not, at least for many years, appreciably affect either the increasing concentration of Negroes in the ghetto or racial segregation in residential areas outside the ghetto.

The Integration Choice

This choice would be aimed at reversing the movement of the country toward two societies, separate and unequal.

The integration choice—like the enrichment choice—would call for large-scale improvement in the quality of ghetto life. But it would also involve both creating strong incentives for Negro movement out of central-city ghettos and enlarging freedom of choice concerning housing, employment, and schools.

The result would fall considerably short of full integration. The experience of

Reprinted from the *Report of the National Advisory Commission on Civil Disorders* (Washington, D.C.: Government Printing Office, 1968), pp. 218-26.

other ethnic groups indicates that some Negro households would be scattered in largely white residential areas. Others—probably a larger number—would voluntarily cluster together in largely Negro neighborhoods. The integration choice would thus produce both integration and segregation. But the segregation would be voluntary.

Articulating these three choices plainly oversimplifies the possibilities open to the country. We believe, however, that they encompass the basic issues— issues which the American public must face if it is serious in its concern not only about civil disorder but the future of our democratic society.

THE PRESENT POLICIES CHOICE

Powerful forces of social and political inertia are moving the country steadily along the course of existing policies toward a divided country.

This course may well involve changes in many social and economic programs—but not enough to produce fundamental alterations in the key factors of Negro concentration, racial segregation, and the lack of sufficient enrichment to arrest the decay of deprived neighborhoods.

Some movement toward enrichment can be found in efforts to encourage industries to locate plants in central cities, in increased federal expenditures for education, in the important concepts embodied in the "War on Poverty," and in the Model Cities Program. But congressional appropriations for even present federal programs have been so small that they fall short of effective enrichment.

As for challenging concentration and segregation, a national commitment to this purpose has yet to develop.

Of the three future courses we have defined, the present policies choice—the choice we are now making—is the course with the most ominous consequences for our society.

The Probability of Future Civil Disorders

We believe that the present policies choice would lead to a larger number of violent incidents of the kind that have stimulated recent major disorders.

First, it does nothing to raise the hopes, absorb the energies, or constructively challenge the talents of the rapidly growing number of young Negro men in central cities. The proportion of unemployed or underemployed among them will remain very high. These young men have contributed disproportionately to crime and violence in cities in the past, and there is danger, obviously, that they will continue to do so.

Second, under these conditions, a rising proportion of Negroes in disadvantaged city areas might come to look upon the deprivation and segregation they suffer as proper justification for violent protest or for extending support to now isolated extremists who advocate civil disruption by guerrilla tactics.

More incidents would not necessarily mean more or worse riots. For the near future, there is substantial likelihood that even an increased number of incidents could be controlled before becoming major disorders, if society undertakes to improve police and National Guard forces so that they can respond to potential disorders with more prompt and disciplined use of force.

In fact, the likelihood of incidents mushrooming into major disorders would be only slightly higher in the near future under the present policies choice than under the other two possible choices. For no new policies or programs could possibly alter basic ghetto conditions immediately. And the announcement of new programs under the other choices would immediately generate new expectations. Expectations inevitably increase faster than performance. In the short run, they might even increase the level of frustration.

In the long run, however, the present policies choice risks a seriously greater probability of major disorders, worse, possibly, than those already experienced.

If the Negro population as a whole developed even stronger feelings of being wrongly "penned in" and discriminated against, many of its members might come to support not only riots but the rebellion now being preached by only a handful. Large-scale violence, followed by white retaliation could follow. This spiral could quite conceivably lead to a kind of urban *apartheid* with semimartial law in many major cities, enforced residence of Negroes in segregated areas, and a drastic reduction in personal freedom for all Americans, particularly Negroes.

The same distinction is applicable to the cost of the present policies choice. In the short run, its costs—at least its direct cash outlays—would be far less than for the other choices.

Social and economic programs likely to have significant lasting effect would require very substantial annual appropriations for many years. Their cost would far exceed the direct losses sustained in recent civil disorders. Property damage in all the disorders we investigated, including Detroit and Newark, totaled less than $100 million.

But it would be a tragic mistake to view the present policies choice as cheap. Damage figures measure only a small part of the costs of civil disorder. They cannot measure the costs in terms of the lives lost, injuries suffered, minds and attitudes closed and frozen in prejudice, or the hidden costs of the profound disruption of entire cities.

Ultimately, moreover, the economic and social costs of the present policies choice will far surpass the cost of the alternatives. The rising concentration of impoverished Negroes and other minorities within the urban ghettos will constantly expand public expenditures for welfare, law enforcement, unemployment, and other existing programs without arresting the decay of older city neighborhoods and the breeding of frustration and discontent. But the most significant item on the balance of accounts will remain largely invisible and incalculable—the toll in human values taken by continued poverty, segregation, and inequality of opportunity.

Polarization

Another and equally serious consequence is the fact that this course would lead to the permanent establishment of two societies: one predominantly white and located in the suburbs, in smaller cities, and in outlying areas, and one largely Negro located in central cities.

We are well on the way to just such a divided nation.

This division is veiled by the fact that Negroes do not now dominate many central cities. But they soon will, as we have shown, and the new Negro mayors will be facing even more difficult conditions than now exist.

As Negroes succeed whites in our largest cities, the proportion of low income residents in those cities will probably increase. This is likely even if both white and Negro incomes continue to rise at recent rates, since Negroes have much lower incomes than whites. Moreover, many of the ills of large central cities spring from their age, their location, and their obsolete physical structures. The deterioration and economic decay stemming from these factors have been proceeding for decades and will continue to plague older cities regardless of who resides in them.

These facts underlie the fourfold dilemma of the American city:

Fewer tax dollars come in, as large numbers of middle income taxpayers move out of central cities and property values and business decline;

More tax dollars are required to provide essential public services and facilities, and to meet the needs of expanding lower-income groups;

Each tax dollar buys less, because of increasing costs;

Citizen dissatisfaction with municipal services grows as needs, expectations, and standards of living increase throughout the community.

These are the conditions that would greet the Negro-dominated municipal governments that will gradually come to power in many of our major cities. The Negro electorates in those cities probably would demand basic changes in present policies. Like the present white electorates there, they would have to look for assistance to two basic sources: the private sector and the federal government.

With respect to the private sector, major private capital investment in those cities might have ceased almost altogether if white-dominated firms and industries decided the risks and costs were too great. The withdrawal of private capital is already far advanced in most all-Negro areas of our large cities.

Even if private investment continued, it alone would not suffice. Big cities containing high proportions of low-income Negroes and block after block of deteriorating older property need very substantial assistance from the federal government to meet the demands of their electorates for improved services and living conditions.

It is probable, however, that Congress will be more heavily influenced by representatives of the suburban and outlying city electorate. These areas will comprise 40 percent of our total population by 1985, compared with 31 percent in 1960; and central cities will decline from 32 percent to 27 percent.[1]

Since even the suburbs will be feeling the squeeze of higher local government costs, Congress might resist providing the extensive assistance which central cities will desperately need.

Thus the present policies choice, if pursued for any length of time, might force simultaneous political and economic polarization in many of our largest metropolitan areas. Such polarization would involve large central cities— mainly Negro, with many poor, and nearly bankrupt—on the one hand and most suburbs—mainly white, generally affluent, but heavily taxed—on the other hand.

Some areas might avoid political confrontation by shifting to some form of metropolitan government designed to offer regional solutions for pressing urban problems such as property taxation, air and water pollution, refuse disposal, and commuter transport. Yet this would hardly eliminate the basic segregation and relative poverty of the urban Negro population. It might even increase the Negro's sense of frustration and alienation if it operated to prevent Negro political control of central cities.

The acquisition of power by Negro-dominated governments in central cities is surely a legitimate and desirable exercise of political power by a minority group. It is in an American political tradition exemplified by the achievements of the Irish in New York and Boston.

But such Negro political development would also involve virtually complete racial segregation and virtually complete spatial separation. By 1985, the separate Negro society in our central cities would contain almost 21 million citizens. That is almost 68 percent larger than the present Negro population of central cities. It is also larger than the current population of every Negro nation in Africa except Nigeria.

If developing a racially integrated society is extraordinarily difficult today when 12.1 million Negroes live in central cities, then it is quite clearly going to be virtually impossible in 1985 when almost 21 million Negroes—still much poorer and less educated than most whites—will be living there.

1. Based on Census Bureau series D projections.

Can Present Policies Avoid Extreme Polarization?

There are at least two possible developments under the present policies choice which might avert such polarization. The first is a faster increase of incomes among Negroes than has occurred in the recent past. This might prevent central cities from becoming even deeper "poverty traps" than they now are. It suggests the importance of effective job programs and higher levels of welfare payments for dependent families.

The second possible development is migration of a growing Negro middle class out of the central city. This would not prevent competition for federal funds between central cities and outlying areas, but it might diminish the racial undertones of that competition.

There is, however, no evidence that a continuation of present policies would be accompanied by any such movement. There is already a significant Negro middle class. It grew rapidly from 1960 to 1966. Yet in these years, 88.9 percent of the total national growth of Negro population was concentrated in central cities—the highest in history. Indeed, from 1960 to 1966, there was actually a net total in-migration of Negroes from the urban fringes of metropolitan areas into central cities.[2] The Commission believes it unlikely that this trend will suddenly reverse itself without significant changes in private attitudes and public policies.

THE ENRICHMENT CHOICE

The present policies choice plainly would involve continuation of efforts like Model Cities, manpower programs, and the War on Poverty. These are in fact enrichment programs, designed to improve the quality of life in the ghetto.

Because of their limited scope and funds, however, they constitute only very modest steps toward enrichment—and would continue to do so even if these programs were somewhat enlarged or supplemented.

The premise of the enrichment choice is performance. To adopt this choice would require a substantially greater share of national resources—sufficient to make a dramatic, visible impact on life in the urban Negro ghetto.

The Effect of Enrichment on Civil Disorders

Effective enrichment policies probably would have three immediate effects on civil disorders.

First, announcement of specific large-scale programs and the demonstration of a strong intent to carry them out might persuade ghetto residents that genuine remedies for their problems were forthcoming, thereby allaying tensions.

Second, such announcements would strongly stimulate the aspirations and hopes of members of these communities—possibly well beyond the capabilities of society to deliver and to do so promptly. This might increase frustration and discontent, to some extent canceling the first effect.

Third, if there could be immediate action on meaningful job training and the creation of productive jobs for large numbers of unemployed young people, they would become much less likely to engage in civil disorders.

Such action is difficult now, when there are about 585,000 young Negro men aged 14 to 24 in the civilian labor force in central cities—of whom 81,000, or 13.8 percent, are unemployed and probably two or three times as many are underemployed. It

2. Although Negro population on the urban fringe of metropolitan areas did increase slightly (0.2 million) from 1960 to 1966, it is safe to assume an actual net in-migration to central cities from these areas based upon the rate of natural increase of the Negro population.

will not become easier in the future. By 1975, this age group will have grown to approximately 700,000.

Given the size of the present problem, plus the large growth of this age group, creation of sufficient meaningful jobs will require extensive programs, begun rapidly. Even if the nation is willing to embark on such programs, there is no certainty that they can be made effective soon enough.

Consequently, there is no certainty that the enrichment choice would do much more in the near future to diminish violent incidents in central cities than would the present policies choice. However, if enrichment programs can succeed in meeting the needs of residents of disadvantaged areas for jobs, education, housing, and city services, then over the years this choice is almost certain to reduce both the level and frequency of urban disorder.

The Negro Middle Class

One objective of the enrichment choice would be to help as many disadvantaged Americans as possible—of all races—to enter the mainstream of American prosperity, to progress toward what is often called middle-class status. If the enrichment choice were adopted, it could certainly attain this objective to a far greater degree than would the present policies choice. This could significantly change the quality of life in many central-city areas.

It can be argued that a rapidly enlarging Negro middle class would also promote Negro out-migration, and that the enrichment choice would thus open up an escape hatch from the ghetto. This argument, however, has two weaknesses.

The first is experience. Central cities already have sizable and growing numbers of middle class Negro families. Yet only a few have migrated from the central city. The past pattern of white ethnic groups gradually moving out of central-city areas to middle-class suburbs has not applied to Negroes. Effective open-housing laws will help make this possible, but it is probable that other more extensive changes in policies and attitudes will be required—and these would extend beyond the enrichment choice.

The second weakness in the argument is time. Even if enlargement of the Negro middle class succeeded in encouraging movement out of the central city, it could not do so fast enough to offset the rapid growth of the ghetto. To offset even *half* the growth estimated for the ghetto by 1975 an out-migration from central cities of 217,000 persons a year would be required. This is eight times the annual increase in suburban Negro population—including natural increase—that occurred from 1960 to 1966. Even the most effective enrichment program is not likely to accomplish this.

A corollary problem derives from the continuing migration of poor Negroes from the southern to northern and western cities. Adoption of the enrichment choice would require large-scale efforts to improve conditions in the South sufficiently to remove the pressure to migrate. Under present conditions, slightly over a third of the estimated increase in Negro central-city population by 1985 will result from in-migration—3.0 million out of total increase of 8.2 million.

Negro Self-development

The enrichment choice is in line with some of the currents of Negro protest thought that fall under the label of "black power." We do not refer to versions of black power ideology which promote violence, generate racial hatred, or advocate total separation of the races. Rather, we mean the view which asserts that the American Negro population can assume its proper role in society and overcome its feelings of powerlessness and lack of self-respect only by exerting power over decisions which directly affect its own members. A fully integrated society is not thought possible until the Negro minority within the ghetto has developed political strength—a strong bargaining position in dealing with the rest of society.

In short, this argument would regard predominantly Negro central cities and predominantly white outlying areas not as harmful but as an advantageous future.

Proponents of these views also focus on the need for the Negro to organize economically as well as politically, thus tapping new energies and resources for self-development. One of the hardest tasks in improving disadvantaged areas is to discover how deeply deprived residents can develop their own capabilities by participating more fully in decisions and activities which affect them. Such learning-by-doing efforts are a vital part of the process of bringing deprived people into the social mainstream.

Separate but Equal Societies?

The enrichment choice by no means seeks to perpetuate racial segregation. In the end, however, its premise is that disadvantaged Negroes can achieve equality of opportunity with whites while continuing in conditions of nearly complete separation.

This premise has been vigorously advocated by black-power proponents. While most Negroes originally desired racial integration, many are losing hope of ever achieving it because of seemingly implacable white resistance. Yet they cannot bring themselves to accept the conclusion that most of the millions of Negroes who are forced to live racially segregated lives must therefore be condemned to inferior lives—to inferior educations, or inferior housing, or inferior status.

Rather, they reason, there must be some way to make the quality of life in the ghetto areas just as good—or better—than elsewhere. It is not surprising that some black power advocates are denouncing integration and claiming that, given the hypocrisy and racism that pervade white society, life in a black society is, in fact, morally superior. This argument is understandable, but there is a great deal of evidence that it is unrealistic.

The economy of the United States and particularly the sources of employment are preponderantly white. In this circumstance, a policy of separate but equal employment could only relegate Negroes permanently to inferior incomes and economic status.

The best evidence regarding education is contained in recent reports of the Office of Education and Civil Rights Commission which suggest that both racial and economic integration are essential to educational equality for Negroes. Yet critics point out that certainly until integration is achieved, various types of enrichment programs must be tested, and that dramatically different results may be possible from intensive educational enrichment —such as far smaller classes, or greatly expanded preschool programs, or changes in the home environment of Negro children resulting from steady jobs for fathers.

Still others advocate shifting control over ghetto schools from professional administrators to local residents. This, they say, would improve curricula, give students a greater sense of their own value, and thus raise their morale and educational achievement. These approaches have not yet been tested sufficiently. One conclusion, however, does seem reasonable: Any real improvement in the quality of education in low-income, all-Negro areas will cost a great deal more money than is now being spent there—and perhaps more than is being spent per pupil anywhere. Racial and social class integration of schools may produce equal improvement in achievement at less total cost.

Whether or not enrichment in ghetto areas will really work is not yet known, but the enrichment choice is based on the yet-unproven premise that it will. Certainly, enrichment programs could significantly improve existing ghetto schools if they impelled major innovations. But "separate but equal" ghetto education cannot meet the long-run fundamental educational needs of the central-city Negro population.

The three basic educational choices are: providing Negro children with quality education in integrated schools; providing them with quality education by enriching ghetto schools; or continuing to provide many Negro children with inferior education in racially segregated school systems, severely limiting their lifetime opportunities.

Consciously or not, it is the third choice that the nation is now making, and this choice the Commission rejects totally.

In the field of housing, it is obvious that "separate but equal" does not mean really equal. The enrichment choice could greatly improve the quantity, variety, and environment of decent housing available to the ghetto population. It could not provide Negroes with the same freedom and range of choice as whites with equal incomes. Smaller cities and suburban areas together with the central city provide a far greater variety of housing and environmental settings than the central city alone. Programs to provide housing outside central cities, however, extend beyond the bounds of the enrichment choice.

In the end, whatever its benefits, the enrichment choice might well invite a prospect similar to that of the present policies choice: separate white and black societies.

If enrichment programs were effective, they could greatly narrow the gap in income, education, housing, jobs, and other qualities of life between the ghetto and the mainstream. Hence the chances of harsh polarization—or of disorder—in the next 20 years would be greatly reduced.

Whether they would be reduced far enough depends on the scope of the programs. Even if the gap were narrowed from the present, it still could remain as a strong source of tension. History teaches that men are not necessarily placated even by great absolute progress. The controlling factor is relative progress—whether they still perceive a significant gap between themselves and others whom they regard as no more deserving. Widespread perception of such a gap—and consequent resentment—might well be precisely the situation 20 years from now under the enrichment choice, for it is essentially another way of choosing a permanently divided country.

THE INTEGRATION CHOICE

The third and last course open to the nation combines enrichment with programs designed to encourage integration of substantial numbers of Negroes into the society outside the ghetto.

Enrichment must be an important adjunct to any integration course. No matter how ambitious or energetic such a program may be, relatively few Negroes now living in central-city ghettos would be quickly integrated. In the meantime, significant improvement in their present environment is essential.

The enrichment aspect of this third choice should, however, be recognized as interim action, during which time expanded and new programs can work to improve education and earning power. The length of the interim period surely would vary. For some it may be long. But in any event, what should be clearly recognized is that enrichment is only a means toward the goal; it is not the goal.

The goal must be achieving freedom for every citizen to live and work according to his capacities and desires, not his color.

We believe there are four important reasons why American society must give this course the most serious consideration. First, future jobs are being created primarily in the suburbs, while the chronically unemployed population is increasingly concentrated in the ghetto. This separation will make it more and more difficult for Negroes to achieve anything like full employment in decent jobs. But if, over time, these residents began to find housing outside central cities, they would be exposed to more knowledge of job opportunities, would have much shorter trips to reach jobs, and would have a far better chance of securing employment on a self-sustaining basis.

Second, in the judgment of this Commission, racial and social-class integration is the most effective way of improving the education of ghetto children.

Third, developing an adequate housing supply for low-income and middle-income families and true freedom of choice in housing for Negroes of all income levels will require substantial out-movement. We do not believe that such an out-movement will occur spontaneously merely as a result of increasing prosperity among Negroes in central cities. A national fair housing law is essential to begin such movement. In many suburban areas, a program combining positive incentives with the building of new housing will be necessary to carry it out.

Fourth, and by far the most important, integration is the only course which explicitly seeks to achieve a single nation rather than accepting the present movement toward a dual society. This choice would enable us at least to begin reversing the profoundly divisive trend already so evident in our metropolitan areas—before it becomes irreversible.

CONCLUSIONS

The future of our cities is neither something which will just happen nor something which will be imposed upon us by an inevitable destiny. That future will be shaped to an important degree by choices we make now.

We have attempted to set forth the major choices because we believe it is vital for Americans to understand the consequences of our present drift.

Three critical conclusions emerge from this analysis.

1. The nation is rapidly moving toward two increasingly separate Americas.

Within two decades, this division could be so deep that it would be almost impossible to unite:

> a white society principally located in suburbs, in smaller central cities, and in the peripheral parts of large central cities; and
> a Negro society largely concentrated within large central cities.

The Negro society will be permanently relegated to its current status, possibly even if we expend great amounts of money and effort in trying to "gild" the ghetto.

2. In the long run, continuation and expansion of such a permanent division threatens us with two perils.

The first is the danger of sustained violence in our cities. The timing, scale, nature, and repercussions of such violence cannot be foreseen. But if it occurred, it would further destroy our ability to achieve the basic American promises of liberty, justice, and equality.

The second is the danger of a conclusive repudiation of the traditional American ideals of individual dignity, freedom, and equality of opportunity. We will not be able to espouse these ideals meaningfully to the rest of the world, to ourselves, to our children. They may still recite the Pledge of Allegiance and say "one nation . . . indivisible." But they will be learning cynicism, not patriotism.

3. We cannot escape responsibility for choosing the future of our metropolitan areas and the human relations which develop within them. It is a responsibility so critical that even an unconcious choice to continue present policies has the gravest implications.

That we have delayed in choosing or, by delaying, may be making the wrong choice does not sentence us to either separatism or despair. But we must choose. We will choose. Indeed, we are now choosing.

7. The Case Against Urban Desegregation

FRANCES FOX PIVEN and RICHARD A. CLOWARD

For years the chief efforts of a broad coalition of liberals and reformers, in dealing with the problems of the Negro, have been directed against segregation. Some significant gains have been made, particularly in the laws governing Negro rights in certain institutional spheres, such as voting and the use of public accommodations. But in some areas the thrust for integration seems to have worked against Negro interests. This is especially true with regard to housing and education of the Negro poor in large cities.

There are two main reasons for this: (1) Efforts to ameliorate basic social inequities, such as deteriorated ghetto housing and inferior educational facilities, have been closely linked to the goal of integration and, since integration measures arouse fierce resistance, proposals to redress these social inequities have usually failed. It is for this reason that, after several decades of civil rights struggle, the lot of the Negro urban poor has actually worsened in some respects. (2) If the Negro is to develop the power to enter the mainstream of American life, it is separatism —not integration—that will be essential to achieve results in certain institutional arenas. Both of these points have implications for both public policy and political action.

DESEGREGATING HOUSING

Reformers oriented to the urban ghetto have generally sought two objectives that they have seen as closely linked—to promote desegregation and to obtain better housing and education for the poor. Restricted housing, they have contended, is the key factor in creating and maintaining racial barriers and, in turn, racial barriers force Negroes into deteriorated slums.

Efforts to desegregate housing, however, have been roundly defeated by massive white opposition. Indeed, residential segregation is increasing rapidly.[1] Moreover, because provision of decent housing for the poor has been tied to desegregation, this end also has been defeated.

Over the next decade or two many central cities could well become predominantly Negro, if the movement of Negroes into the city and the exodus of whites to the

Reprinted with permission of The National Association of Social Workers, from *Social Work* 12, no. 1 (January 1967): 12-21, and with the permission of the authors. Frances Fox Piven is a member of the faculty of Boston University's Government Department, and Richard A. Cloward is a member of the faculty of Columbia University's School of Social Work.

1. The proportion of nonwhites living in segregated census tracts in New York City rose from 49 to 53 percent between 1940 and 1950. In 1910, 60 percent of the Negroes in that city lived in assembly districts that were less than 5 percent Negro. By 1960, 62 percent were in districts that were over 50 percent Negro. "The Program for an Open City: Summary Report" (New York: Department of City Planning, May 1965) (mimeographed). See also Davis McEntire, *Residence and Race: Final and Comprehensive Report to the Commission on Race and Housing* (Berkeley: University of California Press, 1960), p. 41.

suburbs continue, and if the higher Negro birthrate persists.[2] Against these trends, the task of maintaining racial balance in the cities seems insuperable. To offset them, huge numbers of families would have to be shuffled about by desegregation programs. This point has been spelled out by George Schermer, who provides estimates of the number of people who would have to be moved each year in order to insure that a 50-50 population balance would exist in Washington, D.C., in the year 2000. (Washington is now 63 percent Negro.) Assuming that migration trends and birthrates remain constant, 12,000 nonwhite families would have to be dispersed to suburban areas and 4,000 white families induced to return to the District of Columbia *every year until 2000*.[3] Segregation between the suburbs and the central city is only part of the story. Even if whites could be induced to return to the city and Negroes could be accommodated in suburbs, residential integration would not result because Negroes and whites tend to live separately within the city itself. Any public program that would undertake to disperse growing concentrations of Negroes from the ghettos would have to shift formidable numbers to white neighborhoods and resettle whites in present ghetto areas.[4]

Approaches to desegregation have had little effect when the magnitude of the problem is considered. The most popular approach involves legal reforms coupled with education and information programs—legislation is sought to prohibit prejudicial treatment of Negroes, whether by deed restrictions, discriminatory actions of private realtors and landlords, or such governmental policies as the early FHA mortgage underwriting policy, which prescribed racially homogeneous housing developments. It is sobering to note, however, that many such reforms were won years before the civil rights movement but have failed completely to retard segregation.[5] Racial zoning ordinances, for example, were struck down by the courts in 1917.

Special agencies have been developed to hear complaints of violations of antidiscrimination laws.[6] The procedures for achieving redress, however, ordinarily require knowledge and patience on the part of the plaintiff that cannot in fairness be expected of someone merely looking for a decent place to live. Moreover, these agencies are typically charged to negotiate grievances without sanctioning the land-

2. Between 1950 and 1960—for the United States as a whole—the percentage gain in population was 17.5 for whites and 26.7 for nonwhites. The increase in the urban population was 27 percent for whites but 49 percent for nonwhites. In the same decade, the nonwhite population in central cities increased 63 percent while the white population continued to decrease. See *Our Nonwhite Population and Its Housing* (Washington, D.C.: Housing and Home Finance Agency, 1963), pp. 1-3. The nonwhite population in central cities reached 10.3 million in 1960 and may exceed 16 million by 1975, according to McEntire, op. cit., pp. 4-5, 21-24.

3. George Schermer, "Desegregating the Metropolitan Area." Paper presented at the National Housing Workshop, National Committee Against Discrimination in Housing, West Point, N.Y., April 1966.

4. One report on desegregation concluded that housing and redevelopment programs directed to the goal of desegregation could at best only halt the spread of ghettoization. New York City's nonwhite population went from 9.5 percent in 1950 to 14 percent in 1960 and is expected to be more than 20 percent by 1975. (In 1900 it was 1.76 percent.) See "The Program for an Open City: Summary Report."

5. The very proliferation of legal reform measures may account for the prevalent view among liberals that there has been progress in desegregation.

6. In New York City there are two such agencies: the New York State Commission on Human Rights and a parallel city commission. Both agencies recently announced a "great increase" in the number of complaints received. This increase, it turned out, resulted in a *total* of only 528 complaints over a six-month period. Needless to say, a complaint received is some distance from being acted on. "More Negro Families Are Utilizing Fair Housing Law Here and in Suburbs," *New York Times*, October 23, 1966, p. 117.

lord. Thus, although one apartment may be "opened" after torturous procedures, there is no deterrence to further violations—no carry-over effect. Each negotiated enforcement of the law remains an isolated event.

There are many programs that are designed to supplement the antidiscrimination laws by attempting to change the white community's discriminatory attitudes. Thus, "fair housing committees" have been established in receiving communities to over-come community hostility toward entering Negroes. Information and broker services are designed to overcome barriers to the movement of Negroes that result from communication gaps, such as a lack of information regarding housing opportunities outside the ghetto or difficulties in gaining access for inspection. Such programs as the Urban League's Operation Open City combine all these strategies to help Negro families find housing.

However, these efforts tend to reach only middle-class Negroes, because housing in outlying communities generally requires at least a lower middle income. Moreover, even for the Negro middle class such measures do not result in broad-scale deseg-regation. Resistance in the receiving community varies directly with the number of Negro families who are likely to invade it. More important, the majority of housing opportunities are still controlled by the regular institutions of the private real estate market, and these agencies distribute information concerning available housing and provide access for inspection in accordance with class and racial neighborhood pat-terns that reflect the inclinations of the majority of housing consumers.[7]

HOUSING SUBSIDIES

Another general approach to desegregation takes the form of housing subsidies. Both the public housing program and the recent rent supplement program are intended, at least by some of their proponents, to promote integration as a by-product of rehousing the poor. However, it is found that when large numbers of tenants are Negro, low-income whites desert the projects or are reluctant to apply. Projects thus tend to become high-rise brick ghettos rather than outposts of inte-grated living. Programs to further integration by locating projects in outlying white communities have provoked even more serious opposition. Only when white tenants predominate has any degree of community tolerance resulted.[8] The political tension produced by this issue has contributed to the shaky political life of public housing. Indeed, this form of housing subsidy seems to be expiring in many cities.

The new rent supplement legislation so far also shows signs of accommodation in its provisions that enable outlying communities to veto a proposed invasion by low income and minority groups. In any case, current appropriations are adequate only for a few showpiece programs throughout the nation and are likely to be decreased in the next session of Congress. If experience with public housing is any predictor, the opposition that the rent supplement program aroused in Congress, which almost defeated it, will be repeated more fiercely in local communities as

7. A recent large-scale demographic study of the United States concluded, "Residential seg-regation prevails regardless of the relative economic status of the white and Negro resident." Karl E. Taeuber and Alma F. Taeuber, *Negroes in Cities: Residential Segregation and Neighborhood Change* (Chicago: Aldine Publishing Co., 1965).

8. In the city of Newark, N.J., the racial balance in projects is regularly graded from over 90 percent Negro for projects located in the central ghetto ward to over 90 percent white in outlying "country club" projects. Coincidentally, Newark has been able to obtain much more public support for public housing and to build more units per capita than most other cities.

efforts are made to implement the plan. Public subsidies, in short, have failed to reverse the trend toward segregation in urban areas.

EDUCATION AND JOB TRAINING

A third general approach to desegregation is based on this country's hallowed belief in individual mobility. Once Negroes have better jobs and higher incomes, it is asserted, they will be able to bid competitively for housing beyond the ghetto.

However, programs intended to advance Negroes economically by education and job training have only tenuous bearing on their housing. These programs currently reach merely 1 poor person in 10. But even if the scope of these programs was vastly expanded, millions of today's poor would not be helped by attempts to equip them for better jobs. Of the 35 million people below the federal poverty line (i.e., an annual income of $3,100 for an urban family of 4), several million are aged; they are permanently out of the labor force and can be lifted out of poverty only by the direct redistribution of income. One-third of the poor are in families headed by females, and it does not seem reasonable to expect this group to raise itself out of poverty by entering the labor force. Many of the remaining poor are ill, and others are permanently unable to compete for a host of additional reasons.[9]

It must also be recognized that a strategy of enhancing economic mobility—even if it succeeded in lifting large numbers of people somewhat above the poverty line—would not greatly improve their capacity to procure decent housing. In urban areas, adequate housing is difficult to obtain for families with annual incomes of less than $7,000.[10] Indeed, even middle-class whites have required and obtained huge governmental subsidies to bring adequate housing within their reach (e.g., urban renewal, low cost, government-insured mortgages such as FHA, special tax advantages allowed by federal law for builders and realtors, and real estate tax abatements allowed by local governments).

Finally, it should be noted that because of discriminatory patterns, Negroes pay more for housing. They now occupy housing inferior to that of whites with comparable incomes at every income level.[11] For all these reasons it seems unlikely that a strategy predicated on individual mobility will have much effect on the Negro's housing conditions—and surely not on ghettoization—at least not for many decades.

WORSENING OF GHETTO HOUSING

While efforts to get people out of the ghetto have been ineffective, a variety of other measures put forward in the name of desegregation have substantially *worsened* housing conditions within the ghetto itself. Most of the recent housing and redevelopment programs touted as attempts to serve "the city as a whole" by clearing slums, improving the tax base, or retrieving the middle class from the suburbs have had the effect of intensifying ghetto deterioration. Under the general public mandate of meeting

9. See Mollie Orshansky, "Counting the Poor: Another Look at the Poverty Profile," *Social Security Bulletin* 28, no. 1 (January 1965): 3-29.

10. Nationally, it is estimated that an income of over $7,000 (which only 3.4 percent of nonwhites possess) is required to purchase new, privately constructed housing. Housing costs are much higher in urban areas. Schermer, op. cit.

11. In most metropolitan areas nonwhites pay slightly lower rentals than whites in each income group but get vastly inferior housing. McEntire, op. cit., pp. 135-47. In New York City, for example, there are three times as many substandard units occupied by nonwhites as whites at each income level.

the nation's housing needs and redeveloping the urban core, huge subsidies have found their way into the middle-class market and the business community, and have had widespread and devastating effects on low-income residential areas. Urban redevelopment has resulted in the destruction of low-rental housing and low income communities, so that many poor people are pushed farther into the ghetto.[12] Moreover, in the process of redevelopment, owners and tenants on sites scheduled for clearance are placed in a prolonged state of uncertainty and often become either the agents or the victims of quick exploitation. Relocation programs designed to mitigate the effects of redevelopment on low income people and small businesses are ordinarily inadequate.[13] The stalemate now seen in some urban renewal programs may be considered as an achievement in that the poor have finally been spurred by the accumulated abuses of years of dislocation to protest against the further destruction of their homes and communities.[14]

In the housing act of 1949 Congress asserted a national responsibility to provide a decent dwelling for every family. This, however, has not progressed very far. In New York City, for example, Mayor Lindsay's housing task force recently reported that there were half a million unsound units currently occupied (roughly the same number reported through years of new public assaults on the slums) and that the number was on the increase even though *the number of low-rental units* has decreased more than 30 percent since 1960.[15] In Boston, the last family-size public housing unit was built in 1954; the city's nationally acclaimed urban renewal effort diminished by 12 percent the supply of low-rental housing (less than $50 a month) between 1960 and 1965.[16] The federal public housing program has produced only 600,000 low income dwelling units in the 3 decades since it was initiated. The federal urban renewal program and the federal highway program have together demolished close to 700,000 units, most of which were low rental, in less than half that time. Meanwhile, private builders, spurred on by federal tax incentives and mortgage programs designed to encourage construction, have made still further inroads on the supply of low income housing by reclaiming land to erect middle and upper income units. The cheap accommodations that remain in large cities are in buildings that have been permitted to run down without maintenance and repairs or in which rents are pushed to the limit the captive market can afford. High-minded public policies notwithstanding, the dimensions of housing needs among the nonwhites in big cities have, in fact, enlarged.

In summary, attempts to provide better housing for the Negro have failed not

---

12. Criticism of urban renewal has been launched from both the right and the left. See Martin Anderson, *The Federal Bulldozer* (Cambridge, Mass.: M.I.T. Press, 1965); Herbert J. Gans, "The Failure of Urban Renewal," *Commentary* 39, no. 4 (April 1965): 29-37; and the replies to Gans by George M. Raymond and Malcolm D. Rivkin, "Urban Renewal," *Commentary* 40, no. 1 (July 1965): 72-80.

13. For a review of experience with relocation see Chester Hartman, "The Housing of Relocated Families," *Journal of the American Institute of Planners* 30, no. 4 (November 1964): 266-86.

14. James Q. Wilson analyzes the political dilemmas created by renewal programs in "Planning and Politics: Citizen Participation in Urban Renewal," *Journal of the American Institute of Planners* 29, no. 4 (November 1963): 242-49.

15. "An Analysis of Current City-Wide Housing Needs" (New York: Department of City Planning, Community Renewal Program, December 1965), p. 67 (mimeographed).

16. Michael D. Appleby, "Logue's Record in Boston: An Analysis of His Renewal and Planning Activities" (New York: Council for New York Housing and Planning Policy, May 1966), p. 43 (mimeographed).

because anyone has denied the moral imperative of desegregation. Rather, they have failed under the auspices of this moral imperative. It seems clear, therefore, that if the poor are to obtain decent housing, massive subsidies must be granted for new and rehabilitated housing in the ghettos and slums. The Negro is far from possessing the political power to gain subsidies for integrated low income housing. The more relevant question is whether he can even mobilize sufficient pressure to house himself decently wherever he does live.

DESEGREGATING EDUCATION

To emphasize the importance of upgrading ghetto housing is also to accept racially homogeneous elementary schools in large cities, at least for the foreseeable future. Integrated education has been one of the central goals of reformers, and few seem prepared to relinquish this objective. However, the demographic and political realities in large cities cast grave doubts on the feasibility of achieving anything resembling integrated education at the early grade levels.

As a result of the housing patterns described earlier, Negroes are rapidly becoming the largest group (in some cases, the majority) in the central areas of many large cities. Furthermore, they represent an even greater proportion of the school-age population because Negro families are usually younger, larger, and without the resources to place their children in private schools.[17] The white youngsters with whom Negro children presumably are to be integrated are slowly vanishing from inner-city areas, and there is every reason to expect that these demographic trends will continue.

The issue of integrated education is also complicated by socioeconomic factors, particularly in the cities. Recent evidence suggests that diverse economic backgrounds of pupils may be more important than racial diversity in the education of the Negro student. One study of American education, for example, shows that mixing middle-class students (either Negro or white) with lower-class students (either Negro or white) usually has a decidedly beneficial effect on the achievement of the lower-class student and does not usually diminish the middle-class student's achievement.[18] By contrast, the integration of poor whites and poor Negroes does not seem to yield an improved achievement of either group.[19]

But the number of middle-class whites available to be mixed educationally with lower-class Negroes is rapidly declining, and of the whites left in the city with children who attend public schools, an increasing proportion is poor. (As for middle-class Negroes, their numbers are very small to begin with, and many send their chil-

17. Negroes already comprise over 50 percent of the school-age populations in Chicago, Philadelphia, and Washington, D.C. (where they comprise more than 80 percent). In other cities they are rapidly approaching the majority—Detroit, for example, has well over a 40 percent population of school-age Negroes.

18. James R. Coleman et al., *Equality of Educational Opportunity* (Washington, D.C.: Government Printing Office, 1966).

19. Several studies show that by no means do Negroes do uniformly better in integrated schools. They either do better or worse than in segregated schools. One intervening variable appears to be the degree of bigotry exhibited by whites: the greater the bigotry, the more likely that Negroes will achieve less than in segregated schools. Poor and working-class whites have traditionally held the most prejudiced attitudes; integrating them with poor Negroes may actually hurt Negroes. Ibid., especially pp. 330-33. See also Irwin Katz, "Review of Evidence Relating to Effects of Desegregation in the Intellectual Performance of Negroes," *American Psychologist* 19 (June 1964): 381-99.

dren to private schools.) If mixing along class lines is to be achieved, therefore, educational arrangements in which suburban and ghetto children are brought together will be required. Such arrangements are improbable. The defense of the neighborhood school is ardent; it reflects both racial and class cleavages in American society. Efforts to bring about racial mixing, especially when coupled with the more meaningful demand for economic class mixing, run head-on into some of the most firmly rooted and passionately defended attitudes of white families.

Busing versus "educational parks"

Two schemes have been advocated for achieving racial integration while minimizing political resistance. One involves reshuffling children to achieve a racial balance by busing them to distant schools. Aside from the enormous logistical problems this poses, busing usually has met violent opposition from all sides.[20] The second scheme is the development of massive "educational parks," which would centralize upper-grade facilities for children from a wide area. The superiority of these new plants, it is argued, will help to overcome the opposition of white parents to integration. However, even in such plants segregation is likely to persist on the classroom level as a result of the "tracking system," particularly because educational parks are intended only for older children, whose academic levels already reflect wide inequalities in home environment and early schooling. Equally important is the fact that the cost of such educational parks would be enormous. It is improbable that many such parks would be built, and the merits of such an investment must be weighed against alternative uses of funds for the direct improvement of program and staff in ghetto schools.

Improving ghetto schools

The lower-class school, particularly in the large-city ghetto, has always been an inferior institution. Recently the physical facilities in many ghetto schools have improved because of new building programs, but the lower-class Negro school still reflects significant inequalities when it is compared to its white middle-class counterpart. For example, the quality of the teachers has been shown to have a critical influence on the child's learning—lower-class schools, however (especially ghetto schools in large cities), have inferior teachers and are generally characterized by higher staff turnover. To overcome historic inequalities of this kind would be no small achievement.[21]

   The authors conclude, in short, that although schools that are racially and economically heterogeneous are probably superior, removing class inequities in the quality of teachers and programs is also an important goal—and a far more realistic one. Such educational improvements in the ghetto will require public action and expenditure, and these are likely to be achieved only if massive political opposition to demands for class and racial mixing is avoided. As in the case of housing, the coup-

20. There seems to be a somewhat easier acceptance when numbers of Negro children are assigned to white schools than when white children are assigned to ghetto schools. This has not been tried on a sufficient scale to put white tolerance to a genuine test, however. It is also true that Negro parents do not want their children to travel far, either.

21. There have been many studies—including the work of Allison Davis and subsequent studies by August B. Hollingshead—on class biases in the intelligence test and the differential response of the school system to children of different socioeconomic backgrounds. Many other studies document the sharp differences between the low income school and its middle class counterpart. For a recent study of inequalities by class in a large northern urban school system, see Patricia Cayo Sexton, *Education and Income: Inequalities in Our Public Schools* (New York: Viking Press, 1961). See also Coleman et al., op. cit.

ling of measures for integration of education with measures to improve existing conditions in large-city ghettos must lead to the defeat of both. The choice is between total defeat and partial victory; to many, it may appear a difficult choice—but at least it is a choice.

PRIVATE SOCIAL WELFARE: SEPARATIST INSTITUTIONS

In discussing housing and educational reforms for the urban ghetto, the authors have stressed the political futility of integration measures. It is not only the feasibility of integration that is open to question; it is also far from clear that integration is always desirable.

Liberals are inclined to take a "melting pot" view of American communities and to stress the enriching qualities of heterogeneous living—however, the history of ethnic groups in American society belies this view. There have always been ethnic institutions, and these, as has been widely observed, have served important functions in the advancement of different groups. An important precondition for the establishment of such separatist institutions—particularly when the members of the ethnic group are poor—has been the existence of substantial aggregations of people in residential proximity. The current emphasis on integrating people physically in schools and neighborhoods thus deflects attention from a fundamental problem confronting the Negro —the lack of organizational vehicles to enable him to compete with whites for control of major institutions that shape the destiny of the ghetto (housing and educational systems, governmental bureaucracies, corporate economic complexes, political parties, and so forth). Without separatist institutions the Negro is not likely to come to share control in these various spheres, and the powerlessness of the ghetto's population will persist.

The value of separatist institutions is revealed clearly in the field of social welfare. There is, of course, considerable precedent for ethnically based social welfare institutions, which symbolize for many the highest values of self-help. Networks of agencies have been formed by Jews and white Catholics; even Protestants—under the impact of a pluralism that has made them act like a minority as well—have formed essentially white ethnic welfare institutions to advance their interests. Throughout the country these voluntary agencies raise a huge amount of money, which is directed to the less fortunate in their respective ethnic and religious communities (and sometimes to those in other communities as well).

POLITICAL INTERESTS

The point that is not generally recognized about private agencies, however, is that they are as much political as they are social welfare institutions; they serve as organizational vehicles for the expression of the ethnic group's viewpoints on social welfare policy and also as the institutional means for other forms of political association and influence. Religio-ethnic welfare institutions—from hospitals to child care facilities—command enormous amounts of tax money. In New York City, for example, they are now routinely paid over $100 million annually from the municipal budget (exclusive of antipoverty funds). Thus, these agencies are important political interest groups that, in acting upon their own organizational needs, serve the interests of their controlling ethnic and religious constituencies as well.

Exerting pressure for various forms of public subsidy is only one of the political functions of private agencies. They maintain a deep interest in many forms of governmental policy and actively seek to influence the shaping of policy in ways consistent with their interests. These political activities tend to be overlooked because private agencies exert power chiefly at the municipal level—not at the more visible level of national politics. However, large areas of public service *are* controlled locally and, even when programs are initiated and supervised by federal or state authorities, it is primarily at the municipal level that services are organized and delivered to their intended consumers. Public welfare, education, urban renewal, housing code enforcement, fair employment, law enforcement, and correctional practices—all of these are, in large part, shaped by local government.

Nowhere is there a Negro federation of philanthropy—and there are few Negro private social welfare institutions. Consequently, the Negro is not only without an important communal form but also lacks the opportunity to gain the vast public subsidies given for staff and services that flow into the institutions of white communities. In effect, to advocate separatism in this area means to insist that the Negro be given the prerogatives and benefits that other ethnic and religious communities have enjoyed for some decades.

If the Negro expects to influence the proliferating social welfare activities of government, he will need his own organizational apparatus, including a stable cadre of technical and professional personnel who can examine the merits of alternative public policies, survey the practices of governmental agencies, and activate their ethnic constituencies on behalf of needed changes.

COMMUNAL ASSOCIATIONS

Ethnic social welfare institutions serve another important function. This country has faced the problem of assimilating poverty-stricken minority groups into its economic bloodstream many times in the past, and religio-ethnic institutions of various kinds have played a significant part in that process. One of the ways by which such groups effect their rise from deprivation is to develop communal associations, ranging from fraternal and religious bodies to political machines. These communal associations provide a base from which to convert ethnic solidarity into the political force required to overcome various forms of class inequality. They are, therefore, an important device by which the legitimate interests of particular groups are put forward to compete with those of other groups.

The Negro community lacks an institutional framework in private social welfare (as well as in other institutional areas), and the separatist agencies of other ethnic and religious communities are not eager to see this deficiency overcome. When the Negro is concerned, they resist the emergence of new separatist institutions on the grounds that such a "color conscious" development represents a new form of "segregation." This view has frequently been expressed or implied in behind-the-scenes struggles over the allocation of antipoverty funds. In one city after another private agencies have either fought against the development of Negro-sponsored programs or have sat by while Negro groups argued in vain with municipal, county, or federal officials over their right to form autonomous, ethnic institutions to receive public funds.[22]

22. Some OEO funds have been used to stimulate the growth of Negro welfare institutions. Bitter conflicts have inevitably followed—as in the case of New York's HARYOU-ACT and the Child Development Group of Mississippi. Neither of these embattled agencies has received appreciable support from established social agencies.

By and large, private agencies have contended that race is an irrelevant issue in deciding who should mount programs in a ghetto. Existing agencies, it is argued, have the proved professional and organizational competence to operate new programs, and many have succeeded in obtaining public funds to do so. In the end, however, this form of "desegregation" is destructive of Negro interests. Although coalitions of existing ethnic and religious agencies may provide services to the ghetto (especially with the financial incentives of the antipoverty program), these services do not strengthen the ghetto's capacity to deal with its own problems. Rather, they weaken it. Through the "integration" of Negroes as clients in service structures operated by others, political control by outside institutions is extended to one more aspect of ghetto life. Furthermore, the ghetto is deprived of the resources that could encourage the development of its own institutions or bolster them. Existing voluntary agencies could serve the ghetto far better if they lent political, technical, and financial aid to the development of new social welfare institutions that would be under Negro management and control.

Class power in the United States is intimately connected with the strength of ethnic institutions. Powerlessness and poverty are disproportionately concentrated among minority groups—Negroes, Puerto Ricans, Mexicans, and so forth. The success of traditional ethnic and religious social agencies in resisting the emergence of Negro institutions is a reflection of class power differentials. But it also reveals that class power is produced and maintained in part by racial and ethnic power differentials.

NEED FOR SEPARATIST ORGANIZATIONS

A new system of voluntary social welfare agencies in the ghetto can hardly be expected to produce the collective force to overcome the deep inequalities in our society. Ethnic identity, solidarity, and power must be forged through a series of organized communal experiences in a variety of institutional areas. In housing, for example, energy should be directed not only toward improving ghetto conditions but also toward creating within the ghetto the organizational vehicles for renovating buildings and, more important, for managing them.[23] Similarly, educational reforms should mean not only improvements in facilities and staff but also arrangements under which the local community can participate in and influence the administration of the schools.[24]

What the Negro needs, in short, are the means to organize separately and a heightened awareness of the distinctive goals to which his organizations must be directed. The Negro poor in our society do have interests distinct from and, more often than not, in conflict with those of other groups. Unless they organize along

23. In a tentative way, this possibility is now being explored by some groups (e.g., churches), which are receiving loans to rehabilitate ghetto buildings under the federal low cost mortgage program. These groups form local corporations to rehabilitate and later to manage houses.

24. Parent groups in East Harlem recently boycotted a new school (P.S. 201); they abandoned earlier demands for school integration to insist that the Board of Education cede a large measure of control to the local community. The ensuing controversy brought to the fore certain issues in professional and community control. As of this writing, a final resolution has not been reached. Without some administrative arrangement to insure greater involvement by the ghetto community, the schools will continue to be responsive to other, better-organized religious, ethnic, and class groupings that traditionally have been powerful enough to assert the superiority of their claims for educational services and resources over that of the ghetto. There is some indication that such arrangements may also bring educational benefits. A recent study showed a high correlation between the achievement of Negro children and their feeling that they can control their own destinies. See Coleman et al., op. cit.

separatist lines, it is unlikely that they will have much success in advancing these interests. Judging from the history of those ethnic groups that have succeeded in gaining a foothold in our pluralistic society, it seems clear that ethnic separatism is a precondition for eventual penetration of the ruling circles and the achievement of full economic integration. Minority groups will win acceptance from the majority by developing their own bases of power, not by submerging their unorganized and leaderless numbers in coalitions dominated by other and more solidary groups. Once they have formed separatist organizations, participation in coalitions (whether councils of social agencies or political parties) can then be a meaningful tactic in bargaining for a share of power over crucial institutional process in the broader society.

In a recent essay David Danzig observed:

It is, to be sure, a long step from the recognition of the need for power to the building and strengthening of indigenous social and political institutions within the ghetto from which power can be drawn. The Negro as yet has few such institutions. Unlike most of the other religio-ethnic minorities, he lacks a network of unifying social traditions, and this is why he must depend on political action through color consciousness as his main instrument of solidarity. That solidarity entails a certain degree of "separatism" goes without saying, but the separatism of a strengthened and enriched Negro community need be no more absolute than that, say, of the Jewish community. There is no reason, after all, why the Negro should not be able to live, as most Americans do, in two worlds at once—one of them largely integrated and the other primarily separated.[25]

In these terms, then, physical desegregation is not only irrelevant to the ghetto but can actually prevent the eventual integration of the Negro in the institutional life of this society. For integration must be understood, not as the mingling of bodies in school and neighborhood, but as participation in and shared control over the major institutional spheres of American life. And that is a question of developing communal associations that can be bases for power—not of dispersing a community that is powerless.

25. "In Defense of 'Black Power,'" *Commentary* 42, no. 3 (September 1966): 45-46.

8. Public Housing and Urban Policy: Gautreaux v. Chicago Housing Authority

YALE LAW JOURNAL

On February 10, 1969, to the great displeasure of Mayor Richard Daley and others of the Chicago establishment, Judge Richard Austin held that the Chicago Housing Authority had intentionally chosen sites for family public housing with the purpose of maintaining residential separation of the races in Chicago.[1] The judgment order issued five months later generally required future public housing in Chicago to take the form of low-rise, scattered site projects in white neighborhoods;[2] and the fervor of official reaction in both directions underlined the seriousness with which the matter was viewed in Chicago. . . .

The charge before the court in *Gautreaux* was the intentional limitation of sites for public housing[3] to already black areas of Chicago in order to maintain the preexisting residential separation in the city. Had sites not been so limited and had tenants been assigned on a nondiscriminatory basis, placing public housing in white neighborhoods would have resulted in placing blacks in white neighborhoods. Through the exercise of its veto power over site selection, the Chicago City Council had limited project sites to ghetto neighborhoods.[4] Thus, in *Gautreaux* there was no difficulty proving the underlying Fourteenth Amendment violation such placement would create. The court found a direct intent to maintain racial separation. . . .

The remedial purpose applied by the court in *Gautreaux* [is] "to prohibit the future use and to remedy the past effects of CHA's unconstitutional site selection."[5] . . . The court has found an intentional use of public housing to maintain residential segregation, through the building of public housing only in black neighborhoods.

Reprinted by permission of The Yale Law Journal Company and Fred B. Rothman and Company from *The Yale Law Journal* 79 (1970): 712-23 (edited).

1. *Gautreaux* v. *Chicago Housing Authority*, 296 F. Supp. 907 (N.D. Ill. 1969). Mayor Daley was reported as stating that the "ruling . . . could slow up or block future public housing construction." *Chicago Tribune*, March 12, 1969, at 12, col. 1.

2. Judgment Order, *Gautreaux* v. *Chicago Housing Authority*, July 1, 1969. [Hereinafter cited as Judgment Order.]

3. For purposes of the Note, a simplified understanding of the federal housing program is sufficient. Pursuant to state enabling legislation a city first creates a local housing authority. After submission of a planned project, and its approval by HUD, an annual contributions contract is executed by which HUD, through annual grants, agrees to finance the capital costs of the project. Operational and maintenance expenses remain the city's obligation to be covered out of rent. More recently, other federal housing program models have been attempted.

4. Of the family units operated by CHA, 99½ percent were in neighborhoods between 50 and 100 percent black. Gautreaux v. Chicago Housing Authority, 296 F. Supp. 907, 910 (N.D. Ill. 1969). The effect of this has been to limit interest in public housing to blacks, who comprise 90 percent of the current eligibility list. *Id.* at 909. The fact that this exclusion of 188,000 otherwise eligible white families (*id.* at 915) has been willingly borne, even by those excluded, indicates the extent of the fear of placing public housing in white neighborhoods.

5. *Gautreaux* v. *Chicago Housing Authority*, 296 F. Supp. 907, 914; Judgment Order at 1.

As a consequence blacks were denied the opportunity to choose to live in public housing in white neighborhoods. The continuing effect of CHA's discrimination is the continuing unavailability of such a choice. The constitutional duty to eliminate that effect requires the use of public housing to provide an effective opportunity for residential integration. The more difficult question that obviously remains—how one uses public housing for this purpose—is a policy question, not a Constitutional one. It asks how, in practical terms, public housing should be used to provide a ghetto resident with an effective opportunity to live elsewhere.

Although some commentators have maintained that we lack sufficient information to frame workable solutions,[6] there are at least two distinct, though not mutually exclusive, policy positions regarding the most effective use of public housing to provide opportunities for residential integration. The first is the more obvious, and reflects the conventional wisdom of remedial action in civil rights litigation: integrate in the most direct manner possible. In the context of *Gautreaux*, the "integration ethic" directs here the placement of public housing in white neighborhoods to provide black residents with the choice that had been earlier denied them.[7]

There is, however, a second position, purposefully less direct, but still persuasive. It bottoms in the premise that in order for the opportunity for integration to be effective, the merging parties must be equal in fact as well as in law. One provides alternatives to the ghetto by developing it and the people within it. Freedom to integrate will follow as a matter of course. This is admittedly more indirect, but, it is argued, the foundation is stronger. Such a position was taken by the late Senator Robert F. Kennedy in testifying before the Senate Subcommittee on Housing and Urban Affairs. In urging the placement of the great majority of new housing in the ghetto, he went on to say:

> To seek a rebuilding of our urban slums is not to turn our backs on the goal of integration. It is only to say that open occupancy laws alone will not suffice and that sensitivity must be shown to the aspirations of Negroes and other nonwhites who would build their own communities and occupy decent housing in neighborhoods where they now live. And, in the long run, this willingness to come to grips with blight of our center city will lead us toward an open society. For it is comparability of housing and full employment that are the keys to free movement

---

6. See Grier, "The Negro Ghetto and Federal Housing Policy," 32 *Law & contemp. prob.* 550, 560 (1967); see also D. Hunter, *The Slums* 238 (1968).

7. This position has received considerable support in recent governmental advisory committee reports. See *Report of the National Advisory Commission on Civil Disorders* (Bantam ed. 1968).
    Federal housing programs must be given a new thrust aimed at overcoming the prevailing pattern of racial segregation. If this is not done, those programs will continue to concentrate the most impoverished and dependent segments of the population in the central cities. . . .
Id. at 474.
    To date, however, housing programs serving low income groups have been concentrated in the ghettos. Non-ghetto areas, particularly suburbs, for the most part have steadfastly opposed . . . and have successfully resisted the use of these programs outside the ghetto. We believe that federally aided low and moderate housing programs must be reoriented so that the major thrust is in non-ghetto areas. . . .
Id. at 481. A more extensive treatment of the premises underlying the National Advisory Committee's position is found in Anthony Downs, "Alternative Futures for the American Ghetto," 97 *Daedalus* 1331 (1968). See also President's Committee on Urban Housing, *A Decent Home* 13, 48 (1968).
    For nonofficial sources taking a similar position, see, e.g., National Committee Against Discrimination in Housing, *How the Federal Government Builds Ghettos* (1967); J. Kain & J. Persky "Alternatives to the Gilded Ghetto," in *Race & Poverty* 167 (J. Kain ed. 1969).

and to the establishment of a society in which each man has a real opportunity to choose whom he will call neighbor.[8]

Put another way, social equality can be seen as a function of political equality. Where the political process is best characterized as the working out of conflicting group interests, and representation in that process is often geographical, the development of the ghetto provides for the political representation of a group with particular goals and concerns and provides the basis for the equality necessary for a free choice of residence.[9]

The court in *Gautreaux* did resolve this policy debate, and both the direction of its resolution and the skill such resolution displays cast doubts on the wisdom of having courts, in preference to other institutions, so decide.

The judgment order drawn in *Gautreaux* initially divided the city into two sections: a "Limited Public Housing Area" defined to include all census tracts "having 30 percent or more nonwhite population, or within a distance of one mile from any point on the outer perimeter of any such census tract"; and a "General Public Housing Area" which is the remainder of the city.[10] The order then prohibits CHA from constructing any other dwelling units until not less than 700 units are in the process of construction in the General Public Housing Area. Further, no construction of units can take place within the Limited Public Housing Area at all unless 75 percent of the units begun after the initial 700 are within the General Public Housing Area. In short, the next

8. *Hearings on S. 3029 Before the Subcomm. on Housing and Urban Affairs of the Senate Banking and Currency Committee*, 90th Cong., 2d Sess. (1968). It is interesting that the percentages suggested by Senator Kennedy, 75 percent ghetto, 25 percent nonghetto, id., are the mirror image of those in the *Gautreaux* judgment order. See *infra* p. 719. See also Robert F. Kennedy, "Industrial Investment in Urban Poverty," in *Race & Poverty* 153, 157 (J. Kain ed. 1969) (reprinted from a Senate speech of July 12, 1967).

9. The Achilles heel of housing programs has been precisely our insistence that better housing for the black poor be achieved by residential desegregation. This idea glosses over the importance of the ethnic community as a staging area for groups to build the communal solidarity and power necessary to compel eventual access to the mainstream of urban life.

Piven and Cloward, "Desegregated Housing: Who Pays for the Reformers' Ideas," in *Race & Poverty* 175, 181-2 (J. Kain ed. 1969). See also D. Hunter, *The Slums* vi-vii (1968); R. Innis, "Separatist Economics: A New Social Contract" in *Black Economic Development* 50 (W. Haddad & G. Pugh eds. 1969); S. Carmichael & C. Hamilton, *Black Power* 54-56 (1967); H. Cruse, *The Crisis of the Negro Intellectual* 309 (1967); Slayton, "A Racial Policy for Housing Growth," The *N.Y. Times*, Dec. 28, 1969, Sec. 8, at 1, col. 1.

10. Judgment Order id. at 2. The order does make technical allowance for the placement of one-third of the units required for the General Public Housing Area in areas of Cook County outside the City of Chicago. Judgment Order III C & E. However, this provision has no practical effect. It was inserted in the order at the insistence of CHA, who, having such authority under state law, feared that the order might at some time be read as an exclusive statement of their site selection discretion and therefore wanted the order to run coextensive with their statutory grant. Interview with Kathryn Kula, General Counsel, Chicago Housing Authority, in Chicago, November 6, 1969. [Hereinafter cited as Kula Interview.]

Of the total city area of 200 square miles, the General Public Housing Area would cover 75 square miles and the Limited Public Housing Area 125 square miles. The scope of this division is revealed by considering the status under the order of the 10,903 "white" units rejected over the years by the City Council . . . Of these, only 775, less than 10 percent, would fall within the General Public Housing Area under the order and hence be currently developable by the CHA. Memorandum for the United States at 4 (a vague statement of the position of the government, particularly the Department of Housing and Urban Development, on the question of remedy). The number may, however, be significantly fewer. If, as was likely at the time they were proposed, those 775 units on sites still acceptable were slated for relatively large projects, then the number of units such sites could now support would be many fewer under the order's limit of 20 units (120 people) per project.

700 units and 75 percent of all units thereafter have· to be located in white neighborhoods.

The judgment order next regulates CHA's use of the federal leased housing program under which local authorities may lease units in private buildings for use by families eligible for low-rent public housing. The order provides that CHA may make no unit available for occupancy in the Limited Public Housing Area unless, at that time, 75 percent of then occupied leased units are in the General Public Housing Area.

The order then prescribes in detail the type of housing that can be constructed or leased. These provisions, limiting the size and concentration of future projects,[11] are apparently designed to assure stable integration of the new housing into the larger white community. Jurisdiction was retained by the court for the purpose of modifying the judgment order, a procedure which has since been invoked four times on minor points.

The order, by tying the provision of housing in black neighborhoods to that in white, reflects a preference for the "integration ethic" alone. However, even setting aside the argument that ghetto development itself is the best means to achieve eventual integration, the fact remains that large numbers of people prefer to live in an ethnic community we call a ghetto, and that public housing can be one means to make that community a better place to live. Not only does the judgment order make that use impossible until the initial 700 units are built, but, because of interplay among various statutory provisions, the order also makes more difficult the use of other federal programs designed explicitly for ghetto development.

An obvious example of this removal of opportunity is the effect of the judgment order on the leased housing program. A major cause of the decline in quality of ghetto low income housing stock is that landlords cannot afford to maintain a building at rents low income people can afford to pay. In such a situation, a leasing system which provides the private landlord with a reasonable rent helps to forestall otherwise inevitable decay. Yet, in practical terms, the order's requirement that 75 percent of leased units be in the General Public Housing Area will gut the program.

Ninety percent of the families eligible for the leasing program are black, and the participation of a sufficient number of landlords in white neighborhoods is improbable. A lessor who rents 20 percent of his building to low-income blacks is unlikely, given the current market, to be able to rent the remaining 80 percent. Since the vacancy rate in white neighborhoods is so low, he need not take the chance.

---

11. The order specifically provides that no project can be designed for occupancy by more than 120 people, though providing an impossibility exception which, if the application of the exception "will assist in achieving the purposes of this judgment order," raises the limit to 240 people. Judgment Order IVA at 5-6. Given CHA's present estimate of 6 people to family, projects may contain no more than 20 units. Kula Interview. Projects may also not be so concentrated as to constitute more than 15 percent of the total apartments and single-family residences in any census tract. Judgment Order IVC at 6. Finally, no families with children may be placed in an apartment any higher than the third story, the obvious result being that no family public housing may exceed three stories. *Id.*

Limiting the size and concentration of projects reflects a concern articulated by Anthony Downs: "A vast majority of whites of all income groups would be willing to send their children to integrated schools or live in integrated neighborhoods, as long *as they were sure that the white group concerned would remain in the majority* in those facilities or areas." "Alternative Futures for the American Ghetto," 97 *Daedalus* 1331, 1338 (1968) (emphasis in the original). From the other side, a small project, because it would not be socially self-sufficient, assures that its residents will make use of community facilities. Related to this is the 15 percent concentration limit. The limit on the number of stories seems to reflect an idea that low-rise garden type apartments are more likely to fit within the available site neighborhood as well as a belief that it is difficult to raise small children in elevator buildings.

The situation is markedly different, however, in ghetto neighborhoods, where land-lords are eager to use the leasing program. The judgment order's limitation of units leased in black neighborhoods to one-third of those leased in white neighborhoods, when coupled with the unlikelihood that leasing will be successfully used in white neighborhoods, will doom the entire program. Because the end result of the court's interference with the leasing program is to make it unusable by blacks, without any countervailing benefit for whites, the order should not have covered the leasing pro-gram; indeed, nothing in the charge before the court required it to deal with the leasing program at all.

The order also has significant impact on the future use of urban renewal. The "Proxmire Amendment," contained in the Housing and Urban Development Act of 1968, requires that 20 percent of any new housing built in urban renewal projects must be for low income families. Assuming urban renewal will generally take place within the 62½ percent of the city's area represented by the Limited Public Housing Area, public housing could be built on urban renewal land only after both the initial 700 units required by the order were completed and enough additional units in the General Public Housing Area were commenced to create a 75-25 ratio of housing constructed after the first 700 units.

Looking beyond that point, however, the order will continue to make beneficial use of urban renewal difficult, if not in practical terms impossible. Urban renewal has been consistently criticized as being in fact "Negro removal," replacing low income housing with luxury apartments and commercial structures. One response was the "Proxmire Amendment," which gave a new "ghetto development" thrust to the urban renewal program. Yet, the effect of the judgment order is to blunt that thrust, for it sets as a prior condition for the construction of each low-income housing unit on an urban renewal site within the Limited Public Housing Area the construction of three units in the General Public Housing Area.

The Model Cities Program, a program specifically designed for neighborhood development, also suffers from the judgment order's three to one requirement. Of the four model neighborhoods in Chicago, three are within the Limited Public Housing Area. Current proposals for these model neighborhoods provide for the building of 1,950 units of family public housing. Under the *Gautreaux* order, 5,850 units (3 to 1) must be built in the General Public Housing Area before the planned housing can be provided within the model neighborhoods. Such a restraint is directly contrary to the rationale for the Model Cities Act.

These effects on ghetto development were not oversights but were indeed recognized in the drawing of the judgment order. Plaintiff's counsel characterized them as "simply the price one is forced to pay." Ghetto residents are familiar, however, with price gouging. Why should the provision of public housing in white neighborhoods in order to promote residential integration have been thought to be at cross purposes with simultaneous programs for ghetto development?[12] Indeed, an additional factor, the new tenant assignment plan, by acting to slow the order's primary thrust of moving blacks into white neighborhoods, would seem to make concurrent ghetto development even more important. While blacks on the waiting list will retain their priority over

12. . . . One cannot ignore, however, the single argument supporting the judgment order's outcome. Unless something is held out in front of the city—the proverbial carrot and the don-key—it will simply not build housing in white neighborhoods and go on, as before, developing the ghetto. Yet, on this reasoning, one would conclude that the most effective order would be that offering the biggest carrot. Make the availability of the most desirable housing from the city's point of view—housing for the elderly—turn on the provision of family public housing in white neighborhoods. In addition, this would not affect simultaneous ghetto development.

those registering later, an additional priority is created before them: 50 percent of the units available in the new projects both at initial offering and as vacancies occur are reserved for applicants who reside in the community area in which the project is located. The point of the community priority provision, apparently, is to ensure that the individual projects themselves will be integrated. The effect of it is to reduce significantly the number of new units which will be available for blacks.[13] . . .

13. The possibility does remain that the city council will still refuse to approve white sites, and thus eliminate public housing completely. While the thought of jailing the entire City Council for contempt has its appeal, such drastic action might not be necessary, however. One alternative would eliminate the necessity of Council approval by finding the Illinois statute giving the Council the right of approval unconstitutional as applied. While this would in fact take political pressure off the City Council by no longer placing them in the position of having to go on record as approving particular white sites, it does not tie their hands if they are indeed bent on obstruction. They may still refuse to authorize the annual contributions necessary for participation in federal programs. In the event of such outright obstruction in the North, resort to the southern school closing cases would seem appropriate, e.g., *Griffin* v. *County School Board of Prince Edward County*, 377 U.S. 218. And, as first stated, there is civil contempt.

9. Public Housing: The Contexts of Failure

JEWEL BELLUSH and MURRAY HAUSKNECHT

In 1965 Congress passed the Economic Opportunities Act, two aid to education bills, and the Medicare program. The same Congress passed the rent subsidy provision of a housing bill by the barest possible margin, and concluded its session by refusing to appropriate funds for the program. The behavior of Congress is symptomatic of the status of public housing in the United States: while there is an increasing willingness to extend and implement public welfare policies in many new directions, there is no similar willingness to extend and support public housing programs.

The preamble to the Housing Act of 1949 stated:

> To establish a national housing objective and the policy to be followed in the attainment thereof, to provide Federal aid to assist slum-clearance projects and low rent public housing projects initiated by local agencies, to provide for financial assistance by the Secretary of Agriculture for farm housing, and for other purposes.

Despite the clear emphasis on housing, the passage of the act and subsequent ones has had very little effect on the housing situation of the poor. The 1960 Census found one-eighth of all urban households living in dwellings that were dilapidated or lacking in sanitary facilities.[1] Indeed, one housing specialist concludes that:

> . . . the housing problem of the disadvantaged has gradually ceased to be of major concern to those responsible for public policy. Faced with declining ratables and rising costs for municipal services, cities have used federal renewal funds for projects that would shore up local finances.[2]

There is an irony here. Today, as never before in our history, there is a consciousness of the urgency of urban problems, a consciousness that represents a belated triumph for the long line of urban reformers. One of their focal interests was the deplorable state of housing in our cities, and now that we have caught up with their awareness we slight one of their central concerns. This underlines the main problem of explaining the strange neglect of public housing in an era of innovation in welfare policies.

Conventionally public housing is placed in the broad category of "welfare," and so Medicare is assumed to be basically similar to housing as public programs. To the extent that Medicare and public housing represent a recognition of material needs that can only be filled by some sort of government intervention, these are similar programs. But when we ask whom do these programs affect, what proportion of the total population, and which strata of the society, a critical difference emerges.

From *Urban Renewal: People, Politics and Planning*, edited by Jewel Bellush and Murray Hausknecht, pp. 451-57. Copyright © 1967 by Jewel Bellush and Murray Hausknecht. Reprinted by permission of Doubleday & Co., Inc., and of the authors. Jewel Bellush is associate professor of political science at Hunter College of the City University of New York. Murray Hausknecht is a professor of sociology at the Herman Lehman College of the City University of New York.

1. Conference on Economic Progress, *Poverty and Deprivation in the United States* (Washington, D.C.: Conference on Economic Progress, April 1962), chap. X.

2. William Grisgby, "Housing and Slum Clearance: Elusive Goals," *The Annals of the American Academy of Political and Social Science* 352 (March 1964): 109.

Medicare is designed to meet the needs of the aged, and everyone is destined to age. Given the increasing costs of medical care, few people can look forward without anxiety to meeting future health costs from their own resources. Thus Medicare affects almost the entire society and cuts across class lines; almost everyone has either a present or future stake in the program. Public housing, on the other hand, affects only one class and a much smaller proportion of the total population. Equally important, unlike the problem of health and old age, few people see public housing as being important to them in the future.

When we contrast the scholarship aid provisions of the education acts of 1965 with public housing, still another difference among welfare programs emerges. The fundamental premise of the scholarship programs is that no one who can qualify for a college education should miss the opportunity through lack of money, and this applies to the "poor" as well as to those solidly ensconced in the middle class. Once again, then, it is a program that crosscuts class lines. More to the present point is the premise that those who *deserve* it ought to receive aid. In a society that evaluates individuals on performance criteria a distinction is always drawn between the *deserving* and the *undeserving* as measured in terms of individual achievement. Public housing seems to ignore this principle, since it benefits the poor, those who have failed to achieve, i.e., the *undeserving*.

Obviously, other welfare programs, notably those included in the war on poverty, also benefit the poor. But these are related to performance and achievement. The typical poverty program tries to aid the poor to achieve in a society governed by universalistic norms; the program is designed to improve the *performance* of the individual. Public housing has no such apparent instrumental relevance to perform-ance. Moreover, job retraining programs, for example, are self-limiting; that is, once the individual is "retrained," aid stops, and he is once again on his own. Public housing does not have this kind of self-limiting mechanism for the lower class; if a family's income remains below a certain level it still retains its apartment. In other words, if family incomes is an index of achievement, then public aid continues even after lack of achievement has been demonstrated. In this sense, public housing aids the undeserving poor, as do home relief and aid to dependent children. It is precisely these programs that focus on the undeserving poor that become the targets for public criticism and legislative hostility.[3]

The importance of the distinction between the deserving and the undeserving can be seen from another perspective when we contrast general housing policy in our society with public housing policy. Such programs as FHA insured mortgages, GI Bill home loans, and state-aided cooperative housing assist individuals who ordinarily could not purchase homes in the open market. However, the programs aid only the deserving, i.e., those who have accumulated some resources through their own efforts. At the other extreme, the *most* undeserving poor are denied admission to public housing: In almost all communities multiproblem families, for example, are ineligible for public housing. In sum, then, we may say that public housing differs from other welfare programs in that it allocates resources in a manner that ignores performance criteria.

But a home is something more than a "resource"; it has a symbolic significance. Homeownership in our society is a symbol of civic virtue—it is regarded as a prerequisite for the integrity of the social system. It is not surprising to learn that Herbert Hoover once intoned, "The present large proportion of families that own their own homes

---

3. See the stimulating paper by S. M. Miller and Martin Rein, "The War on Poverty: Perspectives and Prospects" (February 1965) (mimeographed).

is both the foundation of a sound economic and social system, and a guarantee that our society will continue to develop rationally as changing conditions demand." Some, however, may be disconcerted to hear this echoed in Franklin D. Roosevelt's assertion that "a nation of homeowners, of people who own a real share in their own land, is unconquerable."[4] But the sentiments will not surprise those who recall Thomas Jefferson's exaltation of the yeoman farmer or the ideological underpinnings of the Homestead Act of 1862. In the 20th century, the virtues of the yeoman farmer and the sterling pioneer are embodied in "the homeowner."

In addition to its civic significance, homeownership also symbolizes individual worth. In our culture the ownership of one's own home is an important symbol of achievement, whether it be a castle at San Simeon, a town house on New York's East Side, or a mass-produced, split-level, or ranch house of the suburban subdivision. It is, in short, a visible sign of individual success, and an important reassurance that the American Dream is not a nightmare. Thus, from a sociological perspective, the home is also a *reward*. But rewards in our society are supposed to be distributed on the basis of achievement, and we have seen that public housing is allocated to those who have failed to achieve.

Public housing, then, runs counter to the implications of traditional notions about virtue. The tradition wraps up home ownership, individual achievement, and "the foundations of a sound economic and social system" into one tightly knit whole, and in this ball of cultural yarn there is no room for public housing. In addition, to provide public housing for the undeserving poor subverts the significance of owning one's own home, be it ever so humble or substandard. This is to say nothing, as yet, of the willingness, in practical political terms, of the latter-day descendants of yeoman farmers and sturdy pioneers to see their taxes go to those so clearly undeserving in comparison with themselves.

Our cultural traditions play into the situation in yet another way. The Jeffersonian idealization of the yeoman farmer is an integral part of the antiurban bias of our society. The yeoman farmer embodies civic virtue because he is a rural man; urban man, by definition, is corrupt. It does not matter that the contemporary homeowner is highly urbanized, or that he may live in the densest part of the metropolitan area. Home ownership makes him the heir to all the rural virtues, or at least a rural bastion against the vice-filled streets of the city. Public housing has historically been provided for the urban mass whose present state and historical antecedents both exemplify and contribute to urban sin. Thus, public housing does not crosscut another great divide of American society, the rural-urban division. And so, by being so securely identified with Sodom and Gomorrah, it manages to mobilize all the traditional negative perceptions of the city and its inhabitants.

Despite their concern for the urban masses, the urban reformers' ideas were not at odds with the cultural tradition we have been describing. Adequate homes for the urban, immigrant masses was a necessary condition for dealing with their poverty; that is, housing reform and the elimination of the slums went hand in hand with education as an instrument or means of social mobility. By 1950, however, it was apparent that the beliefs of the champions of public housing were based on myths rather than facts.[5] It was not simply that the occupants of public housing remained among the poor and that the social ills of the city were not abated as public housing rose in the former slum areas—although this would have been bad enough. During

4. Both statements quoted in Glenn Beyer, *Housing: A Factual Analysis* (New York: Macmillan Co., 1958), p. 249.

5. James B. Conant, *Slums and Suburbs* (New York: McGraw-Hill Book Co., 1961), p. 33.

the fifties observers were also pointing out that the huge public housing projects, while still physically decent, showed all the other characteristics of the slums they had replaced. It was difficult to escape the conclusion that housing made little difference to the situation it was supposed to remedy. Thus, the traditional rationale for public housing was destroyed, and its liberal proponents were thrown into ideological disarray.[6]

Consequently, the liberals were left at a considerable disadvantage on the level of practical politics. But another factor must be noted as well. The decade of the fifties represented for most American liberals "the end of ideology"; it was an era in which one was forced to recognize old beliefs, commitments, and political theories as shibboleths that had no relevance to the world of the "cold war" and the "affluent society." As one shucked off "ideological" orientations one became more "pragmatic," and by 1960 this became central to the "style" of a new Democratic Administration. The new political style was fateful for public housing, because it further weakened and drained off commitment to the program. The basic argument for public housing had been, in any case, a pragmatic one, i.e., it had always been justified in terms of its instrumental functions for alleviating poverty and civic immorality. To continue to advocate a policy and a program that could not be justified pragmatically meant that one was still in the grip of "ideology." Realism demanded that one seek other means of combating poverty and other social ills.

The suspicion of "ideology" and the celebration of a pragmatic politics turned political energies toward other programs, but this was not an inevitable consequence. A pragmatic orientation in these circumstances could lead to a rethinking of the role of public housing. The rent subsidy program shows that, in fact, no attempt was made to seriously reexamine the problem, and it serves as a central clue to another cause of the decline of effective political commitment to public housing.

Public housing programs failed to meet the expectations of their proponents because the programs did not link housing as physical structure with the social and cultural components of a neighborhood. A "slum" is a community as well as a site of substandard housing, and the amelioration of the conditions of life of its inhabitants depends upon dealing with the community as well as the physical dwellings. From this perspective the object of aid is not the individual but the community; the lot of the individual changes with a change in the community. There are two prerequisites that must be met before this perspective can be meaningfully implemented. First, there must be the acceptance of the proposition that the social ills and problems of the slum—where these are empirically correlated—are phenomena linked to the class status of the community rather than to individuals *qua* individuals. That is, the phenomena are the result of structural conditions rather than purely individual problems. Secondly, there must be a recognition that "class" means something more than low income; its means a distinctive subculture and distinctive styles of life related to social position. A total program of aid, of which public housing would be one component, would have to, then, be based on the potentialities and limitations of a specific class community. This orientation would also mean, to revert to an earlier point, overlooking the differences between the deserving and undeserving poor.

It is a perspective, however, that is extraordinarily difficult to achieve in American society. A unique combination of historical circumstances has produced relatively high

---

6. Editors' note: See Harrison Salisbury, *The Shook-Up Generation* (New York: Harper & Bros., 1958), pp. 73-88; Jane Jacobs, *The Death and Life of Great American Cities* (New York: Random House, Inc., 1961), pp. 270-81; Lee Rainwater, "Fear and the House-as-Haven in the Lower Class," chap. 16 in this book.

standards of living for all strata, and these have produced, in turn, a blurring of class lines and distinctions. Consequently, in the public sphere Americans, liberals and nonliberals alike, show little consciousness of class, and they are prone to the myth of classlessness, i.e., that the United States is not "really" a class society— "we are all really middle class." (This does not mean that in the private sphere, e.g., choosing whom one marries or where one lives, Americans are not sensitive to class differences, and do not act on their knowledge of the differences.) The myth is not totally unrelated to reality; from a political perspective, at least, class phenomena in the United States often have a different significance than in comparable European countries. At the same time the myth obscures an important aspect of the American reality, that there are class communities with distinctive subcultures and styles of life to which the assumption and implications that "we are all middle class" do not apply.

In the rent subsidy program we can still see the myth at work and the way the class realities of American life are ignored. The program implicitly assumes that the poor are distinguished from others *only* by a lack of money; that their values, aspirations, and styles of life are not meaningfully different from others; that once the lack of money has been compensated for they will merge relatively easily into their new surroundings. Our class system does produce many individuals for whom these assumptions are appropriate. The rent subsidy proposal, therefore, is quite conventional in its approach, since it concerns itself with individuals and the deserving poor. It demonstrates a failure to see public housing in relation to the poor as members of a community, and to see the community in terms of its class characteristics. Thus, the inability to come to terms with the class dimensions of urban ills leaves the champions of public housing pursuing traditional paths that lead to defeats in the political arena, and to a further weakening of commitment to public housing. For it is in the political arena that the factors of American history and society we have been discussing take on practical significance. . . .

10.   *The Politics of Housing*

CHESTER W. HARTMAN

There is a great deal of ferment in the housing field at present, but not much action. Rhetoric has far outrun (and in a sense diverts attention from) any corresponding commitment to allocate resources. The housing problem is shaking down to an easily identifiable form, following resolutions of the anomalies caused by the Depression and War. Those with adequate income by and large are getting adequate housing, and the private sector, strategically assisted by the government—notably via FHA and VA mortgage insurance and urban renewal—works moderately well to satisfy the housing needs of middle- and upper-income groups.

The vestigial housing problem, although by no means trivial—at a minimum 12 million U.S. families are living below acceptable standards—is composed of specific "types": families and individuals who lack and have little hope of earning adequate income; nonwhite minorities (with and without adequate income); the elderly; rural slumdwellers; and the vague catchall category, "multiproblem families." It is now absolutely clear to all but the most resistant that the vast majority of these 12 million families are not going to secure decent housing through the processes of "normal" mobility, and that existing government programs to aid this sector of the population are hopelessly inadequate to the task, qualitatively as well as quantitatively.

At the present we are being bombarded with new ideas, some good, some not so good, some really innovative, some merely rehashes of old proposals. Model Cities, rent supplements, instant rehabilitation, "turnkey," Percy Plan, Kennedy Plan, Ribicoff Plan are but a few of the terms flying thick and fast over conference tables and speakers' platforms. But it is still a time of rhetoric, not of results, nor even of realistic planmaking. The issue is primarily one of money. The costs of achieving the National Housing Goal, established nearly 20 years ago ("a decent home and a suitable living environment for every American family") are big, and as a nation we just don't seem to want to spend big money these days for anything but killing Vietnamese. We don't even have any good estimates on the costs of attaining this goal (in part due to the vagueness of its definition).

Based on 1960 Census data on the incomes of families presently living in substandard housing and using 1959 Bureau of Labor Statistics figures on the costs of obtaining "modest but adequate" housing in metropolitan areas, a program of housing subsidization for all families in the U.S. who cannot afford decent housing on the private market might cost an additional $7-8 billion a year. This figure would be somewhat higher if housing subsidies were also to be made available to reduce housing costs for families living in standard housing who are devoting an excessive portion of their income to rent. This looks awfully large when compared with present expenditures for housing the poor (less than $400 million annually, plus whatever portion of welfare payments is used—generally speaking, wastefully—for housing). But it represents only

Reprinted from *Dissent* 14 (November-December 1967): 701-14 (edited), by permission of the publisher and author. Chester W. Hartman is senior planning associate, National Housing and Economic Development Law Project, University of California at Berkeley.

1 percent of the nation's GNP and less than four months of warfare in Southeast Asia. Needless to say, there is no immediate prospect of having anywhere near the amount of money required to implement current proposals, except on a token or pilot project scale. This is the basic political fact which must underlie any discussion of housing.

But even if the problem of resource allocation could be solved, there would still be an imposing array of fundamental problems, conflicts, and decisions to be faced. It is these areas and the ways in which they are dealt with under existing and proposed programs that form the hub of this essay.

RACE

Any housing program must face the fundamental fact that the overwhelming majority of white Americans are afraid of and do not want to live anywhere near nonwhite Americans, and that at least a substantial portion of the nonwhite population, if not the majority, does not consider integration into white America (at least on the majority's terms) a very high priority. This situation can only intensify as nonwhites increasingly experience and suffer the effects of second-class citizenship, and as resentment of and insurrection against this status takes ever more hostile and violent forms.

It seems quite probable that we have passed the point where massive integration of the races can be an element of a housing program that will improve the lot of the vast majority of slum dwellers, black as well as white, in a relatively short time span (say, within 5 to 10 years). Existing residential patterns are too firmly fixed, the population shifts and disruptions required would be too massive, and popular resistance to any program of this nature would be staggering. In the December 1966 *New Republic*, Frances Piven and Richard Cloward argue that stress on racial integration as a necessary component of housing programs has drained support for these programs; as a result of a policy of "either integrated housing or no housing," those most in need of better shelter have been denied the benefits of potentially helpful programs, and are in effect paying the price for goals and ideals that are less important to the poor than they are to the reformers.[1] What has undoubtedly been true in the past for relatively meager programs, (*viz.*, congressional curtailment of the rent supplement program and local opposition to public housing projects) will *a fortiori* be true of programs of the magnitude that have recently been suggested by more radical and impatient reformers. If, instead of producing 30,000 units of low-rent public housing annually, we embark on a program which will provide new or rehabilitated housing for a minimum of 800,000 low income families each year, the specter of massive racial shifts would create insurmountable problems with regard to financial appropriations and site selection.

One need only look at current government low-rent housing programs to gain insight into the future. The federal government and many local authorities are now insisting on an end to lily-white public housing projects. In combination with more systematic forces (Negroes apply to public housing in disproportionate numbers because of lower incomes and a narrower range of housing choice), this policy is turning public housing into an all-Negro program, and not too gradually at that. Nationally, 53 percent of all families in public housing are nonwhite (an increase from 43 percent in 1954), and in many cities there are virtually no white families living in housing projects. As projects lose their all-white character, the number of

1. "Desegregated Housing: Who Pays For the Reformers' Ideal?," *The New Republic*, December 12, 1966, 17-22.

white applications decreases and white families move out of the projects in increasing numbers, frequently to worse and/or higher priced—but "safe"—housing. As Negro families apply in ever larger numbers (in Boston, where 26 percent of public housing families are Negro, over half of all applications are now coming from nonwhite families), and as more and more projects "tip"—a process which is surely irreversible—the program will become in fact a Negro institution.

The Department of Housing and Urban Development is trying to induce localities, albeit with much difficulty, to move away from the project approach to public housing (in order to increase the possibility of racial integration, as well as for other reasons of a social and aesthetic nature). At the same time these newer forms of publicly subsidized housing (leasing of private units, public rehabilitation of substandard units, joint public-private developments) are meeting a great deal of local resistance, in no small part due to the possibility of invasion of "good" neighborhoods by "problem" (i.e., Negro) families. Depressing as it may be to white liberals, the truth must be faced: to insist upon racial integration as a sine qua non of housing improvement is to consign millions of American families, white and black, to their present slum conditions for years to come.

This is not to say that a housing program must proceed on a strictly segregated basis: ample opportunity and protection must be provided for those minority-group families who value integrated living highly and are willing to endure the hardship this course may entail. But if we persist in the illusion that improvement of urban living conditions can and must be accompanied by racial integration, 10 years from now we will discover that we have not progressed very far at all in solving the nation's slum problems, just as there has been but little improvement in the past 10 years.

Among the newer programs and ideas, the Model Cities program seems to have accepted this argument, at least implicitly. The program rejected a true "model city" approach that had been initially proposed (attempting, on a pilot project basis, to provide solutions to all urban problems in four or five prototypical cities) in favor of a "model neighborhood" approach—providing these same solutions for an area housing no more than 15,000 persons (or 10 percent of the city's population in the case of large cities).

While this shift was made in part to permit existing funds to go farther in political terms (more cities would get something from the program, thereby increasing its potential support), it also had the effect of allowing cities to compartmentalize the race issue. Most large cities chose one of the worst Negro slums as their model city target area. Given the program's general mandate—to improve conditions *in* the demonstration area *for* the area's residents—the program in effect has become a "gild the ghetto" program (save in those smaller cities where poor white neighborhoods were chosen as target areas, and in the one or two larger cities where a principal objective of the program is to provide open housing opportunities for the area's Negro residents). This critical feature of the Model Cities program has not been universally lamented: in fact the more progressive newcomers to the upper echelons of the HUD hierarchy see it as a sound development. More help will go to those most in need of government assistance, and if integration is ever to come about, it will be only after the ghetto and its residents have developed economic and political strengths.

SOCIAL AND ECONOMIC INTEGRATION

Related to the problem of racial integration is the question of social class integration, or heterogeneity vs. homogeneity. A good deal of overlap exists here; because Negroes tend to have lower incomes and occupational and educational attainments than whites, most whites tend to see Negroes as lower class, regardless of objective economic and social indexes. But the problem is distinct from the racial problem: it comes up as an issue among white families of different social classes and among Negro families of different social classes. And at least among some segments of the population, educational, occupational, and financial attainment are sufficient to erase most barriers imposed by race. In policy terms, the issue comes down to this: should housing subsidies require the grouping of low-income families together, apart from unsubsidized, higher-income families, or should programs be developed which permit or require mixture of subsidized low-income families with families of higher income who do not receive a housing subsidy (or at least the same kind of subsidy, since in our peculiar folk logic such things as FHA insurance and urban renewal land write-downs for middle- and upper-income housing are not regarded as subsidies).

The arguments for and against "mixing" are fairly simple, although they seem to be based more on assumption and ideology than on concrete evidence. It is held by some that the grouping of low-income families creates stigma and reinforces deviant or pathological living patterns, whereas mixing low-income families together with families of higher socioeconomic status (usually conceived of in terms of a marked disproportion, with the subsidized families representing 10-30 percent of the total) will offer incentive, status, and alternative (and assumedly more desirable) models for behavior. Generally, the heterogeneity argument is buttressed by terms such as "more democratic," although why this one manifestation of inequality is chosen as a symbol of nondemocracy in a society with such wide income disparities and such unwarranted poverty is unclear.

Arguments against social and economic integration range from those of the economic conservative worried about the effect on incentive of having persons of different incomes, paying different rents, living in essentially identical quarters—to those of the sociologist, concerned that differences in life-style, child-rearing patterns and the like will in fact exacerbate interclass tensions and conflict rather than create mutual understanding and a "rub-off" effect. There is also a large group to whom such thinking represents cultural imperialism, an attempt to destroy valuable unity and vitality among low-income groups.

Most of the newer forms of public housing, as well as the new rent supplement program, represent an attempt to eliminate the worst forms of isolation and stigmatization that have characterized traditional public housing projects. The "scattered-site" type of development focuses on the problem of scale: projects should be small, located in viable neighborhoods, and designed so as to blend with existing buildings. Rehabilitation programs developed by local housing authorities rely on purchase and remodelling of substandard private buildings and offer public housing that is architecturally no different from housing that remains in the private sector. The "turnkey" approach to public housing, in which site development and construction is done by private developers who then sell the completed project to the local housing authority, also represents an attempt to avoid institutional design. Reliance on the private construction industry is purported to offer significant cost saving, too, but claims to this effect are at present of dubious validity, and if true, may derive from use of nonunion labor paid at less than union scale—a "saving" that may not be in the public interest.

The leased public housing program, under which individual, privately owned units, usually in multifamily buildings, are leased by the housing authority at market rents and then subleased to public housing tenants at reduced rents, is one of the most far-reaching attempts to blur the public-private distinction. The buildings are privately owned and managed, and restriction on the number of public housing tenants in any one structure makes it likely that there will be some form of economic and social mix (although this depends largely on the character of neighborhoods in which the housing authority leases its units). And nascent projects which combine public and private sponsorship of developments with mixed middle- and low-income occupancy also carry the integration idea to an extreme form, relegating the public presence to the background, so as to create no invidious distinction between the subsidized and the unsubsidized.

Finally, the rent supplement program carries this idea one step further in bypassing the housing authority altogether as agent for choosing apartments and tenants. In this program the private developer directly contracts with the Federal Housing Administration to accept a certain number of low-income tenants, and in return receives the difference between the rent established for the low-income family (25 percent of family income) and the market rent for the unit.

A close look at the operations of these new programs provides some insight as to how we can expect the issue of heterogeneity vs. homogeneity to develop in the future. In virtually all cities where these newer programs have been tried, the amount of meaningful social and economic integration has been minimal, and in some cases nonexistent. In brief, where the private sector has been drawn into the public housing program and where mixing has occurred, the utmost care has been taken in tenant selection to choose only the most "worthy," middle-class representatives of the poor: intact, small families at the upper level of the public housing income range, usually white, employed, and educated, with no suggestion of social problems which might cause conflict and resentment among their neighbors who "pay their own way."

These programs attempt to skim the cream off the top of the public housing population and in effect provide no information (except, by inference, negative information) about the impact of and prospects for this kind of mixing. (An ancillary effect, of course, is that by drawing these families away from the housing projects, the remaining public housing population becomes all the more atypical and deviant from the rest of society.) The average family simply is not inclined to live near low-income families which exhibit any "deviant" attributes, such as having no male head of household, having too many children, living on welfare, causing or demonstrating any of a variety of social problems. Sensing that landlords—particularly in the sellers' market that presently exists in the housing field—will not participate in a public program that risks having to rent to lower-class tenants, and that political pressures from unsubsidized families of higher income will lead to extraordinary controversy, administrators of these newer public housing programs have taken the path of least resistance and have avoided any meaningful socioeconomic integration.

An inescapable conclusion seems to be that, desirable as some amount of heterogeneity may be (and whether and in what ways this may be true is still not absolutely clear), political pressures, both overt and internalized, will be such that local administrators will avoid difficulties where possible.

The only way in which low-income families—at least those who wish to do so—will be able to integrate themselves successfully with families of higher socioeconomic status is through a type of program that has not yet been developed: i.e., through creation of sovereign consumers by widespread use of rent or income supplements. The income subsidization approach does not seem feasible at present. Even if we were to achieve a guaranteed annual income (or some version thereof through a negative income tax), the levels presently being discussed would be totally inadequate to secure decent housing at present market rents. The income floors being discussed are on the order of $3,100 for a family of four; yet, using the 20-25 percent rent/income ratio yardstick, decent housing costs at least twice that much in urban areas. (The Bureau of Labor Statistics' 1959 model budget for a family of four in Boston required $6,100; over $1,200 of this sum went for rent, in order to achieve a "modest but adequate" standard of living, and that figure has undoubtedly risen in 8 years.)

A direct and adequate subsidy of the housing expenditures of poor families, through a device such as rental certificates, available for new or rehabilitated standard housing, might permit social and economic heterogeneity, providing mechanisms exist to insure nondiscrimination against certificate holders by private landlords. Such controls over landlords and developers might be secured via incentives to participate in the program provided in the form of low-interest construction and rehabilitation financing or assistance in site acquisition; in exchange for this the private developer would agree to accept as tenants a certain percentage of certificate holders on a first-come, first-served basis.

The present rent supplement program bears some similarities to this suggested program, but has several critical features (apart from its recent Congressional curtailment) which make it unlikely to produce any meaningful residential mixing. The program is tied to the government-assisted market-rate 221 (d) (3) program (for moderate income families); there is, however, no corollary requirement that developers who build with the aid of these government-assisted loan programs also participate in the rent supplement program. Inclusion of low-income families is at the option of the private developer. And in order to induce participation, private developers are given complete discretion in tenant selection, a policy which insures that only the "cream" of the poor will get in. Furthermore, FHA has set no upper limits on the number of rent supplement families which may be included in any one project, with the result that many of these projects (the majority of the first batch to be approved) are using rent supplements for 100 percent of their units, thus creating low-income concentrations similar to those in public housing projects.

Clearly, existing programs are avoiding the issue of economic and social integration (even though there is a nominal attempt in this direction). Current efforts at least make clear the fact that unless low-income families have the effective buying power and concomitant freedom of choice of their more affluent brethren, and unless ways can be found to guarantee that private landlords will in fact not discriminate against subsidized tenants, government housing programs will produce no significant amount of meaningful heterogeneity. A massive program of rent certificates tied to an equally massive program of low-interest development loans will of course meet with substantial political resistance from those who recognize and oppose this potential for social and economic mix. Yet should such a program be passed, it is fairly automatic and self-sufficient in operation and will not meet the repeated political pressures and battles that the local public authority must face each time it wants to move ahead.

PUBLIC VS. PRIVATE

One of the most salient political issues currently under discussion in the field of housing and urban development is the question of private sector vs. public sector: to what extent and in what ways can and will the private building industry meet the pressing housing needs of the country's low-income families? It is indisputable that the realities of land and construction costs have made and will continue to make it impossible for the private sector, unaided, to meet the housing needs of this segment of the population. It is also becoming quite evident that provision of low-rent housing through the public sector has a great many fundamental and inherent defects.

It would be fruitless to go into any great detail about the failures of the public housing program. The litany of social, aesthetic, and administrative defects is already widely known and acknowledged. Many of the program's shortcomings might be effectively remedied through some of the newer forms of public housing described earlier. But it seems virtually impossible for the program to live down the reputation it has acquired over three decades. The very words "public housing" are anathema to too many people, including the program's clientele; the words evoke images of massive, ugly projects, located in the most undesirable parts of the city, teeming with problem families, governed by harsh and arbitrary regulations. The legacy of 30 years of failure is that people are simply turned off to the notion of public housing, no matter how creative and subtle the form in which the public subsidy comes wrapped.

Similarly, we are beginning to recognize the failings of the administrative mechanism through which low-rent housing has traditionally been supplied to the city. Many housing experts are questioning the efficacy (and even the good intentions) of the local public housing authority. We are beginning to see that many of our cherished "good government" institutions (such as draft boards, welfare boards, housing authorities), putatively governed by disinterested civic types, above politics and with only the public interest at heart, in fact consist of a quite biased segment of the population, with their own values, class interests, and preconceptions—all of which render them quite unrepresentative of (and possibly unsympathetic to) the clientele and segment of population served by these programs. In short, local public housing authorities (with very few exceptions) have not been aggressive advocates of a vastly expanded and improved low-rent housing program, have not been true spokesmen for the interests of persons in need of better housing. Nor should we have expected this: although systematic data are not available as of this writing (the author is currently making a survey of the local housing authority commissioners[2]), it is generally known that local housing authorities are governed by boards that are overwhelmingly white (whereas over half of all families in public housing are Negro), upper income (persons in the $10,000 and up income range), and heavily weighted toward business, real estate, insurance, and other occupations that suggest an inherently conservative outlook. In many communities these boards act as a restraint and control on the number, type, and location of low-rent housing developments. Because of who these people are and to whom they owe allegiances, it should not be surprising that they have not been a force pushing for more low-rent housing. In Boston, for example, a city where 20-25 percent of the population lives in substandard housing, not a single unit of family public housing has been constructed in 13 years. Further, there seem to be few, if any, forces in the community that are assuming the advocate role which the local housing authority has abjured.

The local housing authority also builds crucial geographic limitations and distortions into any program for housing reform. With few exceptions, the jurisdiction of these authorities is confined to a single municipality. The clearly metropolitan character of housing problems and housing markets thereby finds no corresponding administrative mechanism for dealing with these issues. The most rational approach to providing decent housing will often involve use of outlying vacant sites and dispersal of families throughout a metropolitan area; yet at present planning and control must stop at the municipal boundary. A study commission of the Illinois legislature has just submitted a remarkable recommendation for abolition of local housing authorities in favor

2. See Chester Hartman and Gregg Carr, "Housing Authorities Reconsidered," *Journal of the American Institute of Planners*, January 1969, 10-21.

of metropolitan and regional authorities and programs, yet the plan is given virtually no chance of passage, due to the complex vested interests in the present, fragmented structure. Since the federal low-rent housing program has traditionally and painstakingly allowed for maximum local autonomy and discretion, there seems little hope of restructuring the present system of local housing authorities. Rather, ways must be found to bypass what has become an administrative roadblock.

It is in large part due to above-mentioned shortcomings that proposals have evolved for "unleashing the private sector," bringing the profit motive back into the low-rent housing field. The argument is based on the need for increased activity and motivation, on the private sector's freedom to maneuver and reduce red tape and political constraints, on the potential that American corporative know-how offers for innovation in the production and marketing of housing.

There is unquestionably a severe shortage of expertise in the housing field, and a large part—if not most—of the technical capabilities regarding all phases of residential development is to be found in the private sector. This expertise refers to questions of financing, land acquisition, legal procedures, design and construction, and management. In a field as complex as real estate development, which involves so many resources—financial, human, and technical—delay and inefficiency become exceedingly costly. The paucity of entrepreneurial talent in the public or quasi-public sector has been amply illustrated in the difficulties which nonprofit organizations have experienced in developing housing under several current government programs. Any program of housing subsidization that can make maximum use of existing talents in the private sector will clearly be that much better. . . .

It should be recognized, however, that part of the motive underlying this move toward the private sector is traceable to some very unrealistic notions regarding the comparative costs involved in public vs. private production of housing. In many persons' minds—back or front—lies the notion that if the private sector can be induced to do the job, this will reduce the need for public funds. Most of the recent private-sector approaches to the housing problem in fact obfuscate the cost issue by underestimating the quantity of public subsidy needed or by offering a deceptive picture of which income groups will be aided by these programs. Thus, Sen. Kennedy's much heralded plan for Bedford-Stuyvesant envisions producing housing that rents for $85-90 per month. Even using the rule of thumb that families should pay no more than 25 percent of their income for rent, these rent levels would require an annual income in excess of $4,000 (in excess of $5,000, if one uses the traditional 20 percent ratio). There are literally millions of families in the country who are unable to afford these rents. One basic fact must be understood, then, in the public/private debate: there is no magic to be achieved—existing income levels and the costs of providing sound housing are "givens" (with little immediate alteration to be expected from programs of job creation and cost-reducing technological innovations in the building industry). If all families are to be housed decently (a National Goal set by Congress that will soon have its twentieth anniversary), the gap between these two "givens" must be bridged, and it must be bridged by government subsidies. No amount of "plans" for the private sector, however ingenious, is going to alter that basic fact. It is axiomatic that if incentives are made sufficiently attractive, the private sector will produce. The infamous FHA Sec. 608 program of the postwar period made this abundantly clear, at the cost of great amounts of jerry-built housing and much bilking of the public. Maximizing profit opportunities can only lead to increased housing costs (and hence to increased public subsidies) and to irresponsible development. The private sector can and should have a crucial role in an expanded government housing program, but only if it is willing to accept moderate profits and to adhere to necessary public controls.

Finally, we must refer to the issue of popular participation and control—that is, who makes and carries out decisions regarding housing programs and conditions for low- and moderate-income families. This issue ranges from broad questions of participation in the planning process to more specific issues regarding changing concepts in the landlord-tenant relationship. There are few areas where it is more imperative to have active and ongoing participation of the prospective clientele than in the area of housing and neighborhood planning. Clearly, questions of preference, life-style, patterns of spatial usage are all crucial to the proper planning of residential areas. Yet there has been a traditional gap between the purveyors and users of housing programs for lower-income groups. There is hardly a housing authority in the country, for example, that includes on its board a resident of a public housing project or a person eligible for residency there. It should not be a matter of great wonder that public housing projects stand as a monument to the insensitivity of program designers to the needs and satisfactions of the program's clientele. The newer, private-enterprise approaches to community development similarly overlook the issue of popular participation and control, or fail to realize the implications of the concept. Thus, Robert Kennedy's two-pronged plan for Bedford-Stuyvesant envisions an indigenous community corporation which is to assert effective control over housing and community facilities planning, plus a "blue-ribbon" board (on which sit men like C. Douglas Dillon and Thomas Watson of IBM) responsible for bringing in the industrial base which will support the community's economic renascence. The Kennedy Plan speaks of the necessity for the community to "create the conditions" under which private corporations and lending institutions will be willing to locate in Bedford-Stuyvesant. Yet there almost certainly will be conflict and contradiction between the set of preconditions demanded by the private sector and the wishes of the local community. If the economic basis of the Bedford-Stuyvesant Plan depends on satisfaction of the investment conditions set forth by the private sector, it is clear that one can speak of meaningful citizen control in only the most limited sense. The new Model Cities approach, which arose out of experience under the urban renewal program, likewise lays great stress on "citizen participation." Yet in only very few places is there the possibility that this will mean true control—the right ultimately to approve or disapprove locally any plan for the area, backed up by a commitment of funds to permit a democratically selected local decision-making body to retain its own professional planning staff to assist in the evaluation of official agency plans and the development of alternative plans.

One of the more advanced notions in true popular control of development programs is the community foundation, a combined governing body and development corporation, to which all local residents would belong. This corporation, or foundation, would be responsible for the administration of government programs for community development and would build up the economic strength of the area by bringing in new employment opportunities and increasing local ownership of housing, stores, and other economic assets. The idea, originally developed by Milton Kotler of the Institute for Policy Studies in Washington, is getting its field test in an area of Columbus, Ohio, and was warmly received and well publicized during the 1966 session of the Ribicoff hearings.[3] If the community corporation, or some variant thereof, became

3. Milton Kotler, *Neighborhood Government: The Local Foundation of Political Life* (Indianapolis: Bobbs-Merrill, 1969).

developer of new and rehabilitated housing in the area, hiring professional contractors and making maximum use of employment opportunities for local residents, the proper sensitivity to residents' needs and desires would be structured into government programs of housing subsidization.

The importance of housing and housing programs now encompasses far more than the traditional realms of health and safety, those basic considerations which so strongly motivated the slum fighters of an earlier generation. Dangers to physical well-being are still a notable part of slum living (ranging from rat bites, fires, and household accidents to certain housing-related diseases such as dysentery and skin ailments). But the issue has now broadened to include the social conditions under which people live: issues of status and dignity; the relation of design to behavior; control over the decisions that affect one's life and over one's own living conditions; location and character of community facilities; real choice with regard to residential location and housing type and a host of other considerations that have not traditionally been defined as "housing" issues *per se*. Any housing program for the 1960s must involve more than a bricks-and-mortar approach, must be prepared to deal with the entire set of living variables that make up residential and community life.

II

Social Aspects

Most of the earlier concern with improving housing conditions, beginning in the late 19th century and continuing through more recent times, involved the effects of poor housing conditions on individual health and welfare. Through observation, knowledge of the etiology of disease, and some statistical inference, it could be fairly well established that unsanitary and unsafe housing conditions directly caused respiratory diseases, infections, fires, accidents and other ills.[1] Out of concern for slum dwellers' welfare as well as self-interest—lest the pestilence and fires spread out of the slum—early social reformers brought into being largely successful housing and health codes, model tenements, and other measures. The present public housing program, begun in the 1930s, stemmed directly from this concept of physical determinism, and it still infuses much thinking about the housing question in this country.

The persistence of a narrow physical determinist approach has been responsible for many of the difficulties in present housing programs and policies. Housing conditions in this country with respect to amount of space, sanitary facilities, and safety conditions now are at a level high enough that the grosser forms of danger and disease produced by 19th- and earlier 20th-century conditions are fairly uncommon. In more recent times the notion of what areas of individual well-being might be affected by improved housing conditions has expanded somewhat, moving beyond the somatic level to such things as psychological welfare, school and work performance, family relationships, and personal aspirations (Greenfield and Lewis, Chap. 14). However, the multiple problems that characterize the ill-housed are attributable to a variety of interrelated factors, only one of which (and probably a minor one) is housing conditions per se (Glazer, Chap. 13). These broader economic and social conditions must be changed simultaneously if individual and group change is to occur, and a housing policy or program that attempts a simple cause-and-effect relationship between provision of good housing and basic personal and social improvement is bound to fail.

The most careful recent study of the effects of housing, by Daniel Wilner and his associates (1965), demonstrates this point well. Over a five-year period two matched samples of families—one had moved from a slum to good housing, the other had

1. For a good summary of these studies, see Alvin Schorr, *Slums and Social Insecurity* (Washington, D.C.: Government Printing Office, 1966).

remained in slum housing—were studied with respect to a wide variety of factors. The group whose housing conditions had improved showed several gains, such as fewer episodes of illness and days of disability due to communicable diseases. In most other areas, however, the results were either inconclusive or ambiguous. For example, the change in housing environment had no significant impact on intrafamilial tensions or on children's performance on school achievement tests. In other words, only a very few changes were brought about by improved housing conditions, particularly outside the narrow sphere of illness and safety factors that may be caused directly by specific physical housing defects.

Perhaps the most interesting observation about the Wilner study is its limited notion of good housing. The experimental group was moved from a slum into a public housing project; thus the only dimension of change was in physical housing conditions —better heat and plumbing, additional dwelling space, structural safety, and modernity. This emphasis would seem to at least partially satisfy some basic housing needs of lower class families that seek refuge from a wide variety of human and nonhuman threats (Rainwater, Chap. 16), but in the public housing program no attempt is made to improve other dimensions of the housing services bundle, such as the social environment, status, and location.

Some analysts have suggested that public housing projects may even exacerbate the social problems of those who live there. In a study of the Pruitt-Igoe project in St. Louis, William Yancey (1971) found that the design provided no safe semiprivate space and facilities around which neighboring relationships might develop. As a result, families retreated into their apartments and lacked the social support, protection, and informal social control necessary to achieve the level of neighborhood and community life that existed in their previous slum neighborhoods.

Although a move to public housing (the experimental group in the Wilner study) may represent an improvement in absolute conditions, the image this new environment evokes may not coincide with the one the residents would like to have of themselves or would like others to have of them (Coleman, 1972). The poor people who occupy public housing may therefore still experience relative deprivation because of the gap between their present level of housing and the level they want, as this in turn is defined and shaped by the housing services others in the society consume (Glazer, Chap. 13; Morrison, 1971). Several studies have indicated that the general preferences of poor and minority group members are for suburban, single-family, owner-occupied houses, which are the norm for middle class white Americans (Hinshaw and Allott, Chap. 17; Ladd, 1972).

To look at housing in this broader sense and to understand the importance of relative housing conditions is to come face to face with the issue of social class in America. Probably the most important defining characteristic of class status is where, how, and near whom one lives; hence urban neighborhoods are stratified according to income and social class as these factors are reflected in housing prices and rents and other sorting mechanisms.[2] To the extent that housing policies and programs influence residential location, they necessarily enter into the area of social class segregation versus integration, but the more controversial issue of racial integration versus

2. For some of the literature on how neighborhoods are defined and their different functions for various social classes, see Milton Gordon, *Social Class in American Sociology* (New York: McGraw-Hill, 1963). For original sources see Robert Park, Ernest Burgess, and Roderick D. McKenzie, *The City* (Chicago: University of Chicago Press, 1967). For more recent efforts see Gerald Suttles, *The Social Order of the Slum* (Chicago: University of Chicago Press, 1968); Suzanne Keller, *The Urban Neighborhood* (New York: Random House, 1968); Elizabeth Bott, *Family and Social Network* (London: Tavistock Institute, 1968).

segregation has tended to overlap somewhat and become identified with the dimension of social class. Several government bodies (most notably the National Commission on Urban Problems and the National Advisory Commission on Civil Disorders) have highlighted the country's growing division into separate and unequal societies along racial and social class lines and have pointed to the dangers posed by this split in terms of the growing mutual hostility among different races and classes. Provision of housing for a cross section of the population in individual communities and neighborhoods is one of the principal recommendations for countering this trend.

Sound arguments exist both for and against such a policy. Herbert Gans and others have pointed to many conflicts that will arise in nonhomogeneous areas with respect to social class differences in such things as childrearing patterns and education (Gans, Chap. 11; Michelson, Chap. 15). Frequent contact among children at the block level is inevitable, and working and lower class modes of strict childrearing will conflict with middle class permissiveness toward children (Gans, 1967). In neighborhood schools, conflict can be anticipated between the working and lower class preference for traditional schooling versus the middle class orientation to more progressive approaches. Class differences in use and function of the neighborhood also can be expected—the working-class orientation toward localism versus the more cosmopolitan patterns of the middle class.

As Gans has noted, these conflicts, which often surface around struggles to control such community institutions as the schools and the police, in actuality refer to control of the allocation of power, wealth, and prestige, and reflect an unwillingness to tolerate other life-styles. Rather than accepting the conflicts of a pluralist society or advocating reduction of the society's inequalities, those who experience social and economic mobility often protect their new life-styles and higher status by moving to smaller suburban enclaves where they have more control over their communities.

Arguments that favor residential heterogeneity are financial and social in nature. As long as community services are supported primarily by local taxes, mixing of this sort can prevent massive disparities in the level of municipal services (schools, fire and police protection, libraries, etc.), which tend to perpetuate social divisions and hinder mobility. Class mixing has also been shown to have some desirable effects. For example, the Coleman Report, an elaborate survey of the effects of school conditions on achievement, found that among black students socioeconomic segregation in the classroom is more likely to produce poor school performance than are such factors as the qualifications of teachers, the quality of school facilities, and the student-teacher ratio (U.S. Office of Education, 1966). Just what degree of heterogeneity is tolerable and desirable is an area that requires much more study.

Residential heterogeneity along racial lines is a somewhat more complex matter than is social class heterogeneity. Some studies have found that personal contacts, particularly among people of equal socioeconomic status, produce attitudinal changes and a reduction of racial prejudice (Simpson and Yinger, Chap. 12). However, whites have greatly resisted the introduction of blacks and other minority groups, of whatever social status, into their neighborhoods. Given the society's prevailing racism, some of this resistance may be due to the assignment of lower class status to blacks of all classes and to the fear of a drop in property values. The complex workings of the social class system also produce the need to see oneself as better than others and thus leads to resistance of newcomers regarded as inferiors.[3] When blacks have moved into white working-class communities in large numbers, integration has been

---

3. For insight into the feelings and conflicts produced by the class system in America, see Richard Sennett and Jonathan Cobb, *The Hidden Injuries of Class* (New York: Knopf, 1972).

only temporary (Molotch, 1969). Often little contact between races has occurred, and generally no new white residents have arrived. Free access of minority groups to all communities might reduce the need for blacks to move in large numbers into white communities adjacent to the ghetto and could thus reduce the tipping phenomenon whereby these communities become predominantly black (Wolf, 1963).

The difficulties of integrating people of unequal resources and status within the context of a hierarchical society are enormous, and it is not surprising that housing policies have by and large not dealt with this issue. Yet it must be recognized that housing programs and policies that do not address some of the fundamental status needs of lower income persons, as these are expressed in and through housing type and neighborhood environment, will have only minimal effect on behavior, welfare, and satisfaction (Glazer, Chap. 13; Gutman, 1970). A housing allowance strategy that attempts to create sovereign housing consumers so that persons can live how and where they want represents an approach that may produce some truly beneficial personal and social effects, but more likely only overall reduction of resource and social class disparities themselves will eliminate the kinds of invidious status distinctions currently embodied in the country's residential patterns.

REFERENCES

Coleman, Richard P. "Explorations in Contemporary Images of Housing and Neighborhood." Cambridge, Mass.: M.I.T.-Harvard Joint Center for Urban Studies, 1972.

Gans, Herbert. *The Levittowners*. New York: Random House, 1967: 22-31.

Gutman, Robert. "A Sociologist Looks at Housing." *Toward A National Urban Policy*, ed. Daniel P. Moynihan. New York: Basic Books, 1970: 119-32.

Ladd, Florence. "Black Youths View Their Environments: Some Views of Housing." *Journal of the American Institute of Planners* 38 (March 1972): 108-115.

Molotch, Harvey. "Racial Change in A Stable Community." *American Journal of Sociology* 75 (September 1969): 226-38.

———. "Racial Integration In A Transition Community." *American Sociological Review* 34 (December 1969): 878-98.

Morrison, Denton. "Some Notes Toward Theory on Relative Deprivation, Social Movements, and Social Change." *American Behavioral Scientist* 14 (May-June 1971): 675-90.

U.S. Office of Education. *Equality of Educational Opportunity*. Washington, D.C.: Government Printing Office, 1966. (James Coleman supervised this study).

Wilner, Daniel; Walkley, Rosabelle; Pinkerton, Thomas; Tayback, Mathew; and associates. *Housing Environment and Family Life*. Baltimore: Johns Hopkins Press, 1962.

Wolf, Eleanor. "The Tipping Point in Racially Changing Neighborhoods." *Journal of the American Institute of Planners* 29 (August 1963): 217-22.

Yancey, William. "Architecture, Interaction, and Social Control: The Case of A Large-Scale Public Housing Project." *Environment and Behavior* 3 (March 1971): 3-21.

11. *The Balanced Community: Homogeneity or Heterogeneity in Residential Areas?*

HERBERT J. GANS

In "Planning and Social Life," which appeared in the May 1961 issue of the *Journal*, I discussed the influence of propinquity and homogeneity on social relations. I tried to show that architectural and site plans can encourage or discourage social contact between neighbors, but that homogeneity of background or of interests or values was necessary for this contact to develop into anything more than a polite exchange of greetings. Without such homogeneity, more intensive social relations are not likely to develop, and excessive heterogeneity can lead to coolness between neighbors, regardless of their propinquity. Homogeneity is even more fundamental in friendship formation, and its presence allows people to find friends nearby, whereas its absence requires them to look farther afield for friends.

These observations can be combined with a variety of value judgments, each resulting in alternative planning recommendations. I argued that positive, although not necessarily close, relations among neighbors and maximal opportunity for the free choice of friends both near and far from home were desirable values, and concluded that a moderate degree of homogeneity among neighbors would therefore be required.

The advocacy of moderate homogeneity was based on a single set of values, those concerning the quality of social life. Communities have many other functions besides sociability, however, and planning must therefore concern itself with other values as well. With such values in mind, many influential planners have advocated the balanced residential area, containing a typical cross section of dwelling-unit types and population characteristics, notably age groups and socioeconomic levels.[1]

Population heterogeneity has generally been advocated for at least four reasons.[2]

1. It adds variety as well as demographic "balance" to an area and thus enriches the inhabitants' lives. Conversely, homogeneity is said to stultify, as well as to deprive people of important social resources, such as the wisdom of the older generation in the suburbs.

Reprinted by permission of *The Journal of the American Institute of Planners*, Volume 27, No. 3 (August 1961) pp. 176-84 and of the author. Herbert J. Gans is a professor of sociology at Columbia University.

1. See, e.g., Catherine Bauer, "Social Questions in Housing and Community Planning," *Journal of Social Issues* 7 (1951): 23; Lewis Mumford, "The Neighborhood and the Neighborhood Unit," *Town Planning Review* 24 (1954): 267-68; Howard Hallman, "Citizens and Professionals Reconsider the Neighborhood," *Journal of the American Institute of Planners* 25 (1959): 123-24; Elizabeth Wood, *A New Look at the Balanced Neighborhood* (New York: Citizen's Housing and Planning Council, December 1960). Reginald Isaacs' critique of the neighborhood plan is based on a similar point of view. See e.g., "The Neighborhood Theory." *Journal of the American Institute of Planners* 14 (1948): 15-23.

2. A fifth reason, the contribution of heterogeneity to aesthetic values is discussed at the end of the article. I shall not deal at all with economic reasons, for example, for the desirability of age heterogeneity in order to prevent tax burdens resulting from the flood of school-age children in suburban communities.

2. It promotes tolerance of social and cultural differences, thus reducing political conflict and encouraging democratic practices. Homogeneity increases the isolation between area residents and the rest of society.

3. It provides a broadening educational influence on children by teaching them about the existence of diverse types of people and by creating the opportunity for them to learn to get along with these people. Homogeneity is thought to limit children's knowledge of diverse classes, ages, and races, and to make them less capable of association with others in later years.

4. It encourages exposure to alternative ways of life—for example, by providing intellectually inclined neighbors for the child from a bookless household, or by offering the mobile working-class family an opportunity to learn middle class ways. Homogeneity freezes people in present ways of life.

These are actually ends to be achieved through population heterogeneity, and should be discussed as such. Two questions must then be answered.

1. Are the ends themselves desirable?
2. Is the balanced community a proper means for achieving them; that is, is it a logically and empirically verifiable means, free of undesirable by-products or consequences?

No one can quarrel with the ends. A society of diverse people taking pride in their diversity, enriching their own and their children's lives by it, and cooperating to achieve democracy and to alleviate useless social conflict is a delightful and desirable vision. I believe that the achievement of this vision is a legitimate planning goal, and the means to achieve it should be explored.

Whether or not the goal can be achieved simply by requiring diverse people to live together is debatable, however. Even if the planning or legislating of population heterogeneity could be implemented—which is doubtful at present—it is questionable whether a heterogeneous and balanced community would result in the envisaged way of life. Many other societal conditions would have to be altered before such a way of life is possible, notably the present degree of economic and social inequality that now exists in the typical metropolitan area's population.

The data needed to determine the ends-means relationships I have suggested are not yet available, so that only tentative conclusions can be reached. The discussion will be limited to heterogeneity of age, class, and race—these being the most important criteria affecting and differentiating community life.[3]

HETEROGENEITY AND SOCIAL RELATIONS

The belief in the efficacy of heterogeneity is based on the assumption that if diverse people live together they will inevitably become good neighbors or even friends and, as a result, learn to respect their differences. The comments about the importance of homogeneity in social relations in my previous article suggest that this assumption is not valid. A mixing of all age and class groups is likely to produce at best a polite but cool social climate, lacking the consensus and intensity of relations that is necessary for mutual enrichment. Instances of conflict are as probable as those of cooperation. For example, some old people who live in a community of young couples may vicariously

---

3. Comments made in the May 1961 article about race as a symbol of class differences (especially on page 137 and in footnote 12) apply here also.

enjoy their neighbors' children—and vice versa—but others will resent the youngsters' noise and the destruction they wreak on flowerbeds. Likewise, some older residents may be founts of wisdom for their younger neighbors, but others are insistent advocates of anachronistic ideas. In a rapidly changing society, the knowledge that the older generation has gathered by virtue of its experience is outdated more quickly than in the past, when social change was less rapid.

Class differences also result in a mixture of good and bad consequences. I noted in the earlier article that most neighbor disputes arise about the children and that they stem from differences in childrearing norms among the classes and among parents of different educational backgrounds. People who want to bring their children up one way do not long remain tolerant of the parents of a playmate who is being reared by diametrically opposed methods. People with higher incomes and more education may feel that they or their children are being harmed by living among less advantaged neighbors. The latter are likely to feel equally negative about the "airs" being put on by the former, although some may want to keep up, especially in matters concerning the children. This can wreck family budgets and, occasionally, family stability as well. Social and cultural mobility is difficult enough when it is desired, but it may become a burden to families who are forced into it involuntarily.

The negative consequences of heterogeneity are not inevitable, but they occur with regularity, even among the most well-intentioned people. As a result, a markedly heterogeneous community that spells enrichment to the planner—especially to the one who sees it only through maps, census reports, and windshield surveys—may mean endless bickering and unsettled feuds to the people who actually live in it.

Indeed, the virtues ascribed to heterogeneity are more often associated with the degree and type of population homogeneity found in the typical new suburb. Much has been written about the alleged dangers of homogeneity, but, frequently, these allegations are based on the false assumption that, because the suburbs as a whole are statistically more homogeneous than cities as a whole, suburbanites are all *alike*. Even if they were alike in age and income—which is not true—they would still be different in occupation, educational level, ethnic and religious background, and regional origin, as well as temperament.

In actual fact, many suburban subdivisions are more heterogeneous than the urban neighborhoods from which some of their residents came. For example, in Levittown, New Jersey, many people felt that they were encountering a greater mixture of backgrounds than where they had lived before.[4] The fact that most people were similar enough in age and, to a lesser extent, income, enabled them to become friendly with people of different occupations, religions, ethnic backgrounds, or regional origins for the first time in their lives. Many felt that they had been enriched by experiencing this diversity. This would not have been possible if marked differences in age and income had also been present. It would seem, therefore, that in the large "brand name" suburbs, at least, the relatively greater homogeneity of age and income provides the cultural and social prerequisites which allow people to enjoy their neighbors' heterogeneity with respect to other, less basic characteristics.

4. Communities like Park Forest and Levittown may be more heterogeneous in class than smaller and higher priced subdivisions. The low house price attracts two types of owners: mobile young couples who will eventually buy more expensive houses as the husband advances in his career; and somewhat older families in which the husband has reached the peak of his earning power and who are buying their first, and probably last, house. These communities are also more likely than smaller subdivisions to attract newcomers to the metropolitan area, which creates a greater diversity of regional origins.

HETEROGENEITY AND DEMOCRACY

Heterogeneity is also thought to engender the tolerance necessary for the achievement of local democracy and for the reduction of social and political conflict. When differences between people are small, residents of an area can develop tolerance toward each other; they can even agree to ignore some important differences that stand in the way of consensus. More extreme population heterogeneity is not likely to have the same result.

Sizable differences, especially with regard to fundamental social and economic interests, are not erased or set aside by the mere fact of living together. For example, many suburban communities today are split over the question of school expenditures. Upper middle- and middle-class residents, for whom high quality schooling is important regardless of price, cannot often find a common meeting ground with lower middle-class residents, who may have different definitions of quality and who place less urgent priority on getting their children into a "good" college, or with working-class residents for whom tax economy is often—and of sheer necessity—the most important consideration.[5] Under such conditions, heterogeneity is not likely to encourage greater tolerance, and the struggle between competing points of view may be so intense that the relatively fragile norms of democratic procedure sometimes fall by the wayside. Homogeneity facilitates the workings of the democratic process, but this is no solution for a pluralist society such as ours. Nevertheless, heterogeneity itself does not facilitate the achievement of the democratic norms of community decision-making.

HETEROGENEITY AND THE CHILDREN

The value of population heterogeneity for children is based on the assumption that they discover other age-groups and classes through visual contact, and that they learn how to live with them through the resulting social contact. In actual fact, however, children develop their conceptions of society and the ability to get along with diverse types from the actions and attitudes of the persons with whom they come into close and continual social contact—especially parents, playmates, and teachers. Mere visual contact does not, however, result in close contact. Although a city child may see all segments of society, he is not likely to come into close contact with them. Even if he does, there is no guarantee that he will learn to be tolerant of differences, especially if he has learned to evaluate these differences negatively at home or elsewhere. Parental attitudes or direct prohibitions can thus discourage a child from playing with other children whom he sees everyday. Conversely, a suburban child, who may not see diverse people in his community, is still likely to learn about them—and to evaluate them—from comments made by his parents. If these parents are well educated, the child may even learn to become tolerant of people he has never seen. (In reality, city children get out of their own neighborhoods much less often than is sometimes imagined, and they may not see people of other ages, classes, and races unless they happen to live in particularly heterogeneous or changing residential areas.)

This issue may be illustrated by the relationship between the races. White city children probably see more nonwhites, at least from a distance, than do suburban children, although even in suburbs like Levittown and Park Forest enough families hire domestic help to insure some visual contact with nonwhites. If community heterogeneity had

---

5. In some suburbs, this conflict is complicated by religious differences. Moreover, Catholic families, who may have to support two school systems, often have lower family incomes than do the members of other religious groups.

the positive effects attributed to it, we should expect that city children, who do see more nonwhites, would exhibit greater racial tolerance than suburban ones. This has not happened, however.

In fact, the opposite is probably true. Children exhibit little or no racial intolerance until they are old enough to understand the attitudes and behavior patterns of their parents and other adults. These reactions reflect the current economic and social inequality of the white and nonwhite populations. If children could be isolated from such reactions, they might grow up with more tolerance than they now do. This is, of course, not possible. Consequently, until the inequality between the races is removed, there is little hope for a pervasive change in interracial understanding, either in the city or in the suburb.

The older city child differs from his suburban peer in that he is more likely to have close contact with children of diverse background, for example, of class and race, because urban schools usually draw from a wider variety of residential areas than suburban ones. Although researchers are still undecided whether close contact will increase tolerance and understanding—or under what conditions it is likely to have more positive than negative effects—such contacts should be encouraged wherever possible.[6] This would suggest the desirability of heterogeneous schools, in the suburbs as well as in the city.

HETEROGENEITY AND EXPOSURE TO ALTERNATIVES

Heterogeneity is also valued for the opportunity it provides for exposure to alternative and, by implication, better ways of life. Elizabeth Wood's recent argument for the balanced neighborhood stresses this value. She is concerned primarily with public housing and argues that middle-class people have generally provided working-class ones with organizational leadership and with models to inspire them to accept middle-class standards. If public housing projects and the neighborhoods in which they are located are homogeneously working class or lower class, the population is deprived of the two functions supposedly performed by the middle class.[7]

Middle-class people have traditionally supplied leadership in settlement houses and similar institutions located in working-class neighborhoods; however, these institutions have not attracted large working-class clientele except from among the socially mobile and from children.[8] The latter tend to use the facilities, while ignoring the middle-class values being propagated by the staff. Middle-class people are also likely to be more active in voluntary associations, such as clubs, civic groups, and tenant organizations, than working-class people, but their activity is usually limited to organizations with middle-class goals, and these are shunned by working-class people. Such organizations do, however, provide leadership to the latter, by offering guidance to the socially mobile, and by pursuing activities which may benefit every class in the area.

6. For an interesting study of the attitudes which young children bring to an interracial nursery school, and of the role of close contact in affecting the interracial relationship, see Mary E. Goodman, *Race Awareness in Young Children* (Cambridge: Addison-Wesley Press, 1952). The general problem is discussed in George E. Simpson and J. Milton Yinger, "The Sociology of Race and Ethnic Relations"; in Robert K. Merton, Leonard Broom, and Leonard S. Cottrell, Jr. (eds.), *Sociology Today* (New York: Basic Books, 1959), pp. 397-98.

7. Wood, op. cit., pp. 18-21.

8. For an analysis of the working-class client's view of the settlement house, see Albert K. Cohen, *Delinquent Boys: The Culture of the Gang* (Glencoe, Ill.: The Free Press, 1955), pp. 116-17.

Occasionally, a middle-class person may also function as a leader of a predominantly working-class organization, although this is rare.

Instances of middle-class leadership abounded in the annals of public housing during the 1930s and the 1940s. Today, however, public housing attracts or accepts mainly the deprived lower-class population, which stays away from middle-class institutions and does not often join voluntary associations of any kind. The deprived population needs and wants help, but so far, it has not often accepted leadership from the types of middle-class institutions and persons who offer it.

No one knows what motivates working-class people to adopt middle-class standards, or whether the presence of middle-class neighbors is likely to do so.[9] The new suburban communities could be studied advantageously from this viewpoint. My own impression is that heterogeneity enables those already motivated toward social mobility to learn from their middle-class neighbors and that, in some instances, the exposure to such neighbors can inspire previously unmotivated individuals to change their ways. As previously noted, close contact can have negative as well as positive consequences, for working-class people are as likely to resent the "uppity" behavior of middle-class residents as they are to adopt it. Success in teaching alternative ways of life seems to be dependent on three conditions. First, the people involved must have the necessary economic wherewithal and the social skills required for the new way. Second, sociologists of social stratification have found that ideas and values are diffused from one class to the one immediately "above" or "below" it, rather than between classes that diverge sharply in income, education, and other background characteristics. Consequently, positive effects are more likely to be achieved under conditions of moderate population heterogeneity. Extreme heterogeneity is likely to inhibit communication and to encourage mutual resentment, whereas moderate heterogeneity provides enough compatibility of interests and skills to enable communication—and therefore learning—to take place. Third, the "teachers" must be sympathetic to the needs and backgrounds of their students, and must have sufficient empathy to understand their point of view.

Wood suggests that heterogeneity be implemented through community facilities and neighborhood institutions, and that these be used to encourage the exposure to alternative ways, since the mixture of classes can be accomplished more easily than in residential arrangements. (A similar use of community facilities has recently been proposed by some planners and community organization officials concerned with the social aspects of urban renewal, in order to aid slum dwellers to adapt to life in nonslum urban surroundings).

I have already noted, however, that such agencies have had little success so far in converting working-class clients to middle-class points of view. Although the lack of success can be explained on the basis of cultural differences between the classes, the existing research has not yet led to policy suggestions as to how these differences may be bridged. My impression is that much of the emphasis—and hope—placed on community facilities and professionally trained staff is naïve. These two elements are important, but success is likely only if the persons chosen to work in such facilities have empathy for their clients' culture and needs. This quality may be more important than professional training, but it is not easily learned, for it entails much more than

9. There is some evidence that students react positively to the exposure to alternatives. Alan B. Wilson found that some working-class high school students adopt middle-class standards if they attend a predominantly middle-class school, and that some middle-class students adopt working-class standards if they attend a predominantly working-class school. See his "Class Segregation and Aspirations of Youth," *American Sociological Review* 24 (1959): 836-45. Students are socially more impressionable than adults, however, and the school is a more persuasive social environment than a residential area or a voluntarily attended neighborhood institution.

sympathy and good intentions. Unfortunately, empathic personalities are rare. Consequently, the encouragement of heterogeneity in community facilities is desirable, but it cannot by itself motivate people to expose themselves to new alternatives.

IMPLICATIONS FOR PLANNING

I have tried to show that the advantages of heterogeneity and the disadvantages of homogeneity have both been exaggerated and that neither is unqualifiedly good or bad. Extreme' forms of either are undesirable. Complete or near-complete homogeneity, as in a company town where everyone has the same kind of job, is clearly objectionable. Total heterogeneity is likely to be so uncomfortable that only those who want no social contact with neighbors would wish to live under such conditions. Even then, it would be tolerable only in apartment buildings in which visual contact between residents is minimal. Both extremes are rarely found in actual communities. In considering planning implications, we need concern ourselves primarily with more moderate forms.

Specific implications for planning policy are best discussed in two steps, at the level of block life and at the level of areawide community life. At the block level, the arguments of this and the earlier article suggest that the degree of heterogeneity advocated in the balanced community concept—which comes close to total heterogeneity—is unlikely to produce social relationships of sufficient intensity to achieve either a positive social life or the cultural, political, and educational values sought through the balanced community. The ideal solution is sufficient homogeneity with respect to those characteristics that will assure: (1) enough consensus between neighbors to prevent conflict; (2) positive although not necessarily intensive relationships between neighbors with respect to common needs and obligations; (3) the possibility for some mutual visiting and friendship formation for those who want it in the immediate vicinity.

This should provide sufficient heterogeneity to create some diversity as well. At the present time, no one knows how this solution could be defined operationally, that is, what mixture of specific characteristics would be likely to provide the kind of homogeneity suggested above. Consequently, existing subdivisions with differing degrees of homogeneity and heterogeneity should be studied, and adventurous builders should be encouraged to experiment with mixing people and housetypes. Planners and students of urban life could observe the results systematically and provide the evidence needed for more specific guides for planning. These guides would not spell out detailed dwelling-unit or population mixtures but would indicate only the types of population compositions which should be avoided because they bring about the undesirable effects of too much homogeneity or heterogeneity.

At the community level, and especially at the level of the politically defined community, population heterogeneity is desirable.[10] It is not a proper means to the ends for which it has been advocated, although a moderate degree of heterogeneity may aid in the achievement of the educational and exposure values. Rather, its desirability must be argued in relation to two other values. First, ours is a pluralistic society, and local communities should reflect this pluralism. Second, and more important

---

10. The planner has traditionally concerned himself more with the neighborhood than with either the block or the political community. The neighborhood is not a meaningful social unit, however, since the significant face-to-face relationships occur on the block. Moreover, it is not a political unit and thus cannot make decisions about its population composition. The neighborhood is therefore not a relevant unit for considering this issue.

as long as local taxation is the main support for community services, homogeneity at the community level encourages undesirable inequalities. The high income suburb can build modern schools with all the latest features; the low income suburb is forced to treat even minimal educational progress as a luxury. Such inequity is eliminated more efficiently by federal and state subsidy than by community heterogeneity, but the latter is essential as long as such subsidies are so small.

The ideal amount and type of heterogeneity can only be guessed at, since so little is known about the impact of population characteristics within various sectors of community life. Two general statements can be made, however.

First, enough homogeneity must be present to allow institutions to function and interest groups to reach workable compromises. In areas with a wide range of population types, the balanced community—that is, a local cross-section of the entire area—would probably experience intense political and cultural conflict. Since local institutions, including government, have little power to affect—and to ameliorate—the basic causes of such conflict, they would be unable to handle it constructively. Conflict itself is not unhealthy, but irreconcilable conflict is socially destructive, and nothing would be gained by instituting population heterogeneity within political units which cannot deal with the negative consequences of conflict.

Second, enough heterogeneity must be provided in the community so that important facilities and services can be financed and enabled to find sufficient clients to allow them to function. Economic or social ghettos, either of the very rich or the very poor, are thus not desirable. (Cultural ghettos, such as those of ethnic groups, are not a problem, as long as they are voluntary ones and are able to provide nonethnic facilities for those who want to get out of the group.)

The generality of these proposals illustrates clearly how little is known about the consequences of homogeneity and heterogeneity. More specific planning guides require a thoroughgoing research program that would explore the consequences of different types and degrees of population mixture for a variety of planning values. No one can now predict the conclusions of such research. For example, I have suggested that schools with heterogeneous student bodies are desirable. Systematic studies may show, however, that children learn better among homogeneous peers. The tracking system that exists in many high schools, and even in elementary schools, suggests this possibility. Moreover, such studies might also show that the heterogeneous elements of the student body come into visual contact, but do not achieve any real social contact. If the learning benefits resulting from homogeneity are greater than the social benefits of a mixed student body, a more homogeneous school system might be desirable. Such a system would, however, conflict with yet another value, that of the school as a symbol and an institution of democratic pluralism. Needless to say, comparison of different types of values is not an easy task. Nevertheless, the importance of the balanced-community concept in contemporary planning thought and the constant rejection of the concept in the housing market suggest that policy-oriented research along this line is badly needed.

AN APPRAISAL OF PRESENT CONDITIONS

It should be clear from the preceding comments that I place little value on heterogeneity as an end in itself. Consequently, I see no overwhelming objections against the patterns of population distribution that exist in today's suburban subdivisions and new communities. I noted earlier the beneficial effects of the kind of population mixture found in Levittown. In addition, the fact that most developments are built in or near older towns, and therefore fall into existing political subdivisions, usually creates additional heterogeneity at the community level.

Thus it would seem that the present system, in which the housing industry supplies subdivisions which are homogeneous in price and where the buyer decides what he can afford or wants to pay, makes for a degree of heterogeneity that is satisfactory both from the point of view of the residents and from that of society as a whole. Three qualifying comments must be added, however. First, acceptance of house price homogeneity should not be interpreted as a justification for accompanying by-products, and especially for racial or religious discrimination. Specifically, if an individual chooses to move into an area where the residents differ from him in age, income, race, religion, or ethnic background, he has not only the right to do so, but he also has the right to governmental support to uphold his action. If this wreaks havoc with the block's social life or the community's consensus, it is an unfortunate but irrelevant consequence. Freedom of choice, civil rights, and the protection of minority interests are values of higher priority than peaceful social life or consensus. Second, the homogeneity of population that results from the homogeneity of house price is on the whole voluntary, differing radically from the enforced homogeneity of slums and public-housing projects, which force deprived people into clearly labeled economic ghettos. Third, the fact that the present suburban housing-market arrangements may be satisfactory with respect to population mixture does not excuse their inability to house low- and even medium-income families.

TOWARD A REFORMULATION OF THE ISSUE

At the present time, population heterogeneity as advocated by planners is not workable. Neither home purchasers nor tenants seem to want it, and the housing market is not organized to provide it. (Planners themselves rarely practice what they preach, and usually reside in areas inhabited by people of like values and class background.) Consequently, it is unlikely that heterogeneity can be implemented through planning or other legislative and political means. Lack of feasibility is not a legitimate objection, per se. However, I have tried to show that heterogeneity does not really achieve the ends sought by its advocates.

Moreover, even if it could be implemented it would not solve the problems that currently beset our communities. *Indeed, the opposite is closer to the truth; population heterogeneity cannot be achieved until the basic metropolitan-area social problem is solved.* This I believe to be the economic and social inequalities that still exist in our society, as expressed in the deprivations and substandard living conditions of the lowest socioeconomic strata of the metropolitan-area population. These conditions in turn produce some of the residential patterns that restrict population heterogeneity. For example, the present homogeneity of the age and class in cities and suburbs results in part from the desire of middle-class and working-class families to avoid contact with the deprived population and with the way it is forced to live. Thus the city—and especially its inner areas—becomes the abode of the very rich, the very poor, and those who cannot get away.

The planner's advocacy of heterogeneity is in part a means for dealing with this problem; he hopes that the mixing of classes will iron out these inequalities. The intent is noble, but the means are inappropriate. What is needed instead is the raising of substandard incomes, the provision of greater occupational and educational opportunities to the deprived population, and the development of institutions that will create opportunities tailored to their needs and cultural wants. These programs should receive first priority in future metropolitan-area policymaking.

The elimination of deprivation cannot be implemented solely or even primarily by city planning as now practiced. Nor are physical planning methods of much relevance. Some policies may fit into the newly emerging field of local social planning, but many can be achieved only through economic and legislative decisions at the national level. Some of the programs in which city planners are involved do, however, bear a direct relation to the basic goal; and changes in city planning policies would, therefore, be helpful in achieving it. For example, urban-renewal programs that give highest priority to the improvement of housing conditions of the poorest city dwellers would be more desirable than, and considerably different from, those presently supported by the city planning profession.[11] Similarly, school planning which seeks better methods and facilities for educating lower-class children—the average as well as the gifted—is more important than concern with space standards that are currently applicable only to high income, low density communities.[12] Also, a more serious attempt to solve the recreation problems of inner-city children should complement, if not replace, the current preoccupations with marinas and with regional parks for well-to-do suburban residents.

I am suggesting that the city planning profession should pay less attention to improving the physical environment of those who are already comparatively well served by private and public means, and pay more attention to the environmental conditions of the deprived population. Such a change in planning emphasis will not by itself solve the problem (even an intensive national program geared to reduce all inequality cannot erase immediately the inequities of a century), but it will be making a contribution toward the eventual solution.

The reduction of inequalities may also have some positive consequences for population heterogeneity. At first, greater social and economic equality would result in greater homogeneity of income, education, and the like. This homogeneity would, however, extend to a larger number of people the opportunity to make choices, and this in turn is likely to result in more heterogeneity of attitude and behavior. Thus, if more people have the discretionary income and the skills to make choices, they will begin to express and to implement preferences. This can create a demand for greater diversity in housing, recreation, taste, and in many other aspects of life.

It must be stressed, however, that the resulting heterogeneity would be qualitatively different from the type that exists today. The disappearance of ways of life based on deprivation would do away with such phenomena as the street life of the overcrowded slum which now provides a measure of variety to the social and physical landscape of a middle-class society. Thus, there would undoubtedly be less clearly visible *cultural diversity*, especially since ethnic differences and exotic immigrant neighborhoods are also disappearing. Conversely, the ability of people to make choices should result in greater expression of *individual preferences*.[13] Even now, homeowners

11. For details, see Herbert J. Gans, "The Human Implications of Current Redevelopment and Relocation Planning," *Journal of the American Institute of Planners* 25 (1959): 23-25. In contrast, it may be noted that the recent AIP policy statement on urban renewal refers only to the removal of blight and has nothing to say about the improvement of housing conditions of those who live in blighted areas. "Urban Renewal," *Journal of the American Institute of Planners* 25 (1959): 221.

12. See John W. Dyckman, "Comment on Glazer's School Proposals," *Journal of the American Institute of Planners* 25 (1959): especially p. 199.

13. The two types of heterogeneity and their implications for American society are explored more fully in Herbert J. Gans, "Diversity is Not Dead," *New Republic* 144 (April 3, 1961): 11-15.

in the Park Forests and the Levittowns make more individual changes in their houses than do the owners of urban row houses.

There is no reason to expect that homogeneity of class and age will ever be totally eliminated in residential areas. But it is possible that a somewhat closer approximation to the kind of residential heterogeneity advocated by planners may be realized when the extreme cultural differences have disappeared and when a greater number of people have more freedom of choice with respect to residence.

APPENDIX

Heterogeneity for Aesthetic Values

My argument has dealt primarily with population heterogeneity, but planners have also advocated heterogeneity of house types, primarily for aesthetic reasons. In the past, it was thought that aesthetic values could be achieved only through custom-built housing, and the discussions of the topic stressed the evils of mass production. Today the issue is: how much heterogeneity should be provided in mass-produced housing to create aesthetic values. No one, including the builder himself, is opposed to beauty; but considerable disagreement exists over priorities and about the definition of aesthetic standards.

The issue of priorities is basically economic, and the debate rages about the price consequences of house-type heterogeneity. I feel that the aesthetic benefits of house-type diversity are not sufficient to justify depriving anyone of a new house because he cannot afford to pay for variations in floor plans or elevations. No one wants what Vernon De Mars has called cookie-cutter developments, although the home buyer with limited means may have no other alternative, and he may subsequently build his own individuality into the house when he can afford to do so. Builders of mass-produced housing should of course be encouraged to vary designs and site plans as much as possible, as long as the added cost does not price anyone out of the market who would otherwise be able to buy. Planners and architects should be able to use their professional skills to help builders to achieve variety; but, too often, their recommendations add too much to costs and prices.

In recent years, planners have advocated a mixture of dwelling-unit types, mainly to cut down suburban sprawl, but also to provide aesthetic variety. Unfortunately, architects have not yet designed salable row-houses or duplexes, and the universal dislike of these house types among most home buyers has not created the incentives necessary for experimentation by builders or their designers. Some sophisticated consumer research to discover what people dislike about the higher density dwelling-unit types is necessary before acceptable new versions can be developed.

The second issue results from the lack of agreement on aesthetic standards. Although everyone seeks beauty, concepts of beauty and of what is beautiful or ugly differ between professionals and laymen, as well as between people of different socioeconomic backgrounds and educational levels. Unfortunately, the American dedication to cultural pluralism specifically excludes aesthetic pluralism. As a result, demands for more beauty in housing usually favor the aesthetic standards of a single group, the well-educated, upper middle-class professional.[14] Indeed, much of the critique of suburban

---

14. It is therefore no coincidence that the illustrations of aesthetically desirable blocks in most planning reports are usually from high-income residential neighborhoods. See, for example, Henry Fagin and Robert C. Weinberg, eds., *Planning and Community Appearance* (New York: Regional Plan Association, Inc., May 1958).

housing and of suburbia generally is a thinly veiled attack by this group on the aesthetic principles and on the overall taste level of the middle- and working-class population.

There is at present no democratic method for reconciling the aesthetic disagreement. Since differences of taste have not been proven to be socially or emotionally harmful, or inimical to the public interest, there is no justification for an undemocratic implementation of a single aesthetic standard. In a democracy, each person is, and should be, free to pursue his concept of beauty. Aesthetic pluralism may hurt the aesthetic sensibilities of the better educated people, but until everyone has the opportunity to acquire their level of education, such hurts must be borne as a price—and a small one—of living in a democracy. No one should be discouraged from advocating and propagating his own aesthetic standards, but public policy must take the existence of taste differences into account. Needless to say, this does not justify promoting ugliness or taking architectural shortcuts under the guise of aesthetic pluralism. Architectural and site designs should, however, respect the aesthetic standards of those people for whom they are primarily intended. This requires some knowledge—little of it now available—about diverse aesthetic standards, and cannot be based on uninformed guesses about such standards by either architect or builder. Public buildings exist for the benefit of all cultural groups, and should therefore appeal to what is common in all aesthetic standards; or better still, promote architectural innovation. Cognizance of the diversity of aesthetic standards will of course add more heterogeneity to the landscape.[15]

15. For a discussion of aesthetic differences and taste levels, see Russell Lynes, "Highbrow, Lowbrow, Middlebrow," in *The Tastemakers* (New York: Harper & Bros., 1954), chap. 13. For an excellent discussion of aesthetic pluralism in a democracy, see Lyman Bryson, *The Next America* (New York: Harper & Bros., 1952), chap. 10. Some of the policy implications of my point of view are discussed in Herbert J. Gans, "Pluralist Esthetics and Subcultural Programming," *Studies in Public Communication*, no. 3 (Summer 1960).

12.   Equal Status, Housing Integration, and Racial Prejudice

GEORGE E. SIMPSON and J. MILTON YINGER

In recent years, in developing strategies for changing prejudiced persons, no factor has received more attention than the effects of contact between members of different groups. It is often said, "If there were only more contact, if people only knew each other better, there would be less prejudice." Yet it is also known that prejudice frequently seems most intense in areas where there is most contact. How effective is contact with members of a minority group in changing attitudes and behavior toward that group? This question requires careful study, for there are many factors that affect the results. It is related to broader questions of international relations, where it is also frequently assumed that contact *per se* will improve understanding. . . .

Contact with the members of a minority group may, of course, be of an unpleasant variety. This is sometimes held to be a cause of prejudice—the attitude is simply a generalization from a few unfortunate experiences. Unpleasant experience with individual members of a minority group, however, can scarcely be the cause of prejudice, because that experience would not be generalized to the whole minority group unless the prejudice were already there. Moreover, we cannot be certain that persons who report more unpleasant memories of contact with members of minority groups have actually had more such contacts. Memory is selective; they may remember (or invent) such contacts *because* they already have a stronger than average prejudice.

Thus we find that prejudice is sometimes explained as a result of the *lack* of contact with members of a minority group and sometimes explained as the result of the *presence* of such contact. Both theories explain only surface relationships.

Such observations do not mean, however, that one's experiences with individual members of a minority group have no effect on his attitudes toward that group. Prejudice does not entirely precede and coerce the interpretation of experience. Unpleasant contacts probably increase the strength of prejudice. Oppositely, *certain kinds of contact* are effective in reducing the strength of a tradition of prejudice. We are learning to examine contact against a background of knowledge of the total personality of the individuals involved, the leadership, the power structure, the place of one attitude in a total value system.[1]

Allport has prepared a valuable outline of the variables that we must have in mind in any analysis of the effects of contact between members of different groups.

Quantitative aspects of contact:
  a. Frequency.
  b. Duration.

Reprinted from George Eaton Simpson and J. Milton Yinger, *Racial and Cultural Minorities* (4th ed.; New York: Harper & Row, 1972), pp. 673-84 (edited), by permission of the publishers and authors. Copyright © 1953 by Harper and Row, Publishers, Inc., Copyright © 1958, 1965, 1972 by George Eaton Simpson and J. Milton Yinger. George Eaton Simpson and J. Milton Yinger are professors of sociology and anthropology at Oberlin College.

1. See Ronald Lippitt and Marian Radke, "New Trends in the Investigation of Prejudice," *Annals of the American Academy of Political and Social Science*, March 1946, pp. 167-76.

   c. Number of persons involved.

   d. Variety.

Status aspects of contact:

   a. Minority member has inferior status.

   b. Minority member has equal status.

   c. Minority member has superior status.

   d. Not only may the individuals encountered vary thus in status, but the group as a whole may have relatively high status (e.g., Jews) or relatively low status (e.g., Negroes).

Role Aspects of contact:

   a. Is the relationship one of competitive or cooperative activity?

   b. Is there a superordinate or subordinate role relation involved—e.g., master-servant, employer-employee, teacher-pupil?

Social atmosphere surrounding the contact:

   a. Is segregation prevalent, or is egalitarianism expected?

   b. Is the contact voluntary or involuntary?

   c. Is the contact "real" or "artificial"?

   d. Is the contact perceived in terms of intergroup relations or not perceived as such?

   e. Is the contact regarded as "typical" or as "exceptional"?

   f. Is the contact regarded as important and intimate, or as trivial and transient?

Personality of the individual experiencing the contact:

   a. Is his initial prejudice level high, low, medium?

   b. Is his prejudice of a surface, conforming type, or is it deeply rooted in his character structure?

   c. Has he basic security in his own life, or is he fearful and suspicious?

   d. What is his previous experience with the group in question, and what is the strength of his present stereotypes?

   e. What are his age and general education level?

   f. Many other personality factors may influence the effect of contact.

Areas of contact:

   a. Casual.

   b. Residential.

   c. Occupational.

   d. Recreational.

   e. Religious.

   f. Civil and fraternal.

   g. Political.

   h. Goodwill intergroup activities.

Even this list of variables that enter into the problem of contact is not exhaustive. It does, however, indicate the complexity of the problem we face.[2] Because of the large number of variables affecting the influence of contact on interracial attitudes and behavior, research conclusions are quite tentative. Yet certain principles are substantially supported. After one of the most intensive reviews of the effects of contact, Williams concludes that ". . . *in all the surveys in all communities and for all groups, majority and minorities, the greater the frequency of interaction, the lower the prevalence of*

___

2. Gordon Allport, *The Nature of Prejudice*, Addison-Wesley, 1954, pp. 262-63. For another useful general statement, see Yehuda Amir, "Contact Hypothesis in Ethnic Relations," *Psychological Bulletin*, May 1969, pp. 319-42.

ethnic prejudice. (Note that the same correlation can be stated: the less the frequency of ethnic prejudice, the more frequent is the interaction.)"[3] Williams does not stop with this statement of a simple correlation. By the introduction of several test variables, he is able to strengthen a causal inference. "*If* contacts can be established"—an interesting and important qualification—even quite marked prejudices cannot nullify the prejudice-reducing influence of interaction.

Brief contacts, however, may not have a measurable impact. Trubowitz divided a group of grade school children into four categories, to participate in interracial contact through a three-day period. The categories were: joint trips and joint discussions; joint trips and separate discussions; separate trips and joint discussions; and separate trips and separate discussions. He hypothesized that planned interracial activity, particularly when heightened by discussion and trips, would produce positive attitude changes. He found, however, that little change occurred.[4]

Nor is pleasurable association by itself adequate to reduce prejudice. What Sherif calls "hedonistic associationism"—people like what is associated with their pleasures—overlooks the human skill in taking the pleasure and maintaining old attitudes. Sherif emphasized the impact of "superordinate goals." When individuals or groups are brought together within a situation that requires their active cooperation to achieve a mutually desired goal, stereotype and prejudice fade.[5]

Selltiz and Cook, in their study of foreign students in the United States, emphasized the importance of opportunities for intergroup contact, the "acquaintance potential" of a situation. Those in smaller colleges, as compared with matched counterparts in intermediate and larger schools, had more personal contacts with Americans, contacts that were more than formal or official.[6] Availability of contacts is not simply a matter of propinquity. Interracial contact in the United States continues to be infrequent, despite the spread of the black population throughout the country. In his careful study of one American community, Molotch found that interracial contacts were infrequent in almost every activity, even in shopping, although there were some exceptions. It has often been remarked that "eleven o'clock Sunday morning is the most segregated time of the week," but he found that eleven o'clock Saturday evening was even more segregated. In those few situations where interracial activity was quite common, as for example a city commission for civic activities, there were status contrasts and, within the commission, contrasts in power (for the blacks were chosen as "representatives," not because of their personal expertise or influence). Such contacts are as likely to confirm stereotypes as they are to create greater sensitivity to members of another race.[7]

The extent of black-white contact in the United States was recently recorded in a Harris survey. A representative cross-section of white people were asked: "Would you say you have a great deal of contact with blacks, some contact, or almost no contact with blacks in the following areas?" The Harris survey cross-tabulated these

3. Robin M. Williams, Jr., *Strangers Next Door*, Prentice-Hall, 1964, pp. 167-68. See chap. 7 of this work for a full discussion of contact.

4. Julius Trubowitz, *Changing the Racial Attitudes of Children: The Effects of an Activity Group Program in New York City Schools*, Praeger, 1969.

5. Muzafer Sherif, *In Common Predicament: Social Psychology of Intergroup Conflict and Composition*, Houghton Mifflin, 1966.

6. Claire Selltiz and S. W. Cook, "Factors Influencing Attitudes of Foreign Students Toward Their Host Countries," *Journal of Social Issues*, First Quarter, 1962, pp. 7-23.

7. Harvey Molotch, "Racial Integration in a Transition Community," *American Sociological Review*, December 1969, pp. 878-93.

results by the expressed fear of violence. Those with least contact are more worried about racial trouble.

The relationship between high contact and less fear of violence does not, of course, show the causal connections. It is perhaps significant, however, that those under 30 were more likely to say they were friendly with blacks and less likely to express fears of racial violence. More intensive community studies, moreover, allow us to speak somewhat more confidently of a causal connection. Warren has shown that suburban whites are not only individually isolated from Negroes, a situation which encourages race tension, but also share a community atmosphere that reenforces that isolation and tends to furnish a community response to the conflict situation. Primary lack of contact generates a secondary, community sustained lack of contact.[8] In another community study, Jeffries and Ransford applied controls for the effects of proximity to the Watts riot and prejudice. They found that contact with Negroes prior to the riot was an important determiner of white attitudes toward the disorder, to some degree independent of the control variables. "Those lacking contact are more fearful of Negroes, cite more outside agitator explanations, evidence more feelings of increased social distance, and voice more punitive responses than those having contact."[9] . . .

EFFECTS OF EQUAL-STATUS CONTACT

The influence that has been most carefully explored in recent research is the degree of status equality or status difference among the participants in intergroup relations. In exploring this issue we must remember how resistant stereotypes are to evidence. Moreover, equal-status contacts are perhaps more likely to involve competition. In his study of an interracial adolescent group, Irwin Katz found that despite its liberal and friendly atmosphere there was the danger that competition for leadership and the other inevitable group tensions—having nothing to do with race—would be seen as racial in origin and meaning.[10] This is especially likely when the surrounding environment in which the equal-status contact occurs does not support the implications of equality.

Nevertheless, there is good evidence that what might be called "stereotype-breaking contacts" reduce prejudice. MacKenzie found that among university students, when several variables that might influence the results were controlled, knowing professional Negroes and having a variety of contacts with Negroes produced statistically significantly more favorable attitudes.[11] In a study which is in better control of the time dimension, Mann assigned 78 graduate students at Teachers College, New York City, to six-person discussion groups. The groups, containing men and women, black and white, southerners and northerners, held four meetings a week for three weeks. At the beginning and at the end they were given sociometric tests and part of the Berkeley

8. Donald I. Warren, "Suburban Isolation and Race Tension: The Detroit Case," *Social Problems*, Winter 1970, pp. 324-39.

9. Vincent Jeffries and H. Edward Ransford, "Interracial Social Contact and Middle-Class White Reactions to the Watts Riot," *Social Problems*, Winter 1969, p. 312.

10. Irwin Katz, *Conflict and Harmony in an Adolescent Interracial Group*, New York Univ. Press, 1955.

11. Barbara K. MacKenzie, "The Importance of Contact in Determining Attitudes Toward Negroes," *Journal of Abnormal and Social Psychology*, October 1948, pp. 417-41.

E-Scale for measuring prejudice. Contact in the group significantly reduced both the E scores and the use of race as a friendship criterion.[12] . . .

In many "contact" studies, there are methodological problems of self-selection and limitation to verbal behavior. Deutsch and Collins report the interesting results of different patterns of interracial housing in which these problems are minimal. In two housing projects Negro and white families were assigned to apartment buildings regardless of race (the integrated pattern); in two other projects different buildings or different parts of the project were used for Negroes and whites (the segregated biracial pattern). Interviews with the housewives in these situations revealed that the integrated pattern reduced prejudice much more sharply.

In the integrated projects only one-third as many women spontaneously expressed prejudice in the interviews as in the segregated projects (13 percent and 10 percent compared with 36 percent and 31 percent). About two housewives want to be friendly for one who wants to avoid contact with Negroes in the integrated arrangement; but in the segregated situation there are 10 who want to avoid contact for 1 who wishes to be friendly. It is particularly interesting to know that 67 percent and 71 percent of the women in the integrated projects have positive attitudes toward the interracial aspects of their communities, many having come to like it more; but in the segregated projects most of the women liked the interracial aspects less than they did before they moved into the community.[13]

TABLE 12.1 *Nature of Housewives' Relations with Negro People in Housing Projects*

| | Integrated | | Segregated | |
	Koaltown (%)	Sacktown (%)	Bakerville (%)	Frankville (%)
Friendly relations	60	69	6	4
Accommodative relations	24	14	5	1
Mixed relations	7	11	2	3
No relations	5	0	87	88
Bad relations	4	6	0	4
Total cases	102	90	100	101

SOURCE: Morton Deutsch and Mary E. Collins, *Interracial Housing*, Univ. of Minnesota Press, 1951, p. 79.

The effects of such types of contact would not be the same, of course, on persons whose prejudices were so strong that they would not join an interracial community; but among families who did accept housing on a biracial basis persons assigned (without regard to their original attitudes, for the type of arrangement was an administrative decision, not an individual choice) to integrated patterns discovered that their prejudices were very inadequate modes of adjustment. Those in the segregated projects had no such opportunity for revising their attitudes.

In a follow-up study of the effects of interracial housing, Wilner, Walkley, and Cook derived evidence that supports many of the findings of Deutsch and Collins, but also introduces some qualifications. In interracial neighborhoods, "the assumption

12. John Mann, "The Effects of Inter-Racial Contact on Sociometric Choices and Perceptions," *Journal of Social Psychology*, August 1959, pp. 143-52.

13. Morton Deutsch and Mary E. Collins, *Interracial Housing*, Univ. of Minnesota Press, 1951, chap. 11.

that segregation is right and inevitable is challenged" by the authority of the community project; and the white resident is confronted with the problem of reconciling the evidence concerning the behavior of actual minority-group members with his stereotypes. Thus contact weakens the supports of prejudice. There are, however, a number of complicating factors:

the relation between *proximity and contact*, and the relation of each to attitude change; the influence of initial attitude on the outcome of the contact experience; the influence of social pressures—or social climate regarding intergroup association—on the outcome of the contact experience, and the ways in which the social climate is established and manifested; the effect that different proportions of minority group members has on the experience associated with proximity or contact; and the dimensions of attitude which undergo change.[14]

The four housing projects studied by Wilner, Walkley, and Cook had a small proportion of Negro residents; none had more than 10 percent. In all four projects, the extent of contact with Negroes was closely tied to proximity. The contacts that occurred were not simply unplanned conversation, but neighborly activities of various kinds —borrowing and lending, helping during sickness, visiting. The white women who lived near Negroes perceived, more often than those living farther away, that the opinions of other white women in the project were favorable to interracial contact. They also held Negroes in higher esteem and were more likely to believe that the races were equal in such things as cleanliness, manners, intelligence, ambition. Although the attitudes toward Negroes which the white women had when they entered the project affected their responses, they were less important than proximity in the project. "Whether we consider the initially more favorable or initially less favorable respondents, those who live near Negroes in a project are more likely than those living farther away to report neighborly contact, to anticipate that white friends in the project will approve of such contact, to have high esteem for the Negroes in the project, to approve of the biracial aspect of the project, and to have a favorable attitude toward Negroes in general."[15]

Without discussing various refinements in the two studies of interracial housing, we can perhaps indicate their major finding.

TABLE 12.2   *Percentage Sharing at Least One Kind of Neighborly Activity*

	%
Two integrated projects of the Deutsch and Collins study (192)	54
Integrated projects of the Wilner, Walkley, and Cook study (91)	50
Two segregated projects of the Deutsch and Collins Study (201)	3
Segregated areas of the Wilner, Walkley, and Cook study (234)	5

SOURCE: Wilner, Walkley, and Cook, *Human Relations in Interracial Housing*, p. 143.

One uncontrolled aspect of these, and most studies of contact is the lack of any measures of selectivity of Negro participants. Are they more "contact prone"? Would the same results occur if a different pattern of selectivity prevailed? A study undertaken in Los Angeles may throw some light on these questions (although there are risks in making inferences through time and space back to the housing studies we have

14. D. M. Wilner, R. P. Walkley, and S. W. Cook, *Human Relations in Interracial Housing*, Univ. of Minnesota Press, 1955, p. 6.

15. Ibid., p. 95.

examined). Bonnie Bullough wondered why there had been a comparatively weak response to the growing opportunities for integrated housing among Negroes. Comparing two samples of Negroes in integrated neighborhoods (n = 224) with one in a solidly Negro area (n = 106), she found that the latter were significantly higher in feelings of powerlessness and anomia.[16] Without panel data, we cannot tell whether these feelings reflect or cause the housing patterns. From our interest here, however, they indicate the need to take account of Negro as well as white attitudes in studies of the effects of contact.

Studies of the effects among children are of great theoretical and strategic importance. It is often possible more nearly to approximate experimental conditions in working with children than with adults, and the effects of intergroup contact on children compete with fewer other stimuli. In a valuable study of intergroup relations in a boys' camp, Muzafer Sherif and his associates reveal the tension-building and stereotype-creating processes; and then indicate how harmony may be established or reestablished.[17] Although this research has no direct interest in majority-minority relations, it skillfully reveals more general principles of intergroup relations that are of wide applicability. The subjects were 22 eleven-year-old middle-class boys. There were no problem children among them; each had a good school record; and all were strangers to one another at the start. So far as possible they were matched into pairs on weight, height, skills, and previous camping experience and then assigned randomly into two groups. For a week the two groups lived separately at an isolated camping site. They were then brought into frequent competitive and often frustrating interaction. At the end of this second stage, there were strong reciprocal prejudices and stereotypes; members of the two groups did not want to associate; there was name-calling and conflict.

How could these expressions of tension and disharmony be reduced? One might make appeals to a common "enemy," break up the groups by individual reward and rivalry, or shift attention to intergroup leaders. Sherif rejected these, however, in favor of an effort to reduce friction by introducing "superordinate goals"—a series of tasks that required, for a mutually esteemed outcome, intergroup cooperation. These tasks were preceded by seven unstructured contact situations. By themselves, these contacts did little to break down the group lines, reduce stereotypy, or end the conflict. When the two groups had to work together, however, to raise enough money to bring a movie to camp or to get water flowing again (after the staff had devilishly disrupted the supply), group lines blurred, antipathies receded, and the differential rating of in-group and out-group disappeared. "Patterns and procedures for intergroup cooperation were laid down at first on a small scale in specific activities. Only during interaction in a series of situations involving superordinate goals did intergroup friction begin to disappear and the procedures for intergroup reciprocity developed in specific situations extend spontaneously to widening areas of activity."[18]

Here is group-building and attitude-forming before our eyes. Undoubtedly new variables are introduced when one deals with group identities that have lasted for years, not weeks. It is valuable, therefore, to follow Sherif's study with one that deals

16. Bonnie Bullough, *Social-Psychological Barriers to Housing Desegregation*, Univ. of Cal., Housing Real Estate, and Urban Land Studies Program and the Center for Real Estate and Urban Economics. Special Report no. 2, 1969.

17. See Muzafer Sherif, *Intergroup Conflict and Cooperation: The Robbers Cave Experiment*, Univ. of Oklahoma Book Exchange, 1961; see also Muzafer Sherif and Carolyn Sherif, *Groups in Harmony and Tension*, Harper & Row, 1953.

18. Muzafer Sherif, op. cit., p. 210.

with an interracial camp. Marian Yarrow and her colleagues describe the interpersonal relationships that develop between Negro and white children during the "equal status contact" of a two-week camping session.[19] Two camps for low-income children had been run on a segregated basis. During the summer of this study, three sessions, the first six weeks, remained segregated, but the last two sessions were integrated. The staff was integrated in all sessions. Six to ten children, chosen to get age homogeneity and to avoid prior friendships, were assigned to a cabin. Out of 32 cabins, 8 were studied intensively during each of the two integrated sessions.

At the beginning of each period, a racial status structure was apparent, with white children definitely holding the top positions—as determined by interviews with the campers—in nine cabins and a more mixed picture in the other seven. By the end of the two-week sessions, this status differential had lessened but not disappeared. In the segregated camps, 45 percent of the children had formed themselves into mutual pairs—each choosing the other as best friend—by the time of the first interview. This had dropped to 35 percent by the end of the period. Almost the same pattern was found in the desegregated groups (44 and 33 percent), and 44 percent of these pairs were interracial, despite the status differential. "At the end of camp, in the eyes of the white children their Negro peers were significantly more desirable as friends than they had been earlier in the session. Indeed, at the end of camp, white and Negro campers were about equally desired as friends by the white children."[20] There was also a significant growth in self-esteem among the Negro children and a reduction in the great sensitivity they showed at first to unfavorable behavior on the part of other Negro children.

In the light of the fact that the situation for Negro girls is often noted to be more favorable than that for Negro boys, it is significant to observe that in a camping setting—and doubtless elsewhere—desegregation held greater initial hazards for Negro girls: they were more likely to internalize their feelings than were the boys; and important camp values—strength and athletic skill for the boys, physical beauty for the girls—put them, but not the Negro boys, at a disadvantage. Nevertheless, there were gains: "For the girls this experience of equal-status contact results in a consistent change toward decreased self-rejection and a relaxation of tight control over their own behavior. . . . At the end of the camp the change is not complete (white girls, for example, still tend to stand as favored ideals for their Negro cabin mates, and the Negro girls still channel most of their aggression toward members of their own race), yet necessary beginnings of change have occurred, particularly changes reflecting an enhancement of the Negro girls' self concept."[21]

Equal-status contact in a two-week camp cannot, of course, offset the influence of years of segregation. A far more important "experiment" is taking place in recently desegregated schools, where hundreds of thousands of white and Negro children are seeing each other for the first time as fellow students. The results are exceedingly complex, varying with the attitudes of school and government officials, the responses of parents, the talents and tensions of the Negro and white children, the grade level, and many other factors. The transition from a segregated to an integrated school, as Robert Coles has recently reported, is undoubtedly easier, from a personality stand-

19. See Marian Radke Yarrow, issue ed., "Interpersonal Dynamics in a Desegregation Process," *Journal of Social Issues*, 1958, vol. 14.

20. Marian Yarrow, John Campbell, and Leon Yarrow, "Acquisition of New Norms: A Study of Racial Desegregation," ibid., p. 27.

21. John Campbell and Marion Yarrow, "Personal and Situational Variables in Adaptation to Change," ibid., p. 36.

point, for first graders than for high school students.[22] Nevertheless, significant changes of attitude occurred even among many of the more segregationist-minded adolescents. Perhaps most important ". . . is the slow development of discretion and selection in the white child, the breakdown of quick and total vision and the beginning of particular vision based on daily experience."[23] Negro children also begin to see whites as individuals, with their varying characteristics. In the learning process, the pull of opposite forces is strong. The ambivalences are nicely shown in the words of one of the white senior boys in Atlanta.

I've really changed a lot of my ideas. You can't help having respect for them, the way they've gone through the year so well. They're nice kids, that's what you find out after a while. They speak well, and are more intelligent than a lot of my friends. You have to understand how we've grown up. They were slaves to us, I mean even after the Civil War. . . . I was taught to expect them to do anything I wanted at home . . . they belonged in the kitchen, or fixing your socks . . . that's the way you grow up and that's what most of us expect . . . and then we're told that they're supposed to go to school with us . . . my daddy nearly died. . . . Mom told him he'd get a stroke if he didn't stop it . . . I sneered a few times the first few weeks, but I just couldn't keep it up, and I felt kind of bad and sorry for them. I used to get nervous when I'd see them eating alone. I wondered how I'd have felt if I were in their shoes . . . next thing I knew I was quiet when some of my friends were calling them all the old names. . . . I felt that I never again would look at them the way I did last September and before. . . .[24]

From the results of such studies as we have reported, we cannot conclude that a decrease in prejudice is the inevitable result of equal-status contact. Ernest Campbell and Ray Schrader studied the attitudes of junior and senior high school students of Oak Ridge, Tennessee, before school integration and then again a year after desegregation. On four scales measuring antiminority attitudes they found a significant shift in a negative direction. Prejudices had increased.[25]

In the face of contradictory findings we must realize the need for a great deal of research to explore the effects of specific conditions. For example, when are there too few members of the minority to break stereotypes (a few can be regarded as "exceptions"), and when are there so many that a sense of threat to status develops? What is the impact of personal insecurity in response to equal-status contact? In a study of 106 white boys from New York, most of them from the lower class, who attended a four-week interracial camp, Mussen found that 28 boys became significantly less prejudiced against Negroes, but 27 boys became significantly more prejudiced. Those whose prejudice increased were those who had more aggressive feelings and needs and greater need to defy authority, felt themselves victims of aggression, felt that others were not kind and helpful, were more dissatisfied with the camp.[26] This might not have been the result had there been a different proportion of Negro campers

---

22. Robert Coles, *The Desegregation of Southern Schools: A Psychiatric Study,* Anti-Defamation League of B'nai B'rith and Southern Regional Council, 1963. This is an intensive comparative study, by a child psychiatrist, concerned primarily with 6- and 7-year-olds in New Orleans and 16- and 17-year-olds in Atlanta.

23. Ibid., p. 10.

24. Ibid., pp. 13-14.

25. Ernest Campbell, "On Desegregation and Matters Sociological," *Phylon,* Summer, 1961, pp. 140-42.

26. Paul H. Mussen, "Some Personality and Social Factors Related to Changes in Children's Attitudes Toward Negroes," *Journal of Abnormal and Social Psychology,* July 1950, pp. 423-41.

(they made up about half the group), had the camp lasted longer, or had various other conditions prevailed. The study points up clearly, however, the need for careful attention to the complexity of the results of equal-status contact.

One can perhaps sum up the present knowledge about the effects of contact on prejudice in these four related propositions:

1. Incidental, involuntary, tension-laden contact is likely to increase prejudice.

2. Pleasant, equal-status contact that makes it unnecessary for the individuals to cross barriers of class, occupational, and educational differences as well as differences in symbolic (nonfunctional) group membership represented by such symbols as "race" is likely to reduce prejudice.

3. Stereotype-breaking contacts that show minority group members in roles not usually associated with them reduce prejudice. It must be added, however, that many people have little capacity for experiencing the members of minority groups as individuals; their stereotypes easily persist in the face of contrary evidence.

4. Contacts that bring people of minority and majority groups together in function-ally important activities reduce prejudice. This is particularly true when those activities involve goals that cannot be achieved without the active cooperation of members of all the groups.

Do We Want Contact, Equal Status or Otherwise?

In recent years there has been some increase in separationist sentiments in the United States, some of it in the name of pluralism—both Negro and white—but much of it renewing established prejudices. In a valuable paper, Thomas Pettigrew summarizes the reasons often given by whites today to support racial separation: (1) each race feels awkward and uncomfortable in the presence of the other and benefits from separation; (2) since whites are superior, they will lose by integration (in schools, for example); (3) contact increases conflict. Black separationists have somewhat match-ing assumptions: (1) yes, each race does feel awkward and uncomfortable in the pres-ence of the other; we're more comfortable by ourselves; (2) most whites *think* they are superior, so white liberals should spend their time working on white racists, not worrying over integration; (3) yes, contact does mean conflict, and it will continue to until after a period of autonomy, when blacks can enter into interaction on a fully equal basis.[27]

We shall refer only briefly to Pettigrew's comments on each of these points. It is true, he notes, that some interracial contacts are awkward, that intraracial contacts may seem more comfortable. But, he asks, at what cost do we gain this comfort? Isolation leads to mutual misinformation and, more importantly, it promotes differ-ences. There has been a sharp reduction in racist beliefs in the United States during the last generation; wise policy should not be based on assumptions of its prevalence or increase. Contact does, under some conditions, increase conflict; but lack of conflict is no sign of progress. "One of the quietest periods in American racial history, 1895-1915, for example, witnessed the construction of the massive system of institutional racism as it is known today. . . ."[28]

Many people argue, Pettigrew notes, that "in the long run" full integration may be desirable, but that for the immediate and foreseeable future, separation is necessary and wise. The "white desegregationist," using some mixture of the three reasons given above, supports some public desegregation, but not extensive integration. This

27. Thomas Pettigrew, "Racially Separate or Together," *Journal of Social Issues*, January 1969, pp. 43-69.

28. Ibid., p. 57.

is basically a moderate version of the older segregationist view. Perhaps more interesting is the argument of some black leaders that autonomy must come first, then integration may be possible. The various positions are charted by Pettigrew as shown in Figure 12.1.

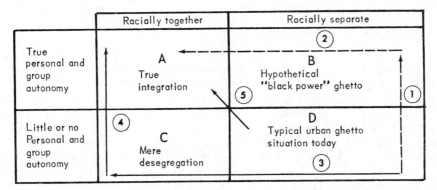

FIGURE 12.1 *Schematic Diagram of Autonomy and Contact-Separation*

SOURCE: Thomas Pettigrew, "Racially Separate or Together" *Journal of Social Issues*, January 1969, p. 58. Dotted lines denote hypothetical paths, solid lines actual paths.

Pettigrew marshalls substantial evidence to support "route 5." With reference to the "3-1-2 route," for example, he writes:

> The black separatist route has a surprising appeal for an untested theory; besides those whites who welcome any alternative to integration, it seems to appeal to cultural pluralists, white and black, to militant black leaders searching for a new direction to vent the ghetto's rage and despair, and to Negroes who just wish to withdraw as far away from whites as possible. Yet on reflection the argument involves the perverse notion that the way to bring two groups together is to separate them further. One is reminded of the detrimental consequences of isolation in economics, through "closed markets," and in "genetic drift." In social psychology, isolation between two contiguous groups generally leads to: (*a*) diverse value development, (*b*) reduced intergroup communication, (*d*) uncorrected perceptual distortions of each other, and (*e*) the growth of vested interests within both groups for continued separation. American race relations already suffer from each of these conditions; and the proposal for further separation even if a gilded ghetto were possible aims to exacerbate them further.[29]

Pettigrew may exaggerate the favorable outcomes of contact and overlook some of the costs.[30] But, in our judgment, he weighs the balance correctly.

29. Ibid., pp. 58-59.

30. See Russell Eisenman, "Comment on 'Racially Separate or Together?' " and Thomas Pettigrew, "Rejoinder," *Journal of Social Issues*, Autumn 1969, pp. 199-206.

13. *The Effects of Poor Housing*

NATHAN GLAZER

To couple together two such terms as "housing policy" and "family" is to immediately suggest something that may not be true—that is, that there are some key effects of one upon the other. That there are such effects is sharply argued in a good deal of both scholarly and popular literature; but the argument as to the effect of housing policy on family is complex and lengthy, because, unfortunately, both terms in the equation themselves are complex. Housing policy on the one side must include local, state, and federal policies (though fortunately the state does not play too large a role in housing policy). It must include both that which is done directly, in an effort to influence or directly control housing, that which is done by indirection (e.g., the impact of tax policies on housing), and that which is not done at all, but which seems a suitable field for public action. Housing policy, too, by extension, includes action in all those fields which affect neighborhood as well as house; there, of course, we must deal with such questions as planning and, even more, with policies in such fields as recreation, health, education, and even police and sanitary services. It is a commonplace that the values of houses and the desirability of dwelling places owe a good deal to neighborhood ambiance and to local services. To speak of housing policies alone, when we consider potential impact on the family, is obviously much too narrow.

On the other hand, the question of impact on the "family" is even more complex. First, we may consider whether, on the simplest level, the family is well housed. We can leave aside for the moment the question of what effects for the family—its stability, its mental health, its capacity to socialize children, its ability to adapt to new conditions —good housing will have and simply take as a given that any society will want to provide a proper setting or stage for family life. However, the question of good housing for the family is not as simple as it appears. Primitive dwellings on Greek isles delight architects and city planners who are horrified by the housing and planning of Levitt and Sons. In Japan, the sixth most powerful industrial nation in the world, and in its wealthiest city, Tokyo, we find that at least three-quarters of the dwellings must be substandard by American census standards, simply because they do not have flush toilets. Or if we consider a country that has what, in common opinion, are among the most enlightened governmental planning policies and highest living standards in the world, Sweden, we find that the number of persons per room is one-third higher than in this country.[1]

Reprinted from the *Journal of Marriage and The Family* 29, no. 1 (February 1967): 140-45, by permission of the publisher and author. Nathan Glazer is professor of education and social structure at the Harvard University Graduate School of Education.

This article was prepared upon request for the *Journal of Marriage and the Family* and was supported by a grant from the Russell Sage Foundation. Kurt W. Back, Alvin Schorr, and William L. C. Wheaton read an earlier draft and gave me valuable suggestions. I wish to acknowledge my indebtedness to them.

1. Paul F. Wendt, *Housing Policy, The Search for Solutions*, Berkeley and Los Angeles, California: University of California Press, 1962, p. 251. On the other hand, Alvin Schorr points out that

So what is "well housed"? Housing experts use three principal measures from the voluminous information provided by the housing census to determine adequacy of housing: whether a housing unit is dilapidated or not, whether it has hot running water and private toilet and bath, and whether it is overcrowded (that is, more than one person per room). Using these measures—and we have indicated by reference to plumbing in Japan and crowding in Sweden how specifically they are the measures of this country, this culture, and this time—we find that 21 percent of nonfarm American families are ill housed and, among specific groups, much larger numbers: 37 percent of those under $4,000, 53 percent of those with nonwhite heads, and 65 percent of those with nonwhite heads and incomes under $4,000.[2]

Thus, American housing, which from one perspective measures in general as the most spacious and best equipped in the world, from another perspective is grossly inadequate.

ON THE EFFECTS OF POOR HOUSING

Up to now we have been considering in our possible equation between housing policy and the family the simple question, is the family well housed? However, our interest in analyzing this equation runs to considerably more than finding the proportion that achieves the standards that housing experts have set. We are also interested in knowing what is the effect of substandard and crowded housing on families? Here we reach the murkiest if, indeed, the most interesting part of our problem. We have indicated how culture-bound are our definitions of the standard and the crowded. We can find examples of entire societies living in housing that by our standards is substandard and crowded and not considering that these conditions create a serious problem for family living. This is understandable and obvious. We are all aware of how the prism of culture transforms the same physical reality into symbolically different settings.

Less understandable and less obvious is the fact that defective conditions in housing in a single society, as defined by that society, seem to have such an irregular relationship to what we may consider good family conditions. We can give no simple and easy demonstration of this point. We do have at hand plenty of studies which correlate poor family conditions with poor housing, but we, of course, have the difficult problem of determining whether poor housing has had any specific impact on the family conditions. Casual observation suggests the effects are limited. Thus, we may observe that in preserves of technically excellent and uncrowded housing that are limited to low income groups—that is, public housing projects—there is no clear and specific relationship between the improvement in housing which the families have undergone and some family condition. Families are neither stronger nor weaker, better nor worse off—except for better housing—in low-rent housing projects. (We are now speaking specifically of housing conditions; we will speak later about other environmental influences in low-income projects on families.) Consider, for example, the most careful study of the effects of good housing of the public housing project variety on family

---

in Sweden such services as laundry and cooking may be performed centrally. Similarly, overcrowding in France is mitigated by the use of cafes for social purposes; in Tokyo, by the use of coffee houses, department stores, etc.

2. For these and some other figures in this paper, I draw upon a convenient summary prepared by the Office of Economic Opportunity for a conference on housing for the poor held by the OEO and the Department of Housing and Urban Development on May 23-24, 1966, *Housing for the Poor: A Factual Background.*

relations, that of Daniel M. Wilner and his associates. Some of their hypotheses "suggested that because of such factors as increased space and other improvements in housing, patterns of within-family activities and quality of family-member relationships might be expected to undergo alterations in the rehoused, test group." (The study design included a control group of slum families that had not been able to get into public housing.) Analyzing comparisons between the two groups on 38 measures showed that on 22 the rehoused group showed more positive family relations than the unrehoused; on 14 the unrehoused showed more positive relationships than the rehoused; and on two they were identical. The authors conclude, "It is not clear from the material presented that the change from bad to good housing has brought with it distinguishable alterations in relations among persons within the family."[3] Equally inconclusive results are found in changes in attitudes and behavior toward neighborhood and community and in a variety of recreational activities. On the other hand, in relations with neighbors and on various rather elusive (to this reader) psychological measures, housing seems to have made some small difference.[4] Also there is a clear, if somewhat small, improvement in health.

If we were dependent on Wilner's study alone—it is clearly the technically most proficient and skillful in the field—to argue for the effects of better housing on family life, our argument would not have much force. However, we must also point out that Wilner studies the impact of housing per se in isolation from all other factors. He is also studying the impact of what is in one perspective—in the light of housing possibilities available to American families—only a small improvement. Alvin Schorr, in his scholarly and insightful summary of the literature on this problem, comes to a balanced conclusion that indicates a somewhat more pessimistic view of the effect of inadequate housing, thus a more optimistic view of what better housing can do. He writes:

> The type of housing occupied influences health, behavior and attitude, particularly if the housing is desperately inadequate . . . [that is] dilapidated or lacks a major facility such as running water.

> Housing, even when it is minimally adequate, appears to influence family and social relationships. Other influences of adequate housing are uncertain. Lack of evidence is not the same as negative evidence. One would hope that eventually research would move on from the iron law of housing research—that research into effects is bound to the lowest housing standards in existence. Research that focuses on the effects of optimum housing . . . also has its place.

> . . . The following effects may spring from poor housing: a perception of one's self that leads to pessimism and passivity, stress to which the individual cannot adapt, poor health, and a state of dissatisfaction; pleasure in company but not in solitude, cynicism about people and organizations, a high degree of sexual stimulation without legitimate outlet, and difficulty in household management and child-rearing; and relationships that tend to spread out in the neighborhood rather than deeply in the family. Most of these effects, in turn, place obstacles in the path of improving one's financial circumstances.[5]

There are four points to which I would draw further attention in this judicious

3. Daniel M. Wilner, *et al.*, *The Housing Environment and Family Life*, Baltimore: Johns Hopkins Press, 1962, pp. 148, 158, 159.

4. Ibid., pp. 170, 198-99, 210-12, 216-19.

5. Alvin Schorr, *Slums and Social Insecurity*, U.S. Department of Health, Education and Welfare, Social Security Administration, Division of Research and Statistics, Research Report no. 1, pp. 31-32.

summary of the available literature: First, the clearest effects come from the "desperately inadequate" housing. Second, many of these ill effects come from *overcrowding* rather than the structural characteristics of housing that we often think of when we speak of poor housing. Third, our studies are as yet studies of the effects of minimal housing and that below it (Wilner); if the differences are small, may it not be because the improvement is small? Fourth, another analyst might argue over whether some of the effects of poor housing ("pleasure in company but not in solitude" and "relationships that spread out in the neighborhood rather than deeply in the family") are entirely negative.

First, desperately inadequate housing is, on the whole, infrequent in this country outside the rural areas. In 1950, 96.4 percent of all nonfarm housing had inside running water; 90.4 percent had baths; 96.6 percent had electricity.[6] Among specific groups, in particular the Negro, it is true that the situation is much worse and the desperately inadequate quite common. Thus, of housing units occupied by urban nonwhites in 1960, 80 percent had inside hot and cold running water; but 15 percent had only cold water, 3 percent had piped water outside the structure, and 2 percent had no piped water. Eighty-five percent had private use of a flush toilet; but 8 percent shared a flush toilet, and 7 percent had none. Seventy-eight percent had exclusive use of a bathtub or shower; but 7 percent shared it, and 15 percent had none.[7]

Where families do not have access to inside piped water, where they cannot easily bathe or use toilet facilities, it would seem there must be an effect not only on health but on the whole ambiance of family life. Yet if one has gotten past the problem of the desperately inadequate, what further losses ensue from poor housing and what gains may we expect from good housing? Certainly housing does not seem to be the most dynamic element in the improvement of family life past this stage, which is why Alvin Schorr's conclusions must be so cautious.

The urban Negro, as we have pointed out (even more so, of course, the rural Negro), suffers from some of the worst housing conditions in the country. Unquestionably for this group there is a decisive relationship between housing quality and family life, and yet other factors are easily capable of overwhelming any positive effects of an improvement in housing.

Some striking improvements have taken place in housing with no impact on significant aspects of Negro family life—e.g., family breakup, illegitimacy, dependency, etc. The proportion of nonwhite couples without their own household—that is, doubled up—dropped from 14 to 5 percent between 1950 and 1960 (white, from 6 to 2); the percentage in substandard units dropped from 72 to 44 (white, from 32 to 13); and the percentage overcrowded (nonfarm only) was reduced more moderately from 32 to 27 (white, from 12 to 8).[8] Meanwhile, various measures of family disorganization increased.[9]

On the same point, we may note that there is no obvious correlation between the quality of housing in low-income Negro areas and the degree of social disorganization. Thus, the housing of more newly built western cities is clearly superior to that of older eastern and northwestern cities (Watts versus Harlem or Oakland versus Chicago's

6. Wendt, op. cit.

7. Housing and Home Finance Agency, *Our Nonwhite Population and its Housing*, 1963, pp. 78-79.

8. Ibid., pp. 10, 11, 60.

9. Daniel P. Moynihan, "Employment, Income, and the Ordeal of the Negro Family," *Daedalus*, Fall, 1965, pp. 765, 768.

south side, to give the picture). In addition to newer, less substandard, less crowded housing, there is certainly in many respects a better neighborhood ambiance (recreational facilities, newer schools, etc.); but other conditions seem to destroy any relationship that might otherwise exist between housing conditions and family life.[10]

Past the threshold of the most inadequate housing, it would appear that crowding has the most serious effects on the family and socialization. Thus, the excessive sexual stimulation, the attitudes toward privacy and self, the irritation of intrafamily relations, the intrusive presence of nonfamily members—all these are consequences of crowding, the simple shortage of space. Oscar Lewis' *Children of Sanchez* describes the incredible crowding of present-day, lower class, urban living in Mexico City, where a dozen or more people, in three or four families, must use the same room for sleeping. Crowding conditions similar to these are described in the literature on the immigrant quarters of New York at the turn of the century. One would think the terrible effects of such crowding could scarcely be overestimated.[11]

However, even under such conditions of room crowding, cultural factors may come into play to mitigate the evil effects. Robert C. Schmitt has studied the effect of room crowding in Hong Kong, which reaches levels as high as any we know. In 1957 three-quarters of Hong Kong households had less than a full room, and the average size of the household was 4.7. The huge concrete resettlement estates average five adults a room, with a child counted as half an adult. "The Hong Kong average of 32 square feet is probably less than one-tenth of the metropolitan U.S. norm."

Despite this, health conditions on some measures are better than in the United States and social disorganization less.

> Death and disease rates, except for tuberculosis, are relatively low. There were 5.9 deaths per 1,000 inhabitants in Hong Kong in 1961, a rate well below the comparable United States figure (9.3). Infant mortality . . . amounted to 37.7 per 1,000 live births, higher than the U.S. rate (25.2). . . . Maternal deaths totaled 0.45 per 1,000 births, compared with 0.32 in the United States. Patients hospitalized for psychiatric disorders as of the end of 1961 amounted to 0.3 per 1,000 population, a rate less than one-tenth as great as that reported in America.
>
> . . . Cases of murder and manslaughter were about one-sixth the U.S. rate. The rate for all "serious crimes" . . . was less than half the American rate. Juvenile delinquency and teen-age violence . . . were still far from reaching U.S. dimensions.[12]

However, presumably even Chinese and Jewish families, whose capacities—at least in the past—to cope with frightfully crowded urban conditions have been legendary, would do better with more space. Certainly families without long urban experience and in a society in which the norms of space are much more lavish than in Hong Kong may be expected to suffer from room crowding. Yet in contemporary America the threshold we now consider crowded is so low that it is questionable whether

10. In 1950 only 19 percent of dwelling units occupied by nonwhites in the Los Angeles SMA were substandard, the lowest proportion in any metropolitan area. Other SMA's showed: Birmingham, 88; New Orleans, 83; Atlanta, 77; St. Louis, 75; Houston, 69; Chicago, 59; Philadelphia, 42; Washington, 34; New York, 34; Detroit, 29; San Francisco-Oakland, 26. Davis McEntire, *Residence and Race*, Berkeley and Los Angeles: University of California Press, 1960, p. 123.

11. The most specific psychosocial account of the impact of crowding, perhaps, is J. S. Plant's 30-year-old account of the slums of Newark, described in *Personality and the Cultural Pattern*, New York: The Commonwealth Fund, 1937, chap. 8.

12. Robert C. Schmitt, "Implications of Density in Hong Kong," *Journal of the American Institute of Planners* 29 (August 1963): 210-17.

it has significant effects on the family. This threshold, as we have pointed out, is one person per room. Two persons per room is considered excessive crowding and is so uncommon that census summary statistics do not give figures for this degree of crowding. It is the nonwhite population—that is, the Negro population—specifically that suffers from crowding. As we pointed out earlier, 27 percent of nonfarm, nonwhite families live under crowded conditions. Thirteen percent have more than 1.51 persons per room.

Can we say that densities of more than one person per room are factors in creating social problems and family disorganization? Perhaps they contribute (everything contributes); yet it is hard to see them as major factors. Consider, for example, the statistics in Table 13.1, which show the proportion of crowded households (more than one person per room) by family income in 1960.

TABLE 13.1   *Percentage of Crowded Households**

Income	Owners	Renters
Under $2,000	6.0	16.0
$ 2,000- 2,999	9.0	20.5
$ 3,000- 3,999	11.0	19.0
$ 4,000- 4,999	11.5	17.5
$ 5,000- 5,999	11.0	16.0
$ 6,000- 6,999	10.0	14.5
$ 7,000- 7,999	9.0	13.0
$ 8,000- 9,999	8.0	11.5
$10,000-15,000	7.0	11.0
Above $15,000	4.5	8.5

*More than one person per room. *U.S. Census of Housing, 1960, Metropolitan Housing*, Final Report HC(2)-1, Table A-3.

Crowding does decline with increase in income (the low crowding of the lowest income levels is accounted for by the high proportion of the elderly). What is striking is how slowly it decreases and how substantial a proportion of the highest income groups still live under crowded conditions. They do this, one must assume, by choice; for they have the ability to allocate their incomes so as to eliminate crowding. Under these circumstances, one wonders whether it should be a major aim of public policy to eliminate crowding of more than one person per room.

Certainly it should be a major aim of public policy to eliminate excessive crowding when it results not from choice, in which privacy is a lesser value than some alternative good that may be purchased, but when it arises because of economic incapacity to purchase space. In 1960, 1,690,000 families of 5 persons or more had incomes under $3,000. In 1960 the median number of rooms in the American housing unit was 4.9, the median value of owner-occupied dwellings was $11,900, and the median gross rent of rented housing units was $71. Most of these large, poor families must consequently live under crowded conditions and without available alternatives; and they form a substantial fraction of the American people.

We have spoken up to now of room crowding alone. Conceivably, room crowding, when measured by the current lavish American standard of one person per room, may have a less serious effect on the family than area crowding, that is, the concentration of too many households in an area and the consequent crowding of streets with children, adolescents, and young adults. Once again, Schmitt has carried through an interesting analysis, correlating various measures of crowding with various measures of ill health and family and social disorganization for the census tracts of Honolulu. "Population per net residential acre"—a measure of area crowding—correlates best with nine measures of ill-health and social disorganization (median r, .63), much better than "dwelling units with more than one person per room" (median r, .37). A third measure of crowding, "couples without own household," shows a median r of .4.[13]

Yet I hesitate to conclude that crowding, whether area or room, in contemporary American cities leads to family disorganization. What, after all, is the range of area crowding we are discussing? When we think of the conditions of the urban poor, we too often think of New York, which is far less typical of the country as a whole than Watts. Schmitt points out: "Statistical subdivisions of American cities seldom exceed 150 inhabitants per gross acre. Analysis of recent census tract statistics indicates the highest densities to be about 450 persons per acre in both Boston and New York, 163 in Chicago, 150 in Philadelphia, 132 in Honolulu, and 62 in Seattle. Several blocks in Manhattan had as many as 1,300 persons per acre of ground space." In contrast, the highest densities in Hong Kong census divisions (equivalent to our census tracts) reach 2,800 per gross acre.[14]

At 150 persons to the acre, assuming four to a household and reserving one-third of the space for streets and open and public use, it would theoretically be possible to give each household a plot of 20 by 40 [feet]. This does not seem excessively crowded for the most crowded urban housing, and these are the most densely settled tracts in American cities, leaving aside the exceptional cases of New York and Boston.

If we are interested in the relationship between housing and the family, the issue may not be whether housing, in terms of any world or absolute standard, is adequate or crowded: It may be, where does one's housing stand in terms of the standards of the system, and what does falling behind that standard mean? In a society in which quarter-acre lots become the norm, anything less will be correlated with a whole range of measures of poor health, family instability, and social disorganization. We may then say that housing has had such and such an influence upon the family, and in some sense it has. However, it is not housing as such that has an effect, but housing as mediated through a complex culture and the expectations it variously distributes among its people. Thus, it is common to read—even in the writing of sociologists—that the housing of the urban Negro is now worse than it was; while it is, by all measures, better. It may be—by some measures—further *behind* the housing of the urban white than it was; even more seriously, the expectations of the urban Negro are no longer—nor should they be expected to be—the expectations of the European immigrant of 1910 or the Negro migrant of 1930. Yet if this is so, we must expect to find paradoxes and ambiguities if we seek clear and determinate effects of poor and crowded housing, by our current standards, on family life: It will only have such effects if the housing reality is symbolically interpreted to mean degradation.

We can be sure that even the measure of one person per room, lavish as it is by world standards, will soon be inadequate, too. If our society begins to define it as the right of every unmarried 21-year-old to have a separate household—and, at least in the upper middle classes, this definition is spreading—and if our society defines it as the right of every older couple or older single individual to live alone and not

13. Robert C. Schmitt, "Density, Health, and Social Disorganization," *Journal of the American Institute of Planners* 32 (January 1966): 38-40.

14. Schmitt, 1963, op. cit.

with his children, then the proportion of American households overcrowded is much, much more than the 12 percent listed as overcrowded by the one-person-per-room measure in the housing census of 1960. ·

The third point to which we drew attention in Schorr's summary was that our studies of the impact of improved housing on health and family life until now have generally contrasted slum living with minimal decent housing provided by public authorities. While it is understandable that this should be the direction of research, it is also possible that in a society such as ours the differences between these two levels may not be very significant. This is because at the slum level itself we have already eliminated the most damaging consequences of poor housing. As we have pointed out, almost all urban dwellings have running hot and cold water and toilet facilities, are connected with sewers, and are relatively uncrowded. Most are covered by public health services and building regulations that prevent the worst abuses. Under these circumstances, the transition to minimal public housing, attractive as it is to many slum dwellers, who now can be assured of modern working appliances, decent structural conditions, and good maintenance, does not introduce a truly radical change. If, on the other hand, the transition were to the housing typical of well-to-do families, with the more lavish inside and outside space they can acquire, we might find more striking differences in family life.

The final point to which I drew attention in Alvin Schorr's summary was that some of the consequences of poor housing, defined from a middle class perspective, might not seem negative consequences from the point of view of those who lived in such housing. Thus, the crowding of the middle classes may be the coziness of the working classes; sitting around the kitchen may be a deprivation to the middle class but a choice for the working class; even the level of noise which may be a deprivation to one group may be the natural accompaniment of a desirable conviviality to another. We must avoid two dangers: one, the danger of a patronizing assumption that the circumstances under which people live are those that they would wish to have and are chosen rather than forced on them; but second, the easy ascription of the tastes of the investigator and the policymaker to others.

. . . [T]he most difficult part of . . . [the problem has yet to be resolved]—what do we (in terms of national policy objectives) want in family life? Do we have in our society some consensus as to what is the "good" family and what is "positive" family life? If we do not, then we can perhaps describe the consequences of different kinds of housing for family life; but we will find it more difficult to prescribe housing policy on the basis of some common national objectives or some widely held common values as to what kind of family life should be encouraged. A policy which encouraged independent living for the young unmarried adult and the older couple or individual might be interpreted by large sections of the population as a policy that encouraged the breakup of families. Measures that might encourage children's independence (and they could be interpreted in policies for homebuilding and neighborhood and urban design) would be interpreted as encouragement for premature sexual experience by large parts of the population. Measures, on the other hand, that encouraged close family living and allowed fewer opportunities for independent experience by children would be seen by other parts of the population as hampering the free development of the child to maturity.

14. An Alternative to a Density Function Definition of Overcrowding

R. J. GREENFIELD and J. F. LEWIS

The influence of environment on the development of social role performance is a central theme of the behavioral sciences. In practice the social, medical, and administrative sciences often converge in an analysis of the influence of housing as an environmental factor on social groups. In the case of the study of the housing environment, a plethora of studies have been done attempting to relate the degree of inadequacy of housing to such diverse variables as mental retardation,[1] juvenile delinquency,[2] social disorganization, mental illness,[3] school performance,[4] and tuberculosis.[5] Among the most seminal sources in the theoretical literature are the writings of William James and J. S. Plant. Plant was concerned with the relationships between living space, socialization, and personality development. He maintains that "persistent and constant crowding from early life destroys the sense of individuality which without doubt is fostered by opportunities for privacy."[6] James, in setting forth his theory of the development of the empirical self, said, "In its widest possible sense, however, a man's self

Reprinted from *Land Economics* 45 (May 1969): 282-85, by permission of the Regents of the University of Wisconsin and of the authors. Robert J. Greenfield is an assistant professor of sociology at Cal State College, San Bernardino, California; June F. Lewis is a research assistant in the Social Science Research Program of the State of California's Department of Mental Hygiene.

This investigation was supported by Public Health Service Research Grant No. MH-08667; Socio-Behavioral Study Center in Mental Retardation, Pacific State Hospital, Pomona, California, and Public Health Service General Research Support Grant No. 1-S01-SR-05632-01; Pacific State Hospital, Pomona, California.

1. J. Tizard and Jacqueline Grad, *The Mentally Handicapped and Their Families: A Social Survey* (London: Oxford University Press, 1961); Sir Cyril Lodowic Burt, *The Backward Child* (London: University of London Press, 1937); R. H. Allardyce, *Statistical Report on the Qualifying Examination*, Glasgow, Corporation of Glasgow, Education Department, May, 1939.

2. C. Dirksen, *Economic Factors of Delinquency* (Milwaukee, Wis.: The Bruce Publishing Co., 1948), p. 91; Howard Harlan and Jack Wherry, "Delinquency and Housing," *Social Forces* 27, no. 1 (October 1948): 58-61; Robert C. Schmitt, "Density, Delinquency, and Crime in Honolulu," *Sociology and Social Research* 41 (1957): 274-75.

3. Benjamin Pasamanick, ed., *The Epidemiology of Mental Disorders: A Symposium in Celebration of the Centennial of Emil Kraeplin* (Washington, D.C.: American Association for the Advancement of Science, no. 60, 1959); William C. Loring, Jr., "Housing Characteristics and Social Disorganization," *Social Problems* 3, no. 3 (January 1956): 160-68; Jean Downes and Katherine Simon, "Characteristics of Psychoneurotic Patients and Their Families as Revealed in a General Morbidity Study," *Milbank Memorial Fund Quarterly* 32, no. 1 (January 1954): 42-64.

4. Marguerite Keller, "Progress in School of Children in a Sample of Families in the Eastern Health District of Baltimore," *Milbank Memorial Fund Quarterly* 31, no. 4 (October 1953): 391-410; and William S. Jackson, "Housing and Pupil Growth and Development," *Journal Educational Sociology* 28 (May 1955): 370-80.

5. L. A. Stein, "A Study of Respiratory Tuberculosis in Relation to Housing Condition," *British Journal Social Medicine* 1, no. 4 (1950): 143-69.

6. James S. Plant, "Family Living Space and Personality Development," Norman W. Bell and Ezra Vogel, ed., *The Family* (Glencoe, Ill.: Glencoe Free Press, 1960), pp. 510-20.

is the sum total of all that he *can* call his, not only his body and his psychic powers, but his clothes and his house. . . ."[7]

The housing environment, then, is a fruitful variable often used as a logically prior, independent, and relatively stable condition. Unfortunately, no standard definition of "adequate" housing has been developed. Much of the difficulty in cross-validating findings of the relationship between housing and behavior is due to the use of different definitions.

This paper is concerned with that characteristic of inadequate housing designated as "overcrowding." Overcrowding is frequently defined in two ways: as a minimum density function of persons per room, including all rooms in the house, minus bathrooms;[8] or, as number of persons per sleeping room.[9] Generally, the person per room ratio uses 1.5 persons or more per room as evidence of overcrowding. This measure includes all rooms in the housing structure minus attics, hallways, alcoves, pantries, and bathrooms. The person per sleeping room measure defines inadequate sleeping arrangements as an excess of two persons per sleeping chamber.

One distinct advantage of the person per room measure is that it is both objective and readily available. The United States Census of Housing reports the median number of persons per room for each census tract, and enumeration district data are available upon special request. Utilizing density measures, investigators often compute associations between housing characteristics of an individual's census tract and characteristics of individuals. But, in our opinion, these measures of overcrowding fail (1) to take into account an individual's need in his own milieu for private living space; and (2) to differentiate between appropriate age and sex relationships in terms of culturally prescribed sleeping arrangements. Partial explanation for the lack may be the hesitancy of behavioral scientists to make explicit value statements as to what is adequate and appropriate since optimal space allocation for maximal social role performance and age-sex cutting points, differentiating compatible sleeping room partners, have never been empirically established. Accordingly, we have constructed a model for room assignment in the individual housing environment which incorporates the value assumptions on which the housing policies of two governmental agencies are based, and also the values expounded in the writings of James and Plant.

The London County Council's Index for allocating accommodations to families in need of rehousing defines "minimally adequate housing." This statement contains several implicit value assumptions. Age-sex compatibility arrangements for a three-room house containing two bedrooms and sitting room illustrates the types of considerations included in their evaluation scheme. They permit: (a) a married couple and one child, or (b) a married couple and two children of the same sex, or (c) a married couple and three children under six, or (d) a married couple and two children of opposite sex if the younger is less than three, or (e) an adult pair not married—brother and sister, father and daughter, et cetera. An extra room is needed for any additional family member where the difference of age would cause difficulty in sharing a room

7. William James, "The Principles of Psychology," in Robert Maynard Hutchins, ed., *Great Books of Western World: Encyclopaedia Britannica*, vol. 53, 1952, pp. 188-259.

8. C. Dirksen, op. cit.; J. Tizard and Jacqueline Grad, op. cit.; Jean Downes and Katherine Simon, op. cit.; and William S. Jackson, op. cit.

9. Daniel M. Wilner, Rosabelle Price Walkley, Thomas C. Pinkerton, and Matthew Tayback, *The Housing Environment and Family Life* (Baltimore: The Johns Hopkins Press, 1962), pp. 143-74; Jean Downes and Katherine Simon, op. cit.; and Marguerite Keller, op. cit.

with a child of the same sex, i.e., grandmother living with the family; water closet and kitchen in addition to the foregoing.[10]

The occupancy standards set forth by the Housing Assistance Administration, United States Department of Housing and Urban Development contain similar, if not identical, value assumptions.

Number of Bedrooms	*Number of Persons* (Minimum)	(Maximum)
1	1	3
2	2	5
3	4	7
4	6	9
5	8	12

Dwellings are to be assigned so that it will not be necessary for persons of opposite sex, other than husband and wife to occupy the same bedroom, except that if necessary at time of admission two children of opposite sex under four years of age may occupy the same bedroom; and if necessary for continued occupancy two children of opposite sex under six years of age may occupy the same bedroom. At admission, one child under two years of age may be permitted to occupy the parent's bedroom; and if necessary for continued occupancy, one child under four years of age may be permitted to occupy the parent's bedroom. Kitchen, bathrooms, and a living room are required. Dwellings will be assigned so as not to require the use of the living room for sleeping purposes.[11]

The theorists, James and Plant, maintain that overcrowded living conditions from early life through childhood hinder personality development. The individual needs a place within his house to call his own, where he may keep his belongings. Formation of a sense of individuality and of the self-concept are fostered, if not dependent upon, opportunities for privacy.

OVERCROWDING INDEX

In order for our model to encompass both governmental policies and the values incorporated in the literature, we have extended the governmental recommendations for minimum housing conditions by adjusting the age-sex limits for sleeping room partners and by giving consideration to the need of privacy for teen-agers and single adults. The basic value assumptions of the resulting overcrowding index are as follows: (a) a married couple may share a room; (b) no more than two children of the same sex may share a room past the age of 12; (c) no more than two children of the opposite sex may share a room past the age of 3; (d) all others must have individual sleeping chambers; (e) 2 additional rooms, one for the preparation of food and the other for general living purposes, are required, as well as bathrooms.

10. J. Tizard and Jacqueline Grad, op. cit.

11. J. A. Crowl, *Occupancy Standards*, Washington, D.C., Department of Housing and Urban Development, Housing Assistance Administration, July 1966.

METHOD

A random sample of 198 housing units was selected from a larger sample of 2,659 households, representing a 10 percent, economically and geographically stratified, random sample of a community of approximately 30,000 housing units[12] drawn for another purpose. A discussion of the survey rationale and methodology of the source study may be found in Mercer, Dingman, and Tarjan.[13] Each household was rated by number of rooms short using the overcrowding index, the procedure as follows: number of rooms minus bathrooms and the age, sex, and relationship to the head of the household of every person living in the house were used as data. Two rooms were subtracted from the total number of rooms reported, one representing a kitchen and one a living room. The remaining rooms were considered available for use as sleeping quarters. Household members were then assigned to rooms so that husband and wife shared a room; no more than two children of the same sex shared a room past age 12; no more than two children of opposite sex shared a room past age 3; and all others were assigned a room of their own. If rooms available were exhausted before all members were appropriately assigned, a count was kept of the number of rooms short and the household rated accordingly. Each household was then evaluated using the two density function models, persons per sleeping room, and our overcrowding index.

RESULTS

Of the 198 households scored by the overcrowding index, 23 had rooms short, a rate of 11.6 percent overcrowded. In comparison, when the density function model of 1.5 persons per room based on federal census housing data was used, 1 percent of the owner-occupied, and 2 percent of the renter-occupied households were defined as overcrowded. The community average was 1.3 percent of all occupied housing units, a rate approximately one-ninth that perceived using the overcrowding index. Only 16 percent of the cases defined as overcrowded by the overcrowding index were defined as overcrowded using the criterion of 1.5 persons per room.

When the density function was calculated by number of persons per sleeping room, 58 percent of the households defined as overcrowded by the overcrowding index were also defined as overcrowded by the number of persons per sleeping room measure. Thus, the person per sleeping room measure yields rates more similar to the overcrowding index than the census measure.

Like many research instruments, the overcrowding index advocated in this paper is more valid in some situations than others. We have constructed it for use in the analysis of the housing environment of the nuclear family. It is less useful in scoring other types of households. For example, two adults of the same sex in the same housing unit would require four rooms, but there are numerous instances where this arrangement is not realistic nor culturally prescribed. A typical case would be two college students sharing an apartment or sleeping quarters with a fold-away bed. For this reason, the index is most useful when built into an interview schedule that provides for coding the type of occupancy configuration of the household and allows for inapplicable situations.

12. United States Department of Commerce, Bureau of Census, *United States Census of Housing: Final Report,* HC (1)-6, 1960.

13. Jane R. Mercer, Harvey F. Dingman, and George Tarjan, "Involvement, Feedback, and Mutuality: Principles for Conducting Mental Health Research in the Community," *American Journal of Psychiatry* 121, no. 3 (1964): 228-37.

SUMMARY

Although person per room and person per sleeping room measures of overcrowding are objective and readily available, both have certain shortcomings. Neither measure takes into account the literature concerning living space needs for adequate socialization, nor do they recognize age-sex configurations in sleeping room arrangements that are culturally acceptable and culturally unacceptable. In answer to these shortcomings, an instrument has been constructed which incorporates both the value assumptions implicit in governmental policies directing the assignment of housing according to family composition and the literature relative to the impact of living space needs on socialization and personality development. Designed to be used in analysis of individual housing units with other variables, the instrument gives a measure of overcrowding expressed as number of rooms short for each individual housing environment.

15. *Determinism by the Urban Environment*

WILLIAM MICHELSON

There is an unwritten rule that anyone writing on the social influence of architecture must quote Winston Churchill's statement upon reopening the House of Commons after its wartime destruction: "We shape our buildings, and afterwards our buildings shape us."[1] While . . . [elsewhere[2]] I have pursued the question of the extent to which selected social characteristics make a difference in the planning of housing and neighborhoods for cities, at this point I should like to explore the extent to which buildings and neighborhoods shape the lives of the people there *regardless* of their personal characteristics.

The question asked here is how much the physical environment influences who comes together with whom. Assuming for the moment that some people are going to have more friends living in their local neighborhood than others, depending on their personal characteristics, to what extent are the people with whom they spend time determined by the arrangement of physical space?

Planners and architects daily draw site plans which specify where people will live with respect to other people. Do they at the same time specify social groupings of the same people? Can designers, if they so desire, intelligently plan "healthy" social lives for people as part of an overall master plan for an area?

Many previous researchers have responded in the affirmative. William H. Whyte, Jr., after studying one prototype suburb, stated:

> Given a few physical clues about the area you can come close to determining what could be called its flow of "social traffic," and once you have determined this, you may come up with an unsettlingly accurate diagnosis of who is in the gang and who isn't.[3]

The principle involved here has been applied to space within buildings as well. It has been widely adopted by office planners and by others whose job it is to satisfactorily arrange people in large interior spaces, such as offices and barracks. For example, I am writing this chapter from an office on the tenth floor of a modern office building, all of whose interior walls are portable and are rearranged yearly, according to current demands. During the most recent reorganization, my office door ceased to open out onto a busy reception area and instead faces a quiet hallway of offices, of which mine is the last. I now find that I see a great deal of one or two people, of whom

Reprinted from William Michelson, *Man and His Urban Environment* (Reading, Mass.: Addison-Wesley, 1970), pp. 168-90 (edited), by permission of the publisher and author. William Michelson is an associate professor of sociology at The University of Toronto.

1. Quoted by R. K. Merton, "The Social Psychology of Housing," in Wayne Dennis ed., *Current Trends in Social Psychology* (Pittsburgh: University of Pittsburgh Press, 1948), p. 204.

2. Editors' note: William Michelson, *Man and His Urban Environment* (Reading, Mass.: Addison-Wesley, 1970), chaps. 3-7.

3. William H. Whyte, Jr., *The Organization Man* (Garden City, New York: Doubleday, 1957), p. 366.

I previously saw only a moderate amount; but on the other hand, I've almost totally lost contact with other people whom I used to see regularly.

Similarly, a very careful study of army barracks brought out that the installation of partitions at regular intervals within barracks influenced the formation of strong friendship groups within the areas bounded by the partitions while at the same time it lessened the formation of social relationships over a wider area—a pattern characteristic of barracks without partitions.[4] Other studies have been conducted with similar results on school libraries, cafeterias, and residences.[5]

To many white-collar workers and GI's, this phenomenon is at least recognized, if not understood. To assess the extent to which it is valid with respect to the home environment, I shall draw on a number of case studies of appropriate areas.

THE CASE FOR SPATIAL DETERMINISM

After World War II, when faced with an avalanche of returning veterans, many of whom were now married, universities commonly produced extensive planned residential developments. One such university was the Massachusetts Institute of Technology. M.I.T. prepared two adjacent areas for married veterans. One of these, called Westgate, contained very small prefabricated single-family and detached homes grouped around an ordered series of courtyards facing away from a central access road. . . . The other facility at M.I.T., called Westgate West, consisted of a number of buildings which had previously been wartime barracks. These buildings were subdivided so as to provide five apartments on each of two floors within each building; access to each apartment was from an outdoor balcony or porch rather than from any central hallway. . . .

Westgate and Westgate West not only served the residential needs of returning veterans, but they also served as the setting for a significant research project.[6] The researchers wished to determine the extent of environmental influence on the friendship patterns and opinions of the residents of these areas. Different influences work in Westgate and Westgate West. Let us examine them separately.

In Westgate, the factor most clearly influencing friendship formation was the physical distance between the front doors of housing units. The fewer the number of feet separating the front doors, the more likely it was that the people behind these doors would become friends. People were likely to make friends with others in the same residential court, and within each court they were likely to be friendly with those living closest to themselves.

In retrospect, such a finding does not appear at all unlikely. The men and their families all arrived at Westgate independently and from all parts of the world. They had no choice in the selection of dwelling units. It is not surprising that their personal contacts were with those with whom they were most easily put into contact. Nonetheless, one must pay full tribute to the influence that space played in this context.

There were few people without close ties to the others in their court, and the majority of these people represented exceptions to the factors operating to produce

4. Robert R. Blake, Clifton C. Rhead, Bryant Wedge, and Jane S. Monton, "Housing Architecture and Social Interaction," *Sociometry* 19 (1956): 133-39.

5. See the work of Robert Sommer. For example, *Personal Space* (Englewood Cliffs, N.J.: Prentice-Hall, 1969).

6. Leon Festinger, Stanley Schacter, Kurt Back, *Social Pressures in Informal Groups* (Stanford, Cal.: Stanford University Press, 1950). . . .

spatial determinism. They were in part people whose front doors looked out on the access road rather than onto the footpath in the interior of the courts. They were also couples in which the wives worked during the day and hence were not around to participate in the daily social life of the court.

The authors discovered, in addition, that friendship patterns were not the end of the process started by spatial determinism. Friendship patterns had *consequences* in the life of the Westgate community. The opinions that people held on issues that were important locally were a function of the particular clique. Indeed the more inbred the friendships of members of any court were, the less likely it was that any of the residents of that area would have deviant opinions on a given issue. Deviation would occur in any given location only inasmuch as a person was not primarily intimate with the others in that court or to the extent that he held membership in a diversity of groups outside the court.

Another consequence of spatially influenced friendship networks is consumer behavior, according to Whyte. *Fortune* magazine studied the purchase of air conditioners among residents of an area of row housing in Philadelphia, most all of whom were white-collar workers in the same age and salary brackets. While 20 percent of the homes had air conditioning, these homes were not randomly distributed. They were located in tight clusters along the sides of streets, which in this case were the physical equivalent of the courts in Westgate. Rows of housing were conspicuous by either the presence or absence of air conditioners, as well as other types of purchases such as awnings and initialed doors, a consequence of communication and social pressures among neighbors. Whyte argues on the basis of this that younger families sell *each other* on major appliances, eliminating part of the need for salesmen who convince or who need to know about the products they sell.[7]

One of my own students reports a "quiet crescent" in a Toronto suburb in which six of the seven homes now have electric organs. One can only wonder what the odds are that this could have happened by chance alone.

In Westgate West, space was equally deterministic. It was, however, a different unit of distance that led to the formation of friendships in Westgate West. On the basis of physical distance alone, one would expect that people who lived in the "same" apartment on the first and second floor . . . would be approximately equally popular and would be friendly with the people in the corresponding apartments on their respective floors. Furthermore, on the basis of physical distance alone, one would not expect differences in the total number of friendships made by all those on the first floor as opposed to all those on the second floor.

But residents of the second floor could not exit from the building in any direction they wished. They were forced to exit via one of two possible paths—by the stairways at either end of the balcony. These stairways brought residents of the second floor directly by the doors of just certain residents of the first floor. This meant that a *few* of the residents of the first floor were well known to those of the second. Thus the patterning of people's movement, as opposed to the simple separation between their doors, led to distinctions in the friendship patterns of residents of the first and second floors in Westgate West. This kind of distance the researchers call *functional distance*; it is an aspect of what I [have] labeled . . . manipulated distance. . . .

In short, the M.I.T. studies brought out two kinds of distance, physical and functional, which determined friendship patterns and consequent opinions except in unusual circumstances among a large number of families. . . .

7. William H. Whyte, Jr., "The Web of Word of Mouth," *Fortune* 50, no. 5 (November 1954): 140-43, 204-12.

Nonetheless, it should be noted that the proximity created by strategic placement of doors could lead just as easily to feuding as it could to friendship. Such spatial proximity, in short, brought about intense relationships, both positive and negative. . . .

Very simply, then, people can be aware of each other's existence in a number of ways, but specific elements of their physical environment, particularly doors, can be designed and oriented so as to expand people's *awareness* of other people into *contact* with them. . . .

A final study to be mentioned in this context strongly suggests that the patterns created by spatial determinism last over relatively long periods of time. William H. Whyte, Jr., studied the town of Park Forest, Ill. over several years.[8] Located approximately 25 miles south of the center of Chicago, Park Forest is a booming town for the up and coming young executive and the professional, the type who has been dubbed by Whyte "the organization man." Such people are generally mobile, both socially and in their place of residence. Of the 17,600 dwellings in Park Forest, approximately 3,000 changed hands every year at the time Whyte was studying this town.[9] There was thus a continual turnover of residents in Park Forest, and therefore it was possible to study the physical aspects of friendship patterns independent of the particular people who happened to be involved in any single point in time.

Some of the Park Foresters lived in two-story garden apartments grouped into courts. Each court developed through time a particular culture of its own. One would be known for its wild parties; another for its emphasis on churchgoing; a third would be actively involved in community affairs; while in a fourth the residents would be typified by their constant complaining. As Whyte observes this situation, the particular interest of any court seems to remain active regardless of the real fact that many residents are being replaced.

Other Park Foresters live in single-family homes on individual lots. Whyte performed an ingenious experiment on one of the single-family home areas. He mapped out which homes participated in various kinds of get-togethers during the period of January to July 1953. . . . [T]he activities were predominantly among those who lived very close to one another. Whyte then returned and obtained the same information for the same months three years later, in 1956. By that time a great number of the original residents had moved away from Park Forest and had been replaced by other people. Nonetheless, practically the same homes were involved with the same other homes in social activity at this later date. . . . [T]he activities had changed in the three-year period, but whatever force was at work in bringing together the original residents of this area also appeared to be at work after these people had been replaced by others.

There were several factors which helped to bring people together, in Whyte's estimation. First, the presence of children and their need to play with other children close at hand would acquaint parents with other adults who happened to be living nearby. In addition, the siting of driveways and stoops, and the presence and situation of lawns (both factors manipulating proximity) helped to bring people together.

Whyte also makes some acute observations about the social life of people living in different locations on the city or suburban block. People living on corners, he asserts, are much more likely to be isolated from other people than are those who

8. Whyte, *Organization Man*, chap. 25.

9. Ibid., p. 335.

live in the middle of blocks. By the same token, the residents of the middle of the blocks are likely to be inundated with friends and friendships just because of the placement of their houses with respect to other houses. This leads Whyte to some overwhelmingly deterministic conclusions. The gregarious person who by ill fortune winds up living on a corner will end up with extremes of frustration and will figuratively wither on the vine; the odds are great that he will want to move to a more "friendly" neighborhood or town. On the other hand, the man who wishes extremes of privacy, who likes to keep his neighbors at a distance, will be beset with problems from living in the middle of a block; life for him will be a constant war to fend off unwanted but persistent intruders.

The city planner, according to Whyte's conception of determinism, therefore has the power to *determine* the nature of intensity of people's social lives or the problems they face from resisting the ascribed intensity. He can shape on his drafting board the length and shape of city blocks as well as the number of homes that will be found at different locations on that block.[16]

CONDITIONS WHICH MODIFY SPATIAL DETERMINISM

We have thus seen that there have been a number of strong statements which support spatial determinism of who neighbors with whom and with what intensity, backed by painstaking and at times ingenious research. Nonetheless, these findings of spatial determinism are now being strongly challenged.

Gans' study of Levittown, New Jersey, for example, repudiates any notion of strict spatial determinism of friendship patterns particularly that based on positioning of front doors.

> If the front door had been significant, owners of the Cape Cod and ranch houses should have chosen their right-hand and across-the-street neighbors most often; those of the Colonial houses should have chosen their left-hand and across-the-street neighbors. The data show that the Cape Cod owners visited most often across the street, but equally between right- and left-hand neighbors; the ranch owners chose left-hand neighbors twice as often as their other neighbors; and the Colonial owners showed a preference for left-hand neighbors.[11]

Dennis, moreover, while in the process of rejecting the possibility that there are social consequences of physical proximity, adds an ideological rejection. He feels that those who advocate neighborhoods planned with interaction in mind in fact act as agents of social control for the "establishment" of the area. If people interact happily with neighbors, they will not try to change basic aspects of societal structure.[12]

Since examples which negate notions of strict spatial determinism are current, then the question of spatial determinism turns into one of a slightly different nature. *Under what conditions* can we find an element of spatial determinism of human friendship patterns?

There is a wide agreement on one such condition: *homogeneity.* The residents must be socially homogeneous or think themselves so. A look at the people who were the subject of the studies that are cited to show the case *for* spatial determinism will show that within each study they were extremely homogeneous. The students

10. Ibid., chap. 25.

11. Herbert Gans, *The Levittowners* (New York: Random House, 1967), p. 158.

12. Norman Dennis, "The Popularity of the Neighborhood Community Idea," in A. E. Pahl ed., *Readings in Urban Sociology* (London: Pergamon Press, 1968), pp. 74-92.

of Westgate, for example, were all married veterans who were studying engineering at a highly prestigious and intellectually demanding university. Those at Princeton were all single freshmen carefully selected on the basis of past accomplishments.[13] The people whom Kuper studied were largely members of the British working class who badly needed housing following the Second World War.[14] The students at the University of Minnesota were so homogeneous that the researchers were unable to find any significant status differences among them in statistical tests;[15] even the most popular residents of that area were indistinguishable in socioeconomic status from the least popular. The residents of Craftown resemble those of Coventry in many ways.[16] Park Foresters fit still another mold so well that Whyte felt justified in assigning them a common label. Homogeneity, then, is singularly common to the examples which support spatial determinism.

Gans suggests how homogeneity, even when not naturally great, can be *induced* by other circumstances. Above and beyond any apparent homogeneity among home buyers in Levittown, for example, Levitt's salesmen had a clear policy of stressing to prospective buyers that everyone in town was approximately the same respectable class and that everyone got along with everyone else extremely well. It was, they said, a friendly town with friendly people. People also tended to think that Levittown was homogeneous because all the eventual buyers had to pass a searching credit check conducted by the Levitt organization; as a result, they felt secure against the potential presence of people with significantly lower status. Finally, the homes were priced at levels similar enough to induce a feeling of homogeneity among their buyers.[17]

In an analysis based on a Detroit Area Study conducted by the University of Michigan, Tomeh showed that the greater the perceived homogeneity of residents in a neighborhood, the greater was their participation within that neighborhood.[18]

But why does homogeneity serve as a condition which helps bring about spatial determinism of friendship? When people first arrive at a new home, they are unlikely to know many or any of their fellow residents. With whom, then, do they establish cordial relations? If all people within a wide area are felt to resemble one another, then the path of least resistance is to strike friendships with those who are closest.

Residential propinquity throws people together. When doors are relatively close and people have no reason to hurry inside (as from a hallway), people are more likely to have sustained eye contact with each other. When people don't think they have to go further out in an urban area to find compatible friends, casual relationships with neighbors can turn into more deeply held friendship relations.

Contact with those in surrounding homes usually comes about through one or more of several ways. First, children often form friendships with other children which subsequently bring their respective pairs of parents together. Some families actively search for children the same age as theirs as potential playmates. In other homes,

13. F. Duncan Case, Jr., "The Influence of Architecture on Patterns of Social Life," unpublished Junior Paper, Princeton University Department of Sociology, 1967.

14. Leo Kuper, "Blue Print for Living Together," in Leo Kuper et al., *Living in Towns* (London: The Crescent Press, 1953), pp. 1-202.

15. Theodore Caplow and Robert Forman, "Neighborhood Interaction in a Homogeneous Community," *American Sociological Review* 15 (1960), p. 357-66.

16. Merton, op. cit. pp. 188 ff.

17. Gans, *The Levittowners*, pp. 13-14. See also his "Planning and Social Life," *Journal of the American Institute of Planners* 27 (1961): 134-40.

18. Aida K. Tomeh, "Empirical Considerations in the Problem of Social Integration," *Sociological Inquiry* 39 (1969): 65-76.

the children bring home these friends themselves. In any case, given a feeling of homogeneity, possessing children the same age, and having easy access to each other, neighbors strike up friendships. Being in the same stage in the life cycle and, beyond that, sharing similar ideas of childraising, are crucial aspects of suburban homogeneity, even when people differ in, say, religion or ethnicity.

Secondly, when people occupy new residences they often find themselves faced with numerous manual tasks, both inside and outside. Few people have either the knowledge or the tools to undertake all the jobs facing them completely on their own. So they ask their neighbors, who are usually doing much the same thing. Again, when there is a feeling that the neighbor is just as good a man as anyone else in town, casual contact has a chance to turn into something deeper.

Furthermore, people moving into new quarters are generally so hyperactive in organizing their own nests that they really don't have much time to go off and find friends among people other than their immediate neighbors. Once people assume that homogeneity is the case, they allow propinquity to specify their immediate choice of friends, almost by default.

As time goes by, however, many of the factors which permitted homogeneity to serve as a condition of spatial determinism cease to be as all-consuming as they once were. Children find friends in institutions such as schools and clubs. Neighbors cease to be as important once their initial advice and aid in emergency situations has been received. People start to meet many other people once they have time to venture forth from their now organized homes. Thus, once people have become relatively settled in a particular area, the more common it becomes for friendships with neighbors to become only a much smaller part of the total friendships the people hold.

Gans, for example, points out that after two years in Levittown about a third of the residents said that none of the couples they spent most of their time with came from the same street. About another third said that less than half of these couples came from the very same street as they. Only 31 percent of Gans' respondents had the majority of their friendships still located on the same street.[19]

Therefore a second condition is necessary in order that spatial determinism of friendship patterns may work. There must be a strong or continued need for mutual assistance or contact, such as that among newly arrived homeowners (particularly those with children) lacking time to seek out friendships elsewhere.

This is the pattern in areas of new housing (for purchase). It is also the case that Whyte describes in the organization man's suburb, where the turnover of population is constant and where almost the entire town might be expected to have changed hands within a period of say, five years. Once people have remained stationary for a period of time they may be in less need of assistance, their children will have found other friends or indeed grown up, and they are able to perceive differences among themselves, which violates conditions of homogeneity.

Shulman presents evidence from Ottawa and Toronto that mutual assistance among selected neighbors *grows* with the length of time a family has lived in one place.[20] This is not incompatible with the foregoing inasmuch as those acquaintanceships that do ripen through time into deeper friendships should show more emotional and

19. Gans, *The Levittowners*, p. 182.

20. Norman Shulman, "Mutual Aid and Neighboring Patterns: The Lower Town Study," *Anthropologica* 9 (1967): 51-60, and "Urban Environment and Social Interaction," unpublished term paper, University of Toronto, Department of Sociology, August 1968. See also E. Pfeil, "The Pattern of Neighbouring Relations in Dortmund-Nordstadt," in R. E. Pahl, ed., *Readings in Urban Sociology* (London: Pergamon Press, 1968), pp. 136-58.

functional dependence among the participants than those which are more newly formed. Nonetheless, friendship patterns which are a microcosm of the physical layout of a neighborhood are more likely to be a function of newly arrived status, when immediate needs are present. The *intensity* of contact with particular neighbors may be less at the moment than it will be later on, but the *concentration* of contact in the local area will be greater when these needs are current and are not ameliorated either by other means or by people already known.

What about the situation when one family moves in and may need help but whose neighbors are long established? Is this mutual or, in fact, unilateral need? According to Shulman's observations, this is still mutual aid as long as the recipient is capable of reciprocating at some future time if necessary. If he isn't, then neighboring contact, despite the need of one party, is more likely to be minimal.[21]

. . . [T]here is a social class difference in what happens next in the search for friends.

NEIGHBORING IN RENTAL SETTINGS

Two conditions thus have been isolated throughout the literature under which proximity becomes a factor in friendship: the first is homogeneity (or at least perceived homogeneity) and the second is the need for mutual aid.[22]

Several settings are popularly known for the lack of neighboring in their confines. One is public housing, and another is the high-rise apartment. The above two conditions may shed some light on behavior in these settings.

First, public housing under most circumstances fails to meet either condition for intense proximate friendship. Several studies agree that prospective tenants of public housing perceive great differences between themselves and other people living in public housing.

Young and Willmott, for example, found that residents of nearby and similar ghetto areas in London consider each other as members of different cultures when placed side by side in a new suburban housing development.[23] They act *with reference to* other people rather than *with* them.

Hartman discovered that Boston's West Enders thought that residents of public housing were not at all like themselves. He found that the environment of the few who subsequently moved to public housing had greatly improved in *condition*. However, those few still did not like living there because, perhaps not surprisingly, they then found their neighbors uncongenial.[24]

Among a sample of Puerto Ricans, Hollingshead and Rogler discovered much the same distrust of fellow tenants (or *potential* fellow tenants) in public housing.[25] Only

---

21. Ibid.

22. For a theoretical discussion of utopias whose conclusions strongly support my current assertions, see Rosabeth Moss Kanter, "Commitment and Social Organization: A Study of Commitment Mechanisms in Utopian Communities," *American Sociological Review* 33 (1968): 499-517.

23. Michael Young and Peter Willmott, *Family and Kinship in East London* (Baltimore: Pelican Books, 1962 [orig. ed. 1957]), pp. 121 ff.

24. Chester Hartman, "The Limitations of Public Housing: Relocation Choices in a Working-Class Community," *Journal of the American Institute of Planners* 24 (1963): 283-96.

25. August B. Hollingshead and Lloyd Rogler, "Attitudes Toward Slums and Public Housing

7 percent of the husbands in public housing think it is a good place to raise children, while 38 percent in a matched sample of slumdwellers think this of their area.[26] 86 percent of the men and 71 percent of the women dislike their public housing, while only 35 percent of the slumdwellers feel this way.[27] At the root of these feelings in this case is the belief that their neighbors will report any slip they might make with respect to the myriad of rules which badger the resident of public housing in Puerto Rico (and elsewhere).

Thus there is a decided *feeling* of heterogeneity among residents of public housing in many places, even if objective data could prove otherwise.

Moreover, even though there may be turnover in the units, there is little to bring people together for mutual aid. They must not make repairs or alterations to their apartments themselves, and their dependence on the city or other level of government is underscored by a welter of regulations. Indeed it often takes promotion of a conflict situation by professional community organizers to bring out a common goal to serve as the basis for organization.

One exception sheds light on this generalization. Bellin and Kriesberg discovered in Syracuse, New York, that husbandless mothers have three to four times the neighboring in public housing as outside it. These are people who *have* a well defined need for mutual assistance, and there are more likely to be people within the same building who are in the same boat in public than in private housing. Significantly, in the four projects studied an appreciably higher number of husbandless mothers than regular mothers (55 percent to 40 percent) put a value on friendliness in neighbors.[28]

In what are normally termed luxury apartments, proximity appears to have little effect on friendship patterns. Again, perceived homogeneity and a need for mutual aid are lacking. While residents may appear homogeneous with respect to superficial economic criteria, they do not perceive this. They are more likely to be cosmopolitan in their urban contacts, and they seldom have even the common possession of children as interests shared with neighbors. They also pride themselves on their *lack* of dependence on neighbors, often a function of newlywed status or, later in life, economic affluence. They *desire* to be on their own.

Only among young singles or families with children in private rental accommodations have I heard reports in North America of any significant neighboring in high-rise buildings, and this is very much a function of perceived homogeneity and certain mutual needs. Reports from Australia strongly support the necessity of perceived homogeneity and mutual need as a function of active neighborhood interaction in such settings.[29]

---

in Puerto Rico," in Leonard Duhl, ed., *The Urban Condition* (New York: Basic Books, 1963), pp. 229-45.

26. Ibid., p. 239.

27. Ibid., p. 238.

28. Seymour Bellin and Louis Kriesberg, "Informal Social Relations of Fatherless Families: A Study of Public Housing and Social Mobility," paper delivered to the 1965 Annual Meeting of the American Sociological Association, Chicago.

29. A. Stevenson, E. Martin, and J. O'Neill, *High Living: A Study of Family Life in Flats* (Melbourne: Melbourne University Press, 1967).

SUMMARY

In short, spatial proximity often based on the position and outlook of doors may determine interaction patterns, but this normally occurs only under conditions of real or perceived homogeneity in the population and where there is a need for mutual aid, which is in many instances caused by population turnover where residents themselves cope with repairs and like problems. . . .

16. *Fear and the House-as-Haven in the Lower Class*

LEE RAINWATER

Men live in a world which presents them with many threats to their security as well as with opportunities for gratification of their needs. The cultures that men create represent ways of adapting to these threats to security as well as maximizing the opportunities for certain kinds of gratifications. Housing as an element of material culture has as its prime purpose the provision of shelter, which is protection from potentially damaging or unpleasant trauma or other stimuli. The most primitive level of evaluation of housing, therefore, has to do with the question of how adequately it shelters the individuals who abide in it from threats in their environment. Because the house is a refuge from noxious elements in the outside world, it serves people as a locale where they can regroup their energies for interaction with that outside world. There is in our culture a long history of the development of the house as a place of safety from both nonhuman and human threats, a history which culminates in guaranteeing the house, a man's castle, against unreasonable search and seizure. The house becomes the place of maximum exercise of individual autonomy, minimum conformity to the formal and complex rules of public demeanor. The house acquires a sacred character from its complex intertwining with the self and from the symbolic character it has as a representation of the family.[1]

These conceptions of the house are readily generalized to the area around it, to the neighborhood. This fact is most readily perceived in the romanticized views people have about suburban living.[2] The suburb, just as the village or the farm homestead, can be conceptualized as one large protecting and gratifying home. But the same can also be said of the city neighborhood, at least as a potentiality and as a wish, tenuously held in some situations, firmly established in others.[3] Indeed, the physical barriers between inside and outside are not maintained when people talk of their attitudes and desires with respect to housing. Rather, they talk of the outside as an inevitable extension of the inside and of the inside as deeply affected by what goes on immediately outside.

When, as in the middle class, the battle to make the home a safe place has long

Reprinted by permission of *The Journal of The American Institute of Planners*, 32, no. 1 (January 1966): 23-31, and of the author. Lee Rainwater is a professor of sociology at Harvard University.

This paper is based in part on research aided by a grant from the National Institute of Mental Health, Grant No: MH—09189 "Social and Community Problems in Public Housing Areas." Many of the ideas presented stem from discussions with the senior members of the Pruitt-Igoe Research Staff—Alvin W. Gouldner, David J. Pittman, and Jules Henry—and with the research associates and research assistants on the project.

1. Lord Raglan, *The Temple and the House* (London: Routledge & Kegan Paul Limited, 1964).

2. Bennett M. Berger, *Working-Class Suburb* (Berkeley: University of California Press, 1960); and Herbert Gans, "Effect of the Move From the City to Suburb," in Leonard J. Duhl, ed., *The Urban Condition* (New York: Free Press, 1963).

3. Anselm L. Strauss, *Images of the American City* (New York: Free Press, 1961).

been won, the home then has more central to its definition other functions which have to do with self-expression and self-realization. There is an elaboration of both the material culture within the home and of interpersonal relationships in the form of more complex rituals of behavior and more variegated kinds of interaction. Studies of the relationship between social class status and both numbers of friends and acquaint-ances as well as kinds of entertaining in the home indicate that as social status increases the home becomes a locale for a wider range of interactions. Whether the ritualized behavior be the informality of the lower middle-class family room, or the formality of the upper middle-class cocktail party and buffet, the requisite housing standards of the middle class reflect a more complex and varied set of demands on the physical structure and its equipment.

The poverty and cultural milieu of the lower class make the prime concern that of the home as a place of security, and the accomplishment of this goal is generally a very tenuous and incomplete one. (I use the term "lower class" here to refer to the bottom 15 to 20 percent of the population in terms of social status. This is the group characterized by unskilled occupations, a high frequency of unstable work histories, slumdwellings, and the like. I refer to the group of more stable blue-collar workers which in status stands just above this lower class as the "working class" to avoid the awkwardness of terms like "lower lower" and "upper lower" class.) In the established working class there is generally a somewhat greater degree of confidence in the house as providing shelter and security, although the hangovers of concern with a threatening lower-class environment often are still operating in the ways working-class people think about housing.[4]

In Table 16.1, I have summarized the main differences in three orientations toward housing standards that are characteristic of three different consumer groups within the lower and working classes. I will elaborate below on the attitudes of the first group, the slum dwellers, whose primary focus in housing standards seems to be on the house as a shelter from both external and internal threat.

ATTITUDES TOWARD HOUSING

As context for this, however, let us look briefly at some of the characteristics of two working-class groups. These observations come from a series of studies of the working class carried out by Social Research, Inc. over the past 10 years. The studies have involved some 2,000 open-ended conversational interviews with working-class men and women dealing with various life-style areas from childrearing to religion, food habits to furniture preferences. In all of this work, the importance of the home and its location has appeared as a constant theme. These studies, while not based on nationally representative samples, have been carried out in such a way as to represent the geographical range of the country, including such cities as Seattle, Camden, Louis-ville, Chicago, Atlanta, as well as a balanced distribution of central city and suburban dwellers, apartment renters, and homeowners. In these studies, one central focus concerned the feelings working-class people have about their present homes, their

4. In this paper I am pulling together observations from a number of different studies. What I have to say about working-class attitudes toward housing comes primarily from studies of working-class life-style carried out in collaboration with Richard Coleman, Gerald Handel, W. Lloyd Warner, and Burleigh Gardner. What I have to say about lower-class life comes from two more recent studies dealing with family life and family planning in the lower class and a study currently in progress of social life in a large public housing project in St. Louis (being conducted in collaboration with Alvin W. Gouldner and David J. Pittman).

TABLE 16.1 *Variations in Housing Standards within the Lower and Working Classes*

Focus of Housing Standard	Core Consumer Group	Most Pressing Needs in Housing	
		Inside the House	*Outside Environs*
Shelter	Slum dwellers	Enough room Absence of noxious or dangerous elements	Absence of external threats Availability of minimum community services
Expressive elaboration	Traditional working class	Creating a pleasant, cozy home with major conveniences	Availability of a satisfying peer group society and a "respectable enough" neighborhood
All-American affluence	Modern working class	Elaboration of the above along the line of a more complex material culture	Construction of the all-American leisure style in terms of "outdoor living" "Good" community services

plans for changes in housing, their attitudes toward their neighborhoods, and the relation of these to personal and familial goals. In addition, because the interviews were open-ended and conversational, much information of relevance to housing appeared in the context of other discussions because of the importance of housing to so many other areas of living.[5] In our studies and in those of Herbert Gans and others of Boston's West End, we find one type of working-class life-style where families are content with much about their housing—even though it is "below standard" in the eyes of housing professionals—if the housing does provide security against the most blatant of threats.[6] This traditional working class is likely to want to economize on housing in order to have money available to pursue other interests and needs. There will be efforts at the maintenance of the house or apartment, but not much interest in improvement of housing level. Instead there is an effort to create a pleasant

5. These studies are reported in the following unpublished Social Research, Inc. reports: *Prosperity and Changing Working Class Life Style* (1960) and *Urban Working Class Identity and World View* (1965). The following publications are based on this series of studies: Lee Rainwater, Richard P. Coleman, and Gerald Handel, *Workingman's Wife: Her Personality, World and Life Style* (New York: Oceana Publications, 1959); Gerald Handel and Lee Rainwater, "Persistence and Change in Working Class Life Style," and Lee Rainwater and Gerald Handel, "Changing Family Roles in the Working Class," both in Arthur B. Shostak and William Gomberg, *Blue-Collar World* (Englewood Cliffs, N.J.: Prentice-Hall, 1964).

6. Marc Fried, "Grieving for a Lost Home," and Edward J. Ryan, "Personal Identity in an Urban Slum," in Leonard J. Duhl, ed., *The Urban Condition* (New York: Free Press, 1963); and Herbert Gans, *Urban Villagers* (New York: Free Press of Glencoe, Inc., 1962).

and cozy home, where housework can be carried out conveniently. Thus, families in this group tend to acquire a good many of the major appliances, to center their social life in the kitchen, to be relatively unconcerned with adding taste in furnishings to comfort. With respect to the immediate outside world the main emphasis is on a concern with the availability of a satisfying peer group life, with having neighbors who are similar, and with maintaining an easy access back and forth among people who are very well known. There is also a concern that the neighborhood be respectable enough—with respectability defined mainly in the negative, by the absence of "crumbs and bums." An emphasis on comfort and contentment ties together meanings having to do with both the inside and the outside.

Out of the increasing prosperity of the working class has grown a different orientation toward housing on the part of the second group which we can characterize as modern instead of traditional. Here there is a great emphasis on owning one's home rather than enriching a landlord. Along with the acquisition of a home and yard goes an elaboration of the inside of the house in such a way as not only to further develop the idea of a pleasant and cozy home, but also to add new elements with emphasis on having a nicely decorated living room or family room, a home which more closely approximates a standard of all-American affluence. Similarly there is a greater emphasis on maintenance of the yard outside and on the use of the yard as a place where both adults and children can relax and enjoy themselves. With this can come also the development of a more intense pattern of neighborhood socializing. In these suburbs the demand grows for good community services as opposed to simply adequate ones, so that there tends to be greater involvement in the schools than is the case with traditional working-class men and women. One of the dominant themes of the modern working-class life-style is that of having arrived in the mainstream of American life, of no longer being simply "poor-but-honest" workers. It is in the service of this goal that we find these elaborations in the meaning of the house and its environs.

In both working-class groups, as the interior of the home more closely approximates notions of a decent standard, we find a decline in concerns expressed by inhabitants with sources of threat from within and a shift toward concerns about a threatening outside world—a desire to make the neighborhood secure against the incursions of lower-class people who might rob or perpetrate violence of one kind or another.

As we shift our focus from the stable working class to the lower class, the currently popular poor, we find a very different picture. In addition to the large and growing literature, I will draw on data from three studies of this group with which I have been involved. Two studies deal with family attitudes and family planning behavior on the part of lower class, in contrast to working-class couples. In these studies, based on some 450 intensive conversational interviews with men and women living in Chicago, Cincinnati, and Oklahoma City, housing was not a subject of direct inquiry. Nevertheless we gained considerable insight into the ways lower-class people think about their physical and social environment, and their anxieties, goals, and coping mechanisms that operate in connection with their housing arrangements.[7]

The third study, currently on-going, involves a five-year investigation of social and community problems in the Pruitt-Igoe Project of St. Louis. This public housing project consists of 33 11-story buildings near downtown St. Louis. The project was opened in 1954, has 2,762 apartments, of which only some 2,000 are currently occupied, and has as tenants a very high proportion (over 50 percent) of female-headed house-

---

7. Lee Rainwater, *And the Poor Get Children* (Chicago: Quadrangle Books, 1960), and Lee Rainwater, *Family Design: Marital Sexuality, Family Size and Family Planning* (Chicago: Aldine Publishing Co., 1964).

holds on one kind or another of public assistance. Though originally integrated, the project is now all Negro. The project community is plagued by petty crimes, vandalism, much destruction of the physical plant, and a very bad reputation in both the Negro and white communities.[8] For the past 2 years a staff of 10 research assistants has been carrying out participant observation and conversational interviewing among project residents. In order to obtain a comparative focus on problems of living in public housing, we have also interviewed in projects in Chicago (Stateway Gardens), New York (St. Nicholas), and San Francisco (Yerba Buena Plaza and Westside Courts). Many of the concrete examples which follow come from these interviews, since in the course of observation and interviewing with project tenants we have had the opportunity to learn a great deal about both their experiences in the projects and about the private slum housing in which they previously lived. While our interviews in St. Louis provide us with insight into what it is like to live in one of the most disorganized public housing communities in the United States, the interviews in the other cities provide the contrast of much more average public housing experiences.[9] Similarly, the retrospective accounts that respondents in different cities give of their previous private housing experience provides a wide sampling in the slum communities of four different cities.

In the lower class we find a great many very real threats to security, although these threats often do seem to be somewhat exaggerated by lower-class women. The threatening world of the lower class comes to be absorbed into a world view which generalizes the belief that the environment is threatening more than it is rewarding—that rewards reflect the infrequent working of good luck and that danger is endemic.[10] Any close acquaintance with the ongoing life of lower-class people impresses one with their anxious alienation from the larger world, from the middle class to be sure, but from the majority of their peers as well. Lower-class people often seem isolated and to have but tenuous participation in a community of known and valued peers. They are ever aware of the presence of strangers who tend to be seen as potentially dangerous. While they do seek to create a gratifying peer group society, these groups tend to be unstable and readily fragmented. Even the heavy reliance on relatives as the core of a personal community does not do away with the dangers which others may bring. As Walter Miller has perceptively noted, "trouble" is one of the major focal concerns in the lower-class world view.[11] A home to which one could retreat from such an insecure world would be of great value, but our data indicate that for lower-class people such a home is not easy to come by. In part, this is due to the fact that one's own family members themselves often make trouble or bring it into the home, but even more important it is because it seems very difficult to create a home and an immediate environment that actually does shut out danger.[12]

8. Nicholas J. Demerath, "St. Louis Public Housing Study Sets Off Community Development to Meet Social Needs," *Journal of Housing* 19 (October 1962).

9. See, D. M. Wilner *The Housing Environment and Family Life* (Baltimore: Johns Hopkins University Press, 1962).

10. Allison Davis, *Social Class Influences on Learning* (Cambridge: Harvard University Press, 1948).

11. Walter Miller, "Lower Class Culture as a Generating Milieu of Gang Delinquency," in Marvin E. Wolfgang, Leonard Savitz, and Norman Johnson, eds., *The Sociology of Crime and Delinquency* (New York: John Wiley, 1962).

12. Alvin W. Schorr, *Slums and Social Insecurity* (Washington, D.C.: Department of Health, Education and Welfare, 1963).

DANGERS IN THE ENVIRONMENT

From our data it is possible to abstract a great many dangers that have some relation to housing and its location. The location or the immediate environment is as important as the house itself, since lower-class people are aware that life inside is much affected by the life just outside.

In Table 16.2, I have summarized the main kinds of danger which seem to be related to housing one way or another. It is apparent that these dangers have two immediate sources, human and nonhuman, and that the consequences that are feared from these sources usually represent a complex amalgam of physical, interpersonal, and moral damage to the individual and his family. Let us look first at the various sources of danger and then at the overlapping consequences feared from these dangers.

TABLE 16.2   *A Taxonomy of Dangers in the Lower-class Home and Environs: Each of These Can Involve Physical, Interpersonal, and Moral Consequences*

Source of Danger	
Nonhuman	*Human*
Rats and other vermin	Violence to self and possessions
Poisons	Assault
Fire and burning	Fighting and beating
Freezing and Cold	Rape
Poor plumbing	Objects thrown or dropped
Dangerous electrical wiring	Stealing
Trash (broken glass, cans, etc.)	Verbal Hostility, Shaming, Exploitation
Insufficiently protected heights	Own family
Other aspects of poorly designed	Neighbors
or deteriorated structures (e.g.	Caretakers
thin walls)	Outsiders
Cost of dwelling	Attractive alternatives that wean
	oneself or valued others away
	from a stable life

There is nothing unfamiliar about the nonhuman sources of danger. They represent a sad catalog of threats apparent in any journalist's account of slum living.[13] That we become used to the catalog, however, should not obscure the fact that these dangers are very real to many lower-class families. Rats and other vermin are everpresent companions in most big city slums. From the sense of relief which residents in public housing often experience on this score, it is apparent that slumdwellers are not indifferent to the presence of rats in their homes. Poisons may be a danger, sometimes from lead-base paints used on surfaces which slum toddlers may chew. Fires in slum areas are not uncommon, and even in a supposedly well-designed public housing project children may repeatedly burn themselves on uncovered steampipe risers. In slums where the tenant supplies his own heating there is always the possibility of a very cold apartment because of no money, or, indeed, of freezing to death (as we were told by one respondent whose friend fell into an alcoholic sleep without turning on the heater). Insufficiently protected heights, as in one public housing project, may lead to deaths when children fall out windows or adults fall down elevator shafts. Thin walls in the apartment may expose a family to more of its neighbor's goings-on than is comfortable to hear. Finally, the very cost of the dwelling itself

13. Michael Harrington, *The Other America* (New York: Macmillan Co., 1962).

can represent a danger in that it leaves too little money for other things needed to keep body and soul together.

That lower-class people grow up in a world like this and live in it does not mean that they are indifferent to it—nor that its toll is only that of possible physical damage in injury, illness, incapacity, or death. Because these potentialities and events are interpreted and take on symbolic significance, and because lower-class people make some efforts to cope with them, inevitably there are also effects on their interpersonal relationships and on their moral conceptions of themselves and their worlds.

The most obvious human source of danger has to do with violence directed by others against oneself and one's possessions. Lower-class people are concerned with being assaulted, being damaged, being drawn into fights, being beaten, being raped. In public housing projects in particular, it is always possible for juveniles to throw or drop from windows things which can hurt or kill, and if this pattern takes hold it is a constant source of potential danger. Similarly, people may rob anywhere—apartment, laundry room, corridor.

Aside from this kind of direct violence, there is the more pervasive everpresent potentiality for symbolic violence to the self and that which is identified with the self—by verbal hostility, the shaming and exploitation expressed by the others who make up one's world. A source of such violence, shaming, or exploitation may be within one's own family—from children, spouse, siblings, parents—and often is. It seems very likely that crowding tends to encourage such symbolic violence to the self, but certainly crowding is not the only factor since we also find this kind of threat in uncrowded public housing quarters.[14] Most real and immediate to lower-class people, however, seems to be the potentiality for symbolic destructiveness by their neighbors. Lower-class people seem ever on guard toward their neighbors, even ones with whom they become well acquainted and would count as their friends. This suspiciousness is directed often at juveniles and young adults whom older people tend to regard as almost uncontrollable. It is important to note that while one may and does engage in this kind of behavior oneself, this is no guarantee that the individual does not fear and condemn the behavior when engaged in by others. For example, one woman whose family was evicted from a public housing project because her children were troublemakers thought, before she knew that her family was included among the 20 families thus evicted, that the evictions were a good thing because there were too many people around who cause trouble.

Symbolic violence on the part of caretakers (all those whose occupations bring them into contact with lower-class people as purveyors of some private or public service) seems also endemic in slum and public housing areas. Students of the interactions between caretakers and their lower-class clients have suggested that there is a great deal of punitiveness and shaming commonly expressed by the caretakers in an effort to control and direct the activities of their clients.[15]

The defense of the client is generally one of avoidance, or sullenness and feigned stupidity when contact cannot be avoided. As David Caplovitz has shown so well, lower-class people are subjected to considerable exploitation by the commercial services with which they deal, and exploitation for money, sexual favors, and sadistic impulses is not unknown on the part of public servants either.[16]

14. Edward S. Deevey, "The Hare and the Haruspex: A Cautionary Tale," in Eric and Mary Josephson, *Man Alone* (New York: Dell Publishing Co., 1962).

15. A. B. Hollinghead and L. H. Rogler, "Attitudes Toward Slums and Private Housing in Puerto Rico," in Leonard J. Duhl, *The Urban Condition* (New York: Free Press, 1963).

16. David Caplovitz, *The Poor Pay More* (New York: Free Press of Glencoe, 1963).

Finally, outsiders present in two ways the dangers of symbolic violence as well as of physical violence. Using the anonymity of geographical mobility, outsiders may come into slum areas to con and exploit for their own ends, and by virtue of the attitudes they maintain toward slum dwellers or public housing residents they may demean and derogate them. Here we would have to include also the mass media which can and do behave in irresponsibly punitive ways toward people who live in lower-class areas, a fact most dramatically illustrated in the customary treatment of the Pruitt-Igoe Project in St. Louis. From the point of view of the residents, the unusual interest shown in their world by a research team can also fit into this pattern.

Finally, the lower-class person's world contains many attractive alternatives to the pursuit of a stable life. He can fear for himself that he will be caught up in these attractive alternatives and thus damage his life chances, and he may fear even more that those whom he values, particularly in his family, will be seduced away from him. Thus, wives fear their husbands will be attracted to the life outside the family, husbands fear the same of their wives, and parents always fear that their children will somehow turn out badly. Again, the fact that you may yourself be involved in such seductive pursuits does not lessen the fear that these valued others will be won away while your back is turned. In short, both the push and the pull of the human world in which lower-class people live can be seen as a source of danger.

Having looked at the sources of danger, let us look at the consequences which lower-class people fear from these dangers. The physical consequences are fairly obvious in connection with the nonhuman threats and the threats of violence from others. They are real and they are everpresent: One can become the victim of injury, incapacitation, illness, and death from both nonhuman and human sources. Even the physical consequences of the symbolic violence of hostility, shaming, and exploitation, to say nothing of seduction, can be great if they lead one to retaliate in a physical way and in turn be damaged. Similarly there are physical consequences to being caught up in alternatives such as participation in alcohol and drug subcultures.

There are three interrelated interpersonal consequences of living in a world characterized by these human and nonhuman sources of danger. The first relates to the need to form satisfying interpersonal relationships, the second to the need to exercise responsibility as a family member, and the third to the need to formulate an explanation for the unpleasant state of affairs in your world.

The consequences which endanger the need to maintain satisfying interpersonal relations flow primarily from the human sources of danger. That is, to the extent that the world seems made up of dangerous others, at a very basic level the choice of friends carries risks. There is always the possibility that a friend may turn out to be an enemy or that his friends will. The result is a generalized watchfulness and touchiness in interpersonal relationships. Because other individuals represent not only themselves but also their families, the matter is further complicated since interactions with, let us say, neighbors' children, can have repercussions on the relationship with the neighbor. Because there are human agents behind most of the nonhuman dangers, one's relationships with others—family members, neighbors, caretakers—are subject to potential disruptions because of those others' involvement in creating trash, throwing objects, causing fires, or carrying on within thin walls.

With respect to the exercise of responsibility, we find that parents feel they must bring their children safely through childhood in a world which both poses great physical and moral dangers and seeks constantly to seduce them into a way of life which the parent wishes them to avoid. Thus, childrearing becomes an anxious and uncertain process. Two of the most common results are a pervasive repressiveness in child discipline and training, and, when that seems to fail or is no longer possible, a fatalistic abdication of efforts to protect the children. From the child's point of view, because his parents are not able to protect him from many unpleasantnesses and even from himself, he loses faith in them and comes to regard them as persons of relatively little consequence.

The third area of effect on interpersonal relations has to do with the search for causes of the prevalence of threat and violence in their world. We have suggested that to lower-class people the major causes stem from the nature of their own peers. Thus, a great deal of blaming others goes on and reinforces the process of isolation, suspiciousness, and touchiness about blame and shaming. Similarly, landlords and tenants tend to develop patterns of mutual recrimination and blaming, making it very difficult for them to cooperate with each other in doing something about either the human or nonhuman sources of difficulty.

Finally, the consequences for conceptions of the moral order of one's world, of one's self, and of others, are very great. Although lower-class people may not adhere in action to many middle-class values about neatness, cleanliness, order, and proper decorum, it is apparent that they are often aware of their deviance, wishing that their world could be a nicer place, physically and socially. The presence of nonhuman threats conveys in devastating terms a sense that they live in an immoral and uncontrolled world. The physical evidence of trash, poor plumbing and the stink that goes with it, rats and other vermin, deepens their feeling of being moral outcasts. Their physical world is telling them they are inferior and bad just as effectively perhaps as do their human interactions. Their inability to control the depredation of rats, hot steam pipes, balky stoves, and poorly fused electrical circuits tells them that they are failures as autonomous individuals. The physical and social disorder of their world presents a constant temptation to give up or retaliate in kind. And when lower-class people try to do something about some of these dangers, they are generally exposed in their interactions with caretakers and outsiders to further moral punitiveness by being told that their troubles are their own fault.

IMPLICATIONS FOR HOUSING DESIGN

It would be asking too much to insist that design per se can solve or even seriously mitigate these threats. On the other hand, it is obvious that almost all the nonhuman threats can be pretty well done away with where the resources are available to design decent housing for lower-class people. No matter what criticisms are made of public housing projects, there is no doubt that the structures themselves are infinitely preferable to slum housing. In our interviews in public housing projects we have found very few people who complain about design aspects of the insides of their apartments. Though they may not see their apartments as perfect, there is a dramatic drop in anxiety about nonhuman threats within. Similarly, reasonable foresight in the design of other elements can eliminate the threat of falling from windows or into elevator shafts, and can provide adequate outside toilet facilities for children at play. Money and a reasonable exercise of architectural skill go a long way toward providing lower-class families with the really safe place of retreat from the outside world that they desire.

There is no such straightforward design solution to the potentiality of human threat. However, to the extent that lower-class people do have a place they can go that is not so dangerous as the typical slum dwelling, there is at least the gain of a haven. Thus, at the cost perhaps of increased isolation, lower-class people in public housing sometimes place a great deal of value on privacy and on living a quiet life behind the locked doors of their apartments. When the apartment itself seems safe it allows the family to begin to elaborate a home to maximize coziness, comfortable enclosure, and lack of exposure. Where, as in St. Louis, the laundry rooms seem unsafe places, tenants tend to prefer to do their laundry in their homes, sacrificing the possibility of neighborly interactions to gain a greater sense of security of person and property.

Once the home can be seen as a relatively safe place, lower-class men and women express a desire to push out the boundaries of safety further into the larger world. There is the constantly expressed desire for a little bit of outside space that is one's own or at least semiprivate. Buildings that have galleries are much preferred by their tenants to those that have no such immediate access to the outside. Where, as in the New York public housing project we studied, it was possible to lock the outside doors of the buildings at night, tenants felt more secure.

A measured degree of publicness within buildings can also contribute to a greater sense of security. In buildings where there are several families whose doors open onto a common hallway there is a greater sense of the availability of help should trouble come than there is in buildings where only two or three apartments open onto a small hallway in a stairwell. While tenants do not necessarily develop close neighborly relations when more neighbors are available, they can develop a sense of making common cause in dealing with common problems. And they feel less at the mercy of gangs or individuals intent on doing them harm.

As with the most immediate outside, lower-class people express the desire to have their immediate neighborhood or the housing project grounds a more controlled and safe place. In public housing projects, for example, tenants want project police who function efficiently and quickly; they would like some play areas supervised so that children are not allowed to prey on each other; they want to be able to move about freely themselves and at the same time discourage outsiders who might come to exploit.

A real complication is that the very control which these desires imply can seem a threat to the lower-class resident. To the extent that caretakers seem to demand and damn more than they help, this cure to the problem of human threat seems worse than the disease. The crux of the caretaking task in connection with lower-class people is to provide and encourage security and order within the lower-class world without at the same time extracting from it a heavy price in self-esteem, dignity, and autonomy.

17. *Environmental Preferences of Future Housing Consumers*

MARK L. HINSHAW and KATHRYN J. ALLOTT

Although considerable housing research has been conducted in recent years, few attempts have been made to measure and assess the preferences of people toward alternative housing environments. There has been much academic speculation concerning what people might or should desire, but few researchers have attempted systematically to determine what people actually do desire. Consequently, in the planning and design of housing, actual preferences of consumers have largely been ignored. The technique we utilized to determine some of these preferences consisted of eliciting reactions to various existing and hypothetical environmental conditions and assessing the responses.

However, there are several drawbacks to this method of analysis. First, people's preferences are biased a great deal by their current and previous life experiences. Because it is difficult for many people to perceive environments foreign to their personal experiences, lack of exposure to a diversity of alternatives limits particular responses. Second, reactions to existing as well as hypothetical environmental situations are influenced by social and economic realities. One may not be able to react in an unbiased manner to a presented alternative if it appears simply beyond reach. Finally, preferences toward living environments undergo changes concurrent with changes in age, family cycle, income level, and so forth. Preferential responses must therefore be evaluated in light of the particular socioeconomic setting of the respondents.

In our study we limited our scope of concern to responses to various schemata and proposals currently enjoying popularity or at least controversy among many professionals involved in urban policymaking and planning. Because our study deals with one particular point in time, other studies need to be conducted in order to determine trends. We are able, however, to compare some of our results with earlier studies involving similar sample populations.

HYPOTHESIS AND RESEARCH METHODOLOGY

In our study we attempted to measure preferences toward alternative housing environments among people soon to become housing consumers. We were also interested in discovering characteristics of the present housing environments of our sample. We hypothesized that preferences would vary according to factors such as socioeconomic status, stage in the family cycle, educational level, age, occupational expectations, race or ethnicity, and life experiences. Because much attention has recently

Reprinted by permission of the authors and the *Journal of the American Institute of Planners* 38, no. 2 (March 1972): 102-7. Mark L. Hinshaw is an architect and urban planner presently co-authoring a book on community design and involved in research concerning urban communication systems. Kathryn J. Allott, formerly with the Community Action Program in Los Angeles, California and the Health Services Administration in New York City, concentrates on social and environmental urban planning.

been devoted to planning for the particular needs of specific urban social and economic groups, we felt it would be valuable to determine what real preferential differences existed among such groups. In addition, because preferences are influenced by the experiences of living in a given type of housing, we wanted to measure any attitudinal differences among inhabitants of various housing environments. We therefore limited our hypotheses to three: first, that preferences vary significantly according to race or ethnicity; second, that preferences vary significantly according to existing family income level; and third, that they vary significantly according to type of housing presently occupied. We made an effort to keep educational level, geographic location, age, and general occupational expectations relatively constant.

A precoded questionnaire was developed that could be self-administered by the sample population. Seventeen questions concerning basic background information were followed by thirty-three questions dealing with future housing preferences. Results were compiled and cross-tabulated.

SAMPLE

Since a large amount of literature has recently concentrated upon social changes affecting the attitudes and behavior of youth (Keniston, 1968; Reich, 1971; Roszak, 1969), we wanted to actually measure their preferences to see to what extent the literature reflects reality. For our study, a sample population was drawn from undergraduate students enrolled at Hunter College of the City University of New York. Because of its "open admissions" and free tuition policies, this institution offered a unique opportunity to survey youths with a wide variety of racial, ethnic, and economic backgrounds.

Our sample consisted of 204 freshmen students enrolled in introductory courses in political science and urban studies. Almost all students were 18 to 19 years old, were living in the homes of their parents, and resided in New York City. Table 17.1 compares the racial-ethnic breakdown of our sample with 1970 population estimates for New York City as a whole.

Most students in our sample came from families consisting of three to six members, the most frequently reported size being four. Blacks and Puerto Ricans tended only slightly more than others to come from larger families, and a relatively large proportion of Irish respondents came from families of seven or more.

Table 17.2 illustrates income levels of our sample population. It can be seen that blacks, Puerto Ricans, and to some extent Italians tended to come from lower-income groups, while no Jewish, Irish, or white Protestants reported family incomes of less than $6,000 per year.

TABLE 17.1   *Percentage Breakdown According to Race-Ethnicity*

	Black	Puerto Rican	Italian	Jewish	Irish	White Protestant	Other*	Did not answer
Sample population	20	12	10	20	8	7	14	9
New York City†	20	11	14	20	9	9	17	. . .

*Cubans, Orientals, Germans, Polish, Jamaicans, and white Catholics, none of which by themselves made up more than 2 percent of the total.

†Figures for New York City from Institute for Public Administration, *Agenda for a City* (Beverly Hills: Sage Publications, 1970), pp. 521-23.

TABLE 17.2 *Percentage of Respondents within Each Income Level According to Race-Ethnicity*

Family income per year	Black	Puerto Rican	Italian	Jewish	Irish	White Protestant
Under 2,000	5	5	. . .	. . .	. . .	. . .
2,000-3,999	6	5	. . .	. . .	. . .	. . .
4,000-5,999	8	23	10	. . .	. . .	. . .
6,000-7,999	18	14	5	7	6	7
8,000-9,999	13	14	24	19	17	13
10,000-14,999	15	9	48	33	50	47
15,000-19,999	15	5	. . .	21	22	13
Over 20,000	3	. . .	10	17	. . .	13
Did not answer	17	25	3	3	5	7

Approximately 40 percent of our sample lived in units that were owned by their families, the remainder coming from rental units. Figures for 1965 for New York City as a whole show 24 percent owner-occupied and 76 percent rental units (New York City, 1965). Ninety percent of our respondents reported that the head of their household was either a blue-collar or service worker. When asked what kind of job they desired in the future, all mentioned job types in the white-collar category.

We found that 75 percent of our sample had lived in New York City all of their lives, while most of the remainder had lived in only one other state. Twenty percent of the black respondents came originally from a southern state; 50 percent of the Puerto Rican respondents came from Puerto Rico. Measurement of intracity mobility revealed that more than half of the blacks and more than one-third of the Puerto Ricans had moved three times or more, while other respondents reported very few moves.

We attempted to determine the relative extent of satisfaction with present neighborhood environments. Respondents were asked to describe their neighborhoods with respect to friendliness of neighbors, safety, attractiveness, locational advantages, suitability for rearing children, and so forth. By averaging responses we were able to arrive at a rough indication of neighborhood satisfaction. Tables 17.3, 17.4, and 17.5 illustrate our findings.

TABLE 17.3 *Percentage of Each Racial-Ethnic Group Satisfied with Present Neighborhood*

Black	Puerto Rican	Italian	Jewish	Irish	White Protestant
45	45	55	70	55	60

TABLE 17.4 *Percentage of Each Income Group Satisfied with Present Neighborhood*

Under $2,000	$2,000 -3,999	$4,000 -5,999	$6,000 -7,999	$8,000 -9,999	$10,000 -14,999	$15,000 -19,999	Over 20,000
40	35	45	50	60	60	60	80

TABLE 17.5 *Percentage of Respondents Living in Different Types of Housing Satisfied with Present Neighborhood*

Single-family	Two-family	Garden apartment	3-5 stories	5-10 stories	10-15 stories	Over 15 stories
65	60	65	40	50	55	40

Most Puerto Ricans, blacks, respondents from income groups below $6,000 per year, and occupants of buildings over three stories tended to be dissatisfied with their neighborhoods. Italians, Irish, white Protestants, and those with family incomes between $6,000 and $8,000 per year were about evenly split. A much larger proportion of Jewish respondents, income groups above $8,000 per year, and occupants of single-family, two-family, and garden apartments appeared to be satisfied with their present neighborhoods. This finding differs from research conducted recently by Yancey (1971), who found that "there was no relationship between social status and neighborhood satisfaction" (p. 7). It must be pointed out, however, that our questions dealt only with selected aspects of the general neighborhood and not with the physical condition or spatial arrangement of the housing itself.

ENVIRONMENTAL PREFERENCES

We limited our questions involving preferences primarily to issues which people concerned with urban planning and design presently view as important. We developed questions to measure neighborhood preferences under the assumption that "neighborhood" is both a useful and a usable concept and that its meaning would be understood by respondents in our sample population. Most of our questions were framed in terms of what the respondents felt they might prefer 10 years hence rather than in the present or near future. This was done to suggest to the respondents that they structure their responses in light of the probability of having a family and its attendant responsibilities by that time.

Respondents were first asked to indicate where they would most like to live: in a central city, suburban area, small town or rural location. There was a strong preference for suburban living among all ethnic groups with the exception of the Irish, the largest percentage of whom (44 percent) expressed a desire to live in a small town environment. We also found a relatively large proportion of Jewish and white Protestant respondents (24 percent in each case) preferring a rural location. Virtually none of the white Protestants wanted to live in a central-city location. With respect to income, the desire to move to suburban areas was equally intense among all groups but particularly high within the two highest income levels. In addition, in contrast to other income groups these two groups had a high percentage of people desiring to move to rural locations.

Next we asked our respondents where they would like to live with respect to their relatives. We were trying to determine the degree of familial dependence or attachment that might affect locational choice or housing arrangement. Almost no one indicated that they would want their relatives to live in their homes. Moreover, few people in any classification indicated a preference even for wanting to live in the same neighborhoods with close relatives. In light of the fact that most of our sample came from working-class backgrounds, our findings do not seem to bear out previous research by Gans (1962) and Keller (1968) that working-class people seem to have strong family ties and a tendency to live within an extended family context. Our results may be indicative of a generational change in attitude. These youth might feel that the opportunities for social mobility offered by their college education diminish their dependence upon family ties (at least in terms of physical proximity) for economic and emotional support.

We then asked our respondents how many children they preferred to have. The most frequent choice was 2 (33 percent), followed by 3 (25 percent). Sixteen percent of the sample preferred 4 children, and about 6 percent preferred each of the following: none, 1, 5, and 6. Black, Puerto Rican, and Italian respondents were only slightly more disposed toward having three or four children than were other groups. If this preference for a nuclear family continues, the next several decades will see a change in the demand for housing.

An overwhelming percentage of our sample preferred to own single-family detached homes. Our findings thus seem to verify other research. It is significant that research conducted a decade ago arrived at precisely the same percentage having such a desire (75 percent) (Meyerson, Terrett, and Wheaton, 1962, p. 85; Foote et al., 1960, pp. 134-166; Michelson, 1966). The only exceptions we found were a small percentage of Italians who seemed to prefer two-family units, and a small group of people presently living in three- to five-story buildings and two-family units who seemed to desire the same. In addition, a relatively large percentage (25 percent) of respondents living in high-rise buildings appeared to prefer high-rise living. However, in all other cases there was no indication of a preference for anything but a single-family detached home.

Respondents were then asked to rate by importance a series of factors they might consider in choosing a neighborhood in which to live. Tables 17.6, 17.7, and 17.8 show the results. Percentage responses were averaged and converted to a five-point scale indicating the relative importance of each factor in the following manner:

1. Very unimportant
2. Moderately unimportant
3. Important

4. Very important
5. Critically important

The point ratings have been averaged to arrive at readings for the sample as a whole.

TABLE 17.6 *Importance of Selected Variables in Neighborhood Choice According to Race-Ethnicity*

	Black	Puerto Rican	Italian	Jewish	Irish	White Protestant	Average
Safe place to live	5	5	5	5	5	4	4.8
Attractiveness	4	3	4	3	3	3	3.3
Near transit stops	4	4	4	4	3	3	3.7
Friendly neighbors	3	4	4	3	4	3	3.5
Near good schools	5	4	5	5	4	3	4.3
Shops close by	4	3	2	3	2	2	2.7
Parks close by	3	4	3	4	3	3	3.3
Near entertainment	2	2	2	2	2	2	2.0
Near place of work	2	2	2	3	3	3	2.5

It can be seen from the tables that, overall, safety and proximity to good schools are considered to be critically important. Attractiveness, proximity to transit stops, friendliness of neighbors, and access to parks are considered important or very important as decisional factors, while proximity to shops, entertainment, and place of work are considered relatively unimportant.

Comparing these findings with other research, we find both similarities and differences. First, in only a few studies involving an evaluation of neighborhood characteristics was the aspect of safety even mentioned. We found it to be of prime importance. Next, although in Keller's study of the urban neighborhood (1968, p. 112) attractiveness was rated high, in our study it was found to be considered only "important." Access to transit stops, also found by Keller to be a highly rated factor (p. 112), was considered

TABLE 17.7   *Importance of Selected Variables in Neighborhood Choice According to Income Level*

	Under 2,000	2,000 to 3,999	4,000 to 5,999	6,000 to 7,999	8,000 to 9,999	10,000 to 14,999	15,000 to 19,999	Over 20,000	Average
Safe place to live	4	5	5	5	5	5	5	4	4.8
Attractiveness	3	4	4	3	3	3	3	4	3.3
Near transit stops	3	3	4	4	4	3	4	3	3.5
Friendly neighbors	3	3	4	4	4	3	3	3	3.3
Near good schools	5	5	5	5	4	4	3	3	4.3
Shops close by	4	3	3	3	3	2	2	2	2.8
Parks close by	2	2	3	4	4	4	4	2	3.3
Near entertainment	2	2	2	2	2	2	2	3	2.1
Near place of work	2	3	2	2	2	2	3	3	2.4

TABLE 17.8   *Importance of Selected Variables in Neighborhood Choice According to Type of Housing Presently Occupied*

	Single-family	Two-family	Garden apt.	3-5 story	5-10 story	10-15 story	15+ story	Average
Safe place to live	5	5	5	4	5	5	5	4.8
Attractiveness	3	4	3	3	4	3	3	3.3
Near transit stops	3	3	3	4	4	4	4	3.6
Friendly neighbors	4	4	3	4	3	3	2	3.3
Near good schools	4	4	4	4	5	5	5	4.4
Shops close by	2	3	2	2	3	4	4	2.9
Parks close by	3	3	3	3	4	4	4	3.5
Near entertainment	2	1	1	2	2	2	2	1.7
Near place of work	2	2	3	2	2	3	2	2.3

to be of only moderately high importance. Next, both Gans (1962) and Keller (1968) indicated that ethnic minorities and working-class people display a great need for friendly neighbors; in our study this need did not appear to be so important. Studies by Michelson (1966) and Keller (1968) found that access to schools ranked extremely high, and on this matter our findings concur.

Black, Italian, and Jewish respondents as well as low-income respondents rated the importance of proximity to good schools very high, while white Protestants and very high income respondents considered this only "important." This difference might be due to a situation in which white Protestants and the higher income groups have ready access to schools of high quality (possibly private) and therefore do not consider proximity to good schools as important as other groups do.

Close proximity to shops seemed to be fairly important to blacks, respondents in the lower-income groups, and people living in high-rise buildings. Since most of our respondents were of working-class background, this appears to confirm Keller's finding that working-class people have a high preference for living close to shops.

Proximity to parks seemed pretty important to people of moderate income as well as occupants of high-rise buildings. Perhaps people who live in high-rise buildings consider parks to be important because they provide recreational amenities which people in other forms of housing have more individual access to.

Living close to place of work was not preferred by anyone. Because most of our respondents were not part of the regular labor force and had not experienced the ordeal of peak-hour commuting, however, this response may be misleading.

The respondents were presented with a hypothetical choice between having a small house with individual private outdoor space or a larger house with outdoor space shared by several other families (sometimes referred to as "cluster housing"). All overwhelmingly preferred the first choice. The proportional desire for the first choice increased along with income. The only groups to be even mildly inclined toward the second option were the Italian and Jewish respondents. Our results, then, seem to support the thesis of William Michelson:

> Many architects and other vocal intellectuals fail to understand why so many people clamor for postage-stamp-sized lots. "Why don't people give up their measley scraps of land, they ask, and combine them into a piece of public open space really worth having." The answer seems beguilingly simple: public open space, no matter how large, does not allow activities that people want to perform on private space, no matter how small [1970, p. 146].

We next measured the willingness of our respondents to live in a neighborhood containing different races and income levels. Italian, Jewish, and Irish people were less inclined than other groups to want to live in a racially mixed area, with the exception of those in the $4,000 to $6,000 income category (mostly comprised of blacks and Puerto Ricans). This may reflect a separatist feeling within these ethnic-income groups.

In contrast to other groups, Italians by and large seemed reluctant to live in communities with mixed incomes. Within the income groups, only those at the $10,000 to $15,000 income level appeared reluctant to live in a mixed income area. People in this income group may feel that their parents have worked hard for a home in a nice neighborhood and that other people will simply have to do the same. Finally, respondents from single-family homes seemed most hesitant about living within mixed income areas.

Next, the concept of New Town living was explained, and the respondents were asked to express their preference for location and general size. Seventy-five percent of our sample accepted the concept of the New Town as a housing possibility. Most totally rejected the South and the Midwest as places to live. The Northeast was by far the most popular with all groups. The western states were considered somewhat desirable by respondents from lower middle income and very high income families and by both Jewish and white Protestant respondents. The West Coast was popular among the highest income groups and Jewish respondents but was markedly rejected by blacks, Puerto Ricans, and Irish.

There seemed to be a general tendency to want to live in New Towns with less than 50,000 inhabitants. Blacks and Puerto Ricans tended to want to live in towns of less than 25,000, with some even reporting a preference for towns smaller than 10,000. Jewish respondents seemed to want to live either in towns of less than 10,000 or in cities of 100,000 to 500,000. Other ethnic groups showed no preference for a particular population size.

We next wanted to see what the interest would be in terms of a "New Town in Town." We used Battery Park City, being built in Lower Manhattan, as an example. People in income groups below $8,000 a year responded favorably to the idea of living in such a development; those above this level did not. Blacks and Puerto Ricans generally responded favorably, while other ethnic groups rejected it. The responses to this question may be unreliable because of the sketchy description that we gave of Battery Park City. (It might have sounded to some like a more fully equipped "housing project.")

We also tried to determine if our respondents might be willing to live in communal housing arrangements in the future. Only 10 percent replied that they would (40 percent were unsure). The greatest percentage of negative responses came from Irish, Italians, and blacks, as well as from middle income groups. Perhaps this is an indication that communes are considered to be only a fad; young people are not thinking of them as a serious housing choice.

The respondents were asked whether they would consider living in Co-op City, the massive high-rise housing development in the Bronx which has been both lauded and criticized by urban housing professionals. Forty-three percent reported that they definitely would not want to live there, another 33 percent said "maybe" and only 12 percent said that they would want to live there. (Twelve percent had not heard of Co-op City.) Surprisingly, Irish, Jewish, and Italian respondents almost unanimously rejected this housing arrangement, although the development is populated primarily by these three groups.

The respondents were asked where they would like to live in relation to where they worked. The choices of living in the same building containing the place of work and of living within 20 minutes walking time were both rejected by all groups. The only group which seemed even moderately disposed toward living close to work were white Protestants. This seems to confirm research by Michelson (1966) showing that few people are interested in living near their place of work.

Another question asked what facilities a neighborhood should contain. Most groups seemed to prefer a neighborhood that was comprised either of residences, small stores, and schools or of this combination plus places of employment. This response appears to contradict our previous findings concerning the workplace. Such an inconsistency might indicate that ideas about living in relationship to work have not been well thought out. Generally, however, our results on this subject coincide with those of Gans (1962), who found that the working class showed a preference for mixed land uses.

Finally, when asked about what types of housing they would like to have in their future neighborhood, the largest proportion of respondents chose single-family homes only. This preference was particularly strong among Irish, Italians, and people from moderate income groups. People in lower income groups generally indicated that it made no difference what types of housing their neighborhood contained.

IMPLICATIONS FOR HOUSING POLICY

Our study indicates that the desire for single-family home ownership is ubiquitous and not in the process of radically changing. This society is therefore faced with the choice of either providing access to this type of housing or of mounting a massive attack on "the American Dream" that is propagated in all forms of media and reinforced by cultural norms involving measures of status and self-worth as well as by traditional antiurban attitudes.

Although our findings do not show a total rejection of the central city, they indicate a general desire to move to outlying areas, particularly suburban areas, but in some cases to small towns or rural environments. (This preference may merely reflect the desire to move to less congested areas as an alternative to life in New York City.) Although suburbia has received tremendous criticism from social scientists and popular writers, it is nevertheless still considered a most desirable environment by the bulk of the population. If our results are indicative, the movement to suburban areas promises to continue through the next few decades, bringing with it an increased demand for housing, community facilities, and high quality services.

Our respondents came mainly from moderate income "working-class" families; yet they appear to be "middle class" in many of their attitudes and aspirations. Possibly we are witnessing an upward social mobility on the part of this generation of urban working-class people, caused in part by expanded educational opportunities. It appears that these people will follow the example of others before them and leave the city as soon as possible, leaving behind only those in lower socioeconomic groups.

Several of our results have implications for the design of housing-related open space. Planners have been trying to satisfy the desire for single-family unit living and to economize on land by proposing cluster housing with common open space. We found, however, that people may be willing to trade off interior space in return for private exterior space. (In a housing development in southwest Washington, D.C., each of the town houses is provided with a semiprivate rear yard in addition to commonly held open areas [Hall, 1966].) Any arrangement of housing and allocation of space must take into account the values of different consumers.

Finally, with the American New Town movement evolving from its gestation period, the generally favorable response we received to this form of urban development seems promising. However, our findings also suggest that concepts concerning optimum population sizes may have to be reevaluated. In addition, measures must certainly be taken now to guarantee equal access to housing and employment in these new centers.

Housing designers and planners must begin to seriously examine consumer needs and preferences rather than simply relying upon accepted formulas and intuitive approaches to housing design. More careful consideration of the aspirations and values of different socioeconomic, racial, and ethnic groups is necessary. Consumers of housing are hardly one monolithic entity, as some would have us believe.

CONCLUSIONS

The results of the study confirmed our first two hypotheses, in that definite differences in preferences toward housing were found among respondents from various ethnic, racial, and income groupings. There were several notable exceptions, however: the almost universal desirability of detached single-family homes, the critical importance of safe neighborhoods, and the generally negative attitude toward communal living arrangements. The third hypothesis was not entirely borne out as few significant contrasts were found among those living in different housing types.

It appears from our sampling that there has been no major shift in housing preferences. The recent attention given to the "counterculture" and its contemplation of alternative life styles is not reflected by our respondents, who seem to prefer housing environments similar to current patterns.

REFERENCES

Foote, N., J. Abu-Lughod, M. M. Foley, and L. Winnick (1960) *Housing Choices and Housing Constraints* (New York: McGraw-Hill).
Gans, H. J. (1962) *The Urban Villagers* (New York: Free Press).

Hall, E. T. (1966) *The Hidden Dimension* (Garden City, N.Y.: Doubleday).

Keller, S. (1968) *The Urban Neighborhood* (New York: Random House).

Keniston, K. (1968) *Young Radicals* (New York: Harcourt, Brace & World).

Meyerson, M., B. Terrett, and W. Wheaton (1962) *Housing, People and Cities* (New York: McGraw-Hill).

Michelson, W. (1966) "An Empirical Analysis of Urban Environmental Preferences," *Journal of the American Institute of Planners* 32 (November): 355-60.

Michelson, W. (1970) *Man and His Urban Environment: A Sociological Analysis* (Reading, Mass.: Addison-Wesley).

Reich, C. (1970) *The Greening of America* (New York: Random House).

Roszak, T. (1969) *The Making of a Counterculture: Reflections on the Technocratic Society and its Youthful Opposition* (Garden City, N.Y.: Doubleday).

United States, Bureau of the Census (1965) *Census Housing and Vacancy Survey, New York City.*

Whyte, W. H. (1970) *The Last Landscape* (Garden City, N. Y.: Doubleday).

Yancey, W. L. (1971) "Architecture, Interaction and Social Control" *Environment and Behavior* (March): 7.

"HOLD ON, NOW — LET'S NOT BE VISIONARY."

III
Economics

Economic analysis of the housing market is the study of the mechanisms for allocating scarce resources to the production of housing and its distribution to consumers. The principal allocative mechanism in the American economy is price, which is a reflection of the demand for and supply of the commodity. The quantity of housing *demanded* depends on its price, the prices of other goods, consumer preferences for housing relative to other goods, consumer income, and the number of consumers (determined by population growth, migration, and the rate of household formation); the quantity *supplied* depends on the price of housing, the costs of production, and the profits to be earned by producing alternative goods and services.

Traditionally the quantity of housing demanded and supplied has been discussed in terms of dwelling units available for habitation. This, however, is an inadequate description of the commodity for sale or rent in the housing market. It is more accurate to think of housing as a bundle of attributes, such as: square feet of living space, number of rooms, structure type (single-family detached, town houses, garden-style apartments, multifamily apartment buildings, accessibility to various activities (employment, recreation, shopping), the quality and quantity of various public and quasi-public services (schools, police, garbage collection, fire protection), type of neighbors (class, life-style, race, education), and neighborhood environment and design. The various attributes of the housing bundle are discussed in greater detail in the general introduction to this book. This introduction is concerned with the residential location choices of households, the functioning of the housing market, and racial segregation.

INTRAMETROPOLITAN RESIDENTIAL LOCATION

The single most important factor in household residential location decisions is employment location. In a study of the moving behavior of San Francisco households from 1955 to 1965, James Brown and John Kain (1970) found that changes in job location led to changes in residential location. The study area was divided into 291 zones. Households whose heads experienced job changes that resulted in job locations in a new zone were nearly three times as likely to change their residence location as were households whose heads experienced no job change.

In the last 50 years employment growth in the suburban rings of metropolitan areas has exceeded that in central cities, and, in fact, many central cities have experienced absolute declines in certain types of employment, especially in manufacturing. This suburbanization of industry has been motivated by technological changes, most importantly changes in transportation and production techniques (Schafer and Pynoos, 1971): the truck and the automobile gave the manufacturing firm more locational freedom; the assembly line and linear materials processing necessitated single-story plants that covered areas larger than were available in the central city. Work forces followed their firms to suburbia, and employees simultaneously received increases in income, which increased their demand for residential space. Federal housing and highway legislation associated with the postwar suburbanization phenomenon was as much a reflection of these forces as a cause of suburbanization. Industries that have not tended to move to the suburbs for the most part (1) require face-to-face communication, or (2) produce unstandardized products, or (3) because of small firm size are dependent on other entities for services. Any central city expansion in employment will be in the area of these selected services, most importantly office activities.

The tie between jobs and residences provides the basis for a model of residential choice based on the transportation costs of the various trips a household makes. Since the dominant trip usually is the journey to work, the model states that households trade the costs of housing consumption against the costs of making a longer journey to work; that is, for a given workplace and bundle of housing attributes, households try to minimize their total location costs and not simply the monetary and time costs of the work trip. In fact, a household that wants a relatively large bundle of housing attributes may generate net savings by incurring increased work trip costs, because that level of housing consumption may be cheaper at the farther distance. Differences in the price of any given bundle of attributes are due principally to spatial variations in land values, which tend to be higher near employment centers.

John Kain (Chap. 18) has empirically tested the accuracy of the journey-to-work model. His data on the locations of high, medium, and low income households in relation to their workplaces indicate that higher income households locate farther from the same workplace than do lower income ones. Since the demand for housing attributes increases with rising income, higher income households consume a larger bundle of housing attributes than do lower income households; consequently, the higher income households will be able to reap net savings from longer work trips. Lower income households that consume a smaller bundle of housing attributes would find that the journey-to-work costs outweigh the housing cost savings they might reap by locating farther from their jobs. The particular bundle of housing attributes that a household demands is not solely a function of its income; it also depends on such factors as family size, the amount of nonhousing goods consumed, and the household's preference for housing relative to these other goods. Professor Kain's study also analyzes the residential locations of families of different size, sex, and housing preference.

HOUSING MARKET DYNAMICS

Location decisions of households are only one aspect of the urban housing market. Several other attributes of the dwelling unit and its environment are important parts of the housing bundle and are related to location decisions. Edgar Olsen (Chap. 19) has applied conventional economic theory of competitive markets to their provision. Perfect competition is a simplifying assumption that economists use to analyze complex problems. One common set of conditions for perfect competition is: buyers and sellers of a good are numerous; the good is homogeneous; resources are mobile; buyers and sellers have full knowledge of the market; there is no collusion. In essence many firms must produce homogeneous products, and the purchases of any one consumer must not be large enough to have an appreciable effect on prices. The number of firms is sufficient if no single firm can foresee the effects of its activities on prices.

In order to view the housing market as one in which a homogeneous commodity is bought and sold, an unobservable theoretical entity called housing service is introduced. Each dwelling (or housing) unit is presumed to yield some quantity of this good during each time period. It is assumed to be the only thing in a dwelling unit to which consumers attach value [Olsen, Chap. 19].

The theory built on these concepts leads to several testable hypotheses. For example, several government housing programs have assumed that tearing down occupied substandard dwellings will reduce the number of families that occupy units in this category. Since these clearance programs do not raise the incomes of the former occupants or decrease the prices they must pay, these households are unable to increase their housing consumption. In a competitive market it will become profitable for some housing owners to allow their units to depreciate in housing services to satisfy this demand. (For a more complete discussion see Olsen, Chap. 19.) One geographical area would be upgraded only to see substandard housing reappear in another area of the same metropolis.

Although a competitive theory of the housing market produces useful insights, it is important to be aware of some of its inadequacies. The more important shortcomings are the following.

1. Heterogeneity and indivisibility. Housing, in fact, is a heterogeneous commodity with a multitude of attributes (such as number of rooms and type of heating system), and probably not one of these attributes or any combination of attributes associated with any dwelling unit is divisible into homogeneous units, even of a theoretical nature. This heterogeneity has led many analysts to divide the housing market into several submarkets along such dimensions as race, tenure, structure type, and lot size, and to analyze each submarket and interactions between various submarkets.

2. Externalities. The amount of housing services that flow from any given dwelling unit depends on the nature of the neighborhood, available public services, and other factors external to the unit. In a perfectly competitive economy such externalities are assumed to be nonexistent.

3. Nonmarket goods. Certain attributes of the housing bundle are not provided through a market system. The principal examples are such public services as police and fire protection, education, solid waste collection and disposal, and street maintenance.

4. Durability. Dwelling units once constructed last a long time, and major alterations are neither easy nor inexpensive to make.

5. Immobility. The stock of housing attributes is not mobile and is nonuniformly distributed within the metropolitan area. This spatial distribution of the commodity has already been described.

The process by which the standing stock undergoes alterations is a crucial part of housing market analysis, because new construction increases the stock of dwelling units by less than 2 percent annually. Although several efforts have been made to analyze *filtering*, the term often used to describe this process of market adjustment, the major result seems to have been increased confusion. Filtering is the process by which a dwelling unit and its environment come to offer more or less housing measured in terms of either quantity or quality; the unit filters up (down) if the bundle of housing attributes increases (decreases). Most of the confusion stems from two sources: efforts to measure the bundle of housing attributes, and attempts to define the process as one that leads to socially desired results.

The first difficulty stems from the heterogeneity and indivisibility of the product; so operational definitions of the process have concentrated on prices, leading to a debate over what price should be the standard for comparison (Grigsby, 1963). Ernest Fisher and Louis Winnick use the dwelling unit's price relative to the prices of all other units in the stock as the standard: if the price of a unit moves up (down) relative to the prices of all other units, the unit is said to have filtered up (down). Ira Lowry compares the price of the dwelling unit to the prices of all other goods: if the price of a dwelling unit moves up (down) more than prices generally, it has filtered up (down). These two definitions can produce different results. For example, under the Fisher-Winnick definition a dwelling unit could filter up while the housing prices generally were experiencing sufficient declines relative to the prices of other goods so that Lowry would conclude that the same unit had filtered down. Such ambiguity can be removed only as more accurate measures of housing attributes are developed.

The second source of confusion has been an insistence that filtering is a process that produces better quality housing for low income families. On the contrary, filtering as a market process provides no guarantee of a socially desirable result. Consider a division of the housing market into two submarkets—high quality and low quality housing; then the demand for units in either submarket is a function of consumer characteristics (e.g., income, family size, education, and age). If the demand for low quality (substandard) housing increases relative to that for high quality units, entrepreneurs will find it profitable to allow some currently high quality units to filter into the low quality submarket. The rents on these units will decline, but so will maintenance expenditures. Ira Lowry (1960) summarized the process as follows.

> The price decline necessary to bring a dwelling unit within reach of an income group lower than that of the original tenants also results in a policy of undermaintenance. Rapid deterioration of the housing stock would be the cost to the community of rapid depreciation in the price of existing housing.

In 1971 the nation became acutely aware that many residential structures in central cities were being abandoned, a phenomenon that can be explained in terms of the filtering process. The definition of housing used throughout this introduction is a key to understanding abandonment: as a household becomes better off it will demand a higher quality environment as well as structure. It is important to note that improvement in a household's welfare need not lead to a change in its welfare relative to all other households; it need only have more resources today than it had yesterday. That real per capita disposable personal income has increased every year since 1958 is evidence that household well-being has improved in this sense.

The standing stock of dwellings, their spatial distribution, and spatial variations in quality of neighborhood and public services limit the ability of certain portions of metropolitan areas to satisfy demands for higher quality. As a result the demand for dwelling units in central cities has declined, and part of the stock has filtered off the market. Some of the structures may be sound by Census Bureau or HUD criteria, but they cannot provide the bundle of attributes now demanded because of their undesirable surroundings and the low quality of public services.

Abandonment is largely a demand phenomenon, and, in fact, the changing character of housing demand has been so great that in the last decade many central cities experienced net declines in population. If a city experiences such a decline it should expect its stock of dwelling units to dwindle and the number of abandoned dwelling units to increase. Chicago, Cleveland, Detroit, Hoboken, Philadelphia, and St. Louis contain sizable numbers of abandoned dwelling units (Linten, Mields and Costen, Inc., 1971; Center for Community Change and National Urban League, 1971; Lilley and Clark, 1972). According to the 1970 *Census of Population*, the population in each of these cities (defined in terms of their 1960 boundaries) declined during the 1960s (U.S. Bureau of the Census, 1971). St. Louis, believed to be the city experiencing the highest degree of abandonment, has also undergone one of the largest percentage declines in population.

One of the most pressing problems in housing policy is the elimination of substandard living conditions (Muth, Chap. 20). The basic question of why such conditions exist has elicited several traditional explanations (Muth, Chap. 20; Schafer, 1971).

1. As a building ages, style and technological obsolescence cause a decline in demand for the building. This decline leads to a price (or rental) reduction. As the price falls, the returns on investment fall, investment declines, and the building deteriorates. Older residents move to new neighborhoods more suited to their tastes in quality and are replaced by lower income households.

2. As the automobile reduced the demand for inner-city residential land and increased the demand for fringe locations, the price of the first declined and the price of the second increased. The decline in inner-city land prices led to reduced maintenance in an effort to maintain returns on investments, thereby fostering deterioration in housing quality.

3. Certain external effects (increased dirt or noise from neighboring industrial or retail firms) caused a decline in demand for the affected areas, again causing price declines, undermaintenance, and quality deterioration.

4. Otto Davis and Andrew Whinston (1966) have described the housing market's prisoner's dilemma as one in which it is profitable for an owner to improve or maintain his building's quality only if all the buildings in the neighborhood are improved. If he proceeds alone he will have a large investment and little increase in rents—his rate of return will fall. His neighbors who have done nothing will have no change in their investment but a small increase in rents—a small rise in return. In the open market the obstacles to coordinating improvement of all the buildings lead to an increase in the supply of low quality housing.

5. Higher interest rates or the unavailability of loans on property in declining areas increases the number of low quality housing units—the capital market imperfections theory.

6. Federal income tax laws on depreciation of residential real estate create incentives for retaining a building in the housing supply beyond its useful life. Depreciation fosters turnovers that extend the building's existence without compensating renovation. As a result, the number of low quality housing units is increased.

7. Local property taxes discourage renovation and maintenance, thus expanding the supply of low quality housing.

More likely the principal explanation for the existence of substandard housing is the inequality of income distribution in the United States. Many consumers' incomes are simply too low to purchase standard housing in the existing market; so fundamental and widespread improvement of housing conditions will occur only through a redistribution of income in favor of households that now occupy substandard housing.

This redistribution can be in the form of income subsidies to households (demand side) or subsidies to producers of housing (supply side) or both. On balance, the demand-side approach would seem preferable because it is more direct, less expensive, possibly less bureaucratic, and more in keeping with the principle of consumer sovereignty. Additional issues need to be considered in recommending an income strategy, chiefly the responsiveness of the supply to an increase in demand. If, as some contend, the housing industry is inefficient, then it might not be able to produce sufficient units fast enough to prevent price increases that would offset the purchasing power of the additional income.

RACIAL SEGREGATION

Some members of society are restricted to certain residential areas on racial or ethnic grounds. As a result, minority households are forced to select their place of residence without reference to employment location (Kain, Chap. 21). The residential choices of blacks have been largely confined to central locations within metropolitan areas; consequently they have been and are being denied access to suburban jobs, a growing segment of the American job market.

Self-segregation, low incomes, and racial discrimination have been cited to explain the concentration of blacks, but it is generally believed that the first two theories are insufficient to explain the degree and continuity of racial segregation in the housing market. One theory of discrimination views the housing market as composed of two submarkets, one for blacks and one for whites. At the boundary the price for an equal amount of housing service is higher for blacks than for whites—a situation maintained through collusive behavior and a high level of market organization. Most empirical research indicates that this price markup is about 5 percent and may be as high as 10 percent in the single-family owner submarket (Rapkin, Chap. 25; Muth, 1969; Ridker and Henning, 1967).

In addition to the price and employment effects, housing market discrimination restricts the housing choices (e.g., structure type and tenure) available by confining blacks to certain geographical areas. Thus black households have less opportunity to accumulate assets through home purchase and value appreciation, a major part of the savings habits of whites over the last 20 years. Since a large proportion of blacks have low incomes, housing market segregation creates disproportionately large concentrations of poor blacks (compared to the distribution of poor whites), which may be a psychologically and sociologically disorganizing force in the lives of the residents and may produce de facto school segregation.

The supply of housing in the nonwhite submarket is expanded at the periphery of the ghetto (Downs, Chap. 22), but there is no clear understanding of what occurs when a neighborhood undergoes transition from one racial submarket to another. One popular belief is that property prices fall when nonwhites enter white neighborhoods. In a careful study of this issue Luigi Laurenti (1960) analyzed actual sales transactions between 1949 and 1955 in seven cities and compared the price movements in neighborhoods undergoing racial transition with those in stable control neighborhoods. The data showed no pattern consistent with the common fear of price decline on racial invasion. When the price effects of nonwhite entry are discussed in the framework of supply and demand within the various housing submarkets and interaction among the submarkets, Laurenti's results, although different from prevailing beliefs, are not surprising.

Very little has been written on the way neighborhoods change their racial composition or the mechanics used to enforce racial discrimination in the housing market. It is known that some real estate agents, known as "blockbusters," earn unreasonably large profits by spreading a fear of black invasion, thus causing panic sales in white neighborhoods at below market prices, and then buying the properties and selling them to blacks at prices above the market value (Rothman, Chap. 23). In addition, some real estate brokers refuse to show houses to white buyers in any area that has so much as one nonwhite resident. The operations of real estate brokers undoubtedly constitute one of the mechanisms for enforcing racial discrimination in the housing market (Helper, 1969).

Existing residents of local jurisdictions often view zoning as a mechanism to exclude from their communities certain uses and persons deemed "undesirable" (not only blacks but also apartment dwellers and the lower and working class generally) (National Commission on Urban Problems, Chap. 24). If the minimum lot sizes established in a zoning ordinance are larger than those that would occur in a market unconstrained by zoning, the effect of the ordinance will be to reduce the supply of land available for development, thus increasing the price of lots and the price of housing above what the "undesirables" can afford. However, the mechanisms that enforce racial segregation in the housing market are more complex than and extend beyond such legal constraints as zoning.

REFERENCES

Brown, H. James, and Kain, John F. "The Moving Behavior of San Francisco Households." *The NBER Urban Simulation Model, Volume II. Supporting Empirical Studies*, ed. John F. Kain. Report to the Department of Housing and Urban Development, December 1970: Chap. 6.

Davis, Otto, and Whinston, Andrew. "The Economics of Urban Renewal." *Urban Renewal: The Record and the Controversy*, ed. James Q. Wilson. Cambridge, Mass.: M.I.T. Press, 1966.

Grigsby, W. G. *Housing Markets and Public Policy*. Philadelphia: University of Pennsylvania Press, 1963.

Helper, Rose. *Racial Policies and Practices of Real Estate Brokers*. Minneapolis: University of Minnesota Press, 1969.

Laurenti, Luigi. *Property Values and Race*. Berkeley: University of California Press, 1960.

Lilley, William, III, and Clark, Timothy B. "Federal Programs Spur Abandonment of Housing in Major Cities." *National Journal* (January 1, 1972): 26-33.

Linten, Mields and Costen, Inc. *A Study of the Problems of Abandoned Housing*. Report to the U.S. Department of Housing and Urban Development, November 1971.

Lowry, Ira. "Filtering and Housing Standards: A Conceptual Analysis." *Land Economics* 36 (November 1960): 362-70.

Muth, Richard. *Cities and Housing*. Chicago: University of Chicago Press, 1969.

Ridker, Ronald G., and Henning, John A. "The Determinants of Residential Property Values with Special Reference to Air Pollution." *Review of Economics and Statistics* 59 (May 1967): 246-57.

Schafer, Robert. "Slum Formation, Race and an Income Strategy." *Journal of the American Institute of Planners* 37 (September 1971): 347-54.

Schafer, Robert, and Pynoos, Jon. "An Introduction to Urban Theory." *Journal of Urban Law* 48 (1971): 361-408.

The Center for Community Change and the National Urban League. *The National Survey of Housing Abandonment*. April 1971.

U.S. Bureau of the Census. *U.S. Census of Population: 1970. Number of Inhabitants*. Final Report PC (1). Washington, D.C.: Government Printing Office, 1971; Tables 6-8.

18. The Journey-to-Work as a Determinant of Residential Location

JOHN F. KAIN

This study presents some empirical evidence on the manner in which transportation costs influence the household's choice of a residential location. It also describes a residential location model which considers the problem of residential location somewhat differently than have models previously presented before the Regional Science Association or available elsewhere in the literature.[1] This model makes it easier to understand the empirical tests offered in this paper. The central hypothesis, suggested by this and similar models, and from which I will obtain a number of subhypotheses, is that households substitute journey-to-work expenditures for site expenditures. This substitution depends primarily on household preferences for low-density as opposed to high-density residential services.

THE MODEL

The model deals with the locational choice of a single household. It is assumed that this household's transportation costs increase monotonically with the distance it resides from its workplace. The reasonableness of this assumption may be seen if the household's monthly expenditure for transportation is broken into its component parts. These outlays may be expressed as the sum of the costs of the journey-to-work, of obtaining residentially oriented services within the immediate residential area—i.e., groceries, elementary school, etc.—and of obtaining other services available only outside the residential area. Included are both dollar expenditures for transportation and dollar valuations of time spent in travel. Unless the distinction is explicitly made, transportation costs here will refer to these combined costs.

The household's monthly transportation costs, T, may then be expressed as the sum of its expenditures for those services obtainable within the residential area, t_r, those which vary with the residence's distance from its workplace, $t(w_1)$, $t(w_2)$, $t(w_3)$, . . . , $t(w_n)$, and those which vary with the residence's distance from other points outside the residential area, $t(o_1)$, $t(o_2)$, . . . , $t(o_m)$, where n equals the number of workplace destinations for the household and m equals the number of other destinations outside the residential area. The household's total monthly transportation cost for each residential site may thus be expressed:

Reprinted from *Papers and Proceedings of The Regional Science Association* 9 (1962): 137-60 (edited), by permission of the publisher and author. John F. Kain is a professor of economics at Harvard University.

1. See, for example, Edgar M. Hoover and Raymond Vernon, *Anatomy of a Metropolis* (Cambridge, Mass.: Harvard University Press, 1959); William Alonso, "A Theory of the Urban Land Market," *Papers and Proceedings of the Regional Science Association* (Philadelphia, Pa., 1960); John D. Herbert and Benjamin H. Stevens, "A Model for the Distribution of Residential Activity in Urban Areas," *Journal of Regional Science* 2, no. 2 (Fall 1960); Lowdon Wingo, Jr., *Transportation and Urban Land* (Washington, D.C.: 1961); Resources for the Future, Inc.; Ira South Lowry, "Residential Location in Urban Areas," unpublished Ph.D. dissertation, Department of Economics, University of California, 1960.

$$T = t_r + t(w_1) + t(w_2) + t(w_3) + \ldots + t(w_n) + t(o_1) + \ldots + t(o_m) \tag{1}$$

For our purposes it may be assumed that t_r is invariant with the household's choice of location. The level of t_r may vary with the kind of residential area the household chooses, i.e., low density versus high density, but there is no reason to expect a significant variation between areas of similar characteristics.

If the costs of residentially provided services—retailing, medical services, schools, etc.,—may be considered as invariant, the accuracy of our assumption depends on the relative weights placed on the trips to workplaces and on the trips made to other points outside the residential area. It is my contention that for the majority of urban households the sum of transportation costs to points other than work or within the immediate residential area is small, and that the costs to any one other single point are almost always trivial. The journey-to-work costs, by way of contrast, are large and significant. Thus if these contentions are correct, no serious violence is done in most instances by considering only journey-to-work costs in our residential location model.

It is not at all difficult, however, to find exceptions to the rule I have proposed. For example, there is the large and probably increasing population of households without a member in the labor force. For such households the worktrip term in our equation is equal to zero. For these households the location of other destinations may be of considerable importance. Many retired people desire to live near their children and grandchildren. Single persons and young married couples may make frequent trips to major cultural and recreational centers. The monthly travel costs of these households may vary significantly with the distance from these centers.

Despite these exceptions to the rule, it is my belief that the assumption used in this model is approximately correct for a very large proportion of the population, perhaps for as many as 80 or 90 percent of households having a member in the labor force.

The data . . . illustrate the importance of the journey-to-work in the household's travel budget.[2] Nearly half of all trips from home are made to work. Of the remainder, some portion of social recreation trips and personal business trips are made to other destinations outside the residential area. The destinations of these trips may be spatially quite separated. Furthermore, many will be to points nearby the workplace, since a large proportion of cultural, recreational, personal business, and other destinations are likely to be nearby employment concentrations. . . .

The Market for Residential Space

It is also assumed that the household is an atomistic competitor in the market for residential space. That is, it is assumed that there is a market for residential space and that the price a single household must pay per unit for space is given. Residential space is defined as the urban land utilized by the household in its residential activities. For single-family dwelling units this would be closely approximated by lot size. For multiple units it would be some proportion of the total amount of land utilized by the structure. (I am glossing over, at this point, a number of complex relationships among the lot layout, overall neighborhood densities, and the substitutability between capital and land and residential space.)

I am assuming that the price the household must pay per unit of residential space varies from one location to another. This price is an economic rent which landlords can obtain from households for more accessible sites. The rents on more accessible

2. Robert E. Schmidt and M. Earl Campbell, *Highway Traffic Estimation* (The Eno Foundation for Highway Traffic Control, 1956), table II-4.

sites arise because of households' collective efforts to economize on transportation expenditures. For this model, I am assuming that these rents, which I will refer to hereafter as location rents, decrease with distance from the household's workplace. Specifically, I am assuming that the unit price the household must pay per unit of residential space *of a stated quality and amenity* decreases monotonically from its workplace. Of course, the magnitude of the location rents is significant only when there is a significant concentration of employment.

It is possible, as Alonso, Wingo, and others have done, to obtain this second result using only the first assumption.[3] Since I am unable to improve on their solutions in what I consider to be the most important directions, i.e., adequate and explicit treatment of time, depreciation, obsolescence, quality, and other problems of housing-market dynamics, I am instead offering this as a provisional hypothesis. Common sense, the excellent theoretical works cited above, and fragmentary evidence support its acceptance; arrayed against it is the opinion of a number of knowledgeable Institutional Real Estate Economists and other urban researchers. A really adequate empirical verification or rejection of the hypothesis has yet to be accomplished or even attempted.

The Household's Consumption of Residential Space

It is further assumed that residential space is not an inferior good and that the household chooses its residential location and its consumption of residential space by maximizing the utility obtainable from a given income. Thus, the quantity of residential space the household will consume depends on the household's income, the price of residential space, and its preference for residential space. These, along with the assumptions about location rents and journey-to-work costs, are the basic components of the model presented in this paper. It will be seen that if the household's workplace and transportation costs per mile are taken as given its residential location can be expressed as a function of its space consumption. Similarly, then, the household's residential location may be expressed as a function of its income, space preference, and the price of residential space. These are the nature of the hypotheses to be tested later in this paper. First, however, it is necessary to spell out the implications of our key assumptions more completely. These key assumptions are: (1) the assumption that the household's transportation cost function increases with distance from its workplace, (2) the existence of a market for residential space in which the price per unit a household must pay for residential space of a given quality decreases with distance from its workplace, (3) a fixed workplace, (4) utility maximization on the part of households, and (5) the assumption that residential space is not an inferior good.

The Location Rent Function

The location rent function or schedule of location rents—i.e., the function which describes the decrease in location rents with distance from the household's workplace—describes the savings per unit of residential space the household may achieve by moving farther from its place of employment. What is of interest to the household in making a locational choice, however, is not this amount but its total savings at various distances. If rents per unit of space decrease as the household moves further from its workplace, the absolute amount of the savings possible through longer journeys-to-work depend on the amount of residential space consumed by the household. Since the household's space consumption has not been specified, the decline in total location rents with distance is described by a family of isospace curves similar to the economist's isoquants. Each curve in Figure 18.1, for example, illustrates the decline in location rents with distance for a given quantity of residential space. From

3. Alonso, op. cit.; Wingo, op. cit.

Figure 18.1, it can be seen that the absolute dollar savings obtainable by a longer journey-to-work clearly become larger as more residential space is consumed. By way of contrast, the household's transportation costs per mile, $t(d)$, are invariant with the amount of residential space consumed.

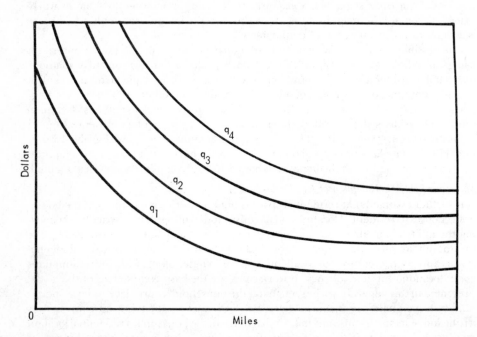

It is, however, the combined outlay for transportation costs and location rents that ought to concern the household in selecting a residential site. Since a given dollar spent for transportation or rents has the same disutility, the household's utility maximization combination of the two is included in the set which minimizes the combined outlay for rents and transportation costs for each quantity of residential space.

*Marginal Savings in Location Rents
and Marginal Increases in Transportation Costs*

The characteristics of the solution we seek can perhaps be more easily understood if we use functions which describe the changes in each of these substitutable costs with the household's distance from its workplace. Figure 18.2 illustrates the incremental savings in location rents obtained by commuting an additional unit of distance for each quantity of space. The area under each curve is equal to the total location rents that would have to be paid by the household if it were to reside at its workplace and if it were to consume the quantity of space specified by a given curve. Since this function describes the manner in which total location rents decrease, the area under each curve to the right of oi equals the total monthly location rents that must be paid to locate at i for each quantity of residential space. For example, the area under q_3 to the right of oi is paid for the quantity of residential space represented by the curve q_3.

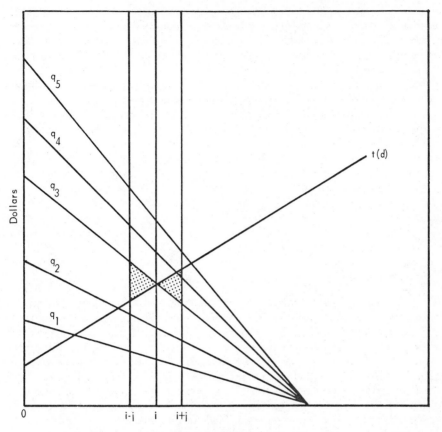

Miles from Workplace

FIGURE 18.2 *Marginal Location Rent and Transportation Cost Functions* [Redrawn with the permission of the author.]

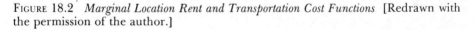

Marginal Transportation Costs

The incremental increase in transportation costs can be illustrated in the same manner. The line $t(d)$ in Figure 18.2 shows the incremental increase in transportation costs with distance. The area under the curve $t(d)$ to the left of *oi* is equal to the expenditures for the journey-to-work required to reside at *oi*.

The minimum cost location for each quantity of residential space is given by the intersection of the marginal cost of transportation function and each of the marginal location rent savings functions. For q_3, the minimum cost location is at *oi*. For larger quantities of residential space, the minimum cost location is farther from the household's workplace; for smaller quantities, nearer.

This solution can be easily verified by using Figure 18.2. Locations farther from the workplace, say *oi+j*, add the area between *oi* and *oi+j* under the $t(d)$ curve to the household's transportation costs. Its savings in location rents amount only to the area under q_3 between *oi* and *oi+j*. Thus, the household's total location costs for the quantity of residential space q_3 are increased by the shaded area under $t(d)$ between *oi* and *oi+j*.

Similarly, if the household locates closer to its workplace, say *oi−j*, it reduces its transportation costs by the area under the *t(d)* curve between *oi−j* and *oi*. At the same time, it increases its rental expenditures by the quantity under the q_3 curve between *oi−j* and *oi*. Thus, the household consuming the quantity of residential space q_3 and residing at *oi−j* rather than *oi*, makes uneconomic expenditures for location which equal the shaded area between *oi−j* and *oi*.

Thus, we have obtained those locations which minimize the household's locational costs for each quantity of residential space. In addition, we have obtained the household's required expenditures for each quantity of residential space. This is all the information we must have to enable us to obtain a unique locational solution for each household.

Total location costs divided by the quantity of residential space is the price the household must pay per unit for residential space. With this price information the household's locational solution is straightforward. Given the price of all other goods and services, the household's preference for residential space, its preference for all other goods and services, and its income, the household's consumption of residential space is uniquely determined. Knowing its consumption of residential space, we have uniquely determined its residential location.

EMPIRICAL TESTING

At the beginning of this paper I stated that the purpose of this model is to provide some testable hypotheses. The variables employed in the model are location rents at each site and transportation costs per mile, from which we obtained a third variable, the price of residential space; incomes; preferences for residential space; and preferences for all other goods and services. I have already stated my willingness to specify the shape of the location rent function. Money costs of transportation are fairly straightforward. The valuation of time is complex. In the empirical tests presented here, it is assumed that similar groups of households place the same valuation on time per mile. Preferences are always difficult to quantify, but we can offer some propositions about the relative space preferences of various classes of households. It is reasonable to assume, for example, that larger households, such as those with children, have higher preferences for space than do smaller households. The income variable is theoretically simple.

Data for the empirical tests presented here were obtained from the origin and destination study conducted in 1953 by the Detroit Area Traffic Study. The data consist of the origins and destinations of worktrips, information on the characteristics of the workers making these trips, information on the characteristics of the households to which the tripmaker belonged, and certain attributes of the trips themselves, for a stratified random sample of approximately 40,000 Detroit households.

THE LOCATION RENT SURFACE FOR DETROIT

For empirical testing of the residential location model, the Detroit metropolitan area is divided into concentric distance rings, numbered from 1 to 6 from the center outward, around the central business district. It is assumed that location rents for a unit of residential space of a given quality and amenity successively decrease from ring to ring outward from the center, with rents very high near the center and very low near the outer circumference. The rate of decrease is assumed to be substantial in the inner rings and very slight in the outer. The surface in the outer rings is assumed to be quite flat, and to decrease only moderately with distance from the central business district.

These assumptions about the shape of the location rent surface are obtained from our premises about the determinants of the surface. It was stated earlier that location rents result from the competition among many workers for residential space near the same workplace or other workplaces nearby. The number of workers employed within each ring may be thought of as representing the number of demanders for residential space within the ring, and the number of acres within the ring as the supply of residential space. Ring 1 includes only 0.2 percent of the available space within the study area, but provides jobs for nearly 11 percent of Detroit's workers. Detroit has 60 percent of its employment located within 6 miles of the central business district, but only 10 percent of the land within the study area is located there. This indicates a substantial excess-demand situation for space within the close-in rings, and a substantial lessening of demand for space in outer rings. The relatively low level of demand for urban use in the outermost ring is indicated by the large proportion of land which is not in urban use within the ring. A full 68 percent of the available land in Ring 6 is vacant; if land devoted to streets and alleys were subtracted, this figure would be even higher.

Thus it is reasonable to expect that location rents in the central business district and nearby would be very high, while in Ring 6 they would be very low. The high level of demand for residential space in inner rings is indicated by the high employment —and, for that matter, high residential densities. The low level of demand for residential space in outer rings is indicated by low employment densities, low residential densities, and the large quantities of vacant land within these rings.

THE ANALYSIS

If workers stratified according to income, sex, race, family size, residential density, or structure type have a common workplace—i.e., the same location rent function—the residential location model would predict different distributions of residence around this workplace for each of these groups. At the same time the model would predict differences in the residential distribution of the same class of workers if the workers are employed at different workplaces, i.e., have different location rent functions.

For the empirical tests presented in this section, the residential distributions of different classes of workers employed within the same ring, having by assumption the same location rent function, are compared with distributions expected a priori from the model. In addition, the residential distributions of workers belonging to the same class but employed at different workplaces—i.e., having different location rent functions—are compared for consistency with the expected relationships.

The first finding which supports the appropriateness of the residential location model is a well-known one. The journey-to-work is predominantly from outer residential rings to inner workplace rings. Furthermore, the proportion of a ring's workers residing within the same or adjacent rings increases with the workplace ring's distance from the central business district.

In terms of the model described above, equal transportation costs are incurred with movement in any direction. Reductions in location rents are to be found only away from the central business district. As a result, the minimization of location rents is always obtained in the direction of the periphery regardless of the household's space consumption. Second, as the schedule of location rents flattens out toward the rural-urban fringe, the space consumption of households becomes less of a constraint and higher proportions of the workplaces' employees live nearby. The model's only justification for a journey-to-work is to reduce the household's total expenditures for location rents. If, as hypothesized for Rings 5 and 6, total location rents do not decrease as the household makes a longer journey-to-work, or decrease only slightly, there is little incentive to make a journey-to-work, at least to economize on rents. Thus, the direction of the journey-to-work is from residences in outer rings where location rents are low to workplaces in inner rings; and larger proportions of worktrips are made to nearby rings as the workplace's distance from the central business district increases.

The distribution of elapsed time spent in reaching work, by workers employed in each ring, also exhibits the expected relationship. The fewest short trips are made by workers employed in the central business district. Few workers employed in Rings 5 and 6 make long trips. For example, 49 percent of workers employed in the central business district make trips more than one-half hour long. By way of contrast, only 17 percent of those employed in Ring 6, where the location rent surface is hypothesized as being nearly horizontal from the workplace, make trips of longer than a half-hour. The proportion is even lower for Ring 5—14 percent. If it is assumed that the distribution of travel time valuations, money costs of transportation, incomes, space preferences, etc., are similar for each workplace ring, the model would predict longer journeys-to-work by workers employed in inner rings than for those employed in outer rings. The longer journeys-to-work made by Ring 6 workers is explained by the fact that much of Ring 6 is rural. Workers employed in isolated establishments within the ring may have to make substantial journeys-to-work to obtain an adequate selection of housing.

These results may seem trivial as tests of the appropriateness of the residential location model. It should be noted, therefore, that the empirical results for nonwhites, who because of housing market segregation are unable to compete freely in the market for residential space as we defined it, are exactly the opposite. The longest trips by Detroit nonwhites are made by those employed in outer rings and the shortest by those employed in inner rings. Similarly the journey-to-work pattern of nonwhites employed in outer rings is from residences in inner rings to workplaces in outer rings. If this economic model lacked relevance, or if residential location resulted entirely from some socioeconomic clustering as many urban sociologists and real estate market analysts have suggested, these regularities would not have to exist. Distributions similar to those observed for nonwhites might be the rule rather than the exception.

Male-Female Differences in Work-Residence Patterns

The work-residence patterns of all workers conceal important differences among the various classes of workers. An understanding of these differences is important for a satisfactory explanation of the relationships between the journey-to-work and the selection of a residential location. Among these is a significant difference in the ring-to-ring movement of male and female workers. . . .

. . . [T]he residential distribution of males around their workplaces is flatter than that of females. Higher proportions of female workers consistently reside in nearby residential rings than do the proportions of male workers.

The tighter locational pattern of female workers is, in terms of the residential location model, consistent with at least three different hypotheses. The first inference that might be drawn is that the direction of causation assumed in the model is wrong for women workers. It might plausibly be argued that the residence is selected for some unspecified reason, and that the wife-and-mother has a greater need to find a convenient job nearby the home. Such an argument would correctly point out that many females, if not most, are secondary wage earners. As such, they tend to seek nearby jobs to augment the family budget, with a more casual attitude in job seeking than that of the primary wage earner. As a result, the place of employment generally has less effect on the choice of a residence. This view suggests that women's selection of a place of employment is more conditioned by the selection of residence.

The second interpretation is that females make shorter journeys-to-work because their workplace is the same as or nearby to that of their husbands. Such households have a stronger incentive to shorten the journey-to-work because the combined journey-to-work costs are higher than for households having only a single wage earner.

Finally, it is likely that a disportionate number of female wage earners belong to households having lower space preference—i.e., to one- or two-person households. For these households both the greater numbers of working wives and the lower space preferences work in favor of shorter journeys-to-work.

I am unable at this time to resolve the question of which hypothesis is most correct; all three, I would expect, contribute to the final explanation. I believe that these three categories include a large proportion of the female working population.

OCCUPATIONAL DIFFERENCES IN RESIDENTIAL DISTRIBUTIONS

The model would postulate that if households had the same location rent function, the same transportation cost function, the same space preference, and the same valuation of time, but different incomes, the length of the households' journey-to-work would increase as an increasing function of income. The Detroit origin and destination study did not obtain household income, but the occupations of wage earners can be used as a crude measure of their incomes.

Figure 18.3 shows the proportion of high-, medium-, and low-income central business district workers residing in each residential ring. Clearly, lower-income workers have the tightest residential pattern; the highest-income workers, the most dispersed.

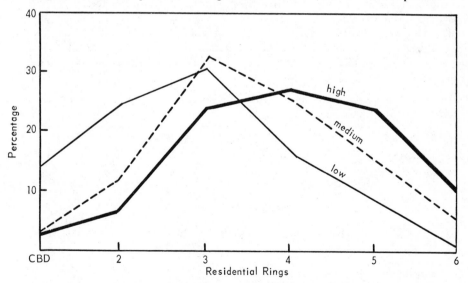

FIGURE 18.3 *Proportion of the Central Business District's Low-, Medium-, and High-income Workers Residing in Each Residential Ring*

Analysis of the Data for Occupations Ranked by Median Income

Similar residential distributions were obtained for employment Rings 1, 2, and 3, using eight occupational classifications. For workers employed in Ring 4, however, these relationships show signs of weakening. The hypothesized relationships have all but disappeared for Rings 5 and 6—an expected result. Since the location rent function is very flat from workplaces located in Rings 5 and 6, space consumption provides less of a justification for a journey-to-work. Additionally, the lower-income workers retain their tight adhesion to the workplace observed for inner rings. Of the service workers employed in Ring 6, 77 percent reside within the same ring. The proportion is nearly as large for male service workers—75 percent. . . .

Family Size by Residence Ring

The relationships between family size and residence are neither as uniform nor as simple to interpret as those between sex and residence and occupation and residence. Family size is employed at this point as an indicator of household space preferences. Larger families undoubtedly spend a greater proportion of their time in the home, using it for a far broader range of social and recreational activities. As a result, it is expected that these households, *ceteris paribus*, would manifest a greater preference for residential space.

At the same time, residential space beyond minimum requirements is to some extent a luxury. When families reach a very large size, the greater desire to consume space is probably partially offset by a lower per capita income. The minimum levels of food, clothing, and other necessities require a larger proportion of the household budget. Thus, there appears to be some tendency for the space consumption of households to fall off as family size increases beyond a certain point.

The Family-Size Residence Pattern for Inner Employment Rings. Table 18.1 . . . shows the cumulative percentages of those employed in Ring 1 . . . who reside in Rings 1 through 6. From Table 18.1 it can be seen that the proportion of one-person families residing in inner rings is substantially higher than that of any other family-unit size. The cumulative percentages residing in Rings 2, 3, 4, and 5 fall as family size increases, until a family size of five persons is reached. For families of six or more, the relationship reverses itself. The proportion of six-person families residing in inner rings exceeds the proportions for all family groups except those having more than six persons or unrelated individuals.

TABLE 18.1 *Cumulative Percentages of Ring 1 Workers Residing in Rings 1 through 6, by Family Size*

| Family Size (No. Persons) | Residence Ring | | | | | |
	1	2	3	4	5	6
1	26.1%	55.6%	86.0%	97.8%	98.5%	100%
2	2.5	14.8	50.3	76.2	93.4	100
3		9.7	39.8	69.3	90.5	100
4	0.4	10.2	38.8	68.8	90.8	100
5		9.8	35.7	67.3	89.5	100
6		11.2	52.0	77.0	93.4	100
More than 6		15.9	46.8	70.7	92.1	100
All	3.7	16.1	46.8	72.9	91.4	100

SOURCE: Tabulated from Detroit Study Deck.

The decreasing proportion of central business district workers residing in inner rings, as family size increases, is consistent with a higher space preference on the part of these households. A higher space preference, *ceteris paribus*, leads to a greater consumption of space and a longer journey-to-work.

The reversal of the relationship for households having more than five members is consistent with their lower per capita income. Beyond a certain size, the greater space preference is offset for many very large families by an income constraint. Household demand for other needed goods and services causes it to forego the higher space consumption.

. . . . [T]hese relationships hold for employment Ring 2 as well, with only one unimportant difference: from Rings 3 through 6 the cumulative percentage of families having more than six persons falls below that of six-person families. The percentages still exceed all but those of one- and two-person families, however. . . .

Family Size by Ring of Residence—Outer Employment Rings. In the outer employment rings, we should expect either a reversal of the pattern observed in Rings 1 and 2 or no discernible relationship between family size and residential location. Table 18.2 shows that one- and two-person families employed in Ring 5 tend to reside in inner rings in the highest proportions of all family-unit sizes. Because of the lower space requirements, living closer to the central business district is less costly for them than for those having higher space preferences. To state that the higher location rents are less of a constraint for these households fails, however, to provide any reason that smaller families should be more willing to pay higher location rents or make a longer journey-to-work in order to reside nearer the center. The more incomplete specification of the transportation costs of these households provides such an explanation.

TABLE 18.2 *Cumulative Percentages of Ring 5 Workers Residing in Rings 6 through 1, by Family Size*

Family Size (No. Persons)	Residence Ring					
	1	*2*	*3*	*4*	*5*	*6*
1	100%	89.1%	78.3%	52.3%	32.6%	10.0%
2	100	99.8	96.6	83.9	63.6	20.9
3		100.0	98.3	85.6	67.8	19.7
4		100.0	98.0	89.2	72.0	23.1
5		100.0	98.8	92.5	72.5	21.2
6		100.0	99.2	88.8	73.1	27.1
More than 6		100.0	97.6	86.6	70.9	26.6
All	100	99.5	97.2	86.2	67.4	22.5

SOURCE: Tabulated from Detroit Study Deck.

It is logical to expect that many of these households make above-average numbers of trips to social and recreational centers located in or near the central business district. Their locational choices, therefore, would be heavily weighted by these trips. This should be true for one-person families as well. Unfortunately, one-person households employed in Ring 6 exhibit the tightest locational pattern of all families but those having more than five persons [Table 18.3]. One-person households employed in Ring 5 exhibit the expected behavior. From Table 18.2 it can be seen that only 33 percent of those employed in Ring 5 reside either in it or in Ring 6. By contrast, 64 percent of 2-person households and 73 percent of 6-person families reside in one of these two rings.

Also, it is likely that a large proportion of two-person families have a second wage earner. If the second member of the household is employed in an inner ring this provides an added incentive for the household to live closer to the center. It should be remembered, for all family sizes, that only small proportions of those employed in Rings 5 and 6 live in Rings 1, 2, and 3.

TABLE 18.3   *Cumulative Percentages of Ring 6 Workers Residing in Rings 6 through 1, by Family Size*

Family Size (No. Persons)	Residence Ring					
	1	2	3	4	5	6
1	100%	93.7%	84.3%	81.1%	79.0%	66.8%
2	100	99.7	96.5	88.0	76.1	56.3
3		100.0	98.7	92.3	81.7	62.7
4		100.0	93.8	93.1	83.5	58.4
5		100.0	97.8	93.4	85.5	62.6
6		100.0	99.6	92.9	90.0	66.4
More than 6		100.0	99.4	95.1	87.3	66.7
All	100	99.6	97.6	91.4	82.2	61.0

SOURCE: Tabulated from Detroit Study Deck.

The final relationship exhibited by Tables 18.2 and 18.3 is an increase in the proportion of a ring's employees residing nearby the workplace as family size increases. This finding is also consistent with the lower per capita incomes of larger families. When changes in total location rents with distance are slight, minimization of transportation costs results in the minimization of total locational costs. Households with lower per capita income may be more sensitive to small differences in transportation costs.

Family Size by Ring of Residence—Rings 3 and 4. Above-average proportions of the very large and very small households employed in Rings 3 and 4 reside in rings near the center. Families with three to six members reside in higher proportions in Rings 5 and 6. The closeness in locational patterns of one- and two-person families employed in Rings 3 and 4 is even more reasonable than is that of the same size families employed in Rings 5 and 6.

Suburban living must be far less attractive to the young married or the childless couple than to those with children; their social and recreational activities are to a much greater degree directed outside the home. For the unattached person, residence in a suburban neighborhood far from the center of activity is even more unsatisfactory.

No adequate explanation in terms of the model can be offered for the locational choices of the very large families. In the case of employment Ring 4, the divergence is great enough that a larger proportion of its workers reside in Ring 3 than in Ring 5. Even so, more workers reside in the two rings away from the central business district than reside in those nearer the central business district.

Space Consumption by Residential Rings

The model of residential location postulates that where location rents are a significant factor households consuming larger quantities of space will, *ceteris paribus*, make longer journeys to work than those consuming lesser quantities. The distance the household resides from its workplace is expressed by the model as a function of the quantity of residential space consumed. The relationship between space consumption and length of the journey to work, like that between income and the length of the journey, should deteriorate for outer employment rings, where the schedule of rents decreases only slightly or not at all around the workplace.

In this paper, structure type is employed as a measure of space consumption. This is an admittedly inadequate index, especially for single-family dwelling units, where the index fails to differentiate between very significant differences in lot size. Regardless of these deficiencies, structure type undoubtedly represents a dimension of the space consumption relationship. It is probably roughly correlated with the measure of space consumption we would wish to employ. For this reason, we will look at the relationships between residential location and occupancy of single-family, two-family, or multifamily dwellings.

The Residence-Space Consumption Pattern for Inner Employment Rings. Table 18.4 shows the percentages of workers occupying each type of dwelling unit in each residence ring, for employment Rings 1, 2, and 3. As might be expected, those choosing higher density structures—two-family dwelling units and multiple dwellings—reside in well-above-average proportions in the close-in residential rings. For example, 30 percent of central business district workers who live in multiple dwelling units reside in the adjacent ring. In contrast, the adjacent ring is elected by only 5 percent of those choosing single-family structures and 13 percent of those selecting two-family structures. This pattern persists through Ring 3, where 50 percent of all central business district workers reside who live in multiple dwelling units. Ring 3 also provides dwellings for 47 percent of those residing in two-family units, as opposed to only 22 percent of those residing in one-family units.

The proportion of those residing in multiple and two-family units in residence Rings 5 and 6, on the other hand, is very low. Less than 2 percent in each case live in Ring 6.

TABLE 18.4 *Percentage of Inner Employment Ring Workers Residing in Each Ring, by Structure Type*

Structure Type	Residence Ring						
	1	*2*	*3*	*4*	*5*	*6*	*Total*
Percentage of Ring 1 (CBD) Workers							
One-family	—	5.4%	22.1%	29.8%	28.9%	13.8%	100%
Two-family	—	13.1	46.7	32.8	5.8	1.5	100
Multiple	2.4	29.5	50.2	14.7	2.1	1.1	100
All	3.8	12.6	31.1	26.3	18.4	7.8	100
Percentage of Ring 2 Workers							
One-family	—	8.7%	25.5%	28.1%	25.1%	12.5%	100%
Two-family	0.2	26.2	46.8	21.4	4.0	1.4	100
Multiple	1.2	43.6	43.4	9.3	1.7	0.7	100
All	1.0	20.1	34.1	22.4	15.6	7.7	100
Percentage of Ring 3 Workers							
One-family	—	5.3%	27.0%	29.7%	24.1%	13.9%	100%
Two-family	0.1	13.8	60.0	21.4	3.7	1.0	100
Multiple	0.8	25.2	59.9	11.2	2.0	0.8	100
All	0.7	10.9	39.3	24.3	15.9	0.9	100

SOURCE: Tabulated from Detroit Study Deck.

The Residence-Space Consumption Pattern for Outer Employment Rings. The differential pattern of residence by structure type for outer workplace rings is also in basic conformity with the model. These patterns are shown in Table 18.5. A large proportion of these residents of all three structure types reside in their workplace rings or adjacent rings. Employment Ring 6 encompasses the residences of 64 percent of all single-family households, 40 percent of the two-family households, and 52 percent of households choosing multiple units who work in that ring. Where the rent schedule is relatively flat, as in Ring 6, we would postulate a short journey to work regardless of space consumption. In the case of employment Rings 4 and 5, a similar pattern exists: the residential distribution is tighter than for inner rings, but less tight than for Ring 6. . . . In terms of the model, households employed in Ring 6 tend to live nearby, regardless of space consumption. Those employed in Ring 2, by comparison, tend to live nearby only if they consume limited quantities of residential space. They tend to make a journey-to-work to outer rings if they consume larger quantities of residential space. Very few of those consuming small quantities of space live in Rings 4, 5, and 6.

Somewhat larger proportions of those employed in Ring 6 and consuming small amounts of space reside in interior rings.

TABLE 18.5   *Percentage of Outer Employment Ring Workers Residing in Each Ring, by Structure Type*

Structure Type	Residence Ring						
	1	2	3	4	5	6	Total
Percentage of Ring 4 Workers							
One-family	—	2.6%	13.4%	34.2%	30.7%	19.1%	100%
Two-family	—	8.2	39.4	42.8	7.1	2.5	100
Multiple	—	21.5	43.2	25.5	5.1	4.7	100
All	0.5	6.0	21.4	34.5	23.3	14.4	100
Percentage of Ring 5 Workers							
One-family	—	0.7%	6.0%	16.3%	51.8%	25.1%	100%
Two-family	—	5.2	27.0	31.8	30.2	5.9	100
Multiple	—	12.9	34.4	24.2	17.9	10.5	100
All	0.3	2.2	10.5	18.4	46.8	21.8	100
Percentage of Ring 6 Workers							
One-family	—	0.8%	3.4%	7.3%	24.0%	64.5%	100%
Two-family	—	3.2	21.2	25.7	10.2	39.8	100
Multiple	—	9.8	18.2	10.3	9.5	52.2	100
All	0.4	2.0	6.2	9.2	21.2	61.0	100

SOURCE: Tabulated from Detroit Study Deck.

Income and Substitution Effect

It was pointed out previously that, in terms of the way the problem is formulated in this paper, the price of residential space is determined by location rents and transportation costs. As a result, the households employed in inner rings, confronted by higher and steeper schedules of location rents, must pay a higher price for residential space than must be paid by those employed in outer rings. If the assumption of similar incomes, tastes, and transportation costs for those employed in each successive ring is reasonably adequate, it would be expected *a priori* that the relatively lower price of residential space for those in outer rings would lead to higher space consumption.

From Table 18.6 it can be seen that this pattern generally holds. A smaller proportion of central business district workers and those employed in Ring 2 reside in single-family units. A larger proportion select two-family and multiple units. The proportion employed in Rings 5 and 6 living in one-family structures in turn exceeds those for Rings 3 and 4. Similarly, the proportion residing in multiple and two-family living quarters is smaller.

TABLE 18.6 *Percentage Residing in Each Structure Type, by Employment Ring*

Structure Type	Employment Ring					
	1	*2*	*3*	*4*	*5*	*6*
One-family	58.4%	56.9%	60.6%	69.0%	79.2%	78.1%
Two-family	18.2	21.7	20.8	18.4	11.8	10.4
Multiple	17.4	17.2	15.4	10.4	6.9	7.5
Other	5.9	4.2	3.2	2.4	2.2	4.0
Total	100.0	100.0	100.0	100.0	100.0	100.0

SOURCE: Tabulated from Detroit Study Deck.

DERIVED DEMAND FOR RESIDENTIAL SERVICES

There is one final question which I am unable to evaluate with any degree of adequacy, but which should, I feel, be at least alluded to in this paper. A large number of researchers have emphasized the role of good schools and public services, and the supply of new and high quality dwelling units, in determining residential location. It is an empirical fact that the mean quality level of the housing stock, and most likely of government services, increases with distance from the central business district. My intuition, based partially on the findings presented here and those of related research, are that an explanation of residential location in these terms is at best an oversimplification and at worst may be basically incorrect. It is my belief that housing quality is less of a determinant of residential choices than are collective residential choices a determinant of the quality of housing services and of the quality of governmental services. Among other things, this paper solves for a spatial distribution of demand for residential space by different income groups. If, as I would assert, the demand for housing quality and quality of governmental services is a derived demand, the distribution of quality predicted by my model and to some extent supported by the evidence presented in this paper would be very similar to that observed empirically. This leads me to the tentative conclusion that observed distribution of housing quality is the result of the long-run operation of an admittedly imperfect market, but one which is possibly less imperfect than supposed.

There is one major exception to my remarks: racial discrimination represents a major market imperfection which distorts the spatial demand for residential space by both whites and nonwhites.

Nevertheless, my suggestion is that the market for residential space has as a whole operated in the direction expected a priori. With the major exception I have stated, it seems probable to me that many of the *so-called* ills of our central cities are the result of a spatial concentration of employment and insufficient housing expenditures by our low-income population.

There is no need for me to tell anyone that this is an extremely complex problem. My remarks at this point should be taken as highly conjectural. The correct explanation is far more complex than what I have presented here; however, it is my opinion that the findings of this paper suggest the desirability of a rather thorough rethinking of these problems.

CONCLUSIONS

In this paper I have presented a theory or model of residential location and have evaluated this model by examining residential distributions for Detroit whites employed in six concentric rings around Detroit's central business district. These same six distance rings are also used as the residential subareas in the analysis. I have hypothesized that workers employed in each ring participate in a different market for residential space from that of workers employed in every other ring. These markets are differentiated by the fact that the schedule of prices per unit of urban space in each differs with distance and direction from the workplace. It is my contention, therefore, that differences in the length of the journey-to-work and in the locational choices of workers employed in each ring may be comprehended only when the characteristics of the metropolitan schedule of location rents is specified. I postulated, for Detroit, that the surface of location rents tends to decrease with distance from the central business district, and that the rate of decrease was greatest near the center and least near the periphery.

In addition, although housing quality was not explicitly included as a variable in the empirical work, I offered some conjectures about the relationships between the distribution of housing quality and the selection of residential locations by households. These observations were based on the most intuitive of theorizing but justify, I feel, a rather careful rethinking of a number of our policies of public intervention in the housing market.

The empirical findings are generally in conformity with those expected a priori from the model of residential location. This model would predict that where the market for residential space has the characteristics ascribed to the inner rings in Detroit, households will locate at varying distances from their workplaces according to their transportation costs, space consumption, space preferences, and incomes.

It was determined that the commuting pattern was largely from residences in outer rings to workplaces in inner rings, that the average length of the journey-to-work decreased with the workplace's distance from the central business district, and that the proportion of a ring's workers residing in the same or nearby rings increased as the workplace ring's distance from the central business district increased.

Workers employed in higher-income occupations and working in inner rings tended to make longer journeys-to-work and reside in outer rings. When employed in outer rings they made much shorter journeys-to-work and lived within the same ring and adjacent rings at very high rates. Lower income workers made short journeys-to-work and resided within the workplace ring and in nearby rings regardless of the location of workplace.

Family size as an indicator of space preference had a similar effect on residential location. The smallest and largest families were found to make the shortest journeys-to-work. For the smallest families, I attributed this to low space preferences; the shorter journeys-to-work by the largest families I attributed to a per capita income constraint.

Structure type is used as a measure of the household's space consumption. The longest journeys-to-work were made by those residing in one-family units and the shortest by those residing in multiple units. A marked difference between the locational choices of males and females was also discovered. Female workers, regardless of workplace ring, made shorter journeys-to-work than male workers and resided within the workplace ring and nearby rings in much higher proportions. Finally, it was determined that the proportion of workers residing in low-density structures increased as the workplace ring's distance from the central business district increased.

All the relationships summarized above were very clean-cut for rings near the central business district, where the location rent function with distances from the workplace is believed to be very steep. For peripheral workplace rings, where the function is believed to be very flat, the relationships were much weaker.

In general it is my opinion that the evidence presented in this paper bears out the appropriateness of the theoretical framework employed. The findings are generally consistent with our a priori views on the problem as obtained both from this model and similar models by Alonso, Wingo, and others. The issues evaluated in the paper are still far from settled, however, and will remain so until we are able to take into account more explicitly the dynamics of the housing market in both our models and our empirical work.

19. *A Competitive Theory of the Housing Market*

EDGAR O. OLSEN

In his article on the demand for nonfarm housing, Richard Muth (11) rigorously developed a competitive theory of the housing market.[1] Muth used this theory in the statistical estimation of the demand function for housing service and of the speed of adjustment to long-run equilibrium in this market. His theory also makes possible the translation of some of the idiosyncratic concepts used by housing specialists into the familiar terms of microeconomic theory. A secondary purpose of this article is to make these translations. More importantly, this theory has implications for a number of crucial issues in government housing policy. The primary purpose of this article is to derive these implications and use them to suggest additional tests of the competitive theory of the housing market. In order to achieve these purposes, it is first necessary to explain the crucial simplifying assumption which makes it possible to view the market for housing service as a competitive market in which a homogeneous good is sold.

THE ASSUMPTIONS

Let us assume that the following conditions are satisfied in markets for housing service: (1) both buyers and sellers of housing service are numerous, (2) the sales or purchases of each individual unit are small in relation to the aggregate volume of transactions, (3) neither buyers nor sellers collude, (4) entry into and exit from the market are free for both producers and consumers, (5) both producers and consumers possess perfect knowledge about the prevailing price and current bids, and they take advantage

Reprinted from the *American Economic Review* 59 (September 1969): 612-22 by permission of the American Economic Association and the author. Edgar Olsen is an assistant professor of economics at the University of Virginia.

This paper was written while the author was a postdoctoral fellow in The Institute for Applied Urban Economics at Indiana University. He is indebted for helpful criticisms of earlier drafts to H. James Brown, David Greytak, W. David Maxwell, J. W. Milliman, Richard F. Muth, and R. L. Pfister. The author is also grateful to Resources for the Future for the grant which financed his postdoctoral fellowship.

1. There are clearly two housing markets. There is a demand for and supply of a consumer good which we shall call housing service. There is also a derived demand for and supply of an investment good which we shall call housing stock. These two markets are integrally related. Indeed, Muth (11, p. 32) defines one unit of housing service to be that quantity of service yielded by one unit of housing stock per unit of time. Thus, he assumes that housing stock is the only input in the production of housing service. Although all buyers of housing stock are also sellers of housing service, there are many people who participate in one market but not in the other. Consumers who occupy rental housing are not typically in the market for housing stock. They are not buyers or sellers of this capital asset. Builders who construct housing for sale are sellers of housing stock but not of housing service. This paper will focus primarily on the market for housing service. Finally, it must be emphasized at the outset that this paper abstracts from consideration of the land on which dwelling units stand.

of every opportunity to increase profits and utility respectively, (6) no artificial restrictions are placed on demands for, supplies of, and prices of housing service and the resources used to produce housing service, and (7) housing service is a homogeneous commodity.

This set of conditions is nothing other than a conventional statement of one set of conditions sufficient for a perfectly competitive market.[2] While objections to all of these assumptions can be found in the housing literature, most scholars would probably find (7) to be the least plausible assumption. Noting the great variations among residential structures as to size, type of construction, and other characteristics to which consumers attach value, many presume that a very heterogeneous good is traded in the housing market. This paper presents a theory with a very different view of the good being traded. An understanding of this theory of the housing market requires an elaboration on its conception of housing. Therefore, we will now focus our attention on this crucial simplifying assumption.

In order to view the housing market as one in which a homogeneous commodity is bought and sold, an unobservable theoretical entity called housing service is introduced.[3] Each dwelling (or housing) unit is presumed to yield some quantity of this good during each time period. It is assumed to be the only thing in a dwelling unit to which consumers attach value. Consequently, in this theory there is no distinction between the quantity and quality of a dwelling unit as these terms are customarily used.

This conception of housing is bound to raise objections. It will be argued that housing is a complex bundle of technically independent attributes. However, since housing service is not observable directly, it is not possible to argue for or against this assumption directly.[4] Hence, it is not possible to test this theory other than by reference to its implications. The competitive theory of the housing market does contain bridge principles which relate housing service to observable phenomena, and it does have testable implications in terms of these phenomena. Muth (11) has already tested some of these implications. Other implications will be derived in this paper. Eyesight is not a satisfactory judge of the question of homogeneity. The assumption of a homogeneous good called housing service can only be rejected if theories of housing market without this assumption have greater explanatory power.

THE TRANSLATION OF CONCEPTS

Based on the assumptions of the preceding section, four concepts—dwelling unit, slum, filtering, and shortage—traditionally used in housing market analysis can be translated into the jargon of conventional microeconomic theory.

What is a dwelling unit? *A dwelling unit* is a package composed of a certain quantity of a capital asset called housing stock. Some dwelling units will contain 10 units of

2. This set is a composite taken from three standard price theory textbooks. See Richard Leftwich (7, pp. 23-25), George Stigler (14, pp. 87-89), and James Henderson and Richard Quandt (6, pp. 86-89). As Stigler clearly explains, this is by no means the weakest set of assumptions sufficient for perfect competition. A strong set of assumptions is used in order to obtain clear-cut implications of the competitive theory.

3. Carl Hempel (5, pp. 70-84) gives an elementary but lucid explanation of the role of unobservable theoretical entities in scientific theories.

4. Intuitively, it does seem more reasonable to conceive of the difference between an apartment renting for $50 and one renting for $100 in the same city as more akin to the difference between $50 and $100 worth of oranges than to the difference between $50 worth of oranges and $100 worth of golf balls. However, arguments of this sort are not scientific.

housing stock, other dwelling units will contain 20 units of housing stock. By definition, these dwelling units will be said to yield 10 and 20 units of housing service per time period respectively.[5] In long-run competitive equilibrium only one price per unit applies to all units of housing stock and another price to all units of housing service regardless of the size of the package in which these goods come. Hence, if we observe that one dwelling unit sells for twice the amount of another dwelling unit in the same market, then we say that the more expensive unit contains twice the quantity of housing stock and, hence, involves twice the total expenditure. This distinction between price, quantity, and total expenditure is not usually made in housing market analysis where it is simply said that the price of one dwelling unit is twice that of the other dwelling unit. Similarly, if we observe that one dwelling unit rents for twice the amount of another dwelling unit, then we say that the more expensive dwelling unit yields twice the quantity of housing service per time period and, hence, involves twice the total expenditure per time period. Here again, traditional housing market analysis uses a price theory concept, in this case "rent," in a way far removed from its original meaning. Despite the fact that housing service and housing stock are not directly observable, the competitive theory of the housing market contains bridge principles which permit us to compare the relative amounts of housing service yielded by different dwelling units.

What is a slum dwelling unit? A *slum dwelling unit* is one which yields less than some arbitrary quantity of housing service per time period. Using the relationship established between total expenditure and quantity, we might decide to call all dwelling units in a particular locality renting for less than $60 per month slum dwelling units. What is a slum area? A *slum area* is a contiguous area which contains a high (but arbitrary) percentage of slum dwelling units.

It would be possible to give the word "slum" a welfare economics definition in which a slum dwelling unit would necessarily represent suboptimal resource allocation. Otto Davis and Andrew Whinston (3, pp. 111-12) have provided such a definition. At least one other distinctly different definition of this sort is possible.[6] However, the definition provided above is more in keeping with the use of this word in both popular and scholarly writings.

What is a housing shortage? The most frequently used unit of quantity for housing market analysis has been the dwelling unit. As a result, a housing shortage has usually been defined as a situation in which everyone who is willing to pay the market price for a separate dwelling unit is not able to obtain a separate dwelling unit. This is a unnecessarily narrow definition of a shortage which results from the acceptance of the dwelling unit as the unit of quantity. The unit of quantity introduced by Muth allows us to take a broader view of a housing shortage. To be precise, *a short-run housing shortage* is said to exist if, and only if, the quantity of housing service demanded at the existing market price is greater than the quantity of housing service supplied. Short-run shortages will be eliminated by a rise in the price of housing service for bundles of the size which are in excess demand initially. A *long-run housing shortage*

5. Dwelling unit means the same thing as housing unit. Therefore, a housing unit is quite different from a unit of housing stock or housing service. The term dwelling unit is used throughout this paper to avoid this natural confusion.

6. Some people care about the housing occupied by low income families for altruistic and more selfish reasons. The market will not properly account for these preferences and, hence, low income families may consume too little housing service by the criterion of efficiency. We might call the dwelling units occupied by these low income families slum dwelling units. Clearly, with this definition slumness is not a characteristic of the housing alone.

is said to exist if, and only if, the quantity of housing service demanded at the long-run equilibrium price is greater than the quantity of housing service supplied. Long-run shortages are eliminated by maintenance, repairs, alterations, and additions as well as by new construction. Clearly, a housing shortage can exist by these definitions even if everyone who wants to occupy a separate dwelling unit at the relevant price is doing so because everyone may want to occupy better housing (i.e., to consume a greater quantity of housing service) at this price than they presently occupy and none may be available.

Although the concept of filtering has been used in housing economics for many years, a rigorous definition of this term has only recently been proposed. Ira Lowry (8, p. 363) defines filtering as " . . . a change in the real value (price in constant dollars) of an existing dwelling unit." Lowry uses this definition together with a theory of the housing market to demonstrate that filtering is not a process which necessarily results in all families occupying housing above certain minimum standards. With the competitive theory of the housing market, it is possible to define filtering slightly more rigorously and in a manner which significantly clarifies the meaning of the concept and the method of detecting the process. Using this new definition and a competitive theory of the housing market, it is easy to demonstrate the result which Lowry showed with great difficulty.

A dwelling unit has *filtered* if, and only if, the quantity of housing stock contained in this unit has changed. A dwelling unit has *filtered up* if, and only if, the quantity of housing stock contained in this unit has increased. A dwelling unit has *filtered down* if, and only if, the quantity of housing stock contained in this unit has decreased.[7] Within the theory presented in this paper, Lowry's definition is the same as the new definition if he intended to deflate money values by the cost of construction. This is true because in a perfectly competitive housing market in long-run equilibrium the price per unit of housing stock equals the minimum long-run average cost of production and, hence, the quantity of housing stock contained in a particular dwelling unit is equal to the market value of this dwelling unit divided by the cost of production.[8] For example, if the cost-of-construction index was 100 in 1960 and 110 in 1962 and if a particular dwelling unit sold for $6,000 in 1960 and $6,050 in 1962, then we would say that this particular unit has filtered down between 1960 and 1962 because our index of quantity of housing stock fell from 60 to 55.[9]

To determine whether particular dwelling units have filtered is of far less importance than understanding the function of filtering in the operation of the housing market. In essence, Lowry set out to demonstrate that filtering is not a process that insures that all consumers will purchase greater than an arbitrarily chosen quantity of housing service per time period. If the housing market is perfectly competitive, then this result is trivial since there is nothing in the operation of such a market which insures

7. In these definitions, "housing stock contained in" could be replaced by "housing service yielded per time period by." These definitions are stated in stock terms to facilitate the comparison with Lowry's definition.

8. Lowry does not say what he intends to use as a deflator.

9. This method abstracts from changes in the price paid for a particular structure attributable to changes in the relative desirability of its location. Since I do not want to include these changes in my concept of filtering, the market value of the land must be subtracted from the total price of structure and land in determining whether a dwelling unit has filtered. Practically, this might be done by observing the sale price per square foot of nearby vacant land and assuming that the land containing the structure of interest has the same market value per square foot.

that all individuals will consume greater than an arbitrary quantity of the good.[10] As will be shown in the next section, filtering is a process by which the quantity of housing service yielded by particular dwelling units is adjusted to conform to the pattern of consumer demand. The profit incentive leads producers to make these adjustments.

None of the definitions in this section corresponds exactly with previous usage of the terms. No simple definitions could. These definitons have been offered in order to bring housing market analysis within the realm of standard microeconomic theory where advantage can be taken of the accumulated knowledge in this field. The value of this transformation should be strongly emphasized. Even as eminent a price theorist as Milton Friedman (4, pp. 178-80) reaches an undoubtedly fallacious conclusion about public housing simply because he did not apply the conventional distinction between the very short run and the long run to the housing market.[11]

THE WORKINGS OF THE MARKET

The workings of the market for housing service under the set of assumptions introduced in the first section can best be illustrated by beginning from a situation in which the price per unit of housing service for bundles of all sizes but one is equal to the long-run average cost of production. For the one bundle size, the price is assumed to be greater than the long-run average cost. In this situation, producers will be making profits (i.e., they will be making more than a normal rate of return on capital) only on this one size bundle of housing service.

Owners of housing stock can change the quantity of housing stock contained in and, hence, the quantity of housing service yielded by their dwelling units through maintenance, repair, alteration, and addition.[12] In the absence of maintenance, dwelling units deteriorate with use and over time, which means that they yield smaller and smaller quantities of housing service per time period. Normally, producers of housing service find it profitable to invest in maintenance (although not enough to halt deterioration completely). If bundles of some particular size become more profit-

10. For any given positive quantity, there exists a set of admissible indifference curves, relative prices, and income such that the consumer associated with these will choose less than the given quantity.

11. Friedman (4, p. 179) concludes that " . . . far from improving the housing of the poor, as its proponents expected, public housing has done just the reverse. The number of dwelling units destroyed in the course of erecting public housing projects has been far larger than the number of new units constructed." Aside from the factual question of whether far more units have been destroyed than constructed and aside from Friedman's use of numbers of gainers and losers rather than the values of gains and losses, Friedman ignores the fact that the displaced families will lose over a few years while housed families will gain over the much longer physical life of the project. As will be demonstrated . . . , in long-run equilibrium the displaced families will occupy the same type of housing and pay the same rent as prior to the public housing project. According to Muth (11, pp. 49-52), the market for housing service adjusts at a rate of one-third of the difference between the present situation and long-run equilibrium each year. Hence, there is a 90 percent adjustment in 6 years. By comparison, the physical life of public housing projects is likely to be far in excess of 50 years. From Edgar Olsen's calculations (12, pp. 83-87) it can be estimated that the average public housing tenant received benefits from public housing which he valued at $263 in 1965. This benefit would be received each year by some poor family during the entire physical life of the project.

12. In the remainder of this paper, the word "maintenance" will be used to denote all four of these phenomena.

able than bundles of other sizes, then some producers with larger bundles of housing service will allow their housing units to deteriorate more than they would otherwise. That is, they will allow their dwelling units to filter down to the bundle size which is most profitable. This is accomplished by following a lower maintenance policy than would have been followed had all bundle sizes been equally profitable. By the same token, some producers of smaller bundles of housing service will follow a higher maintenance policy than otherwise resulting in a filtering up of their dwelling units.

The supply of the most profitable size bundle having increased, the price per unit of housing service for bundles of this size will decrease. Since initially there were zero profits for bundles of housing service slightly greater and slightly less than the profitable size bundle, the filtering down of larger bundles and the filtering up of smaller bundles will create short-run shortages, higher prices, and profits for bundles of these sizes. This will result in filtering down of still larger bundles and filtering up of smaller bundles. Eventually the process will reach bundles of sizes which can be provided by the construction of new dwelling units. This new construction will continue until there are no profits to be made on bundles of any size. This requires the price per unit of housing service for bundles of all sizes to be the same.

THE POOR-PAY-MORE HYPOTHESIS

A popular claim in current policy discussions is that the poor pay more for many goods including housing. If the housing markets are perfectly competitive and if it is neither more costly to provide small quantities of housing service nor to provide housing service to low income families, then the poor will not pay more for housing service. It is instructive of the workings of a perfectly competitive housing market to demonstrate this result.

We begin by interpreting the poor-pay-more hypothesis in terms of the theory presented in this article. For some reason the price per unit of housing service is greater for dwelling units yielding small quantities of housing service than for dwelling units yielding large quantities. This price difference is not attributable to differences in cost.[13] For large bundles of housing service, the market works efficiently. The price of housing service tends toward the minimum long-run average cost of production of housing service. Consequently, the price per unit of housing service for small bundles exeeds the minimum average cost. As a result, owners of dwelling units yielding small quantities of housing service make economic profits. For some reason, these profits do not stimulate an increase in the supply of these small bundles of housing service. As a result, the consumers of these small bundles (i.e., primarily the poor) consume a smaller quantity of housing service than required for efficient resource allocation.

Participants in a competitive housing market would not allow this situation to persist. Suppose that owners of bundles of housing stock yielding quantities of housing service less than x received a higher price per unit for their production than owners of bundles which yield greater than x units of housing service. These slum landlords would be making higher profits per dollar invested than other landlords. In this case, some owners of dwelling units yielding slightly more than x units will follow

---

13. If the price difference is solely attributable to differences in cost, then no market imperfection is involved and government action on grounds of efficiency is not required. A recent study by the U.S. Bureau of Labor Statistics (15) has shown that the poor do pay more for food, but that this difference is fully explained by difference in cost. The poor tend to shop in small stores where merchandising cost per unit is high.

a lower maintenance policy than otherwise, allowing the quantity of housing service yielded by their units per time period to fall below x. The supply of dwelling units yielding less than x units of housing service per time period will increase, and the price per unit for these small bundles will fall. Eventually, new construction will be induced. Only when the price per unit of housing service for bundles of all sizes is equal to the minimum long-run average cost of production will there be no incentive for change.

If we actually observe that the poor consistently pay more per unit of housing service than the rich and that it is not more expensive per unit to provide small packages of housing service or to provide housing service to low income families, then we have evidence contrary to the assumption that the housing market is competitive. This is one of the testable implications of the competive theory.[14]

WILL SLUM CLEARANCE AND URBAN RENEWAL RESULT IN A NET REDUCTION IN SLUMS?

Slum clearance is the destruction of slum dwelling units by government with or without compensation to the owner. It is required by the Housing Act of 1937 as part of the public housing program. It is undertaken independently by many local governments. Finally, slum clearance is the first stage of urban renewal. Slum clearance and urban renewal have been premised in large part on the naïve belief that the physical destruction of slum dwelling units results in a net reduction in the number of families occupying such units. Many writers have questioned this presumption and have suggested that slum clearance merely results in the transfer of slums from one location to another.[15] Indeed, this argument should suggest itself to all economists since slum clearance does not increase the incomes of or decrease the prices of any goods to the former residents of the cleared areas. If the market for housing service is perfectly competitive, then this argument can be made completely rigorous.

We have defined a slum dwelling unit as a dwelling unit yielding a flow of less than x units of housing service. Starting from a situation of long-run equilibrium in the housing market with normal vacancy rates, the immediate effect of slum clearance is to decrease the supply of slum dwelling units. Some of the former residents of the destroyed dwelling units will move into vacant dwelling units providing the same quantity of housing service. Others will have to move into dwelling units which provide slightly more or slightly less housing service than they prefer to buy at the long-run equilibrium price. The owners of slum dwelling units will realize that they can both charge higher prices and have lower vacancy rates than before slum clearance. They will take advantage of the short-run shortage to raise prices in order to increase their profits. This, however, is only the very short-run impact of slum clearance.

14. A recent study by the BLS (16) has shown that the quality of housing occupied by richer families is superior to that occupied by poorer people in the same rent range. Unfortunately, it is almost certainly true that within each rent range the higher the income range, the higher the average rent. The higher rent may completely explain the differences in quality. This author is trying to obtain the BLS data to check this possibility with regression analysis. Finally, the BLS study does not consider the possibility that it is more costly per unit of housing service either to provide small bundles or to sell to low income families. For example, it is reputed to be much more difficult to collect rents from low income tenants. This involves extra costs in time and nonpayment. Furthermore, the existence and enforcement of building and occupancy codes with penalties for violations increase the long-run equilibrium price of low quantity housing in a competitive market because there exist some producers and consumers who will have an incentive to violate the code. (I owe this point to Richard Muth.)

15. For example, see Martin Bailey (2, p. 291), Davis and Whinston (3, p. 112) and Martin Anderson (1, pp. 8-9).

In the long run the owners of slightly better than slum dwelling units will allow their dwelling units to filter down to the level of slum dwelling units in order to take advantage of the profits to be made on such units. This adjustment will continue until the rate of return on capital invested in bundles of housing stock of all sizes is the same. In long-run equilibrium the price per unit of housing service must be the same for bundles of all sizes. Since neither slum clearance nor urban renewal subsidizes housing consumption by low income families, and since neither results in a lower cost of production of housing service, therefore, neither results in a lower price of housing service to the former residents of slum clearance or urban renewal sites in the long run. Neither slum clearance nor urban renewal results in change in the incomes of or the prices paid for nonhousing goods by the former residents. Consequently, the former residents of the cleared area will, in long-run equilibrium, consume exactly the same quantity of housing service as before slum clearance or urban renewal. Slum clearance and urban renewal do not result in a net reduction in the occupancy of slums in the long run.

This implication of the competitive theory is testable. To conduct this test, we might observe the characteristics of the housing occupied by former residents of slum clearance sites and their incomes just prior to slum clearance and for six years afterward. With respect to each characteristic, we shall probably observe that the percentage of families occupying housing with that characteristic is different immediately after slum clearance from what it was immediately before. For example, the percentage of families in dilapidated dwelling units might have been 90 percent before slum clearance and 50 percent afterward. The competitive theory suggests that in long-run equilibrium we will again find 90 percent of these families in dilapidated dwelling units if these families experience no change in real income. Therefore, if we determine the percentage of families occupying dwelling units with each particular characteristic by income groups, then we should observe that within each income group the percentage of families occupying housing having the particular characteristic should, over time, approach the before slum clearance percentage. This convergence provides a weak test of the competitive hypothesis. As mentioned before, Muth (11, pp. 49-52) estimates that we get a 90 percent adjustment in the housing market in 6 years.[16] Consequently, we expect that the difference between the percentage at the end of 6 years and the percentage immediately after slum clearance will be roughly 90 percent of the difference between the percentage immediately before slum clearance and the percentage immediately afterward. A test of the statistical significance of the difference between these two variables is a strong test of the competitive theory.[17]

There have been, and continue to be, many instances of slum clearance, especially associated with urban renewal. It is quite feasible to conduct studies of displaced families at least partly for the purpose of testing this implication of the competitive theory of the housing market. Since the nature of the housing market is very relevant to the choice of government housing policies, these data might reasonably be collected by the U.S. Department of Housing and Urban Development in conjunction with urban renewal and public housing.

If the housing market is perfectly competitive, then slum clearance and urban re-

16. Specifically, Muth's estimates indicate that individuals seek to add about one-third of the difference between desired and actual stock during a year, which implies that for the adjustment of the actual housing stock to be 90 percent completed, 6 years are required.

17. If there is much variation in the speed of adjustment among the housing markets in the United States, then it would be desirable to estimate Muth's equation with data from the particular local housing market to obtain the speed of adjustment for that market and to use this estimate for our test.

newal result only in a shift in the location of slums rather than in a net reduction in slums. Consequently, we should expect neither urban renewal nor slum clearance to lead to a reduction in the social costs of slum living or to net beneficial spillover effects for properties not on the slum clearance site. Cost-benefit analyses of urban renewal typically find that measured benefits are far less than measured costs.[18] The authors of these studies usually do not attempt to calculate the alleged benefits from these two sources, but they claim that the benefits from the reduction in social costs of slums and the net beneficial spillover effects on neighboring properties might well overcome the excess of measured costs over measured benefits.[19] If the housing market were perfectly competitive, then the expected value of these alleged benefits would be zero and, hence, almost all slum clearance and urban renewal projects would be extremely wasteful.

THE EFFECT OF RENT CERTIFICATES ON THE HOUSING OCCUPIED BY THEIR RECIPIENTS

If it is desired either to decrease the number of occupied slum dwelling units or to improve the housing occupied by low income families and if the housing market is competitive, then slum clearance and urban renewal are not the answers. They would have neither of these effects. The most direct ways of obtaining these results are to tax (or prohibit) the occupation of slum dwelling units or to subsidize the housing of low income families. The former method would make the occupants of slum dwelling units worse off as they judge their own well-being. Consequently, to the extent that the desire to decrease the amount of slum housing and to increase the housing consumption of low income families is motivated by a desire to help these people, to that extent the tax (or prohibition) alternative can be dropped from consideration.

Probably the most efficient method of subsidizing the housing of low income families is to allow these families to buy certificates which they could use to pay the rent or make mortgage payments up to an amount equal to the face value of the certificate.[20] The low income family would purchase this certificate for an amount less than the face value.[21] These certificates would be redeemed by the government from sellers of housing service. It would be illegal to exchange these certificates for other than housing service.

Given the amount of public money likely to be spent for such a program and the amount that might be reasonably charged for these certificates, the face values of rent certificates will not be large enough to induce many low income families to move to newly produced housing because new housing typically comes in relatively

18. For example, see Jerome Rothenberg (13, p. 341, Table 4) and Stephen Messner (9, p. 78, Table 13). In each study, costs and benefits for three projects were calculated. Total benefits for the 6 projects were only 27 percent of total costs. The highest benefit-cost ratio was .37 and the lowest was .05. Rothenberg's calculations were intended to be illustrative only, but Messner's calculations based on Rothenberg's framework are very careful and detailed.

19. See Rothenberg (13, p. 340). Messner (9, p. 78) takes a much more guarded view of the likelihood of significant benefits from these two sources.

20. Olsen (12, pp. 69-116) has made estimates which strongly suggest the rent certificate plan to be significantly more efficient than public housing.

21. Under the principle of benefit taxation, each recipient should be charged an amount equal to average expenditure on housing service prior to the program by families of the same size and with the same income. See Olsen (12, pp. 110-16). This result follows primarily from Muth's finding (11) that the price elasticity of demand for housing service is roughly constant and unitary.

large bundles of housing stock. Since a rent certificate plan does not directly increase the supply of newly constructed housing and since few of the recipients are likely to demand new housing, many people wonder how a rent certificate plan could result in an increase in the total quantity of housing stock. They suggest that since there will be no increase in housing stock, the only result of the increase in demand stemming from the rent certificate plan will be higher prices for housing service purchased by the low income families who use rent certificates.[22]

By now it should be clear that if the market for housing service is perfectly competitive, then this is only the very short-run effect of a rent certificate plan.[23] In the long run, the owners of the smallest bundles of housing stock will either increase their maintenance expenditures (and thereby increase the quantity of housing service yielded by their units) or convert their buildings to other uses. There would no longer be any demand for dwelling units which provide less housing service than can be purchased with rent certificates of the smallest face values.

Some owners of dwelling units presently providing bundles of housing service larger than could be purchased with rent certificates of the highest face value will allow their units to filter down to the relatively more profitable sectors initially affected by rent certificates. As a result, there will be shortages and, hence, economic profits for these larger bundles of housing service. Owners of dwelling units yielding still larger quantities of housing service will allow their units to filter down. Eventually shortages will result for bundles of housing stock which can be provided by new construction. Construction of new dwelling units will continue until there are no more excess profits in the market for housing service. In long-run competitive equilibrium all consumers must pay the same price per unit of housing service. Consequently, purchasers of rent certificates with a face value of x dollars per month should be able to consume the same quantity of housing service as individuals who spent this much per month for housing service prior to the program.

This result leads to yet another testable implication of the competitive theory of the housing market. If the competitive theory is correct, then we should observe that the buyers of rent certificates with a face value of x dollars will occupy housing as good as the housing which rented for x dollars prior to the rent certificate plan.[24] This is the long-run equilibrium situation. The adjustment of this equilibrium will take several years. As already pointed out, Muth's evidence suggests a 90 percent adjustment in 6 years. Hence, we should observe that the characteristics of the housing occupied by recipients (e.g., whether the dwelling unit has hot and cold running water) should approach the characteristics of the housing occupied by individuals who spent the same amount on housing prior to the program.

It should not be necessary to wait until a national rent certificate plan is adopted to test this implication. According to Meyerson, Terrett, and Wheaton (10, p. 71), " . . . welfare agencies in many states in this country do issue rent certificates to families on relief. During the Depression, millions of families received such payments."

22. For a lucid statement of this position taken by many housing specialists, see Martin Meyerson, Barbara Terrett, and William Wheaton (10, pp. 71-72).

23. Indeed, since a rent certificate plan would undoubtedly be discussed by Congress for some time before passage, it would be anticipated by sellers of housing service who would find it profitable to adjust their maintenance policy in advance of passage. Consequently, there might be little price inflation immediately after implementation.

24. It would be necessary to correct for changes in the general price level, but we should not expect the relative price of housing to rise in the long run because of the increase in the total demand for housing service which is a result of the rent certificate plan. Muth (11, pp. 42-46) finds the supply curve to be perfectly elastic.

There may already be data from these experiences to test this implication of the competitive theory of the housing market. Given the demonstrated inefficiency of urban renewal and public housing, it would also seem reasonable for a city to propose and the federal government to accept a rent certificate plan in place of the two other programs on a demonstration basis. The experience of the buyers of rent certificates in this city could be used to test the competitive theory.

CONCLUSION

In this article, the assumptions of Muth's competitive theory of the housing market are stated and the nature of the good called housing service is elaborated upon. This theory is used to translate four familiar terms of housing market analysis—dwelling unit, slum, shortage, and filtering—into the standard concepts of microeconomic theory. If the housing market is perfectly competitive and if it is not more costly per unit to provide housing to low income families or to provide small packages of housing service, then (1) the poor would not pay more per unit for housing, (2) slum clearance and urban renewal would not result in a net reduction in the number of occupied substandard units, and (3) the recipients of rent certificates would enjoy housing just as good as the housing occupied by others who spent as much on housing as the face value of the certificates. These results and their implications for government policy are deduced. In each of the three cases, testable implications of the assumptions are derived and the nature of the test made explicit. It is hoped that this article will serve to bring housing market analysis within the realm of conventional economic theory and to suggest additional tests of one particular conventional economic theory of markets.

REFERENCES

1. M. Anderson, *The Federal Bulldozer*. Cambridge 1964.
2. M. J. Bailey, "Note on the Economics of Residential Zoning and Urban Renewal," *Land Econ.*, Aug. 1959, *35*, 288-92.
3. O. A. Davis and A. B. Whinston, "Economics of Urban Renewal," *Law and Contemp. Prob.*, Winter 1961, *26*, 105-17.
4. M. Friedman, *Capitalism and Freedom*. Chicago 1964.
5. C. G. Hempel, *Philosophy of Natural Science*. Englewood Cliffs 1966.
6. J. M. Henderson and R. E. Quandt, *Microeconomic Theory*. New York 1958.
7. R. H. Leftwich, *The Price System and Resource Allocation*. New York 1961.
8. I. S. Lowry, "Filtering and Housing Standards: A Conceptual Analysis," *Land Econ.*, Nov. 1960, *36*, 362-70.
9. S. D. Messner, *A Benefit Cost Analysis of Urban Redevelopment*, Bureau of Business Research, Indiana Univ., Bloomington 1967.
10. M. Meyerson, B. Terrett, and W. L. C. Wheaton, *Housing, People, and Cities*. New York 1962.
11. R. F. Muth, "The Demand for Non-Farm Housing," in A. C. Harberger, ed., *The Demand for Durable Goods*, Chicago 1960, pp. 29-96.
12. E. O. Olsen, "A Welfare Economic Evaluation of Public Housing," unpublished Ph.D. dissertation, Rice Univ. 1968.
13. J. Rothenberg, "Urban Renewal Programs," in R. Dorfman, ed., *Measuring Benefits of Government Investments*, Washington 1966, pp. 292-341.
14. G. J. Stigler, *The Theory of Price*. New York 1966.
15. U.S. Bureau of Labor Statistics, "A Study of Prices Charged in Food Stores Located in Low and High Income Areas of Six Large Cities, February 1966," mimeo. report, June 12, 1966.
16. ———, "Differences in the Characteristics of Rental Housing Occupied by Families in Three Income Ranges Paying Approximately the Same Rent in Six Cities," mimeo. report, Sept. 1966.

20. *The Determinants of Dwelling-Unit Condition*

RICHARD F. MUTH

Despite the widespread concern over poor quality housing or slums, the many pages written on the subject, and the large sums of money and resources devoted to improving housing quality by federal and local governments, surprisingly little attention has been given to the causes of poor quality housing. Books on slums and urban renewal typically devote only a few pages to examining the causes of slums before turning to ways of dealing with the problem. This is probably the case because slums seem so obviously bad that the need for taking action against them is clearly established. And yet, without proper diagnosis, any proposed treatment may be largely ineffective. In my study of the slum problem I have become convinced that this is the case. Most arguments commonly given are defective for one or more of a variety of reasons and ignore the basic cause of poor housing quality, which is the poverty or low incomes of its inhabitants. With the possible exception of public housing, most suggested remedies for slums do little or nothing to remove or reduce poverty, and they may even tend to increase it. Hence, they are likely to be ineffective in the long run.

Certain arguments for the existence of slums are obviously incomplete and of little value. Thus, it is very often said that slums result from the greed of landlords and their neglect to maintain their properties in good condition. But one might justifiably argue that all landlords desire to earn as large incomes as they can from the properties they own or manage. The relevant question to be asked, and most fail to ask it, is why some landlords find it profitable to maintain their properties in good condition while others do not. Likewise, it is frequently asserted that slums result from the failure of cities to enforce building, occupancy, and similar codes.[1] But this second assertion quite obviously begs the question of why the need for enforcement exists.

While many other arguments for the existence of slums are logically complete, they are inconsistent with at least one of three fairly simple empirical facts. I will discuss these arguments in the first section of this chapter, and the facts upon which they founder in the second. In the third section I will outline a theory which is consistent with these basic facts. Finally, in the last section I discuss spatial aspects of poor housing quality and the effects of housing quality on the spatial pattern of land-use intensity.

THE AGE AND NEGLECT AND OTHER TRADITIONAL THEORIES OF SLUMS

Many frequently cited theories of slum formation are based upon a decline in the demand for housing in what were once good neighborhoods. While the reasons for

Reprinted from Richard F. Muth, *Cities and Housing* (Chicago: University of Chicago Press, 1969), pp. 115-30 (edited) by permission of the publisher and author. Copyright © 1969 by the University of Chicago Press. Richard Muth is a professor of economics at Stanford University.

1. This point is heavily stressed by the Subcommittee on Urban Redevelopment of the President's Advisory Committee on Government Housing Policies and Programs, *A Report to the President of the United States* (Washington: Government Printing Office, 1953), pp. 108-9.

the assumed decline in demand are varied, its effects are quite similar in all these theories. I shall discuss these theories first. Next, I shall discuss several closely related theories whose emphasis is on factors inhibiting investment in housing or new assets generally and which lead to much poor quality housing. In the following section I discuss three important facts with which these theories are in conflict.

Perhaps the most commonly advanced reason for the decline in demand for housing in once good quality neighborhoods which is believed to initiate slum formation is age and obsolescence. It is frequently argued or implied that physical deterioration and obsolescence by itself inevitably makes the housing in older areas progressively less desirable for places of residence.[2] This might be the case if the cost of maintaining structures in good repair increased over time, so that maintenance expenditures on any given building or its neighbors would decline with age.[3] Or, it might be argued that, even if maintained in good condition, old housing becomes progressively less desirable over time as new types of dwellings and more attractive neighborhood patterns are developed. Other forces which affect the demand for residences might be closely associated with the age of a neighborhood and its buildings. In discussing the origin of cheap residential areas in Chicago, Hoyt observes that:

> Workingmen's cottages tended to grow up in all sections of the city between the belts of fashionable land and the industries and factories along the Chicago River. . . .The tracts they occupied were close to the noise and dust of factories but not directly contiguous to water or rail transportation. Such sites were poorly provided with street improvements and surface car transportation.[4]

While such dwellings may have provided satisfactory accommodation to their original inhabitants, because of rising incomes or for other reasons the demand for housing in these areas has fallen over time. Many writers also stress the neglect by municipal governments of older residential areas as a cause of the decline in the demand for housing. Failure to plan effectively and to enforce zoning laws as well as the lack of parks and other recreational facilities and inattention to street maintenance and lighting are mentioned as specific instances of this neglect.[5]

While the reasons given for the decline in the demand for housing in older neighborhoods are varied, the effects of this decline noted by those who consider explicitly the process of slum formation are quite similar.[6] The decline in demand reduces the price of housing in old neighborhoods. With the fall in housing prices, investment in existing dwellings declines because of the fall in returns to such investment, and the quality of housing deteriorates. If quality deterioration itself caused the initial decline in demand, the latter accelerates the deterioration of the neighborhoods. With the fall in demand and quality deterioration, older residents move to newer neighborhoods where the available housing is more suited to their tastes and circumstances. Their places are taken by lower income households, who

2. See, for example, Thomas F. Johnson, James R. Morris, and Joseph G. Butts, *Renewing America's Cities* (Washington: The Institute for Social Science Research, 1962) pp. 3-5; Richard U. Ratcliff, *Urban Land Economics* (New York: McGraw-Hill, 1949), p. 402; and *Slums, Large Scale Housing, and Decentralization*, Report of President's Conference on Home Building and Home Ownership, ed. John M. Gries and James Ford (Washington: U.S. Government Printing Office, 1932), p. 2.

3. Ratcliff, *Urban Land Economics*, p. 402.

4. *One Hundred Years of Land Values in Chicago* (Chicago: University of Chicago Press, 1933), p. 311.

5. Subcommittee on Urban Redevelopment, *Report to the President*, pp. 108-9.

6. These effects are best described by Ratcliff, *Urban Land Economics*, pp. 402-3.

have less aversion for poorer quality housing than higher-income groups, and dwellings may be converted to smaller units more suitable to the size quarters these lower income groups wish to occupy. The relative, and in some cases absolute, decline in population in the older, more central parts of cities is often attributed to the decline in housing demand due to age and/or related factors.

Another frequently cited cause of the decline in demand for housing in the older, more central parts of cities is the fall in transport costs brought about by the automobile.[7] I have . . . argued . . . [elsewhere[8]] that the fall in the marginal costs of transport which accompanied the automobile reduced the relative rate of decline of housing prices with distance from the city center. . . . [T]he effect of this decline in the price gradient will be a fall in housing prices in residential areas near the city center and an increase in the outer parts of the city. The fall in prices near the center reduces the returns to investment in housing, and for this reason expenditures for maintenance and repair are reduced, and housing deteriorates. The effects of the deterioration in quality are much the same as in the age and neglect theory discussed above: housing prices fall further, higher income groups move out of the older areas, and lower income households move in.[9]

Of course, one might ask why the older areas closest to the city center are not converted to other uses if returns to residential uses have declined. Apart from factors peculiar to real property which inhibit redevelopment generally, two classes of reasons might be given.[10] First, if anything, it would seem that land in the CBD [Central Business District] has become more intensively used. It is sometimes argued that factors such as improved construction methods and the development of better elevators have reduced the relative costs of taller buildings. (Such changes, however, may merely reflect that taller buildings have become relatively more profitable for other reasons.) In addition, while the introduction of the automobile and truck may have reduced the marginal cost of transport outside the CBD, the increased traffic congestion in the center may have actually increased marginal transport costs there. Second, with the auto era the central parts of the city no longer have as great a comparative advantage as they once did for many nonresidential activities. With residential populations more widely dispersed in the city and circumferential travel relatively less costly than radial movement, the advantage of the CBD as a place for retail and service business has probably declined. As another example, wholesaling and some types of manufacturing may no longer find locations close to rail freight terminals near the center as desirable as they did prior to truck transportation. For reasons such as these, in many instances conversion of the deteriorated residential areas to other uses is not profitable.

A third set of reasons sometimes advanced for the decline in the demand for housing in the older, more central parts of cities can be classified under the heading of external effects. Several kinds of such effects can be distinguished. An expansion of manufacturing firms out of a neighboring industrial district or retail and service firms beyond their original locations along major streets may make housing in surrounding areas less desirable because of increased dirt, noise, or for many other reasons.[11] Or the owner of a parcel in a neighborhood of, say, single-family residences may find it

7. This is emphasized by Gries and Ford, *Slums*, p. 2; and Hoover, *The Location of Economic Activity* (New York: McGraw-Hill, 1948), pp. 208-11; and hinted at by Mabel L. Walker, *Urban Blight and Slums* (Cambridge, Mass.: Harvard University Press, 1938), p. 17.

8. R. Muth, *Cities and Housing* (Chicago: University of Chicago Press, 1969), Chap. 5.

9. Gries and Ford, *Slums*, p. 2; and Walker, *Urban Blight*, p. 17.

10. These are best discussed in Edgar M. Hoover, *The Location of Economic Activity*, pp. 209-11.

11. Gries and Ford, *Slums*, p. 2.

profitable to him to convert it to a grocery store, filling station, or a rooming house. However, by so doing he may reduce the desirability of surrounding residences, with the already familiar effects of declining housing demand.[12]

Closely related to the decline in demand theories discussed above are external factors which are said to operate so as to limit the amount of investment in housing generally and, hence, to increase the supply of poor quality housing. As many of the above arguments imply, the demand for the housing provided by any particular type of structure depends upon the nature of the surrounding structures as well as the quality of structure actually inhabited. This means that the owner of any particular residential parcel in making an investment produces benefits not only for himself in the form of the increased rental value of his property but also for the owners of surrounding properties by making their housing more desirable and thus increasing its rental value. If individual owners carry investment in their properties only to the point where the marginal returns to them equal marginal cost, too little investment will be made from the social point of view since the marginal social returns exceed marginal social cost by the marginal increase in the rental value of surrounding properties.[13] This argument, of course, applies to all types of neighborhoods, regardless of their age, location, and quality. In fact, if, as seems not unlikely, higher income and other households inhabiting better quality housing are more influenced by the external character of the neighborhood in which they live, it would apply with special force to better neighborhoods. However, by limiting investment in housing generally, such external effects would result in a large number, both absolutely and relatively, of dwellings being below any given level of quality, and hence more slum housing.

Now there are several reasons why the effects noted in the preceding paragraph might not occur. In the first place, it would be in the interest of a single owner to acquire a group of contiguous properties. Under the conditions assumed by the argument, a group of contiguous properties would be worth more under common than under fragmented ownership. The principal obstacle to so internalizing these external effects would seem to be the difficulties of land assembly. . . . Another obvious method of dealing with the problem of external effects is cooperation among owners of contiguous parcels. However, cooperation is likely to break down since any individual owner has the incentive to avoid making the extra expenditure on his property and to reap the benefits of the extra expenditure of others. Finally, collective action in the form of zoning or other municipal land-use controls might be mutually beneficial. But such controls may be expensive to enforce, and, indeed, it is frequently asserted that existing controls are inadequate and poorly enforced.

Several other forces might also increase the supply of poor quality housing. It is sometimes argued, for example, that dwellings in certain parts of a city may be poorly maintained because of capital market imperfections which raise interest rates or make loans unavailable to property owners in these areas. I have never seen a convincing explanation of why such capital market imperfections exist, and, indeed, there is good reason to believe that interest rates would be high or loans unavailable for investment in changing or slum neighborhoods. In either kind of neighborhood there is likely to be more risk attached to investment than in neighborhoods of better housing quality—in slums because of the risk of loss of income due to code enforcement and in changing neighborhoods because of uncertainty about the future of the area.

12. Clarence Arthur Perry, *The Rebuilding of Blighted Areas: A Study of the Neighborhood Unit in Replanning and Plot Assemblage* (New York: Regional Plan Association, 1933), p. 8.

13. For a fuller discussion see Otto A. Davis and Andrew B. Whinston, "The Economics of Urban Renewal," *Law and Contemporary Problems* 26 (Winter 1961): 105-17.

Furthermore, if otherwise socially desirable and privately profitable investment in housing is not made because of capital market imperfections which affect the availability of funds to certain property owners, others—perhaps insurance companies—not affected by these imperfections would find it profitable to buy up the properties and make the investment themselves. The failure of such purchases to be made might result, however, from difficulties in land assembly.

Certain features of the tax system are sometimes cited as contributing to slums. It is argued that slum properties are taxed at lower effective rates than others, perhaps because assessments are based primarily on outward appearance rather than the income the property produces or perhaps because of differential underassessment by some related factor such as age. Or it may be argued that taxation of site and improvements rather than site value only results in too little investment on sites generally, and hence too much poor quality housing. Finally, depreciation provisions in the federal income tax structure are sometimes mentioned as a cause of poor quality housing. . . . [F]or federal income tax purposes allowable deductions for depreciation exceed the true rates at which properties depreciate. For this reason, it is argued by some, dwellings are retained in the housing stock longer than they otherwise would be, or the housing stock is older than would otherwise be the case. (This argument, of course, applies equally to physical assets other than dwellings.) More poor quality housing than otherwise will result, however, only if there is a tendency for dwellings to be of poor quality purely for reasons associated with age.

The effects of depreciation provisions in the federal tax structure are similar to several other arguments which are often mentioned as inhibiting socially desirable redevelopment and causing slums.[14] The crudest of these is the assertion that owners place unrealistically high values on their properties and refuse to sell for redevelopment at "reasonable" prices.[15] As with most such glib explanations of economic phenomena, further examination in the third section suggests good reasons why seemingly unrealistic values may, in fact, be quite consistent with market conditions. Or Hoyt argues that once a neighborhood acquires the reputation as a poor quality one, builders prefer to invest in other sections.[16] But this merely says either that demand for new housing in the area is not strong enough to make redevelopment privately profitable or that other factors inhibit redevelopment on a small enough scale to be undertaken privately. One of these inhibiting factors is the possibility that redevelopment, to be privately profitable and socially desirable, must include a new street system or new schools, parks, and other services commonly provided by municipal governments. . . . Especially important is the fact that the assembly of large tracts of contiguous properties under diverse ownership may be too expensive and time-consuming to undertake except where, as in urban renewal projects, properties may be acquired using the power of eminent domain. Factors such as these, like the external economies, capital market imperfection, and tax-related arguments, tend to increase the supply of poor quality housing and prevent private individuals from undertaking socially desirable redevelopment.

SHORTCOMINGS IN THE TRADITIONAL THEORIES OF SLUMS

The theories of slums discussed in the first section are, or can be made, logically complete, and some—the declining transport-cost argument in particular—have a

14. These are given special emphasis by Ratcliff, *Urban Land Economics*, pp. 427-31.
15. Ibid., p. 430; and especially Walker, *Urban Blight*, p. 17.
16. *One Hundred Years of Land Values in Chicago*, p. 311.

certain a priori plausibility. My empirical analysis[17] . . . suggests that some of the forces stressed by these theories might have some empirical relevance. But, almost without exception, the traditional theories are deficient in that they are inconsistent with, or at best fail to provide an explanation for, three simple but important empirical facts. These are: first, that slum housing seems to be expensive in relation to its quality; second, that urban renewal projects lose money; and, third, that contrary to widespread opinion, housing quality seems to have improved markedly over the decade of the fifties. I wish to discuss these facts in relation to the theories discussed previously in more detail in the present section.

The theories of slums discussed in the preceding section all imply that the increase in the relative quantity of slum housing, which the theory attempts to explain, results from an increase in the supply of slums relative to that of good quality housing in the city as a whole. The age and neglect, decline in transport cost, and encroachment of hostile land-uses theories assert that this occurs because of a fall in the demand for housing generally in some particular area or areas of the city. Because of the decline in demand, the returns to investment in structures in the affected areas fall, and housing is allowed to deteriorate. With this deterioration, the fraction of the whole city's housing stock which is poor quality tends to increase. The external economies, capital market imperfection, tax, and barriers to redevelopment arguments, however, all stress factors which increase the supply of poor quality housing directly. In either case, with an increase in the relative supply of poor quality housing such as any of the above-noted forces may produce, the price per unit of housing service[18] of poor quality housing will fall relative to that of good quality housing, provided that the relative demand for the two types of housing is not perfectly elastic.

The traditional theories thus imply that with the increase in the relative quantity of slum or poor quality housing, the rental values of slum housing would decline. This decline results primarily from the fall in the price per unit of housing service for properties used to produce poor quality housing prior to the change. For properties converted to slum use, rental values will also decline because the converted dwellings now contain fewer units of housing services than prior to their conversion. With the fall in the price of the services of slum housing, the returns to properties used to produce slum housing before the change would fall. These properties would thus become less profitable to their owners when evaluated at property prices which prevailed prior to the change or at their estimated reproduction cost less depreciation. Hence, the prices of properties used to produce slum housing prior to the change would fall. The same is true for properties converted to poor quality use because of the changed conditions, except perhaps for certain of the tax arguments cited earlier, even though these properties tend to be worth more when converted than if they were to remain in the good quality use.

The implications of the traditional theories developed in the two preceding paragraphs would seem to be at variance with common popular beliefs that slum housing is expensive in relation to its quality and highly profitable to its owners. Slum housing provides fewer units of housing services per unit of time and can have a high rental value in relation to its quality only if the price per unit of housing service for slum

17. R. Muth, *Cities and Housing*, pt. II.

18. I stress the qualification "per unit of housing service." Since poor quality dwellings provide fewer units of housing services per unit of time than good quality ones, expenditure on or rental value of poor quality dwellings per unit of time would be smaller than for good quality dwellings if the prices per unit of housing service of the two types were the same.

housing is greater than that for good quality housing. But, as can be seen from the above, the traditional theories fail to provide any reason why this last should be the case.[19] These theories also imply that the profitability of slum housing, evaluated at previously existing property values or at estimated reproduction cost less depreciation, would have declined with the increase in the relative quantity of the slums. For the profitability of slum housing to be greater than average, in the sense described above, and at the same time to have fallen, it must have been higher still prior to the increase in the relative quantity of slum housing. But none of the theories described in the first section give any indication why this should be so.

Now, of course, since there is almost no good empirical evidence on the price per unit of housing services and on rental and property values in slum versus other areas, the profitability of slum housing may be more apparent than real. Direct evidence on housing prices in relation to quality is quite difficult to obtain. The difficulties are largely the same as those discussed in the preceding chapter in regard to evidence on housing prices in relation to race. In addition, it is quite possible that rentals may be higher in relation to housing quality in slums than in better neighborhoods because of greater operating and/or depreciation costs, a more rapid turnover of tenants, or because of higher rental collection costs and/or delinquencies.[20] Furthermore, even if rentals net of the costs listed above were higher in slums after taking account of quality differences, slum operation would not necessarily be especially profitable. The higher rentals might merely reflect the greater risks inherent in slum properties, such as the possible losses of income from sporadic occupancy and building code enforcement. . . .

Another fact which is inconsistent with many of the theories discussed earlier is that urban renewal projects almost universally lose money or require a governmental subsidy. By this I mean that the expenditures for acquiring properties plus costs of planning, demolition, and improving the site exceed the receipts from the resale of the cleared site to private redevelopers. Indeed, acquisition costs alone generally exceed the resale value of the cleared site by a wide margin.[21] Now if the decline in demand for housing which is alleged to have caused the deterioration of an area came about because of obsolescence, because of encroachment or introduction of hostile land uses, or because the area was originally poorly planned or poorly supplied with municipal services, then a renewal program which corrected these deficiencies should certainly result in an excess of receipts from resale of the redeveloped site over acquisition costs. And, if external effects, capital market imperfections, or various barriers to private redevelopment prevent socially desirable redevelopment, then governmental renewal projects employing powers of eminent domain

19. Of the writers cited earlier, Walker, *Urban Blight*, p. 17, is one of the few to recognize this difficulty. She observes that in some slum areas properties may yield good returns "because of the sheer density of population forced by necessity to live in the most undesirable surroundings." In discussing barriers to redevelopment, Ratcliff, *Urban Land Economics*, p. 429, argues that property owners may earn good returns by overcrowding or by deferring maintenance expenditures. Gries and Ford, *Slums*, p. 2, also note that "In some cases a slum has become economically profitable because of the high rents that can be obtained for improper use . . ." Neither of the latter two works indicates why the apparently high returns can be earned.

20. Hoyt, *One Hundred Years of Land Values in Chicago*, p. 314, asserts this is the case.

21. For example, in those parts of the Hyde Park-Kenwood program in Chicago known as Hyde Park A and B, acquisition costs were of the order of $10 million and receipts from resale of the cleared site $1 million. For information on the costs of federally supported urban projects in the nation as a whole see Martin Anderson, *The Federal Bulldozer* (Cambridge, Mass.: M.I.T. Press, 1964), pp. 19-23 and table A.1.

should result in a surplus, or at least not in a subsidy.[22] To reconcile the existence of a governmental subsidy to renewal projects with these traditional arguments for slum formation, one would have to argue that renewal has been premature or poorly planned and executed, that slum properties are taxed at rates which are too low, or that condemnation awards for properties acquired for the programs are too high.[23]

The third major fact with which most traditional theories of slum formation are inconsistent is that in recent years the quality of the housing stock in cities appears to have improved markedly. Data on the quality of the housing stock which permit comparisons over time are quite limited, partly because data on housing condition were first obtained by the census in 1940 and partly because for each succeeding decennial census there has been a change in the definition of housing condition. Furthermore, comparison of data from the 1950 Census of Housing and the 1956 National Housing Inventory, which employed identical definitions of housing condition, is made difficult by the nonreporting of quality for some dwellings and by the fact that the classification of individual dwellings by condition is not wholly reliable. Nevertheless, estimates made by Beverly Duncan and Philip M. Hauser[24] using these data point to a great quality improvement from 1950 to 1956. Of the six Standard Metropolitan Areas they studied, only in New York does it appear that the number of substandard dwelling units—units which are dilapidated or lack private bath—has increased. In the five other SMA's—Boston, Chicago, Detroit, Los Angeles, and Philadelphia—and in the cities of Chicago and Philadelphia, the number of substandard dwellings declined on the order of one-third from 1950 to 1956.[25] About 90 percent of this reduction was due to improvement in the quality of given units and only about 10 percent to demolitions, mergers, and other changes.[26]

It is quite difficult, if not impossible, to account for this great improvement in quality on the basis of the hypotheses discussed in the first section. In fact, on the basis of some of these arguments one would expect an increase in the proportion of dwellings that are substandard. Most neighborhoods and dwellings aged six years during the period of quality improvement; the building of express highways and other improvements in transportation would have further reduced marginal transport costs, and property tax rates increased in many cities.

Thus, the traditional theories of slums seem to be seriously deficient. Some of these theories, however, may have some empirical relevance. . . . If age of dwellings or factors related to it were responsible for the existence of slums, one would expect the proportion of substandard dwellings to vary with age, both among census tracts

22. Note that such factors as enumerated may result in too much poor quality housing even though renewal is not justified because of conversion costs.

23. Also note that the existence of a governmental subsidy need not mean that urban renewal projects are socially undesirable. Such projects may yield external benefits in the form of increases in the value of surrounding properties, a reduction in the cost of municipal services, or, perhaps, a reduction in crime and disease. These social benefits would not be reflected in the offers of private redevelopers for the cleared sites.

24. *Housing a Metropolis–Chicago* (Glencoe, Ill.: The Free Press, 1960), pp. 56-58.

25. Data such as these which point to housing quality improvement are frequently discounted as being unreliable. The evaluation of the U.S. Bureau of the Census, however, suggests that census data provide an accurate estimate of the decline in the number of occupied substandard dwellings from 1950 to 1960. It also concludes that census tract data on substandard housing provide a ranking of tracts according to housing condition which is relatively free from error. See U.S. Bureau of the Census "Quality of Housing: An Appraisal of Census Statistics and Methods," pp. III-8 to III-10.

26. Duncan and Hauser, *Housing a Metropolis*, pp. 63-68.

in a given city and among cities. Likewise, if slums and blight have resulted from a decline in transport costs, one would expect the proportion of substandard dwellings in a census tract to be inversely related to the tract's distance from the CBD. This is because the extent of the decline in housing prices that resulted from a fall in marginal transport costs would be greater in relative terms the smaller the distance to the CBD. . . . And, if the encroachment or mixture of hostile land uses is an important determinant of the condition of residential structures, one would expect to find a higher proportion of substandard dwellings in tracts close to manufacturing or retail centers. Finally, to the extent that these theories offer any explanation at all for the association between the condition of dwellings and the incomes of their inhabitants, it is that dwelling-unit condition is an important determinant of the locational choice of households. . . .

AN ALTERNATIVE THEORY OF SLUMS

In order to account for the apparently high price and profitability of slums one must consider factors which tend to increase the demand for poor quality housing or limit its supply. I now turn to the consideration of such factors and will attempt to show how they are consistent with those three facts with which theories discussed earlier are not.

. . . [R]ecent evidence indicates that housing demand increases at least in proportion to income. The increase in housing consumption which follows an increase in income may take various forms: more rooms per dwelling, larger rooms, better quality materials, more attractive and frequent interior decoration, larger lot sizes, and so forth. Indeed, casual observation would suggest that higher income households would typically consume more housing in most or all of these ways. It would certainly not seem strange, therefore, if the lower income households tended to occupy poor quality housing and to use smaller amounts of space per person. In fact, the strong association between poor quality housing and crowding may be mostly due to the fact that these are merely different aspects of a small per household consumption of housing.[27]

Now there is nothing very novel in an economist's suggesting that poor quality housing is purchased by low income households, or, indeed, that poor quality housing results from poverty rather than the reverse. What is surprising, however, is that in popular or even in scholarly discussions of slums, this fact is so rarely mentioned. Walker is one of the few writers discussed in the first section who mention poverty as a cause of slums, and she argues that poverty and blight need not be closely related.[28] Furthermore, these writers have generally argued that poor quality housing exists primarily for other reasons and that low income households have less of an aversion to living in it than do higher income ones. An alternative hypothesis . . . is that the location of lower income households is determined primarily by other forces and that the quality of the housing stock in the neighborhoods low income households choose to inhabit is adapted to their circumstances. This would be done primarily

27. Viewing, say, space and quality as inputs into the production of satisfactions called housing, they will tend to vary directly so long as they reflect variations in the quantity of housing demanded. However, under certain circumstances space and quality may vary inversely if their relative prices as inputs into the production of housing vary. Thus, near the centers of cities where space is relatively expensive, rooms may be small though of high quality. Conversely, in older areas houses with large or many rooms may be relatively cheap but of below-average quality for their size.

28. *Urban Blight*, p. 23.

through conversions of existing structures to a larger number of smaller units and allowing these units to deteriorate by deferring maintenance and repairs.

While previous research has clearly established that income is one of the most important determinants of housing consumption, other variables have an important effect on the quantity of housing a household consumes. One of these is the relative price of housing. Just as a decline in income, so an increase in the relative price of housing could be expected to lead to poorer quality housing. Since I have argued earlier that housing prices tend to decline with distance from the CBD, one might expect to find that the proportion of dwelling units which are substandard declines for this reason. Also, one would expect to find that in cities where construction costs are relatively high, the price per unit of housing service would also be relatively high, and thus the proportion of substandard units would be higher than average. Along these lines, if housing prices paid by Negroes are higher than those paid by whites for comparable quarters, I would expect that at any given level of income a higher proportion of Negroes inhabit poor quality housing and less space per person than whites. Indeed, it is frequently said that a higher proportion of Negroes live in poor housing because of residential discrimination.[29] In discussion of the question, however, the fact that Negroes' incomes are, on the average, lower than those of whites is frequently overlooked.

It is not difficult to account for a strong and rising demand for poor quality housing in the central cities of our metropolitan areas on the hypothesis that it is but an aspect of a low per household consumption of housing. During the first half of this century the per capita stock of nonfarm housing showed relatively little increase in the United States. I would attribute this primarily to the fact that the relative price of housing has risen greatly during this period.[30] Low-income migrants to this country have tended to congregate in cities. While the flow of migration from abroad was greatly reduced following 1920, large-scale migration of lower-income persons from the rural South—many of them Negroes—has taken place. This migration was especially heavy during the 1940's. In addition, the natural rates of population growth of Negroes and perhaps of other lower-income groups have tended to be higher than for others. During the same time, higher-income households have tended to move away from central cities to their suburbs. Thus, while on the average the per capita consumption of housing showed but little increase, the central cities of our metropolitan areas came to be increasingly inhabited by persons of lower than average income and housing consumption.

The relative price of slum housing and the proportion of dwelling units which are poor quality also depend upon conditions of supply. If the supply of poor quality relative to good quality housing were perfectly elastic, an increase in demand would increase the proportion of poor quality dwellings but, after adjustment to the new equilibrium position, would not raise the price of such dwellings relative to that of better ones. There is good reason to think, however, that the relative supply of slum housing is less than perfectly elastic. Slum housing in American cities today is rarely newly constructed as such; rather, it tends to be produced primarily through the conversion of existing dwellings to smaller ones and, by deferring maintenance and repair, allowing them to deteriorate in quality. But surely dwellings differ in the ease and cost with which they can be converted or, stated differently, they differ in the relative amounts they can earn as good versus poor quality housing. I would

29. For example, see Subcommittee on Urban Redevelopment, *Report to the President*, p. 109.

30. For a more complete discussion see my "The Demand for Non-Farm Housing," in *The Demand for Durable Goods*, ed. A. C. Harberger (Chicago: University of Chicago Press, 1960).

expect, for example, that single-family dwellings on large lots and newer dwellings generally would be more costly to convert than would apartment buildings and older dwellings. In addition, enforcement of building and occupancy codes by local governments tends to limit the conversion of existing dwellings to smaller or poorer quality ones, and these codes may be enforced more strictly in certain areas of cities than others. Under these conditions a growth in demand will tend to raise the relative price of slum housing as well as the proportion of poor quality dwellings. And, under these conditions, the ownership of slum dwellings will tend to become more profitable with an increase in demand for slum as opposed to good quality housing. If this analysis is correct, then it is easy to see why urban renewal programs lose money. In effect, they shift sites from a high to a low price market.

But, one might ask, if the above is correct, how can one account for the marked improvement in housing quality that took place during the early fifties? I suspect this was due mainly to a decline in the demand for poor quality housing. Unlike what happened in the first half of this century, a substantial increase in housing consumption took place during the early fifties. Data from the 1956 National Housing Inventory suggest that the number of occupied dwelling units in the United States increased by 16.5 percent from 1950 to 1956, while population increased by only 12 percent.[31] The increase in average quality per unit was much greater during this same period. The median value of one-unit, owner-occupied nonfarm dwellings increased by 54 percent and the median contract rent of tenant-occupied nonfarm units by 47 percent, as compared with an increase in construction costs of only 27 percent.[32] Raymond W. Goldsmith's[33] estimates of the stock of private, nonfarm housekeeping units (including land) in 1947-49 prices point to a similar conclusion, increasing by about 23 percent from the end of 1949 to the end of 1955. Migration from the rural South slowed down noticeably during the 1950s. In addition, even the incomes of the lower income groups rose rapidly during the forties and early fifties. But, because of rent controls, many lower-income households may have been prevented from acquiring better accommodations or preferred to remain in dwellings with low, controlled rentals before 1950. While the area inhabited by the lowest fifth, say, of a city's households by income level no doubt expanded in the early fifties, and some housing may have deteriorated in the process, with rising incomes and per household consumption of housing the absolute level of housing quality of the lowest relative income group would tend to improve. Hence, the number of dwellings substandard, or below a given absolute level of quality, would decline.

The existence of rent controls during the forties may also have tended to increase the relative supply of poorly maintained housing. To the extent that rent controls are successful in preventing increases in nominal rentals during periods of rising prices, real rentals decline as does the profitability of maintaining properties. With the removal of controls and the subsequent increase in rentals, the profitability of maintenance is increased. In this regard it is interesting to note that of the six SMA's examined in the study by Duncan and Hauser cited above, New York, the only one

31. Data on number of units, median value and median contract rent cited here are from U.S. Bureau of the Census, 1956 *National Housing Inventory*, vol. 3, pt. 1 (Washington: U.S. Government Printing Office, 1959).

32. As measured by the Boeckh index of residential construction costs, brick. Because of the removal of rent controls prior to 1950, the above increase may overestimate the quality improvement of tenant-occupied dwellings.

33. *The National Wealth of the United States in the Postwar Period* (Princeton: Princeton University Press, 1962), table B-12, p. 235.

where rent controls were still in existence, is the only one to show an increase in the number of substandard units. Other factors which may have reduced the supply of poor quality housing during the early fifties are more vigorous enforcement of building and occupancy codes resulting from greater concern over housing quality, demolitions for expressways, renewal programs, and other purposes. These latter could not have been very important, however, since Duncan and Hauser's results indicate that most of the reduction in the number of substandard dwellings took place because of an improvement in quality of given dwellings.

In sum, while considerations such as those discussed above do not necessarily constitute an "airtight" case for the hypothesis that slums are merely an indicator of low housing consumption, they clearly indicate that this alternative hypothesis can more easily explain the apparent high price and profitability of slum housing and the recent improvement in housing quality than can the traditional explanations for slums cited earlier.

IMPLICATIONS OF SLUM HOUSING FOR THE SPATIAL PATTERN OF LAND USE

Another important fact about poor quality housing is that it tends to be spatially concentrated, frequently in areas close to the center of the city. . . .

The reasons for the spatial concentration of poor quality housing, not surprisingly, depend partly upon the reasons for the existence of this poor quality housing. If slums result from a decline in demand for housing in older areas of the city, concentration of slums in the more central parts of today's cities could readily be explained by the fact that the central parts of today's cities are generally the oldest. If slums result because of a decline in transport costs, as described earlier, then the areas hardest hit would be those closest to the city center. Or, if slums result from the encroachment of hostile land uses, they would tend to be located near areas of concentration of these uses. Such areas are frequently in the older, more central parts of the city. Finally, if, contrary to the above, slums are the result of the low incomes of their inhabitants, the location of slums will be governed by the locational determinants of low income households as well as those of dwellings which are cheapest to convert. . . .

21. *Effect of Housing Market Segregation on Urban Development*

JOHN F. KAIN

This paper is concerned with the residential segregation of Negro Americans and the effects of this segregation on housing markets and on patterns of urban development. Existing theories of residential location ignore this serious market imperfection almost entirely. Yet it is hard to conceive of any factor that has a greater effect on either residential location decisions or the pattern of urban development. Until very recently economists concerned with urban problems paid very little attention to race. Exceptions to this generalization were studies sponsored by the Committee on Race and Housing and research by economists at the University of Chicago, whose particular sensitivity to the problem is perhaps understandable.[1] In contrast, considerable empirical research on residential segregation and discrimination was carried out by sociologists and, to a lesser extent, by urban planners. Unfortunately this work, published in sociology and planning journals, had little influence on urban economics.

This paper is an attempt to synthesize existing "economic" theories of location and the considerable body of empirical and descriptive research on housing market discrimination. The discussion begins with a brief survey of the empirical research on the extent and causes of residential segregation in American cities. Then a modest beginning is made at introducing racial discrimination into "economic" models of residential location. The final section uses the results of these explorations to comment on the prospects of our cities and what I regard as appropriate policy responses.

BLACK CENTRAL CITY CHOKED BY WHITE SUBURBS

Any discussion of the contemporary role of racial discrimination in influencing the behavior of housing markets and the patterns of urban development should begin

Reprinted from *Savings and Residential Financing: 1969 Conference Proceedings*, ed. Donald P. Jacobs and Richard T. Pratt (Chicago: United States Savings and Loan League, May 8-9, 1969), pp. 89-108, by permission of the publisher and author. John F. Kain is a professor of economics at Harvard University.

I would like to acknowledge the numerous suggestions as to both substance and exposition offered by H. James Brown, Mitchell Stengel, Clifford Kern, Joseph J. Persky, John M. Quigley, Eric A. Hanushek and Molly Mayo.

1. Davis McEntire, *Residence and Race: Final and Comprehensive Report to the Commission on Race and Housing* (Berkeley: University of California Press, 1960); Gary S. Becker, *The Economics of Discrimination* (Chicago: University of Chicago Press, 1957); Beverly Duncan and Philip M. Hauser, *Housing a Metropolis–Chicago* (Glencoe: The Free Press of Glencoe, Inc., 1960); Otis D. Duncan and Beverly Duncan, *The Negro Population of Chicago–A Study in Residential Succession* (Chicago: University of Chicago Press, 1957); Martin J. Bailey, "Effects of Race and Other Demographic Factors on the Values of Single-Family Homes," *Land Economics* 42, no. 12 (May 1966): 215-20; Martin J. Bailey, "Note on the Economics of Residential Zoning and Urban Renewal," *Land Economics* 35 (August 1959): 288-90; and Richard F. Muth, "The Variation of Population Density and Its Components in South Chicago," *Papers and Proceedings of the Regional Science Association* 11 (1964).

with a clear understanding of the extent and nature of residential segregation prevalent today in American cities. This proposition may seem self-evident, but previous experience with many discussions of these issues suggests the undesirability of proceeding without a clear statement of the available evidence.

An important aspect of housing market segregation is the token representation of Negroes in suburban areas. Black Americans have not participated in the rapid postwar suburbanization of the population. Unfortunately, there is more than a germ of truth to the characterization of an increasingly black central city being strangled by a noose of white suburbs. In 1960 the 216 metropolitan areas of the United States were 11 percent Negro. However, 17 percent of central city populations was black as contrasted with only 5 percent of suburban populations.[2] If southern metropolitan areas, with their suburban (agriculture) Negro population, are omitted, the underrepresentation of blacks in the suburbs is even more apparent. In 1960 Negroes were over 15 percent of the population of central cities of metropolitan areas outside the South, but less than 3 percent of their suburban populations. Much has been made recently of data from the current population surveys which suggest that suburban black populations may have grown more rapidly in the past few years. These data should be regarded with considerable caution, however, since small sample sizes do not permit any meaningful evaluation of these aggregate changes. For example, it is not possible from these statistics to determine whether the aggregate increases in black suburban populations are occurring in all SMSAs, are limited to a few SMSAs or particular sections of the country, or whether they take the form of a dispersed (integrated) pattern of settlement, an acceleration in the growth of small suburban ghettos, or simply the spilling over of central city ghettos into the suburban ring. It should be clearly understood that the implications of these aggregate changes cannot be determined without more information about the nature of the changes.

Housing market segregation does not end with the exclusion of blacks from suburban areas, because Negroes also are intensely segregated within central cities. Karl and Alma Taeuber have calculated segregation indexes for central cities in 1940, in 1950, and in 1960 using census block statistics. These indexes, which assume values between 0 and 100, measure the extent to which observed racial patterns of residence by block differ from a pattern of proportional representation. A value of zero indicates a completely even distribution of Negroes, that is, the proportion of Negroes on every block is the same and equal to the proportion of the entire central city. A value of 100 indicates the opposite situation of a completely segregated distribution, or, each block contains only whites or blacks but not both. The higher the value of the index, the higher the degree of residential segregation. Values for the 156 central cities analyzed in 1960 ranged from 60 to 98 with only a few cities having values in the lower range of observations—only 5 cities have values below 70.[3]

LOW INCOME ONLY ONE FACTOR OF SEGREGATION

Numerous explanations have been offered for the virtually total segregation of blacks. One of the most common is the contention that Negroes are concentrated within particular neighborhoods because they are poor, spend too little on housing, or differ

2. U.S. Bureau of the Census, *U.S. Census of Population: 1960. 1960 Selected Area Reports. Standard Metropolitan Statistical Areas*. Final Report PC (3)-1D (Washington, D.C.: U.S. Government Printing Office, 1963), table 1.

3. Karl E. Taeuber and Alma F. Taeuber, *Negroes in Cities: Residential Segregation and Neighborhood Change* (Chicago: Aldine Publishing Co., 1965).

systematically from the majority white population in terms of other characteristics affecting their choice of residence. This socioeconomic hypothesis is easily evaluated empirically, and several studies have examined it.[4] Without exception these studies have determined that only a fraction of the observed pattern of Negro residential segregation can be explained by low incomes or other measurable socioeconomic differences.

Although many tests of the socioeconomic hypothesis rely on elaborate statistical methods, even the most primitive analyses are sufficient to raise serious doubts. If low income explains the concentration of Negroes in central cities, it also should be true that most low-income whites live in central cities and that most of the small Negro middle class live in the suburbs. Yet, as the data presented in Table 21.1 illustrate, almost as many low-income whites live in the suburban rings of the largest metropolitan areas as live in the central cities. For example, 45 percent of Detroit's poor white families live in suburbs, but only 11 percent of its poor Negro families. In fact, the proportion of low-income whites living in the suburbs is not very different from the proportion of all whites.

TABLE 21.1 *Percent of White and Negro Families Living In the Suburban Ring of the 10 Largest Urbanized Areas**

	WHITE			NEGRO		
	All Families	Families with Income Under $3,000	Families with Income Over $10,000	All Families	Families with Income Under $3,000	Families with Income Over $10,000
New York	27.8%	16.3%	39.2%	9.4%	8.2%	13.9%
Los Angeles-Long Beach	59.5	53.5	57.7	25.1	20.7	28.5
Chicago	47.6	37.2	54.7	7.7	5.9	9.0
Philadelphia-Camden	47.7	32.7	42.2	11.5	10.1	13.8
Detroit	58.9	44.9	63.3	12.1	11.3	12.6
San Francisco-Oakland	57.8	48.8	60.8	29.2	25.8	31.5
Boston	74.3	64.0	82.4	19.2	13.9	37.7
Washington	75.7	59.6	77.3	9.8	10.4	8.4
Pittsburgh	70.5	63.3	73.6	29.4	27.1	29.4
Cleveland	59.2	39.3	75.2	3.1	2.4	4.3

*For New York and Chicago the suburban ring is the difference between the SMSA and the urban place (central city). For all other cities it is the difference between the urbanized area and central city. San Francisco-Oakland, Los Angeles-Long Beach, and Philadelphia-Camden are counted as two central cities.

SOURCE: U.S. Bureau of the Census, *U.S. Census of Population: 1960, vol. I, Characteristics of the Population*, pts. 6, 10, 16, 23, 24, 32, 34, 37, and 40, chap. C, "General Social and Economic Characteristics," tables 76 and 78.

The situation is completely different for Negroes. Relatively few high-income (over $10,000 per year) Negroes live in suburbs. Indeed, the percentage of high-income

4. Ibid.; A. H. Pascal, "The Economics of Housing Segregation," Memorandum, RM-5510-RC (Santa Monica: The RAND Corp., November 1967); John R. Meyer, John F. Kain, and Martin Wohl, *The Urban Transportation Problem* (Cambridge, Mass.: Harvard University Press, 1965), chap. 7; and Davis McEntire, op. cit.

Negroes living in suburban areas is considerably less than that of *low*-income whites. In Chicago 9 percent of *high*-income Negroes live in the suburbs as compared with 55 percent of high-income whites and 37 percent of low-income whites. Clearly, income is not the explanation for the underrepresentation of high-income Negroes in the suburbs.

Another "explanation" holds that the segregation of Negroes is the result of a desire "to live with their own kind" and that this is a "normal" and "healthy" manifestation of a pluralistic society. The immigrant colonies that are evident even today in many cities are offered as evidence of the "normality" of this behavior. It is true that a number of identifiable ethnic and nationality groups have exhibited some degree of segregation in American cities. However, the differences between their experience and that of the American Negro are so marked as to invalidate the historical analogy.[5]

The intensity of Negro residential segregation is greater than that documented for any other identifiable subgroup in American history. Moreover, segregation of these other groups has declined over time, while that of Negroes has remained at a high level, and possibly increased. Finally, metropolitan areas are very different places than they were 30 or 50 years ago. They are far less compact, and employment is much more dispersed. These widely scattered employment centers impose heavy commuting costs on many ghetto residents. No comparable disincentives existed when the ethnic colonies flourished.

VOLUNTARY SELF-SEGREGATION NOT REALLY VALID

To conclude that "voluntary" self-segregation is responsible for much of the current pattern of Negro residential segregation it is necessary to assume that Negroes have much stronger ties to their community than other groups. Although there is evidence of a growing cultural pride and a sense of community among blacks in recent years as evidenced by the apparent appeal of slogans such as "Black Power" and "Black is Beautiful," it is impossible to assign much weight to this increased awareness as an explanation of these durable segregation patterns. Recognizing the difficulties of interpretation, recent surveys of Negro attitudes provide little support for the self-segregation hypothesis. In 1966, 68 percent of a random sample of U.S. Negroes interviewed by the Harris poll indicated a preference for living in integrated neighborhoods. This fraction is somewhat larger than the 64 percent expressing this opinion in 1963, in spite of the growth of Black Power rhetoric during the period. Similarly, only 20 percent of Negroes interviewed in 1963 and 17 percent in 1966 indicated a preference to live in all-black neighborhoods. The fraction of northern Negroes preferring Negro neighborhoods was even smaller (8 percent in 1966); and the fraction of middle and upper income respondents in the North was still smaller (6 percent).[6]

In spite of the lack of any systematic evidence which supports the self-segregation hypothesis, it is difficult to dispose of. The problem is that it is virtually impossible to determine finally the role of self-segregation as long as strong traces of community

5. The most comprehensive comparative study of the segregation of Negroes and other ethnic groups is by Stanley Lieberson, *Ethnic Patterns in American Cities* (Glencoe: The Free Press, 1963). Similar findings are reported in: Otis Dudley Duncan and Stanley Lieberson, "Ethnic Segregation and Assimilation," *American Journal of Sociology* 64, no. 4 (January 1959): 364-74; and Karl E. Taeuber and Alma F. Taeuber, "The Negro as an Immigrant Group," *American Journal of Sociology* 69 no. 4 (January 1964).

6. William Brink and Louis Harris, *Black and White* (New York: Simon & Schuster, 1967), pp. 232-33.

(white) antagonism toward Negro efforts to leave the ghetto remain. The physical dangers of moving out of the ghetto probably are less today than in the past, but many subtle and indirect forms of intimidation and discouragement still exist.

Evidence of the methods used to enforce housing market segregation is more difficult to obtain today than in the past. Open-occupancy laws, which forbid discrimination in the sale and rental of housing on the basis of race, and a decline in clear-cut community approval for such practices, have caused opponents of open housing to resort to more subtle and secretive methods. This is a new situation. Until very recently the most important devices used to enforce segregation could hardly be called subtle. Deed restrictions (racial covenants), the appraisal practices of the FHA and private lending institutions, the actions of local officials, and the practices of real estate agents were among the most important of these.[7] Because residential patterns have a great deal of inertia, the effect of these now discredited devices will long be felt.

Even if there were no future resistance to Negro efforts to leave the ghetto, the cumulative effects of decades of intense discrimination will have long-lasting impacts. If these inimical patterns of housing market segregation are to be destroyed, strong laws, vigorous enforcement, and powerful incentives for integration will be necessary. In determining the range of corrective action both needed and justified, it is important to recognize the extent of discriminatory actions and particularly the complicity of government and law.

COMMUTER COSTS DO NOT HOLD WHITES IN CORE

"Economic" theories of residential location "explain" the locational choices of urban households by means of a trade-off between savings in location or site rents obtained by commuting further from work and the larger transportation costs thereby incurred.[8] Edgar Hoover and Raymond Vernon, in their analysis of the spatial structure of the New York region, depicted this choice in terms of "spacious living vs. easy access."[9] For a particular household, the amount of the location rent savings obtained from commuting any particular distance increases as its consumption of residential space (the inverse of net residential density) increases. The metropolitan surface of location or site rents in these theories results from competitive bidding among households for sites that are more accessible to certain desirable locations, particularly workplaces.

7. Davis McEntire, op. cit.; Charles Abrams, *Forbidden Neighbors: A Study of Prejudice in Housing* (New York: Harper & Bros., 1955); and Robert Thompson, Hylan Lewis, and Davis McEntire, "Atlanta and Birmingham: A Comparative Study in Negro Housing" in *Studies in Housing and Minority Groups*, Nathan Glazer and Davis McEntire, eds. (Berkeley: University of California Press, 1960).

8. William Alonso, *Location and Land Use* (Cambridge, Mass.: Harvard University Press, 1965); Lowdon Wingo, Jr., *Transportation and Urban Land* (Washington, D.C.: Resources for the Future, Inc., 1961); John F. Kain, "The Journey-to-Work as a Determinant of Residential Location," *Papers and Proceedings of the Regional Science Association* 9 (1962); Richard Muth, "Urban Residential Land and Housing Markets," in *Issues in Urban Economics*, Harvey S. Perloff and Lowdon Wingo, Jr., eds. (Washington, D.C.: Resources for the Future, 1968); Richard Muth, "Economic Change and Rural-Urban Conversions," *Econometrica* 29 (January 1961); and Edwin S. Mills, "An Aggregative Model of Resource Allocation in a Metropolitan Area," *American Economic Review*, May 1967. Each of these authors formulates this problem in a somewhat different manner. Only the first three depict the consumer trade-off in the precise manner described here. The remaining two authors obtain similar results by means of a capital-land substitution in the production of housing services. These theories provide an explanation for declining densities and land values from the core, but do not explain locational choices in the manner of the first three theories.

9. Edgar M. Hoover and Raymond Vernon, *Anatomy of a Metropolis* (Cambridge, Mass.: Harvard University Press, 1959). Doubleday-Anchor Paperback.

Most of these theories assume there is only a single workplace center in order to simplify obtaining an analytical solution for the surface of location rents. However, the solution is not changed markedly by a more complex employment distribution. All that is required is that residential space be more expensive in central than in outlying areas.

In general, households choosing to live at low density will be encouraged by these larger location rent savings to travel further from work, leaving the sites near large workplace concentrations for those consuming more modest quantities of space. The principal exception to this general rule will be those households having both an effective demand for large quantities of residential space and exceptionally large transportation costs savings.

The latter might result when an unusually high value is placed on commuting time or from a need to make unusually frequent trips to central locations. These, typically high income, households will live in central locations despite their consumption of large amounts of residential space. Still it appears that only a few households have commuting costs that are high enough to reside in central areas while consuming large quantities of residential space. Thus, "economic" theories of residential location "explain" the tendency for high income households to live in suburban areas by the fact that, on average, any upward effect of higher incomes on journey-to-work costs is not great enough to offset the effect of income on residential space consumption.

RESIDENTIAL ECONOMIC THEORIES ARE INCOMPLETE

While these economic theories of residential location unquestionably provide some insight into the residential choices of urban households, they are very incomplete. Even if there were no evidence of racial discrimination in housing markets, serious questions could be raised about their realism and appropriateness. However, given the evidence presented previously, the failure of these models to consider the effect of housing market discrimination on the metropolitan surface of location rents and on the location decisions of both whites and blacks must be regarded as their most glaring deficiency.

Despite some recent improvement in the access of Negroes to previously closed portions of the housing supply, limitations on the residential choices of Negro Americans remain great enough to justify the working assumption of separate black and white submarkets. Blacks can purchase or rent property outside of neighborhoods which convention and practice have sanctioned for Negro occupancy only with great difficulty, inconvenience, and costs. These black residential areas hereafter will be referred to as the black submarket or simply the ghetto. By contrast, whites may purchase or rent dwelling units anywhere, including the ghetto, although because of prejudice or other reasons most live in predominantly white residential areas. This creates a situation whereby location rents for equally accessible sites need not be the same within the two markets.

IMPORTANCE OF STOCKS MAKES MARKET ANALYSIS DIFFICULT

One factor that makes the analysis of housing markets so difficult is the importance of stocks. In no area of economics is the role of stocks treated adequately. Unfortunately, this general inadequacy of economic theory is considerably more serious in the case of theories of urban location, since residential and nonresidential structures are so durable. New construction each year is but a fraction of the total housing supply.

For all metropolitan areas, 29 percent of the dwelling units occupied by whites in December 1959 had been constructed during the previous decade. Stocks are an even more important portion of the housing supply in the black submarket. Only 13 percent of the units occupied by blacks in 1959 had been built during the previous 10 years. These averages are strongly weighted by southern metropolitan areas, where Negro neighborhoods are more dispersed and often contain vacant land on which some new construction for blacks takes place. In the northeast only 8 percent of the black supply was newer than 10 years old, and the fraction was even smaller (5 percent) in the north central region.

Most of the increased supply needed to house the rapidly growing ghetto populations consists of units shifted from the white market, generally at the periphery of existing ghettos. For example, in the north central region, during the decade 1950-1960, units formerly occupied by whites are nearly 10 times as important as new construction in terms of additions to the black submarket (Table 21.2). The 10-1 ratio is obtained by allocating the "other" category in Table 21.2 (primarily units changed through conversions and mergers) in the same proportion as units whose previous occupant is known. Based on this assumption, more than half of north central Negroes in 1959 lived in dwelling units that were occupied by whites a decade earlier. In contrast, few units shifted from black to white occupancy during the same period. For example, in the north central region only about 7 percent as many units shifted from white to black occupancy as shifted from black to white.

Although the term *location rent* will be used in references to the Negro submarket, it is not a pure accessibility payment as in the white submarket. The level of location rents in ghetto areas results primarily from restrictions on Negro residential choice rather than from transport savings between a particular location and the periphery. Given the unimportance of new construction as a source of additions to the black submarket, the level of location rents in ghetto areas is determined almost entirely by the price at which units are shifted from the white market. The price of new additions to the black submarket will depend on the price level prevailing in the white market and whether black buyers are able to buy or rent units at the white submarket price, must pay a premium, or obtain them at a discount.

TABLE 21.2 *Ghetto Housing Supply by Source and Region*

Region	New Construction	Previously Occupied by Whites	Previously Occupied by Negroes	Previously Occupied by Other	Total
Northeast	7.5%	35.3%	36.6%	20.6%	100.0%
North Central	5.3	33.2	29.2	32.3	100.0
South	19.7	14.6	44.9	20.8	100.0
West	21.8	32.1	30.4	15.7	100.0
United States	13.4	30.1	36.7	19.8	100.0
Inside Central City	10.6	34.1	36.8	18.5	100.0
Outside Central City	24.0	15.0	36.2	24.8	100.0

SOURCE: U.S. Bureau of Census, *U.S. Census of Housing:* 1960, vol. IV, *Components of Inventory Change*, Final Report HC (4), pt. 1A, no. 1 (Washington, D.C.: U.S. Government Printing Office, 1962).

UNIT SHIFT TO BLACK SUBMARKET REQUIRES PREMIUM

Whether blacks must pay a premium in order to add units to the ghetto is similar to, but not identical with, the question of whether blacks pay more than whites for housing of otherwise identical characteristics. Most researchers have concluded that blacks do pay more than whites for housing of comparable size and quality, but this view is by no means unanimous.[10] This is, of course, a factual question, and while many factual questions are easily resolved, determining the "facts" in this instance is not so simple. To determine whether there is a difference in prices paid by whites and blacks for comparable housing, it is necessary first to standardize the complex and heterogeneous bundle of residential services. Further complications are introduced by the fact that the magnitude of such discrimination would be expected to differ among metropolitan areas and over time in the same area. The size of the premium blacks must pay to shift housing from the white to the black market will depend on the extent of prejudice, the degree of organization of the market, and the instruments available to those wishing to contain the expansion of the black submarket. No one has been able to carry out the standardization in sufficient degree to demonstrate conclusively that measured price differences are not simply the result of systematic differences in the housing consumed by whites and blacks. In spite of the serious methodological and empirical problems, I conclude from my assessment of the existing evidence that a premium is required to shift units to the black submarket. This conclusion is based partially on several empirical studies referred to previously, but it is also based on a broader range of descriptive material and a priori theorizing.

Prices at active margins of the ghetto then may be depicted as being equal to the price in the white submarket plus a premium or discrimination markup. This markup might be some constant amount, as in Equation 1, or be proportional to value, as in Equation 2.

$$p^n = p^w + \alpha \tag{1}$$
$$p^n = p^w (1 + \beta) \tag{2}$$

The concept of a discrimination markup bears a close resemblance to the concept of a discrimination coefficient employed by Gary Becker in his classic work, *The Economics of Discrimination*.[11] However, there is a crucial difference. Becker's discrimination coefficient is a measure of the individual seller's taste for discrimination and indicates the amount of money he would be willing to forego to avoid selling to blacks. The discrimination markup in this formulation depends only in part on an *individual* seller's unwillingness to sell to blacks. Becker's model depicts atomistic sellers with God-given tastes acting independently. The model presented here depicts much more collusive behavior and a relatively high level of market organization. Individual sellers may be motivated in part by individual prejudice, but real or imagined "com-

---

10. Chester Rapkin, "Price Discrimination Against Negroes in Rental Housing Market," *Essays in Urban Land Economics* (Los Angeles: University of California, 1966); Ronald G. Ridker and John A. Henning, "The Determinants of Residential Property Values with Special Reference to Air Pollution," *The Review of Economics and Statistics* 44, no. 2 (May 1967); Chester Rapkin and William Grigsby, *The Demand for Housing in Racially Mixed Areas* (Berkeley: University of California Press, 1960); Luigi Laurenti, *Property Values and Race: Studies in Seven Cities* (Berkeley: University of California, 1960); Duncan and Duncan, op. cit.; Duncan and Hauser, op. cit.; McEntire, op. cit.; Muth, "The Variation of Population Density and Its Components in South Chicago"; and Bailey, "Effects of Race and Other Demographic Factors on the Values of Single-Family Homes."

11. Gary Becker, op. cit.

munity" pressures and the behavior of intermediaries are hypothesized to play a central role in effecting the white seller's willingness and opportunities to sell or rent to a Negro. In the not-so-distant past, these transactions were well organized and openly enforced by codes of "ethics" among market agents and even by FHA appraisers. Today the degree of organization appears to be less, or at least less visible.

This formulation also provides a mechanism for peripheral expansion of the ghetto, something which is entirely absent from Becker's model. When excess demand within the ghetto becomes too great—that is, when the price within the ghetto exceeds the white submarket price plus the markup ($p^w + \alpha$ or $p^w (1 + \beta)$)—units are shifted from white to black occupancy at the periphery of the ghetto. Sales by whites to blacks other than at the periphery of the ghetto either are not permitted at all or only at much larger discrimination markups—markups that for all blacks exceed the potential transportation cost advantages of all other locations. Markups for dwelling units far from the ghetto exceed the markups for units on the boundary of the ghetto because there is a greater consensus about keeping blacks out of these neighborhoods. When rapid growth of the black population makes it apparent that expansion must take place somewhere, it is channeled into adjacent neighborhoods. In the past, real estate agents, lenders, and local and federal officials openly enforced these rules. Although these overt enforcement activities have become less prevalent, it would be foolhardy to conclude they have disappeared entirely.

PSYCHIC, MONETARY COSTS HIGH FOR LEAVING GHETTO

The discrimination markup is a monetary difference in either the rent or purchase price paid by blacks in order to add a unit to the ghetto. In addition to these monetary differences there are, of course, the psychic costs of moving into a hostile environment, the transaction costs of finding a suitable dwelling and persuading the owner or landlord to make a transaction, and problems of acquiring information. These transaction and information costs also operate systematically to discourage blacks from obtaining residences outside of or far from the ghetto. If a black chooses a dwelling within the ghetto, he can expect to be courted by both white and black real estate agents and lenders. If he tries to locate outside the ghetto, the reception he receives from these agents is likely to be far less enthusiastic. There are two other explanations of ghetto expansion and price determination that are worthy of mention. The first of these, like the hypotheses outlined above, produces a positive discrimination markup. The second also provides for peripheral expansion of the ghetto but produces a negative discrimination markup.

A positive discrimination markup and peripheral expansion of the ghetto might occur if blacks prefer to live in or near the ghetto and are therefore willing to pay more for adjacent properties. In the case of blacks employed at suburban workplaces, this preference for ghetto locations must be great enough to offset the transportation cost savings available from residing in suburban areas. Under these circumstances, rents would be higher in the black submarket because blacks regard the ghetto as a more desirable location.

The other alternative hypothesis produces a negative markup. It postulates that whites residing on the periphery of the ghetto are more willing to sell to blacks than whites living further from the ghetto because of a preference not to live near blacks, a fear of racial invasion, and a belief that property value will plummet with Negro entry. Black entry into a white neighborhood located on the periphery of the ghetto is interpreted as the first step in an inevitable process whereby the neighborhood will rapidly become all black. Since this expectation does not arise in the case of Negro entry into a white neighborhood distant from the ghetto, whites do not panic and prices remain firm. If white fears were great enough, blacks might be able to purchase or rent dwellings in these transitional neighborhoods for substantially less than in the white market. Under these circumstances, the value of the discrimination markup would be negative and the ghetto would expand as long as blacks were willing to pay a price equal to the white submarket price on the periphery of the ghetto minus the negative markup. Bargains obtainable at the periphery of the ghetto would discourage blacks from paying higher prices to reside in all-white neighborhoods far from the ghetto.

THREE FACTORS CAUSE GHETTO EXPANSION

All three of the above hypotheses provide mechanisms for peripheral expansion of the ghetto. The first and second produce higher housing prices in the ghetto than outside, while the third produces lower prices in the ghetto. The second hypothesis seems highly implausible, given the preceding discussion of self segregation. A choice between the first and third can be made by empirically determining whether blacks must pay a premium or obtain their units at a discount. As I indicated previously, the evidence suggests that they typically pay a premium.

The fact that the level of location rents in the Negro market depends primarily on the level in the white market and the discrimination markup does not mean that accessibility considerations may play no part in determining the surface of location rents within the ghetto. In a manner parallel to conventional models of residential location, the location rent surface within the ghetto would depend on the distribution of Negro jobs and the transport costs savings afforded by various residential locations. Given a rapid redistribution of Negro jobs, it is possible that some parts of the ghetto might become more accessible to the new employment centers and location rents would be bid up in these residential areas, causing the shape of the surface within the ghetto to deviate from that outside. However, these situations should be temporary if the previous discussion of the processes that shift housing from the white to the black submarket is valid. As long as the markup for shifting units to the black submarket is the same everywhere at the periphery, the location rent surface within the ghetto should in general resemble that in the white market plus a markup. Deviations would occur only if the markup (alpha) was larger at some boundaries than others.

There is reason to believe that differences of this kind exist. Some ethnic neighborhoods resist Negro entry more strongly than the general public. Also suburbs with small Negro ghettos may be more successful in limiting their expansion through zoning and other political means. Forces such as these would increase the discrimination markup. Similarly, if the ghetto is bounded by groups sympathetic to the plight of the Negro, the markup might be lower.[12]

12. For example, the tendency for the ghetto to expand through Jewish neighborhoods has been noted by a number of observers. Ernest W. Burgess commented on this question in an early paper and remarked that "No instance has been noted . . . where a Negro invasion succeeded in displacing the Irish in possession of a community. Yet, frequently . . . Negroes have pushed forward in the wake of retreating Jews . . . ," Ernest W. Burgess, "Residential Segregation in American Cities," *Annals of the American Academy of Political and Social Science* 140 (November 1928): 112.

DEMAND FOR CENTRAL CITIES PROPERTIES TIED IN WITH SEGREGATION

The impact of the ghetto on the metropolitan surface of location rents is not limited to its effect within the Negro market. By reducing the white submarket supply of residential sites in particular parts of the metropolitan region, it affects the level and spatial distribution of location rents in the white market as well. The central location of the ghetto causes location rents in central areas to be higher than if this pattern of housing market discrimination did not exist. It is true that some centrally employed blacks would choose to live in these centrally located residential areas, even if there were no discrimination. However, many blacks employed at central workplaces and nearly all blacks employed in suburban areas would not bid for these central locations were it not for restrictions on their residential choices. Of course, this also means that the current demand by blacks for suburban sites is less than it would be if no housing market discrimination existed. The net effect of the present restrictions is to increase the demand for sites in central areas, where the ghetto is located, and to decrease somewhat the demand for suburban locations. The rapid growth of the Negro market represents a source of demand for central city properties that would not exist in the absence of segregation.

HETEROGENEITY, IMMOBILITY IMPORTANT TO HOUSING DURABILITY

The preceding discussion of the effects of residential discrimination on metropolitan housing markets, while responding to some serious deficiencies of existing "economic" theories of residential location, fails to consider a number of factors that influence the behavior of urban housing markets and that reinforce the effects of residential segregation. Existing "economic" theories of residential location entirely ignore stocks, despite the fact that they are more important than in almost any other market. The particular importance of stocks (the durability of housing) arises from two other characteristics of the bundle of residential services—dwelling units and their associated environments are very heterogeneous and difficult to move. Were it not for this heterogeneity and immobility, the durability of housing would be much less important. For example, if dwelling units were indistinguishable, the bundle of housing services obtained by households would be the same, at all locations. Similarly, if dwellings were durable, but cheaply moved (such as automobiles), neither heterogeneity nor durability would affect the location problem in any important respect since households could locate a particular kind of dwelling unit at any location. The fact is, however, that residential structures are at once durable, heterogeneous, and difficult to transport, and these attributes complicate the residential location problem greatly.

It is also a characteristic of the bundle of residential services that external effects and collective goods are highly important. A household's preference for and valuation of a particular dwelling unit depends not only on its characteristics, but on the characteristics of surrounding structures, the attributes of the neighborhood and its residents, and the quality and quantity of services provided—for example, public and parochial schools and police and fire protection.

GHETTO DISCOUNT EXISTS FOR SOME PROPERTIES

Given a heterogeneous and durable housing stock, different price relationships may exist between the black and white submarkets for various kinds of housing. It is not hard to imagine circumstances where blacks have to pay a premium for adding certain types of dwelling units (of a particular size, quality, or other characteristics) to the ghetto, while other types of dwelling units may be cheaper in the ghetto. Such a result could arise if dwellings become less desirable to whites once they become part of the ghetto. It seems likely that few whites will wish to live in all-black neighborhoods, and particularly deep within the ghetto. Thus, bundles of residential services located in the ghetto might be cheaper than otherwise identical ones outside the ghetto without causing large numbers of whites to buy or rent them. This difference, which might be termed the ghetto discount, could exist for some kinds of properties at the same time blacks were finding it necessary to pay a premium to add other kinds of units to the ghetto.

Assume there are only two kinds of dwelling units—high quality and low quality. The conditions outlined above could produce an excess supply (defined in terms of the white market price) of low-quality dwelling units within the ghetto at the same time there existed an excess demand for high-quality units. For this excess supply condition for low-quality dwelling units to be consistent with the continued expansion of the ghetto and the payment of a premium for high-quality units, it is only necessary that the supply price of providing high-quality units by means of ghetto expansion (the price of high-quality units in the white market plus the discrimination markup) be less than the cost of providing such units through the conversion of low-quality units (the price of low-quality units in the black submarket plus the cost of upgrading). In order for this condition to persist, it may be necessary for the depreciation rate or the filtering of high-quality units to be more rapid inside the ghetto than outside.

"GHETTO SUBURBS" LACK MIDDLE-INCOME BUFFER

While the growth of the ghetto has not been systematically studied in these terms, most descriptive accounts seem consistent with mechanisms of this kind. These accounts indicate that the ghetto expands into some of the best portions of the surrounding stock and that disproportionate numbers of blacks moving into previously white neighborhoods are members of higher-income groups.[13] This peripheral expansion of the ghetto serves high-income blacks in very much the way that the flight to the suburbs serves upper-income whites. A major difference, however, is that upper-income blacks are less able to protect their "ghetto suburbs" from the incursion of lower-income groups. This could provide the more rapid depreciation of high-quality units in the ghetto needed to produce a permanent discrepancy in relative prices between the ghetto and the white submarket.

"Ghetto suburbs" do not have the buffer of middle-income housing that separates high-income white suburbs from low-income neighborhoods. With the continued growth of the ghetto, the neighborhoods of well-to-do blacks are continually invaded by lower-income groups. This causes a decline in neighborhood quality, and upper-income blacks are forced to migrate to a new "ghetto suburb." Since they are unable to leapfrog and establish high-quality, high-income residential neighborhoods far from the adverse influences of low-income households in the manner of high-income whites, they pass houses down to lower-income groups more rapidly than do whites.

GHETTO IS BOTH BLACK AND POOR

It is well to remember that the ghetto is not simply black. It is also poor. The concentration of poverty in central city ghettos produces a host of adverse environmental condi-

---

13. The most detailed analysis of ghetto expansion is found in Duncan and Duncan, op. cit.

tions that make the central city and its core (both ghetto and nonghetto) less attractive to both middle-income whites and blacks. The only difference is that the former need not live there; they can move to independent political subdivisions a safe distance from the ghetto where they may vote service-taxation packages appropriate to their tastes and incomes. Blacks do not have this option.

In the postwar period, white central city residents, unable to obtain the desired services-tax packages by political means, voted with their feet and moved out of central cities by the millions. Today, the concentrated poverty of the ghetto makes it difficult, if not impossible, for central cities to provide the quantity and quality of services demanded by middle- and upper-income whites and blacks.

Chicago's experience is typical of large northern metropolitan areas. During the decade 1950-1960 the central city lost 399,000 whites and gained 320,000 Negroes. The suburbs gained 1,076,000 whites but only 34,000 blacks. Similar data for other metropolitan areas are presented in Table 21.3. These trends, noticeable earlier in the century, became pronounced with the rapid migration of blacks northward beginning with World War II. Between 1940 and 1960 the white populations of the 24

TABLE 21.3   *Change in White and Nonwhite Central City and Suburban Ring Populations 1950-1960 (in thousands)*

Rank		Central City		Suburban Ring	
		White	Negro	White	Negro
24	Atlanta	91	65	140	− 6
12	Baltimore	−113	100	324	7
7	Boston	−130	23	278	3
3	Chicago	−399	320	1,076	34
21	Cincinnati	− 32	31	166	3
11	Cleveland	−142	103	367	2
20	Dallas	171	72	111	−17
5	Detroit	−363	182	904	19
16	Houston	250	90	87	7
22	Kansas City	− 9	27	204	2
2	Los Angeles-Long Beach	388	169	1,668	77
17	Milwaukee	61	41	133	−
14	Minneapolis-St. Paul	− 47	8	366	−
1	New York	−476	340	1,177	67
13	Newark	− 97	63	226	27
18	Patterson-Clifton-Passaic	3	15	286	6
4	Philadelphia	−225	153	700	38
8	Pittsburgh	− 91	18	257	7
9	St. Louis	−168	61	429	18
23	San Diego	212	20	231	3
6	San Francisco-Oakland	−148	67	554	25
19	Seattle	70	11	171	−
10	Washington, D.C.	−173	131	553	18
15	Buffalo	− 83	34	259	4

SOURCE: U.S. Bureau of the Census, *U.S. Census of Population: 1960, Selected Area Reports, Standard Metropolitan Statistical Areas*, Final Report PC (3)—1D (Washington, D.C.: U.S. Government Printing Office, 1963), Table 1.

metropolitan areas of over a million in 1960 increased by 12 million and their Negro populations by 4.2 million. Even though these 24 included rapidly growing cities such as Los Angeles, San Diego, and Houston, only 0.2 percent of the white population increase (net) occurred in the central cities as compared to 83 percent of the Negro increase (net). These changes became even more pronounced during the decade 1950 to 1960 when the Negro population of these 24 central cities increased by 2.1 million. Large numbers of whites were displaced by this growth of central city ghettos, and these same cities lost more than 1.4 million whites during the decade. Finally between 1960 and 1968, these same central cities lost an additional 2 million whites while gaining an additional 1.9 million Negroes.[14] During the same 8 year period the white population of the suburban rings of these metropolitan areas increased by 6.8 million, while the Negro population increased by .6 million.

DEMAND FOR LOW-QUALITY HOUSING GROWING

In summary, housing market segregation modifies the logic of "economic" models of residential location in several important respects. It creates a demand for certain locations (typically the inner part of large central cities) that is unrelated, or only weakly related, to their access advantages. Negro households, physically limited in their choice of residential locations, must bid sites in the segregated market away from whites who wish to be near their places of employment. The result is a radically different pattern of price (or location rent) determination than is derived in most theories of residential location. In most large U.S. metropolitan areas there exists a rapidly growing "captive" demand for residences within the ghetto. This demand is principally for low-quality housing. These locations are accessible to the workplace of many Negroes, but for an increasing number of Negroes they confer no such advantages. Indeed, for those Negroes employed in peripheral areas the ghetto is perhaps the poorest location possible.

In evaluating the effect of the growing central ghetto on metropolitan development, it is crucial to keep in mind that because so many blacks have low incomes, the growth of the central ghetto also implies an increased concentration of poverty, a growing aggregation of low-quality housing, and an impaired capability on the part of cities to provide urban services. These factors make the city still less attractive to higher income groups and increase the relative desirability of the suburbs.

These factors, important in a static analysis, assume even greater significance in a dynamic framework. The rapid dispersal of employment from the central parts of metropolitan areas is amply documented elsewhere.[15] The effect of employment dispersal should be to reduce the demand for centrally located residences and cause a downward shift in the location rent surface in central areas. If centrally located units become less expensive, the location rent savings from commuting to suburban locations would become much less. Under these changed circumstances, many more centrally employed middle- and upper-income groups would find it more advantageous to choose centrally located neighborhoods. The fact that many units would be of lower than desired quality provides no serious obstacle, providing the units can be obtained cheaply enough. The most structurally sound of these units could be renovated and modernized, while the least valuable could be demolished and be replaced by

14. U.S. Bureau of the Census, Current Population Reports, Series, P-23, Special Studies (formerly Technical Studies), no. 27, "Trends in Social and Economic Conditions in Metropolitan Areas" (Washington, D.C.: U.S. Government Printing Office, 1969), p. 2.

15. John F. Kain, "The Distribution and Movement of Jobs and Industry," in *The Metropolitan Enigma*, James Q. Wilson, ed. (Cambridge, Mass.: Harvard University Press, 1968).

new structures. However, these possibilities have not been realized since the rapid increases in the black population for the most part have largely offset the effects of employment dispersal.

URBAN DEVELOPMENT GREATLY AFFECTED BY SEGREGATION

Were it not for Negro residential segregation, the postwar pattern of U.S. urban development would have been much different. If the suburbs had been open to low-income blacks, many would have moved to suburban areas along with their jobs, much in the fashion of whites of similar socioeconomic status. This would have affected the central city housing market in two ways. First, central cities would have had a very different image. A slower rate of growth of the poverty population would have affected the prestige of central city residential areas. If more middle- and high-income families had remained in the central cities, the public schools and other facilities would have been maintained better and the quality of services and other aspects of the environment of their neighborhoods would have been much higher. Second, as noted previously, the prices of suburban properties would have been somewhat higher and the prices of central city properties somewhat lower if blacks had been allowed to compete for the former. The exact magnitude of these price changes is difficult to predict, but their direction is indisputable. Given these changes in relative housing prices, many more centrally employed whites would have found it to their advantage to live in the central city. Similarly, few blacks employed at suburban work-places would commute long distances back to the central city core in order to pay more for housing. Increased Negro residence in the suburbs would also reduce the underrepresentation of blacks in suburban plants. It is hardly necessary to detail the way in which these changes in the distribution of the population by race and income would have ameliorated the problems of our cities.

So much for the counterfactual question of what might have been if there had been no housing market discrimination or if the pattern of Negro residential segregation had taken a different form. The relevant policy question is whether the situation can be retrieved by removing the barriers to Negro residential choice. Devising solutions to these problems will be difficult and will require the most vigorous efforts to undo what has been done. Turning the present situation around will be immensely more difficult than preventing it from happening in the first place would have been.

The present pattern of residence by race has created a number of adverse environmental effects that will be most difficult to correct. Because of the collective nature of many aspects of the bundle of residential services, many needed improvements cannot be made a dwelling unit at a time. Under existing political arrangements the quality of services provided the residents of a particular neighborhood cannot be markedly better than those provided the residents of another neighborhood within the same jurisdiction. Thus, it is far more difficult to provide high-quality bundles of residential services within the central city than outside, since in order to do so it is necessary to raise all city services to that level. Many recent and well-motivated actions to force school districts and local governments to provide equal services to all neighborhoods and to balance their schools racially may accelerate the departure of middle- and upper-income families from the central city. By comparison, the even more recent interest in decentralization, while born in the ghetto, may provide the means by which upper-income neighborhoods will be able to provide higher levels of services than less fortunate neighborhoods. It seems likely that conserving or renewing central city neighborhoods requires the development of new institutions that allow the provision of higher levels of services.

SUBURBAN HOUSING MUST BE OPENED TO NEGROES

While the above changes in the provision of services are essential, the first requirement is devising methods for opening suburban housing to blacks. Only when the city loses its monopoly on black poverty will it have a chance. As long as the ghetto continues its rapid growth, prices in central cities will remain at high levels and the expectation that the city will become a lower-class slum will persist. If the growth of the ghetto can be arrested, positive programs aimed at making the central city attractive to middle-income families, be they white or black, have a chance. Without this change in the dynamics of metropolitan development there is no way in which the trends outlined in this paper can be reversed.

22. *An Economic Analysis of Property Values and Race (Laurenti)*

ANTHONY DOWNS

Do property prices fall when nonwhites move into a neighborhood? Probably no other question concerning real estate has created so much controversy or played such an important a role in determining the ethnic ecology of our cities. Yet objective evidence about the answer has been so scarce that the controversy has consisted mostly of hearsay, opinions, and prejudices rather than facts. But now the Commission on Race and Housing has sponsored a study in which a mass of data has been gathered and analyzed by Luigi Laurenti and set forth in a new book entitled, *Property Values and Race.*[1] . . .

The study's major conclusion can be stated as follows: when nonwhites enter a previously all white neighborhood consisting primarily of single-family residences, and no other changes in neighborhood character occur, then prices of residential property in the area will probably not decline and may very well rise in comparison with prices in similar neighborhoods that have remained all white.[2] In other words, nonwhite entry alone—as distinguished from such changes in physical use as increased density—rarely causes residential property to fall in price, and quite often causes it to rise.

This conclusion is so directly opposite to traditional opinions that it deserves extremely careful analysis. Therefore we shall examine at some length the methods used to derive this result in order to discover whether they are truly valid. Then we shall discuss the study's limitations and its implications for all cities.

THE METHODOLOGY

Although the subtitle of Laurenti's work is "Studies in Seven Cities," its real meat is an analysis of neighborhoods in San Francisco, Oakland, and Philadelphia. In order to isolate the influence of nonwhite entry upon prices of property, he chose 20 neighborhoods in which entry had occurred at some time during the past 15 years and compared price movements in each one with price movements in one or more similar neighborhoods which had remained all white. Nineteen such "control" neighborhoods were used, but some were compared with more than one "test" neighborhood. Thus a total of 34 comparisons was made. In each one the two areas being compared were similar in size, reputation, type and price of homes, and character

Reprinted from *Land Economics* 36 (May 1960): 181-88 (edited), by permission of the publisher and author. Anthony Downs is a senior vice president of Real Estate Research Corporation, a national consulting firm with headquarters in Chicago.

1. Luigi Laurenti, *Property Values and Race* (Berkeley: University of California Press, 1960). Although Laurenti uses the term *value* as equivalent to *price* I have retained the traditional distinction in this review article. Therefore, since his study concerns sales *prices* of properties, I use the term *price* in many places where he refers to *value*.

2. In the areas studied by Laurenti, 95 percent to 100 percent of the nonwhites were Negroes and almost all the whites were Caucasians.

of residents; hence the only major difference between them was the entry of nonwhites into the "test" neighborhood.

For each area Laurenti obtained the sales prices of as many transactions as possible for the six-year period from mid-1949 to mid-1955. In San Francisco and Oakland these prices were procured from multiple-listing services; in Philadelphia they were provided by real estate directories. Over 9,700 sales prices were analyzed—a total comprising about 40 percent of all sales during the 6 year study period in the areas considered.

Two methods of comparison between prices in the paired neighborhoods were employed. Where properties in both areas had very similar prices and price ranges within each area were not large, average sales prices for each quarter were compared directly. When these conditions did not apply, quarterly comparisons were made of the average ratio of prices to 1950 assessed values. In either case the end result was a series of quarterly averages for each neighborhood, which was then graphed and analyzed numerically.

The most significant results of this analysis are derived from the ratio of test-area prices to control-area prices, which was computed both before and after nonwhite entry into each test area. Changes in this ratio serve as indicators of the effect of nonwhite entry on property prices. . . .

. . . [B]efore we examine those results, one significant limitation of the study should be mentioned. Almost all of the neighborhoods selected consisted primarily of single-family residences occupied solely by their owners. This was true both before and after nonwhite entry. Furthermore, most of the test neighborhoods were not contiguous to other areas of nonwhite population. Some were as far as two miles from the nearest nonwhite resident when entry first occurred.

THE RESULTS

. . . *[I]n almost half of the price comparisons made, prices in the racially mixed neighborhood increased significantly, relative to those in the all white neighborhood.* Positive changes in the test-price/control-price ratio ranged from 5.1 percent to 26.3 percent and averaged 11.7 percent. In 38.3 percent of the comparisons, no significant change in the ratio was observed. *Thus in only one out of seven cases was nonwhite entry followed by a significant decline in test-area prices relative to control-area prices.* These declines ranged from 5.1 percent to 9.1 percent and averaged 6.7 percent. . . .

WHY PRICES DID NOT FALL

Since the purpose of Laurenti's study is simply to present the facts, he does not attempt to explain in detail why his results are so different from prevailing beliefs. However, the evidence he amasses points to certain basic causes of this discrepancy, which we shall try to illuminate.

Two arguments are usually advanced to uphold the belief that nonwhite entry depresses property prices. The first states that such entry converts neighborhoods from low density and high quality maintenance to high density and low quality maintenance, resulting in rapid physical deterioration and a depreciation of even those homes that have been well maintained. However, this argument was completely inapplicable to the neighborhoods in Laurenti's study. In these areas the entering nonwhites kept up or improved the standards of density and maintenance that their white predecessors had exhibited. As noted previously, these neighborhoods consisted mainly of single-family residences.

The second argument declares that nonwhite entry reduces prices because of panic selling. According to this view, as soon as a nonwhite buys a home in an all white neighborhood many white owners become frightened and try to sell their homes immediately. This floods the market and causes a sharp fall in prices. Contrary to this view, Laurenti's graphs reveal no consistent pattern of either relative or absolute price declines immediately after nonwhite entry. This is true even though entry was completely unexpected in many areas. There were a few instances in which such panic occurred, but even in these cases test-area prices usually regained their relative position shortly and sometimes climbed even higher than control-area prices in the long run. But in most areas, there was no panic whatsoever; therefore this argument was also completely inapplicable.

One reason why so few white owners panicked was undoubtedly the widespread awareness that nonwhite entry would not lead to high density and lower maintenance standards. Thus the absence of the first factor usually cited as a cause of declining prices partially explains why the second factor also failed to appear.

The foregoing analysis shows clearly why property prices did not react to nonwhite entry in the way most people in the real estate profession expect them to react. Neither of the price-depreciating factors usually associated with nonwhite entry was present in the majority of test areas studied. Thus it is incorrect for anyone to argue that nonwhite entry *always* leads to either high density use or panic selling or both. These outcomes *may* result but they are not inevitable consequences of nonwhite entry. Laurenti's study proves conclusively that no simple generalizations about the effects of nonwhite entry upon prices are valid; hence such effects can be predicted only after a careful analysis of the factors operative in each specific area of entry.

THE MARKET SHIFT AND ITS EFFECTS

One important aspect of such specific analysis is the degree to which nonwhite entry causes the market for future sales to shift from white to nonwhite buyers. Because of prevailing attitudes toward race the market for housing does not consist of a single set of available properties on the supply side and single set of buyers on the demand side. Instead, both supply and demand are divided into white and nonwhite segments. Nonwhite buyers either exclude themselves from access to the white housing supply because they do not want to live among whites, or they are involuntarily excluded by tacit collusion among realtors and sellers and by fear of violence. On the other hand, whites typically exclude themselves from access to the nonwhite housing supply because they do not wish to live in nonwhite areas. But as the nonwhite urban population grows it must be housed somehow—either by new construction on vacant land or by the shifting of extant housing from white to nonwhite use. Since most vacant land exists only in all white areas, new housing has been built mostly within the white segment of the market, except for public housing which is usually built on land cleared for this purpose. Therefore most additions to the supply of nonwhite housing have come about through shifts of "used" housing from the white segment of the market to the nonwhite segment.

Such a shift usually starts to occur soon after nonwhites first enter an all white area. In the areas Laurenti studied white residents rarely left *en masse* when nonwhites started moving into an all white area; thus there was no sudden increase in the supply of homes offered for sale by whites. However, there was almost always a decrease—sometimes a sharp one—in the demand for housing by whites seeking to move into the area. This fall in white demand was invariably accompanied by the appearance of nonwhite demand for housing in the area. Once the racial "barrier" had been penetrated, nonwhites no longer felt excluded from this portion of the white housing supply and began offering to buy houses there. In fact, such transition areas were considered especially desirable by many nonwhites because they offered both decent housing and escape from nonwhite ghettos.

It is apparent from this analysis that the impact of nonwhite entry upon prices depends upon two factors: (1) the degree to which such a shift from white to nonwhite market segments takes place, and (2) differences between white and nonwhite demand for housing of a given type. The first factor simply determines the degree to which the second factor becomes operative: the more an area is shifted from one market to the other, the greater will be the effects of whatever differences exist between these markets.

Two factors in the nonwhite segment of the housing market distinguish it from the white segment: an artificial restriction of supply and a lower centered distribution of income among buyers. The very existence of market segments creates an artificial restriction of supply for nonwhites: they cannot satisfy their demand for housing anywhere it is available, but must confine their search to areas already penetrated by nonwhites (except for the rare individuals who "pioneer" initial entry into all white areas). This fact creates pent-up housing demand all across the nonwhite income distribution. In those sections of the distribution where the greatest number of nonwhites are clustered, the backlog of demand is greatest. Since very low incomes are most numerous, demand for low-income housing is very high—in fact, it creates a great pressure to convert decent housing into small units accessible to low-income consumers. Thus the artificial restriction of supply in the nonwhite market is partially responsible for the tendency of transition to cause increases in density which eventually result in physical deterioration of property.

But there is also a high demand among nonwhites for decent low-density housing accessible to middle income consumers. An increasing number of nonwhites are skilled workers, businessmen, and professionals capable of purchasing moderate priced homes and just as eager as whites to maintain decent housing standards. Their total number is much smaller than the number of whites who can afford the same level of housing, but because the supply of such housing available to nonwhites is so small, the intensity of demand among nonwhites is much greater. Thus when a given area of middle price housing shifts from the white segment of the market to the nonwhite segment, the intensity of demand for it is likely to increase. This tends to raise prices relative to similar housing still in the white market segment.

On the other hand, the intensity of demand for high priced housing is likely to be less among nonwhites than among whites. In this case the effect of restricted supply for nonwhites is outweighed by the effect of their lower incomes. So few nonwhites can afford high priced housing that when an area of such housing shifts from the white to the nonwhite market segment, its value is likely to decline in comparison with similar housing still in the white segment. This is exactly what happened in the one high-priced neighborhood studied by Laurenti.

THE EFFECTS OF A GENERAL HOUSING SURPLUS

Thus the effect of nonwhite entry upon prices in a specific area can be predicted by analyzing two basic aspects of the ensuing change in the area's "market location": the degree to which the area shifts from the white market to the nonwhite market, and the differences between these two markets at the relevant price level. Both of these aspects are markedly influenced by the relation between supply and demand in the housing market as a whole.

Although the supply of housing in the United States has grown rapidly since 1945, not until 1958 did it catch up with the demand generated by the backlog from World War II and the large number of families formed during the postwar period. Thus from 1945 to 1958—the period in which Laurenti conducted his study—there was a relative shortage of housing. But during the past two years, a surplus of supply has caused the housing market to become relatively "soft." This shift from shortage to surplus will affect nonwhite impact upon property values in two ways.

First, because the surplus of supply is mainly in the white segment of the market the intensity of demand for housing among whites will decline in all neighborhoods. But demand among nonwhites for housing available to them will remain relatively high because of the artificial restriction of supply explained above. Thus for white sellers in any low- or middle-income neighborhood, the relative attractiveness of selling to nonwhites will increase. If financing is available to nonwhites, they will be willing and able to offer more for desirable property than whites will if it is not in the high price range. As a result, nonwhite entry should occur in more predominantly single-family neighborhoods not adjacent to ghettos than it has in the past.

The second effect will take place once nonwhite entry occurs. Since whites looking for homes have more alternatives than they had in the period of shortage, and since most whites do not wish to live in transition neighborhoods, fewer will offer to buy homes in such neighborhoods. Once a nonwhite citizen enters a previously all white area, the "normal turnover" demand among whites for homes in that area will fall off much faster than it did in periods of shortage. Whites living in the neighborhood who wish to move will find few white buyers who can match the prices that nonwhite buyers will be offering; therefore they are more likely to sell to nonwhites. In other words, the "soft" condition of the white housing market will cause any area where nonwhite entry has occurred to shift into the nonwhite market faster than it would have under conditions of shortage. This is precisely what happened in one of the Oakland neighborhoods which Laurenti studied, where white demand had already sagged before nonwhites entered and reversed the falling trend of values.

Essentially, a surplus in the white housing market increases the difference between the intensity of demand found in the white market and that found in the nonwhite market. Because nonwhites are denied access to most of the housing supply the intensity of their demand is not immediately affected by additions to supply made in the white sector. This changes the "terms of trade" in favor of nonwhites and should result in wider entry of nonwhites into all white areas and faster transition of those areas to high levels of nonwhite occupancy once entry has occurred. However, these tendencies could be largely offset by a decline in the rate at which nonwhites migrate into northern and western urban areas. If this rate subsides, as it shows signs of doing, then the intensity of demand in the nonwhite market may decline also.[3] This would tend to make the white and nonwhite markets more alike, since a fall in demand in the latter would have the same effect as the increase in supply in the former. In any case, Laurenti's study has proved that the effect of nonwhite entry upon prices can be determined only by specific analyses of supply and demand, rather than by shibboleths about the inevitable relations between race and property prices.

3. Very few accurate data are available on the rate of migration of nonwhites into northern and western cities. However, Real Estate Research Corporation makes annual surveys in Chicago to determine the number of blocks which have more than 25 percent nonwhite occupancy. Yearly changes in this total provide a crude measure of changes in the overall rate of growth of the nonwhite population. Such growth is caused by both natural increase and net immigration, but the former should provide either constant or increasing annual population increments.

(continued on p. 272)

LIMITATIONS OF THE STUDY'S APPLICATION

Although Laurenti's conclusions cannot, in my opinion, be strongly challenged on methodological grounds, this does not mean they will be universally accepted. In fact, a basic objection is sure to be raised against applying these conclusions to cities other than the ones he studied. This objection states that, since every city is unique, conclusions derived from San Francisco, Oakland, and Philadelphia are not necessarily applicable elsewhere. Such a view is most likely to be encountered in the form of remarks like, "it may be true on the West Coast, but in *my* city, when nonwhites move in, property prices fall." How valid is this criticism? Its validity depends upon two factors: (1) whether nonwhite entry in any given city occurs under conditions significantly different from those studied by Laurenti, and (2) if so, whether it can be proved that the differences involved mean nonwhite entry will always cause property prices to fall.

The first factor is certainly operative in a great many cities. In Chicago, for example, nonwhite expansion nearly always occurs on the edge of a giant ghetto and usually (though not invariably) involves increases in density and decreases in income and occupational status levels in the transition neighborhoods. None of these conditions were extant in the neighborhoods Laurenti studied. The same differences in accompanying conditions exist in New York, Detroit, Milwaukee, Newark, and many other cities with significant nonwhite minorities. In fact, these particular differences are really the only relevant grounds for arguing that the conclusions Laurenti derived in three cities are not applicable to all others. The question then becomes: does the fact that these particular conditions have usually coincided with nonwhite entry in certain cities mean that such entry must lead to declining property prices in those cities?

Surprisingly enough, the answer can be derived from Laurenti's study even though he did not base his conclusions on neighborhoods where the above conditions existed. His methodology is designed to isolate the effects of racial change upon property prices from the effects of all other causal factors. Where racial transition is accompanied by increased density or lower levels of income and occupational status the effects of these factors upon property prices cannot be analytically separated from the effect of race *per se*. This intermingling of effects may lead people to "blame" racial change for results actually caused by other factors. For example, in some cities racial transition is usually accompanied by conversion of old single-family dwellings to multifamily occupancy. This causes a rise in population density and rapid physical deterioration of the converted properties. The whole neighborhood becomes downgraded, and

---

Hence any decline in growth rates can be attributed to declines in net immigration. The number of blocks per week converted from less than 25 percent nonwhite occupancy to more than 25 percent nonwhite occupancy for various periods from 1950 to 1959 is as follows:

Period Covered	Average No. Blocks Changed per Week
April 1950 (Census)—October 1952	2.96
October 1952—October 1953	2.85
October 1953—April 1955	2.15
April 1955—April 1956	2.35
April 1956—July 1957	3.78
July 1957—August 1958	2.59
August 1958—July 1959	1.94

These figures indicate a significant decline in the rate of nonwhite expansion from its peak in 1956-1957.

even well-maintained homes still used by only one family decline in price. Such declines are frequently attributed to racial change; whereas they are really caused by the higher density and lower economic status of the incoming population.

To escape the analytical difficulties inherent in such multiple causation, Laurenti studied only neighborhoods where racial change was not accompanied by increases in density or declines in maintenance standards. He therefore omitted neighborhoods on the periphery of nonwhite ghettos and instead selected those into which nonwhites had "leapfrogged" over sizable distances from the nearest previous nonwhite residences. But in many American cities such "leapfrogging" is very rare; almost all nonwhite expansion occurs on the borders of large ghettos. Therefore in such cities realtors and homeowners can argue that Laurenti's conclusions simply do not apply since racial change is almost always associated with higher density and lower maintenance standards. Under these conditions, nonwhite entry seems to lead directly to neighborhood deterioration, with its ensuing declines in property prices.

Although this argument contains an important kernel of truth, it is still essentially false. The kernel of truth is that racial change is indeed bound up with other changes in many cities, for a variety of reasons. But one of the most significant of these reasons is the belief that nonwhite entry *always* leads to falling prices—a belief which Laurenti's study decisively disproves. When this erroneous belief is accepted by white homeowners, they strongly oppose entry of nonwhites into all white areas of decent housing because they fear falling prices. Such opposition keeps nonwhites bottled up in ghettos and makes the density in them so high that whenever a new border area opens up for nonwhite settlement it is flooded with residents far beyond its capacity to house decently. This process tends to confirm the original (but erroneous) belief that nonwhite entry is invariably accompanied by rising density and falling values. A vicious circle is created, founded on what Robert Merton has labeled a "self-fulfilling prophecy:" "A *false* definition of a situation evoking a new behavior which makes the originally false conception come true."[4] If "leapfrogging" by middle and upper income nonwhites into decent all white neighborhoods were permitted in all cities (as it has been in San Francisco and Oakland) then at least some instances of nonwhite entry without higher density or falling maintenance would occur everywhere. Such universal evidence would destroy the belief that nonwhite entry *inevitably* means deteriorating neighborhoods. But at present this belief remains unchallenged in many cities because its continued existence blocks the creation of situations which would disprove it.[5]

4. Robert K. Merton, "The Self-fulfilling Prophecy," *Antioch Review*, Summer 1946, p. 208.

5. Such a "self-fulfilling prophecy" recently occurred in Deerfield, Illinois. When a builder revealed his plans to sell some new homes to Negroes, local residents caused a furor, stating that they feared falling property prices. This furor was so great that two other builders who had been planning to construct all white housing withdrew from the area, thereby causing land prices to fall. They did not depart because they feared the entry of Negroes (none have yet entered and perhaps none will) but because the reaction of the community, and especially of the city building department, created what they believed was an unfavorable climate for any builder. Thus it was the uproar about falling prices that turned demand away from the area and caused prices to fall—not the appearance (or potential appearance) of Negroes. Yet the result will undoubtedly be cited as confirmation of the original fear that Negro entry would cause prices to fall—even though not one Negro has entered the area.

23. *The Ghetto Makers*

JACK ROTHMAN

Meet a group of ugly Americans you probably don't know—the "Ghetto Makers." They are found primarily in the real-estate and money-lending worlds, and their stock in trade is racism for a profit. These are the men who control and manipulate the housing market in integrated areas of our cities. They specialize in panic salesmanship—the rumor, the racial argument, the prejudicial insinuation. They engage in a variety of pernicious financial practices, both legal and extralegal, taking the Negro home buyer for a ride in the process. Through their pressure-cooker tactics, whole neighborhoods are induced to change from white to colored—and segregated —in short order and at great cost in human terms.

Racially changing neighborhoods have in recent years reached widespread and troubling proportions. Almost every city dweller can call to mind some neighborhood that was transformed almost overnight from a solidly white to a solidly Negro district. Such rapid dislocation stirs up a torrent of intergroup tensions and a welter of social and welfare problems. And this is a problem that holds geography in disregard; it is as much prevalent and malevolent in the North as in the South.

One of the chief causes of rapid neighborhood change (and consequently of residential segregation) is the presence of prejudice in so many of our white citizens. No sooner does the first Negro family move into a white area than large numbers of whites move out. But this prejudice constitutes only the most obvious starting point in attempting to understand the dynamics of the change pattern. What is less known is that in addition to this "spontaneous" process, there are purposeful, efficiently organized "unspontaneous" influences at work—the Ghetto Makers, who consciously trigger off these personal predispositions and channel them into large-scale movements. These Ghetto Makers play at least as large a part in fostering segregation as do public attitudes, and their role needs to be laid bare and understood if we are ever to make headway in coping with the problem.

Standing at their head are a core of unethical or prejudiced real-estate brokers. In the course of directing an experimental citizens' project aimed at stabilizing a racially changing neighborhood, I had a chance to observe a representative group of these brokers at first hand. The project, sponsored by the community planning division of the New York City Youth Board, was centered in the middle class residential community of Springfield Gardens in the Borough of Queens.

The brokers I observed seemed to fall into two categories, which may be described as the "blockbusters" and the "lily-whiters." The blockbusters are the more deliberately destructive. Once a Negro somehow manages to move into a white neighborhood, these brokers make their entrance and work over the area. Through house-to-house canvassing, relentless telephone solicitation, use of the mails and by various other means, they create an atmosphere of panic in the neighborhood and high-pressure

Reprinted from *The Nation*, October 7, 1961, pp. 222-25, by permission of the publisher and author. Jack Rothman is a professor in the School of Social Work at the University of Michigan.

the white residents into selling. They open up one block at a time, saturating block A with Negroes and then going on to block B. "Do you want your kids to play with colored kids?" goes their sales talk. "Do you want to be the last white family left on the block? Do you want to lose a fortune on your house?" Characteristically, they approach a homeowner with a cash offer and the (often fallacious) news that Mrs. Jones down the street is selling to a Negro family. Emphasis is placed on the urgency of selling immediately, before the value of the house nose-dives. Occasionally "decoys,"[1] such as a Negro woman wheeling a baby carriage, are paraded up and down the street to set the proper psychological climate.

For the realty salesman, the wholesale turnover of an entire area is a happy and enormously profitable prospect. By panicking homeowners, the broker can pocket an even greater return by entering the market he is manipulating, buying low and selling high. Negro brokers as well as white avail themselves of the blockbusting technique; actually, the Negro brokers are even more insidious, since they are so heavily relied on by their Negro clients.

The blockbusting real-estate men show homes in integrated districts such as Springfield Gardens only to prospective Negro buyers; I have known them deliberately to turn down prospective white buyers. For them the steady and total segregation of the neighborhood is a desirable goal.

Meanwhile the other real-estate brokers, the lily-whiters, are operating in white areas adjacent to the changing community. Their clientele is usually entirely white. I saw them operating in Laurelton, adjacent to Springfield Gardens. If these Laurelton brokers had made an effort to show homes in contiguous integrated areas to their clients (as indeed had been their custom prior to integration), there would have been a greater possibility of counterbalancing the influence of the blockbusters and maintaining a racially mixed community. However, we found that these lily-white brokers consistently failed to show homes in these areas to white clients and turned down listings from Springfield Gardens which were offered to them. Just a few Negro families in an area marked it off-limits to these brokers for showing homes to white buyers. Their reasons for taking this position range from their own conscious or unconscious prejudices ("What decent person would want to live in that area anyway?")[1] to realistic economic considerations (it takes less time and effort to place the average white buyer in a white community than in an integrated one; and time is money).

Because of the extensive activity in the integrated areas of the blockbusters and the abandonment of the areas by the lily-whiters, each time a house is placed on the market it is sold to a Negro family. This results usually in a gradual and unswerving rise in the percentage of Negro residents in a given community.

Banks and lending institutions also play their unsavory part in this operation. They not only make it difficult for nonwhites to obtain a mortgage when they attempt to buy in a white area; they also discriminate against whites who want to buy in a changing neighborhood. The banks take the view that a white individual who moves into a mixed area will soon find himself part of a small minority and will consequently move out within a short period of time, thus diminishing the duration of the loan.

---

1. In one instance a white woman who was moving for reasons of health called one of these brokers specifically because she wanted to see racial balance kept in the community—even though she knew it would be more difficult to sell her home to a white person and that it might take a longer period of time. The broker turned her listing down cold. "Nobody but white trash would want to live in that neighborhood," was his caustic comment. This is in an "enlightened" northern city.

In one case, our committee had to contact a dozen banks before the enlightened Bowery Savings in downtown Manhattan agreed to make a loan to a financially solid white family.

Advertising in the Negro press is still another facet of Ghetto Making. Extensive and dramatic advertising directed at the Negro community is placed by brokers who specialize in changing communities. Brokers located in the major districts of Negro settlements like Harlem, and Bedford-Stuyvesant in Brooklyn, play up these areas with gigantic signs, flyleafs, etc. Since often such locations are the only sources of decent residential property for Negroes, this activity is entirely understandable. It tends, however, to make more difficult the process of orderly neighborhood change, and to foster segregation.

In advertisements in the Negro press (placed by both white and Negro brokers), one detects a pattern of unethical, even fraudulent, practices. Homes are advertised at unrealistically low prices to attract naïve purchasers. Example of a typical ad:

> Magnificent home, $29.00 a month pays all. Detached 2-family, plus a rentable 3-room basement apartment. Really living rent free. Situated in a tremendous garden plot. Modern kitchen, Cadillac-size garage, automatic heat, three bedrooms and extras galore. $890.00 down.

When a Negro teacher acquaintance of mine responded to such an ad, he was first told the property was located in an isolated swamp area near Idlewild International Airport and that he wouldn't really be interested in it. Later the broker admitted that the ad was a "come-on." The objective is to entice the prospective buyer into the office by any suitable means at hand. Then an attempt is made to sell him a more expensive home.

The uninformed buyer is encouraged to overcrowd the house by using the attic and basement to take in roomers, boarders, foster children, etc., often in direct violation of existing housing ordinances. This tends to attract to a middle class area large numbers of working-class families—which in turn causes a stampede of the remaining middle-class white families from the area. It also disheartens middle class Negro families who, in the usual sequence of events, are the first to enter an all-white neighborhood, seeking a community of middle class character. Most brokers who speak loftily of "neighborhood homogeneity" when it comes to keeping a neighborhood white, do not at all respect the concept of a homogeneous *middle-class* neighborhood when applied to Negroes. They willingly inject lower-class and "problematic" elements into an evolving middle class Negro or interracial community, thus thwarting the efforts of colored teachers, doctors, lawyers, and businessmen to enjoy the benefits of a reasonable standard of community living for themselves and their children.

As people who cannot afford payment for homes are deliberately enticed into brokers' offices, funding companies associated with the brokers make loans through devious and highly questionable financing methods. The result is that the purchasers are led into debt over their heads and find it necessary to overcrowd their homes for extra income. Again, a middle-class area tends to break down into a segregated slum.

On one occasion, members of the citizens' committee with which I was associated visited the publisher of one of the country's largest Negro dailies to call to his attention how some brokers were using the classified pages for their own ends—ends which we found wholly incompatible with the well-being of the Negro people. The approach we used was a friendly, interested, tactful one. Our delegation, an interracial group, was shocked at the cold, unsympathetic, even cynical reception we received from the publisher. A newspaper, we were told, is in the business of reporting news and bringing in an income. It is not a social welfare institution. The use made of its want-ad columns is not the concern of the newspaper so long as the wording of ads does not violate existing laws. Any interference with the manner of advertising, the publisher informed us, would be an affront to the "free enterprise system." Ghetto Making for profit, it would appear, operates on both sides of the color line.

The intricate financial machinations of the Ghetto Makers could make up a field of study in its own right. I will describe here only techniques I personally witnessed in the project area. Similar techniques, with appropriate local adaptations, have been put into effect in communities across the country and have been amply documented in the recent multivolume survey of the Commission on Race and Housing, sponsored by the Fund for the Republic (University of California Press, 1960).

In the Queens instance, funding companies affiliated with brokers required a large number of "points" to complete the purchase of a home. Each point is 1 percent of the mortgage (for example, $150 on a $15,000 mortgage) and consists of a kind of service charge for making the loan. Since often the Negro purchaser, drawn into the broker's office through one of the beguiling hawking methods described above, does not have enough money for the down payment, he cannot obtain a loan directly from an ordinary bank, which might require only one or two points. He is therefore at the mercy of the funding companies, which in some cases have been known to demand up to 12 percent of the mortgage (12 points) merely for making the loan. This is independent of any interest rates on the loan. Later the funding company may pass the loan over to the bank. (Actually, the seller is supposed to be responsible for payment of the points, but this is circumvented by incorporating them into the purchase price. Through the point system, and by inflating the purchase price, brokers can charge exorbitant interest rates without technically violating usury laws.)

But this is not the end of the story. We now have a Negro buyer paying a high number of points and unable to afford even a sufficient down payment. A contract of sale is made, permitting the purchaser to occupy the house; he must, however, pay a monthly bill until he has met the down payment. There is no actual transfer of title or deed until the down payment is completely paid off—ordinarily a matter of some five to seven years. Only then do the payments on the actual mortgage begin. During these first years, the monthly payment includes not only the down-payment installment but also interest on the down payment, interest on the old mortgage, carrying charges on the house such as taxes, insurance, water and sewage bills, etc. All this time *the purchaser has no security whatever*. Should he fail to meet a monthly payment, he may lose the house and every cent he has so far put into it.

The whole operational scheme of the Ghetto Makers makes sense only in the light of the undemocratic and socially debilitating ground rules under which our racial minorities live. While choked for space in depressed slum areas, Negroes are rigorously restricted in the housing market, with almost no new housing being constructed to meet their needs.[2] At the same time, their economic position is rising significantly, and their attitudes are increasingly influenced by the middle-class values which pervade our society. It is no wonder that as a particular area of the city opens up for nonwhite occupancy, the Negro market will flow in that direction, all other channels being

2. Of the 9 million new homes built nationally between 1935 and 1950, *less than 7 percent* were available to non-whites: See *Social Progress* (September 1958), organ of the Board of Christian Education, The Presbyterian Church in the United States of America.

blocked. Thus, the slightly integrated community rather quickly becomes the changing community and, with a solid assist by the Ghetto Makers, eventually becomes the totally segregated Negro community.

This pattern can be reversed only when our cities achieve an open-occupancy status compatible with our democratic precepts. Under these circumstances, Negro families could disperse themselves widely into many neighborhoods in accordance with their economic resources.

Such an end can be achieved only by eliminating racial restrictions on home owner-ship and, simultaneously, striking hard at the Ghetto Makers, the shysters and manip-ulators of the housing market. No legislation currently on the books is geared toward specific control of the Ghetto Makers' practices I have described. There are fair housing practices bills in some cities (notably New York and Pittsburgh) and states (notably Colorado, Connecticut, Massachusetts, and more recently New York) which deal with discrimination in housing.

But none has a fair selling practices clause which effectively regulates the blockbusters until a state of open occupancy is achieved. (The blockbusters do not discriminate per se against Negroes in the housing field. As a matter of fact, to a certain extent they may be said to open up new areas for Negroes to live in. But they do so by use of inflammatory selling practices and in such a way as to heighten racial tensions and create new racial ghettos.) Likewise, no existing law can deal adequately with some of the elaborate, racist financing and advertising techniques devised by the Ghetto Makers. An encouraging recent breakthrough has been the attempt by the license-issuing bureaus of New York and Pennsylvania to regulate blockbusting through administrative directives.

Some liberal and minority groups, caught up and frustrated in this complicated housing web, have thrown the full weight of their energies and emotions into the school integration issue. Still, as former National Urban League Director Lester Gran-ger stated, clamoring for school integration in these circumstances is like whistling in the dark. He reminds us, "If we spend our time battering school boards over the head, we overlook the real villains of the place—Jim Crow-minded property owners and real-estate brokers and developers."

The Ghetto Makers exert power in present-day America. They decide whom you may live next to and who may live next to you. For this service they extract a huge profit. The power of these men may be broken by legal means coupled with the weight of an enlightened public opinion.

24. *Restrictive Zoning*

NATIONAL COMMISSION ON URBAN PROBLEMS

THE ZONING ORDINANCE

Regulated Subjects

A zoning ordinance typically prescribes how each parcel of land in a community may be used. Most regulations cover at least the following subjects.

Use. First, zoning ordinances designate permitted "uses" (activities). Many divide uses into three basic categories: dwellings, businesses, and industry. These basic categories are usually divided into subcategories. It is common practice, for example, to distinguish between one-family detached houses and apartment buildings, between "light" and "heavy" industry. Over the years ordinances have tended to establish more and more use categories. Ordinances with more than 20 different use categories are now common, and many ordinances now make specific provision for hundreds of listed uses.

Population density. A limitation on population density is also part of today's accepted zoning pattern. Most ordinances establish this limitation by setting a minimum required size for each lot. Alternatively, they may limit the number of families per acre or set a minimum required lot area for each dwelling unit on a lot. Some, particularly in large cities, establish more refined density controls that try to take account of the likelihood that more people will live in larger apartment units than in smaller ones.

Building bulk. Zoning regulations also limit building bulk. Usually, they do this by requiring yards along lot boundaries, by limiting building height, and by limiting the proportion of lot area that may be covered by buildings. Refinements of these devices have become common, in recent years, as communities have recognized that rigid yard and height requirements often deter imaginative design. "Floor area ratio" and "usable open space" requirements are among the increasingly common refinements.

Offstreet parking. As an addition to the original pattern, most zoning ordinances now contain offstreet parking requirements. These are intended to assure that new development provides for at least some of its own parking needs rather than adding to the number of parked cars on already crowded streets.

Other subjects. Many other requirements also appear in zoning regulations. Minimum house size, landscaping, signs, appearance of buildings, offstreet loading, view protection, and grading are just a few of the other subjects sometimes regulated.

Reprinted from National Commission on Urban Problems, *Building the American City* (Washington, D.C.: Government Printing Office, 1968), pt. III, chap. 1 (edited).

The Zoning Map

In recognition of differing conditions and planning policies in different parts of each community, zoning regulations establish "zones" or "districts." Within each of these districts a uniform set of regulations dealing with uses, bulk, and the like apply. Thus, for example, stores may be permitted in one district but not in another. To show the location and boundaries of these districts, the ordinance includes a zoning map. . . .

Administration

To apply substantive requirements, every regulation needs an administrative apparatus. The originators of zoning anticipated a fairly simple administrative process. They thought of the zoning regulation as being largely "self-executing." After the formulation of the ordinance text and map by a local zoning commission and its adoption by the local governing body, most administrations would require only the services of a building official who would determine whether proposed construction complied with the requirements. This official was not expected to exercise discretion or sophisticated judgment. Rather, he was to apply the requirements to the letter. In the case of new construction, he was to compare the builder's plans with the requirements governing the particular land and either grant or deny a permit. Even today, this nondiscretionary permit process is at the heart of zoning administration.

Nevertheless, it was recognized from the outset that the permit process was not enough. Zoning statutes and regulations commonly provide for the following additional kinds of administrative action.

Appeals. First is the appeal from a decision of the building official. The applicant may allege, for example, that the official has misinterpreted the ordinance or applied it arbitrarily. In most states, such appeals are taken to a local board of zoning appeals (or adjustment).

Variances. Because of special conditions, strict application of ordinance requirements sometimes causes hardship that is unnecessary to achievement of the public purposes of the ordinance. A lot may be oddly shaped, for example, or topography may be unusual. To alleviate these hardships, and also to safeguard the constitutionality of regulation where strict application of requirements would amount to a "taking" of land, zoning regulations have traditionally provided for "variances." The variance power, too, most often belongs to the board of appeals. To qualify for a lawful variance, the applicant is normally required to show that strict application of the rules would cause "unnecessary hardship" due to "unique circumstances."

Special exceptions. The third type of administrative decision is the "special exception," which has now grown to include many types of discretionary decisions bearing such names as "conditional uses" and "special-use permits." The zoning ordinance will list particular uses (e.g., airports or cemeteries or gas stations) and permit them only with some sort of discretionary review in each case. The review may be by the board of appeals or governing body (or sometimes by a planning commission or a zoning administrator). The ordinance may set up specific standards to guide the discretionary review. Often, however, standards are very general.

Amendments. Finally, the administrative apparatus of zoning includes a provision for changing the rules. It was foreseen from the outset that both the text and the map would occasionally become out of date, and provision was made for revision of both by the local governing body. Although statutes normally require notice and hearing, the amendment process is otherwise much the same as that used to amend other local laws. The vast majority of amendments are changes in the zoning map, commonly called "rezonings."

To assure that regulatory actions stay within the limits set by constitutions, statutes, and ordinances, zoning statutes further provide for review by the courts.

THE SUBDIVISION REGULATION

While conventional zoning normally applies to individual lots, subdivision regulations govern the process by which those lots are created out of larger tracts.

Regulated Subjects

Site design and relationships. Subdivision regulations typically seek to assure that subdivisions are appropriately related to their surroundings. Commonly, they require that the subdivision be consistent with a comprehensive plan for the area (e.g., by reserving land for proposed highways or parks). Requirements normally assure that utilities (local streets, sewers) tie into those located or planned for adjoining property. Other requirements are intended to assure that the subdivision itself is related to its own site and that it will work effectively. The widths of streets, the length of blocks, the size of lots, and the handling of frontage along major streets, are among commonly regulated subjects.

Allocation of facilities cost—dedications and fees. Second, subdivision regulations may contain provisions that effectively allocate costs of public facilities between the subdivider and local taxpayers. Commonly, regulations require subdividers to dedicate land for streets and to install, at their own expense, a variety of public facilities to serve the development. These often include streets, sidewalks, storm and sanitary sewers, and street lights. In recent years, more and more subdivision regulations have also been requiring subdividers to dedicate parkland and sometimes school sites, or to make cash payments in lieu of such dedication. Some regulations go further still, requiring payment of fees to apply toward such major public costs as the construction of sewage disposal plants.

Administration

Subdivision regulations contemplate a more sophisticated administrative process than do conventional zoning regulations. Instead of prescribing the precise location of future lot lines, for example, subdivision regulations provide more general design standards (based in part on local plans). The local planning commission or governing body then applies these standards, at the time of subdivision, to preliminary and final plats submitted by property owners.

THE NATURE AND EVOLUTION OF CONVENTIONAL REGULATIONS

Responsibility: Local

Regulatory power was given to local governments. Although state enabling legislation prescribed the general nature of the regulations and established the administrative process, regulatory initiative and discretion were local. Regulations responded to local policies and were administered by local officials.

Technique: Self-executing, Noncompensative, Negative

Like the building and other codes whose form they resembled, these regulations were self-executing, noncompensative, negative.

Self-executing. The detailed zoning requirements—down to the last zone boundary and side-yard width—were to be determined in advance. (Subdivision regulations, as already noted, established both specific requirements and more general standards to be applied to the facts of each individual case.) Once adopted, the zoning ordinance was to be basically self-enforcing. Provisions for administrative relief and rezoning were thought of more as occasional adjustments than as parts of the day-to-day regulatory process.

Noncompensative. The regulations did not provide for compensation to property owners. Affected property remained in private ownership, and regulatory limitations on its use were authorized under the state's police power to protect the public health, safety, and welfare. This approach had the advantage of resembling established codes. It also saved public funds and avoided the administrative complexity of purchasing or condemning interests in affected property.

Negative. The role of the regulating government was essentially negative. Similar in concept to the law of nuisance, regulations were normally intended to prohibit inappropriate development—to keep out the bad rather than to achieve the good. Development initiative was left with private builders.

Policy: Limited Control

Finally, most early regulations were remarkably lax by today's standards. Even in the most restrictive residential district, some early regulations prohibited only a handful of specified commercial and industrial uses, and many district regulations provided neighborhoods only minimal protection against incompatible intrusions. Permissiveness was revealed even more clearly by zoning maps. Substantial areas in some communities were placed in unrestricted districts, in which all uses were allowed. "Overzoning"—particularly for business and industry—was the rule rather than the exception. Out of local optimism, an absence of planning, and a concern not to depress speculative property values came zoning maps in many towns that provided for development beyond the dreams of land promoters. . . .

Preventing Change in Established Residential Neighborhoods

The primary demand behind zoning in thousands of communities was to protect established neighborhoods—especially residential ones—from the intrusion of incompatible uses. Zoning in these situations was intended more to prevent change than to guide it. The location of residential districts on zoning maps could largely reflect established development patterns. And the lists of permitted uses and bulk standards could largely be derived from what was already on the ground and from what was traditionally considered compatible with what was on the ground. In effect, regulations for this purpose could follow the broad directions already established by the market. . . .

More Restrictive Requirements

. . . [One] widespread tendency of recent regulations has been toward increased restrictiveness. In part, this has stemmed from greater public acceptance of land use regulations. Particularly in well-to-do suburban communities, newer regulations

are likely to remove some of the undeveloped "strip commercial" zoning that characterizes so many regulations. Sign regulations may be tightened up. Much higher standards may be established to achieve quality development in commercial and industrial
areas.

The most dramatic increase in restrictiveness has been a widespread reduction of
permitted residential densities. In recent years, communities across the nation have
amended their ordinances to require larger and larger lots. "Acreage" zoning, the
extreme situation, is now common, and lot sizes in community after community are
being raised across the board.

The objectives of these density restrictions vary from place to place and time to
time. Because real objectives are sometimes unspoken, it is often difficult to know
which ones predominate in any particular situation. All of the following are important.

First is a disturbing group of exclusionary objectives, discussed in detail later. . . .
For a variety of reasons, citizens of some communities want to prevent as much development as possible for as long as possible, or to increase development cost to provide
locations for people who choose low density living, or to prevent people of low or
moderate income from being able to afford homes in the community.

Second, density restrictions often represent a simple desire to raise development
quality or carry out conventional local plans. When detached houses are built on
the narrow lots permitted by many regulations, there is little space for adequate side
yards. As houses increase in size, space for yards is smaller still. The intent of many
regulations is, in effect, to assure adequate space between detached dwellings in the
interest of privacy, amenity, and compatibility.

Even the one- and two-acre zones that fill so many zoning maps may simply express
a municipal intention that the land be developed for one- and two-acre lots (perhaps
coupled with a hope that no building will occur). Such requirements may be intended
to carry out a community plan that designates locations for various development
intensities. Essentially they may carry out community policy relating to development
timing—channeling development pressures of today into higher density areas elsewhere in the community with the intent of changing the zoning later, after those
areas are developed. In each case, density regulations can be an essential adjunct
of plans for the location and timing of public facilities.

Third, large-lot zones may be symptomatic of the "wait and see" regulatory approach,
serving to assure that any future development receives discretionary review by the
municipality. (Indeed, large-lot zoning may achieve this result whether or not this
was its original intent.) Large-lot zoning can effectively prevent economically attractive
development until the municipality grants rezoning. When the owner applies for
that rezoning, the municipality has an opportunity to look over the proposal and
give it the broadest of discretionary review. Such a "wait and see" approach to regulation
is now gaining acceptance very rapidly.

Changes in Administration: "Wait and See"

The "wait and see" approach to regulations represents a change in the administrative
procedure applied to proposed development. In place of the older "self-executing"
regulations, the approach contemplates discretionary public review of development
proposals shortly before development occurs. In essence, the traditional administrative
process in zoning is giving way to the more general standards and administrative
discretion traditional in subdivision regulations. The developer proposes, and the
municipality disposes. Sometimes the process is guided by useful plans and standards,
but often not. Increasing reliance on discretionary review may well represent a more

fundamental change in land-use regulations than any changes in substantive requirements. . . .

EXCLUSIONARY LOCAL LAND-USE POLICIES

. . . [M]any of the most serious problems facing the nation's cities are metropolitan in scope. Problems of air and water pollution, transportation, open space, solid waste disposal, housing, and employment do not end at municipal borders. At the same time, land-use controls, which are important factors in the creation and solution of such problems, are lodged in local governments with virtually no supervision by metropolitan or state agencies.

The constituency served by local officials making land-use decisions is quite different from that of the metropolitan area as a whole, whose concerns are affected by those decisions. It is hardly surprising that the interests and desires of one small jurisdiction do not always conform to the needs of the larger area of which it is a part. It is understandable, for example, that local officials—and their constituents—may not want a regional waste disposal plant within their own borders. Indeed, many officials would prefer to have as little development as possible of any kind—to keep the community just as it is. The inevitability of regional development may be obvious; but to local officials and their constituents it may be equally obvious that much of it should be located somewhere else. Similarly, there may well be a recognition that low and moderate income families within the metropolitan area need to be housed somewhere; that they need to be housed within any given jurisdiction in the area is far less readily accepted.

The problem takes on momentous proportions when compounded by the reliance of local governments on the property tax as their major source of revenue. How land within their borders is used becomes not merely a question of esthetic and social sensitivity, it is a matter of governmental solvency. Land-use controls have become a major weapon in the battle for ratables.

The game of "fiscal zoning" requires the players—i.e., zoning jurisdictions—to attract uses which add more in property taxes or local sales taxes than they require in expensive public services and to exclude uses which do not pay their own way. In essence, this means that jurisdictions are influenced to seek industrial and commercial uses and luxury housing, and discourage or prohibit such uses as housing for low and moderate income persons.[1] A further refinement is the desire to exclude housing which attracts families with many children in favor of housing with no children or as few as possible—all this because children require schools, the most significant expenditure item of local governments. Low income housing is bad from a purely fiscal perspective because it does not add to the tax rolls the same amount of assessed value as luxury housing and because it often brings large families into a community. In addition, the families occupying such housing may require welfare and, it is widely believed, more of other services from the local government than higher income families require.

Of course, there are sometimes important nonfiscal policies behind certain types

---

1. The implications of this for job opportunities are obvious. In Part I [of the Commission's Report] there is a description of the growing disparity between new job locations, and especially blue-collar jobs, and the surplus labor force. Fiscal zoning would appear to contribute significantly to the problem. [See National Commission on Urban Problems, *Building the American City* (Washington, D.C.: Government Printing Office, 1968).]

of exclusionary land-use decisions. "Undesirable" uses such as junkyards are not very attractive. "Undesirable" people—minority groups and the poor—would not "fit in." Indeed, for many suburban dwellers it was just such "undesirable" aspects of the city that drove them out; and for central city dwellers who have managed to find neighborhoods which satisfy them, it may well be the absence of such "undesirables" that keeps them in.

Attracting industry and commerce in competition with neighboring jurisdictions is not new. Many localities have developed it into a fine art, using such magnetic devices as the issuance of municipal bonds to help private companies finance land acquisition and plant construction. The land-use control contribution is overzoning for such uses, which is common practice, or adoption of a permissive policy with respect to requests for rezonings and special exceptions for such uses. The exclusionary side of fiscal zoning takes a variety of forms which are considered below.

LARGE-LOT ZONING

The most widely discussed form of exclusion is large-lot zoning, by which a jurisdiction attempts to limit development in substantial portions of its territory to single-family residences on very large lots. The actual effects of this practice are not easy to isolate. Many factors determine the price which a particular lot will command in the market. In a weak market, large-lot zoning may make little difference, with a four-acre tract selling for little more than a two-acre tract, and both sizes providing sites for shacks. In a strong market, a change from a four-acre minimum to a two-acre minimum may not lower the price per lot since potential developers are concerned primarily with the number of units that can be built on a given tract and will bid up the price of the rezoned tract. Comparisons of different properties are difficult. A two-acre lot may be more valuable than a four-acre lot because of factors unrelated to size—location, topography, etc. Broad comparisons thus become extremely suspect. Nevertheless, it does appear that land prices per lot do diminish as minimum lot size is reduced, though usually not commensurately with the change in size. That is to say, a half-acre lot will cost less than a one-acre lot, but will cost more than half the price. . . .

Even where prices per lot do not differ markedly from zone to zone, it does appear that large-lot zoning can have significant effects on the cost of housing. *First*, extensive large-lot zoning in a given area has the effect of substantially reducing the total amount of housing that can be accommodated. If demand for new housing is strong, this restriction of the supply of housing sites will increase residential land costs generally. Moreover, by limiting the amount of land for housing on smaller lots and multifamily units below that which the market demands, the prices for these sites may be increased.

Second, the increase in the total house-and-lot price may be greater than the increase in land price caused by large-lot zoning. Some builders will simply not build the same house on a large lot that they will on a smaller lot, believing that a larger house is necessary. Furthermore, many builders observe a rule of thumb that the price of a lot should be some specified percentage of the total price of house and lot—e.g., 20 percent. If such a rule is strictly observed, a $1,000 increase in lot cost will result in a $5,000 increase in the price of the finished house and lot.

Third, large-lot zoning generally results in added costs for land improvements. Depending on specific requirements in the zoning ordinance regarding lot width, the effect can be to increase significantly the required linear feet of streets, sidewalks, gutters, sewers and water lines. Table 24.1 suggests the magnitude of such added costs.

TABLE 24.1   *Land improvement costs per lot by residential zoning category in St. Louis County, Mo., and Montgomery County, Md.*

Zone	Minimum Area per Dwelling Unit	Average Frontage per Lot (Feet)	Improve- ment Cost per Lot*
St. Louis County, Mo.:			
R-1 .... 1 acre		125	$4,375
R-2 .... 15,000 sq. ft.		100	3,500
R-3 .... 10,000 sq. ft.		80	2,800
R-4 .... 7,500 sq. ft.		65	2,275
R-5 .... 6,000 sq. ft.		55	1,925
Montgomery County, Md.:			
R-A .... 2 acres		150	5,250
R-E .... 40,000 sq. ft.		125	4,375
R-R .... 20,000 sq. ft.		100	3,500
R-150 .... 15,000 sq. ft.		80	2,800
R-90 .... 9,000 sq. ft.		75	2,625
R-60 .... 6,000 sq. ft.		60	2,100

*Estimated locally at $35 a foot of frontage.
SOURCE: Study prepared for the Commission by Department of Urban Affairs, Urban Research Center, Hunter College of the City University of New York.

In some instances the fiscal objectives behind large-lot zoning are quite clear. In St. Louis County, for example, the Parkway School District has calculated that any home costing less than $26,274 does not pay its own way in educational costs. On this basis, district officials oppose any change in zoning to permit lots of less than a quarter-acre, below which they believe housing costing less than this amount can be built.

But the motives for large-lot zoning are generally not clear-cut. Rather they are a mixture of fiscal and nonfiscal factors. Where a community does not wish to bear the cost of extending water and sewer lines beyond present development, it may limit new development to large lots so that it can be served by septic tanks and wells. Some communities think of large-lot zoning as a means of retarding development or preserving rural character or open space. And, in some instances, it is clearly viewed as a technique for keeping out "incompatible" people—lower income groups and minorities.

Large-lot zoning is a common and widespread practice in many major metropolitan areas. Data are scarce, however, since few metropolitan planning agencies or other regional groups have attempted to make consolidated area zoning maps or compile data on the total zoning pattern in the area. A Commission survey shows that 25 percent of metropolitan area municipalities of 5,000-plus permit *no* single-family houses on lots of less than a half-acre. Of these same governments, 11 percent have some 2-acre zoning; 20 percent have some 1- to 2-acre zoning; 33 percent have some ½- to 1-acre zoning; and more than 50 percent have some ¼- to ½-acre zoning.

In the New York metropolitan area (as defined by the Regional Plan Association), 90 percent of the vacant land zoned for single-family residences calls for lots of one-fourth acre or more, and two-thirds of this land is zoned for lots of at least one-half acre. For 5 of the counties in the metropolitan area, the average lot size increased from 9,000 square feet in 1950 to 19,000 square feet in 1957. Major increases in the average size of building lots in these years took place in Bergen County (7,674 square feet to 20,614) and in Westchester County (13,068 square feet to 24,955) and to a lesser extent elsewhere. Since 1960, major portions of Monmouth, Suffolk, and Orange Counties have been rezoned from one-fourth acre and one-eighth acre lots to one-half and one-acre lots. The town of Brookhaven, in eastern Suffolk County, rezoned substantially all of its vacant land for one-half acre lots or larger; moreover, it appears quite possible that the town's remaining vacant land will be further rezoned to one-acre lots or larger. The town of Riverhead, which is also in Suffolk County, recently rezoned its vacant land from one-fourth-acre to one-acre lots.

In Connecticut, more than half of the vacant land zoned for residential use in the entire state is for lots of one to two acres. In Greenwich, Conn., a community of about 65,000 within mass-transit commuting distance of New York City, more than four-fifths of the total undeveloped area is zoned for minimum lots of 1 acre or more—39 percent for 4 acres, 25 percent for 2 acres, and 17½ percent for 1 acre.

In Cuyahoga County, which contains the city of Cleveland, 85,200 acres of vacant land are zoned for single-family residential use. Of this amount, only 28,425 acres, or 33 percent, are zoned for ½ acre or less; 42,225 acres, or 50 percent, are zoned for ½ to 1.9 acres minimum lot sizes; and 14,550 acres, or 17 percent, are zoned for 2 acres or more. Thus, 67 percent of the vacant land zoned for single-family development in the core county of the Cleveland SMSA is zoned for minimum lots of one-half acre or more. In outlying Geauga County, for example, 85 percent of the residentially zoned area requires lots of 1 acre or more.

EXCLUSION OF MULTIPLE DWELLINGS

Perhaps an even more important form of exclusionary zoning is the limitation of residential development to single-family houses. Again, motives are undoubtedly mixed. Apartments are viewed by many suburban dwellers as central city structures, having no place in the "pastoral" setting of suburbia. Apartment dwellers are sometimes stereotyped as transients who, not having the permanent ties to the community which homeownership provides, will not be sufficiently concerned about the community or their own residences. But fiscal motives are also present. There is a concern that apartments—especially those which have large units and thereby can accommodate large families—will not pay their way. Where low or moderate income units are involved, both fiscal and social concerns increase.

Multifamily housing units generally provide the best opportunities for housing persons of low and moderate incomes. The rental nature of such housing, and the savings produced by spreading land costs over a greater number of units, place such housing within the means of many who could not afford new single-family houses. Furthermore, many of the publicly assisted housing programs are multifamily programs and depend on the existence of zoning for multifamily structures.

Most jurisdictions have some zoning for multifamily structures, and it appears that more suburban zoning jurisdictions are permitting them than in the past. A Commission survey shows that 87 percent of municipalities and New England-type townships of 5,000-plus have at least 1 district in which multifamily housing can be built. But the figure fails to reveal the way in which such zoning comes about. In many suburban jurisdictions zoning for multifamily housing occurs only through a piecemeal rezoning process. There is at any one time little undeveloped land available for multifamily construction. The price of land zoned for such purposes is thus inflated because of the uncertainty about the total amount of land that may become available. Of the undeveloped land zoned for residential purposes in the New York metropolitan area, for example, 99.2 percent is restricted to single-family dwellings.

MINIMUM HOUSE SIZE REQUIREMENTS

The most blatant, though not most extensive, exclusionary practice takes the form of excluding housing which fails to contain a minimum floor area as set out in the zoning ordinance.[2] Such requirements raise the lower limit of construction costs, and thus can be the most direct and effective exclusionary tool. An extreme application of the technique is found in Bloomington, Minn., an affluent suburb of the Twin Cities. Bloomington imposes a 1,700-square-foot minimum floor area. At a square foot construction cost of $15.82, the average for FHA Section 203 housing in the Minneapolis area in 1966, the smallest house permitted would require $26,894 in construction costs alone.

Table 24.2 shows the results of the Commission's nationwide survey on minimum house size requirements.

TABLE 24.2 *Percent of zoning municipalities and New England-type townships of 5,000-plus having selected minimum floor area requirements in their zoning for 1-story, single-family houses, by size, type, and location of government: 1967*

		Within SMSA's				Outside SMSA's		
Minimum floor area	All Zoning Govern- ments	Total	Municipalities 5,000		Town- ships	Total	Munici- palities	Town- ships
			50,000 Plus	to 49,999				
1,000 sq. ft. or more	7.6	8.8	6.5	11.4	4.8	5.8	4.5	12.2
800 to 999 sq. ft.	13.5	17.5	5.5	17.7	23.1	7.4	5.1	18.7
600 to 799 sq. ft.	15.8	17.6	9.7	12.3	32.4	13.0	13.4	11.0
Under 600 sq. ft.	3.9	3.6	5.8	2.9	3.9	4.4	4.0	6.5
Applicable, but areas not reported*	4.4	4.6	1.0	6.0	3.7	3.9	3.8	4.9

*These governments had a minimum floor area requirement but did not specify its size in response to the survey.
SOURCE: Allen D. Manvel, "Local Land and Building Regulation," Research Report no. 6, National Commission on Urban Problems, 1968.

EXCLUSION OF MOBILE HOMES

Exact figures are not available on the extent to which mobile homes are excluded from zoning jurisdictions, but it appears that a large number of governments exclude them entirely or limit them to industrial and commercial areas. A study in 1964

2. Such provisions are to be distinguished from minimum floor area requirements in housing codes. Housing codes provisions, applying both to new and existing housing, plainly purport to deal with minimum health and safety requirements and not with maintaining neighborhood character or property values. They are stated in terms of minimum floor area per occupant, and typically they are lower than the minimum requirements in zoning ordinances. The American Public Health Association model housing code, for example, requires that a dwelling unit have a minimum floor space (limited to habitable room areas) of 150 square feet for the first occupant and 100 square feet for each additional occupant.

showed that in New York State, of 237 zoning ordinances reviewed, over half excluded mobile homes either explicitly or by imposing minimums relating to floor area, height, or other factors which mobile homes could not meet. Only 82 communities permitted mobile homes on individual lots, as distinguished from mobile home parks; and in all but 12 of these communities such lots had to be in areas zoned for industrial or commercial uses. Only 11 communities permitted mobile home parks to locate in residentially zoned areas.

The exclusion of mobile homes in large part reflects a stereotyping of their appearance and of their occupants. Many see mobile homes as unattractive and occupied by people who do not take care of their homes or neighborhood. Such images are often derived from viewing mobile homes in the midst of industrial districts, to which they are so often relegated. Moreover, there are sometimes fiscal reasons for exclusion in addition to those generally applicable to housing which might accommodate low and moderate income families. In many areas mobile homes are not taxable as real property. And in some states they are not subject to local personal property taxes because of special state levies, the imposition of which may exempt them from local taxes. In New York State, mobile homes are taxable as real property, and the fiscal motive for exclusion is accordingly reduced. The high exclusion rate in New York may thus indicate an even greater amount of exclusion in other States.

UNNECESSARY HIGH SUBDIVISION REQUIREMENTS

Land improvement costs are becoming an increasingly important part of housing costs. Zoning, as discussed above, affects such costs by determining the number of linear feet of various improvements which are required to serve a given house. Subdivision regulations determine the precise specifications of such improvements, as well as the amount of land within a subdivision which can actually be devoted to housing. The more expensive these requirements are, the greater the cost of housing.

Subdivision regulations differ widely from locality to locality. By demanding higher quality improvements, a jurisdiction can effectively increase the cost of housing and thereby exclude a greater number of potential home buyers from the market.

ADMINISTRATIVE PRACTICES

Some of the most effective devices for exclusion are not discoverable from a reading of zoning and subdivision ordinances. Where rezoning is, in effect, necessary for many projects or where apartment development requires a special exception (as it does in some suburban communities), officials have an opportunity to determine the intentions of each developer with some precision. How many bedrooms will the units in his apartment house contain? What will be the rent levels? To whom does he plan to rent or sell? "Unfavorable" answers in terms of the fiscal and social objectives of such officials do not necessarily mean that permission will be denied outright. They may, however, mean long delays, attempts to impose requirements concerning dedications of land and provision of facilities over and above those which are properly required under the subdivision ordinance, and the like.

25. *Price Discrimination Against Negroes in the Rental Housing Market*

CHESTER RAPKIN

In the mid-1960s, residential segregation and its accompanying economic inequities remains as one of the last major barriers to the cultural integration of Negroes in American life. . . . Because it has created a type of price discrimination inimical to the principles of a free market, it has also had a direct effect on the quality of housing and on our ability to achieve a major national goal of a sound and attractive dwelling for every American family.

It should not come as news that Negroes as a group occupy inferior housing, but the prevalence of such inequality may be astonishing to some. The census of 1960 showed that 44 percent of Negro households then lived in substandard quarters (i.e., in housing units that were in need of substantial repair or that lacked necessary plumbing facilities). Nevertheless this disturbing situation represented an improvement over previous years, for as recently as a decade earlier 72 percent of Negro households were in substandard units. Thus a comparison of the two decades does show that the average quality of American housing is moving upward and that the Negro people are sharing in the benefits. Despite its marked improvement, however, the Negro housing situation is far worse than that of white households, for whom the incidence of substandard occupancy was 13 percent in 1960 and 32 percent in 1950.

Many explanations can be offered for the inferior housing status of the Negro people. The most obvious is their limited purchasing power when compared with the rest of the nation; the median Negro income is approximately 55 percent of that of the white. And since the income gap is so great, it seems reasonable to assume that differences in purchasing power alone can account for the greater incidence of substandard units. But although there is no doubt that the quality of housing correlates negatively with income, the incidence of substandard units is higher in every income category, for owners as well as for renter Negro families.

It has been further suggested that the poor condition of housing occupied by Negroes is due to the fact that, compared with that of whites, housing occupies an inferior position in the scale of Negro consumer preference. If this were generally true, then the housing expenditures in each income class would be less for Negroes than for whites. And this is so in many housing market areas. The trouble with this thesis,

Excerpted and reprinted from *Essays in Urban Land Economics* (Los Angeles: Real Estate Research Program, University of California, 1966), pp. 337-39, 342-45 (Copyright Number A896711, dated August 18, 1966), by permission of the publisher and author. Chester Rapkin is a professor of urban planning at Columbia University.

I wish to express my appreciation to Dr. Grace Milgram, for her invaluable assistance during the entire course of this study; and to Mr. Gene Milgram. Certain original data used in this paper were derived from a punch card file furnished under a joint project sponsored by the U.S. Bureau of Census and the Population Council and containing selected 1960 census information having a 0.1 percent sample of the population of the United States. Neither the Census Bureau nor the Population Council assumes any responsibility for the validity of any of the figures or the interpretations of the figures published herein.

however, is that in many other areas the reverse is also true. The problem, then, is to explain the departure, regardless of its direction, assuming of course that it is not random; for, given a free market, there is no prior reason why any variance should occur. If there were a tendency to spend less on housing, it would imply a greater social preference, or a physical need for more of other commodities, or that the tendency to save is the greater; all three assumptions, however, are difficult to establish.

The only thesis that explains these statistical anomalies is the flat statement that the poorer condition of Negro housing arises from discriminatory treatment in the housing market, so that the purchasing power of the dollar spent by nonwhites is less than that of the dollar spent by whites. This view has been widely held by housing economists, as well as by students of race relations. Possibly the only dissenting opinion has come from Margaret Reid,[1] who holds that if permanent income is considered, income for income Negroes pay the same rent and receive the same space and quality as whites. Any exception results from their recent immigration into large cities, she maintains, rather than from operation of a discriminatory or segregated market. Their recent urbanization, she believes, has produced disadvantages in knowledge and the ability to acquire housing from the sitting population. Not only is Dr. Reid's major conclusion at variance with the body of opinion and evidence, but data presented later in this paper cast doubt on the exception to her general statement.

If price discrimination is assumed to exist, then the differences, positive or negative, between the rent-income ratio of Negroes and whites can be explained by dividing Negro households into two groups. Where the Negro families seek the same housing standards as whites in comparable income brackets, they are compelled to pay more to obtain accommodations of the quality available to whites at lower rentals, which of course will lead to higher rent-income ratios. This economic consumption phenomenon is all the more pronounced because Negroes of lower occupation and income status than whites in comparable groups tend to adopt middle-class patterns of life. It may therefore be suggested that the greater the upward social mobility of the Negro, the higher his rent-income ratio is likely to be, compared with the ratios of whites in similar income categories.

Where there is relatively little social mobility, or where Negroes lack middle-class aspirations, there will be a tendency for their rent-income ratios to be lower than those of whites in similar income categories. The Negro in this group acts as an economic man attempting to obtain a dollar's worth of goods for every dollar expended. His expenditures on food, consumer durables, automobiles, clothing, and other commodities are in the general American market, whereas he suffers from price discrimination in the housing market, where he gets less than a dollar's worth of goods for a dollar. Under these circumstances, housing cannot compete successfully for the Negro consumer's dollar, and he will therefore be inclined to spend less of his income on housing than will whites in similar income groups.

But despite the many variations that are found in rent expenditure patterns, the overall average across the metropolitan United States shows that in every rent class the median rent-income ratio of Negro renters is higher than that of whites, and regardless of income Negroes show a higher proportion of substandard units than do whites (Table 25.1).

Another possible explanation for this apparent inequity lies not in discriminatory treatment but in the amount of space used. Since Negro households are on the average

1. Margaret Reid, *Housing and Home* (Chicago: University of Chicago Press, 1962), p. 389.

larger than white, it is possible that they prefer more space to better quality. There are no three-way tabulations of housing units by number of rooms, condition, and rent available in the standard published material of the Census of Housing. The published data of the median number of rooms by rent for United States metropolitan areas in 1960 show that Negroes, on the whole, obtain smaller units than whites. This would lend credence to the belief that some Negroes, at least, receive worse housing and less space for their money than whites; but the questions of whether such discrimination is widespread or limited to certain rent classes and the degree to which discrimination operates have remained open.

TABLE 25.1   *Characteristics of Renter-Occupied Housing Units, Total and Nonwhite, Inside SMSA's for the United States: 1960*

Monthly Gross Rent	Median Rent-Income Ratio		Percent Substandard		Median Number of Rooms		Percent more than One Person/Room	
	Total	Nonwhite	Total	Nonwhite	Total	Nonwhite	Total	Nonwhite
Total	24.9	26.1	20.7	41.2	3.8	3.2	14.0	28.5
Less than $30	19.8	22.3	50.3	62.1	2.4	2.2	17.3	25.8
$ 30-$ 39	20.8	24.2	42.9	56.3	2.7	2.4	16.5	28.5
$ 40-$ 49	19.6	24.3	36.8	50.9	3.1	2.6	17.3	29.2
$ 50-$ 59	19.0	23.9	29.3	44.5	3.4	3.0	17.0	30.0
$ 60-$ 69	19.2	24.8	23.2	39.1	3.6	3.2	16.5	29.9
$ 70-$ 79	19.8	24.8	17.8	33.9	3.8	3.4	14.5	28.3
$ 80-$ 99	20.4	26.2	12.9	30.6	4.1	3.7	12.7	27.9
$100-$119	21.8	28.1	8.6	27.4	4.3	4.1	11.2	27.9
$120 and over	22.1	29.4	4.5	23.9	4.6	4.7	7.8	25.7

SOURCE: U.S. Bureau of the Census, U.S. Census of Housing: 1960, vol. II, Metropolitan Housing, pt. 1, United States and Division.

The availability of the one-in-a-thousand sample from the 1960 census has made possible a further examination of the questions of the extent and location of differences in the quality of housing of the same room count occupied by Negroes and whites at the same rent levels, as well as consideration of the degree to which recent migration to metropolitan areas might explain the existing variations in quality.[2]

Because the emphasis in this study lay not so much in the differences in housing, per se, as in whether the housing market operated in a discriminatory fashion, an effort was made to examine housing quality in comparable submarkets. Access was gained to the sample on IBM cards, which contain somewhat less information than the tapes. Limitations of available data forced a number of decisions on how to narrow the variables so that influences affecting both white and nonwhite housing were as nearly alike as possible.

The data presented by the census could be distributed only by the four major regions of the country, and within each region only by size of metropolitan area. Although older suburbs with housing in poor condition exist, for the most part there

2. For details on the composition of the sample see: U.S. Census of Population and Housing: 1960, *1/1000 and 1/10,000, Two National Samples of the Population of the United States, Description and Technical Documentations.*

are both environmental and quality differences between housing in central cities and in other sections of the metropolitan area. Consequently housing conditions have been examined only for the central cities of metropolitan areas, separately for those in areas above and below 500,000 population, within each of the 4 regions. To eliminate influences which might tend to mask major differences in treatment, the study was limited to an examination of the condition of the housing of Negroes, rather than of all nonwhites, and of whites without Spanish surnames, rather than all whites. Study was further restricted to households paying monetary rent; those living in a unit without payment of cash rent, and owners whose annual housing expenditures cannot be learned from the housing census, were both excluded. Renters were divided into 9 classes: those paying under $50 a month gross rent, those paying rents from $50 to $79, and those paying $80 and over; and within each rent class those living in 1 and 2 rooms, 3 to 5 rooms, and 6 or more rooms were included in the study.

In each region, and for each metropolitan size class separately within a region, within each of the nine classes, a comparison was made between the proportions of Negro and white households living in substandard units and, similarly, between the proportions living in units of "low quality." Low quality was defined to include, in addition to substandard units, those classified as deteriorating yet having all plumbing facilities and those lacking central heat or private cooking facilities. A chi-square test was performed to determine the statistical significance in each cell of the differences in the proportion of substandard and of low quality units occupied by whites and Negroes.

After screening all the cards, 9,126 observations remained. Despite this large number, the great detail into which the sample was distributed resulted in several cells in which the number of observations was very small. In most instances the differences between the white and Negro figures were statistically significant; in some cases they were not. Virtually all of the differences proved to be in the same direction, however, with all exceptions noted in the ensuing discussion.

When the proportion of substandard units is examined, certain patterns emerge which hold with minor variations throughout the country, and in both metropolitan area size classes. Separate tables were prepared for each region of the country. The three regions outside of the South show much the same pattern. The lower housing quality obtained by Negroes when renting dwellings is pervasive; it persists in virtually all rent classes and all size units, except 1- and 2-room units renting for less than $50, in center cities of larger metropolitan areas outside of the South (Table 25.2). Despite this major exception, it is more than evident that Negroes spending the same rent as whites to rent the same number of rooms obtain a substantially greater proportion of substandard units.

The exception is in itself interesting, exemplifying two other strands of the pattern. Throughout the country, regardless of the race of the occupant, there is a sharp distinction between the quality of one- and two-room units and units with a higher room count. This is particularly true of the low-rent small units, over 70 percent of which in center cities of all metropolitan areas are substandard. In fact, in the smaller metropolitan areas all one- and two-room units occupied by Negroes in the South, and over 80 percent of those in the rest of the country, are substandard. In more expensive units, the incidence of substandard units is not so great, but even in the middle range, a quarter of those occupied by whites and over half of those occupied by Negroes are substandard, as are one-tenth of white-occupied and two-fifths of the Negro-occupied small units renting for $80 or more a month.

TABLE 25.2 *Percentage of substandard units by rent class and number of rooms, for center cities of metropolitan areas with less and more than 500,000 population, by race: South, U.S. other than South, and U.S. 1960*

| | Number of Rooms | | | | | |
| | 1-2 | | 3-5 | | 6 and over | |
Rent Class	White	Negro	White	Negro	White	Negro
I. Center Cities in Metropolitan Areas with 500,000 or more						
A. Total U.S.						
Less than $50	72.0	71.4	20.7	33.0	11.5	14.3
$50-$79	23.6	57.8	7.9	18.6	4.9	25.0
$80 and over	8.7	41.7	1.4	9.4	2.0	15.5
B. South						
Less than $50	63.8	77.1	18.3	38.6	33.3	50.0
$50-$79	16.2	41.2	7.3	22.3	8.3	41.2
$80 and over	4.8	25.0	.5	—	5.3	17.4
C. U.S. other than South						
Less than $50	73.1	69.0	21.0	27.8	8.7	—
$50-$79	24.9	60.4	8.0	16.9	4.6	17.9
$80 and over	9.1	43.8	1.6	10.9	1.7	14.9
II. Center Cities in Metropolitan Areas with less than 500,000						
A. Total U.S.						
Less than $50	70.6	97.4	26.5	53.8	20.0	14.3
$50-$79	27.5	46.7	10.5	43.1	12.8	55.6
$80 and over	16.7	—	.7	4.3	2.2	44.4
B. South						
Less than $50	55.8	100.0	19.7	55.9	25.0	16.7
$50-$79	17.6	66.7	6.5	48.1	16.7	83.3
$80 and over	12.5	—	—	—	2.4	33.3
C. U.S. other than South						
Less than $50	77.4	83.3	30.4	33.3	16.7	—
$50-$79	32.4	33.3	12.6	28.0	11.7	—
$80 and over	18.8	—	1.1	6.3	2.1	50.0

Since the proportion of substandard units among the larger apartments is considerably lower, there arises the question of why anyone would rent a small substandard unit when apparently he could obtain a larger standard accommodation for the same rental. In part, the answer may lie in the complete unavailability of larger units. The more likely explanation, however, is the fact that small units frequently offer quite different services, providing not only space but furniture, weekly rather than monthly rent payments, and the possibility of not being bound by a lease. The price for these additional services may be met not only by cash rent but also by low quality. Finding the explanation, however, lies beyond the scope of this study.

The group of one- and two-room units renting for less than $50 a month shows the impact not only of the difference in the small unit market, but also of the low rent. Not surprisingly, the incidence of substandard quality in central cities across the nation is greatest in units renting for less than $50, averaging 44 percent for white-occupied units and 53 percent for Negro-occupied; in the $50 to $79 rental class, the figures drop to 11 and 29 percent; and for rentals of $80 and over the drop is to 2 and 14 percent.

While the variation displayed between rental classes is to be expected, the lack of a consistent pattern within rental classes is surprising. It has been assumed generally that more rooms could be obtained at the same rental only at the cost of poorer condition; and the question that was to be examined, of course, was whether Negroes substituted space for quality to a different degree than did whites. Thus it might be expected that within any rental class the proportion of substandard units would be higher, the greater the number of rooms rented. We have already seen that one- and two-room units do in fact have the highest proportion of substandard units, and we have assumed that they therefore represent a distinct submarket offering services different from those of the rest of the rental housing stock. But it is only in the South that the expected increase between proportion substandard in three-to-five and six-room units occurs.

Another explanation for quality differences which was tested was the possibility that recent immigrants to the metropolitan area had greater difficulty in obtaining standard units than did the sitting population. The condition of housing occupied by those of the same race who had moved to the metropolitan area from a noncontiguous state within the preceding five years was examined separately from housing occupied by all others. The results are shown in Table 25.3 for the central cities of the entire United States. As can be seen, there is no regular difference between the proportion of substandard dwellings occupied by those resident for five years or more and those of less than five years; nor are the differences in the cells of either Negroes or whites statistically significant. Length of residence, then, would not seem to have any systematic effect upon the quality of housing obtained.

TABLE 25.3 *Percentage of Substandard Units, by Rent Class and Number of Rooms for Sitting Population and Inmigrants of Central Cities of Metropolitan Areas, by Race: United States, 1960*

| | Number of Rooms | | | | | |
| | 1 and 2 | | 3-5 | | 6 and over | |
Rent Class	Sitting Population	Inmi-grants*	Sitting Population	Inmi-grants*	Sitting Population	Inmi-grants*
			A. White			
Less than $50	71.4	76.2	21.3	30.0	14.8	11.1
$50-$79	24.6	18.5	9.1	3.4	8.6	2.8
$80 and over	9.0	20.0	1.3	1.9	2.0	3.1
			B. Negro			
Less than $50	78.7	62.5	39.7	73.7	14.3	—
$50-$79	57.1	33.3	22.5	29.2	30.6	—
$80 and over	38.2	66.7	8.9	12.5	19.2	—

* Inmigrants were defined as all households headed by persons whose place of residence in 1955 had been in any noncontiguous state. All others, including households headed by persons whose place of residence was in the same metropolitan areas, in the same state, or in a contiguous state, were included in the sitting population.

From a social viewpoint, possibly the most important observation which can be made from these tables is not the fact that discriminatory treatment exists, a confirmation of a view long held by housing economists, but rather that the degree of discrimination appears to increase markedly as Negroes approach middle-class status. The data show that in general the incidence of substandard housing decreases as rent paid increases, for both whites and Negroes, but the decrease is considerably greater for whites than for Negroes. If all cities are examined, the proportion of substandard among the smallest units was almost equal in the lowest rent class, approximately twice as great for Negro-occupied units renting for $50 to $79, and over four times as great in those renting for over $80. In the three-to-five-room units, the ratio of the proportions of substandard units increased from under twice as much to over seven times as great. In the largest units, the proportion decreased among whites, but actually increased for Negro-occupied units, as rent rose from less than $50 to $50-$79; then it decreased in the highest rent category, but not quite to the level of the group under $50. In all units in central cities of the country, taken as a whole, the proportion of substandard in Negro units was approximately one-fifth greater than in white-occupied units, for those renting under $50, and 6 times greater for those renting for over $80.

Increased price discrimination in the higher rent brackets may be accounted for by the fact that middle-class Negroes seeking accommodations commensurate with their income and attainments find it either difficult or against their taste to select an accommodation in a segregated area; they are therefore compelled (or impelled) to seek an apartment in an area that is largely or entirely occupied by white families. Although race restrictions are disappearing in some cities in the North, it is usually extremely difficult for a Negro family to obtain quarters under these circumstances, because the mechanisms of exclusion are powerful and difficult to combat. Moreover, they are used with great frequency because the landlord fears his white tenants will resent a new neighbor of a different color. Resistance to Negro occupancy is likely to be less marked if an apartment has been vacant a long time and if the prospect of renting it to a white family in the near future is slim. Apartments in this category are usually poor value for the money, which means that their rent is in excess of the market level for apartments of similar size, quality, and location.

The intensification of price discrimination in the higher rent ranges has undoubtedly fortified the great impulse to homeownership among the middle-class Negroes. The enhancement of status which accompanies homeownership would undoubtedly have motivated many middle-class Negroes, even if their treatment in the rental market had been the same as for whites. Price discrimination makes the purchase of a home virtually the only way in which the middle-class Negro family can obtain a superior accommodation in a better neighborhood. In the cities of the North, homeownership rose between 75 to 150 percent during the decade of the 1950s; in the West, the increase was from 125 to 175 percent; and in the South, from 50 to 100 percent.[3]

As far as the upwardly mobile Negro is concerned, the results of this study understate the discrimination practiced against him and the difficulties placed in his way by the housing market. Even within center cities, neighborhoods differ in the community facilities available to them and the undesirable uses which impinge upon the residential structures. Though low-rent housing occupied by whites may be in as unpleasant a location as that available to Negroes, neighborhoods in which more expensive housing restricted to whites is located are generally superior to those in which equally expensive housing is available to Negroes. And insofar as Negroes able to afford more expensive

3. For a discussion of the housing problems of the middle-class Negro, see Chester Rapkin, "More Housing For Negroes," *The Mortgage Banker*, February 1964.

housing share the customary American middle-class view that the suburban environment is preferable to that in the center city, even those Negroes who succeed in finding housing of standard quality are obtaining less desirable units than those of whites who move to suburbia or who voluntarily rent in the city because they prefer it. Thus, the Negro who achieves middle-class status is rewarded in the housing market by an increasing burden of price and locational discrimination.

IV

Production

The housing industry is a complex system that involves many actors—financial institutions, architectural and engineering firms, insurance companies, federal, state, and local governments, builders, contractors and subcontractors, real estate agents, and others. Housing is a durable asset and a costly capital good, and as such is too expensive for most consumers and producers to finance with their own resources. They borrow a large share of the cost of housing, usually 70-80 percent or more of the value, primarily from banks and insurance companies; so movements in the monetary sector of the economy have severe impact on housing production.

An increase in interest rates affects housing production in two ways. (Commission on Mortgage Interest Rates, Chap. 26). First, higher interest rates increase the carrying costs of purchasing and owning a house, and a sustained increase in the cost of borrowing capital would also be reflected in higher rents in the rental submarket. These higher carrying costs reduce the market for new housing in that fewer people have sufficient incomes to afford the increased prices. Second, when interest rates are rising the rates on mortgages tend to lag behind the increases on other securities, such as commercial paper; so lending institutions turn to these other areas, and the amount of credit available to the housing sector declines. In addition, the amount of mortgage lending is curtailed relative to other uses of borrowed funds (mostly by business corporations and for shorter terms) because rising interest rates tend to divert funds from thrift institutions, such as savings and loan associations, which are the major source of residential mortgages.

In 1966 and again in 1969-70 inflation and antiinflationary policy produced rising interest rates. In 1970 interest rates on residential mortgages rose to over 8 percent, a full 3 percentage points above the mid-1950s level, which constitutes a $425 increase in the annual payments ($36 per month) on a $17,000, 30-year mortgage.[1] If families are expected to spend no more than 25 percent of their incomes on housing costs, a family would need $1,700 in additional annual income to afford a mortgage with the same principal and term at these higher interest rates.

1. The average mortgage amount insured by the Federal Housing Administration in 1970 was $21,283 for new single-family homes and $17,004 for existing single-family homes. U.S. Department of Housing and Urban Development, *1970 HUD Statistical Yearbook* (Washington, D.C.: Government Printing Office, 1971), table 200.

A major cause of inflation in the 1960s was increased war expenditures in Southeast Asia. The federal government's insistence on restricting the money supply to control inflation has increased interest rates and aggravated the problems of the housing sector (Commission on Mortgage Interest Rates, Chap. 27), which tends to suffer a disproportionate share of the burden of these controls in part because of the effects on credit availability. Although restrictive monetary policy restrains capital expenditures of all types, housing is the only major capital investment that is also a major consumer good; hence the effects of monetary policy are more readily transmitted to the consumer in housing than in other goods.

Several institutions, however, have some power to reduce the inequitable impact of antiinflationary measures on the housing sector by making available more funds for new mortgages. For example, the Federal Home Loan Bank Board (FHLBB) provides a credit reservoir to over 4,600 member savings banks. In 1969-70 the FHLBB loaned funds to member banks to offset savings withdrawal. The Federal National Mortgage Association, since 1968 a private corporation on the stock exchange, can increase its purchases of existing mortgages from banks, insurance companies, and other mortgage holders, thus providing them with funds for new lending activities. The Government National Mortgage Association is able to guarantee bonds that mortgage lenders issue, thus increasing funds in tight times. However, none of these operations occur automatically, and increasing interest rates still make it more expensive to purchase homes in an inflationary period. Hence fiscal as well as monetary policy seems necessary to guarantee stable housing production.

Several important characteristics of the housing industry are: (1) localization of production because of the uniqueness of home sites and the relatively high costs of shipping large housing components over long distances; (2) fragmentation of the building process into a number of producing units, such as masonry, carpentry, plumbing, electrical, painting, roofing, and landscaping; (3) subcontracting of many construction tasks to other firms rather than performance by a single general contractor (according to a 1962 Bureau of Labor Statistics survey an average of 14 subcontractors combine to construct a single-family house); (4) the small size of the firms involved in housing production. These characteristics have been held responsible for the industry's inability to innovate; they also account for the housing industry's being one of the most competitive segments of the American economy.

Before a detailed examination of the question of technological innovation, some description of housing producers is in order. The President's Committee on Urban Housing (Kaiser Committee) divided producers into five categories: (1) merchant builders (who build on their own land), (2) general contractors (who build on land others own), (3) home manufacturers, (4) mobile home manufacturers, (5) owner-builders. Table IV.1 contains rough estimates of the share of production in each category. Figures on firm size indicate that no firm or group of firms dominates any category. Levitt and Sons, one of the largest merchant builders, produced only 5,100 units in 1967, less than 0.4 percent of the total number of homes built that year. National Homes, the largest home manufacturer, produced 11,500 units in 1967. The largest mobile home producer manufactured only 18,000 units in 1967.

Three major trends have been evident in housing production. (1) Mobile homes have been rapidly increasing their share of the market (see Table IV.2). (2) Owner-builders once produced one-third of the starts; today they produce less than 10 percent. (3) Multifamily units have increased their share of the market from 6 percent of private nonfarm housing starts in 1956 to 41 percent in 1970 (U.S. Bureau of the Census; Neutze, 1968).

TABLE IV.1 *Approximate Share of Annual Housing Starts, By Type of Producer, in the United States For the Middle 1960s*

Type of Producer	Approximate Number of Units, Annually	Percent of Total Annual Production
Merchant builders:		
One-family (not including factory built)	450,000	26
Multifamily	260,000*	15*
General Contractors:		
One-family units for private owners (not including factory built)	170,000	10
Multifamily construction for private owners	260,000*	15*
For public agencies	30,000	2
Factory built:		
Home manufacturers.............................	180,000	11
Mobile homes	200,000	12
Owner-built one-family homes intended for ultimate occupancy of the owner and built with the owner acting as general contractor and often doing some or all of the work	150,000	9
Total..	1,700,000	100

*There are no data on the split in multifamily starts between merchant builders and general contractors. These units were split evenly between the two simply to minimize the possible error.

SOURCE: President's Committee on Urban Housing, *A Decent Home* (1968), table 4-20, p. 151.

Several independent studies have projected that in order to eliminate substandard housing the United States will need 26 million new and rehabilitated housing units by 1978—a goal that Congress adopted in the Housing and Urban Development Act of 1968. The National Commission on Urban Problems (Douglas Commission) has made a conservative estimate that at least 2.25 million new dwelling units must be built annually to meet this target. Until 1971 housing starts never exceeded 2 million per year and approached this level in only one earlier year (Table IV.2). During 1970-71 restrictive monetary policies were substantially eased with a view to stimulating a growth in Gross National Product, and price and wage controls were implemented in an effort to keep inflation under control. One result was a large increase in loanable funds, which in turn led to lower interest rates and a short-term increase in housing production.[2] Housing starts may not continue at their 1971 level because of the short-run nature of the underlying economic policies and because those policies have not significantly reduced inflation and unemployment.

Richard Muth (Chap. 20) and Edgar Olsen (Chap. 19) have argued that substandard housing exists because some families have insufficient purchasing power, which must be increased either through income supplements or price reductions. Income supple-

2. The interest rate on prime commercial paper (4- to 6-month notes) dropped from 8.78 percent in January 1970 to 4.19 percent in March 1971, and the secondary market yield on Federal Housing Administration residential mortgages dropped from 9.25 percent in the first quarter of 1970 to 7.32 percent in the first quarter of 1971. Board of Governors, Federal Reserve System, *Federal Reserve Bulletin*; U.S. Bureau of the Census, *Business Conditions Digest*.

ments are examined by Lee Rainwater and Dick Netzer in Section V. Price reductions can be achieved through cost-reducing industry reorganization, through cost-reducing innovations in production techniques, or through governmental price subsidies. Industry reorganization assumes that housing production is inefficient and that more efficient organization will lead to lower prices and greater investment in research and technology. However, is the housing industry inefficient? Has it experienced technological change comparable with other industries? Can the costs of housing production be significantly reduced?

TABLE IV.2   *New Housing Starts 1945-1972*

Year	Total Nonfarm Housing Starts* (Thousands)	Mobile Home Production (Thousands)	Farm Housing Starts (Thousands)	Total Starts (Thousands)
1945	326			326
1946	1,023			1,023
1947	1,269			1,269
1948	1,362			1,362
1949	1,466			1,466
1950	1,952			1,952
1951	1,491			1,491
1952	1,504			1,504
1953	1,438			1,438
1954	1,551			1,551
1955	1,646			1,646
1956	1,349	125		1,474
1957	1,224	119		1,343
1958	1,382	102		1,484
1959	1,531	121	22	1,674
1960	1,274	104	22	1,400
1961	1,337	90	28	1,455
1962	1,469	118	24	1,611
1963	1,615	151	27	1,793
1964	1,535	191	27	1,753
1965	1,488	216	24	1,728
1966	1,173	217	23	1,413
1967	1,299	240	23	1,562
1968	1,524	318	24	1,866
1969	1,482	413	18	1,913
1970	1,449	401	20	1,870
1971	2,032	497	20	2,539
1972p	2,335	572	20	2,927

*Government figures on housing starts generally exclude mobile homes.

P These figures are preliminary. The division into farm and nonfarm starts for 1971 and 1972 is estimated from the divisions reported in previous years.

SOURCES: Economic Report of the President, February 1970, table C-41; and U.S. Bureau of the Census, *Construction Reports: Housing Starts*, Series C-20.

It is frequently asserted that fragmentation of the building process is irrational and inefficient. Through analysis of the administration of construction work and comparison with bureaucratic functions in mass production industries, Arthur Stinchcombe (Chap. 28) concludes that the decentralized, unstable, and small-scale mode of production and task administration is a rational, efficient response to the economic and technical constraints the housing industry faces. Large-scale homebuilding is shown to represent an advance more in marketing techniques than in housing production. It should be noted that the article deals with on-site construction and not with factory production of homes and home components, which is accounting for an increasing proportion of United States housing construction.

Perhaps the most frequent criticism of the construction industry is that it is technologically stagnant and that various institutional rigidities and barriers (mostly unions and building codes) have been major impediments to technological change. Christopher Sims (Chap. 29) rigorously analyzes construction industry efficiency over the period 1929-65 and concludes that the industry was stagnant until 1947, but since then it has experienced technological change comparable to that of other industries. While significant barriers to technological advance in the construction industry may still exist, the industry's sensitivity to new technology indicates that new materials and processes would be utilized. Therefore, one policy conclusion that emerges from Sims' analysis is the need for greater research on building technology, which logically, given the fragmented nature of the construction industry, the government should conduct. Sims also notes that price distortions may lead to disincentives to the development of technological innovation. For example, the "wage bargain" that the seasonality and short-term nature of demand for construction labor produces may hinder the development of technological methods for elimination of seasonal fluctuations. It should also be noted that a successful attack on this price distortion would alter one of the basic economic and technical constraints Stinchcombe describes—instability in the volume of construction work.

Building codes were designed to eliminate hazards inherent in poor quality construction, but each local jurisdiction has its own building code, and great variation exists in the standards that developers are asked to meet. Some local governments use these codes to prevent the introduction of new materials and methods (National Commission on Urban Problems, Chap. 30). The lack of code uniformity makes large-scale housing production and marketing extremely difficult, and the archaic quality of most building codes retards technological innovation.

A related issue is whether union practices produce inefficiencies in the construction industry and whether those practices retard the introduction of new methods and materials (National Commission on Urban Problems, Chap. 31). Charges of archaic union practices fall into three categories: (1) rules requiring certain work to be performed on the construction site; (2) restrictions against the use of certain tools and devices; (3) rules that result in an excessive manpower requirement, known in the railroad industry as featherbedding. While many instances of restrictive labor practices exist, much myth and exaggeration also exists in this area; many of the restrictions result from legitimate demands for safety and proper working conditions. Nor are restrictions in the job preservation category wholly reprehensible. Better social mechanisms must be devised to protect individual workers against job loss as housing construction industrializes and their skills become obsolescent. A higher, steadier volume of construction and less seasonal and cyclical variation in the industry may reduce the unions' use of overly restrictive practices. Exclusion of minority workers from union membership may also be lessened with a higher and steadier volume of construction, but even in the absence of such changes this discriminatory practice must be eliminated (Dubinsky, Chap. 33).

Increased efficiency may not lead to substantial cost reductions because general increases in material prices, wages, land costs, and finance charges may offset any cost reductions from improved technology or industry organization. Table IV.3 analyzes the components of the increase in housing costs. The largest increases have been in site values, which have risen 10 times as fast as house size (floor area). Although housing cost reductions might follow improved technology, they are unlikely to substantially reduce the price to the housing consumer (Stegman, Chap. 32). However, the benefits of increased efficiency may show up in greater production capacity, perhaps in the ability to achieve the official goal of 26 million additional units of standard housing in a 10-year period. Innovations of this magnitude require time to take effect, and it is doubtful whether the national commitment necessary to achieve these goals exists.

TABLE IV.3   *Diagnosis of Rise in Price of Houses–1948-66*

| | Percent Increase to 1966 from: | | |
Component	1948	1957-59	1958
Site	259	60	61
FHA value	100	24	25
Ratio, site/value	71	29	30
Construction cost/sq. ft.	46.1	10.6	11.1
Closing costs	na	33	27
Sale price	na	22	23.5
Floor area	24.5	6	6.5
BLS building trades wages, all	118	36.9	37
Helpers and laborers	144	41.4	44
Construction workers, earn/day	126	38	38
earn/week	124	40	40
BLS Wholesale price index:			
Building materials	32	3.9	5.1
Lumber	23.4	8.5	12.0
Millwork	36.8	10.0	12.2
Plywood	(-16.3)	(-7.2)	(-6.2)
Building cost indexes:			
American Appraisal	76	27	27
Boeckh, Residential	54	20	21
Engineering News-Record	88	23.3	24

SOURCE: Elsie Eaves, *How the Many Costs of Housing Fit Together,* Research Report no. 16 to the National Commission on Urban Problems (1969) table 28, p. 52.

Another avenue to price reduction is government subsidies to producers, which can be direct, such as subsidized interest rates, or indirect, such as preferential tax treatment. In Section V Lawrence Friedman, Robert Schafer and Charles Field, and Eli Goldston analyze several methods of direct subsidy. The indirect route of tax incentives has been a frequent suggestion; the late Senator Robert F. Kennedy was a principal exponent of such legislation. A selection from the report of the National Commission on Urban Problems (Chap. 34) describes the important workings of the federal income tax system in relation to housing production. Until 1969 the tax laws did not channel investment into low-income housing because they made no distinctions within classes of residential apartment development nor any distinctions between residential, commercial, and industrial real estate. In two basic ways the Tax Reform Act of 1969 took some small steps toward making tax incentives work for improving the housing conditions of low-income families. (1) The depreciation recapture rules and the availability of accelerated depreciation were revised to favor residential apartment development over other real estate activities and to favor low- and moderate-income rental housing over other rental housing. (2) Rehabilitation expenditures were made depreciable over a five-year period regardless of their useful life. One important drawback of this approach is the tax loopholes it provides developers and high-income investors, with subsequent loss of tax revenue.

REFERENCES

Neutze, Max. *The Suburban Apartment Boom.* Baltimore: The Johns Hopkins Press, 1968.
U.S. Bureau of the Census. *Construction Reports: Housing Starts.* Series C-20. (An annual publication.)

26. Mortgage Market Developments in the Postwar Period

COMMISSION ON MORTGAGE INTEREST RATES

Homebuying and homebuilding are among the most credit-dependent activities undertaken in our economy. Because of the sheer size of the financial outlay, most homebuyers require some external financing—allowing the payment to be spread out over time. Thus, of all new one-family homes sold, about 95 percent are partly financed by a mortgage. It is not surprising, then, that residential construction has proved to be highly sensitive to changes in interest rates and credit availability.

Changing credit conditions affect the housing sector in two general ways. (1) As interest rates rise, other things equal, some prospective homebuyers are priced out of the market by the high cost of borrowed funds. (2) Historically, an even greater adverse effect results from periodic limitations on the availability of mortgage credit.

This sensitivity to changing credit conditions is clearly apparent in the record of ups and downs in the homebuilding sector during the past 20 years. In all, there have been four distinct cycles in homebuilding activity in the postwar period, and a fifth is now in process, as shown by the various measures charted in Figure 26.1.

The two most severe postwar disturbances in the housing market, in 1956-57 and 1966, amply illustrate the effects of changing credit conditions on homebuilding activity. In both periods, the mortgage market was squeezed between heavy demands for credit from other sectors, particularly corporations, and a sharply curtailed credit supply resulting from efforts by the Federal Reserve to fight inflation. Net mortgage lending fell from an annual rate of nearly $16 billion in mid-1955 to less than $11 billion in the last half of 1957, and would have dropped even further except for an injection of nearly $1 billion of additional funds from the federal government (mostly through FNMA). During the same interval, the number of new housing units started fell from 1.7 million to less than 1.2 million (annual rates). In the second period, net mortgage lending fell from an annual rate of $26 billion in late 1965 to only $13 billion a year later, in this case despite $2.4 billion of *extra* Government support in 1966 compared with 1965; meanwhile, the number of housing units started dropped by 40 percent.

Although these cycles in homebuilding have generally helped to stabilize overall economic activity by countering opposing cycles occurring in other sectors, the damage to the housing sector has been quite significant. The on and off nature of business has limited the rate of increase in productivity and contributed to a high rate of business failures in the construction industry. Capital, skilled labor, and management know-how have been lost to other areas. And housing needs have been met erratically.

As long as monetary policy continues to be the main tool used to damp swings

Reprinted from the *Report of the Commission on Mortgage Interest Rates to the President of the United States and to the Congress* (Washington, D.C.: Government Printing Office, 1969), pp. 15-26 (edited)

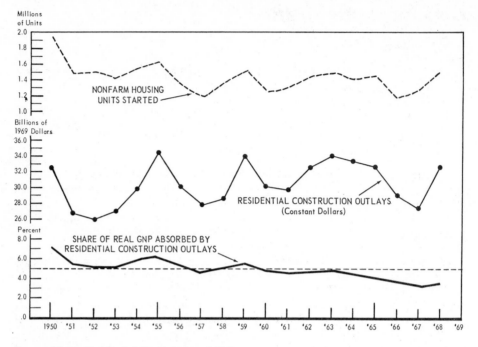

FIGURE 26.1   *Residential Construction Activity*

in overall economic activity, the mortgage market and homebuilding activity will continue to be subject to cyclical instability. The financial reforms enacted in the past three years plus implementation of the steps recommended in this report should help keep the cycles from becoming as extreme as in the past. The basic solution to the cycles in the housing sector, however, is to make greater use of fiscal policy as a stabilizing force, so that monetary policy is freer to maintain an even flow of credit at reasonable rates of interest that American families can afford.

THE MORTGAGE MARKET: ITS SIZE AND KEY PARTICIPANTS

In 1968, the typical single-family home purchased with an FHA-insured mortgage cost around $18,000—a little higher if newly constructed, less if used. The average family paid about 7 percent in down payment, and took out a mortgage of about $16,500 to cover the remainder of the cost. For many families, this loan was the largest single financial transaction they ever undertook.

The national mortgage market which supplied such loans is correspondingly large. Total mortgage debt of all types outstanding at the end of 1968 amounted to nearly $400 billion, as shown in Table 26.1. The major share (63½ percent) of this total represented debt on 1-4 family homes, with debt on multifamily residential apartment buildings accounting for another 12 percent, and debt on office buildings, stores, factories, and the like amounting to a fourth of the total. In the residential mortgage sector, most of the mortgages carry "conventional" terms; only 20 percent of all residential mortgages outstanding were FHA-insured, with another 11½ percent VA-guaranteed.

TABLE 26.1 *Mortgage Loans, 1968 (Billions of Dollars)*

	Amount Outstanding at Year End	Net Change during Year	Originations	Repayments
Residential mortgages	298.5	18.7	51 e	32 e
1-4 Family	251.5	15.4	44 e	29 e
FHA-insured	50.6	3.2	6.5	3.3
VA-guaranteed*	34.5	1.1	3.9	2.8
Conventional	166.3	11.1	34 e	23 e
Multifamily	47.0	3.3	7 e	3 e
FHA-insured	9.0	0.7	1.1	0.4
Conventional	38.0	2.6	6 e	3 e
Nonresidential mortgages	98.4	8.4	15 e	7 e
Total—all mortgages	396.9	27.1	66 e	39 e

*Includes direct VA loans.

e—estimated by Commission staff, based on assumption that annual repayments as a percent of outstandings were about 12 percent on 1-4 family mortgages and about 8 percent on multifamily and nonresidential mortgages.

SOURCES: Federal Reserve Board, FHA, VA, and Commission on Mortgage Interest Rates.

The $18.7 billion net increase in residential mortgage debt during 1968 absorbed slightly less than a fifth of the total amount of funds raised in U.S. credit and equity markets last year.[1] This was an unusually low share of total borrowing going to residential mortgages. . . . In most years of the postwar period, residential mortgage borrowing absorbed a third or more of total funds raised, and thus represented the largest single element of demand pressing on the capital markets. Variations in the share of total borrowing going to residential mortgages have generally reflected (inversely) the varying strength of business demands for credit—though in 1968 heavy credit demands from the U.S. Treasury to finance a huge budget deficit added to the squeeze on the mortgage market.

The bulk of residential mortgage credit comes from four groups of private financial institutions: savings and loan associations, mutual savings banks, life insurance companies, and commercial banks. Together these institutions supplied nearly 85 percent of the total residential mortgage debt outstanding at the end of 1968, and also 85 percent of the mortgages on 1-4 family homes, as shown in Table 26.2. The federal government (including FNMA and other government-related institutions) is another big supplier of mortgage funds, though it tends to play a somewhat residual role in the market.

As shown in Table 26.3, savings and loan associations have the strongest commitment to the mortgage market, as they regularly invest 85 percent or more of their assets in mortgages. The other institutions, however, have gradually been devoting a larger fraction of their assets to mortgages, though in each case the permissible range of alternative investments is far wider than for savings and loan associations: commercial banks have 22 percent of their assets in business loans and another 13 percent each in Treasury and state and local government securities; life insurance companies hold nearly half of their assets in corporate bonds and stocks; and even mutual savings

1. A small part of the overall increase represented some mortgage loans that were only in process.

banks, which have become the second biggest source of residential mortgage loans, sometimes (as in early 1968) invest heavily in high-yielding corporate bonds.

TABLE 26.2   *Percent of Mortgages Outstanding Held by Key Lenders, 1968*

	All Mortgages	Residential Mortgages	1-4 Family Mortgages
Savings & loan associations	33.0	40.4	43.7
Mutual savings banks	13.4	15.7	13.9
Life insurance companies	17.7	14.2	11.9
Commercial banks	16.6	13.9	15.4
Subtotal	80.6	84.1	84.9
Federal government	5.5	5.1	5.2
All other	13.9	10.8	9.9
Total	100.0	100.0	100.0

SOURCE: Federal Reserve Board.

TABLE 26.3   *Percent of Lenders' Total Assets Invested in Mortgages*

	All Mortgages		Residential Mortgages		1-4 Family Mortgages	
	1950	1968	1950	1968	1950	1968
Savings & loan associations	80.5	85.6	78.7	79.0	77.5	72.0
Mutual savings banks	37.1	74.9	31.7	65.6	19.2	49.0
Life insurance companies	22.5	38.2	17.7	23.1	13.6	16.3
Commercial banks	9.2	15.0	7.0	9.4	6.4	8.8
4 lenders combined	19.9	37.8	16.8	29.7	14.1	25.2

SOURCE: Federal Reserve Board.

INTEREST RATES

Since the end of World War II, U.S. interest rates have risen by 4 to 5 percentage points, and now stand at the highest levels since at least the mid-1800s. This rise in interest rates came in five specific spurts, each brought on by a tightening of monetary policy to fight inflation; intervening periods of monetary ease brought only a partial retracement of the previous upswing in rates. . . .

A number of factors have been suggested to explain this basic uptrend in interest rates. In part, it clearly represents a return from the low interest rate levels brought on by the depression of the 1930s and then artificially maintained during the 1940s. Inflation was not a threat during the 1930s, with so much of the nation's capacity idle; and in the early 1940s, price and wage controls were imposed to keep inflation within bounds while the nation was at war. Although inflationary pressures emerged soon after World War II, monetary policy did not provide much restraint on the economy until the early 1950s. In subsequent economic expansions of the 1950s, monetary policy was directed toward fighting inflation, and interest rates rose to new postwar highs.

Secondly, the rise in U.S. interest rates has partly reflected a movement toward equilibrium with interest abroad. Prior to 1958, interest rates abroad did not have much effect on U.S. rates since capital could not and did not move freely in international financial markets. During the early 1960s when unemployment was high, a fall in interest rates might have been expected. But with convertibility permitted among the main international currencies, high interest rates in Europe and elsewhere began to pull funds out of the U.S. in the late 1950s and early 1960s. To stem this drain on the U.S. balance of payments, U.S. monetary policy in the early 1960s consciously sought, among other things, to raise short-term rates in this country to a level more in line with rates prevailing in Canada and Europe.

An additional factor exerting upward pressure on short-term interest rates around this time was an intensified competition for time and savings deposits among the nation's thrift institutions—facilitated by changes in Regulation Q ceilings governing the rates that banks may pay on their deposits. The shift in the flow of funds that resulted from this competition was generally favorable to homebuilding: it produced some overall easing of long-term interest rates, including mortgage rates. In some areas, however, the high rates paid on thrift deposits tended to set a floor under mortgage rates, and the search for investments led to a sharp easing in lending standards in the mortgage market. This, in some cases, fostered considerable overbuilding.

Finally, the especially sharp run-up in interest rates during the past four years can be traced for the most part to the surge in federal expenditures that began in mid-1965 and the inflationary expectations generated by that expansion. For much of the past four years, unusually large federal budget deficits have imposed a heavy burden on the capital market. And in the inflationary environment prevailing, this has been accompanied by unusually heavy demands for capital from private businesses eager to finance expansion of their plants and equipment before prices rise even higher. The available pool of national saving was far from adequate to meet these inflated demands.

INTEREST RATES AND HOUSING DEMAND

Whatever the cause of the uptrend in interest rates generally and mortgage rates in particular, the effect clearly adds to the monthly payments required to amortize a mortgage and thus increases a family's monthly housing expense, as shown in Table 26.4. Incomes have also, of course, increased over the years, thereby reducing the "burden" of any given dollar amount of housing expense. A gradual lengthening

TABLE 26.4 *Mortgage Rates and Monthly Payments on a $20,000, 30-year Mortgage*

Mortgage Interest Rate	Monthly Payments to Princ. & Int.	Total Monthly Housing Expense*	Housing Expense as a Percent of Typical Family Income†
5 %	$107.37	$195.37	19.8%
5½	113.56	201.56	20.5
6	119.92	207.92	21.1
6½	126.42	214.42	21.8
7	133.07	221.07	22.4
7½	139.85	227.85	23.1
8	146.76	234.76	23.8

*Column 2 plus $88, which is the approximate average amount of other monthly expenses incurred in existing houses financed with a $20,000 FHA mortgage in 1968.

†Based on annual income of $11,825, which is the approximate average (before tax) income of families taking out $20,000 FHA mortgages on existing houses in 1968.

SOURCE: Commission on Mortgage Interest Rates.

of the loan maturity helped keep down monthly mortgage payments during the 1950s; but maturities have not changed much in recent years, as most lenders now offer the maximum permitted by law. At a given 30-year maturity on a mortgage, each 1 percentage point rise in the interest rate increases monthly payments for principal and interest by approximately 12 percent; the dollar increase is the same—though the percentage rise is smaller—in total monthly housing expenses.

At any given moment in time, an increase in interest rates may lead some families to make a larger downpayment than they would otherwise in purchasing a home in order to keep down their monthly mortgage payments. Others may seek to earn additional income by moonlighting in order to meet the higher payments, while some will look for a somewhat less expensive house. Some are simply priced out of the market.

Systematic studies have confirmed that the *demand* for mortgages does decline with rising mortgage rates (assuming that other things remain the same); i.e., a rise in rates does price some homebuyers out of the market—though quantitative estimates of the effect vary. In the actual world, of course, the "other things equal" assumption generally made in presenting such estimates does not hold true. In particular, to the extent that a rise in interest rates reflects a general inflationary psychology, borrowers may well be willing to pay the higher interest costs now before the price of houses becomes even more expensive. This kind of psychology has clearly been at work in the past several years of very high mortgage rates.

CREDIT AVAILABILITY

An even greater problem for the housing sector than the effects of high interest rates on demand lies in the variations in availability of mortgage credit. Such variations can generally be traced to changing relationships among various key interest rates.

Interest Rates and Savings Flows

The relations among short-term interest rates in the open market and the rates offered by thrift institutions on time and savings deposits were shown by the experience of 1966 to be particularly crucial in determining the volume of resources these institutions have available for mortgage lending. In each past period of rising interest rates, rates in the open market rose faster than rates paid by the thrift institutions. This at times induced savers to invest their savings in open market securities rather than in savings deposits.

In the second half of 1958, for example, households bought $4.5 billion (annual rate) of open market securities and then bought an additional $7.5 billion the following year. Meanwhile, mutual savings banks experienced a sharp slowing in the growth of their deposits. An even more dramatic illustration occurred in the first half of 1966, when rising interest rates attracted $14.5 billion (annual rate) of household funds into open market paper. This, combined with aggressive competition from commercial banks, cut the deposit growth at savings and loan associations to less than half that of the year before.

Such diversions of household savings away from thrift deposits mean that these institutions have that much fewer resources to lend. In the case of the specialized lenders, the result is inevitably an enforced curtailment of mortgage lending operations. Figure 26.2 clearly shows the strong tie between growth of deposits and growth of mortgage portfolios at the key lending institutions, with the 1966 problems at the savings and loan associations particularly evident.

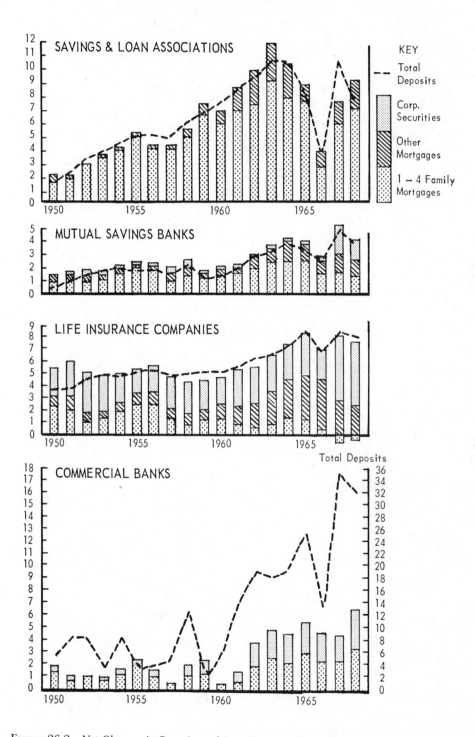

FIGURE 26.2   *Net Changes in Deposits and Investments, Selected Lenders (Billions of dollars)*

Interest Rates and Investment Flows

The relations among mortgage interest rates and yields on alternative investments are an important factor influencing how much of an institution's resources will be invested in mortgages. As shown in Table 26.5, yields on corporate bonds have consistently risen more than mortgage yields in periods of rising interest rates. This occurs because corporations, for a variety of reasons, are generally more able and willing than other private borrowers to pay whatever it costs to obtain funds: in an inflationary environment, corporations see prospects for profitable use of the borrowed funds far outweighing interest cost considerations; in addition, the after-tax cost of borrowing at a given interest rate is less for corporations than for most other private borrowers.

The result is that, as corporate bond yields rise relative to mortgage yields, some lenders switch some of their portfolio investments away from mortgages and toward corporate bonds. Some also shift to equities. Life insurance companies and mutual savings banks shifted their portfolios in these ways in 1957 and in the past two years, as shown in Figure 26.2.

TABLE 26.5   *Cyclical Changes in Selected Yields (Percent)*

	Yield on Conventional Mortgages	Yield on FHA-Insured Mortgages	Yield on New Issues of Aaa-rated Corporate Bonds
June 1955-September 1957	+.85	+1.00	+1.49
September 1957-June 1958	−.45	− .26	− .90
June 1958-December 1959	+.75	+ .86	+1.23
December 1959-June 1965	−.50	− .69	− .37
June 1965-December 1966	+.85	+ .33	+1.16
December 1966-April 1967	−.25	− .48	− .32
April 1967-June 1968	+.85	+1.23	+1.23
June 1968-September 1968	+.05	− .24	− .35
September 1968-May 1969	+.45	+ .78	+ .92

SOURCES: FHA and Federal Reserve Board.

Net Results

Through these effects on both the flow of savings deposits to financial institutions and their choice of investments, shifting relations among various interest rates induced by changes in monetary policy and credit demands have led to marked variations in the overall availability of mortgage credit. And, as shown in Figure 26.3, the wide cyclical swings in the net amount of new mortgage lending have been closely accompanied by wide swings in homebuilding activity. When mortgage funds were plentifully available, as in the early 1960s, homebuilding proceeded at a rapid clip—indeed, at times more rapid than warranted in terms of basic demand factors. On the other hand, the sharp curtailments in mortgage availability, as in 1956-57 and 1966, quickly led to sizable reductions in homebuilding.

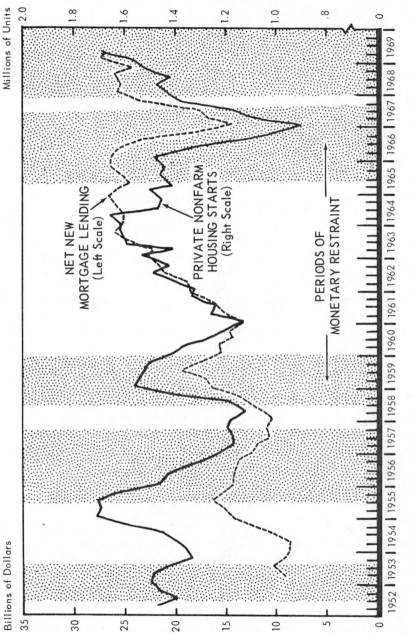

Billions of Dollars

Millions of Units

FIGURE 26.3 *Mortgage Lending and Housing Starts (Seasonally Adjusted Quarterly Data at Annual Rates)*

27. *Fiscal and Monetary Policy*

COMMISSION ON MORTGAGE INTEREST RATES

As emphasized at several previous points in this report, the balance struck between fiscal and monetary policy is the key to establishing the economic and financial preconditions essential to achieving the national housing goal.

Experience has made it abundantly clear that housing simply is not produced at the needed pace under tight monetary policy conditions. The declines in homebuilding in 1956-57, 1959-60, and 1966 were all directly related to the tight money policy then being pursued with its resulting sharp rise in interest rates and curtailed credit availability. And even now a new round of tight money is preventing the economy from meeting its tremendous housing needs. On the other hand, easy monetary policy environments have generally been accompanied by a high level of homebuilding activity—indeed, sometimes too high relative to basic demand factors. This was amply illustrated in the 1961-65 period.

Some variation in monetary conditions is to be expected as part of any balanced approach to stabilizing aggregate economic activity. All too often, however, there has been an undue reliance on tight monetary policy as a means of controlling inflation. This has arisen for one simple reason: even when the need for economic restraint is widely acknowledged, the Administration and the Congress have generally been unwilling or slow to take the necessary fiscal actions—increasing taxes, reducing federal expenditures, or both—to curb the inflationary forces. In such situations, monetary policy has little choice but to take up the slack. The result has been a series of counter-cyclical swings in homebuilding. Although this may have made some contribution to aggregate stabilization policy, *the Commission believes* that it has had serious adverse effects on the efficiency of the housing sector. Greater stability in the housing sector is essential if the housing goal is to be met.

THE NEED TO END INFLATION

The primary factors currently restraining housing production clearly have their roots in the general inflationary environment prevading the economy during the past four years. Since the middle of 1965, the combination of a sharp rise in federal defense expenditures to meet the nation's expanded commitment in South Vietnam and heavy demands from the private sector—especially from businesses eager to expand their plant and equipment capacity—have pushed aggregate demand beyond the economy's supply capabilities. In this situation something had to give: price stability has been one unfortunate casualty; and, in terms of real economic activity, homebuilding has absorbed most of the squeeze needed to fit total demands within the bounds of the nation's capacity.

Reprinted from the *Report of the Commission on Mortgage Interest Rates to the President of the United States and to the Congress* (Washington, D.C.: Government Printing Office, 1969), pp. 55-61 (edited).

Economic history for these past several years would have been far different had a timely and adequate measure of fiscal restraint been imposed to offset the effects of the rise in federal defense expenditures. A request for a general rise in taxes was considered early in 1966, but was never submitted to the Congress; and the formal request that was finally submitted in August 1967 was not enacted until nearly a year later. In the meantime, the budget deficit increased sharply to nearly $9 billion in fiscal year 1967 and to more than $25 billion the following fiscal year.[1]

As in the past, the absence of adquate fiscal restraint placed an undue burden on monetary policy to damp the excessive expansion of demands. Indeed, because inflationary psychology became so pervasive as to mute even the massive dose of fiscal restraint that finally was imposed, monetary policy has now had to become extremely restrictive. As a result, interest rates are at the highest levels in more than a century, and the availability of mortgage credit is sharply limited. Under these conditions, it is virtually impossible to assure financing of the needed housing construction—except through direct government lending or stringent controls on private lenders.

For the present, because the inflation is so deeply entrenched, there is little choice but to maintain the present restrictive monetary policy. But the inappropriate expansionary element that was previously in the federal budget has been removed by the expenditure cuts and 10 percent income tax surcharge enacted last year. This brought the budget into surplus in the fiscal year just ended, and present estimates point to another surplus in the current year. So long as the budget does in fact remain in surplus, the cumulative effects of fiscal restraint will ultimately restore a more balanced economic environment in which the present wage-price spiral can and will begin to unwind. As this occurs—but only then—monetary policy can begin to ease and thereby facilitate a reduction in interest rates and a return to financial conditions conducive to expanding housing production.

To help curtail inflation and permit a reduction in interest rates from their current unprecedentedly high levels, the Commission urges in the strongest possible terms that the federal budget be kept in surplus until the current inflation is brought under control.[2]

SHIFTING RESOURCES TO HOMEBUILDING

A longer run prescription for fiscal and monetary policy cannot, of course, be given in such simple and definite terms. The objective that must be sought is clear, however. Presently, the housing sector is obtaining a share of national output that is about 1 percent less than estimates suggest is needed on average over the next 10 years to achieve the housing goal. .... Only by shifting the allocation of resources somewhat more toward the housing sector can this housing goal be reached.

With respect to fiscal and monetary policy, two interrelated steps are necessary to accomplish the needed shift of resources. First and foremost, the total amount

1. Senator McIntyre [a member of the Commission]: The Commission received no evidence that earlier congressional enactment of new taxes would have in anyway moderated the current inflationary environment.

2. Senator McIntyre: I want to stress that there are ways to maintain a budget surplus other than through the continuation of the income tax surcharge: (1) enacting basic reforms in the income tax structure, which would eliminate or substantially reduce unfair and unjustified loopholes and special privileges, would bring in new revenues to the Treasury; and (2) reordering of budget priorities could result in the reduction of less essential expenditures. Under no circumstances should a budget surplus be achieved at the expense of increased expenditures for such essential programs as housing.

of saving generated by the economy must be sufficient to meet the housing needs and other investment demands within a noninflationary, full-employment environment. Secondly, this saving must flow into the appropriate channels so that an adequate share reaches the housing sector.

The size of the surplus or deficit in the federal budget directly affects the total flow of saving available. If aggregate national saving is insufficient to meet all investment demands at full employment without inflation, the saving total can be increased simply by increasing the surplus in the federal budget through either a rise in taxes or a cut in federal expenditures or both. Any expenditure cutting in such a situation should, of course, come out of only low priority programs in the budget and must avoid the housing programs and other programs essential to domestic well-being. If enough saving cannot be found in the budget, there may simply be no alternative but to raise taxes or force private saving in some other way. Such an increase in taxes would curtail consumer and business spending and—provided that budget expenditures are kept under control—create a large enough surplus in the federal budget to assure that national saving is adequate to meet housing needs and other investment demands.[3]

Most long-range estimates that the Commission has seen are not optimistic about prospects for developing a large volume of saving in the private sector over the years ahead, while all see very heavy investment demands. Such estimates are, of course, always subject to question. If they prove at all accurate, however, it may well be necessary to maintain a rather persistent *surplus* in the federal budget over coming years to assure that total saving is sufficient to meet the investment demands without inflation. In such a situation, achievement of the housing goal would hinge directly on the government's willingness and ability to maintain the appropriate budget surplus without allowing it to be dissipated through unduly rapid increases in expenditures or reductions in taxes, or both.

If fiscal policy is appropriately adjusted to provide enough total saving, monetary policy can also be adjusted to provide reasonable assurance that this saving will flow into the channels that reach the housing sector—at reasonable levels of interest rates. Essentially, this involves maintaining an appropriate balance (1) between interest rates in the open market and the rates paid by thrift institutions—the key mortgage lenders —on their deposits, and (2) between rates on mortgages and rates on competing investments. An easy monetary policy has always in the past been accompanied by ample availability of mortgage credit, and *the Commission is confident* that this condition can be brought about again once the current inflation is halted.

This emphasis on creating ample credit availability should not be taken as implying that the Commission is totally unconcerned about the possibility of a recurrence of the kind of environment prevailing for a time earlier in the 1960s when easy access to credit seemed to be facilitating undue real estate speculation in some areas across the country. In view of the tremendous housing need now facing the nation, however,

---

3. Mr. Jones [a member of the Commission]: A surplus budget does not create savings, It does free funds invested in Treasury issues for investment elsewhere and can, thereby, increase the availability of funds for mortgage investment. If business and consumer demands for credit remain large, the budget surplus required to assist homebuyers may have to be so large that it is destructive. Under these conditions, the shift in federal expenditures must be the result of a conscious effort to reduce federal expenditures in low-priority areas and increase expenditures in high-priority areas. This is the hard decision that neither Congress nor the Administration can avoid. If we fail here, inflation will become a permanent characteristic of the American economy, and housing will continue to suffer disproportionately.

such a problem seems unlikely to arise in the near future. Moreover, the most efficient way of coping with this kind of problem, if it should recur, would seem to be through stronger supervisory powers of the key agencies regulating financial institutions rather than through curtailment of overall credit availability—assuming, of course, that prevailing credit conditions can be maintained without generating inflationary pressures.

Over the long run, then, the Commission urges formulation of fiscal and monetary policy with a view to changing the present allocation of national output in such a way that the share of output required to meet the nation's housing needs is shifted away from other sectors and into homebuilding.

COUNTERCYCLICAL STRATEGY

The discussion in the preceding section assumes that an "appropriate" fiscal policy somehow can and will be maintained. It especially assumes much greater reliance than in the past on fiscal policy for general economic restraint when such is needed. This is the crucial element in the basic strategy of shifting the allocation of national output so that homebuilding obtains a greater share than at present, and in assuring that monetary policy is free to maintain financial conditions conducive to the creation of enough credit to meet the housing goal at rates of interest American families can afford.

The Commission recognizes that these "ideal" conditions are in reality unlikely to be achieved at all times. Even now, with the lessons of 1966 and 1968 still fresh, there was a lengthy delay in extending the 10 percent income tax surcharge, which is so crucial to preserving the present fiscal restraint. *The Commission does urge,* however, that—even in situations when a restrictive monetary policy is necessary to "make up" for insufficient fiscal restraint—appropriate steps be taken routinely by the government and the Federal Reserve to protect the housing industry from absorbing an undue share of the burden of this restraint.

. . . [T]he Commission feels . . . the government in such situations . . . [should] establish . . . some formal standby mechanism for pumping special assistance funds into the mortgage market through GNMA whenever the assisted housing programs are falling short of production targets because of shortages of mortgage credit.

With respect to monetary policy, the key is for the Federal Reserve to pay more attention than in the past to the distribution as well as the total amount of credit created. In the first half of 1966, one of the key factors diverting funds from nonbank thrift institutions and thereby from the mortgage market was the aggressive bidding for savings deposits by commercial banks that developed after the December 1965 increase in the Regulation Q ceiling on interest rates payable on bank time and savings deposits. Meanwhile, a lack of "depth, breadth, and resiliency" in the market for federal agency securities hindered efforts by the Federal Home Loan Banks and other agencies to obtain funds that could be funneled directly into the mortgage market. *The Commission believes* that the Federal Reserve should take these kinds of considerations more into account than previously has been the case in formulating and carrying out a restrictive monetary policy.

During periods when overall economic restraint is necessary to curb inflationary forces, the Commission urges that appropriate steps be taken both by the government—through a responsive mechanism that can pump special assistance funds into the mortgage market—and by the Federal Reserve—in the general conduct of its operations—to avoid imposing an undue share of the burden of such restraint on the homebuilding industry.

One final issue should be raised. The record throughout the postwar period and especially of the last several years clearly underscores the need for greater flexibility in fiscal policy than is now possible.

This is partly a question of finding some way to expedite decisions. A long process was required to enact the investment tax credit in 1962 and the general income tax reduction in 1964 when the economy clearly needed economic stimulation; the more recent long and costly delay in raising taxes has already been noted.

But a more basic issue is also involved. The Commission has stressed the need for maintaining a consistently appropriate overall fiscal policy. It sees no reason to expect that this can be achieved at ever-constant tax rates. Any given set of tax rates will generate constantly rising tax revenues as overall economic activity expands over time. This can produce undue "fiscal drag" on the economy unless the revenue growth is kept within appropriate bounds by reductions in tax rates, or properly offset by rising budget expenditures, or both. Similarly, an overly rapid expansion in government spending—such as occurred after mid-1965 when the economy was already operating virtually at full capacity—will generally necessitate a rise in tax rates.[4]

For the most part, a change in general tax rates—like the present surcharge, or its equivalent in terms of tax reduction—probably would be sufficient to maintain the kind of overall economic environment conducive to price and interest-rate stability and thereby to expansion of homebuilding. There are situations, however, in which the source of economic difficulty is concentrated in one particular sector of the economy. The current boom in business spending for new plants and equipment is the latest illustration of a long history of spurts and lapses of activity in one especially volatile sector.

In the past, undue reliance on monetary policy for purposes of economic stabilization often produced a countercyclical fluctuation in homebuilding which moderated or offset a concurrent swing in some other sector—such as business investment. *The Commission believes* that a better approach would be to use some form of tax instrument to influence activity in that sector which is the source of difficulty. The aim would not be to create offsetting cycles in any particular sector, but rather to smooth excessive fluctuations that might otherwise develop. Sweden has such an instrument specifically designed to moderate excessive swings in business investment, and it seems to have worked quite well on the few occasions that its use has been necessary to stem an inflation that could not otherwise be stopped efficiently.

To provide a more realistic framework for continuous maintenance of appropriate fiscal policy, the Commission urges increased flexibility in setting federal tax rates: the Administration and the Congress should explore possible procedures for changing general income tax rates speedily within prescribed limits and subject to prescribed conditions; and consideration should be given to using tax instruments to moderate directly excessive swings in activity in particular sectors of the economy—when broad fiscal measures are unable to accomplish this efficiently.

4. Such adjustments should be designed, of course, to maintain the appropriate budget surplus (or deficit), as discussed earlier.

28. *Bureaucratic and Craft Administration of Production*

ARTHUR L. STINCHCOMBE

Administration in the construction industry depends upon a highly professionalized manual labor force.[1] The thesis of this paper is that the professionalization of the labor force in the construction industry serves the same functions as bureaucractic administration in mass production industries and is more rational than bureaucratic administration in the face of economic and technical constraints on construction projects.

Specifically we maintain that the main alternative to professional socialization of workers is communicating work decisions and standards through an administrative apparatus. But such an apparatus requires stable and finely adjusted communications channels. It is dependent on the continuous functioning of administrators in official statuses. Such continuous functioning is uneconomic in construction work because of the instability in the volume and product mix and of the geographical distribution of the work. Consequently the control of pace, manual skill, and effective operative decision (the essential components of industrial discipline) is more economical if left to professionally maintained occupational standards.

After presenting evidence and argument for these assertions, we will try to show why work on large-scale tract construction of houses continues to be administered on a nonbureaucratic, craft basis. Tract housing turns out to be a major revision in the *marketing* of construction products rather than a revision in the *administration of work*.

Our method will be to reanalyze certain published demographic and economic data for their administrative implications. Since the data were collected for other purposes, they fit the requirements of our problem only roughly. The gaps in the information and the gross character of the categories make it necessary, therefore, to use very rough statistical procedures and to limit the data to a suggestive role. . . .

BUREAUCRATIC ADMINISTRATION AND CRAFT ADMINISTRATION

Craft institutions in construction are more than craft trade unions; they are also a method of administering work. They include special devices of legitimate communications to workers, special authority relations, and special principles of division of work, the "jurisidictions" which form the areas of work defining labor market statuses. The

Reprinted from the *Administrative Science Quarterly*, September 1959, pp. 168-87 (edited), by permission of the publisher and author. Arthur L. Stinchcombe is a professor of sociology at the University of California at Berkeley.

1. "Professionalized" here means that workers get technical socialization to achieve a publicly recognized occupational competence. "Public recognition" involves preferential hiring (ideally to the point of excluding all others) of workers who have proved their competence to an agency external to the hiring firm or consumer. Often this agency is a professional association composed exclusively of qualified persons and more or less exhaustive of the occupation. This professional association itself often enforces preferential hiring rights of its members. The professional's

(continued on p. 322)

distinctive features of craft administration may be outlined by contrasting it with mass production manufacturing administration.[2] The object of this section is to show that craft institutions provide a functional equivalent of bureaucracy.

Mass production may be defined by the criterion that *both* the product *and* the work process are planned in advance *by persons not on the work crew*. Among the elements of the work process planned are: (1) the location at which a particular task will be done; (2) the movement of tools, of materials, and of workers to this workplace, and the most efficient arrangement of these workplace characteristics; (3) sometimes the particular movements to be performed in getting the task done; (4) the schedules and time allotments for particular operations; and (5) inspection criteria for particular operations (as opposed to inspection criteria for final products).

In construction all these characteristics of the work process are governed by the worker in accordance with the empirical lore that makes up craft principles. These principles are the content of workers' socialization and apply to the jobs for which they have preferential hiring rights.

This concentration of the planning of work in manual roles in construction results in a considerably simplified communications system in the industry; but the simplification does not markedly reduce the number of people in administrative statuses. Administrative statuses are roughly equivalent to occupations in census categories: proprietors, managers, and officials; professional, technical, and kindred workers; and clerical and kindred workers.

The proportion of administrative personnel in the labor force in various fabricating industries does not vary widely. In construction the proportion of the labor force in the three administrative occupations is 15.5 percent; in manufacturing as a whole it is 20.6 percent; in iron and steel primary extraction, 15.5 percent; motor vehicles and motor vehicle equipment, 17.6 percent; in chemicals and allied industries, 33.4 percent.[3] But these rough similarities in proportion of administrative personnel conceal wide differences in the internal structure of the communications system. . . .

The proportion of administrative personnel who are clerks in various fabricating industries is presented in Table 28.1.

Clearly the proportion of all administrative personnel who are clerks is considerably greater in manufacturing generally than it is in construction, and the typical mass production industries tend to have even greater development of specialized communications processing structures. The centralized planning of work is associated with this development of filed communications, with specialized personnel processing them. . . .

The engineering of work processes and the evaluation of work by economic and technical standards take place in mass production in specialized staff departments, far removed from the work crew in the communications system. In the construction industry these functions are decentralized to the work level, where entrepreneurs, foremen, and craftsmen carry the burden of technical and economic decision.

---

permanent labor market status is not to be confused with permanent firm status (preferential hiring or continued employment of the current employees of a firm). This definition, therefore, differs somewhat from that of Nelson Foote in "The Professionalization of Labor in Detroit," *American Journal of Sociology* 58 (1953): 371-80.

2. This account of mass production institutions is derived from Peter Drucker, *The New Society* (New York, 1950), and his *The Practice of Management* (New York, 1954), along with the work of David Granick, *Management of the Industrial Firm in the U.S.S.R.* (New York, 1954).

3. *Characteristics of the Population*, pt. 1 (U.S. Summary) (*Census of the Population*, 2 [1950]), table 134, pp. 290-91.

TABLE 28.1 *The proportion of administrative personnel* who are clerks in selected fabricating industries, U.S., 1950*

Industry or Industry Group	Administrators' Clerks
Manufacturing	53%
Motor vehicles and accessories	63%
Iron and steel primary extraction	60%
Chemicals and allied	45%
Construction	20%

*Proprietors, managers, and officials; professional, technical, and kindred workers. *Characteristics of the Population, pt. 1, pp. 290-91.*

This decentralization of functions of the firm to the work level in construction, and the relative lack of information about and professional analysis of work processes at administrative centers, is accompanied by a difference in the types of legitimate communication.

In the construction industry, authoritative communications from administrative centers carry only specifications of the product desired and prices (and sometimes rough schedules). These two elements of the communication are contained in the contract; first, the contract between the client (with the advice of architects or engineers) and the general contractor,[4] and, second, between the general contractor and subcontractors. Subcontractors do the work falling within the "jurisdiction" of the trade they specialize in.

In mass production, where both the product and the work process are centrally planned, we find a system of legitimated advice on work and legitimate commands from line officials to foremen and workers to do particular work in particular ways. This more finely adjusted communications system depends on the development of specialized communications positions (clerks) and staff advice departments (professionals). . . .

Craft administration, then, differs from bureaucratic administration by substituting professional training of manual workers for detailed centralized planning of work. This is reflected in the lack of clerical workers processing communications to administrative centers and less complex staffs of professionals planning work. It is also reflected in the simplification of authoritative communications from administrative centers.

VARIABILITY AND BUREAUCRATIZATION

In this section we try to demonstrate that professionalization of manual labor is more efficient in construction because bureaucratic administration is dependent on stability of work flow and income, and the construction industry is economically unstable.

Bureaucratization of administration may be defined as a relatively permanent structuring of communications channels between continuously functioning officials. This permanent structuring of channels of legitimate communications, channels defined by the permanent official status of the originator of the communication and of its receiver, permits the development of routine methods of processing information

---

4. This step is omitted in the case of operative builders, but otherwise the authority structure is similar.

upward and authoritative communication downward. That is, it permits administration on the basis of files and the economical employment of clerical workers.

Routine processing of administrative communications and information is economical only when the overhead cost of specialized information-processing structures is highly productive; this productivity will be high only if rules concerning the route of communication can be taught to clerks. Otherwise, if it is necessary to use discretion in the choice of the receiver of a communication, it is cheaper to rely on visual supervision and executive or professional discretion.

The Case of Mass Production

Bureaucratization of administration depends therefore on the long-term stability of the administration. Of bureaucratic industrial administrations Peter Drucker says:

> The central fact of industrial economics is not "profit" but "loss"—not the expectation of ending up with a surplus . . . but the inevitable and real risk of ending up with an impoverishing deficit, and the need, the absolute need, to avoid this loss by providing against the risks. . . . The economic activity of an industrial economy is not "trade" taking place in the almost timeless instant of exchange, but production over a very long period. *Neither the organization* (the human resources) nor the capital investment (the material resources) *are productive in the "here and now" of the present.* It will be years before the organization or the investment will begin to produce, and many more years before they will have paid for themselves.[5]

It is clear that he cannot be talking about construction organizations, which have to be productive "here and now."

This association between orientation to stability and large-scale bureaucratized firms reflects the social requirements of complex communications systems between designated officials. Administrations faced with critical problems of instability and flexibility, such as those in the construction industry, will not find it economical to teach clerks rules for channeling communications. For it is impossible to hire a clerk on the labor market who will know the firm's communications channels, so clerks have to be kept on even when they are not productive.[6] And it is difficult to specify rules for channeling communications in advance when volume, product mix, and work force composition change rapidly, as they do in construction.

The Case of Construction

The variability of the construction industry, its intimate dependence on variations in local markets, makes the development of bureaucracy uneconomical. Table 28.2 shows the relationship between one type of variability and the employment of clerks.

Data are for some types of construction firms, for all firms in Ohio large enough to have to report to the State Employment Office (those normally employing three or more persons). In the first column the mean size of firms in the branch is reported (computed here), and the branches are classified by mean size. In the second column

---

5. *The New Society*, p. 52 (our italics). Veblen said the same thing in a different moral vocabulary: "Under the changed circumstance [the replacement of the 'captain of industry'] the spirit of venturesome enterprise is more than likely to foot up as a hunting of trouble, and wisdom in business enterprise has more and more settled down to the wisdom of 'watchful waiting.' Doubtless this form of words, 'watchful waiting,' will have been employed in the first instance to describe the frame of mind of a toad who had reached years of discretion . . . but by an easy turn of speech it has also been found suitable to describe the safe and sane strategy of that mature order of captains of industry who are governed by sound business principles" (Thorstein Veblen, *The Portable Veblen*[New York, 1950], pp. 385-86).

6. Also the class position of clerks makes it more difficult to hire temporary clerks.

is an index of seasonality of employment for the years 1926-1936 (computed in the source[7]). In the last column the average proportion of the labor force who were clerks in 1939 is reported (computed here).

TABLE 28.2 *The relationship between mean size of firm, seasonality of employment, and the percentage of the labor force clerks, for branches of the construction industry.*

Type of Contractor	Mean Size of Firms (1939)	Index of Seasonality of Employment (1926-1936)†	% of Clerks in Labor Force‡ (1939)
More than 8 employees per contractor			
Street, road, and sewer	12.3	73	4.8
Sand, gravel, excavation	9.9	43	7.6
Ventilating and heating	8.2	29	11.7
4-8 employees per contractor			
Brick, stone, and cement	5.5	47	3.3
General contracting	6.9	43	5.2
Sheet metal and roofing	4.9	29	11.7
Plumbing	5.1	20	10.9
Electrical	6.3	13	12.5
Less than 4 employees per contractor			
Painting and decorating	2.5	59	3.9

*Taken from Viva Boothe and Sam Arnold, *Seasonal Employment in Ohio* (Columbus: Ohio State University, 1944), table 19, pp. 82-87. Plasterers are omitted from this table, because the number employed was not large enough to give a reliable figure on seasonality of clerks' work, the original purpose of the publication. There were less than 50 clerks in plastering enterprises in the state. Consequently the needed figure was not reported in the source. Plasterers' employment is very unstable, so the omission itself supports the trend.

†See footnote 7.

‡Excluding sales clerks.

The relationship between the development of clerical statuses in administration and the stability of the work flow is clear from Table 28.2. The strength of the

7. The index of seasonality was computed in the source in the following way: The monthly index of employment in firms reporting was computed for each year of the 10 year period, to the base of the mean employment of that year. Then the 10 indexes (one index for each of the 10 years) for each month were arrayed, and the median taken. The 12 monthly medians give an overall picture of seasonality for the category for the 10 years. Scatter diagrams of these monthly indexes, standardized for the general level of employment during the year as outlined above, are presented in Viva Boothe and Sam Arnold, *Seasonal Employment in Ohio* (Columbus, 1944), chart 16, pp. 83-86. Graphs of seasonality are presented by drawing lines through the median monthly indexes. This prcedure eliminates between-years (presumably cyclical) variations in employment level.

After this array of 12 monthly indexes is found, the index of seasonality reported in Table 28.2 is computed by the formula: $\frac{\text{max} - \text{min}}{\text{maximum}}$ x 100, where the maximum is the largest median monthly index, and minimum the smallest. This gives an index ranging from zero (no seasonality) to 100, which would be the result of no employment at all in the minimum month. From the scatter diagrams, this might result in an underestimation of the short-time instability only for electrical contracting firms. But other evidence indicates that electrical construction firms have very stable employment. See W. Haber and H. Levinson, *Labor Relations and Productivity in the Building Trades* (Ann Arbor, 1956), p. 54. They rank construction occupations by percentage working a full year. Electricians work less than proprietors but more than any other occupation, including "foremen, all trades."

relationship within the industry can give us confidence in asserting that instability decreases bureaucratization. There are only two inversions, and these are of insignificant size: sheet metal and roofing should have been less bureaucratized than plumbing; and painters should have been less than brick, stone, and cement firms. This is a strong support for the hypothesis that the lack of bureaucratization in the construction industry is due to general instability.

We do not have space to document adequately the sources of variability in the work flow of construction administrations. The main elements may be outlined as follows:

1. Variations in the volume of work and in product mix in the course of the business cycle.[8]

2. Seasonal variations in both volume and product mix.[9]

3. The limitation of most construction administrations, especially in the specialty trades, to a small geographical radius. This smaller market magnifies the variability facing particular firms according to well-known statistical principles (individual projects can form a large part of a local market).[10]

4. The organization of work at a particular site into stages (building "from the ground up"), with the resulting variability in the productive purpose of any particular site administration.[11]. . .

THE IMPLICATIONS OF MARKETING REFORM

There is a good deal of careless talk about the bureaucratization of construction and the introduction of mass production by operative building of tract homes. The central innovation of operative building is in the field of marketing and finance rather than in the administration of production. The similarity of productive administration in operative building and other large-scale building is well summarized by Sherman Maisel.

> Many popular assumptions about subcontracting—that it lowers efficiency, raises costs, and leads to instability—are contradicted by our study in the Bay area of the reasons for subcontracting and its efficiency relative to its alternatives. Building appears to be one of the many industries where vertical disintegration increases efficiency and lowers costs without lessening stability. The fact that most large [operative housebuilding] firms have tried integrating various of the processes normally subcontracted but have usually returned to subcontracting them is of great

8. Miles L. Colean and Robinson Newcomb, *Stabilizing Construction* (New York, 1952), pp. 18-20, 49-50, and appendix N, pp. 219-42. Also Clarence Long, *Building Cycles and the Theory of Investment* (Princeton, 1940).

9. The data reported from Boothe and Arnold show both great seasonality and differential seasonality by trade. Their data show construction to be one of the most seasonal industries (op. cit., pp. 23-27).

10. Cf. Colean and Newcomb, op. cit., pp. 250-51, for the ecological limitations on administrative scope. For data on variations in volume in local areas, see U.S. Bureau of Labor Statistics, *Construction during Five Decades* (Bulletin no. 1146 [July 1, 1953]), pp. 22-25.

11. Cf. Gordon W. Bertran and Sherman J. Maisel, *Industrial Relations in the Construction Industry* (Berkeley, 1955), pp. 3-5.

importance because it shows that the present prevalence of subcontracting is the result of a policy deliberately adopted by builders after testing alternative possibilities. . . .

The logic of trade contracting has developed as follows. (1) Efficiency reaches its maximum effectiveness under specialized labor. (2) Specialized labor reaches its maximum effectiveness when applied regularly on many units. . . . (3) The problem of sustaining specialized jobs as well as the coordination of the movement of men among them requires special supervision, usually performed by trade contractors. . . .

Given a need for specialized mechanisms, the builder gains greater flexibility and a decrease in the problems of supervision through subcontracting.[12]

The central limitation on supervision is the increase in overhead when mediated communication is introduced. "A disproportionate increase takes place [in overhead in the largest construction firms] because production has spread beyond the area of simple visual control by the owner or owners [of the firm]."[13]

In fact, the characteristic of mass production administration, increasing specialization of tools and other facilities at a planned workplace, does not take place with increasing size. Most machinery added in large firms consists of hand power tools and materials-handling machinery.[14]

The low development of distinctively bureaucratic production-control mechanisms, such as cost accounting, detailed scheduling, regularized reporting of work progress, and standardized inspection of specific operations, is outlined by Maisel.[15] What happens instead of centralized planning and bureaucratic control of work is an increase in the fineness of stages on which crews of workers are put. This results in the development of more efficient, but still quite diversified, skills. And most important, these skills still form a component of a labor market rather than an organizational status system.

Operative decisions are still very important at the work level, rather than being concentrated in production engineering and cost-accounting departments. Modification of tools for special purposes is done by workers (e.g., the making of templates which provide guides for standardized cutting operations, or the construction of special scaffolds for the crew). There is no large element in the administration with the specialized task of planning technological innovation in the work process. And stable communications between work crews and decision centers are poorly developed.

The central consideration is that variability of work load for the administration is not very much reduced, if at all, by operative building. And it is not necessarily economical to take advantage of what reduction there is, when the subcontracting system and structured labor market are already in existence.

What is changed, what makes the economies possible, is the place of the goal-setting function. The productive goals in the past were set by clients with architectural advice, who quite naturally did not set goals in such a way as to maximize productive efficiency. In operative building productive goals are set autonomously by the administration. This means that they can choose, among the products they might produce, those which are technically easier. The main reduction of costs, of course, comes from the planning of the construction site so as to minimize transportation and set-up

12. *Housebuilding in Transition* (Berkeley and Los Angeles, 1953), pp. 231-32.

13. Ibid., p. 102.

14. Ibid., p. 103.

15. Ibid., pp. 123-30.

costs. Sites next to each other minimize costs of moving men, materials, and equipment to the site. Warehousing of materials can be planned to fit the individual site, rather than burdening builders' supply places. Uniformity of design reduces the complexity of materials distribution, reduces design costs, and so forth.

The main innovation, then, is the planning of the *product* for ease of production, rather than in the planning of the *productive process*. This is the introduction of the conceptions of Eli Whitney on *standardized parts* into construction, rather than of Henry Ford's innovation of *standardized tasks*. . . .

29. *Efficiency in the Construction Industry*

CHRISTOPHER A. SIMS

PRELIMINARIES AND PREVIEW

The efficiency of a producer or an industry can be defined in two ways: as an ability to economize on inputs, or as an ability to obtain high output with given inputs. From the first point of view, the rate of advance in efficiency is the rate of decline in real costs. From the latter point of view, the rate of advance in efficiency is the rate of growth of input productivity.

In order to improve its efficiency, a producer or an industry must be capable of continual changes in production technique. As we will be using the term, a production technique is a combination of inputs in certain quantities used to produce a certain quantity of output. An efficient producer will be changing techniques over time for two reasons: in order to substitute inputs with slowly rising prices for those with more rapidly rising prices, and in order to take advantage of new techniques which become available as knowledge advances. Only the latter type of change in techniques is properly called technological change,[1] but both lower costs and, hence, raise efficiency. Efficiency growth is related to technological change, but it is not the same thing. The analysis and conclusions of this paper will be concerned with efficiency in construction, and will not be directly translatable into conclusions about technological advance in construction. We will aim at detecting historical changes in construction technique, not (directly) changes in construction technology.[2]

A number of studies in the 1950s concluded that technique in the construction industry had shown little change since the turn of the century. Prices of construction industry output seemed to have risen relative to other commodity prices, and labor productivity (output per man or per man-hour) in the industry seemed to have shown little change. This picture of the construction industry as technically stagnant has even recently had wide currency.

On the other hand, some people familiar with the industry have pointed to apparent changes in construction technique during the postwar period—shift of work off-site

Reprinted from the *Report of the President's Committee on Urban Housing, Technical Studies*, vol. II (1968), pp. 149-74 (edited), by permission of the author. Several of the more technical parts of the original paper are omitted in this version. Christopher A. Sims is an associate professor of economics at the University of Minnesota.

1. See the first two chapters of Edwin Mansfield's book (10) for a good discussion of the distinction between change in technology and change in technique. [The numbers in parentheses refer to the bibliography at the end of the article.]

2. The formal definition of a technique—a certain combination of inputs used to produce a given output—has been given above. What economists mean by the technology of a good's production is the array of all techniques which would give lowest unit costs for some combination of input prices. A change in technology occurs when one of the techniques in this array is replaced by a previously unknown technique with lower input requirements. It is not always possible to determine whether a newly adopted technique is a previously unknown technique (a technological advance) or a known but previously unused technique which has only now become profitable.

by the use of prefabricated components and increased application of machinery such as cranes, for example.

This paper examines the basis for the conclusion that construction has been technically stagnant, and finds that the conclusion is justified, but only for the period up to around 1947. There is some basis for believing that since 1947 the price of construction industry output has risen no faster than other prices in the economy. Since 1947 labor productivity in construction has clearly begun to rise. There is also statistical evidence in industry balance sheets that the proportion of fixed assets in total construction industry assets has increased substantially since 1947, another indication that industry technique has changed. It is clear that the picture of construction technique as stagnant is not justified for the postwar period.

The techniques of analysis applied in this paper are limited in some ways. They do not allow us to determine precisely the physical nature of the changes in technique which have been taking place or the reasons for the change in behavior beginning around 1947. The evidence is consistent with the possibility that use of prefabricated components may have shifted many construction operations off-site, that there may have been increased use of heavy machinery, and that there may have been a reduction in working capital costs through more rapid construction and improved scheduling. The reasons for these changes could have included the accelerated rise in the costs of financial capital over the postwar period, the reduction in the variability in demand for construction industry output with the end of the war, and a possible advance in construction technology. What this paper proves is that construction technique has begun to change since 1947. To determine exactly how or why it has changed would require more detailed research.

Two other limitations on the results are discussed in more detail below: the difficulty of applying results for the whole of construction to its residential component, and the shadow cast over all the results by the sparseness and lack of coordination in federal government statistics on construction.

The fact that construction is not rigidly tied to 19th-century techniques, but instead seems to shift technique in response to economic pressures, has some modest implications for policy. It means, for example, that a government-sponsored or government-run research program to advance construction technology could be undertaken without fear that it would be fruitless because the industry might have an institutional structure which bars change in technique. It means also that well-conceived tax or subsidy programs might be effective in influencing industry behavior, or again, that seasonal and cyclical variability in construction activity is important because it may affect technique and costs as well as employment.

MEASURING EFFICIENCY CHANGE IN CONSTRUCTION

The most direct way to measure efficiency growth in the production of a commodity is to look at the rate of rise of the commodity's price. If we are comparing efficiency growth across commodities, production of commodities with lower rates of price growth might be said to show greater rates of growth of efficiency.[3] One problem with using this measure is that shifts in demand may produce apparent relative changes in effi-

3. Denison, in (3), uses an index of "total input" productivity which is a ratio of a price index for all inputs to a price index for a particular commodity. When compared across commodities, Denison's index gives the same results as the direct price comparisons suggested here.

ciency even if all production techniques remain fixed. If demand shifts toward labor-intensive commodities, for example, the relative price of labor will rise; and, if no changes in production technique take place, prices of labor-intensive commodities will rise relative to prices of other commodities. But shifts in demand would make comparisons of efficiency across commodities ambiguous in any case. In practice, this objection is not of great importance.

A more serious problem is that direct use of prices in measuring efficiency is possible only where we are measuring the efficiency of the entire economy in producing a particular commodity. But policy in most cases will deal with a production unit, a firm, or an industry. Therefore, for policy purposes it makes a great deal of difference whether the source of efficiency growth is in the construction industry itself or in the materials-supplying industries.

In fact, not only is the efficiency of the economy in producing a commodity different in principle from the efficiency of the industry most strongly associated with that commodity, but also changes in efficiency may occur which are not uniquely allocable to any industry. Reductions in labor requirements in the construction industry might be made possible by innovations which, from a technological point of view, appear to have originated in the construction materials-producing industries. In such a situation there is no unique "theoretically correct" way to allocate the cost reduction. One could unambiguously say that the economy's efficiency in producing new construction had increased and that labor productivity in the construction industry had increased, but the question of what industry should be credited with the cost reduction would be unanswerable in principle. . . .

A last objection to price as a measure of efficiency in construction is perhaps the most important. The notion of a "unit of output," and hence of price and unit cost, is difficult to apply to construction. Most existing price indexes for construction are based on some indirect measure of output rather than on market prices of standardized products. The price deflator for structures in the U.S. GNP accounts is based on an assumption that output growth is a weighted average of the growth in inputs. Hence it assumes that there is no technological change to allow increased output with given inputs. An alternative price index which will be mentioned below, Gordon's Income-Dacy index, assumes that output is proportional to constant dollar materials input; thus the Income-Dacy index is biased if there is any change in real unit materials requirements. These two price indexes behave quite differently, yet it is difficult to say which is to be preferred. Therefore, considerable uncertainty inevitably surrounds any measure of efficiency in construction based on price.

Another approach to efficiency measurement is based on productivity ratios. A productivity ratio is a ratio of an amount of output to the amount of a certain input required to produce it. The most commonly computed productivity ratio is output per man or per man-hour labor productivity. The productivity of an input measured in this way is clearly a property of the production process, not the input itself. Labor productivity and labor quality are not the same thing.[4]

Input productivities have one advantage over prices as an efficiency measure: they can be computed on an industry basis. Statistics on labor input in the construction industry are available. If the construction industry's technique were stagnant, we would expect that the ratio of construction output to man-hours in the construction industry

---

4. For example, the use of higher quality machines might reduce labor requirements (and hence raise labor productivity) without any associated change in labor quality.

would remain unchanged, even though output price might be influenced by advances in efficiency in materials-supplying industries.

However, computing productivity ratios involves the measurement of "real" output so that measurement of efficiency growth by productivity growth is as dependent on accurate price indexes as measurement techniques based directly on prices. To get away from dependence on accurate price measurement, one can look at the ratios between inputs of various types. An industry with stagnant technique should show a fixed ratio of labor to materials inputs, for example, so that if this ratio changes, we can be sure that technique is not rigid. Furthermore, if it can be shown that the changing ratios reflect a substitution of inputs with slowly growing prices for those with more rapidly growing prices, this would indicate that efficient response of production technique to changing input prices is taking place. This kind of analysis can provide no absolute measure of the rate of advance in efficiency, and it is difficult to use it to make comparisons across industries which start out with different input ratios. On the other hand, the limited conclusions it can provide are more solidly grounded than those based on output price movements or productivity ratios.

CONSTRUCTION AS A BACKWARD INDUSTRY: THE CONSENSUS OF THE 1950s

[Professor Sims reviews several postwar studies of construction: Grebler, Blank, and Winnick (7); Colean and Newcomb (1); R. J. Gordon (6); Denison (3); and Milton Gilbert and Associates (5). In general all of these studies support the view that relative to the rest of the economy construction efficiency grew slowly prior to the 1950s. Professor Sims also presents evidence of his own to support the same conclusion (Tables 29.1, 29.2, and 29.3). (All tables are located at the end of the chapter.)]

On balance, the available statistical evidence agrees with the hypothesis that the production process was stagnant over 1929-47, showing little or no efficiency growth. However, statistics on the construction industry are somewhat questionable even since 1947. Prior to that time they may be extremely unreliable.[5] It may be that some of the apparent change in the behavior of construction technology since 1947 simply reflects an improvement in official statistics beginning in that year.

RESIDENTIAL VERSUS NONRESIDENTIAL CONSTRUCTION

The evident differences in technology between highway construction and housebuilding are enormous; yet up to this point we have made no attempt to examine the behavior of residential construction separately from that of other sorts of construction. United States government statistics on the contract construction industry do not provide separate price or employment data for residential and nonresidential components, so that distinguishing productivity movements for these two subsectors is impossible. What little evidence there is, however, suggests that the stagnation of construction technology over 1929-47 holds if anything more strongly for residential than for other construction.

Reliable price indexes are available for certain types of heavy construction with relatively easily measured output. R. J. Gordon ([6], Table A-4) presents several such

5. In 1964, the series for the value of residential construction (one-third to one-half of all construction) in the national accounts was revised upward by amounts as large as 30 percent over a number of post-war years. The revisions were not extended back beyond 1946, leaving a frankly admitted "break" in the accuracy of the series in that year. . . .

indexes applying to highway construction, excavation and similar nonstructural heavy construction; all rise much less over 1929-47 than does Gordon's index of overall construction price. . . .

CONSTRUCTION PRODUCTIVITY SINCE 1947: A TECHNOLOGICAL EXPLOSION?

. . . The Gordon index implies that total input productivity has, since 1947, grown slightly more rapidly in construction than in the economy at large (Table 29.3). A version of the Gordon index (Gordon's Final Price of Structures, or GFPS), which he prepared by removing the nonstructures component and deflating it separately, also grows more slowly than the GNP deflator, so the result cannot be attributed to developments in earthmoving and roadbuilding alone.

As can be seen from Table 29.2, physical output per employee grew slightly less rapidly over 1947-65 in construction than in manufacturing, but it did show substantial growth. Deflation by the Department of Commerce Composite would reduce the apparent growth of physical output per worker in construction from 50 percent to 23 percent. Note that even the Department of Commerce Composite implies some labor productivity growth since 1947.

The movements of labor share in value added and in income originating shown in Table 29.1 seem to continue the pre-1947 pattern, with labor share in construction showing a slow but steady rise. It should be noted, however, that in the light of the movement of relative input prices shown in columns 5 and 6 of Table 29.1, it is not clear that this rise in labor share reflects a lack of response to input price movements. We will give more attention to this point below.

The rapid rise of physical productivity in construction since 1947 does not reflect rapid substitution of capital for labor within the construction industry. Real value added per employee and real income originating per employee both increased more slowly in construction than in manufacturing over 1947-65, again continuing the pre-1947 pattern.

On the other hand, costs for capital and labor within the construction industry have, since 1947, fallen along with other construction costs. The rise in current dollar income originating as a proportion of value of output over 1929-47 is not repeated over 1947-65. The proportion rose by 11 percent over the earlier period, but remained practically unchanged over 1947-65.[6] Constant dollar income originating, the real value of capital and labor employed in construction, fell as a proportion of physical output in construction. . . . This contrasts not only with the rapid rise in that ratio over 1929-47 but also with the continued rise in the corresponding ratio for manufacturing.

THE IMPORTANCE OF THE OUTPUT MEASURE

One of the widely recognized postwar changes in construction technology . . . is the movement of construction operations off-site through the use of prefabricated components. The I.L.O. study (8) . . . lists the movement of costs off-site as one part of the recent "technological explosion" in construction. The postwar retardation in the growth of value added as a share of the value of construction output is in line with the hypothesis that costs might be moving off-site; and if one accepts the GFPC deflector, the postwar decline in constant dollar value added and income originat-

6. Based on figures from (20) not shown separately in the tables at the end of this paper

ing as a proportion of real product . . . provides even stronger support for the hypothesis. To the extent that substitution of off-site for on-site capital and labor has been going on, one would expect that the constant dollar value of materials per unit of construction output might have been rising. It is possible that total input productivity has been rising rapidly enough in construction so that a shift of costs off-site has occurred without any substantial increase in constant dollar unit materials costs. However, without an independent measure of output price we have no way of determining what changes in constant dollar unit materials costs have been. If, as seems quite possible, constant dollar materials costs per unit of construction output have risen since 1947, Gordon's Income-Dacy index may also underestimate price rises in residential or building construction. . . .

The procedure adopted in this study, in the absence of any reliable alternative, is to apply the GFPC to all construction, recognizing that the picture of postwar technological "explosion" in construction which this approach produces may give a somewhat overoptimistic picture of cost changes if it is applied to residential construction.

SOME EXPLANATIONS AND HYPOTHESES

Examination of statistics will by itself allow us to draw no substantive conclusions. The statistics can be useful only in providing a check on substantive hypotheses about what has been happening to construction technology. We have already confronted the statistics with two hypotheses: the first, that construction is still a stagnant industry, conflicts with the statistical evidence; the other, that construction operations have tended to move off-site, finds support in the statistics. In this section we will set forth some additional, less familiar hypotheses to explain some of the changes in construction technology.

Several lines of evidence suggest that the changes in construction technology since 1947 may reflect substitution responses to input price changes. A relatively large part of the capital in construction has always consisted of nondepreciable assets. Figures from 1964 tax returns (28) show the net value of depreciable assets to make up 17.1 percent of total assets for corporations in construction, as opposed to 30.5 percent for manufacturing. Therefore, it is especially important in analyzing construction technology to distinguish financial capital inputs from depreciable assets. As can be seen from the last two columns of Table 29.1, the rise in interest rates over 1947-65 has been more rapid than the rise in compensation per employee, so that there has been no input price pressure to substitute financial capital for labor. The Department of Commerce price index for construction machinery, on the other hand, has risen slightly less rapidly over 1947-65 than has compensation per employee in construction ([20] p. 165 and pp. 107-9). Furthermore, compared to the great swings in construction demand caused by World War II and the depression, postwar variability in construction demand has been mild indeed.[7] Financial capital is mobile. It can be rather quickly shifted into new uses with shifts in demand. Most sorts of depreciable assets are

---

7. A logarithmic trend fit by least squares to constant dollar residential construction output (deflated by the official deflators, since there is nothing else available and the deflator makes little difference here) over all of 1929-65 shows a trend growth rate of 6.2 percent and a standard deviation about the trend (approximately, the standard deviation of proportional deviation from trend) of .49. For the postwar period alone, the trend growth rate is 1.9 percent, with a standard deviation of .088. . . .

less mobile than either financial capital or labor, so that increased stability in demand favors the introduction of more fixed capital in place of labor and financial capital.[8]

In sum, interest rates have risen relative to both wages and the price of capital goods, with wages rising slightly faster than capital goods prices. Efficient substitution responses should tend to replace financial capital with labor and fixed capital. The construction industry responded by more than doubling the ratio of depreciation to gross margins over 1947-65[9] . . . That ratio rose in manufacturing as well, but less sharply. Balance sheets for corporations shown in *Statistics of Income* (27) show that the ratio of gross capital assets (fixed capital)[10] to total assets averaged .285 over 1947-48 in construction, as compared to .586 in manufacturing. The corresponding figures for 1964 were .367 in construction, .671 in manufacturing. The ratio increased by 29 percent in construction, by 17 percent in manufacturing. The movement of construction value added off-site can also be regarded in part as a response to relative input cost movements. Prefabricated components produced in factories are, in effect, a vehicle for the application of more fixed capital in construction.

In light of the high proportion of financial capital in total construction assets, the continued rise in the labor share in income originating since 1947 might represent an appropriate substitution response rather than continued stagnation of input proportions.

It has been suggested[11] that one reason for the inadequacy of labor productivity as an index of efficiency in construction is that the cost advantages of speed in construction might result in apparent decline or retardation in labor productivity growth. Increased speed of construction is probably the most direct way to substitute other inputs for financial capital. Returns to inventories and notes and accounts receivable, together accounting for over 45 percent of total assets in construction corporations in 1964, (28) would both be directly reduced as a proportion of total current costs by speedier construction. A trend toward more rapid construction would fit well into the general pattern of input substitution we have suggested here, and in principle it should be possible to obtain more direct evidence on this point. A similar effect on financial capital costs might be obtained by increased managerial emphasis on scheduling deliveries of materials to coincide with their use.

Indirect, and probably rather flimsy, evidence on the substitution of fixed for variable inputs . . . [is] the proportion of corporations in total income originating. For construction, this ratio has shown a slight tendency to move countercyclically in the short

8. It may be that technical and managerial labor is not so mobile as other labor. If returns to managerial labor include returns to "expertise" or "experience," highly unstable demand could attach a risk premium to the price of such labor by discouraging talented individuals from "investing" themselves in construction. Since many of the managerial and technical workers in construction are attached to separate architectural and consulting firms not included as part of the construction industry in the statistics, it would be difficult to test the hypothesis that the relative stability of demand in postwar construction has increased the use of this type of labor.

9. *Statistics of Income* (28), shows that "Rental of Business Property" was about 36 percent as large as depreciation in construction in 1964, as compared to a corresponding figure of 26 percent in manufacturing. Hence it is important to verify that the rise in depreciation as a proportion of total construction costs does not reflect a shift from equipment rental to equipment purchase. The 1947-48 average for the ratio of rental costs to depreciaton was 29 percent in construction, 28 percent in manufacturing. Rentals in construction increased relative to rentals in manufacturing—in other words, meaning that the figures . . . probably understate the difference between construction and manufacturing over 1947-65.

10. Depreciable, depletable, and intangible assets.

11. The importance of this point was first suggested to the author by John T. Dunlop.

run. The reason could be that corporate organization tends to be associated with higher investment in fixed managerial and/or capital inputs, in which case the secular increase in corporate share since 1947 is another evidence of substitution of fixed for variable inputs in construction since that year. However, the trend movement in corporate share is more interesting in itself than as a weak support to this paper's input-substitution analysis.

CONCLUSIONS: POLICY IMPLICATIONS AND SUGGESTIONS
FOR FURTHER RESEARCH

The evidence examined up to this point shows clearly that production techniques in construction can no longer be characterized as stagnant. According to even the most conservative estimates, output per worker has risen since 1947. Furthermore, the pattern of cost movements suggests that the postwar changes in the construction production process may in part be substitution responses to changing input prices.

As long as the picture of construction as technologically rigid was accepted, there was some justification for assuming that policy to reduce construction costs should be aimed at eliminating "institutional rigidities" and "barriers to innovation." The discussion of labor productivity in Colean and Newcomb's book ([1], loc. cit.) is one example of an approach emphasizing union work rules and building codes as limiting productivity growth. The I.L.O. study from which we have lifted the phrase "technological explosion" (8) also takes an institutional approach to policy, emphasizing small scale and lack of "coordination" as barriers to the dissemination of information in the industry.

But the evidence that construction technology has not been rigid since 1947 makes continued exclusive emphasis on eliminating "rigidities" and "barriers" inappropriate. However important such factors may be (and they may indeed be important), they did not prevent construction technology from responding to market pressure over 1947-65. There is no reason to fear, therefore, that (for example) a government subsidized or operated program of research related to housing technology would be fruitless because the inflexible structure of the industry would prevent adoption of new techniques resulting from the research.

Relatively little attention has been given to price distortions in construction industry input markets and to how such price distortions might reduce efficiency in the industry.[12] If construction technique does not respond to input prices, as the pre-1947 stagnation implied, then there was little policy relevance in such issues, since input price distortions could be expected to leave technique unchanged. But the evidence presented in this paper suggests that input price distortions could indeed affect construction technique, and conversely, that policy measures which eliminate such distortions could have important effects on construction costs.

It may be useful to list here some unresolved questions concerning the structure of construction input markets, together with brief indications of their importance to policy. It seems possible that a peculiar conjunction of market characteristics and

---

12. There is, of course, one major exception to this generalization. A great deal of attention has been focused on wage distortions introduced by possible monopoly elements in unionized labor markets. Even here, however, the pattern has been to emphasize the direct effect of possible wage distortions on money costs, rather than on the distortions in the choice of input techniques which artifically high wages could create. How often has it been pointed out that if unions really do maintain construction wages at an artificially high level the effect must be to put artificial pressure on producers to raise labor productivity by increasing capital or materials input?

institutional factors may hold hourly labor costs in construction too high *as seen by the producer*. The seasonality and short-term nature of demand for labor in construction impose unusual costs on construction workers, and the construction labor market seems to have balanced these special costs by arriving at an hourly wage in construction which remains persistently higher than hourly wages for workers in similar occupational categories in other industries.[13] D. Q. Mills, in (13), pp. 20ff, has shown that seasonality in construction employment has shown no decline over the postwar period, despite geographical shifts and technological developments which might have been expected to reduce seasonality. These two sets of facts may be related. The traditional form of the wage bargain, with its concentration on hourly rates of pay and standard work weeks, provides no pressure on individual employers to take into account the important part of "labor costs" which arises from the need for employees to search for a new job. Because these costs are important, they are paid for in the total construction wage bill, but there is no incentive for individual employers to take them into account. If this picture of the construction labor market is accurate (and it is partly conjecture at this point) the structure of the wage bargain may be responsible, by charging employers only indirectly for the consequences of seasonality, for the failure of seasonal fluctuations in employment to moderate. Such a situation, where a real cost fails to be priced directly in the market, is known technically as an externality. Where externalities are present, market forces do not necessarily lead to efficient production decisions, and intervention in the market by public authorities may therefore be justified.

A variety of methods to reduce employment seasonality in construction have been proposed and applied in Canada and various European countries. An extensive discussion of the subject appears in a recent OECD publication by Jan Wittrock (29). If the analysis presented here proves on further study to be correct, good results might be obtained by altering the wagesetting process so that employers pay labor costs due to seasonality directly rather than indirectly. One approach might be to institute or encourage state or union-run unemployment benefit programs in which an employer's annual contributions are keyed partly to the difference between the number of his employees averaged over the three months in the year of highest and of lowest employment. A detailed proposal along these lines would of course require a more elaborate analysis of the construction labor market than has appeared in this paper.[14] The point of discussing this proposal here is to show how analysis of input market structure may provide insights into the nature of policy problems and suggest policy solutions.

Equally important distortions might be present in the construction capital market. Cyclical and seasonal variability in demand, as has already been noted above, imposes special costs on owners of fixed assets. Construction, especially residential construction, has a highly variable pattern of aggregate demand. In fact, residential construction is the most variable of the six major components of private domestic demand—durable goods consumption, nondurable goods consumption, services consumption, nonresidential structures, plant and equipment, and residential construction. Of these six components, residential construction in constant dollars (from [20], pp. 4-5) shows the highest proportional standard deviation about a logarithmic trend both over 1929-65 and over the postwar 1947-65 period (though for the latter period the proportional

13. Evidence on both these points appears in D. Q. Mills' thesis (13), pp. 170ff.

14. It might be difficult, for example, to devise a scheme which charged more directly for seasonality in employment without penalizing employers for hiring workers who genuinely desire short-term employment or who in a recession are happy to have any employment.

variance of plant and equipment was nearly as high—the standard deviation was about 8.7 percent for both these components). . . .

It has been suggested that the structure of financial markets makes residential construction demand especially variable, that in fact the sensitivity of construction to monetary policy is a major reason for the effectiveness of monetary policy. If this is so (and let it be emphasized that we present this notion here as an exemplary hypothesis, not a conclusion), changes in the pattern of regulation of financial markets might improve construction efficiency by reducing the risk premium on the cost of fixed assets. Other possible sources of artificially high fixed capital costs in construction are the high regional variability in construction demand[15] and the substantial risk involved in construction projects relative to the size of the assets of most firms in construction.[16] Both of these distortions (again, if they indeed exist) might be corrected or alleviated by appropriate measures of policy. Regional demand variation might be reduced by more careful coordination among public agencies in the timing of public construction projects. Risk premiums on capital costs due to small firms undertaking large, risky projects might be reduced through a government-run or government-sponsored insurance program.[17]

The possible market distortions and hypothetical policy response to them discussed in this section are not carefully worked out proposals. They are meant to illustrate a kind of question which has taken on fresh importance for policy now that it is clear that construction technique may be influenced by relative prices. Little is currently known about these questions of market structure. Increased knowledge in this area is of first importance to intelligent formation of public policy related to construction costs.

REFERENCES

1. Colean, Miles and R. Newcomb, *Stabilizing Construction*, McGraw-Hill, New York, 1952.
2. Dacy, Douglas C., "A Price and Productivity Index for Non-Homogeneous Products," *Journal of the American Statistical Association*, June 1964.
3. Denison, Edward F., *The Sources of U.S. Economic Growth and the Alternatives Before Us*, Brookings Institution, 1962.
4. ———, *Why Growth Rates Differ*, Brookings Institution, 1967.
5. Gilbert, Milton & Associates, *Comparative National Products and Price Levels*, OEEC, 1958.
6. Gordon, Robert J., "A New View of Real Investment in Structures, 1919-65," presented to the Econometric Society Meetings, December 1967.
7. Grebler, Leo, D. M. Blank, and L. Winnick, *Capital Formation in Residential Real Estate*, Princeton University Press, Princeton, New Jersey, 1956.

15. Some evidence on regional variability appears in D. Q. Mills' thesis (13).

16. An article in the *Survey of Current Business* (17) showed that the average annual ratio of new firms and discontinued firms to total firms over 1959-62 was higher in construction than in manufacturing, retail trade, or services (the average ratio for construction was .27).

17. This latter proposal is more speculative than the others presented in this section. One could argue that if risk premiums were in fact very large and if an insurance program were practically feasible, a private firm or trade association would already have set one up. Government action might be justified, however, if the economical scale for such a program is extremely large.

8. International Labor Organization, Building, Civil Engineering, and Public Works Committee, 7th Session, Report II, *Technological Changes in the Construction Industry and Their Socio-Economic Consequences*, Geneva 1964.

9. Lund, P. J., "Building Statistics: Construction Time and the Measure of Work Done," *The Manchester School*, September 1967.

10. Mansfield, Edwin, *The Economics of Technological Change*, W. W. Norton, New York, 1968.

11. McCarthy, Michael D., "On the Aggregation of the 1958 Direct Requirements Input-Output Table," *Review of Economics and Statistics*, November 1967.

12. Mills, D. Q., "Data on Construction," unpublished manuscript.

13. ———, *Factors Determining Patterns of Employment and Unemployment in the Construction Industry in the U.S.*, unpublished Ph.D. dissertation, Harvard University, 1967.

14. Nelson, R., M. Peck, and E. Kalachek, *Technology, Economic Growth, and Public Policy*, Brookings Institution, 1967.

15. Salter, W. E. G., *Productivity and Technical Change*, 2nd Edition, Cambridge University Press, Cambridge, 1966.

16. U.S. Department of Commerce, Bureau of the Census, "Construction Reports —Series C30, Value of New Construction Put in Place: 1946-63, Revised," U.S. Government Printing Office, 1964.

17. U.S. Department of Commerce, Office of Business Economics, "Business Population in 1962 Continues Its Slow Growth," *Survey of Current Business*, June 1963.

18. U.S. Department of Commerce, Office of Business Economics, *Business Statistics: 1967 Biennial Edition*, U.S. Government Printing Office, 1968.

19. ———, *National Income 1954 Edition*, U.S. Government Printing Office.

20. ———, *National Income and Product Accounts of the U.S., 1929-65*, U.S. Government Printing Office, 1966.

21. U.S. Department of Labor, Bureau of Labor Statistics, *Bulletin No. 1390*, "Labor and Materials Requirements for Civil Works Constructed by the Corps of Engineers."

22. ———, *Bulletin No. 1402*, "Labor and Materials Requirements for Public Housing Construction."

23. ———, *Bulletin No. 1404*, "Labor and Materials Requirements for Private One-Family House Construction."

24. ———, *Bulletin No. 1517*, "The Consumer Price Index: History and Techniques."

25. ———, *Bulletin No. 1554*, "The Consumer Price Index: Technical Notes, 1959-63."

26. U.S. Office of the President, *Economic Report of the President, 1968*, U.S. Government Printing Office, February, 1968.

27. U.S. Treasury Department, Internal Revenue Service; *Statistics of Income, Part II: Corporation Returns*, 1947-48.

28. ———, *Statistics of Income, 1964: U.S. Business Tax Returns*.

29. Wittrock, Jan, *Reducing Seasonal Unemployment in the Construction Industry*, O.E.C.D., Paris, 1967.

TABLE 29.1 *Relative Shares and Relative Prices of Labor and Capital, Construction and Manufacturing (Indexes, 1947 = 1.00)*

	1.	2.	3.	4.	5.	6.
1929	.908	.953	.914	.989	.462	.433
1930	.910	.965	.924	1.022	.452	.446
1931	.921	1.063	.950	1.170	.402	.449
1932	1.016	1.197	1.101	1.418	.305	.385
1933	1.028	1.180	1.119	1.373	.333	.415
1934	.930	1.087	.972	1.173	.374	.459
1935	.917	1.036	.946	1.094	.447	.534
1936	.901	1.000	.912	1.039	.571	.632
1937	.947	1.014	.959	1.043	.602	.657
1938	.919	1.046	.927	1.102	.589	.650
1939	.966	1.018	.972	1.057	.672	.735
1940	.969	.950	.970	.974	.734	.804
1941	1.015	.908	1.005	.916	.856	.882
1942	1.064	.943	1.047	.948	.995	.936
1943	1.054	.977	1.038	.978	1.096	1.052
1944	1.020	.988	1.010	.996	1.116	1.108
1945	1.004	1.011	.999	1.029	1.130	1.125
1946	.987	1.038	.981	1.038	1.017	1.038
1947	1.000	1.000	1.000	1.000	1.000	1.000
1948	.965	.974	.967	.976	.940	.942
1949	.943	.959	.953	.969	1.030	1.029
1950	.957	.933	.969	.938	1.076	1.112
1951	1.004	.937	1.016	.941	1.026	1.050
1952	1.011	.982	1.024	.993	1.040	1.054
1953	1.033	.999	1.048	1.015	1.010	1.021
1954	1.049	.998	1.070	1.027	1.126	1.136
1955	1.051	.961	1.078	.989	1.075	1.126
1956	1.051	.989	1.077	1.020	1.003	1.050
1957	1.039	.998	1.067	1.035	.882	.917
1958	1.051	1.019	1.083	1.069	.910	.952
1959	1.060	.992	1.094	1.032	.812	.860
1960	1.080	1.013	1.113	1.056	.832	.866
1961	1.073	1.018	1.103	1.065	.864	.894
1962	1.075	1.003	1.104	1.055	.894	.931
1963	1.079	.997	1.110	1.048	.931	.968
1964	1.079	.987	1.106	1.038	.930	.968
1965	1.094	.956	1.118	1.002	.931	.961

1. (Compensation of Employees)/(Value Added), Construction.
2. (Compensation of Employees)/(Value Added), Manufacturing.
3. (Compensation of Employees)/(Income Originating), Construction.
4. (Compensation of Employees)/(Income Originating), Manufacturing.
5. (Compensation per Fee*)/(Interest Rate), Construction.
6. (Compensation per Fee*)/(Interest Rate), Manufacturing.
*Full-time equivalent employee.

Column 1: Source: (20), Table 6.1 for Compensation of Employees. These figures include Supplements to Wages and Salaries. Value added is income originating in construction plus corporate capital consumption allowances plus noncorporate capital consumption allowances from (20), Tables 1.12, 6.18, and 6.9, taking the GNP deflator into account.

Column 2: Same as Col. 1 in sources and derivation.

Column 3: Same as Col. 1 in sources and derivation except for replacement of Value Added by Income Originating.

Column 4: Same as Col. 3 in sources and derivation.

Column 5: Sources: Numerator = Compensation of Employees ([20], Table 6.1) divided by GNP deflator, further divided by Number of Full-Time Equivalent Employees ([20], Table 6.4). Denominator = Corporate Aaa bond interest rate as given in (26), Table B-54.

Column 6: Same as Col. 5 in sources and derivation.

TABLE 29.2 *Labor Productivity Ratios, Construction and Manufacturing*
(Indexes, 1947 = 1.00)

	1.	2.	3.	4.	5.	6.
1929	1.225	.880	.922	.823	.916	.793
1930	1.135	.859	.865	.805	.852	.761
1931	1.129	.931	.765	.741	.742	.673
1932	1.035	.909	.576	.617	.532	.521
1933	1.077	.844	.557	.605	.512	.519
1934	1.044	.823	.616	.647	.590	.600
1935	1.121	.879	.673	.711	.653	.674
1936	1.204	.936	.786	.785	.777	.755
1937	1.269	.919	.794	.810	.784	.787
1938	1.411	.973	.784	.759	.777	.721
1939	1.428	.981	.802	.833	.798	.802
1940	1.404	1.007	.824	.921	.823	.898
1941	1.215	.965	.895	1.031	.904	1.022
1942	.991	.914	1.014	1.076	1.031	1.070
1943	.740	.952	1.087	1.126	1.105	1.124
1944	.620	1.061	1.141	1.169	1.151	1.160
1945	.734	1.152	1.130	1.117	1.136	1.098
1946	1.063	1.049	.999	.969	1.005	.970
1947	1.000	1.000	1.000	1.000	1.000	1.000
1948	1.022	1.015	1.053	1.045	1.050	1.043
1949	1.134	1.066	1.114	1.094	1.102	1.082
1950	1.301	1.117	1.129	1.197	1.115	1.190
1951	1.039	1.119	1.120	1.228	1.107	1.222
1952	1.055	1.129	1.167	1.217	1.152	1.204
1953	1.130	1.133	1.198	1.253	1.181	1.234
1954	1.244	1.160	1.193	1.265	1.170	1.229
1955	1.333	1.230	1.199	1.375	1.170	1.335
1956	1.171	1.220	1.228	1.367	1.198	1.325
1957	1.209	1.229	1.265	1.369	1.232	1.320
1958	1.328	1.282	1.257	1.356	1.219	1.292
1959	1.437	1.315	1.285	1.455	1.246	1.400
1960	1.421	1.350	1.301	1.444	1.262	1.386
1961	1.498	1.394	1.343	1.464	1.306	1.398
1962	1.528	1.453	1.380	1.541	1.344	1.464
1963	1.513	1.506	1.408	1.585	1.369	1.506
1964	1.498	1.578	1.453	1.653	1.417	1.572
1965	1.505	1.612	1.464	1.729	1.432	1.649

1. Physical Output Per Fee,* Construction.
2. Physical Output Per Fee,* Manufacturing.
3. Value Added Per Fee,* Construction.
4. Value Added Per Fee,* Manufacturing.
5. Income Originating Per Fee,* Construction.
6. Income Originating Per Fee,* Manufacturing.
*Full-time equivalent employee.

SOURCES: Denominators are in each case Number of Full-Time Equivalent Employees from (20), Table 6.4. Physical output is derived by deflating Gordon's estimate of value-put-in-place in contract construction by GFPC price index for construction output from (6), Table A-8. For value added and income originating, see Table 29.1.

TABLE 29.3   *Construction Price and Cost*
(Indexes, 1947 =1.00)

	1.	2.	3.	4.	5.	6.	7.	8.
1929	.560	.552	.538	1.243	.724	.537	—	.678
1930	.525	.537	.505	1.210	.733	.522	—	.661
1931	.455	.493	.435	1.146	.706	.482	—	.601
1932	.380	.433	.367	1.028	.684	.407	—	.539
1933	.398	.463	.367	.885	.616	.407	—	.527
1934	.452	.522	.421	.830	.701	.443	—	.565
1935	.449	.508	.422	.828	.708	.433	—	.571
1936	.482	.522	.458	.849	.606	.447	—	.572
1937	.501	.552	.486	.888	.686	.501	—	.597
1938	.464	.552	.450	.916	.656	.515	—	.589
1939	.462	.522	.449	.917	.686	.528	—	.579
1940	.478	.537	.469	.920	.661	.542	—	.589
1941	.552	.582	.544	.936	.608	.586	—	.632
1942	.684	.657	.662	.956	.510	.619	—	.711
1943	.809	.702	.789	.956	.585	.646	—	.761
1944	.905	.687	.917	.959	.716	.702	—	.780
1945	.841	.716	.847	.962	.889	.753	—	.800
1946	.804	.836	.790	.968	.889	.826	—	.894
1947	1.000	1.000	1.000	1.000	1.000	1.000	—	1.000
1948	1.110	1.120	1.109	1.066	1.121	1.125	—	1.067
1949	1.068	1.105	1.069	1.112	1.191	1.097	—	1.060
1950	1.052	1.149	1.057	1.151	1.218	1.156	—	1.075
1951	1.238	1.254	1.234	1.198	1.322	1.246	—	1.148
1952	1.259	1.284	1.253	1.240	1.465	1.278	—	1.173
1953	1.250	1.314	1.251	1.314	1.517	1.301	1.313	1.184
1954	1.210	1.314	1.216	1.361	1.475	1.291	1.336	1.201
1955	1.210	1.343	1.223	1.380	1.517	1.330	1.349	1.219
1956	1.336	1.418	1.344	1.405	1.598	1.389	1.371	1.260
1957	1.367	1.478	1.370	1.431	1.620	1.415	1.437	1.307
1958	1.304	1.493	1.302	1.457	1.661	1.428	1.463	1.341
1959	1.289	1.523	1.295	1.479	1.681	1.475	1.477	1.362
1960	1.291	1.538	1.302	1.501	1.744	1.500	1.511	1.385
1961	1.281	1.552	1.288	1.520	1.777	1.504	1.521	1.402
1962	1.320	1.597	1.326	1.539	1.842	1.530	1.538	1.418
1963	1.355	1.627	1.361	1.555	1.945	1.561	1.559	1.437
1964	1.379	1.672	1.387	1.569	1.980	1.606	1.589	1.460
1965	1.415	1.732	1.421	1.585	2.007	1.658	1.623	1.487

1. Gordon's Final Price of Construction.
2. Department of Commerce Composite.
3. Gordon's Price Index for Rent.
4. Consumers' Price Index for Rent.
5. Dodge Value per Square Foot, Residential.
6. Boeckh Input Cost Index, Residential.
7. Consumers' Price Index for Homeownership.
8. GNP Deflator.
Column 1: Source: Gordon (6), Table A-8. Derivation described in (6).
Column 2: Gordon (6), Table A-2. Derivation described in Gordon (6) and in (16), Appendix C.
Column 3: Source: Gordon (6), Table A-9. Derivation described in (6).
Column 4: Source: (18). An index of rental prices paid by consumers of rental housing.
Column 5: Source: Gordon (6), Table A-9.
Column 6: Source: Gordon (6), Table A-2.
Column 7: Source: (18).
Column 8: Source: (20), Table 8.1. The GNP deflator indicates the movement of the general level of all prices.

30. *Building Codes*

NATIONAL COMMISSION ON URBAN PROBLEMS

A building code is a series of standards and specifications designed to establish minimum safeguards in the erection and construction of buildings, to protect the human beings who live and work in them from fire and other hazards, and to establish regulations to further protect the health and safety of the public. Building codes are formulated and enforced through the police powers of state governments, ordinarily delegated to and exercised by local governments, usually municipalities. In one form or another, codes go back to the earliest days of civilized society, and serve an essential purpose.

In modern America, a plethora of codes has been promulgated by various organizations. In the building construction field, there are four major groups known as the model code groups. The Building Officials' Conference of America (BOCA) is most prominent in the East and North Central areas of the country, but also has membership elsewhere. Its code is called the Basic Building Code.

The International Conference of Building Officials (ICBO) is the most influential of the code groups in the Western States, but like BOCA is not limited exclusively to that region. Its code is known as the Uniform Building Code.

In the South, the Southern Standard Building Code is the major code but, like the others, it does not have exclusive jurisdiction. The BOCA, ICBO, and National codes overlap it in many areas.

The National Building Code is the code published by the American Insurance Association. It is estimated to have been adopted in about 1,600 communities.

In addition to codes confined strictly to building, there are mechanical codes, mainly plumbing and electrical but also including codes for elevators and boilers, and the special codes, usually promulgated by states, for hospitals, schools, theaters, factories, nursing homes, and other special categories.

Of the mechanical codes the two best known are the National Electrical Code and the National Plumbing Code. Recently the model code groups have adopted their own plumbing codes as well.

PROBLEMS

Complaints against building codes, building code organizations, and local officials are widespread. It is alleged that unneeded provisions and restrictions in locally adopted codes add significantly to the cost of housing, that they delay construction, that they prevent the use of the most up-to-date and modern materials, that they inhibit creative design, that their provisions are antiquated and outdated, and that the procedures for modernizing and amending them are slow, laborious, lacking in objective standards, and dominated by a very small group in the industry; namely, building code officials

Reprinted from National Commission on Urban Problems, *Building The American City* (Washington, D.C.: Government Printing Office, 1968), pt. III, chap. 3 (edited).

and officials of the trade associations in the building materials field. It is charged that other directly interested parties, including qualified building, producing, and professional groups, are excluded from the decision-making bodies, and that the general public and the public interest are represented inadequately, if at all.

Additional complaints against building codes and their administration include:

the lack of uniformity of both provisions and administration at the local level and in metropolitan areas characterized by large numbers of independent cities, towns, and counties;

the inadequacies of training and the absence of proper qualifications for local building officials;

the arbitrary actions of local building officials;

the lack of proper appeal procedures;

the inhibitions against marketing of mobile homes and prefabricated housing;

the prevention of large-scale building and selling by conventional builders. which could achieve economies of mass production and the standardization of production;

the abandonment by the states to the localities of responsibilities and functions that should properly be exercised at the state level; and

the diverse standards and regulations of various federal agencies responsible for building construction, with resulting confusion and added costs.

ESTABLISHING THE FACTS

Past controversies on these subjects have been heated but lacking in basic information. Building code officials representing national construction code groups complain that they are charged with local abuses over which they have no control. Complaints by innovators whose materials or methods are not accepted in the codes are often said to be unfounded because the innovations have not been properly tested. Model code groups also point out that while provisions of the national model codes may include a specific product or practice, producers of competing materials or methods may influence its exclusion from local codes. In other instances, it is said that complaints against a state or city plumbing or electrical code provision are unfairly charged against the national construction model code.

In order to establish the facts of these charges and countercharges, the Commission embarked on a planned and meticulous inquiry through a program of hearings, meetings, interviews, inspections, and detailed research studies. . . .

Of prime importance, however, was a major survey on building codes undertaken for the Commission by the Census Bureau.[1] The survey results show what codes are being used and where; to what degree local government units had adopted one of the model codes and when it was adopted; *whether and to what degree it had been amended*; whether procedures existed for updating the code; and what specific provisions were in effect in the case of a number of actual materials and practices.

The survey was designed to obtain the facts in an objective, quantitative manner. Past assertions that the codes restricted the use of Romex or plastic pipe, for example, have been denied on the grounds that the national model codes included these items. Because of that, some claimed there were no problems. What are the facts? What is done? What codes are in effect? What are the real practices?

1. Allen D. Manvel, *Local Land and Building Regulation*, National Commission on Urban Problems, Research Report no. 6.

WHAT WAS SURVEYED

The survey of building codes dealt with 17,993 units of local government. Of these, 7,609 were within the standard metropolitan statistical areas of the United States, including 404 counties, 2,228 townships, and 4,977 municipalities. All of the 314 municipalities above 50,000 in population were surveyed. All 404 metropolitan counties were surveyed. Samples of the remaining metropolitan units were taken.

Of the total sample, 10,384 units were outside the standard metropolitan statistical areas. Unlike the units within SMSA's, those with 1,000 persons or less were omitted. The survey dealt with a sample representing 2,645 counties, 2,732 townships, and 5,007 municipalities outside SMSA's.

WHO HAS BUILDING CODES?

Of the almost 18,000 units of government represented in the sample, 46.4 percent, or just under half, had a building code. Almost 54 percent had no such code.

Of the 7,609 units of government within SMSA's, 4,527—59.5 percent—had a building code. More than 40 percent did not.

Of the 10,384 units outside SMSA's, only 3,817—36.8 percent—had a building code.

The breakdown of counties, municipalities, and townships, both within and outside SMSA's, which have a building code is given in Table 30.1.

TABLE 30.1 *Number and Percent of Units of General Government According to Survey Sample Which Have a Building Code*

	Within SMSA's		Outside SMSA's	
	Number	Percent	Number	Percent
Counties	159	39.4	256	9.7
Municipalities	3,434	69.0	3,050*	60.9*
Townships	934	41.9	511*	18.7*

*Units of under 1,000 omitted.

PROLIFERATION OF CODES

The survey obtained extensive details on the practices of municipalities and townships, both within and outside SMSA's, which had a population of 5,000 or more. These are the areas where building codes and the provisions of building codes are most important.

There were 4,067 such units of government. Of these, 80.5 percent (3,273) had a building code. But almost 20 percent did not.

In addition to a building code for construction, many jurisdictions reported both an electrical code and a plumbing code to cover mechanical work. Of these, the National Electrical Code dominated the electrical code field. The survey showed that of the 3,273 governments which had a building construction code, 78.1 percent (2,556 units) had also adopted the National Electrical Code.

The National Plumbing Code has been of primary importance in that field. Recently, however, other plumbing codes, such as the BOCA and the Western Plumbing Codes, have become important because of the failure since 1955 to revise the National Plumbing Code. The survey found that the National Plumbing Code was used by only 43.9 percent (1,438) of the 3,273 units which had adopted a building construction code. This means that many local governments (2,629 or 65 percent of all units) either do not have a plumbing code or use the BOCA, Western, or a plumbing code other than the National Plumbing Code.

When builders and architects complain about the lack of uniformity, the absence of clear standards, or the proliferation of provisions, their complaints are confirmed by the facts above merely concerning the coverage of codes.

One of the frequent complaints heard by the Commission was that local codes actually bore little relationship to the model construction codes on which they were sometimes said to be based. This fact was said to add to the lack of uniformity and the absence of clear standards. The facts gathered by the Census survey for the Commission bore out these complaints.

Of the surveyed government units which were over 5,000 in population, only 1,717 or 52.5 percent of model code governments (42 percent of all units of government) had a building construction code which "substantially incorporated" a national or regional model code. By that is meant that the local building code incorporated the entire model code except for possible departures involving only administrative or enforcement provisions.

Other local codes were merely based on such a code (482 of these governments), *or based on a state model code* (589), *or were not related to any model* (383), *or the relationship was not reported* (105).

FAILURE TO REVISE

Each year the national model code groups meet and consider changes and revisions in their codes. While there are complaints about the procedure, the fact is that the model codes are revised from time to time leading to ultimate acceptance of many—if not the most controversial—new products and methods. Most of the national model codes or their plumbing code or plumbing chapter counterparts actually allow plastic pipe for drain, waste, or vent, wall board, and Romex cable, to name only a few of the more prominent products which building codes are said to exclude.

But a major complaint is that the codes at the local level, even when based on a national model code, do not provide for the use of such products and new procedures. The survey undertaken for this Commission attempted to determine the extent to which local codes are kept up-to-date.

One of the basic problems is that only two-thirds of the building code governments (i.e., only about half of all these governments, including those without codes) either substantially incorporate or base their codes on the model codes to begin with.

But of these, only 1,278, or 58 percent, of the model code governments had procedures for the annual consideration of changes or updating.

Of the model code governments, *only 28 percent had adopted as much as 90 percent of the recommended changes of the model code groups during the previous 3 years.*

Of all the governments which have a building construction code of any kind, 45 percent either had not adopted or comprehensively revised their codes in the previous 4 years.

Thus, while strong arguments are made concerning the quality of the national model construction codes, the facts are that their provisions do not apply without substantial amendment on a widespread basis at the local level.

Based on this survey, the following conclusions can be drawn: *Only about 15 percent of all the municipalities and townships above 5,000 in population had in effect a national model building code which was reasonably up-to-date; about 85 percent of the units had no code, did not use a model code, or had failed to keep the code up-to-date.*

RESTRICTING NEW PRODUCTS AND PRACTICES

The Commission did not limit its survey merely to general questions. It asked about specific products and specific practices. It did this because some materials are reasonable alternatives, serve the same purpose, take less time to install, or provide a means of reducing costs.

The Commission chose 14 specific products or practices where complaints about costs, prevention of preassembly, or excessive requirements are most commonly heard. Most of the practices or products complained against are not prevented by the national model codes. In general, the model codes allow the product or practice. But quite different results were found locally, not only for building code governments in general but also for the model code governments.

Plastic Pipe

Perhaps the most controversial building code issue in recent times has been the use of plastic pipe in drain, vent, and waste systems in one-to two-story housing units. This practice is now allowed, at least technically, by most of the major model building codes or their plumbing code counterparts.

Of all governments which had a building code, 63 percent prohibited the use of plastic pipe in drainage systems. In model code governments, 62 percent prohibited this product. In practice, additional restrictions are placed on the use of plastic pipe through administrative action.

With regard to plastic pipe, it is an understatement to say that there is a vast gulf between the provisions of the national model code or their plumbing code counterparts, on the one hand, and local practice on the other.

Preassembled plumbing and electrical units

Among the more important methods of reducing building costs is the prefabrication or offsite assembly of plumbing or electrical units. This makes the use of mass production and assembly line techniques possible; work can be done more efficiently through specialization and the division of labor; and much of the work is freed from the added costs due to time lost because of inclement weather because it is done indoors.

The survey showed, however, that of the 3,273 governments which *had a building code, 42 percent prohibited offsite preassembled combination drain, waste, and vent plumbing systems for bathroom installation (plumbing trees).*

Preassembled electrical harnesses were entirely prohibited by 46 percent of the governments surveyed.

In other words, in almost half the areas which had a building code, preassembled plumbing and electrical units were completely prohibited. With respect to these items, the builder and the consumer have no freedom of choice.

Two-by-fours in non-load-bearing partitions

Any objective standard or test indicates that the requirement for the use of 2 by 4's every 16 inches in non-load-bearing partitions is an excessive one. They are not required to bear the stress and weight of the building or ceiling. Experts agree that

2 by 3's can be used just as effectively in interior partitions and in non-load-bearing walls, and that 2 by 4's spaced every 24 inches would be just as safe. There seems to be no expert or scientific data to refute these facts. The requirement for 2 by 4's every 16 inches in non-load-bearing walls clearly adds to both material costs and labor costs.

Nevertheless, nearly half (47 percent) of the building code governments surveyed entirely prohibited 2 by 4-inch studs every 24 inches on interior partitions.

Two- by three-inch studs of whatever spacing were entirely *prohibited* on interior or non-load-bearing partitions by 36 percent of the building code governments.

Local acceptance of model code provisions

The problem of local acceptance of the provisions of the national model codes can be further illustrated by an example. One of the four major national building code groups has an eight-member committee which passes on such issues as the use of plastic pipe for inclusion under the provisions of the model code. On the basis of evidence presented to the committee, its members voted unanimously to accept the use of plastic pipe in the drainage systems of nonmultifamily residential construction. They recommended that such use be incorporated locally as a part of the plumbing chapter provisions of their building code.

Even today, however, the use of plastic pipe for this purpose is allowed under the local code in the jurisdiction of only one of the eight members who voted to include or accept it in the national code.

This example highlights how local practice or local amendment to a code takes precedence over the provisions of a national model code even in those jurisdictions where such a model code is adopted as the basis of the local code.

Table 30.2 gives the results of the survey of the 14 specific products or practices.

LACK OF UNIFORMITY

What conditions face the local builder, the industrial prefabricator, the mobile home company, or the architect who wishes to build, sell, or design housing or housing products in the metropolitan areas of the United States? Can he market his preassembled plumbing or electrical unit? Can his new product, approved by a model code group, be used locally? Can he obtain approval from the local building code official to sell his factory-built housing unit? Can the preassembled panels be installed or must they be ripped apart in order that factory-installed electrical wiring can be inspected? What are the facts with respect to both the requirements and the practices under local codes?

Building codes in the big cities

First of all, the central city of a metropolitan area would in most cases have a building code whose provisions were essentially unique to the city involved. This would tend to be true even when that code was originally based on one of the model codes. This is not to say that the code would be either less or more restrictive than codes of other cities. It merely means that in its totality it would be less like a model code. With a more active building department and a wide variety of conditions which create

TABLE 30.2 *Proportions of Local Building Codes That Entirely Prohibit Various Features in Residential Construction: 1968*

(Based on data for municipalities and New England-type townships of 5,000-plus)

Construction Feature Prohibited	Percent of governments with build-Codes*		Percent of building code governments Specifically reporting†	
	All‡	"Model code" governments§	All‡	"Model code" governments§
Plastic pipe in drainage system	62.6	61.7	68.9	67.6
2 in. by 4 in. studs 24 in. on center in non-load-bearing interior partitions	47.3	43.5	50.6	46.1
Preassembled electrical wiring harness at electrical service entrance	45.7	44.8	51.2	49.1
Preassembled combination drain, waste, and vent plumbing system for bathroom installation	42.2	39.6	46.8	43.2
2 in. by 3 in. studs in non-load-bearing interior partitions	35.8	34.7	38.3	36.9
Party walls without continuous air space	26.8	27.4	30.6	30.7
Single top and bottom plates in non-load-bearing interior partitions	24.5	23.5	26.2	24.8
Wood frame exterior for multifamily structures 3 stories or less ‖	24.1	22.0	26.7	23.5
½-in. sheathing in lieu of corner bracing in wood frame construction ¶	20.4	21.1	22.0	22.3
Prefabricated metal chimneys	19.1	16.9	20.5	18.p
Nonmetallic sheathed electric cable	13.0	13.0	14.5	14.4
Wood roof trusses 24 in. on center..........	10.0	10.3	10.7	11.1
Copper pipe in drainage systems	8.6	9.4	9.3	10.0
Bathroom ducts in lieu of operable windows	6.0	5.3	6.4	5.6

*Units so reporting as a percent of all building code governments in each group (including those that did not specifically report yes or no for particular construction features).

†Units so reporting as a percent of those reporting either yes or no (i.e., excluding those not giving this information for particular construction features).

‡These data pertain to the 3,273 municipalities and New England-type townships of 5,000-plus that have building codes.

§These data pertain to the 2,199 units (of the 3,273 total) that have building codes reportedly based primarily upon 1 of the 4 national or regional model codes).

‖ Calculation excludes governments that entirely prohibit frame residential construction (77 altogether, including 59 "model code" governments).

¶ Plywood or fiberboard.

SOURCE: "Local Land and Building Regulation," by Allen D. Manvel, Commission Research Report No. 6.

problems and issues to be acted on, the larger city has both the staff and the opportunity to judge, change, and amend its code. In some smaller communities, on the other hand, a code may stay essentially unchanged for years, except for a few items where strong economic interest groups have a stake.

The Commission collected detailed data for the 52 largest cities through a special tabulation in its census survey. Each of the 52 had a population of over 250,000 in 1960. Only four of the 52 did not provide detailed reports. For many key items, the gaps in information were filled from other sources. . . .

These cities had 40 million inhabitants in 1960, or more than 20 percent of the total population. They contained more than one-third of the population of all the governments in the country which had planning, zoning, or building regulation activities. They accounted for about one-third of all the funds spent for such activities. The findings are, therfore, of considerable importance.

From the survey it was possible to determine the relationship of the local building code to the various model codes. The results were as follows:

Substantially incorporating 1 of the 4 national or regional model codes 14
Based upon such a code but with some substantive departures 20
Based upon a state-recommended model code 1
None of the foregoing 13

A closer look, however, indicates that the codes may be more unique than this would indicate. For example, of the 34 major cities whose building codes are said to be related explicitly to a national or regional model code, only 25 report "an established procedure for local consideration, at least annually, of changes proposed by the pertinent national or regional code organization." However, only 9 of these indicate that official action during the past 3 years has led to local acceptance of 90 percent or more of the changes proposed by the model code organization, and for 7 cities the estimated proportion of local acceptance was less than 50 percent.

Thus, only 9 of 48 governments, or 19 percent, had a building code which either substantially incorporated the model code or was based upon such a code but with more substantive departures, and which had incorporated as many as 90 percent of the recent model code changes. Furthermore, the 20 cities where the code was merely based on a model code but with substantive departures from the model code further reduce the degree to which uniformity with model code provisions would exist.

At least 43 of these major cities have reportedly adopted the National Electric Code, but the corresponding minimum number that have enacted the National Plumbing Code is only 16.

Expenditure. Of the $97.5 million that these major cities expended in fiscal 1967 for planning, zoning, and building regulation activities, more than three-fourths ($77.5 million) was directly for the administration of codes, including inspection work. This figure includes expenditures for both building code and housing code activities.

Residential construction regulations. The building codes of the largest cities typically reflect somewhat less rejection of the specific residential construction practices listed in the survey inquiry than was found for building-code governments generally. Substantially complete reports on this subject are available for 48 of the 52 cities. These show a numerically smaller fraction of them prohibiting seven construction features, as follows (with the percentages for all building-code governments shown parenthetically, for comparison):

29 percent (versus 47.3 percent) for 2-by 4-inch studs 24 inches on center in non-load-bearing interior partitions;

27 percent (versus 42.2 percent) for preassembled combination drain, waste, and vent plumbing system for bathroom installation;

21 percent (versus 35.8 percent) for 2- by 3-inch studs in non-load-bearing interior partitions;

19 percent (versus 26.8 percent) for party walls without continuous air space;

13 percent (versus 24.5 percent) for single top and bottom plates in non-load-bearing interior partitions;

13 percent (versus 20.4 percent) for use of one-half inch sheathing in lieu of corner bracing in wood frame construction; and

6 percent (versus 19.1 percent) for prefabricated metal chimneys.

On the other hand, these 48 of the 52 largest cities show an even higher proportion of rejection for several items, including these:

73 percent (versus 62.6 percent) for plastic pipe in drainage systems;

44 percent (versus 24.1 percent) for wood frame exterior walls in multifamily structures of three stories or less;

21 percent (versus 13.0 percent) for nonmetallic sheathed electric cable; and

13 percent (versus 8.6 percent) for copper pipe in drainage systems.

For the other three construction-practice items, the large city percentages of rejection were generally similar to overall averages. These included "preassembled electrical wiring harness," outlawed by building codes in 40 percent of the reporting large cities as against 45.7 percent of building-code governments as a whole.

Codes in the suburbs

In the various towns and suburbs outside the central city, the builder faces a variety of conditions. Some towns have a model code on their books. In a few towns or cities it might even have been adopted without amendment and be reasonably up-to-date. In most towns or cities with a model code, it would contain amendments or restrictions and would be out-of-date. In the major metropolitan areas of the country, different towns would have different model codes, both with and without amendments.

Furthermore, some towns would have no code at all, or their own code, or a code based on a state code. In some places a combination of a model building code and the National Plumbing Code would be in effect. In other places, both the model building code and model plumbing code would apply.

In some large metropolitan areas where no one national model code is dominant but where the model code areas overlap, the number of combinations and permutations could number in the thousands.

Chaotic conditions. This chaotic condition prevents the effective application of modern mass production methods and the adoption of new products and techniques. It is localism, provincialism, and so-called home rule gone wild.

The authority under which a local government formulates and administers building codes is the police power of the state—that is, the power of a sovereign government in a federal union to legislate for the public health, safety, morals, and general welfare. Under the Constitution of the United States, the police power resides in the states; and though it is permissible for the states to delegate various police power functions to localities, the localities exercise those functions as agents of the state and not by virtue of any inherent powers of their own.

The localities therefore have no constitutional or inherent right to inflict these chaotic conditions on the public, as some apologists for the building code mess assert. What police powers the state delegates to the locality to exercise, the states can properly withdraw. The situation has no constitutional sanction nor was it ordained in heaven.

Local interpretation. Even where a model code has been adopted over a relatively large number of jurisdictions or relatively wide area with no or few amendments, local inspectors often interpret the code in a way which differs from the language and often even more from the interpretations of inspectors in the neighboring city or suburb.

One builder at the Commission's St. Louis hearing gave a list of varying local interpretations, building code amendments, and regulation in the 95 jurisdictions in the St. Louis area which he said could add as much as $1,000 to the cost of building a home there.

At the St. Louis hearing, the following questions were asked of a builder witness:

Q. If you built a standard house, say a $22,000 house, in each of the 95 jurisdictions, with a standard set of plans, in how many communities could you build that house without having to make some basic change in it or some costly change in it due to the building codes? Could you build the same house in each of the 95 communities in this county, or would you have to go to a building code inspector in each of them and get approval and have changes made? What is the kind of situation you would face in trying to build the same house in each of these 95 communities?

A. One, you definitely would have to submit it on an individual basis to each one of these municipalities and, two, I would say that in the majority of them you would have to make some changes, very few real changes, but some change that would increase your costs.

Specialization and mass production, and the savings which accompany them, depend on the extent of the market. Building codes as now administered and applied hinder specialization, the use of modern technology and mass production methods in the housing industry. They limit the application of new materials and methods even in a metropolitan area, let alone over a state or geographic region or throughout the United States. . . .

A CASE HISTORY: BUILDING CODE PROBLEMS OF HOME MANUFACTURERS

To determine the impact of local building codes on home construction, the Commission undertook a detailed study of code problems confronting home manufacturers producing "prefabricated houses." Their operations were selected for study because they are concerned with the distribution of a product that is more or less uniform and must be approved by building officials within relatively large regions. Their market area may contain hundreds of governmental jurisdictions, each with its own codes and administrative agencies. In contrast, the average conventional builder usually operates in a limited local market, constructing homes of varying style and construction and conforming to only a handful of different building codes and local administrative agencies.

The Commission secured the cooperation of the Home Manufacturers Association, which agreed to assemble the necessary information on local problems. An advisory committee to the Commission was established and a survey was made of all firms engaged in prefabrication. A large body of data was assembled, identifying the specific code problems and the added costs resulting from local building regulations.

The study produced findings in the following three categories:

1. An extensive list was assembled indicating specific local code requirements which exceeded those in national model codes and the FHA minimum property standards. The extra costs per house attributed to *each* of these items ranged from $25 to $640. The list, assembled from 126 reports submitted by 20 home manufacturers, cites code requirements of 32 counties and 109 cities and towns in 20 States.

2. Based on the total list (reported only by those home manufacturers participating in the study), the home manufacturers' advisory committee prepared a list of excessive code requirements most frequently encountered by home manufacturers, as shown in Table 30.3. If a manufacturer were forced to incorporate every item in his product, there would be "extra costs" of $1,838 per house *if* he marketed in 20 States. The home used for estimating costs was assumed to be a 1,000-square-foot family unit that would cost $12,000 without improved lot, under model code or FHA requirements.

TABLE 30.3 *More Frequent Code Requirements in Excess of Model Codes or FHA Minimum Property Standards*

	Extra Cost Added
Foundation footings to clay, when piers and grade beam would do as well ...	$150.00
Special bolts	15.00
Unnecessary bridging and ties	76.00
Extra number and sizing of joints above FHA requirements	63.00
Conventional floor rather than stress skin floor	40.00
Extra thickness of subfloor	30.00
Extra sheathing above FHA requirements	125.00
Extra studs above FHA requirements	30.00
Extra window and door headers above FHA requirements	20.00
Extra thickness of gypsum board	22.00
Plaster instead of gypsum board	200.00
Extra fire wall requirements in frame construction above model codes	50.00
Extra roof sheathing ($25-$50)	37.50
Extra roof trusses ($25-$50)	37.50
Requirement of a masonry chimney when a Class B flue would do a better job	150.00
Special fire protection in furnace room not needed when approved heating for zero clearance is used	100.00
Extra plumbing above first floor over National Plumbing Code ($135-$250) ..	192.00
Extra plumbing below first floor over National Plumbing Code	100.00
Extra electric over National when no conduit	50.00
Extra electric over National when rigid conduit required	300.00
Extra heating duct requirements (return metal plenum over gypsum) and insulation beyond 6 feet from hot air plenum	50.00
Total...............	1,838.00

3. The most significant information was revealed in an analysis of the problems of one manufacturer who must adjust his product to all codes in the region within which he operates.

The Commission staff analyzed the reports submitted by that manufacturer relating to code requirements of 19 counties and six cities included in the six states of Georgia, Maryland, Kentucky, North Carolina, Virginia, and Ohio, within which the manufacturer conducted his business. Within a relatively small market area of 25 code jurisdictions, cited by the manufacturer, there are reported 75 *different* code requirements considered to be excessive. The reported excessive code items for each one of the

25 individual code jurisdictions ranged in number from 1 to 13, with extra costs ranging from $50 to $520 per house within each jurisdiction.

If the single manufacturer attempted to produce a standard product which would meet the code requirements of the 25 areas, he would have to introduce 75 separate extra factors in materials and/or methods of construction exceeding the normal requirements in model codes and FHA regulations. The cost of each basic home would thus be raised by $2,492.

TECHNICAL STANDARDS AND NEW PRODUCT REVIEW

Technical standards in building codes originate in the mainstream of the building industry. One of the key problems is the segmented nature of that part of the building industry which generates and maintains standards. There are more than 150 associations and technical groups producing standards to which the building industry is asked to conform. Some of these groups are affiliated with industrywide organizations such as the American Society for Testing and Materials and the United States of America Standards Institute. Others carry on work associated with the operations of the National Bureau of Standards. In the latter instance, the technical groups may not actively participate in the technical activities of ASTM or USASI.

Interlocking of standards and product approval

It is significant that half of these standards-generating groups carry on some type of product approval or certification program. Among them are private agencies, such as Underwriters Laboratories, which test products, inspect factories, and grant manufacturers the right to apply their label or seal on approved products. They also publish lists of materials and equipment which meet their standards. Included in this group are organizations which provide inspectional and grading services, such as the West Coast Lumber Inspection Bureau.

Very few of the standards-generating groups are in the business of stimulating the development of technological innovations. Their primary activities are concerned with reacting to the work of others. Yet, it is inevitable that the innovators must sooner or later obtain the approval of these technical groups before their products are accepted for building construction.

The promulgation of product standards by the building industry, for its own use and guidance, is closely intertwined with the development of building code standards. There is an interlocking of procedures and decisions, involving representatives of industry and government and affecting product and building code standards. The resulting interaction makes it difficult to delineate independent courses of judgment and action. These conditions have been caused by the ever-growing complexity of technology and the structure of the industry. The nature of building construction dictated the establishment of some type of framework that could guide the development, review, and acceptance of new methods and materials. A system was required to serve manufacturers, designers, and builders, who must deal with thousands of disparate building products, to enable them to fit the pieces together in structurally sound, weathertight buildings with effective supply and disposal systems. Through trial and error, various institutions were developed by different sections of the industry, with government participation at times. Procedures evolved to guide and control the development and acceptance of innovations in construction.

The framework that goverment and industry have developed has proved inadequate for coping with the increasing demands for expeditious processing and acceptance of technological innovations. The ever-growing complexity of building technology and the increasing need to adopt new methods and materials of construction make it necessary to seek a more rational system than the current arrangement.

Hurdles for new products

By examining the process by which new products are now developed, reviewed, and accepted by industry and government, it is possible to appraise not only the current product approval system but also the role of building codes. The following is a brief outline of the steps that currently must be taken to secure acceptance of a new product, assuming that it can meet existing standards.

1. The manufacturer undertakes a program of research and development of a new product, intended to meet specific needs and performance requirements that have been established by experts in that particular field. Reviewing this phase, his engineers will consult all available technical literature describing the requirements, standards and conditions which may affect the proposed product, as well as reports on similar products.

2. The product is tested by a recognized testing laboratory with established test methods and measurement tools to determine whether it meets specific performance criteria. The criteria and standards are established by recognized industrywide technical groups and organizations of building officials.

3. The product specifications and test data are reviewed and approved by a national trade association, or technical group, or building officials' organization, or technical institution, or certification laboratory.

4. Local building officials are requested to review and accept the new product under building code procedures.

5. An educational program is undertaken by the manufacturer to acquaint the design professions, builders, and officials with the value of the new product.

Weaknesses in present procedures

There are very serious weaknesses in the current framework for carrying out the above activities. The following is a brief critical review of the process, listing the more conspicuous inconsistencies between theory and practice for each item in the above outline.

1. (*a*) There is no single point of reference to assist designers and manufacturers in determining whether technical papers have been published in a particular subject area. (*b*) There is no single point of reference to acquaint manufacturers, institutions, investors, and professionals with research projects undertaken by others—and their results. (*c*) To a large extent, performance requirements based upon user needs, which could guide innovations in the building industry, are absent and await development.

2. (*a*) There is no single set of nationally accepted criteria for testing building materials and methods. (*b*) Testing laboratories do not conform to a single set of nationally accepted procedures. (*c*) Test methods in key areas of inquiry, such as accelerated aging, await further development.

3. (*a*) There is no single institution or national system to which members of the building industry could apply for review and acceptance of new methods and materials. (*b*) There are over 80 different associations, institutions, technical groups, and laboratories that now establish standards, inspect, certify, grade, or issue seals of approval for proprietary materials and equipment.

4. *(a)* As a general rule, local building officials lack the appropriate facilities and technical personnel to judge the merits of new products or methods. *(b)* Manufacturers must apply separately to hundreds communities for product acceptance because approval in one area is no guarantee that others will follow suit.

5. *(a)* Educational programs by producers require large expenditures which increase the cost of the product. Innovators and small manufacturers cannot afford the required expenditures during the initial high-risk period for product promotion, after underwriting high costs for research, development, testing, and review by national product reviewing groups. *(b)* There is no single source to which designers, builders, and material suppliers could refer to learn about the development of new products.

The big hurdle–local building codes

Short of contending with competing forces in the marketplace, the greatest hurdle to overcome in the product approval process is the local building code. This is more difficult because code standards are neither uniform nor clearly defined. This phase is usually singled out for discussion by dissatisfied members of the building industry because it contains the most conspicuous barriers and applies to every innovative producer. The other phases are voluntary in nature and often provide alternative routes for approval.

The acceptance of new methods or materials depends primarily upon the judgment of local building officials. Except in those rare instances when standards are defined in performance terms, approval is usually based upon opinion and not upon accepted technical criteria. Control over new materials and methods of construction in a building code is usually defined in language similar to the following (italics added for emphasis).

> Nothing in this code shall be construed to prevent the use of any material or method of construction whether or not specifically provided for in this code *if*, upon presentation of plans, methods of analysis, test data, or other necessary information to the building official by the interested person or persons, *the building official is satisfied that the proposed material or method of construction* complies with specific provisions of or *conforms to the intent of this code.*
>
>   . . . Where no appropriate test method is prescribed in this code, *the test procedure shall be determined by the building official.* (Sections 100.7 and 101.2, National Building Code, American Insurance Association.)

Many building officials try conscientiously to protect the public's best interests. But a community cannot expect its public servants to be fully conversant with all developments in this era of revolutionary technological advances. The rapid growth of specialization in engineering and architecture reflects the inability of the average professional to keep up with all changes.

Except for those rare instances in which the official has special training or experience, he must either seek the assistance of more knowledgeable experts or base his judgment of a new product's merits on his own attitudes. The objective local official who recognizes the shortcomings of inadequate technical staff and facilities will seek the advice of technicians who operate at regional and national levels. But this is not the typical case. One of the serious weaknesses in the present framework is the lack of a single mechanism to which code officials, builders, and professionals can refer such problems and from which manufacturers and material suppliers can obtain universally accepted judgments.

SUMMARY OF THE PROBLEMS

Local level

What is needed at the local level is a system which provides for the following.

1. The uniform application of up-to-date building and mechanical codes over an area large enough to allow mass production methods and specialization. At the minimum such an area should cover any of the major metropolitan areas of the United States such as Greater New York, including the contiguous areas of New Jersey and Connecticut; Chicago and its adjoining counties, including Lake County, Indiana; Greater Los Angeles, including Orange County; St. Louis and the East St. Louis and Madison-St. Clair County industrial complex, and similar areas throughout the country.

2. Minimum standards below which no community might fall and maximum limits in order to prevent restrictive practices. Then the mobile home industry, the prefabricated housing industry, the manufacturers of preassembled plumbing and electrical units, and the producers of new products could be guaranteed an opportunity to build and sell on a competitive price-cost basis provided only that their product or method met minimum standards of performance or specifications established by competent and reliable testing groups through the application of objective standards.

3. An appeals procedure whereby any arbitrary decisions of a local inspector could be appealed quickly, and without prejudice to the builder or manufacturer, to a body composed of both competent technical personnel and individuals representing the broad public interest.

State level

The role of the states in these matters is first of all to exercise their police power in useful and constructive ways or to see to it that those to whom they have delegated such authority exercise it properly.

The states should also provide for the uniform application of an up-to-date building and mechanical code over the state as a whole, to apply in those areas where no local code has been adopted or where a community or region fails to adopt uniform code practices and insists on keeping restrictive practices.

The states have a role to play in licensing and training personnel in order to bring about uniformity in applying code provisions and standards.

Finally, the states should provide an appeals procedure, not dominated by either a single person, or the industry, or groups and narrow factions within the industry.

National level

At the national level the major problems are of a somewhat different order. The contents of the four national model building codes—BOCA, ICBO, Southern, and National—are more up-to-date and progressive than is generally assumed. Most of the controversial materials and methods of production are now included under their provisions.

This is not to say that there are no serious defects in model codes. The system for adopting new products and methods has shortcomings. For example, the Southern Standard Building Code turned down plastic pipe as late as 1966 without giving any reason, and its inclusion in that code under two recent modifications is under legal attack which has delayed acceptance. One may raise the question of why a letter ballot should be used by a trade association of building officials to determine approval of a product.

The system is often far too slow. A product which is accepted by one code group is often not accepted by another until a producer has complied with a second or third set of procedures.

Another very proper complaint is that decisions are made by the building code officials and not by a more representative group of the industry, let alone of the general public.

Furthermore, there are no uniform objective standards or tests, or groups of certified agencies for testing, which would make the acceptance of a product or method a question of objective analysis.

Nonetheless, the contents of the national model construction codes have at times received more criticism than they deserve, and sometimes the criticism has been unfounded and misinformed. If these codes could be applied over wide geographic areas without amendment, the present chaotic situation would be remarkably improved.

While there are many problems, most of the basic ones do not now lie with the provisions of the model construction codes as such. Similar generalizations can be made about the National Electrical Code.

But the same cannot be said for the National Plumbing Code which has not been updated since 1955. The slowness in the amending procedure, brought about in part by the conflicts between competing economic interest groups, has led to a proliferation of plumbing codes so that BOCA now has its own plumbing code and the Western Plumbing Code is used in many areas where the ICBO code is in general use.

What is needed, therefore, at the national level, is a system whereby standards of performance based upon the most objective and scientific methods are set by bodies with the highest reputation and prestige. These bodies should represent not only the industry but the general public. The purpose is to make it possible for a producer of a new product or the innovator of a new method or system to have objective standards against which to test his product and to get speedy action.

The system should also provide for a means of certification so that private builders, government officials, and building code groups and experts would have an unimpeachable scientific basis on which to make judgments about products and methods. The assurance by such an objective group that basic performance standards were met should lead to the almost immediate and universal acceptance of a new product or method, both in the building codes themselves and by building officials at the Federal, state, and local levels.

With regard to the federal government, it is estimated that at least 35 different agencies are directly or indirectly concerned with construction. The standards which they insist upon differ from agency to agency and from department to department. The chaos which exists between and among federal government groups mirrors the greater problem of building codes in the nation. But it ill-behooves the federal government and federal agencies to preach to states, localities, and model code groups until they move to put their own house in order.

CONCLUSION

In brief, the facts disclosed by the exhaustive inquiries of this Commission at local, state, and national levels, and the problems faced by producers, builders, and professional people in the building industry, show unmistakably that alarms sounded over the past years about the building code situation have been justified. If anything, the case has been understated. The situation calls for a drastic overhaul, both technically and intergovernmentally. . . .

31. *Restrictive Union Practices*

NATIONAL COMMISSION ON URBAN PROBLEMS

What part do building practices play in slowing progress in home construction? As a result of such practices, are Americans denied cheaper, better housing?

Because of the Commission's central concern with generating a vastly increased supply of decent housing at the lowest possible cost, this issue had to be faced squarely. Probably no other single issue confronted the Commission with greater complications. . . . Apart from the emotional setting which frequently clouds labor questions, the analysis of this subject had to surmount such difficulties as the following.

Apparent restrictive building practices often result not only from the efforts and interests of unions but from those of contractors and producers as well.

Assertions that unions typically raise costs unnecessarily are made so often and so forcefully that the public tends to take claims as facts, although numerous claims are not borne out on closer scrutiny.

Generally, both union leaders and builders are unwilling to discuss restrictive practices publicly, even in response to charges of specific restrictions.

Even those with intimate knowledge of working conditions often find it difficult to distinguish between restrictive practices and legitimate safety or job security requirements.

The fragmentation of the building industry into many craft unions and the multitude of local and regional trade agreements make generalizations hazardous.

The Commission made an extensive effort to surmount these various difficulties and to gather and assess the facts. We believe we took neither a prolabor nor antilabor, proindustry nor antiindustry posture in this work, but rather a propublic posture—a position intended to open to consumers the fullest benefits of housing technology consistent with the legitimate interest of the main participants in the productive process. Several general findings and conclusions lend perspective to the more detailed discussion that follows.

1. Unions have been active partners in a number of breakthroughs involving new products and methods. The circumstances under which labor is more likely to cooperate than to react defensively in the face of innovation need to be more widely understood.

2. Many restrictive practices do exist. They vary greatly from place to place. Beneath these variations from place to place and from trade to trade are certain practices that, in their totality, retard the adoption of new materials and improved systems of handling old materials, thereby adding to housing costs.

3. Too microscopic a view of restrictive practices draws a curtain over the larger problem: the need for a much higher rate of home construction along with continuity of work for the labor force throughout all seasons. Many of the onerous practices that seem insoluble in the framework of widely fluctuating employment and construction patterns could more readily be resolved if the construction industry were expanded and stabilized.

Reprinted from National Commission on Urban Problems, *Building The American City* (Washington, D.C.: Government Printing Office, 1968), pt. III, chap. 4 (edited).

SEARCHING FOR THE FACTS

Public hearings, private interviews, staff research, university surveys, and research and studies by outside consultants were among the means used by the Commission to throw light on the state of local building practices. . . .

. . . [U]nlike the situation in many industries where the management or corporate concentration of power is as great or greater than that of the unions with which they deal, the home construction industry is characterized by enterprises that, in the major cities, have less power than the building trade unions. Elsewhere, homebuilding labor tends to be unorganized and hence the upper hand most often lies with the builder, despite the fragmentation of the industry. . . .

PROGRESSIVE ACTION

Any overall view of the housing industry today must take note of many technological changes. Some changes have been adopted almost universally. Many others are used only by the pathfinders of the industry. But the fact that these products and processes are in evidence, and that the craftsmen doing the work are typically members of building trade unions, refutes some of the oft-quoted charges that unions oppose and prevent all progress.

This is not to make any special case for the virtues of labor which, like almost all other elements in our economy, is motivated in part by self-interest. But technological progress often is in the self-interest of a union group. A craft, in these times of industrial change, can be priced out of the market if it too stubbornly resists change. The competition between products and between different craft unions often is the spur to progress.

In recent decades, the most dramatic change has been the acceptance in the homebuilding process of many more prefabricated components, reducing time-consuming and costly on-site production.

From California to New York, the Commission also heard builders and designers of whole new building concepts praise the labor unions for giving invaluable help in seeing these projects through to successful completion. These included instances of revolutionary approaches to the whole building, and of massive rehabilitation efforts.

In these instances, the trade union leaders were brought into the projects at the outset. Potential jurisdictional disputes and other difficulties were avoided by anticipating likely trouble spots and by ironing them out in advance. New methods and materials were not suddenly set before workers without warning, in a way that would arouse their fears of abandoning established patterns, or the greater fears of losing their livelihoods. In short, both the union leadership and rank-and-file workers felt that they were participants in a worthwhile experiment. Their ideas and enthusiasm were capitalized on by assuring at the outset that their vital interests also would be respected.

These instances, however, are far from universal. They show what can be accomplished. They reveal the potential for progress. But to take heart from the silver lining is not to deny that many restrictive practices still remain very much a part of the current scene.

NARROWING DOWN THE CATALOG OF COMPLAINTS

In canvassing the building industry for complaints, the Commission wanted to obtain those which were unique to the industry.

In the wide-ranging catalog of complaints received, one of the first jobs was to eliminate those which the Commission, in consultation with labor-management specialists, believed to be encountered generally in many industries and not unique to homebuilding. More importantly, these are the complaints which experts believe can best be resolved through normal collective-bargaining arrangements. In any event, because these are such common complaints, they are receiving widespread attention in the labor-management field. These include questions about responsibilities of shop stewards, hiring halls, coffee breaks, lunch periods, seniority, wages and hours, grievance procedures, cleanup, travel time, maintenance allowances, and tools and storage.

The Commission, let it be emphasized, neither discounts the importance of such questions nor passes on the validity of the charges and countercharges it heard about them. But the Commission decided that its limited time could be put to best use by concentrating on complaints directly related to advances in building technology and costs.

OFFENDING PRACTICES

The work rules practiced at the local level and incorporated in agreements between management and labor that impede the use of technological innovations appear to fall chiefly into the following categories: on site rules, requiring certain work to be done on the premises and prohibiting or limiting the use of prefabricated products; restrictions against the use of certain tools and devices; requirements for excessive manpower on the job, including what appear to be irrational limits on the variety of work certain categories of workers may perform.

While there are honest differences of opinion about the seriousness or cost impact of any specific example of such practices on any particular construction project, the existence of them in many forms and variations is beyond question. They are imbedded in custom and contract. It strains belief to think that the totality of these practices would not increase the cost, impair the quality, or decrease the supply of housing.

However, the conclusion that these practices are completely without justification, or that they can be remedied in some simple fashion, is not supported by the facts. Even the abbreviated examples of charges and response below give an inkling of the complexities involved.

What one man sees as a wasteful procedure or use of manpower, for example, may turn out to be a genuine, necessary safety feature in the light of experience. *We do not recognize as restrictive practices work rules designed to protect men from undue hazard* in an industry which is risky at best. But this may be abused. Everything called a safety rule is not necessarily that.

To cite restrictions in a few places does not automatically mean they exist uniformly. The trade unions, like their employers, are still very fragmented. They possess a good deal of local autonomy. Unusual patterns develop from region to region.

The Commission attempted to collect instances of restrictive practices in a responsible way, insisting on substantiation with specific details rather than accepting broad, generalized attacks. Yet it seems evident that antipathy toward trade unions in general was reflected in some of the charges received.

Many practices incorporated in work rules may be more the responsibility of the employers than of the unions who negotiated the agreement. In the bargaining process, the union may be seeking x dollars an hour. The contractors may succeed in getting the union to accept 20 cents an hour less, for instance, by offering the union one or more of the work rules that, from a public perspective, appear restrictive. And the benefit, as well as the responsibility, may be greater for the employer.

In other instances, dealt with in great detail elsewhere,* restrictive practices embedded in building codes may be and often are largely the result of the influence of interested manufacturers. Sometimes the contractors, too, lend their support to these restrictions. And at times the manufacturers, contractors, and labor are all working in harmony in behalf of these restrictions.

Many of the charges and countercharges examined by the Commission concern big construction, not the typical small home. Furthermore, a large portion of the homebuilders employ nonunion workers. These facts are noted as a further complexity in understanding how these matters relate to housing. Big-city construction projects, particularly high-rise buildings, are typically union. Nonunion labor in a metropolitan area often receives the pay and abides by many of the work rules that apply to unionized labor in the same area. Some homebuilders who employ both union and nonunion labor testified that the major difference is that the former tend to be more efficient.

A final note before looking at a sampling of alleged restrictions is that the construction industry is vastly different from the average industry. The differences will be examined later in an attempt to explain why restrictive practices persist.

On-site production versus prefabrication

Contractors contend that various craft unions require work to be done on the site when factory-cut or assembled products would be both better and cheaper. It is further claimed that such rules in the long run tend to stifle the development of new construction techniques.

Charge 1. Plumbers allow only stock items to be brought to the site. They further limit the size of pipes permitted to be prefabricated. When it is not practical to do the cutting on the job, permission must be obtained from the union to use prefabricated pipe.

Item. The following language is extracted from a plumbing agreement.

Pipe 2 inches and under shall be fabricated on the job by plumber mechanics to whom the work belongs. In cases where it is not practical to cut pipe on the job, it shall be discretionary with the employer to have pipe 2 inches and under fabricated elsewhere; provided, however, that permission is obtained by the employer from the business manager of the local union.

Charge 2. Builders and contractors contend that carpenters prevent the use of precut cabinets, hung doors, doors cut for hardware, moldings, etc.

Item. The Supreme Court case concerning prehung doors (discussed later) substantiated some of these practices beyond any doubt.

Response. The United Brotherhood of Carpenters & Joiners of America did not deny the specific charges but justified them in four words, "Work preservation. Gross exaggeration." But the union discussed the general charge as follows:

Comments made to this item are basically too generalized, lacking both premise and conclusion in order to adequately reply to. Therefore, any statements will be in a generalized nature. It is true that there are certain provisions within collective

*Editors' note: See the article on building codes, Chap. 30 in this book.

agreements which restrict the use of certain machines and devices, but the instances revealed within the text are completely false. The United Brotherhood of Carpenters & Joiners of America does not restrict or prohibit the use of manufactured or milled cabinets. The fact of the matter is, the united brotherhood has within its membership several hundred thousand members who are employed in large and small industrial plants who earn their livelihood from such manufactured goods, so it would hardly be realistic or practicable to prohibit such products and highly discriminating to a large segment of this organization's membership. The united brotherhood has traditionally advocated that such products be manufactured under reasonable standards and working conditions. This policy, however, has never restricted the use of manufactured products. It merely encourages employers to deal with fair manufacturers. Such activity has contributed greatly to the economic standards enjoyed in this country. True, there are restrictions over the use of certain devices: however, such prohibitions or restrictions generally fall in the form of safety or work preservation insurances. Each of these matters have been or are to be discussed in their appropriate subject matter in detail. Certainly the Commission has no intentions of diluting time-honored safety standards nor does it wish to come in conflict with the United States Supreme Court concerning "the work preservation concept." The implications of both these factors are far reaching and are entitled to a broader view of discussion than to be submerged within the extension of these discussions.

Charge 3. Ironworkers in several localities were said to require *(a)* the on-site bending of reinforcing rods. In addition, the union itself recognized charges in many localities by contractors that *(b)* the welding of studs as shear connectors on the top surface of beams must be performed in the field.

Item. In Commission sessions builders have cited specific examples from New York City that rods must be bent on-site.

Response. The International Association of Bridge, Structural & Ornamental Iron Workers noted in regard to *(a)* the bending of rods, "there are one or two minor restrictions on this." But the union insisted: "The general rule is that whatever work can be fabricated in the shop and by practical work operations moved to the field, such materials are accepted and handled. . . . The total tonnage of reinforcing installed in the United States would be under conditions that 99-plus percent of all reinforcing would be shop bent. Secondly, there has been a new technological development (and) within the very near future, the bending of reinforcing rods will be a thing of the past." In regard to *(b)*, the studs, the union said, "When these studs are installed in the shop, it is extremely dangerous to walk on the top surface of the beam since the studs catch the cuff of the ironworkers' overalls, and many injuries and deaths have resulted." The union said many states are adopting safety laws supporting the union position of on-site welding.

Charge 4. A number of allegations pointed to instances in which prefabricated products are accepted by the unions, but accepted in connection with two practices which negate the cost savings: *(a)* the unions disassemble the prefabricated materials on the site and put them together again; and *(b)* the unions handle the materials but charge a premium rate for so doing.

Item. Electricians were said to rewire certain fixtures on the site, but specific citations were not received about this. This is a matter that would be the responsibility of the electrical subcontractor rather than the general contractors who furnished most of the evidence gathered.

Response. We received the following reply from the president of the International Brotherhood of Electrical Workers. . . .

I am sure that members of your Commission have sufficient knowledge and background in the construction industry to realize that it is a natural reaction of any construction worker to be resentful upon seeing work, which he has traditionally done at the jobsite, gradually being fragmented and diminished through new methods, changing technology and prefabrication offsite. Since a typical construction worker has in all probability completed at least a 4-year apprenticeship training course, devoted his life to his trade and has relied on said trade to provide a livelihood to his family and permit him to be a good citizen, he instinctively takes a defensive attitude either individually or insists that his bargaining representative do so on his behalf. This type of reaction resulted in such extremes as civil cases up to and including Supreme Court action.

Devices and tools not allowed

Many unions are alleged to prohibit the use of specific devices, tools, or equipment on the job.

Charge 1. One of the oldest and most persistent charges is that painters often limit the width of brushes or, in the case of rollers, the width of rollers and the length of handles.

Item. The following language is taken from a Baton Rouge contract:

Brushes not over 4½ inches will be used when painting structural steel. Brushes over 5 inches shall be used in water emulsion paints only.

Also, interview testimony pointed to instances where rollers over nine inches and with handles six feet or over were prohibited.

Further prohibitions cited in the case of painters included the use of sprays for floors, doors, offices, cafeterias, dispensaries, and recreation places.

Response. The painters replied as follows.

Attention is hereby called to article 17 of Painters District Council No. 22's labor agreement, wherein it will be noted that spray painting is performed on an extensive basis on both old construction as well as new construction.

Topeka, Kans., was referred to as having restrictions on the use of devices, and in this connection, article IV, section 4 of the labor agreement for Painters Local Union No. 96 of Topeka, Kans., clearly sets forth the procedure for performing spray painting, and, as will be noted, a joint trade board for both contractors and union members issues the decision for the use of paint sprays governed by the health and safety considerations that must accompany the proper and safe use of paint sprays. The last paragraph of article IV, section 4, clearly sets forth certain materials which may be sprayed without obtaining a permit.

The Brotherhood of Painters, Decorators & Paperhangers replied as follows to the

. . . reference of "brushes not over 4¼ inches will be used when painting structural steel," said provision appearing in the collective bargaining agreement of Painters Local Union 728 of Baton Rouge, La. While painting erected structural steel, bridges, and towers the use of a 4½-inch paint brush is the very maximum of brush size which could be used with any degree of safety. Anyone who possesses any conviction to the contrary is simply not informed as to the hazards in the performance of such work. Across the land painters are required to paint steel buildings, and, in some cases over a hundred stories in height, some towers over 600 feet in height, and a more hazardous work assignment does not exist in this Nation than that which is involved in the painting and repainting of bridge structures. In addition to complying with State and local safety codes, plus the safety measures taken by the local unions of the brotherhood, a quick look at the hazards involved in this work will reveal that the very highest casualty and fatality rate within the overall construction industry prevails in connection with steel painting, which is, by the way, made even more hazardous by weather conditions, especially moisture and frigidity. Steel painters are required to serve a 3-year apprenticeship, and, while so doing, they are quite naturally taught to employ the use of the proper tools. This fact is recognized by the management and always this fact is reflected by the collective bargaining agreements. If one would make a realistic survey of this matter, they would be early to learn that a steel painter actually performs more work and a better quality of work by using a paint brush not more than 4 or 4½ inches in width. The civil engineers and inspectors responsible for the proper coating and painting of steel structures would be quick to prevent the use of paint brushes too large to perform the application, and if such practice were employed, the steel would not be properly protected.

They also replied to the allegation that:

. . . "interviewed testimony pointing to instances where rollers over 9 inches and with handles over 6 feet were prohibited." Such testimony was surely not taken from anyone familiar with the use of paint rollers. No mechanic could efficiently produce quality finishes using paint rollers wider than 9 inches.

Anyone attempting to use a wider paint roller would practice false economy. The labor and time necessary for cleanup would far exceed any advantage of a wider roller. Also, even the manufacturers of the roller realize that a roller in excessive length would fail to apply coatings and paints with the proper adhesion. In fact, there are many paint roller assignments which require even less than 9 inches on certain types of work.

With regard to the handles exceeding 6 feet in length, please be advised that a vast majority of the employers who perform high quality work will not permit the use of any roller handles other than the 12 or 18 inch produced by the roller manufacturers. Handles which are 6 feet in length are the very maximum which could be efficiently used.

The survey . . . should have been made with the counsel and advice of someone familiar with the painting and decorating industry, or, such survey could have been made by engineers or architects who have a knowledge of the work and the tools involved in the painting and decorating industry.

Charge 2. On jobs of less than a certain size, some roofers prohibit the use of mechanical aids for installation, and some of this equipment again is prohibited on new construction.

Item. From a roofer's contract:

On all new jobs of less than 300 squares per building no machinery of any sort, including slagging in machinery, felt laying machinery, whether run by motor or operated by hand, shall be used or permitted, except for hoists, pumps, hot buggies (one man shall be assigned to each hot buggy when in use), tank trucks and conveyors. Hand-operated slag spreader may be used for hauling only in lieu of wheelbar-row. . . . On all new jobs of 300 squares or more per building no motor driven machinery of any sort including slagging in machinery, felt laying machinery, cranes and any and all other types of motor operated machinery shall be used or permitted except for hoists, pumps, tank trucks, and conveyors.

Response. The United Slate, Tile & Composition Roofers replied as follows.

The most common practice in the roofing industry is not to limit the use of mechanical equipment.

The size of jobs plays an important part in whether or not it is profitable to use equipment. To make statements that mechanical equipment could be used on roofs, regardless of size, denotes a lack of knowledge of roofing designs whereby a roof can have 1,000 squares, yet equipment would be cumbersome and not practical.

Other factors that must be considered before irrational statements are made, are safety to the roofers and men working underneath and what harm is done to the roof by running equipment over the finished felts.

Charge 3. Operating engineers were said to restrict the use of machinery.

Item. No substantiation of this was offered, although it arose in a different light to be noted under discussion of restrictions related to excessive manpower.

Response. The Operating Engineers conceded the practice but responded as follows.

New tools and equipment should not be arbitrarily introduced into use in the construction industry. Frequently, tools and processes which are perfectly valid and safe in an industrial plant are real hazards under the conditions that obtain on many construction sites. Careful investigation and discussion of possible problems with the tradesmen who will have to use the tools is essential.

Charge 4. Cement masons, while not forbidding the use of machine tools, nevertheless are said in many instances to demand that hand troweling go over the machined work.

Item. In a number of states from New Hampshire to Oregon, the survey pointed to the cement finishers as requiring the following.

There shall be no restriction on the use of machinery but all cement floating or finishing machinery shall be operated by cement finishers and all hand work shall be also done by cement finishers. *Under no circumstances shall work be left under machinery finish.* [Italic added.]

In one instance, hand finishing was required both *before and after* the machine finishing, raising the question in some contractors' minds of why they should use the machine at all.

Response. The Operative Plasterers & Cement Masons replied as follows.

We wish to point out that power troweling machines and power floating machines were never conceived with the idea of replacing hand finishing methods. The power machine was primarily inteded to serve as an aid to enable the placement of low slump concrete, increase volume of placement, densify and compact after placement and increase the speed of the finishing process with reduced effort. The troweling machine cannot produce the final fine finish that is specified for a troweled surface. This can only be achieved by hand work. . . . Many unethical contractors frequently substitute a machine finished surface for a troweled surface. Ignorance or lack of knowledge on the part of many architects and almost all owners cannot distinguish between a machine finish surface and a troweled surface and, thereby, unwittingly encourage this policy to the detriment of the concrete industry.

Alleged excessive manpower requirements

The charges of excessive manpower, and of manpower used nonproductively, are numerous. What was said about restrictive practices in general needs to be doubly emphasized in introducing this matter: it is very complex, far more so than meets the eye.

Charge 1. Some complaints stem from jurisdictional difficulties between two or more crafts, and with the complexity of modern materials, the nature of the job is admittedly far from clear.

Item. A claim that best illustrates the charge (although it does not apply to housing, and is lacking in substantiation) concerned a special hospital table in Pittsburgh that had fittings for gas, electricity, and water. It was alleged that sheet metal workers, electricians, and steamfitters all had to take part in moving the table from the truck in order to get it delivered to the hospital.

Response. None required, because item was not verified.

Charge 2. Some of the strongest feelings on this issue were directed at the engineers. Contractors stated that although electrical equipment may often be started with nothing more than the push of a button, contracts nevertheless call for operating engineers to man it. Air compressors and pumps that run for 24 hours, it was asserted, must be manned by separate engineers during three shifts, even when other engineers are at the site.

Item. A Minnesota contract requires an oiler for almost all equipment even if it is stationary throughout the duration of the project. In Massachusetts the following instance was cited.

> When a single diaphragm pump or one electric pump of not more than one-half inch is used more than 2 hours in any one day, an engineer shall be employed at a minimum of a day. Single diaphragm pumps and one-bag mixers, gasoline or electric power, may be grouped on jobs as follows: (1) Two or three of these machines, one engineer. (2) Four of these machines, two engineers.

Response. The International Union of Operating Engineers replied as follows.

> The practice of shifting an engineer from one machine to another has long been a hazard where it has been uncontrolled. Much of good operating practice depends on familiarity of the operator with the placement and direction of action of control levers, pedals, and other operating appurtenances. In addition, even outwardly identical models of machines frequently have highly individual idiosyncrasies. Machines which are totally different in function usually require a completely different set of reflexes for safe operation. Under no circumstances should an engineer operate more than two different machines on one shift and even then should exercise caution. . . .
>
> There are many excellent reasons for requiring oilers on cranes, shovels, hoes, and similar equipment. Among these are the fact that this is virtually the only source of trained and experienced operators. In addition, there are many, many circumstances in which an engineer must have someone who knows the machine immediately available to him to secure essential information about items he cannot see or read during operation. Often the oiler must act as signalman both for operating signals and for warning personnel in the vicinity of an operation. He keeps an eye on the machinery while the attention of the engineer is entirely devoted to operations. All these factors are essential to even minimally safe operation and are in addition to his function of assuring proper lubrication and cleanliness of the machine. . . . It is difficult to imagine a more hazardous practice than allowing

another trade to start a machine. Inspections *must* be made before each start and the engineer must assure himself that all controls are in safe position.

Charge 3. Elevator constructors were frequently mentioned in connection with the issue of standby workers. Contractors have said that, since all new elevators today are self-operating, either manually or automatically, they do not need an operator, much less a highly paid worker, to run an elevator.

Item. The survey included charges that elevator constructors claim jurisdiction over elevators up to the time of final inspection. In addition, it was claimed that having an elevator constructor on hand during drilling operations could be very expensive if these took a long time.

Response. The International Union of Elevator Constructors replied as follows.

The report should have been more explanatory and stated that the cars are of a temporary nature or an incompleted car wherein some equipment, usually of a safety factor, such as car doors, electrical interlocks on said doors are inoperative (or in the elevator language "jumped out"); hoistway doors being manually opened and closed instead of automatically; other factors such as the automatic leveling are usually only roughly adjusted; nonpermanent cab liners are used to protect the finished product, thereby having an operator on to prevent damage which surely would occur with no operator present; cars set at a speed below normal for safety reasons, such as no car doors on and to prevent accidents to riders; and if same car is run at normal speeds, the operator prevents overloading of car which is a constant threat on constructon work. . . . With regard to the part of the report that the Elevator Constructors require a man to simply "stand by" while a hole is being dug that will receive the casing of a hydraulic elevator, that can stand some clarification. This item was actually a concession on the part of the Elevator Constructors, in our last standard agreement, to allow our employers (the elevator contractor) to subcontract a part of our jurisdictional grant in order to permit them to do the work more expediently and economically, especially in certain areas where granite, rock, etc. were in the soil to be dug. We do require that at least one elevator constructor be on the job site, not only to protect our jurisdiction, but to lay out the hole, aid in setting up the drilling rig, supervise the drilling and setting of the casing, and perform any other work required in the process of digging the hole, and then in the dismantling of the drill rig so the man cannot be classified as window dressing as the report infers. The report also infers that the man remains after the hole is completed until the start of the installation of the remainder of the elevator equipment which is not true as normally the hole is dug before the walls of the building are up and hence they pull off until it is possible to install the remainder of the elevator. Actually, the subcontracting of the hydrohole is a very small part of the industry and many, if not the majority, of our employers have their own drilling equipment and then the work is performed exclusively by Elevator Constructors.

Charge 4. Cement finishers, it was claimed, must stand by when concrete is being poured although they are not actually used in this operation.

Item. A New Orleans contract states that cement masons shall be present at the site of the pour at the time the contractor shall commence the pouring of concrete.

Response. The Operative Plasterers' & Cement Masons' International Association replied as follows.

The allegation about cement masons being on standby is a joke. This sort of reminds me of calling up a surgeon and requesting his arrival in 15 minutes because you will have the patient on the operating table at that time. How can he be expected to know the patient's symptoms, the tools required or anything else? This is not to equate a cement mason with a surgeon, but it makes a good analogy. If the concrete is important enough to require a cement mason, it sure is important enough to have a cement mason there when the operation begins, in order for him to become aware of the type of material being used, the grades and elevations, the tools needed, the type finish desired, and also some idea of the concrete setting up rate.

RESTRICTIVE PRACTICES IN PERSPECTIVE

Investigation of work rules cannot stop with one round of claims and counterclaims. A deeper look reveals that facts and fictions are easily confused because rules that sound restrictive may be ignored in practice or because progressive positions taken by the national unions sometimes are ignored in one or more localities.

But even when the facts of a given case are clarified, how does one decide whether the obstruction of a work rule to new devices or to cost reductions outweighs the value of that rule toward safeguarding the immediate, short-run interest of a worker in his job and in certain working conditions?

This question leads to the view that no fair judgment can be reached by looking at these practices in isolation. They must be judged, rather, in terms of their peculiar industry. Many of the work rules cited seem ridiculous or indefensible to people familiar only with other industries. Yet the case against these rules grows weaker and weaker within the perspective of the unique aspects of the construction industry as it exists today.

Some of these aspects are: wide fluctuations in productivity, year to year, season to season; high rate of unemployment; fairly high hourly wages, relatively lower annual incomes; highly competitive employers; highly competitive craft unions; jumping from employer to employer and from place to place; weather a constant source of uncertainty; difficulties in attracting and keeping apprentices.

The highly segmented homebuilding industry is surpassed only by the retail trade in the number of bankruptcies. The entrepreneur in this insecure industry produces, on the average, less than 25 homes a year. Even the largest homebuilder, in this era when so many industries are dominated by giants, accounts for only a fraction of 1 percent of the total volume of homes produced in a single year.

From the worker's perspective, unemployment rates in this industry have been twice as high as in other industries. Problems of seasonal employment are intense. During the course of any year, the total number employed in the building industry rises and falls 30 to 35 percent. . . . In recent years, between 800,000 and 1 million more workers have been employed in the building industry in August than in February. These seasonal fluctuations vary with climate and region; the warm states of Florida and California experienced employment differences of only 10 percent in 1966 while Minnesota, in the same year, employed 65 percent more construction workers in August than in February.

On an annual basis, unemployment in construction has almost doubled other fields. In 1966, the unemployment rate for construction workers in February (the low point) was 13.1 percent compared to 4.1 percent for all wage and salaried workers, and in August (the high point) the construction unemployment rate was 4.9 percent, compared to 3.9 percent in all other work. That year, as compared with a 7.3 percent unemployment rate for all nonfarmworkers, construction workers experienced an annual unemployment rate of 11.9 percent.

At a theoretical standard of 2,000 hours of annual employment (based on a 40-hour week less holidays), the AFL-CIO estimates that construction workers are employed an average of 1,400 to 1,600 hours. The *Labor Review* of September 1967 reported lower annual earnings for contract construction workers than for other manufacturing industries. In 1964, average earnings were $8,078 for petroleum workers, $7,386 for motor vehicle workers, and only $6,305 for construction workers. One further study on this aspect: in New Jersey in 1964, the operating engineers found that whereas their members had an average annual employment of about 1,600 hours, 20 percent of these workers enjoyed 2,000 hours or more of work, but another 22 percent were employed for less than 1,000 hours during the year.

For the average American employee who goes day after day and possibly year after year to the same indoor place of employment, it is easy to forget that the man in the building trades may be denied work by inclement weather; that each time he finishes a job he is likely to lose his employer; that he may work on many separate projects during the year; that to find work he not only must find a new job but often go to a new community; that in some seasons he can expect prolonged unemployment, and that for some of these reasons he often does not want his sons to follow in his footsteps. In fact, parents in general are not urging their sons to be carpenters, bricklayers, and so forth.

What many of these aspects of the building industry add up to is an understandable effort on the part of unions to give their members security in the midst of an essentially insecure system. To propose simplistic solutions to dilute security measures could move back the clock in terms of social concern. And while bringing greater insecurity to members of the construction work force, it could leave the industry itself with more severe shortages of skilled manpower.

Certainly some of the seemingly restrictive measures are attempts by the unions to require employers to carry as high a load as possible of apprentices. From the short view, these apprentices may seem to be excessive laborers for the job at hand. But for the long view, these are the people who must be trained if enough skilled workers are to be available to carry on the work of the future. . . .

RESTRICTIVE WORK PRACTICES AND THE LAW: RECENT DEVELOPMENTS

Several recent court decisions and certain National Labor Relations Board decisions have clarified some long-standing questions about the legality of restrictive work practices. Most significant is the 1967 Supreme Court decision in *National Woodwork Manufacturing Association* v. *NLRB* (386 US 612, 1967), often referred to as the Philadelphia prehung door decision. The case involved a provision in a work agreement between the local carpenters union and the contractors association, which provided that "no members will handle any doors which have been fitted prior to being finished on the job." The provision was attacked as an illegal secondary boycott under the Landrum-Griffin Act by the plaintiff association, which represented the manufacturers of prehung doors.

The Supreme Court held that the agreement was legal. Such agreements according to the Court, will be upheld where the primary object is to preserve and protect the job security of the union involved. Job security, being a legitimate subject of collective bargaining, may be protected by work preservation provisions even though such provisions incidentally may have the effect of excluding the product of some third party.

A companion case, *Houston Insulation Contractors Association* v. *NLRB* (386 US 664,

1967), involved a similar job security provision prohibiting the use of precut insulation around pipes and fittings. The collective-bargaining agreement was upheld against the contention that it constituted a secondary boycott.

The Supreme Court has, unfortunately, been widely misunderstood in these rulings. The door case often is cited as holding that prefabricated components are considered bad by the courts or that a union at any time may refuse to work on a job which uses such components. In fact, the decision states only that exclusion of such products, *where they threaten job security*, may be a legitimate subject of a collective bargaining agreement and enforceable as such.

Later decisions by the NLRB have emphasized that, for such agreements to be legal, they must in fact be directed at protecting the job security of the union which is a party to them. In a number of cases, union action to enforce provisions which exclude various prefabricated components have been held illegal because the provision of the collective bargaining agreement was either not primarily aimed at protecting job security or not for the protection of the particular union signing the agreement.

A WAY OUT AND A WAY FORWARD

To try to deal with restrictive practices on a case-by-case basis and in the context of the building industry as it exists today offers little hope of success. However, the Commission recognizes the widespread existence of restrictive practices from a variety of sources and believes they must be minimized now if the rising cost of housing is to be checked and production rate radically increased.

We must deal with the basic weaknesses of the building industry by greatly increasing the production of housing, and by doing this in such a way as to assure maximum stability to the manufacturers, employers, and workers in the industry.

We further believe that government, as the primary consumer of one-third of all construction put in place annually, and as chief provider of housing for the poor, has important leverage power to help accomplish these purposes. Not only the federal government, but state and local governments as well, can play a significant role in this stabilization effort. Of the approximately $75 billion worth of construction money that goes to contractors in a year, $25 billion comes from the three levels of government.

To meet the nation's dire housing needs, underscored so strenuously in other parts of this report, we must increase housing production from the present level of between 1.3 and 1.6 million a year to an annual production of over 2 million units throughout the next decade. In mounting that effort, problems of work preservation by the unions may well be overshadowed by problems of meeting a serious labor shortage.

32. *Reducing the Cost of New Construction*

MICHAEL A. STEGMAN

Because substantial reductions in the cost of new construction will enable more families to be adequately housed in the private market and permit a given level of federal support to produce a larger number of subsidized dwelling units, both the Kaiser and the Douglas panels investigated the relationships between the construction industry and homebuilding technology.[1] Indirectly, they both tackled the question of whether the industry is as resistant to change and as anachronistic as is so commonly alleged.

Both analyses begin with some basic facts about the industry and the nature of the homebuilding process. Briefly, there are today some 322,000 homebuilders, more than half of whom employ fewer than 3 persons; more than 93,000 general construction contractors employing almost 1 million persons; and 200,000 special trades contractors employing an additional 1.5 million individuals. The industry is localized and fragmented, but it is not dominated by a few giants as is so often the case in modern industry. A 1964 survey by the National Association of Home Builders, which claims that its membership produces 75 percent of all single-family houses and 65 percent of all new housing, indicates that the vast majority of its members maintain relatively small operations, with an average production of 49 single-family units a year. About 27 percent of the membership constructs 11 to 25 units, both single-family and multifamily, while another 37 percent produces less than 10 units a year. It should also be noted that the construction industry is extremely volatile, accounting for 19 percent of the total number of business failures in 1967.

Most critics would argue that the construction industry was "out-to-lunch" during the industrial revolution, and that it belongs in the nonprogressive sector.[2] The most serious problem with such an assertion is the policy implication that if we could encourage greater use of mass production techniques, we could substantially lower the cost of new construction.

REDUCING ON-SITE LABOR

Such a proposition is fine as far as it goes. Unfortunately, however, the housebuilding industry is probably not as archaic and anachronistic as many would like to believe. The unique and complex nature of the housing commodity is such that, by increasing the productivity of on-site labor involved in building homes in the more traditional

Reprinted by permission of the *Journal of the American Institute of Planners* 35, no. 3 (November 1969): 423-24, and of the author. Michael A. Stegman is an associate professor of city and regional planning at the University of North Carolina, Chapel Hill.

1. Editors' note: Report of the President's Committee on Urban Housing (The Kaiser Committee), *A Decent Home* (Washington, D.C.: Government Printing Office, 1968); National Commission on Urban Problems (the Douglas Commission), *Building the American City* (Washington, D.C.: Government Printing Office, 1968).

2. See, William J. Baumol, "A Macro Economic Model of Unbalanced Growth," *The American Economic Review*, June 1967, pp. 415-26.

manner, or by replacing on-site labor with more productive, off-site labor, the costs of new construction would not be appreciably lowered. Nor, for that matter, could anything less than a complete and totally unanticipated breakthrough in the development and use of new building materials meaningfully reduce the cost of housing.

It would be unwise to expect to lower housing costs through the industrialization of the housebuilding process which is taken here to mean a reduction in the proportion of on-site labor costs to total building costs, because the existing construction industry is currently far more industrialized than one might think. It has been estimated by the Department of Labor, for example, that only about one-third of all labor costs that go into the construction of a house can be attributed to on-site labor.[3] Thus, if we were to reduce the unit cost of on-site labor by as much as 50 percent, we would only be reducing the total cost of labor by 17 percent, and the total cost of new construction by proportionately less, since labor is but a single component of building cost.

Table 32.1 shows the distribution of builders' construction cost dollar among such expenditure classes as on-site labor, materials, profits, and the like. If, as the table indicates, on-site wages account for approximately 19 percent of the total cost of a new single-family dwelling, then by reducing that component of construction cost by half, the cost of the finished house could be lowered by only 9 percent.

TABLE 32.1   *Percent Distribution of On-Site Wages, Materials, and Other Costs, Including Improved Land, for Single-Family Dwelling, 1968*

Expenditure class	Percent of builder cost
On-site wages	19
Materials and equipment	36
Profit, overhead	14
Improved land	25
Miscellaneous	6
Total	100

SOURCE: Report of the President's Committee on Urban Housing, *A Decent Home* (Washington, D.C.: Government Printing Office, 1969), p. 118.

The dilemma confronting the construction industry can be summarized: even though union hourly wages approximately doubled between 1950 and 1967 while the wholesale cost of materials increased by only 27 percent, the fact that on-site labor contributes less than one-fifth to the final building cost of a house sets an upper limit on the extent to which an exchange of off-site for on-site labor can contribute to the production of less expensive dwellings.

CONSTRUCTION COST AND NEW BUILDING MATERIALS

If a shift to a more industrialized housebuilding process, making use of the same basic materials currently used in residential construction, will not significantly reduce the cost of housing, what about development and application of new building materials as a path to cost reduction? The difficulties here derive from the broad array of materials and components that go into the typical dwelling unit, no single one of which accounts for a truly significant component of building costs. As indicated in

3. *House and Home* 26, no. 4 (October 1964): 108.

Table 32.2, the average single-family house consumed $482.20 in materials for every $1,000 of building cost, exclusive of land. Of the 11 materials categories included in the table, lumber and lumber products ranked the highest, accounting for approximately 40 percent of the total cost of materials.

TABLE 32.2   *Cost of Selected Material Components for Each $1,000 of Construction Price of Surveyed Private One-Family Houses for the Nation, 1962*

Selected products and product groups	Cost ($)
All products	482.20
Lumber and lumber products	193.10
Stone, clay, and glass products	115.30
Metal products (except plumbing and heating)	52.80
Plumbing products	26.80
Heating and ventilating equipment	19.60
Electrical equipment, fixtures, and wire	16.50
Fixed house equipment (ovens, ranges, and so on)	13.70
Petroleum products (asphalt shingles and so on)	11.10
Paints and other chemicals	10.30
Construction equipment (depreciation)	9.80
All other categories	13.30

SOURCE: "Housing Facts and Trends," *House and Home* (New York: McGraw-Hill-Dodge, 1965), p. 77.

Assuming that a synthetic material should become available as an alternative to lumber, possessing all of its desirable attributes, but costing only one-third as much, how great a reduction in the cost of housing might we expect? Such a materials breakthrough would reduce the cost of materials from $482.20 per $1,000 of building cost to $317.10, or by 27 percent. But, since *all* building materials account for only 36 percent of the cost of a house and lot, a 27 percent reduction in materials cost results in only a 10 percent reduction in the total cost of housing. As a matter of fact, if we were able to reduce the cost of housing by developing costless substitutes for asphalt shingles, paint, ovens, ranges, and refrigerators in addition to the above-noted wood substitute, housing cost would be lowered by no more than a total of 15 percent.

In short, a dwelling unit is unlike a television set or other such commodity that might benefit from a single scientific advance, such as the development of the transistor, or from an individual production breakthrough. Too many diverse elements and components go into the residential package, each accounting for only a small portion of total cost.

In the judgment of both the Kaiser and the Douglas panels, reductions in construction costs can be brought about by improved management techniques in the industry itself and through increasing reliance on off-site fabrication. Such efforts, however, can reasonably be expected to bring about no more than a 10 percent reduction in building cost, which can, of course, be completely wiped out by continued increases in land costs that have doubled since 1956 or by further increases in the cost of money—currently at an historical peak. While the development of entirely new building systems utilizing new materials, tools, equipment, and labor skills might yield substantial cost savings, it is concluded in a supporting study undertaken for the Kaiser Committee that the "likelihood of finding an all new system . . . is not very good."[4]

Thus, construction is a reasonably responsive industry that must satisfy a traditional clientele, "building code jurisdictions (which are) thousands of little kingdoms, each having its own way," and discriminatory zoning ordinances. Additionally, restrictive building practices, such as on-site rules requiring particular work to be done on the premises, restrictions against the use of certain tools, and devices and requirements for excessive manpower on the job, impede technological innovation.[5]

Finally, as between the two groups, one would have to conclude that the Kaiser Committee, on the whole, is more satisfied with the technologic advances of the post-World War II construction industry than is the Douglas Commission. At one point, the final Kaiser report suggests that "While the construction industry still lags somewhat behind manufacturing . . . , it had an annual growth rate of 2.3 percent in output per employee from 1947-65 . . . [and] there is evidence too that the construction industry has been more responsive to postwar changes in prices of inputs than has the manufacturing sector."

4. The Report of the President's Committee on Urban Housing, *Technical Studies*, vol. II (Washington, D.C.: Government Printing Office, 1969) p. 59.

5. Editors' note: See the article on restrictive union practices, Chap. 31 in this book.

33. Trade Union Discrimination in the Pittsburgh Construction Industry

IRWIN DUBINSKY

Black Americans have an unemployment rate twice as high as whites, while the construction industry claims there are severe shortages of skilled manpower. Blacks contend the trade unions discriminate against them, while the unions claim they must maintain "high standards" of craftsmanship. Although it is important to identify the charges and establish the "facts," not enough attention has been paid to analyzing this problem based upon a sound understanding of how the construction industry and trade unions operate.[1] This researcher has participated in numerous discussions between blacks, unionists, and industrialists, which have produced much heat but little light. All too often, ideologies, policies, strategies, and programs are built upon a misunderstanding of the construction industry "system."

The objective of this paper is to detail how and why the manpower system in the construction industry operates. In examining this process, we will contrast trade unions and industrial unions, as well as describe black participation in the trade unions, especially in Pittsburgh. Finally, based upon the analyses, a number of recommendations will be suggested to increase black participation in the trade unions.

TRADE UNION DISCRIMINATION

The discrimination against Negroes by unions is not a unique phenomenon. The "white racism" the Riot Commission described permeates all our institutions. The unjust treatment of blacks by the labor unions only reflects what is apparent in other organizations and institutions (Jacobs, 1966: 166). Blacks often have found it exceedingly difficult, if not impossible, to go from entry-level jobs up the employment ladder, as whites have done. Major institutions, the universities, corporations, foundations, and government are attempting today either to compensate blacks for past injustice (compensatory or preferential treatment) or, at least, establish equal employment opportunity.

The irony of union discrimination is that what began as an equalitarian, open, protest movement for the underdog has been changed by success. While there are differences among unions, the movement in general has become autocratic, closed, and conservative.[2] What began as a protest movement, furthermore, has now become the object of protest (O'Hanlon, 1968: 104).

"Trade Union Discrimination in The Pittsburgh Construction Industry" by Irwin Dubinsky is reprinted from *Urban Affairs Quarterly*, 6, 3 (March 1971): 297-318, by permission of the publisher, Sage Publications, Inc., and of the author. Mr. Dubinsky is currently a doctoral candidate in urban affairs at the Graduate School of Public and International Affairs at The University of Pittsburgh. He has been director, Research and Planning Division, Community Action Pittsburgh, Inc.

1. Trade union and craft union are used interchangeably.

2. The concern of revitalizing the labor movement to obtain its original ideals, expand its membership (which is decreasing), and ferret out corruption and discrimination is covered in two recent publications: Jacobs (1966) and Tyler (1966).

The blacks account for roughly 2 million of 18 million members of organized labor (O'Hanlon, 1968: 104). Their numbers are greatest in the lesser skilled and lesser paid unions, which are generally called the "trowel trades." Over the past 30 years, the status of the Negro in the noncraft union sector has generally improved—industries, once segregated, are now at least relatively integrated.[3] The "elite" craft union group of labor, however, has remained unchanged. The trade unions, which are comprised of a little over 2 million members, have become a symbolic target of civil rights groups. The crafts represent the last major barrier in a long struggle to integrate the labor movement.

The protest against the trade unions results from the relatively low participation of blacks as journeymen or apprentice craftsmen. While national statistics on race in the trade unions are not available, there are census estimates which calculate that 3 to 5 percent of all the union journeymen are blacks.[4] The percentages vary depending on sections of the nation and the type of craft union. The South has the worst record, but the other sections are not too much better. The electricians, ironworkers, and plumbers have generally the poorest records.

THE PITTSBURGH SCENE

Pittsburgh was cited in a recent study on discrimination in the trades as having the worst record of eight major cities. The study (Marshall and Briggs, 1966: 204) noted:

> In no other city have these figures [black participation] been so small. Thus, neither the union [commercial and industrial] or non-union [residential] sector of the industry [construction] have [sic] afforded opportunities for Negroes to find any meaningful degree of employment.

In 1965, the Pittsburgh Human Relations Commission published a study entitled *Status of Negroes in Craft Unions*. The data from 1963 have been updated for 1969. In Table 33.1 appear membership figures for the Pittsburgh trade unions and their percentages of blacks. Besides the teamsters and construction laborers, who are really not part of the skilled trades, the percentages of blacks range from a high of 8 percent for the cement masons to 0 for the electricians, asbestos workers, boilermakers, bridge and ironworkers, tile setters, elevator constructors, terrazzo helpers, and marble polishers. Two trade unions have only a fraction of 1 percent—the plumbers and steamfitters. The operating engineers and carpenters have 2 and 1 percent, respectively. It is clear that blacks, about 21 percent of the city population, are scarcely represented in these trade unions.[5]

3. Black status in labor unions, though improving, is not equal to white. Discrimination through seniority, as well as other factors, tends to relegate blacks to lesser skilled and lesser paid positions. The discrimination, though, is more pronounced in the construction industry trade unions. One researcher has made two interesting hypotheses, supported by some historical evidence. First, that unionization has inhibited the growth of nonwhite employment opportunities. Second, the stronger the bargaining position of a union (craft unions are strongest due to monopoly over a skill), the higher the wages, and the fewer black opportunities. See Rapping (1969).

4. The "guesstimate" was made by an official in the U.S. Department of Labor's Office of Information to me in an interview in March 1969. He informed me about the inaccuracy of using census data, due to the lack of standardization of occupational definitions of journeymen and apprentices. There are no national figures at this time.

5. This population estimate is based on the Home Interview Survey in 1966-67 by the Southwestern Regional Planning Commission, Pittsburgh, Pennsylvania.

There exists a small core of skilled black craftsmen who are either unwilling or unable to obtain union membership.

These men tend to view union membership with distrust and uncertainty. They feel that through contracting their own jobs they can earn as much as their organized fellow workers without having to capitulate to the restraints of the craft unions. They feel, too, that the unions might discriminate against them because of their race in the allocation of available work [Status of Negroes in Craft Unions, 1965: 12].

In fact, however, these nonunion men generally work for "scab" wages, below journeyman scale, on small and inconsistent projects. Their earnings are low, relative to union journeymen.

In apprenticeship training—the "formal route" to becoming a journeyman—the record is not too different. Many programs do not have blacks, have a small percentage, or do not use the apprenticeship system as illustrated in Table 33.1.

TABLE 33.1 *Black Participation in Trade Unions in the Greater Pittsburgh Area*

Name of Union	Year	Total Members	Total Black Members	Percent Black Members	Total No. of Apprentices	No. of Black Apprentices	Percent Black Apprentices
Asbestos Workers Local 2	1963	212	0	0	27	0	0
	1969	217	0	0	22	0	0
Boilermakers Local 154	1963	610	0	0	12	0	0
	1969	n.r.	n.r.	n.r.	n.r.	n.r.	n.r.
Bricklayers Local 2	1963	979	12	1	32	0	0
	1969	980	35	4	35	2	6
Bridge and Ironworkers Local 3	1963	1937	2	1	1	0	0
	1969	2000*	0	0	n.r.	0	0
Carpenters District Council of Pittsburgh and Vicinity (33 County Western Pa. Area)	1963	7500*	50*	1	115	3	3
	1969	8000*	100*	1	n.r.	n.r.	n.r.
Cement Masons Local 526	1963	748	35-40	5	15	3	20
	1969	700	55-60	8	30	8	31
International Brotherhood of Electrical Workers Local 5†	1963	1000	1	1	18	0	0
	1969	1000	0	0	20	1	5
Engineers Local 66 (33 County Western Pa. Area)	1963	5880	120	2	19	0	0
	1969	7000	131	2	185	7	2
Lathers Local 33	1963	180	14	8	15	1	7
	1969	159	9	6	3	1	33
Painters Local 6	1963	800	22	3	22	1	5
	1969	1039	24	2	16	2	13
Plasterers Local 31	1963	254	5	2	6	1	17
	1969	n.r.	n.r.	n.r.	n.r.	n.r.	n.r.
Plumbers Local 27‡	1963	886	0	0	27	0	0
	1969	1075	6	.5	74	3	4
Roofers Local 37	1963	186	4	2	10	0	0
	1969	214	6	3	5	0	0
Sign Painters Local 479	1963	147	0	0	6	0	0
	1969	149	2	1	NAP	NAP	NAP
Sheetmetal Workers Local 12	1963	1200	20	2	50	2	4
	1969	n.r.	n.r.	n.r.	n.r.	n.r.	n.r.

TABLE 33.1   *Black Participation in Trade Unions in the Greater Pittsburgh Area, Continued*

Name of Union	Year	Total Members	Total Black Members	Percent Black Members	Total No. of Apprentices	No. of Black Apprentices	Percent Black Apprentices
Steamfitters Local 449	1963	1400	0	0	50	0	0
	1969	1785	3	.2	26	0	0
Stone and Marble Masons Local 33	1963	238	2	1	5	0	0
	1969	n.r.	n.r.	n.r.	n.r.	n.r.	n.r.
Tile Setters Local 26	1963	79	0	0	1	0	0
	1969	n.r.	n.r.	n.r.	n.r.	n.r.	n.r.
Construction General Laborers Local 373	1963	2500	1300	52	NAP	NAP	NAP
	1969	2750	1359	49	NAP	NAP	NAP
Elevators Constructors Local 6	1963	227	0	0	NAP	NAP	NAP
	1969	225	0	0	NAP	NAP	NAP
Glaziers Local 751	1963	185	1	.4	NAP	NAP	NAP
	1969	185	2	1	8	0	0
Terrazzo Helpers Local 64	1963	33	0	0	NAP	NAP	NAP
	1969	n.r.	n.r.	n.r.	NAP	NAP	NAP
Tile Layers and Helpers Local 20	1963	68	4	6	NAP	NAP	NAP
	1969	n.r.	n.r.	n.r.	n.r.	n.r.	n.r.
Teamsters Local 341	1963	1225	350	29	NAP	NAP	NAP
	1969	1700	400	24	NAP	NAP	NAP
Plumbers Laborers Local 347	1963	240	0	0	NAP	NAP	NAP
	1969	241	3	1	NAP	NAP	NAP
Marble Polishers and Helpers Local 15	1963	30	0	0	Unknown	Unknown	Unknown
	1969	n.r.	n.r.	n.r.	n.r.	n.r.	n.r.

SOURCE: Status of Negroes in Craft Unions . . . Pittsburgh Labor Market, Special Report of the Pittsburgh Commission on Human Relations, June 1965. The 1963 figures are published in the report cited above, and the 1969 figures were obtained from the Commission's contract compliance section in May 1969.

n.r.—no response.

NAP—no apprenticeship program.

*An estimated figure.

†The number of journeyman electricians has been the same for the past 25 years.

‡Plumbers Local Union No. 27 was not surveyed, as the Commission has been in litigation with this union since October 29, 1963. Figures are based upon the testimony of the Local's officials in Rule Hearings held November 27, 1963, and January 23, 1964.

THE TRADITIONAL EXPLANATION OF TRADE UNION DISCRIMINATION

Trade unions have been accused of discrimination by many public and private groups and individuals. The general charges are based upon the low percentages of racial or ethnic members. The question of discrimination, though, is not as simple as the percentages might indicate, and is extremely difficult to prove legally. For example, a group may not be represented because it is aspiring to other occupations.

The blue-collar field is traditionally the lower end of the occupational ladder in our nation. Blue-collar workers hope their children will become white-collar workers. This trend is evident today in many "ethnic" locals which no longer recruit sons and relatives, because the members want their children to be college-educated and become white-collar employees (Manpower, 1969: 8). For blacks, however, the access to skilled blue-collar work has not been an available alternative. Many trade unions have had in their by-laws and constitutions clauses forbidding the admission of blacks.

The Civil Rights Act of 1964 deemed this illegal, and the clauses have subsequently been dropped. The practice, though, has remained, as is evident by the statistics.

The causes of trade union discrimination, which vary by trades and locations, have generally been attributed to trade union/guild tradition, economic security, and discrimination by default (Kheel, 1965: 193). The trade union evolved from the guild in the Middle Ages, and some claim it goes as far back as the ancient Egyptians. The skilled craftsman and his apprentice took great pride in their work. Today, their pride is translated into the enthusiasm among trade unions to keep their skill levels high in order to maintain their high wage and demand. An influx of poorly trained workers, they believe, will force management to seek alternative techniques or to pay lower wages. Out of the guild tradition also comes the idea that the trade union is a private association, whose members alone can decide who will be admitted. It is natural that sons and relatives, as well as friends, have received preferential treatment. It is not accidental that early trade unions were closely tied to ethnic groups. For example, there were the Swedish carpenters, Italian stonemasons, Irish bricklayers, German machinists, and English cabinetmakers (Manpower 1969: 8).

The second cause, economic security, is based on the idea of maintaining high demand, wages, and job security for the members. The unions, traditionally, have feared "flooding the market" with journeymen. They want to keep their numbers in high demand or, conversely, short supply. Trade unions, thus, take an active role in controlling or "rationing" the number of journeymen in the labor force. Journeyman training programs, over which the unions have no control, are greatly feared and detested.

The third cause, discrimination by default, occurs when people do not know about opportunities. Since many trade unions were (and are) quite secretive—byzantine in some cases—in their recruitment and selection processes, few people are informed about them. Due to these policies, coupled with their traditional treatment of blacks, it is no wonder recruitment of blacks into the trade unions is beset with skepticism and failure. In 1965, the Pittsburgh Human Relations Commission tried to recruit for operating engineers. Of the 60 prospective blacks, only 5 came to take the test, 2 passed, and only 1 elected to stay (Marshall and Briggs, 1966: 214).

Moreover, craft unions have resented the blacks, aside from outright racism, because of the traditional scab-strikebreaking role blacks have played in the movement. When unions went on strike, management would hire blacks. This scenario caused the historic race riot in East St. Louis in July 1917. The company brought in southern Negroes to break a strike, and the "AFL leaders provoked a veritable hysteria of race hatred." The outcome was more than 200 black dead, 8 white dead, 10,000 black homeless, and $7 million in property damage (Hill, 1968: 481).

A commission after the 1919 Pittsburgh Steel Strike found that "Negroes come to believe that the only way they could break into a unionized industry was through strike breaking" (Hill, 1968: 483). An important factor in the inclusion of blacks into the labor movement, undoubtedly, was their role as strikebreakers. A strong labor movement needs all labor, not just white.

THE TRADE UNION-CONSTRUCTION INDUSTRY MANPOWER SYSTEM

Trade unions in the construction industry form a distinct training and employment pattern, unlike management-labor relationships in U.S. industry in general.[6] It is

6. For a discussion of the differences as they apply toward blacks, see Marshall and Briggs (1966).

primarily this unique system which has prevented blacks from attaining the level of integration they have in industrial or plant unions. The system characteristics reflect the distinct nature of the industry and tradition of the craft unions.

Thus, it is important to contrast the trade and industrial unions. Craft unions operate in an industry of many small firms, short-term and seasonal employment, one-skill unions, union control over labor supply, and independent locals of a loose federation (e.g., the International Brotherhood of Electrical Workers [IBEW]). In contrast, the industrial unions operate in a few large firms, long-term and steady employment, multiskill unions, no control over labor supply, and centrally controlled locals (e.g., United Automobile Workers [UAW]).

The construction firms use the union as their principal "employment" agency. Contractors will call, detailing the numbers and types of men (skill specialties) they require, and the union will notify its members and nonmembers who are on the waiting list about the openings. This union function is called "the hiring hall." Since a given firm generally requires a number of distinctly skilled men, such as electricians and carpenters, it deals with a number of trade unions in obtaining its work force.

In contrast, the industrial unions operate in a market of a number of large firms, such as the steel and automobile companies. A company generally maintains a steady flow of work all year round. Employment rolls are stable and steady. The firm, moreover, recruits and trains men itself. The union represents the entire work force, which includes different skills and levels of the work force.

The concerns of the union, in both of these cases, closely reflect the nature of its employment. Trade unions are interested in wages, job training, and recruitment, so they can supply the craftsmen when and where needed to the many small firms. If the unions cannot supply the men, the firms will hire scabs who will undercut the wages and skill level of the craft. The industry expects men to be already trained, because all journeymen receive about the same wage. Industrial unions are concerned with wages, job security, and seniority. The industry itself upgrades training and wages. In some cases, the unions have taken an interest in social issues affecting the diverse membership.

The nature of the unions' power structure and political processes differs in the trade and industrial unions. In the craft union, the members work in small groups on the job. Except for union meetings, the membership is not together but scattered through many companies. The business agent and his office are the prime sources of information and contact for the members. The union office, through job referral, has great power, and it is jealously guarded. Generally a small group can run the union, accept whom they want, and award the steady overtime jobs to friends. That is why trade union elections are, and can become, intensely competitive.

The local craft union operates autonomously from its international union. The AFL is essentially a loose federation of many "international" trade unions which are likewise a loose federation of local unions. Union power emanates from the local level. The Internationals of AFL do not have much authority or power to enforce. The international organizations are used by locals to lobby collectively to protect their craft. Local autonomy is jealously guarded, and international intervention greatly detested, regardless of the issue.

The local industrial unions, in contrast, have their members working together within the plant. Since the company recruits men, the unions' power is limited to issues affecting the selected work force. These unions tend to be more open, because the members have the ability to communicate easily and quickly and information is more "public." The international unions also can exercise a greater degree of control, because an individual-industry union usually cannot effectively act alone, as can a local trade union.

The local trade union, by virtue of its exclusive representation of a craft, can delay progress on large projects requiring many interrelated and interdependent craftsmen from many trade unions. The industry local can shut down a plant, but other similar plants can increase their production to lessen the impact of the "wildcat" strike.

The levels of discrimination in the two types of unions, as noted before, are significantly different. The industrial union experience is dependent primarily upon the policies of the employer. The union organizes the work force that was selected, white or black. It is in the interest of the union to include everyone, or its bargaining power through its principal weapon—the strike—would be diminished. Through the manpower shortages from the war, urbanization, black migration, governmental policies, and social pressures, employers have adopted, to varying degrees, open and fair employment practices which have increased black participation markedly. Southern industry, though, still remains anti-black and anti-union in many cases.

The construction industry's record, however, reflects a situation in which the craft unions, not the employer, can exercise a great degree of control over the type of work force created. Trade unions, as tightly knit groups, have tended to favor father and son, anti-Negro, or pro-ethnic policies. The power of the union to issue certification of union journeyman status and do job referrals gives the leadership great power and autonomy from local groups or individuals outside the union who seek training, certification, and employment.

This is not to say that the industry has no control over the hiring practices. Management can hire whom it wants, but it prefers not to threaten the union. If a firm independently recruits men, especially nonunion, the union could pull its men from the work project, picket the firm's projects, or send the firm, in the future, the least skilled and experienced journeymen available when men are needed. Firms facing these possibilities usually try to establish a "good working relationship" with the trade unions. The industry frequently declares that the union discriminates, and, alternately, the union discloses that the industry does not want any blacks. The complex nature of the employment and training process makes it difficult to put the blame on any one aspect.

Thus far, the discussion has centered on the unique characteristics of the trade union/management labor relations. It is important also to detail the means by which the construction industry manpower system works; that is, how are people recruited, trained, selected, and certified in this industry? An examination of this system can give us the basis for understanding the training and employment process, evaluating the impact of measures to remedy discrimination.

THE SYSTEM

The manpower flows in the construction industry, for the purposes of analysis, can be seen as a system. There are flows of men through a number of distinct and often interrelated training processes that produce skilled journeymen with their union book. Figure 33.1 illustrates this system. Men are the inputs; recruitment, selection, and training are the process; and journeyman status is the output of the system.

Inputs

The inputs can be classified into two nonexclusive groups, one limited to 18-26-year-old men and the other 18 and above. Age requirements for apprenticeship specify 18 and 26 as lower and upper limits.

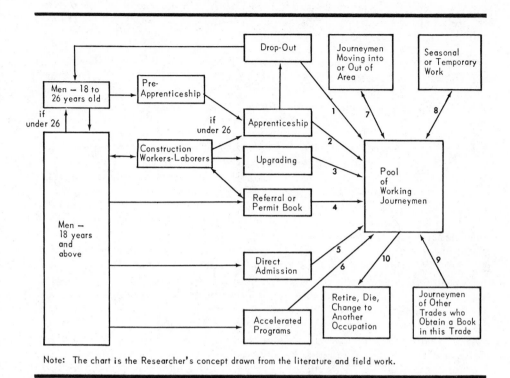

Note: The chart is the Researcher's concept drawn from the literature and field work.

FIGURE 33.1 *Trade Union–Construction Industry Manpower System*

The selection standards of the trade union vary by trade, location, and market conditions. Trade unions have generally controlled selection by often requiring new members to be related to old, pass an apprenticeship exam, pass a journeyman exam (set up by the union), or be sponsored by industry (Kovarsky, 1967: 101-2). This system works to the benefit of relatives and friends of those in the industry—both in the union and in management. When openings become available, both groups seek to fill manpower needs through an informal system which is common throughout all occupations.

Quite frequently, the contractors were originally trade union craftsmen and likely of the same ethnic and racial group as the rest of the trade union. For example, there are many Italian craftsmen who work exclusively for Italian contractors. An Italian, friend of either union men or the contractor, will find it easier to obtain a job than someone not so closely related. Regardless of his ability, a person outside the circle of friends and relations may find insurmountable problems in seeking acceptance.

Although blacks are not alone in being discriminated against, they suffer most, because they are traditionally the last ones hired and the first to be fired. Since few blacks are union members, they benefit little from the informal selection system.

The system of preferences, however, is breaking down, as journeymen desire their sons to pursue white-collar professions and not blue-collar work. But blacks still receive last preference in competing against whites. With these biases in selection, it is little wonder that few blacks become journeymen.

Processes. There are nine nonexclusive ways a man can become a journeyman in a given craft. Six approaches emanate from training or placement programs that flow from left to right in Figure 33.1. The other three methods, which are to the right of the journeyman box, entail journeymen moving into or out of the area or the skill.

Apprenticeship Dropouts and Completions (1 and 2). The first two processes (1 and 2) involve apprenticeship training. The members of the pool of recruited men compete with other applicants for a limited number of slots in an apprenticeship class. Preapprenticeship is an optional two- to three-month program that is being increasingly adopted. The program simply helps prospective apprentices prepare for the apprenticeship admission examination. The program concentrates on verbal and quantitative skills that are demanded on the exams.

The apprenticeship program is a three- to five-year program, depending upon the trade. The apprentices are required by law to attend 144 hours of related school instruction during each year of apprenticeship.[7] The bulk of the training, however, is done on the job, where the apprentices work alongside skilled journeymen. In many cases, apprentices drop out of the program before completion. Some drop out to become journeymen, method (1), while others go into some other field of work. The procedure of leaving apprenticeship to become a journeyman is more common than is generally admitted by trade unions.

A study of the California apprenticeship system found that for 200 recruited apprentices, only 100 (or 50 percent) completed the program. Of the dropouts, 37 (or around 20 percent of the total) eventually became journeymen (Strauss, 1965: 322). Dropout ratios vary considerably by trades. In 1960, 64 percent of the apprentice electricians finished, while only 33 percent of the carpenters finished (Foltman, 1964: 1118). The variation in percentages among the trades, as well as the variation year by year, is due to a number of factors, such as the skill level of the craft, wage-rate differential, and the level of industry unemployment.

In certain crafts, such as the electricians, a high degree of skill is necessary to become a qualified craftsman. The length of the apprentice training, thus, gives ample time to thoroughly learn the trade. But other trades, such as the "rough" carpenters, do not require the four years to learn the trade. Many authorities believe that two years is sufficient time. Carpenters, with some apprentice experience, can often drop out of their program, obtain a union book, and get a journeyman's position.

The wage-rate differential is the difference between the journeyman's and the apprentice's salaries.[8] Apprentices start at 50 percent of the wage rate of craftsmen and receive periodic raises until, by the end of the program, they have obtained full journeyman wages. The attraction of earning $2.00 to $3.00 an hour in hope of earning double that amount is less palatable to the young apprentices, especially poor ones who cannot afford to wait. Why wait, when you can earn full wages now?

A third major factor influencing the movement is the level of unemployment (Farber,

7. For a critique of related instruction and high attrition in apprenticeship training, see Ginzburg, (1966).

8. For an examination of the wage-rate differential, see Farber (1967).

1967: 84). If the economy is in a period of prosperity and people in the construction industry are in short supply, apprentices can move into journeyman status easily. In periods of unemployment, apprentices remain securely in their programs.

The outputs of apprenticeship, however, account for a minor proportion of the total number of journeymen. The National Manpower Council has estimated that only about one-third of all journeymen participated at all in apprenticeship (Strauss, 1965: 321). The majority of journeymen who participated in apprenticeship, moreover, did not complete the program. The other two-thirds had no "formal" training; they became journeymen "informally," through methods 3 through 8 described in Figure 33.1. Indications are that this percentage of apprentices, if anything, will decline and has always been a small proportion in the training of journeymen (Barbash, 1968: 77).

The decline in apprenticeship as a mode of training seems puzzling, especially since trade unions publicly push apprenticeship so much. One researcher contends the paradox is due to "the tension between the long- and short-term" admission policies (Strauss, 1965: 320). In the long run, the unions want to maintain a high demand for the trade; in the short run, however, they must meet cyclical and seasonal demands which make it "less cumbersome and more flexible to do it through temporary permits and direct admissions" (Barbash, 1968: 77). Thus, ostensibly, their policy stresses apprenticeship as the sole means, which gives them control over long-run programs. Unions realize, though, that if they cannot meet manpower needs employers will seek nonunion or substitute materials, which will hurt the trade union.

The real function of apprenticeship is "to train the cadre and the leadership, the core of really skilled men who provide guidance to the others" (Strauss, 1965: 327). Apprentices become supervisors, foremen, and some even contractors. The all-around training of apprentices is not desired for all men by the firms. Firms need specialists, not generalists, whom they can train to suit their needs. "The myth that every journeyman should be fully trained makes it impossible to develop training programs leading to semiskills. The only acceptable program is one which brings a man to the top skill as quickly as possible" (Strauss, 1965: 330). The irony is that, while the union talks so much about apprenticeship, most of its journeymen have not used it at all. While the myth perpetuates high wages for skilled, it does so also for the unskilled trying to steal the trade. Trade union insistence on this double standard may eventually price them out of the market. If wages are too high, substitute methods may be adopted by industry which will probably require less skill and pay lower wages.

The high-waged bricklayers, once a growing trade, are now declining partly due to the attractiveness of cheaper, substitute building techniques and materials. Plastic plumbing and prefabricated electrical circuits could revolutionize the construction costs, materials, and manpower skills. It is highly probable, with the adoption of large-scale, prefabricated units in construction, the journeyman of the future will need to be only semiskilled to assemble the units. The skilled craft union journeyman may soon be "overskilled."

Upgrading Laborers and Referral Book (3 and 4). The upgrading of the laborer is the method most favored by contractors. They reason that the laborers have already been exposed to the industry and know what will be expected of them as skilled craftsmen. Moreover, laborers who have worked closely with craftsmen have frequently already learned the trade but cannot practice it due to the union regulations.

The laborers "steal" a trade, by watching and practicing during lunchtime and other breaks. The laborer's ability to learn the trade and become part of the union usually depends on: (1) his ability to make friends and particularly to find a "sponsor" who will help him out; (2) his relationship to his first line supervisor, who is in a position to assign him to jobs on which he performs there; (3) fortuitous circumstances, such as an emergency or rush order, when usual occupational barriers are down [Strauss, 1965: 327].

The laborer, too, if he is under 26, can apply for apprenticeship training. This route is not frequently taken, because laborers earn more than first-year apprentices. The laborer has a third possible avenue through the use of a referral or permit book as a vehicle to journeyman status. This method, though, as will be discussed soon, is very uncertain and risky. The permit book, which allows a craftsman to work on a job and receive union wages, is good for a specified time period, often 30 to 60 days. The permit holders are literally the "last hired and first fired." They have no job security, and are at the bottom of the union job assignments. Blacks are often given referral books as a means of appeasement, especially when unions are being threatened by various groups and organizations. The books, though, run out and the man is soon out of a job again.

Whereas the contractors may prefer upgrading as a means of quickly and efficiently training men, unions often use the permit book as a means of controlling the numbers of journeymen.

> Short of closing membership rolls outright, the union may issue temporary work permits, either to new entrants or to union members from areas of slack employment. The craft union prefers the union man over the apprentice because the former is expendable when demand slackens; the apprentice represents a permanent obligation for employment, regardless of demand [Barbash, 1968: 43].

Direct Admission (5). Direct admission is the practice whereby the man, skilled or not, becomes a union journeyman at once. This practice varies considerably in different trades, locations, and market conditions. In this way a son, relative, or friend can immediately join. There is a good deal of opposition to this method—often called back-door entry. "Those who 'steal the trade' in this way are called 'Joe McGees' " (Strauss, 1965: 326). Direct admission, though, like permit books, "enables the union to take on men when they are needed. Apprenticeship involves a forecast as to the future and many unions fear to expand their apprenticeship programs too fast, not knowing what business conditions will be 3 to 5 years later when the men finish their course" (Strauss, 1965: 326).

Accelerated Programs (6). Due to much pressure on trade unions and construction industry to integrate, there has been an effort to improve substantially the level of black participation. This has forced a number of trade unions and contractors in the nation to set up some accelerated programs. Some programs are linked with Model Cities development projects in Boston and St. Louis. These programs intend to upgrade nonunion craftsmen and laborers, and train unskilled youth from the areas under the builder's contract. These programs are being run by industry and the unions.

Operation Dig, located in Pittsburgh, was an accelerated program outside the union and industry training structure, which trained a small number of the black hard core to become heavy-equipment operators and carpenters. The Operating Engineers locals in Pennsylvania have also initiated a new program to train 100 hard core in 6 months. This program was called Operation Ben Franklin. There is a Project Justice in Buffalo which also trains journeymen from varying backgrounds.

Such programs are generally looked upon unfavorably by both labor and industry. The unions do not like their lack of control on the number and the training of new journeymen coming through some of these programs. They also complain that one cannot make instant journeymen and that some programs may only produce half-trained craftsmen. Companies fear that such programs will produce many semi-skilled workers who will still be receiving full journeyman wages. Both organizations, moreover, dislike being pushed into programs which violate their traditional autonomy.

Journeymen Moving into and Leaving Area (7). The seasonal and cyclical nature of the construction industry has made mobility an asset for journeymen. The mobile can go where the work is. Journeymen can freely move about to other regions and have their union books recognized by an affiliated local union of their trade. For example, an electrician can arrive in Pittsburgh from New York and have his union book easily converted into a Pittsburgh book. This movement—in and out—thus affects to an extent the number of journeymen of a given skill in a given area local.

Journeyman Movement into and out of Work Force (8). During the winter months, when construction work is scarce, many laid-off journeymen take other jobs to supplement their incomes. When the construction season is on—April to October—they return as journeymen. In their absence, they keep paying union dues.

Journeymen Switch Matrix (9). It is not uncommon for journeymen in one skill to seek another journeyman's book in another skill. In fact, a man may obtain a number of journeymen's books to assure him greater job opportunity and security. To obtain the book in another skill, the journeyman will try to obtain a "direct admission." Sometimes he accepts a temporary work permit when he cannot obtain a book and needs the work. Due to the common problems and the nature of the trade unions, there is a great deal of mutual cooperation. Granting a book to other members is sort of a mutual job insurance program for all.

Attrition Pool (10). Thus far we have generally discussed how people move into and out of journeyman status. Journeymen also leave their trade, as in any other occupation, due to death, retirement, accidents, changing professions, and the like.

Outputs

The attainment of journeyman status, as has been noted in our examination, is multifaceted, involving a number of different methods. The system seeks to maintain an equilibrium between supply and demand for trade union craftsmen. The seasonal and cyclical nature of the construction industry forces continual readjustment by the industry at large. The industry expands during the summer and contracts during the winter. Firms, too, besides seasonal layoffs, increase their work force to fulfill projects and reduce the force after the work is done.

The journeymen, thus, operate in an ever-changing market. Their prime source of security is not the firm (unless they are some of the few continually retained by a firm), but the trade union, which seeks to adjust the supply of journeymen to the needs of industry. The union, along with industry, uses apprenticeship to train the needed master craftsmen, but also uses temporary work permits, direct admissions, and transfers as more flexible and rapid sources to expand and contract its work force.

The lack of black journeymen is understandable, since few enter this system at all. Skilled blacks are often relegated to nonunion-scale work or given temporary permit books. Apprenticeship testing, too, in effect discriminates against blacks. Their inferior educational background proves to be a handicap in these academically oriented tests. Finally, skilled blacks, seeking union membership, often are barred certification until they can pass a journeyman exam set up by the union. These often arbitrary exams prove little. A Pittsburgh city official claims most journeymen could probably not pass them, because the tests are theoretically, not work, oriented. An electronics teacher is better prepared for the electrician's exam than a skilled craftsman.

The continual flux in the journeyman system makes it difficult to pinpoint the roadblocks for blacks. Trade unions, of course, bias their selection to bring in relatives and friends. The companies also exercise control because, in the last analysis, they must hire union members and accommodate employers who do not wish blacks on the job (Greer, 1959: 28). When the discrimination problem is brought up, companies accuse the union, and the union, the companies. Both groups bear the onus of responsibility.

The rhetoric on the virtues of apprenticeship training to all craftsmen and the inability to produce "instant journeymen" belie the facts. Sincere unionists and industrialists interested in improving the situation can best do so by first disposing of the myths and then concentrating upon the reality. The fluctuation of the system itself makes it difficult to plan long-range programs to improve black journeyman status. Recalcitrant trade unions run the risk of ruin by government and racial policies and pressures because myths guide policy determination more than facts do.

Restrictive policies, intent on increasing the number of black journeymen, may inadvertently "flood the market" in a given trade. In such a case, blacks lacking seniority would be "last hired, first fired." A surplus of journeymen might also mean less work and money for all, and a loss of the union's bargaining position, which is based upon a tight labor supply. The effectiveness of the construction industry manpower system lies in its flexibility, which is threatened when restrictions are imposed.

CONCLUSION

The integration of the discriminatory trade unions in the construction industry cannot be accomplished through one measure alone. There is no "quick solution" to correct past injustices. If barriers were abolished today, few blacks could qualify for journeyman status, many would be disinterested in the type of work, and others would lack the necessary work attitudes and behaviors.

Black protest, a growing phenomenon, along with other public and private efforts, is directed toward trying to remedy trade union discrimination. There are many approaches being attempted. The purposes of these, or any efforts, should be the *long-run* institutional change and not just temporary or token measures. This will be no mean achievement. The fluid nature of the industry's hiring and employment practices makes it quite difficult to make long-run changes affecting the level of black participation.

This researcher believes that immediate efforts should be focused on substantially increasing the numbers of blacks in the trade union movement. Only when blacks represent a sizable number will they be able to have some control over replacements. The replacement system, as in many occupations, depends to an important extent on referral by relatives and friends. "Objective criteria" may operate in apprenticeship selection, but these account for less than one-third of all new entrants. Others are recruited by the informal system in which groups often "help their own" first.

The problem is not so much changing the system as allowing other groups to enter the system and rise through the same mechanism as everyone else. This may not be in the ideal of American democracy and opportunity, but it is in the American reality. At the bottom of the socioeconomic ladder, survival of family and clan comes first. As people's status improves, they generally adopt a less parochial view of life.

The question, however, remains: How can the blacks break into the journeyman system so they can begin to benefit from it and generate subsequent black replacements? As noted before, no one policy can accomplish this. A combination of efforts—public and private, legal and economic—promises the best alternative. This study suggests the following strategies.

1. Continued government financing and support of outreach work programs and preapprenticeship.[9] These programs, along with beefed-up apprenticeship information centers, will contribute much toward developing interest in skilled trades and capability to meet apprenticeship entrance requirements for black youths.[10] Such programs should be tied more closely to the existing vocational high schools. Recruiting blacks as apprentices, though they account for a relatively small percentage of journeymen, is important because apprentices traditionally become the foremen, supervisors, and even contractors in the industry.

2. Efforts for black craftsmen should cautiously emphasize training and employment in growing trades, excluding the declining. Demands should be based upon the concept of developing jobs for blacks in trades which will need men. It must be patently clear that blacks will not replace whites on existing jobs. There is no surer way to sabotage sincere efforts to help increase black participation than to do it at the expense of whites already in the system. Vigorous efforts must be made to assess which trades are growth trades in a given area, as well as to convince white journeymen that their jobs are not in peril. The threat of job security could conceivably cause race riots (as in the past) which will only hurt the black minority more.

3. There should be standardized and vigorous enforcement of Executive Order 11246.[11] This order's contract compliance section provides probably the greatest lever in forcing both contractors and trade unions to integrate the work force. By refusing bids, suspending or terminating government contracts, the federal, state, and local

9. The U.S. Labor Department has funded an apprenticeship outreach program in 51 cities, including Pittsburgh. The outreach is a preapprenticeship program using the "tutor and cram" method to assist minority youth in preparing for specific examinations in the building and construction trades. The concept was developed from the Workers Defense League's pilot program in New York (see Marshall and Briggs, 1968). The Labor Department claims that in the past two years, "minority apprenticeship has risen 68 percent from 9,300 to 15,600," while the total apprenticeship numbers have increased only 16 percent (see U.S. Department of Labor, 1969).

10. The purpose of apprenticeship information centers is to provide an easily accessible source of information, guidance, and counseling concerning apprenticeship opportunities, particularly to minority youth who usually had no knowledge that such openings existed. These centers are located in most major cities, including Pittsburgh (see Manpower, 1969: 8).

11. In 1965, President Johnson issued Executive Order 11246, which has changed the usual approach to discrimination in employment. Previously, discriminatory practices had to be proved in the courts or improved through persuasion. There were punitive penalties. This Executive Order, however, changed the burden of proof from the aggrieved to the employer, on federally funded contracts. The contractor must prove that he is not discriminating or that he is taking "affirmative action" to correct past racial imbalances. The failure to comply with this order can result in the cancellation, termination, or suspension of a contract or any part of it.

The most ambitious interpretation of the Executive Order to date has been the "Philadelphia Plan." This plan, initiated by the OFCC (Office of Federal Contract Compliance) in Philadelphia, will require bidders on all construction projects receiving federal assistance in excess of $500,000 to submit affirmative action plans setting specific goals for the utilization of minority employees

(continued on p. 390)

authorities have a powerful weapon against the unions through the contractors. Simply, when the money stops, their source of income stops. Cut the money and their income is cut. Economic rationales, hopefully, will displace racist appeals which have occurred in numerous other instances in our history. When the *cost* of lost income exceeds the small *benefits* derived from "racial superiority," most men will opt for minimizing their losses.

4. The government at all levels, if vigorous in enforcing affirmative action programs, must also provide most of the funds to pay for upgrading programs. Government assistance will make these programs more palatable for reluctant contractors and unions which are unwilling to bear the burden themselves. Support of these programs would appear consistent with current manpower funding policies.

Traditionally, the nation's manpower program has worked toward helping job seekers find employment. The state employment services would refer individuals, just as in an employment agency, to job vacancies. The jobs were generally of secondary or marginal types. The new approach is trying to provide a "suitable job for each man or equipping the man to fill a suitable job" (Levitan and Mangum, 1967: 4).

5. Citizen groups, community organizations, and public and private agencies need to exert continued pressure on both the government and the construction industry. Without pressure, the best programs and intentions probably will not be fully implemented. Some agencies should continue to monitor the progress and publish periodic reports to inform the public regarding the status of black craftsmen.

6. The government, too, must make a concerted effort to help develop black contractors who can hire and train blacks as the ethnic white contractors have done in the past. Efforts to assure bonding of contracts and financial aid may go a long way toward developing a core of black contractors. In the final analysis, it is the contractor who hires and must pay the journeymen. Therefore black contractors, as whites have, can exert direct influence on those whom the union sends them.

7. Further research and study should be directed at using legal procedures against unions under the 1964 Civil Rights Act and perhaps under the antitrust acts as well. This procedure is a slow one, but it may help provide a legal basis for integrating the unions. Currently it is the discriminating union that benefits from the *protection* of the law against the protesting blacks. This was vividly demonstrated in Pittsburgh in September 1969, when the Pittsburgh Black Construction Coalition was directed by the courts through an injunction to refrain from trying to stop construction.[12] The police were brought in to enforce the injunction. The issue for the judge was blacks preventing contractors and workers from building a stadium, in the "public interest"! Attempts to present the issue of unions denying blacks opportunities were declared "irrelevant" to the concerns of the judge. This may be law, but it certainly is not justice.

In conclusion, much needs to be done. More efforts should be made to develop more effective dialogue among all the parties concerned, and more factual information should be published so that decisions and policies reflect realities and not biases, which in the end will hurt everyone.

---

based on federally established standards. It is anticipated that the plan will be put into effect in all the major cities across the nation as soon as possible (see Kuttner, 1969; Presidential Documents, 1965).

12. This researcher is currently writing a larger study evaluating "Operation Dig," a black militant program to train the black hard core. In the study, the Black Construction Coalition and the "Pittsburgh Construction Crisis" of September 1969 will be examined.

REFERENCES

Barbash, J. (1968) "Union interest in apprenticeship and other training programs." *Journal of Human Resources* 3 (Winter): 63-85.

Farber, D. J. (1967) "Apprenticeship in the United States: labor market forces and social policy." *Journal of Human Resources* 2 (Winter): 70-96.

Foltman, F. F. (1964) *Public Policy in Apprenticeship Training and Skill Development in the Role of Apprenticeship in Manpower Development: The U.S. and Western Europe.* Washington, D.C.: Government Printing Office.

Ginzburg, E. (1966) *The Development of Human Resources.* New York: McGraw-Hill.

Greer, S. (1959) *Last Man In: Racial Access to Union Power.* Glencoe: Free Press.

Hill, H. (1968) "Labor unions and the Negro," in J. Grant (ed.) *Black Protest: History, Documents and Analyses.* New York: Fawcett.

Jacobs, P. (1966) *The State of the Unions.* New York: Atheneum.

Kheel, T. W. (1965) "Increasing employment opportunities in the printing and electrical trades," in H. R. Northrup and R. L. Rowan (eds.) *The Negro and Employment Opportunities: Problems and Practices.* Ann Arbor: Univ. of Michigan Press.

Kovarsky, I. (1967) "Racial barriers in apprentice training programs," in E. B. Jakubaukas and C. P. Baumel (eds.) *Human Resources Development.* Ames: Iowa State Univ. Press.

Kuttner, R. (1969) "The rusty fair employment machine." *Washington Monthly* (April 1): 63-73.

Levitan, S. A. and G. L. Mangum (1967) *Making Sense of Federal Manpower Policy.* Ann Arbor: Institute of Labor and Industrial Relations, University of Michigan.

Manpower (1969) "Reaching out for apprentices." 1 (June): 8-13.

Marshall, R. F. and V. M. Briggs, Jr. (1968) *Equal Apprenticeship Opportunities: The Nature of the Issue and the New York Experience.* Washington, D.C.: Institute of Labor and Industrial Relations and National Manpower Policy Task Force.

———. (1966) Negro Participation in Apprenticeship Programs, Washington, D.C.: OMAT, U.S. Department of Labor.

O'Hanlon, T. (1968) "The case against the unions," in *The Negro and The City.* New York: Time-Life.

Pittsburgh Commission on Human Relations (1965) "Status of Negroes in craft unions . . . Pittsburgh labor market." Special Report, June.

Presidential Documents (1965) "The President's Executive Order 11246." Title III. Federal Register 31 (September 28).

Rapping, L. A. (1969) "Union induced racial entry barriers." Monograph. Pittsburgh: Graduate School of Industrial Administration, Carnegie-Mellon University.

Strauss, G. (1965) "Apprenticeship: an evaluation of the need," in A. M. Ross (ed.) *Employment Policy and the Labor Market.* Berkeley: Univ. of California Press.

Tyler, G. (1966) *The Labor Revolution: Trade Unions in a New America.* New York: Viking.

U.S. Department of Labor (1969) "Minority group apprentices increase by more than twice all opportunities." News (March 13).

34. *Federal Income Taxation and Urban Housing*

NATIONAL COMMISSION ON URBAN PROBLEMS

Taxes on individual and corporation income, which provide the bulk of the federal government's tax revenue (83 percent in 1967), have a tremendous impact upon both the demand for housing and its supply, character, and condition. These taxes materially affect: consumers' capacity to own or rent housing, and their choice between these alternatives; investors' capacity and willingness to provide funds for housing construction and rehabilitation; builders' and developers' choices among alternative types of residential development; property owners' practices in buying, holding, maintaining, and selling residential property. . . .

In view of the "striking power" of federal income taxes, it is not surprising that many of those concerned with unmet urban housing needs would seek to place primary reliance upon tax-incentive devices in order to meet such needs. We share both their concern and their expressed interest in making the utmost possible use of "the private sector" to expand and improve the urban housing supply and to bring adequate housing within the reach of all Americans. As more fully explained below, however, we are convinced: (1) that special tax preferences should not be relied upon as the sole or even the primary instrument to deal with urban housing problems; (2) that, however, some changes in federal income tax laws and regulations should be made as soon as possible; and (3) that there should be vigorous official exploration of certain other potentially significant changes that might improve the tax climate for urban housing.

The Commission's consideration of these matters has benefited from an intensive scholarly study, "The Federal Income Tax in Relation to Housing," which was carried out for us by a recognized authority in the field of federal taxation, Dr. Richard E. Slitor, professor of economics of the University of Massachusetts. The following discussion draws heavily upon that study, previously published as Commission Research Report No. 5. . . .

INCOME TAXATION IN RELATION TO HOUSING CONSUMPTION

All taxes—not just the individual income tax—tend to reduce the public's effective demand for housing and other goods or services, as compared with what it would be if there were no need to apply some of the nation's productive effort to governmental requirements. However, many taxes do this only indirectly; for example, to the extent that sales taxes are shifted forward in the form of higher prices, they reduce the buying power of consumers' income, rather than cutting it directly. As by far the largest direct tax in the American revenue system, the federal individual income tax has a particularly strong and visible impact upon the effective demand for housing. Because of its provision for exemptions and its graduated-rate structure, this tax

Reprinted from National Commission on Urban Problems, *Building The American City* (Washington, D.C.: Government Printing Office, 1968), pt. IV, chap. 7 (edited).

operates "progressively"—i.e., imposing little or no burden at the low end of the income scale and taking larger proportions as it applies to larger incomes. In this respect, it differs from the rest of the federal-state-local tax system which, altogether, operates "regressively."[1]

Poor families typically spend a considerably higher-than-average proportion of their income for housing, and the affluent a less-than-average proportion for this purpose. The individual income tax, in hitting harder at the rich than at the poor, cuts the total effective demand for housing much less than would a comparably productive but less progressive or even regressive "tax package," as typified by the remainder of the American revenue system. Since housing is, at least over a broad range of family incomes, a form of consumption that is especially desirable from a social stand-point, this is a very strong "plus" for the federal individual income tax as compared with alternative tax forms.

But the individual income tax affects housing consumption in more direct ways, especially in providing different treatment for renters and homeowners. It gives distinct advantages to the housing consumer who chooses (and is able) to own rather than rent. The principal income tax advantage of the owner is that the rental value of his home is not legally recognized as part of his gross income (although he is allowed to deduct from his tax base any property tax paid on the property and any interest paid on mortgage debt, as if these were costs associated with his acquisition of income). As one observer has put it:

> A person who resides in his own house or apartment obtains an income in the form of consumer services. . . . A homeowner is an investor who takes his return in the form of services. If he wishes to do so, he can convert his imputed return to a cash return by moving and letting his house.[2]

The discrimination can perhaps best be seen by noting the different tax treatment with these alternative courses of action: the investor-renter must count as part of his gross income the interest he receives on his nonhouse investments, so that the amount he has left to pay rent is reduced by the tax due upon that interest, but the owner's benefit in the form of gross rental value does not go through the taxation "wringer."[3]

These provisions, according to a recent careful study, provide federal income tax savings to the "typical" taxpaying homeowner (at 1965 rates) that offset about 15 percent of his annual housing costs, rising to a considerably larger proportion at high incomes (e.g., nearly one-third at the $50,000-income level).[4]

Another advantage to the homeowner is the availability of special tax treatment upon the sale of his home. If within a year after selling his principal residence he buys another costing at least as much, there is no current tax on any gain he may have realized. Even otherwise, any realized gain is taxable at only half the rate applied to "ordinary" income, with a 25 percent ceiling; and, as in the case of other asset

1. See National Commission on Urban Problems, *Building the American City* (Washington, D.C.: Government Printing Office, 1968), table 15, chap. 8.

2. Richard Goode, *The Individual Income Tax* (Washington, D.C.: The Brookings Institution, 1965), pp. 120-21.

3. The discrimination does not directly depend upon whether the owned home is mortgaged or debt free (although the resulting amounts may be affected). For example, note 3 taxpayers differing in home tenancy but each with $25,000 "invested" in various ways, and each identical in other income status, as follows: (see p. 394)

4. Richard Goode, op. cit., p. 122.

Continued on p. 394

holdings, no income tax applies to any increase in the value of the homeowner's property from its acquisition to his death. Accordingly, only a very minor proportion of all increases in the value of owner-occupied homes ever enters into the federal income tax base, and the gains that do so are taxed at preferential rates.[5]

These tax advantages have undoubtedly contributed—along with other important factors, including the general rise in real income—to the spread of homeownership during recent decades. In 1945, only about half of all nonfarm housing units were owner occupied, but by 1960 the proportion had risen to 61 percent, and it is undoubtedly still higher today.

The homeowner-favoring features of the individual income tax result in some significant biases:

They reduce the progressiveness of the tax, both because they especially benefit households that have enough income (and initial capital) to become homeowners, and because the resulting cut in tax base is "worth more" at the marginal rates paid by higher income taxpayers.

They tend to discriminate against families that—even aside from economic capacity—must rent their housing because of job mobility.

They benefit a smaller fraction of large-city residents (many of them apartment dwellers) than the population elsewhere.

In the light of such facts, it has sometimes been proposed that the tax preferences available to homeowners be curtailed (for example, by requiring the homeowner to count the gross rental value of his housing as reportable income), or that they be offset by giving renters some equivalent kind of tax-base deduction. It would seem most realistic, however, to expect the former type of change, and an offsetting preference for those who rent—assuming that some workable formula might be devised—to add further to the many loopholes that already make income tax rates considerably higher than they would otherwise need to be. Moreover, any such "renters' benefit" arrangement would obviously provide little or no saving to families in the lowest income groups—those so poor they incur no income tax liability and those somewhat better off who pay only at the minimum marginal rate.

It should also be emphasized that the ownership-favoring features of the federal

	Renter	Owner A (100-percent equity)	Owner B (60-percent equity)
Total investment	$25,000	$25,000	$25,000
In own home		25,000	15 000
Other investments	25,000		10,000
Investment return at 7 percent	1,750		700
Earned income minus personal exemptions and miscellaneous deductions	10,000	10,000	10,000
Plus: investment income	1,750		700
Minus: house-related deductions:			
Property tax (2 percent on $25,000)		500	500
Mortgage interest (6 percent on $10,000)			600
Taxable income	11,750	9,500	9,600

5. Specially generous provisions apply to homeowners aged 65 or over, and to homeowning members of the armed services. Homeowner benefits are not limited to owners of single-family structures but are available also to owners of "condominium" property and to taxpaying tenant-shareholders in cooperative apartments. For more detailed information, see chap. 2 of Richard E. Slitor, *The Federal Income Tax in Relation to Housing.* . . . National Commission on Urban Problems, Research Report No. 5, 1968.

income tax tend to encourage a form of housing occupancy which has important social advantages. As expressed in Dr. Slitor's study for this Commission:

Homeownership encourages social stability and financial responsibility.
It gives the homeowner a financial stake in society with a built-in inflation hedge.
It encourages better maintenance. . . .
It helps eliminate the "alienated tenant" psychology.
It helps reduce the cost of housing, which necessarily includes in the case of rented quarters a substantial rate of return on risk capital . . . the homeowner can in effect earn this return on his own commitment rather than having to pay it to a landlord investor.[6]

Dr. Slitor concludes:

. . . The federal income tax benefits for homeownership [should] be retained. Many of the criticisms of the tax treatment of homeowners as compared with tenants . . . are in reality triggered by the "vertical tax differentiation" (as between higher and lower incomes) which results from excessive benefits for wealthy homeowners and the inability of lower income taxpayers to secure the benefits.

Retention of the basic income tax encouragement to homeownership could be reconciled with appropriate maximum limitations where the present benefits are so large as to go beyond their ordinarily understood objectives . . . [for example, by] dollar limits on allowable deductions for residential property tax and home mortgage interest payments. However, such an approach would face some important problems. . . . While such restrictions have an appeal on equity grounds, it may be preferable to leave the delicate task of ironing out excesses or misapplications of the homeowner deductions to comprehensive tax reform . . . (such as) the minimum-maximum tax approach discussed in recent years.[7]

It is our considered judgment that, while the provisions of the individual income tax which favor homeownership are not ideal in all respects, their net effect is clearly desirable. These provisions make little or no contribution to the housing needs of relatively poor families. But the best way to deal with this situation is not by changes in the income tax law but, instead, through other efforts to bring homeownership within reach of a larger proportion of the population.

INCOME TAXATION AND INVESTMENT IN RENTAL HOUSING

Tens of millions of new housing units will have to be provided within the next two decades, because of the growth of the nation's population (now adding a million new households a year), its shifting location (toward metropolitan areas and to the West), and generally rising standards of living, which make increasingly evident the inadequacy of much of the existing stock of housing.

The bulk of this additional housing will be private housing, even if—as we urge elsewhere in this report—there is an enlargement of governmental efforts to meet the housing needs of poor families. Furthermore, even with further growth of home-ownership, a large proportion of all urban housing will still have to be supplied on a rental basis. It is important, then, to consider how the federal income tax system affects the attractiveness of investment in rental housing, and how it may influence the production, ownership, and upkeep of such housing.

---

6. Ibid., p. 109.

7. Ibid., pp. 109-10. The "minimum-maximum tax approach" referred to would seek to limit interpersonal differentials in effective federal income tax rates that arise from excessive deductions or exempt forms of income of various types. This approach was described in an address by Stanley S. Surrey, Assistant Secretary of the Treasury, before the Boston Economic Club, May 15, 1968, as reported in a Treasury Department news release of that date.

The starting point is to note the rate pattern of federal income taxation. Ordinary taxable income of individuals (i.e., excluding tax-exempt income and above allowable personal exemptions and authorized deductions) is subject to tax at graduated rates—at 1967 levels, starting at 14 percent and rising to a maximum marginal rate of 70 percent. Corporations are taxed at a uniform rate on their ordinary net income above a low minimum amount—at 1967 levels, 48 percent except for the first $25,000, which is taxable at 22 percent. In both instances special treatment is given to income from "realized capital gains" from assets held more than six months. Such gains are taxable at only half the rates for ordinary income, up to a top rate of 25 percent.

The capital gains features of the law are especially important for the real estate investor. The owner of rental residential property can obtain "income" in two forms—(1) as any excess of rental receipts over his expenses, and (2) as any increase in the market value of the property. On the latter form of income there is no tax liability until a capital gain is "realized" by disposition of the property, and the tax on any such gain is then computed at a lower rate (never more than half) than that on the taxpayer's ordinary income. Furthermore, in computing his current property expense, the investor is permitted to deduct for depreciation an amount that is likely to be considerably more than the actual reduction in property value it is theoretically intended to measure.

The owner thus has considerable incentive and opportunity to concentrate his overall return from the investment, for tax reporting purposes, into the form of capital gains, which are taxable later and at considerably lower rates. Furthermore, if he is able to show for tax purposes a current operating loss, this can be used to offset his taxable income from other sources. The benefits the property owner can obtain from such an effective shifting of ordinary income into capital gains form, for tax reporting purposes, are typically enlarged by another factor—"leverage." His equity in the property is often only a minor fraction of the entire building value against which depreciation is being taken as a deductible expense. As more fully described in Dr. Slitor's study:

> A combination of key factors . . . results in important tax savings and related investment gains in rental real estate. These advantages arise from favorable tax depreciation, and the use of relatively thin equity and heavy mortgaging, with reduced or deferred taxation of gains on the disposition of the investment.
>
> The major tax features favoring the real estate investor are:
>
>> Accelerated depreciation formulas: an investment in real estate can be recovered tax free by depreciation deductions which in the case of new construction can be taken at a rate which recovers two-thirds to three-fourths of the depreciable cost in the first half of the useful life of the building and more than 40 percent of the cost in the first quarter of the useful life.
>>
>> Ability to depreciate the entire building cost, including the part financed by mortgage: since depreciation deductions are computed on the whole building cost although the investor's equity interest is a modest fraction of the total investment, the tax-free capital recovery may be further enhanced relative to the owner's equity investment. . . .
>>
>> Gain and loss treatment: When rental real estate is sold at a loss, the loss may be fully deductible as an ordinary loss from ordinary income; when sold at a gain, the gain may qualify for the favorable capital gain treatment.
>>
>> Limited recapture rules: unlike transactions in machinery and equipment, gain on which is taxable as ordinary income to the extent of depreciation previously taken, real estate sales are subject to very limited recapture, so that all gains, regardless of prior depreciation taken, are capital after a 10-year holding period.

Deferment of gain: tax on the gain arising from sale or exchange of real estate may be postponed by various forms of installment or deferred payment sale. . . .

Repair and maintenance: the owner of real estate may sometimes build up the value of his property by judicious repair and maintenance expenditures which qualify as currently deductible expense although they more than compensate for physical deterioration and obsolescence. (On the other hand, outlays which would hardly be reflected in the value of some slum properties may be treated as nondeductible capital expenditure.)[8]

The importance and complexity of these features of the tax system are attested by the abundance of popular "get-rich-quick" publications that trace means by which real estate investors can seek shelter from the winds of federal income taxation, as well as by the attention given to real estate investment matters in numerous more sophisticated tax guides and services. The "loophole" flavor suggested by some such sources may make it tempting to urge drastic tightening of existing provisions and rules. From the standpoint of equity and adequate governmental financing, this *is* undoubtedly one portion of the federal tax system—along with others—that merits critical review and significant adjustment. But our special concern here is with the effect of present arrangements upon incentives for investment in housing, and it seems clear (1) that existing tax provisions have been "institutionalized" into a complex set of economic relationships that involve a large volume of investment as well as the provision of rental housing for about one-third of all American families, and (2) that any "loophole-closing" efforts, if applied only or more strenuously to this than to other competitive investment fields, would probably curtail the flow of resources and managerial efforts into this area. Concern for tax equity and productivity, then, must be carefully tempered in the light of these considerations.

In one way, real estate investment has some disadvantage from the standpoint of federal income taxation, as compared with investment in other forms of income-producing property. This involves the "investment credit" device that has been in effect since 1962, and which is substantially limited to equipment. By this device, business firms can deduct from their tax liability (within certain limits) 7 percent of amounts they invest in facilities having a service life of at least 8 years.[9] For assets with a shorter life, specified fractions of the full credit are allowed. With minor exceptions, these benefits do not extend to investments in land and buildings, which make up nearly all the value of residential property.

Even though largely excluded from the "investment credit" system, housing investment clearly benefits by important tax-sheltering provisions. It should be noted, however, that these are not limited to rental housing, but apply similarly to other forms of income-producing real estate—office buildings, stores, shopping centers, and the like. The nation has an obvious stake in adequate investment in commercial as well as residential plant. However, there is a *particular* public and social concern with housing—an interest expressed by the Housing Act of 1949 and by many pronouncements and laws, including the act authorizing this Commission. Accordingly, it is reasonable to ask whether the income tax system should include some specific preference for housing investment, as compared with that in other real estate. . . .

Another feature of the tax benefits available to real estate investment should be

8. Ibid., pp. 12-13.

9. Tax credits can materially reduce the effective rate of corporation income tax, as illustrated in Joseph A. Pechman, *Federal Tax Policy* (Washington, D.C.: The Brookings Institution, 1966), p. 121.

emphasized: they involve only minor differences of treatment for investment in new or rehabilitated structures as compared with that in unchanged older structures. (In contrast, the investment credit arrangement designed to encourage other forms of productive investment apply only to business expenditures for new or additional equipment.) In the field of real estate, the only distinction is that the owner of a new structure has the option, for tax reporting purposes, of using depreciation formulas that write off cost somewhat more rapidly. But since a shorter remaining life expectancy is generally recognized for used structures, the actual rate of write-off may be similar.[10]

INCOME TAXATION AND OWNERSHIP PRACTICES

Present income tax arrangements operate strongly to inhibit long-term ownership of income-producing real estate. Important tax advantages can in most instances be obtained by sale after a rather brief interval of holding—commonly 10 years or less —because the tax-saving depreciation allowances are highest in the first few years. As described in Dr. Slitor's study:

> One of the most clearly established investment responses to the federal income tax law is the careful and generally quick timing of the turnover of properties once the investor has skimmed off the cream of the depreciation deduction. . . . In 1963, prior to the partial recapture legislation of the Revenue Act of 1964, a *Wall Street Journal* writer described it as follows:
> "At present a real estate company can buy or build a structure, quickly write off its cost against taxable income, and distribute the untaxed income to stockholders; the stockholders pay no tax because the distributions are considered a return of capital rather than dividends. The company can then sell the building to a new owner who can start the same process over again. The selling company would pay a capital gains tax on the difference between the building's depreciated value at the time of sale and the price it received."
> . . . The rapid turnover syndrome is not limited to luxury apartments or financial district office buildings. A recent description of slum property investment activities indicates that they follow different patterns . . . [which] include (1) repeated rounds of ownership to restore depreciable basis, (2) preoccupation with the creation of quick capital gains through the conversion of older property for overcrowding, higher revenues and subsequent deterioration, and (3) rapid turnover due to concentration of depreciation allowances in the early years. . . .
> The essence of skilled tax management of real estate in the hands of high bracket, tax-conscious investors is apparently optimal timing of turnover. This calls for resale after depreciation attrition unduly exposes cash flow to tax, and after recapture has ceased to be a significant factor. . . . While powerful nontax motives such as the prospect of future rapid appreciation in the property's value may counterbalance the tax motive, it seems evident that the present tax structure in its application to depreciable real estate contributes to frequent turnover and instability of tenure. The old-fashioned motives of careful stewardship, conservation, and rational long-range management of investment are apparently subordinated in the tax

10. The "fastest" depreciation method authorized for investments in used properties is the "150-percent declining balance" formula, while investments in new properties may be depreciated according to the more rapid "200-percent declining balance" formula or the "sum-of-the-years-digits" formula. In the first 10 years of holding for a property with a 40-year estimated life, the latter two would respectively provide about one-fourth and one-third more depreciation than the "150-percent declining balance" formula. However, the 150-percent method in combination with a 25-year-life "used" property provides the same depreciation deduction and after-tax rate of return as the 200-percent method with a 33-year-life new property, and would be more favorable than the 200-percent method with a 40-year-life new property.

shelter operation which often characterizes multiple-unit rental housing development, luxury or slum.[11]

There is, of course, nothing immoral or socially undesirable in frequent turnover as such. Whether the tax features which now work in that direction should be seriously questioned from a housing supply standpoint (rather than on grounds of tax equity) depends upon whether property turnover has desirable side effects—in particular whether it results in poorer maintenance of rental residential property than would otherwise apply. Even the limited-period owner of a rental housing property may often find it economically advantageous to provide a high standard of maintenance. On the other hand, some observers have reported a high correlation between frequent turnover and poor maintenance practices, especially for "slum" housing.[12] It is difficult to see how frequent turnover would specifically *encourage* better maintenance. Thus the net effect—whether it applies to such rental housing or only to limited portions of it—is no doubt in a socially undesirable direction.

For rental housing in older city neighborhoods at least, the income tax system also contributes in another way to poor maintenance practices. Understandably, the laws and regulations differentiate between owners' expenditures for property repairs and for property improvements. Repair costs can be entirely deducted from gross property revenue as a current expense, while improvement expenditure can only be added to the cost base against which depreciation is computed. These distinctions, although generally reasonable, are likely to be unrealistic in the case of slum housing. What the tax law recognizes as "improvements" may actually represent long-overdue repairs, made necessary by past neglect and deterioration. Thus, as Dr. Slitor points out:

> The existing tax barriers to rehabilitation expenditures reinforce the underlying economics of "mining" or "milking" of older low-income housing. The rehabilitation expenditures of the particular taxpayer often add little to the current earning power of the property and possibly little to its anticipated resale value. Yet in addition to failing to qualify for a current income tax deduction, rehabilitation outlays may: lengthen the estimated useful life of the property and thus reduce depreciation rates and increase exposure to federal income tax; and result in a higher local assessment and thereby increase property tax costs. . . .[13]

A closely related problem is the tendency of the income tax to operate less favorably for investment in remodeling or renovation of run-down properties than for investment in new housing. This is especially unfortunate because (1) renovation may often be more economic or socially desirable than new construction, especially to deal with housing needs in deteriorating city neighborhoods; and (2) financing and market conditions may be less favorable for the renovator. For example, heavy debt financing—with its potential tax benefits—is generally less available for fix-up costs. Yet the income tax is likely to add further disincentives to renovation. As Dr. Slitor points out:

> Unless the administrators of the tax law make fine and sophisticated distinctions, expense elements in housing remodeling may be capitalized. The fact that slum housing rehabilitation is sometimes in part an accumulation of neglected past repairs or that it frequently fails to prolong life or to be reflected in immediate capital

11. Richard E. Slitor, op. cit., pp. 36-37.

12. For example, see Jerome Rothenberg, *Economic Evaluation of Urban Renewal* (Washington, D.C.: The Brookings Institution, 1967), pp. 49-50.

13. Richard Slitor, op. cit, pp. 105-6.

values despite bearing the superficial earmark of a capital improvement may well be ignored.

. . . The tax effects are likely to be more onerous if the capitalized amount is added to the tax basis of the building to be depreciated at a composite rate based primarily on the building life. . . . The administration of the tax laws may fail in practice to distinguish between the life of the building shell which may run to 40-60 years and the lives of interior (equipment and decoration) which would be 5-8 years or even less under the low-income urban conditions of use. . . .

Wherever the tax law errs on the size of capitalizing expense or of unduly slowing the write-off of short lived improvements, the resulting retardation of capital recovery tends to raise the effective rate of taxation above the nominal rate. It restricts cash flow and enhances risk by lengthening the capital pay-off period. . . .

[In addition,] substantial improvement on an existing building may subject gain on sale to ordinary income [rather than capital gains] treatment, even though the old property had been held for more than the 10-year period normally required to eliminate recapture.[14]

CONCLUSIONS AND RECOMMENDATIONS

Elsewhere in this report, we have emphasized the pressing need for governmental programs and policies that will (1) encourage a large and relatively stable volume of overall housing construction and (2) greatly enlarge the volume of adequate housing available for families of moderate and low incomes. The second of these objectives can be met only if there is a considerable amount of public subsidy. The additional housing involved clearly cannot be financed entirely from rental or purchase payments within the reach of the households that need it. But the subsidy might take any of various forms. Conceivable alternatives include governmental provision of housing (either publicly owned or leased) at less than full cost; financial aid to households, to help them meet essential housing costs they could not otherwise afford; explicit subsidies to developers, builders, rental-property owners, or financial institutions, designed to enable and encourage them to provide housing that would not otherwise be economically feasible; or "indirect" subsidies through preferential tax treatment of income from investments in housing for low or moderate income families.

It is understandable why some people concerned with urban housing needs urge that primary reliance be placed upon the tax-incentives route. They argue that, as compared with alternative types of subsidies: (1) this approach should be more feasible to enact, since any public costs involved would be indirect (in the form of a revenue loss) rather than involving an increase in federal expenditures; (2) once built into the federal tax system, such subsidies would have far more chance of continuity than would subsidy programs subject to the usual process of specific statutory authorization and annual budgeting and appropriations; and (3) tax-incentive subsidies could operate with far less detailed governmental control than direct subsidies, since most of the decisions about the tax-preferred housing to be provided would be left to private investors and builders.

On the other hand, it seems clear that the indirect subsidy approach through tax preferences would be economically inefficient, since some—perhaps even a very large part—of the tax benefits would go for residential investment that would have occurred anyway. This approach may also be socially wasteful in stimulating residential construction of types, or in locations, that rank low in priority from the standpoint of the urban housing needs intended especially to be served. If an effort were made to

14. Ibid., pp. 34-35.

minimize these problems by limiting the prospective tax benefits to rather narrowly defined categories or locations, the program would confront many of the problems of detailed specification and "bureaucratic" control which the tax-incentive approach is alleged to avoid. The claim for "cost invisibility" and political appeal can also be questioned, in view of the growing awareness by the Congress (and particularly by some key members of its revenue and appropriations committees) that revenue-sacrificing tax concessions are similar in their budgetary and economic effect to federal expenditures involving similar sums. Finally, with the federal income tax system already far too riddled with preferential provisions that materially impair its equity and productivity, proposals for the introduction of sizable new "loopholes"—even for socially desirable purposes—surely deserve the most critical and cautious scrutiny.

The study made for this Commission by Dr. Slitor included an intensive analysis of various tax-incentive approaches to deal with urban housing needs. We accept and share his conclusion that governmental efforts to encourage the construction and rehabilitation of housing for low and moderate income families should rely *primarily* upon direct subsidy programs rather than upon special tax benefits.

This is not to say, however, that no change should be made in federal income tax provisions that particularly affect the housing supply. As the foregoing discussion has pointed out, the important tax benefits now available to the investor in real estate include the following questionable or undesirable features.[15]

1. Tax provisions make no distinction between investment in rental housing and in other income-producing real estate, despite the special public concern for housing.

2. They provide little or no effective preference of tax treatment for investment that actually enlarges the stock of usable housing (through new construction or renovation), as compared with investment that merely involves ownership of existing structures.

3. They stimulate relatively frequent changes in the ownership of rental housing, and thereby in at least some instances work against acceptable standards of maintenance of such housing.

4. They tend to reinforce, rather than to offset, the unfortunate economic and social conditions that inhibit adequate maintenance and renovation of rental housing in deteriorating city neighborhoods.

5. They include no preferential treatment for investment in low and moderate income housing, relative to other rental housing.

---

15. Editors' note: Several of the Commission's objections were dealt with in the 1969 Tax Reform Act, as noted in our introduction to section IV. The 1969 Tax Reform Act tightened the recapture rules applicable to real estate transactions. Residential rental property must be held for 16-2/3 years before all the gains on a sale or exchange are taxed as capital gains; all other depreciable real estate is always subject to recapture of the excess depreciation (above straight-line depreciation) for taxation at ordinary income tax rates. In addition, capital gains in excess of $50,000 are now taxed at a rate higher than 25 percent but no higher than 35 percent.

"OH, PETE, WHAT FUN WE COULD HAVE DOING OVER ONE OF THOSE BROWNSTONES!"

V

Policies and Programs

Apart from a few scattered efforts in the late 19th and early 20th centuries, nothing that could be seriously described as national housing policies or programs emerged in this country until the Depression years, which saw the establishment of low-rent public housing and the Federal Housing Administration. Since that time, however, numerous programs and approaches have been tried, illustrating S. M. Miller's observation that "we are a nation of panacea hoppers."[1] Although some of the attempted approaches have been clearly proved mistaken, there is little unanimity about what should be done to implement the National Housing Goal of "a decent home and a suitable living environment for every American family." A detailed review of each and every program undertaken at the federal, state, and local levels would itself take a book; so we have confined ourselves to a review of what appear to be the more important housing programs and to a selection of some of the more salient issues of housing policy.[2] The articles in this section cover such specific programs as homeownership for the poor, rent control, low-rent public housing, rehabilitation, enforcement of minimum standards of habitation, the property tax, and new towns. Some of the policy issues discussed are the bias of American housing policy, public sector intervention versus reliance on the private sector, and whether housing programs in themselves make sense, as opposed to a policy that seeks to provide people with sufficient income to obtain decent housing on their own. A more complete list of articles that deal with specific programs may be found in the Bibliography. As far as possible these programs and policies should be evaluated in light of the economic, social, and political considerations discussed in the previous sections.

1. "Poor Corporations," *New York Advocate* 1 (December 1968): 23.

2. One important housing program not covered in this section is urban renewal, which might more accurately be termed a "dehousing program" for the poor. For a good treatment of the housing aspects of the renewal program, see James Q. Wilson, ed., *Urban Renewal: The Record and the Controversy* (Cambridge, Mass.: M.I.T. and Harvard, 1966); and Jewel Bellush and Murray Hausknecht, eds., *Urban Renewal: People, Politics and Planning* (Garden City, N.Y.: Doubleday, 1967).

35. *The Bias of American Housing Policy*

NATHAN GLAZER

What should be the goals of housing policy? Nathan Glazer suggests a policy that "maximizes choices," but he is quick to point to several constraints on its implementation: scarcity of resources, the visibility of past mistakes, and the American bias in favor of the single-family, owner-occupied house. Glazer traces the influence of these factors on the directions of housing policy, and against this background inquires whether the poor have benefited from federal housing policy and whether the federal policy has encouraged segregation by social class, race, and family life-style.

There is an easy verbal solution to the problem [of what shall constitute America's housing policy]: Allow all choices to be available, and then let people choose freely what they want. . . .

. . . [T]here are always—there must inevitably be—serious constraints on the attempt to implement a policy that "maximizes choices." The first major constraint is that economic resources are limited, and housing policy in any society, including ours, operates within a larger economic policy which limits, directly or indirectly, the resources that can be placed into housing. . . .

Aside from these general economic considerations, there are some special problems in establishing a housing policy that maximizes freedom of choice as to the kind of housing and the kind of community desired. In any public policy that involves building relatively expensive physical facilities, the constraint on a program that maximizes choices—that is, offers many different possibilities—is particularly great. The fact that one poorly conceived work training program may operate at 80 percent of capacity (what is capacity anyway?) could hardly make a serious public issue. However, when a public housing project operates with 20 percent vacancy rates or when 20 percent of the buyers in a government-insured development default on their mortgages, this becomes a visible problem which cannot be concealed and which subjects the policymakers and administrators to the greatest embarrassment. Nor are they permitted to make too many such errors. . . .

. . . In the first quarter of 1966, 7.5 percent of all rental units and 1.4 percent of homeowner units were vacant. The available for-rent vacancy rate (that is, units not deteriorated, available for year-round occupancy) was lower but still substantial—2.7 percent and .8 percent. From the point of view of providing a desirable level of choice in the search for housing, these rates are still too low for many groups and in many areas. However, from the point of view of builders and housers, the vacancy levels are too high, and they are higher than in any other major industrial nation.

Reprinted from *Journal of Marriage and The Family* 29, no. 1 (February 1967): 145-63 (edited), by permission of the publisher and author. Nathan Glazer is professor of education and social structure at the Harvard University Graduate School of Education.

Under these circumstances, just as the private builder of rental units or the developer of units for sale knows he may be courting disaster when he builds and is therefore cautious, so too are the shapers and administrators of government policy cautious. In effect, choices are already so wide that a new choice, a new approach, must compete with many existing alternative possibilities. This is perhaps one of the chief constraints on American housing policy. On the other hand, where shortages are or have been more severe and where more of the elements of investment policy are in the hands of the government (as is true of Western Europe, Eastern Europe, Japan, and the developing world), one can operate with some assurance that almost any policy one decides upon will produce houses that are occupied, even if they come in a shape and style and community that are less attractive than some conceivable alternative.

. . . Thus, paradoxically, scarcity may permit greater freedom and experimentalism in policy; while affluence, the presence of surplus, may impose greater caution.

This is one constraint, a very contemporary one, on an American housing policy that would attempt to maximize choice. It operates with another constraint, perhaps the most distinctive constraint on American housing policies. This is the consistent bias in this country in favor of the owner-occupied, single-family, freestanding house with a bit of land around it. When we speak of housing problems in this country, we tend to think of the city tenement, crowded with the poor. If this is our focus, we tend to consider how to rehabilitate it or replace it with more spacious and better planned multiple-family dwellings. Yet in the range of American housing problems and American housing policies, neither the crowded slum nor the type of multifamily housing that may potentially and has in some cases actually replaced it is central. Both have received the chief attention of reformers, writers, and analysts. But it is the single-family, owner-occupied home—getting it built, getting it financed, saving it from the banks, reducing its cost, and increasing its amenities—that has received the chief attention of elected officials, administrators, and, one suspects, the American people, even the poor among them.

The overwhelming preference of the American family in housing is the single-family home, preferably owned, preferably detached. Our housing policy at local and federal levels has been designed to facilitate its building, to protect its environment, and to make it accessible to more and more people at lower economic levels. . . .

Thus, if we look at American housing policy, we will see that it consists of two large segments; and both are overwhelmingly directed toward facilitating the building, financing, and protection of the single-family home. On the *local* level we find zoning regulations, building codes, and health codes. All of these, in their origins in the early 20th century, were designed to protect the low income, immigrant- and working-class population from frightful housing conditions and to protect, too, the middle and upper income population from the evil consequences in health and amenities that flowed from these conditions. New York City was the pioneer, for it contained the greatest concentration of tenements.[1] Paradoxically, all these mechanisms of housing policy soon outgrew their origins; and, as their use spread to all the cities and many of the towns of the country, in their expansion they became adapted to the

---

1. For the history of early housing reform, see Roy Lubove, *The Progressives and the Slums* (Pittsburgh: University of Pittsburgh Press, 1962). "Except for New York, Pennsylvania was the only state to enact a housing law before 1900. The other cities had to depend upon local building and health ordinances, and most of them had decreed some such ordinances in the 1880's and 1890's. These dealt with the same problems of light, air, ventilation, sanitation, fire protection and construction as the New York State measures" (p. 142).

housing conditions and housing desires of the greater part of the population—that is, they became policies for protecting the single-family home.[2]

On the federal level, we may trace a similar emphasis in policy. The first federal action in the field of housing was a survey of slums in 1892. During World War I the federal government, directly and through loans to private builders, put up war housing. These initial forays into policy had no lasting consequences, but, beginning in the early thirties with the President's Conference on Homebuilding and Home Ownership, federal policy was set on the path of the encouragement of homeownership through the development of the amortized long-range mortgage, federal insurance of home mortgages, encouragement of large-scale development of single-family homes, and guidance of the supply of long-term housing credit. The Federal Home Loan Bank system in 1932, the Home Owners' Loan Corporation and Federal Farm Mortgage Corporation of 1933, and the National Housing Act of 1934, setting up the Federal Housing Administration, were all steps to the creation of a federal policy which facilitated homeownership.[3] Should we say these policy developments "encouraged" homeownership by providing incentives and subsidies which forced many families into the kind of dwelling conditions they would have preferred to avoid, or should we say this course of policy "satisfied" widespread desires and needs for this type of housing? This is a question around which there has been a good deal of controversy.

As against these two major forms of governmental policy—zoning, building and health codes at the local level, and the encouragement of homebuilding and homeownership at the federal level—other major thrusts of policy have been relatively minor. Federally financed public housing (the United States Housing Act of 1937) was in its origins designed to combat the Depression by encouraging building as well as to clear slums and provide housing for the poor. It has always been operated on such a small scale that its achievement in all these areas has been minor. Today public housing makes up only a little more than 1 percent of the housing units of the country and accommodates 1 percent of the population. (For certain parts of the population, of course, public housing is more important. In New York City, where public housing is most prominent, about 7 percent of the population and a quarter of the Negro population live in public housing.) Urban renewal, which began in 1949, even with the large areas that have been cleared in some American cities, is small potatoes compared to the central policy of encouraging single-family homebuilding and ownership. In contrast to some 600,000 units of public housing that have been built during the history of that program and 80,000 that have been built under urban renewal, over 5,000,000 units have been built under FHA home mortgage

2. Building, housing, and health codes and zoning regulations, of course, still perform their original functions: preventing the building of inadequate and unsafe houses, assuring light and air to streets and rooms, preventing unpleasant intrusion of commercial and industrial facilities in residential areas. However, in each case there seems to have been a shift in emphasis, as suggested in the text, from concern with the worst dwellings and the poorest living conditions to protection of a higher norm. My references here are hardly authoritative or fully satisfactory (the history of building, housing, and health codes and zoning regulations, from the point of view of the social values they attempted to realize at different times, would be a fine subject for an urban historian); but see, in addition to Lubove, op. cit., to begin with: Burnham Kelly, et al., *Design and Production of Houses* (New York: McGraw-Hill, 1959), chap. 9; Glenn H. Beyer, *Housing and Society* (New York: Macmillan, 1965), pp. 219-20, 448-54; Edward C. Banfield and Morton Grodzins, *Government and Housing* (New York: McGraw-Hill, 1958), pp. 93-98.

3. Paul F. Wendt, *Housing Policy: The Search for Solutions* (Berkeley and Los Angeles: University of California Press, 1962), pp. 145-50.

programs.[4] It can hardly be denied this has been and remains the chief emphasis of American housing policy, but how do we evaluate its impact on the family?

This overwhelming central tendency in American housing policy undoubtedly reflects certain characteristics of the actual American family and of the models, conscious or unconscious, that are held as to the ideal family life. Thus, the emphasis on a room for every individual and on space between the houses reflects an emphasis on familial privacy and individual privacy within the family. Certainly there is no support in this approach for the extended family, which is one reason why those ethnic and cultural groups that favor extended family ties are unhappy at being forced out of denser urban areas and required to take up residence in spread-out suburbs. Having, however, decided to foster this ideal, American housing policy, because of the type of housing it encourages, does make it harder to maintain other styles of family life—such as, for example, an extended family. It thus encourages further the consequences of the initial bent to privacy and individualism, encouraging, for example, a situation in which children are raised in the expectation of earlier and earlier independence and in the expectation of less and less effective control by parents over the development of their lives. If parents lose power, the loss of power of other older family figures is of course even more radical and more complete.

Thus, housing policy, reflecting tendencies in family life, pushes those tendencies further, and yet there is no question this is what the family—for the most part—*wants*. William Slayton and Richard Dewey, summarizing 11 opinion studies in 1953, assert simply that, "whenever given the opportunity, most American families express their desire to own their own homes."[5] . . .

[That] this has been the taste of the American family . . . . can hardly be argued with, since the choice has a certain amount of face validity. It means more space for children, inside and out; it means the opportunity to invest one's resources, if they are available, in newer equipment and better upkeep; it means a generally rising investment; it means freedom to alter the home at will and to keep pets and animals; and one may proceed from there to various more subtle gains, all of which quite overwhelmed the demonstrations of housing experts 20 years ago that ownership was often financially unwise.[6] Together with the housing policies we have outlined, this preference has resulted in a homeownership rate of 62 percent of all housing units in 1962.

Even this understates the prevalence of the single-family house, for many are rented. In 1960 no less than 70 percent of all housing units in this country were one-family houses, detached; another 6 percent were one-family, attached; 13 percent were in structures with 2 to 4 units; another 11 percent were in structures with more than 5 units. Even in metropolitan areas the apartment house was—statistically—a relatively rare phenomenon. Sixteen percent of all housing units in SMSA's were in structures containing more than 5 units; 17 percent were in structures with 2 to 4 units. However, the single-family structure dominated overwhelmingly: 60 percent of all metropolitan

4. *Annual Report of the Housing and Home Finance Agency* (1964), pp. 16, 52, 75. These figures relate to the end of 1964, but the relative dimensions of the programs have not changed since.

5. William M. Slayton and Richard Dewey, "Urban Redevelopment and the Urbanite," in Coleman Woodbury (ed.), *The Future of Cities and Urban Redevelopment* (Chicago: University of Chicago Press, 1953), pp. 323-26.

6. E.g., John P. Dean, *Homeownership: Is It Sound?* (New York: Harper, 1945); Louis Winnick, *Rental Housing* (New York: McGraw-Hill, 1958) p. 60, and elsewhere, showed that in the postwar period it was a better buy than rental. On the official opinion that favored rental in the early postwar period, see Lloyd Rodwin, *Housing and Economic Progress* (Cambridge, Mass.: Harvard University Press, 1961), pp. 5, 50, 192-93.

housing units were single-family, detached; another 8 percent were one-family, attached.[7]

New York is the unique city which, for reasons of culture, or crowding, or land value, breaks with this pattern. It contains the bulk of the apartment houses of the country—in 1950, 51 percent of apartment units in structures of more than 20 units were in New York City![8]

Presumably, homeownership and the single-family detached dwelling have now reached most of the family units that might find them desirable. Of our 53 million households, 41 percent hold 2 persons or less; and many of these, we must assume, would not be interested in homeownership. Of our 45 million families, only 52 percent contain children under 18, and many of the remainder, too, might find homeownership less attractive than renting. Indeed, after dominating the housing markets of the 1960s overwhelmingly (92 percent of all private housing units started in 1956 were single-family homes), the proportion of single-family homes has been dropping steadily; and in 1964 only 62 percent of all new units begun were single-family homes.

THE CRITICISMS OF AMERICAN HOUSING POLICY

Criticism I: Does Housing Policy Neglect the Poor?

The first criticism is, to my mind, the most serious. How did the poor fare under federal housing policy? One can look at the census figures . . . and point out a good deal of improvement in the overall housing picture in upgrading quality and in reducing crowding. We have pointed to this improvement in particular for the part of the population that is most poorly served, the Negro population.[9] Private building, with the form of government assistance represented by mortgage insurance, improved and increased the housing stock. Yet if we look at the direct impact of government policy, did it not serve only the wealthier? . . .

Varying judgments were possible, at the same time, as to how far down in the income distribution the government insured and guaranteed new home reached: only the top 30 percent, according to Charles Abrams; 80 percent, according to Sherman Maisel.[10]

Someone who is not an expert on the economics of housing might well strike a median. Indeed, it seems that the median income of families purchasing FHA houses hovers about $1,000 above the median income of urban families. Thus, in 1958 the median income of buyers of new FHA houses was $7,733; the median income of buyers of existing homes on FHA mortgages was $7,447. In 1959 median family income was $5,660, but urban husband-wife families had a median income of $6,454.[11] In the early postwar period, the median income of FHA purchasers was about the same as the median income of all families, for in those years it was possible to get mortgages at lower interest rates; and the FHA or VA house was cheaper, owing to smaller size, less equipment, and smaller lots.[12] This suggests that the FHA house

7. *U.S. Census of Housing, 1960, States and Small Areas, U.S. Summary*, pt. I, p. xxxiv.

8. Winnick, op. cit., p. 29.

9. Editors' note: See the first part of this article, Chap. 13 of this book.

10. Wendt, op. cit., pp. 210-11.

11. HHFA Annual Report, 1964, p. 127; *U.S. Census of Population, 1960, United States Summary*, table 224.

12. Wendt, op. cit., pp. 177-80.

is within the means of the median American family, if we have in mind the urban, husband-wife family at which this policy aims. What it leaves out are the substantial numbers of families that fall below the median, for example, the nonwhite family, whose median income (again, urban and husband-wife families) was in 1959 only $4,329. It certainly leaves out the family headed by a woman, the elderly couple without resources, and other poor families. Yet we should avoid a position which often becomes polemical and exaggerated: in 1963, 13 percent of new single-family homes were priced under $12,500, and in 1964, 11 percent. This substantial part of the new home market was available to families earning well below the median that year.[13]

Of course, for the bottom half of the distribution there were other programs. There was, in the postwar period, a great deal of rental housing under an FHA program which created a scandal and which was abandoned. In effect, the program bribed builders to put up rental housing by making it possible for them to "mortgage out"— that is, to recover their entire investment and, indeed, more from the government guaranteed mortgage. After the revival of multifamily housing in the late fifties, however, new rental housing was too expensive for poor families. In New York City, where the apartment is still the norm, state and city funds made possible various kinds of subsidized apartment houses for middle income and lower middle income populations, and these have included enormous developments of cooperative apartments, sponsored by trade unions and other nonprofit organizations. However, these were not popular elsewhere. The federal government moved into this field of subsidizing lower middle income (or upper lower income) apartment units with its 221 (d)3 program, offering federally insured mortgages to nonprofit or limited profit builders at lower than market interest rates; but this program, which has a good deal of promise for the future, numbered only 15,000 units at the end of 1964.

The major federal program for the poor has been public housing. We have indicated above its relatively small scale. It has been starved by Congress; and low cost units have been built in recent years at a rate of only 20,000 units a year, less than 2 percent of all housing starts. However, if Congress has been unsympathetic, so too has been a substantial part of the group for which it was ostensibly designed—the poor family. Thus, while poor families on urban renewal sites have priority in entering public housing projects, only a minority do so.[14] Public housing has been much discussed but as yet little studied. Some of the best studies have been of public housing in Puerto Rico, where the program operates under the same federal laws as on the continent, but where the prevailing conditions of poverty and the prevailing influence of rural patterns of living make public housing something quite different. The best studies of public housing on the continent are yet to come, but it seems clear they will come after the country as a whole—both Congress and a large percentage of those for whom the program was designed—have indicated their sharp rejection of it. Admittedly, the middle-class liberal and the radical ally of the poor (along, of course, with older critics of the right) seem to be more sharply opposed to public housing than those who live in it and for whom it is designed. As we can see from the long waiting lists in most cities, many families are delighted to get into public housing; but this acceptance of public housing is based on the fact that it is a bargain

---

13. HHFA Annual Report, 1964, p. 51.

14. *Relocation: Unequal Treatment of People and Business Displaced by Governments* (Advisory Commission on Inter-governmental Relations, January, 1965), p. 25; Chester Hartman, "The Limitations of Public Housing: Relocation Choices in a Working-Class Community," *Journal of the American Institute of Planners* 29 (November 1963): 283-96.

(about $500 a year subsidy for an apartment) and that for many people it is the best buy available. Although we do not have the evidence that could give complete assurance for such an assessment, it seems clear that many who live in public housing also have sharp criticisms and find it easy to think of something better.

Public housing has survived to the extent it has only because it has begun to serve a number of special elements in the population who either find it unobjectionable or who have no alternatives available. Thus, after 1956—and owing to its unpopularity with Congress and local communities—public housing began to accept single elderly persons and began to build for the elderly. After World War II, the proportion of nonwhites in public housing began to increase; and in some cities public housing is now largely Negro, which makes it more difficult to attract white families. Also, public housing has increasingly provided dwelling places for families without fathers. Thus, in 1964, 53 percent of families in public housing were nonwhite; 28 percent were elderly.[15] In individual projects, such as that under study by Lee Rainwater in St. Louis, as much as 50 percent of the families may consist of women and children, without husbands.[16] There are, of course, complete families with children in public housing, and perhaps half or more of the units are occupied by them; but white families are a declining proportion, and in most cities they are concentrated in a few projects that are known as "good" projects.

If public housing has "failed"—and we mean that it is unpopular among those who pay for it and those who are supposed to be benefited by it—what explains its failure? The following seem to be the most important explanations.

1. It has been limited to the poorest. Thus, in 1964 the median income of public housing families was under $2,500. Inevitably, these families must include large proportions of families on relief, large proportions of broken families, large proportions of families without wage earners, and large proportions of families with problems that prevent earning. This is not true of all projects; but, when the concentration of the unfortunate and the miserable becomes too large, other families shun the project, and then, despite the attractiveness of good housing (physically speaking) at low rents, a too-high vacancy level may develop. The income limits checked annually have also meant that the more productive are required to leave.

2. Administration has been rather more restrictive and intrusive than in alternative housing, and this has both limited the number of those who would enter and perhaps created a restrictive and unpleasant atmosphere among those who have remained. Studies as to the reasons that people do not like public housing often refer to these restrictions: the inability to keep animals in apartments and conduct businesses in them (in Puerto Rico); the restrictions on painting, alterations, and even on pounding nails into walls (sometimes these restrictions do not actually exist, but the fact that tenants believe they do is itself evidence of the restrictive atmosphere); the prohibition on overnight guests (again, this may be an illusion); and the fact that rents rise with income (which again makes administration—by law and of necessity—intrusive). Under these circumstances, the helpless, fatherless families on welfare flock to the projects.[17]

15. HHFA Annual Report, 1964, p. 19.

16. Lee Rainwater, "Fear and the House as Haven in the Lower Class," *Journal of the American Institute of Planners* 32 (January 1966): 26.

17. On the objections to public housing see Hartman, op. cit.; Kurt W. Back, *Slums, Projects, and People* (Durham, N.C.: Duke University Press, 1962); A. B. Hollingshead and L. H. Rogler, "Attitudes Toward Slums and Public Housing in Puerto Rico," in Leonard J. Duhl (ed.), *The Urban Condition* (New York: Basic Books, 1963). The last two items deal with Puerto Rico. I am also grateful to Professor Back for making available to me unpublished studies done for

(continued on p. 412)

3. Public housing architecture and siting as well as its regulations and its clientele have often marked it off from other housing, stamping it as separate, institutional, and deviant. One can find little evidence that the architecture as such has had unpleasant consequences: the same buildings, more or less, that house low income families in New York seem to provide what is considered reasonable family housing for that city when they house middle income families. Unquestionably, those public housing projects that approximate most closely in their design the housing of the neighborhoods in which they are set—and this means, for most of the country, single-family housing—are most attractive to the public housing resident.

Yet the jungle is not created by the 20-story apartment house. It is created by the social circumstances of the families who live in them. The physical setting only contributes to some undetermined extent, largely as it becomes symbolic of life set apart—of placement in a ghetto. Thus, it would be difficult to argue that curtains instead of doors over clothing closets, or toilet seats without covers, or elevators that stop on every other floor in themselves lead to an unhappy life; but they become symbols of an unhappy life and develop an exaggerated importance. Ironically, any form of physical deviance can be used to symbolize the social deviance. Thus, Marin City, north of San Francisco, which represents the efforts of the Public Housing Administration to break away from institutional architecture and which is a daring creative solution to the problem of building apartment houses on a hill, has had more problems than many architecturally conventional public housing projects (though not for that reason!). Deviant architecture, even when deviant in a progressive direction, is taken to symbolize the deviant social condition of the population and becomes a target of their aggression.

4. Critics have also pointed to the fact that public housing projects are set in old and dilapidated neighborhoods (originally it was hoped the new building might help

---

the Baltimore Housing Authority. On the tendency for public housing to become attractive to fatherless families, see Back, op. cit., pp. 28-29 and elsewhere; Helen Icken Safa, "The Female-Based Household in Public Housing: A Case Study in Puerto Rico," *Human Organization* 24 (Summer 1962): 135-39.

William L. C. Wheaton points out that these restrictions are not as severe as those in the huge middle income projects, cooperative and limited dividend, in New York, where also pets are not allowed, walls are protected, income must not exceed a certain limit, number of occupants must not exceed the limit set by management, business cannot be conducted, and where, in addition, private police forces question all visitors. I have often wondered why the same physical characteristics (tall apartment buildings and apartments arranged along long corridors) that social critics point to as having dehumanizing effects on public housing project residents do not have the same effects on middle income housing project residents—who, in New York City, live in buildings almost undistinguishable from the public housing projects. As Professor Wheaton points out, the management restrictions are also severe. I can think of a number of answers, but the subject is certainly worth research. I would suggest that the residents of the middle income housing projects of New York City are generally Jewish and/or unmarried couples—the young or old—and either because of culture or stage of life may not feel the physical characteristics and management restrictions as severely as Negroes and Puerto Rican females of rural background, where freedom accompanied poor housing. Second, the cooperative tenant and even the tenant in a limited-dividend development, such as we have in New York City, do see that the restrictions are for their own benefit: maintaining the value of their investments or permitting the reasonable rents of the limited-dividend housing project. Third, much of the intrusion in the low income project is designed to search out those who exceed the income limit; in the middle income projects, while there may be an income limit too, there is little policing of income to find out who has exceeded it. Yet all this still does not answer the intriguing question of why the same physical characteristics and management restrictions have different effects in middle income and low income projects. Unquestionably, we would also have to consider Oscar Lewis' "culture of poverty."

improve the neighborhoods) and are cut off from the middle-class areas, which resent their intrusion but which might serve to encourage social mobility among the project population if public housing could be placed among them.

Much of this criticism is unfortunately undocumented with research, and this last point is perhaps least well supported. In New York, in Washington, and elsewhere, there have been efforts to place public housing adjacent to middle income housing developments. It is not clear what effect, if any, this has had on the low income population, as compared with projects that are placed in low income neighborhoods. One may feel confident that the poor prefer to live in a less poor neighborhood; there are more facilities, better stores, and less crime. One must be less confident when one asserts that proximity to middle-class, residential areas will have some specific social and psychological effects on the project dwellers. Indeed, Kriesberg and Bellin, in their careful study of four Syracuse housing projects, suggest the opposite.

> Integration within a project network of friends and mutual aid is facilitated by prior acquaintance with another project tenant, by previous residence in the neighborhood near the project, and by project homogeneity. But these conditions are most likely to be maximized when projects are located in predominantly low-income neighborhoods. The integration and support then may be most likely to further the maintenance of low-income life styles.[18]

Thus, racial and class integration may mean less psychological support; but psychological support may mean less motivation to change. Even more alarmingly, they suggest,

> The support and aid of low-income housing can give an incremental benefit to being husbandless rather than enduring a distressful marriage. (Welfare also has such an effect.) A husband can feel less sense of responsibility if he sees husbandless mothers managing very well with the support of a variety of formal and informal networks.[19]

Thus social policy and the support of the incomplete family can serve to encourage family breakup.

The dilemma is a familiar one: to support the broken family means to make it easier for the family to be broken. Kriesberg and Bellin suggest the housing project has certain virtues for the broken family.

> It appears that many husbandless mothers living in the small projects of Syracuse derive social and emotional support from residence in the projects. Depending upon the characteristics of the projects, this can also mean more active lives, with more involvement in community activities.[20]

We all feel that the concentration of the poor is bad and will have bad effects. Yet what if this concentration gives "social and psychological support" to the unfortunate and permits "more active lives"?[21]

Are there solutions to these problems of public housing? Many earnest efforts have failed, and others have been partially successful. Thus, consider the efforts to create balanced communities within the projects. The New York City Housing Authority has tried to limit the number of families on welfare, and this leads to the ironic

18. Louis Kriesberg and Seymour S. Bellin, "Fatherless Families and Housing: A Study of Dependency," Syracuse University Youth Development Center, unpublished final report, U.S. Department of Health, Education and Welfare, Grant Number 042, 1965.

19. Ibid.

20. Ibid.

21. Ibid.

necessity of the welfare department paying inflated rents for slum dwellings for its clients because it cannot place them in public housing. The objective of balanced communities means, too, that the Housing Authority may favor a family that financially is in lesser need over one that is in greater need, because the first family will make a larger contribution to creating a balanced community. The Housing Authority has tried to create racially and ethnically mixed projects; and this, too, has led to the ironic conclusion that it will favor an elderly white couple (because whites are in short supply in public housing) over a Negro family with children (because Negroes are all too plentiful in public housing). It has tried to protect its families from potential and actual criminals and drug addicts and has therefore set up a checklist for applicants; this has meant that it has had to exclude those whose need is greatest. It has rehabilitated brownstones and older apartment houses so that its dwellings would blend into the New York scene, but the costs, in administrative time and money, of rehabilitation to government standards have been frighteningly high and have forced it to depend on large projects. It has tried to break up its projects and spread them into middle class communities; consequently it has roused the protests of middle class community dwellers who are convinced that public housing will make their neighborhoods less attractive, less safe, and less desirable.

Public housing is a graveyard of good intentions, some of which succeed partially. Some projects are maintained as good communities; some are racially balanced; some rehabilitated dwellings are added to the public housing supply; some small projects are sited in middle class areas. However, to turn public housing into sound, low cost family housing seems enormously difficult. Indeed, the government has put its hopes for low income family housing into rent supplements, which perhaps will overcome the major problems I have outlined. Yet while Congress has accepted the principle, it has resisted the appropriation of the funds required to put a large rent-supplement program into effect. Rent supplements themselves raise a host of intriguing problems for the sociologist of the future; for if the homeowner and the middle income renter have resisted the low income housing project coming into their neighborhoods, how will they feel about the subsidized low income family? What stigma will it bear? How will its relations with unsubsidized (or less subsidized) neighbors be affected? If there is stigma, will it be because of the program under which the family is subsidized, the low income which makes it necessary, or some social or cultural attributes correlated with low income?

My own conclusion is that while both traditional public housing and the new rent-subsidy program have a place in providing housing for the poor, they are not the final or the best answers to the problem. In an egalitarian society, where the single-family home, under homeownership, is the *norm,* it must also become the *objective* of the poor family; and less than that will generally become a sign of discrimination and degradation. This will not be true in situations where a substantial number of middle income families live in apartments (as in New York), but it will be true in most of the country. Charles Abrams has argued that homeownership, in houses indistinguishable from those of other Americans, should become the norm for the low income family in our cities. . . .

I would argue that one must avoid the danger of building for the poor under regulations or in a style very different from that which the middle class is accustomed to. The housing for the poor of the nations of northwestern Europe, whether the Council housing of England or the apartments of Scandinavia, is in effect the housing that most people in those countries have; and it is not marked by any stigma of deviance. In New York, public housing is not that different from the housing of other New Yorkers; and there public housing is politically popular, and various types of public housing are built with city and state funds as well as federal funds. Sam B. Warner, describing the history of two philanthropic projects to provide working-men's homes in late 19th century Boston, provides a cautionary tale for us in considering what kind of housing to provide for the poor.

The first project, put up through the efforts of Robert Treat Paine, provided two-story, row, brick houses. Warner writes:

> Though Paine's houses and narrow streets may have been suitable in Philadelphia, where there was a long and continuous tradition of row housing, in Boston these buildings had a strong philanthropic air. They were brick and fireproof and had a full set of plumbing facilities, but for all their safety and sanitation they remained mean, cramped row houses built a full decade after the main body of the middle class had ceased building row houses for itself. Like the wooden barracks and tenements of the neighborhood, these houses were suited to the momentary needs and capabilities of their inhabitants—all too suited to them, and not at all suited to their aspirations. . . . Because Paine had built minimal structures, and built without regard to some of the important middle class aspirations of the day, his houses suffered the fate of all the other homes in the area. For the last forty years they have served as slum dwellings, and, despite Paine's careful construction, they are falling to the ground.[22]

Paine's second undertaking was

> . . . a cheap project . . . but the streets do follow the contours of the land and are designed to make a traffic cul de sac . . . such site planning was just then coming into vogue for expensive subdivisions in Brookline and other parts of greater Boston. . . .
>
> The houses themselves came in several styles of detached frame single and two-family structures. A variety of contemporary ornament was also offered. . . . The houses were more than twice as big as the little row houses of the 1880's and sold for twice as much. . . .The whole suburban "cottagey" effect of this hundred-house subdivision was underlined with street names of "Round Hill" and "Sunnyside". . . .
>
> Paine's houses are still kept up because for sixty years they have been the best choice of the neighborhood. They have been the best choice because they were more in keeping with the housing aspirations of Bostonians than any of the other cheap alternatives of the 1890's.
>
> The success of Paine's experiment suggests that slum housing is one of the prices that a society pays for allowing any major amount of its building to proceed at a level below its common understanding among the middle class as to what constitutes a satisfactory home environment.[23]

This is an intriguing conclusion, but is this not what we have allowed to happen with public housing? Also, is this not part of the reason that we are faced with the contradiction of social slums in what are some of the best built structures in our housing stock?

Criticism II: Does Housing Policy Destroy Urbanism?

The second major criticism of American housing policy—that it is destructive of urbanism—has , . . . a number of parts. Part of the criticism is of the design of the

22. Sam B. Warner, *Streetcar Suburbs* (Cambridge, Mass.: Harvard University Press and MIT Press, 1962), pp. 103-5.

23. Ibid. There are pictures of both developments; contemporary architects would un-questionably prefer the clean lines of the row housing.

communities that have been built with federal subsidy and support, both new suburban communities and new developments within the city. This design criticism is linked with social criticism of insufficient density and variety. Finally, we have placed under this criticism the charge that federal policy has encouraged the separation of the races.

Certainly we can point to few creative achievements in the field of urban design except for the shopping center, and that has been built without federal aid. Yet it is equally true that the demand for the kinds of design that urban designers have most favored has not been very great. Thus, urban designers have been attracted to the row house, which combines an economy in the use of space with a relatively high degree of privacy for the family. It offers the possibility of a common use of some of the saved space. It gives a larger opportunity to the architect to create a space than does the single-family detached house and links current building with the great tradition of urban architecture.

Yet there tends to be a conflict between the interest of the designer and the interest of the family. Regardless of its great historical associations for the architect, for the family seeking space and good living row housing generally means more cramped conditions than the detached house.[24] Where land is expensive—the land of urban renewal developments in central cities and of near-in older areas in New York—the row house will be widely used, but it is clearly a second best. For most of this country, land costs are still so reasonable as to permit most families to realize their first choice in the amount of space they consider desirable.

The variety that is so attractive to the architectural critic or urban designer is less attractive to the homeowner as well as the family. If the variety means only varied ornamentation on houses of the same basic style or price, that is fine with the homeowner. If it means the introduction of apartment houses, homeowners will object; if it means nonresidential uses, they will object again. They do not want the convenience of corner shopping. They often do not even want the presence of a too-nearby church, regardless of the mildness of its activities. The use of the automobile is so widespread that the family prefers to put all these things at a distance and approach shopping, work, worshipping, and most other activities by automobile. Only for the elementary school is an exception made, because children do not drive.

The variety favored by the urban designer may not imply any social heterogeneity. He may want to mix uses for a single economic level, and, even so, he is often resisted. The social heterogeneity of mixed income groups is fought even more vigorously (even though it may do nothing to break physical heterogeneity). An as yet unpublished study of new communities in California by Werthman, Mandel, and Dienstfrey demonstrates the strength of the resistance to the nearby presence of cheaper residential developments. The homeowner is also an investor, and cheaper housing nearby (any mixing of economic levels means that some of the housing will be cheaper) will be resisted. Thus, even the homeowner at the $21,000 level will resist the intrusion of development, if he can, at the $17,000 level. Ironically, one of the meanings—indeed the chief meaning—of "planning" to the homeowner, according to this study, is that the homeowner will be protected from the intrusion of cheaper housing, which he fears will reduce the value of his own investment, and that he will be protected from nearby nonresidential uses. To the planner and new community developer, on the other hand, what planning means is just the opposite—that, instead of the enormous

24. Herbert Gans, "Effects of the Move from City to Suburb," in Duhl (ed.), op. cit., pp. 184-200.

tract in one style for one income group, he will be able to introduce a variety of groups and a variety of uses.[25]

The charge that federal housing policy has contributed to the separation of the races is certainly the most serious part of this criticism. That residential segregation of Negro and white in the American city is extensive and spreading is undeniable.[26] On the other hand, it is difficult to trace this segregation to federal policy. Charles Abrams has sharply criticized the FHA for encouraging segregation. From 1935 to 1950 its official handbooks warned against the stability of areas that held both Negroes and whites and discouraged guaranteeing mortgages in such areas. Certainly Abrams has demonstrated that the federal government did nothing for many years to encourage integration.[27] Where the local political situation permitted—e.g., New York—public housing was integrated. Where it did not (in the South) it was segregated. In other parts of the North, it was informally segregated. Yet almost everywhere the normal practices of real estate agents and mortgage lenders prevailed. The federal government rationalized these procedures and enormously expanded the possibilities of home-ownership. In this sense, it encouraged segregation, but this encouragement was a by-product of its facilitation of homeownership.

Could it have used its powers, along with its aids to homebuilding, to have moved the country along to integration? Technically, yes; politically, this was unpopular; and, practically, measures to overcome segregation are difficult to implement. Even today, with all the power that the civil rights movement has developed in the years since 1960, the integration of residential areas does not have the highest priority for civil rights activists. Since President Kennedy's executive order of 1962, all federal aid to housing and community development has been on the condition that discrimination will not be practiced. In 1964 the Civil Rights Act prohibited discrimination and segregation in any program that uses federal funds. Many states and cities have had laws against discrimination in rental and sales of housing for some years. Yet the total effect of these measures in creating integrated neighborhoods has been hardly visible. Integration exists in some residential areas but generally as a result of the operation of the housing market rather than as a result of express governmental action.

To produce integration in residential areas requires the most persistent and sophisticated measures of administration and enforcement before any major effect is produced, and even in New York City, where such laws have been in existence for the longest period and with the widest support, one cannot be optimistic about the results. Neither federal, state, nor local action can create integration by fiat. Segregation is an outcome that is shaped by complex forces on many levels: ignorance and prejudice; the differing economic levels of whites and Negroes; economic fears as to the loss of property values by homeowners and other propertyholders; social fears as to the decline of the neighborhood, which seems to refer to such elements as the quality of schools, level of public safety, degree of littering, and social patterns in the use of open space; the institutionalization of discriminatory practices and procedures in all the agents of the housing market—renters and buyers, builders and lenders, banks and appraisers, and local government officials and employees; and personal choice

25. "Planning and the Purchase Decision," by Carl Werthman, Jerry Mandel, and Ted Dienstfrey, unpublished study of the Community Development Project, Edward P. Eichler, Director, Center for Planning and Development Research, University of California, Berkeley.

26. Karl E. and Alma F. Taeuber, *Negroes in Cities* (Chicago: Aldine, 1965).

27. Charles Abrams, *Forbidden Neighbors* (New York: Harper, 1955); and *The City is the Frontier* (New York: Harper & Row, 1965), p. 61.

by Negro and white. On the whole, in this area federal policy has followed local practice, and, on the whole, local practice has been discriminatory.[28]

The executive order of 1962, the Civil Rights Act of 1964, and many local and state laws now call on government to do more; but in this area—as in so many areas of social policy—it is not easy to find the Gordian knot to be cut at one stroke. One can find principles, policies, and approaches. Perhaps the single most important principle that emerges from the literature on this question is that it is possibly too much at this time to try to integrate both different economic levels and Negro and white in the same areas. When one keeps these two forms of integration separate and tries to integrate middle income Negro and white groups and lower income Negro and white groups, the problems may be manageable, even if difficult and delicate.

It is clear that the builder who is willing to accept a few losses and a somewhat lower rate of sale can successfully sell to both groups. However, as we know from experience in other areas—such as higher education and the higher civil service—in which there has been no discrimination for some time, it requires active measures of recruitment to proceed from nondiscrimination to integration. As against the cases of the civil service and some universities and.corporations, builders and developers who have gone out of their way in an attempt to create an integrated community are rare indeed. A few experiments have been conducted on a small scale. With a rising Negro middle income housing market, it should be possible to extend the scale of these undertakings.[29]. . .

It will take political muscle on the federal level to make residential integration a reality, more now than before the summer of 1966. For some time, it would appear, that muscle, if it is available, will be directed to the objectives of reducing unemployment, raising welfare and social insurance levels, desegregating and improving urban education, and increasing Negro political representation. Indeed, one may question the overall importance of the residential integration aim. Unquestionably, housing must be available; discrimination should be illegal (though, when the discrimination is that of the individual homeowner, we have a serious clash of principles). However, the task of creating a fully integrated residential pattern raises such overwhelming difficulties and the gains to be achieved by it are so questionable that I wonder how far governmental power in this direction should reach. Government should prevent active discrimination. But should it go beyond this to actively promote integration? In the light of the persistent tendencies of ethnic and racial groups in the past to prefer some degree of concentration—though nowhere the degree that is imposed on the Negro—I doubt it.[30]

If we were to move ahead to a major policy of homebuilding for the poor, then we would have an even larger problem. We would be faced with the same difficulty of achieving residential racial integration for low income Negroes that we now find in public housing. The concentration of Negro families in the low income population in the worst housing is so great that any program designed to accommodate poor

---

28. On the mechanisms that produce segregation, see among others, Davis McEntire, *Residence and Race* (Berkeley and Los Angeles: University of California Press, 1960); George and Eunice Grier, *Privately Developed Interracial Housing* (Berkeley: University of California Press, 1960); Nathan Glazer and Davis McEntire (eds.), *Studies in Housing and Minority Groups* (Berkeley: University of California Press. 1960).

29. On experiences in this field, see *Equal Opportunity in Housing* (Housing and Home Finance Agency, June, 1964).

30. For further discussion on this point, see *Beyond the Melting Pot* (Cambridge, Mass.: MIT Press, 1963), passim.

families in new housing would be a program largely for Negro families. The difficulties of distributing such housing in higher priced neighborhoods would be immense. The tendency of any program that hoped to make an impact on this problem rapidly would be to bypass the subtle and time-consuming political and administrative procedures required to distribute low income housing among an upper income population and build large tracts designed specifically for those whose housing needs were greatest—that is, poor Negro families. Thus, once again we would have the specter of racially segregated areas built with federal funds.

Any proposal to eliminate the worst family housing along the lines I earlier suggested—single-family housing—would come into conflict with the aim of integration. One American New Town project trying to achieve a balanced community of middle and low income, white and black, has attempted to analyze, with help of social scientists, how heterogeneity of this type could be introduced and has concluded that some minimal degree of separation of income levels and races would in effect take place. Those who bought the more expensive housing would want the neighborhood benefits that came from more prosperous neighbors, and the poor neighborhoods would inevitably be largely Negro.

I would conclude that, while it is possible to integrate the races of the same economic level, to carry through such an integration when the whites are (mostly) prosperous and the Negroes are (mostly) poor would be enormously difficult; and no measures that we can project give hope that such integration on a major scale can take place in the near future. Under these circumstances, we must expect for some time to come that poor areas will be largely Negro and that more prosperous areas will be largely white, with some small degree of integration. This further raises the prospect that cities will become inhabited by majorities of Negroes and that suburbs will remain overwhelmingly white, with slowly rising proportions of Negroes. At one time this prospect appeared disastrous; now that we know that we must undergo it, further analysis and reflection and experience suggest that it need not be.[31] Growing Negro economic capacity will destroy this pattern, and, if this develops rapidly enough, conceivably this pattern of Negro central city and white suburbs will be limited to only a few metropolitan areas.

In considering this question of racial integration, as in our consideration earlier of the complex problems of creating a "balanced community" in a housing project, the question must come up, who wants balanced and integrated communities and what are their virtues? Obviously this question would not arise if such a community developed as a result of the unguided play of economic and technological forces. Thus, the Middletown of the 1920s had workers and businessmen, community leaders and casual laborers, Negroes and whites. It had grown as a service and industrial city; and, in contrast to a Levittown of the same size 30 years later, seemed to have clear and obvious virtues. The classes could learn from each other by direct observation and contact something of the whole complex structure of society. Children growing up could see men at work, the aged, and the houses of the rich and the poor.

On the other hand, Levittown and the housing project also came into existence for clear and sufficient reasons: one, to house rapidly great numbers of relatively low income young families; the other, to house great numbers of truly poor people. We have seen why it has been difficult to introduce a great range of social variation in such communities. The homeowners of Levittown would not want cheaper houses, and buyers of more expensive houses would not want to live there. The poor in the housing projects would be deprived of their right to subsidized housing if some

31. On the earlier view, see Morton Grodzins, *The Metropolitan Area as a Racial Problem* (Pittsburgh: University of Pittsburgh Press, 1958); on the latter, see Edward P. Eichler and Marshall Kaplan, *The Community Builders* (Center for Planning and Development Research, University of California, Berkeley, forthcoming).

substantial portion of this housing went to those who economically did not need it, whatever their presumed social virtues for the community. Some degree of variation comes into effect even under these circumstances. Wealthier professionals will be willing to live in Levittown. Some of those who become more prosperous will add to their houses rather than leave for a higher level community.

The question remains, what efforts of social policy are justified in introducing a greater social variety into these communities? If this social variety is maintained by the exclusion of racial groups, it is in large measure illegal and it is certainly immoral. Beyond this, however, should we—using the test of the family and what is good for it—introduce a greater social variety through insisting on a wide range of economic levels and through a positive effort to recruit families of minority groups? One is cognizant of the fact that even where such variety exists (in the crowded central city), the mere fact of geographical proximity may lead to very little social contact. *Dead End*, in which the slum kids interact with the swells, is still fiction; most such interaction occurs through the intermediary of the police. Puerto Ricans and Negroes in the shadows of the expensive apartment houses of New York scarcely have any interaction with the wealthy; they generally use different stores, schools, churches, and open spaces.

Geographical proximity may lead to little of that social interaction that we want and which we try to achieve when we press for communities with representatives of different economic levels and racial groups. On the other hand, the new monumental scale of our metropolitan areas and subareas does not necessarily isolate economic and racial groups more. Interaction between our larger ghettos and larger suburban communities may be in some ways more intense than when low income and middle income groups shared the same small community. This interaction today occurs through politics, the press, and the mass media and through riots and demonstrations. It may be an interaction appropriate to our new urban scale.

Nor have we truly examined the gains of the one-class or one-race community. Herbert Gans has unemotionally and unideologically pointed out that middle-class families like to have people like themselves as their neighbors; and he has questioned what gains would follow from imposing on them a random selection of unlike-minded neighbors.[32] We pointed earlier to the advantages for even fatherless families of some degree of concentration. Certainly ethnic groups, even 40 years after the end of mass immigration, still seem to want to cluster together. Consider the Italians of Boston's late West End or the East European communities of Chicago that are resisting Martin Luther King's integration campaign.

I think we have good social grounds for imposing a certain amount of discomfort on people who would prefer to live in communities of like and like-minded people. We can impose this discomfort when this common desire restricts others' rights to housing; we may impose this discomfort when some larger social end dictates a new and different use for the land of the community in which they live. However, I would stop at imposing this discomfort out of our Western, Protestant ideology that progress is that result of being uprooted from the familial and tribal wombs. One hesitates to use a sociological theory as the basis for social policy.

Aside from racial and economic segregation, our new communities show another form of segregation—by family life-cycle. Young families with children live in new suburban single-family home areas; older families will live in the older sections of the city. When children are grown and gone, elderly couples or single survivors will occupy a variety of specialized buildings or communities for the aged. Young couples without children occupy the new suburban apartment houses, and, with more money

32. Herbert J. Gans, "Planning and Social Life: Friendship and Neighbor Relations in Suburban Communities," and "The Balanced Community: Homogeneity and Heterogeneity in Residential Areas," *Journal of the American Institute of Planners* 27 (May and August 1961): 134-40, 176-84.

and a different style of life, the new inner-city apartment houses. Certainly we find a degree of segregation by family life-cycle that is more extreme than in the past, and that must have certain consequences for children and family life. It encourages the peer-group society, reduces the role of the generation of grandparents in the rearing of children; it also encourages a more rapid geographical mobility, for some neighborhoods are appropriate to one section of the family cycle, others to another part.

Has housing policy encouraged this segregation? In some degree it has. It has encouraged it simply because programs are defined in terms of certain specific needs: we have the standard FHA and VA programs which are designed for the family with children, special programs for senior citizens, and special programs for apartment building. Theoretically, a developer could mix all these and other building types in the same development. Practically, he does not have the overhead resources for planning and negotiating with various federal agencies that this requires. It is hard to think of any good reason that the segregation should be as pronounced as it it. Perhaps senior citizens are annoyed by children's noise and prefer the company of others like them. Does this mean we should build communities of thousands of units for senior citizens alone? We cannot refer to any definitive studies—indeed, there are hardly any studies at all—but it does seem that, just as we have decided it was inhuman and murderous to segregate the mentally ill in vast institutions of many thousands, we may in time decide that the scale of some of our communities and developments for the aged is far too large. We may find that there are drawbacks in communities that recruit all their residents from the young family stage in the life-cycle. One can only speculate as to the social and psychological effects, but we can point to inefficiencies in such communities—enormous pressures on schools followed by underutilization, for example. On the other hand, the drawbacks are not yet so obvious as to lead to any clear or strong demand that our policies be reviewed in the light of their effects in fostering or discouraging developments limited to one stage in the family life-cycle. . . .

Aside from the immediate impact, urban renewal also reduced the quantity of low cost housing and raised rents for the poor. On the other hand, the overall housing stock was rising faster than the number of households; the average quality of the housing stock was rising; and the number of vacancies was slowly increasing. Thus, this increase in housing costs was, overall, matched by an increase in housing quality. Was this increase in housing quality essential, when there were so many poor who would have preferred their poorer housing at lower rents? One may take this side of the argument. However, those who take it do not always realize that a necessary implication is that, in doing so, one accepts the legitimacy of a range of freedom of choice in housing for people which a wealthy and socially conscious society tends to restrict at the lower end. Thus, we do not allow people in cities to live in shacks without plumbing. Yet if we want to give them the freedom to spend only a small proportion of their income on housing, then we must give them this freedom. One cannot take both sides of the argument, insisting that we should not undertake housing policies that improve housing and increase housing costs and insisting, at the same time, that we should not tolerate slums.

The increase in housing costs for the poorest as a result of urban renewal's destruction of cheap housing (which plays only a small role actually in eliminating cheap housing —other public and private investment policies have a much larger effect) has been to some extent matched by a general increase in income. However, urban renewal raises sharply the need either to establish minimum incomes so that people can afford the minimum housing that society insists they occupy or to subsidize the housing costs directly. . . .

CONCLUSION

I would conclude that our housing policy has permitted the majority of American families to improve their living conditions and to gain family settings for themselves that are superior to those they left. We have done little for a substantial minority of poor families who have not had the resources to achieve what the society considers (and they, too) minimally desirable housing; for them, we must devise income maintenance policies or housing subsidies that permit them to achieve such housing. Nor has this policy been attractive to urban designers, architects, and all those sensitive to the value of maintaining or achieving subtle unities in the relationships between home, community facilities, workplaces, transportation, and natural setting. Just as we are rich enough to provide decent minimal family settings for the economically deprived in our population, so, I believe, we are rich enough to provide some resources to the aesthetically deprived so as to maintain our more successful urban settings and to devise new ones. However, both new directions of policy must be fed, of course, through the complex procedures of a democratic society; and their proponents must convince the majority that they too will benefit from these extensions of our major policy commitments.

36. Federal Housing Policy: A Political-Economic Analysis

MICHAEL E. STONE

Analysts often tend to view housing in a parochial manner, without questioning the overall implications of government policy for the type of economic system we live in. Since the 1930s government involvement in the housing sector has increased significantly, particularly in respect to its role in the mortgage market. Housing experts have identified deposit insurance, mortgage insurance and guarantees, the secondary mortgage market, and housing subsidy programs as the key elements in providing for homeownership and the upgrading of the housing stock. Michael Stone, however, contends that this transformation has served only to augment the power and profits of ↑ mortgage lenders and has entrenched them as major components in our modern capitalist system. Moreover, he finds that this pattern of government involvement has caused many families to pay exorbitant rents and to live in substandard housing.

The United States is in the midst of a severe housing crisis. There are not enough dwelling units in decent condition, at appropriate locations, with required amenities and secure tenure and at bearable prices. While the present situation is particularly severe and great public concern is being voiced about it, this country has had a persistent housing problem which it has never shown itself capable of solving. Even at the times when the absolute number of housing units has been nearly sufficient, families have still had to pay an enormous percentage of their incomes for housing and millions still have had to live in squalid, miserable conditions. The housing problem is not new; it has just persisted and worsened. Indeed it is unlikely that much progress will be made toward its solution unless widespread political and economic changes take place in America.

The crucial decisions in the housing sector—as in most major areas of this society—are not made primarily on the basis of human needs. Instead, the important decisions revolve around the flow of investment capital into housing, and these decisions of course are made on the basis of opportunities for profit. Due to the intrinsic nature of housing and to the structure of ownership in this country, housing investment is primarily by means of mortgage borrowing. Mortgage-lending institutions are the dominant force in the housing sector and contribute directly to the existence and maintenance of the housing problem.

THE HOUSING MARKET

Housing possesses certain characteristics which, taken together, make it quite distinctive as an economic good. These characteristics make housing particularly vulnerable to the profit-making structure of capitalism and therefore make housing a particularly good example of the injustices and inefficiencies of the present economic order.

The Price of Housing

One of the most distinguishing qualities of housing is its durability. If reasonably well built and maintained, housing can last for generations. As a result, the stock of housing turns over and is replaced only very slowly. In any given year newly constructed housing is only about 2 to 3 percent of the total supply. In 1968, for example, there were about 66 million dwelling units in the United States and a total of about 1.5 million housing starts—2.3 percent of the housing stock was therefore new.[1] Last year housing starts reached the highest rate this country has ever seen—nearly 2.1 million units.[2] Since there was a total of about 69 million units at the beginning of the year,[3] new housing was 3 percent of the total stock. Even if the stated national goal of an average of 2.6 million housing starts for the 10-year period 1968-1978 were met (it was met last year, if mobile homes are included), each year new housing would still be less than 4 percent of the total.[4]

In addition, housing is an extremely bulky commodity—a characteristic with two important aspects. First, the total construction time for new housing tends to be at least a year. Second, housing is tied to land and possesses locational advantages or disadvantages. Together, the durability and bulkiness of housing make its supply extraordinarily stable and unresponsive to changes in demand. They also make it extremely hard for equivalent or comparable replacement housing to enter the market.

The relative fixity of housing supply would probably not be terribly significant were it not for certain important features of the demand for housing. First, the need for housing is constantly expanding. The number of households is continually growing, while at the same time housing is being lost through age, neglect, disasters, and clearance for highways and urban renewal. Growing competition for the existing housing drives up its price, but, in the short run at least, there is no compensating increase in supply. The market mechanism is thus rather ineffective in adjusting housing supply to housing demand.

In addition, housing is a necessity in this society. As demand increases and prices rise as a result, consumers generally have no choice but to pay. Because of climatic and social conditions in this country, people cannot choose to do without housing and live on the streets or in the woods. Because of legal constraints they cannot successfully opt out of the housing market by squatting in vacant buildings or erecting their own structures on vacant land.

The increasing and unavoidable need for a bulky commodity of relatively fixed supply inevitably drives housing expenses up as high as consumers can possibly bear—that is, to a very high proportion of every family's income. Housing is by far the largest single consumption expenditure in this country. For the population as a whole, on average 15 percent of family income goes for housing[5], not including utilities, furniture, and other household operations. For most poor families, housing

1. U.S., President's Committee on Urban Housing, The Report of the Committee, *A Decent Home* (Washington, D.C.: Government Printing Office, 1969), pp. 39, 48.

2. *Housing Affairs Letter*, no. 73-3, January 21, 1972, p. 1.

3. U.S., Bureau of the Census, *Statistical Abstract of the United States: 1971* (92nd ed.; Washington, D.C.: Government Printing Office, 1971), p. 675, table 1112.

4. *A Decent Home*, p. 3.

5. *Statistical Abstract*, p. 308, table 490.

expenditures exceed 25 percent of their already meager incomes. Over 80 percent of the residents of metropolitan areas with annual incomes of below $2,000 spend more than 35 percent of their incomes for rent. About two-thirds of households with incomes between $2,000 and $3,000 (and nearly half of households between $3,000 and $4,000) must spend over 25 percent.[6] At the same time, these poor families are relegated by the market to the worst housing because of their inability to compete for more costly better housing. For no other item, except perhaps medical care, are the injustices of the market economy so great and the burdens so heavy.

The Financing of Housing

Given the market-determined system of monthly housing expenses, who benefits from these housing payments? Many studies reveal that typically, for both renters and so-called homeowners, about one-quarter of monthly occupancy expenses goes for property taxes and one-quarter for utilities, maintenance, repairs, and overhead. The other half represents profits for the investors in the property—the owner of record and the mortgage lender or lenders.[7]

At present nearly every purchase of residential real estate is financed in part by mortgage loans. Because of the long economic life of most housing and as a result of state support for mortgage lenders, the loans usually amount to about 70 to 90 percent of the purchase price and are for terms of 20 to 40 years. This means that during the first few years of ownership nearly all the investment profits go directly to the mortgage lender in the form of interest payments. Indeed, over the entire period of the loan, total payments for interest are generally much greater than the loan principal itself. For example, on a 30-year 7-percent loan, the borrower will pay in interest 1.4 times the amount of the loan.

Mortgage lenders are clearly major beneficiaries of the scarcity and resulting high prices of housing. The political significance of these benefits becomes clearer when the scope of the housing sector and the nature of mortgage lenders is considered. Dwellings and the land they occupy comprise almost one-third of the wealth of this country, and despite the slow turnover of stock, new housing represents over one-quarter of the nation's annual capital investment.[8] Residential mortgages outstanding at the end of 1971 were worth nearly $375 billion, about $50 billion more than total publicly held federal debt and more than twice the value of all outstanding long-term bonds of nonfinancial corporations.[9] In a typical year over 4 million new mortgages are written, with a net increase of residential mortgage debt of about $20 billion.[10] With the sudden easing of the money market, the net increase in 1971 jumped to $36 billion, by far the largest annual increase in history.[11]

The collective power of mortgage-lending institutions is obviously enormous. What makes this power even more formidable is its distribution. Rather than being dispersed among a diverse and heterogeneous group of relatively small investors, it is concentrated in five major types of savings institutions. Three of these are "depository institutions"—savings and loan associations, mutual savings banks, commercial banks

6. U.S., President's Committee on Urban Housing, *Technical Studies*, vol. 1 (Washington, D.C.: Government Printing Office, 1969), p. 14; p. 32, table A-6.

7. *A Decent Home*, p. 118.

8. Ibid., p. 114.

9. U.S. Savings and Loan League, *Savings and Loan Fact Book: 1972* (Chicago: U.S. Savings and Loan League, 1972), p. 32, table 23.

10. Ibid., p. 34, table 25.

11. Ibid.

—and together they hold about 70 percent of outstanding mortgage debt.[12] The two others are "contract savings institutions"—life insurance companies and retirement funds.

Each type of lending institution has an enormous scope and power. In addition, the different types have much in common and wield their power very much in concert. What is especially noteworthy about all of them is that their enormous power comes from control of wealth which they do not even own. They collect and direct the savings of tens of millions of people. Thus, the power over this wealth and much of the profits that flow from it accrue to those who do not even own it. This is a remarkable feature of modern capitalism in general as well as of the housing sector, and it has come about only relatively recently and with the active support of the federal government.

Changes in Housing Supply

Although mortgage lenders are the principal beneficiaries of the large expenditures which people must make for housing services, it might be argued that these burdensome expenditures are simply the result of excessive demand relative to supply and not the result of any action by mortgage lenders. If the supply of housing were to increase significantly, consumers would have more choices available, and sellers of housing would have to compete for buyers by lowering their rents and sale prices. In fact, there are definite reasons why a housing shortage persists, and mortgage lenders play a crucial role in maintaining this shortage.

Although the supply of housing is relatively fixed, the supply does gradually change as builders and developers pursue profit opportunities created by increasing demand. What determines whether new housing gets built, however, is the cost of producing new housing relative to the price of existing housing. Thus, even though a shortage of housing drives up the price of existing housing and apparently creates a market for new housing, not much new housing will get built if production costs also rapidly increase and sharply reduce developer's potential profits. This is in fact what has been happening.

As rents rise in response to scarcity, housing investment becomes attractive to would-be landlords who hope to profit from high rents and would-be homeowners who want to escape from paying rent. As the demand for residential real estate increases, sales prices rise and the size of and demand for mortgage loans increase. Although mortgage interest rates are largely determined by the overall supply of and demand for credit in the economy, increased demand specifically for mortgage money does tend to push up interest rates. Higher interest rates and larger loans combine to produce higher monthly mortgage payments. These higher payments will partially offset the financial attraction of buying property and thereby reduce demand somewhat. This in turn has a depressing effect on the price of houses. Mortgage lending thus prevents scarcity-induced rent increases from being fully translated into increases in sale prices for existing housing. Mortgage lending therefore inhibits the impact of increased demand on new construction.

The Cost of New Housing

In producing new housing, a developer's costs, both for single-family and multifamily housing, are roughly distributed as follows:[13]

12. *A Decent Home*, p. 130.

13. U.S., President's Committee on Urban Housing, *Technical Studies*, vol. 2 (Washington, D.C.: Government Printing Office, 1969), p. 9; Elsie Eaves, *How the Many Costs of Housing Fit*

Site		20%
Land acquisition	10%	
Grading, sewers, etc.	10%	
Building		55%
Labor	20%	
Materials	35%	
Developer's overhead and profit		15%
Construction Financing		10%

It is commonly believed that labor is the main factor causing increased housing-production costs. The cost increases are allegedly attributed to the archaic closed-shop practices of the unions, low productivity and high wage settlements. This is in fact a union-busting tactic designed to divide the working class and divert attention from the major sources of cost increases—profiteering by land speculators and bankers.

Hourly wages of workers in the building trades have risen extremely rapidly when compared with other industries. What is never added though is that the average construction worker has a job only two-thirds of the year, and for the past few years there has been little enough construction work of any sort. Indeed, ever since World War II the annual average unemployment rate in the construction industry has been about twice as high as in all nonagricultural industries; since the mid-1950s it has been even more than twice as high.[14] The apparently high wage settlements have in fact not kept annual incomes of construction workers up with workers in manufacturing.[15]

In addition, careful studies have revealed that from 1947 to 1965 real output per man-hour in the construction industry actually increased at an average annual rate of 3.4 percent—quite comparable with manufacturing.[16] According to the President's Committee on Urban Housing, labor today represents only about 20 percent of the cost of new housing, and between 1950 and 1966 the labor share of housing costs actually decreased. This relative decrease can be attributed to "rising labor productivity, transfer of many activities formerly performed on building sites back into factories, and extremely rapid increases in land prices."[17] The assertion that labor has been the prime source of construction-cost increases is clearly a myth.

The most rapidly rising components of housing costs in recent years have actually been land costs, financing charges and closing costs. During the last few decades land has been the fastest rising major element in the cost of new housing. On average, each parcel of urban land in the U.S. more than doubled in value between 1950 and 1965.[18] This increase refers to raw land alone and does not reflect additional increases in the cost of land development and site preparation. In the same period,

---

Together, U.S. National Commission on Urban Problems, Research Report no. 16 (Washington D.C.: Government Printing Office, 1969), p. 5. This distribution does not include closing costs and any discounts on permanent mortgage loans, which effectively increase the selling price but are not a direct part of production costs.

14. *Technical Studies*, vol. 2, p. 250.

15. Ibid., p. 260; "Black Monday," *Pacific Research and World Empire Telegram*, November-December 1969, p. 21.

16. *Technical Studies*, vol. 2, p. 250.

17. *A Decent Home*, p. 120.

18. Ibid.

for single-family FHA homes, site value (including land development) went on average from 12 to 20 percent of total house value.[19]

As land prices rise, there is a multiplier effect on total construction costs. Developers generally tend to put more expensive or larger houses on higher-priced land.[20] In addition, increases in land prices are generally related to increases in housing demand and housing prices. As the value of housing goes up, the value of both occupied and potentially occupied land also goes up. To the extent that land speculation is financed by mortgage borrowing, lenders contribute to and profit from increased land values.

The incredible inflation in urban land values can also be traced in a very direct way to the changes in mortgage-lending practices caused by federal intervention in the housing sector. By inducing the creation of long-term, low-down-payment mortgage loans, which resulted in the postwar boom in single-family home construction, state intervention encouraged land speculation, created the present scarcity and high price of land in metropolitan areas, and yielded immense profits to speculators and lenders.

The other area of major cost increase is associated with profits made by the financial institutions that invest in housing production. Since housing developers rarely supply much of the capital themselves, they must go through an elaborate process to obtain the funds to build. A study by the National Association of Home Builders of housing-cost increases from 1960 to 1964 directed sharp attention to construction financing in attributing "the greatest percentage cost increases to the factors of financing (higher interest rates and larger discounts on interim loans) and closing costs (title search, recording fees, escrow fees, title insurance, and the like)."[21]

The market for construction financing tends automatically to limit the rate of construction of new housing. As developers compete for construction money, interest rates and/or discount points rise. Depending upon the general scarcity of money and upon the total time of construction, financing charges can add 5 to 12 percent to the cost of new housing.[22] In addition, interim lenders, which are usually commercial banks, often will not make a construction loan unless a developer already has a commitment from another lender for a long-term mortgage loan following construction. In view of the vested interest of lenders in limiting the rate of construction so as to protect the values of their investments in existing housing, this commitment process can have a great deal of leverage over new construction.

Finally, closing costs may add another 10 percent to the price of housing.[23] These costs, which largely represent fees received by banks and lawyers for excessive and often unnecessary paper work, of course add to the price of existing housing as well as new housing. However, the effect of these costs is to increase the price of housing to potential buyers without passing on any of the increase to potential sellers. The net result is thus to stifle housing-market activity and thereby reduce incentives to developers for new construction.

19. Ibid.

20. Eaves, op. cit., p. 1.

21. *A Decent Home*, p. 120.

22. Eaves, op. cit., p. 5.

23. Hugh L. Morris, "Closing Title Costs Prompt Probe," *Boston Sunday Globe*, August 22, 1971.

THE STATE AND THE HOUSING SECTOR

The Emergence of Mortgage Finance

The controlling influence of mortgage-lending institutions on housing has not always existed. In fact, it really began at the start of this century and has grown mainly during the past 40 years, primarily as a result of federal intervention. In this process, an incredible thicket of agencies, structures, programs, devices, and regulations has been created, designed to make housing investment profitable and secure especially for the mortgage lender.

The importance of mortgage financing for residential real estate developed from the quest for new profit opportunities by banks. According to Charles Abrams, "With the dawn of the twentieth century, funds of financial institutions swelled. New outlets for their investment had to be found. Undermortgaged real estate provided one source, new building another."[24] Buyers still had to put up a sizable share of the purchase price and faced the traditional risks of business ventures, while mortgage terms were only three to five years, much less than the economic life of the mortgaged buildings.[25]

The growing importance of mortgage credit for housing was at the time exerted most strongly through the supply side. By the 1920s suppliers of mortgage credit, mostly banking institutions, had already become the locus of power in housing production. As Abrams has said, "Concentration of lending power in institutions having a common interest and a common idiom gave them the power to stimulate or depress building activity. Since building activity vitally influences recovery and depression, the decisions of these institutions to lend or not to lend react upon the national welfare."[26] Inevitably then, when the depression of the 1930s occurred, lending institutions were in the key position for action in the housing sector.

The Trigger for State Intervention

The initial shock of the Depression struck the housing sector, and especially the system of mortgage finance, with particular severity. The collapse was essentially a simple cycle that fed on itself. When the Depression struck, homeowners lost their sources of income and landlords could not command high rents. Property owners therefore could not keep up their mortgage payments without drawing on their savings. But when they went to the banks to withdraw their savings the banks did not have the cash. Their assets were frozen in outstanding mortgage loans.

Unable to make their mortgage payments, owners had their properties foreclosed by the banks, and the banks were then left with houses that they could not sell. In addition, in those cases where banks did have some funds available to satisfy depositors, the withdrawal of these funds eliminated the possibility of new mortgage loans and thereby brought the housing market to a virtual standstill. The need for retooling and for state assistance was therefore obvious and compelling.

In the housing sector the restructuring took place primarily through the creation of permanent supports for the institutions supplying mortgage credit, with no benefits for the masses of people. Apart from a few minor alterations and several additions, the basic form of these supports has remained as originally conceived.[27]

24. Charles Abrams, *The Future of Housing* (New York: Harper & Row, 1946), p. 109.

25. Ibid., pp. 109-10.

26. Ibid., p. 114.

27. Charles M. Haar, *Federal Credit and Private Housing: The Mass Financing Dilemma* (New York: McGraw-Hill, 1960), p. 1.

The Federal Home Loan Bank System

Federal attention toward the housing sector in the 1930s resulted in three main types of structures to aid mortgage lenders. First was the creation of a central banking system for home-loan banks, comparable to the Federal Reserve System for commercial banks, along with governmental insurance of deposits for all types of banks. This system was designed to create a national mortgage market by centralizing, stabilizing, and insuring mortgage-banking operations. Its purpose was to make mortgage banking more efficient, predictable and profitable and at the same time to free mortgage lenders from liability to their depositors, the very people whose money they profit from.

Passed in 1932, the Federal Home Loan Bank Act was the first major federal support for the housing sector. The act created the Federal Home Loan Bank Board which oversees a system of 12 regional Home Loan Banks and also directs the Federal Savings and Loan Insurance Corporation. Membership in the system is open to all state and federally chartered financial institutions other than commercial banks that engage in long-term financing.[28] Savings and loan associations have made up the great majority of membership in the system. The various regional banks act as reserve banks for their members, accepting deposits from them and making loans to them as they pursue profitable investments. Thus the system puts the credit of the federal government behind the member banks, enabling them to borrow cheaply to maintain their profit position.

In addition, the Federal Savings and Loan Insurance Corporation was intended to attract funds into member banks by promising savers that they could get their money back, virtually on demand, regardless of how poorly the bank has operated. As a result, the member banks have been able to obtain greatly increased funds for investment while at the same time reducing their obligation to the suppliers of these funds.

Since 1945 the total capital in savings and loan associations has increased over 20-fold to almost $175 billion in 1971.[29] This fantastic growth has provided needed funds for housing, but has done so at great cost in the form of lenders' profits. And it has done so at virtually no risk to the lending institutions because of the second main feature of federal assistance—mortgage insurance.

Mortgage Insurance

The Federal Housing Administration (FHA) was established by the National Housing Act of 1934. It is in the business of insuring mortgage lenders against the risk of financial loss occurring from default on approved mortgage loans. The costs of running the business and the funds for paying off claims do not come from taxes nor from the lenders who receive the insurance. They come from the borrower, who is insured against nothing. Once again, the federal government created a device to stimulate the housing sector by reducing risk and guaranteeing profits.[30]

The FHA mortgage-insurance system and Veterans Administration (VA) mortgage-guarantee system which was added in 1944 were together an ingenious device for greatly increasing the power and profits of mortgage lenders. Essentially the scheme was one of promoting a boom in housing sales and increasing the role of approved

28. Arthur M. Weimer and Homer Hoyt, *Real Estate* (New York: Ronald Press Co., 1966), p. 456.

29. *Savings and Loan Fact Book*, p. 15, table 4.

30. Abrams, op. cit., p. 233.

mortgage lenders in each housing transaction. To promote purchases the system reduced the down payment to 10 percent or less and greatly extended the loan term to at least 25 years. This in and of itself would have vastly increased the relative importance of lenders, but lenders would not liberalize their loan terms in this way unless their risk could be reduced as well.

Risk reduction was provided by the insurance or guarantee of the mortgage by a federal agency, and so the system was built around this feature. Its results are well known: the vast postwar suburban boom, creating the illusion of homeownership for millions of people, while the actual owners are the mortgage lenders. The putative homeowner pays rent to the bank and also pays an insurance premium to the government. Then if he cannot make his mortgage payments, the government insurance repays the outstanding part of the loan to the mortgage holder, and the government is left owning the property.

The FHA scheme has been very successful in enlarging and consolidating the power of institutional mortgage lenders. By standardizing the mortgage instrument and requiring mortgages to meet certain standards for approval, the system facilitated participation by large-scale institutions and discouraged or prevented individual lenders from participation.

It was originally expected, or at least declared, that the ceiling on interest rates for insured loans would tend to keep down interest rates on conventional loans. In fact, conventional rates have driven up insured rates, attesting to the power of mortgage lenders and their quest for profits. Part of the power over interest rates is revealed in real adjustments up and down of the maximum interest rates FHA will permit on insured loans. A more subtle and profitable adjustment is effected, though, by the lenders themselves—throught the institution of "points," a system of hidden surcharges on VA and FHA-backed mortgages which effectively circumvents the interest ceiling.

The FHA housing-subsidy programs have been built around the established formula and represent no real departure from the basic mortgage-insurance system. In these programs FHA not only provides the mortgage insurance but also pays part of the interest on the mortgage loan. The loan is made by an approved mortgagee at the market rate, and so the lender's profits are as high as ever. Although the home buyer or tenant pays less, the lender receives his usual share. The programs thus use tax dollars to subsidize the profits of mortgage lenders, an approach quite consistent with the basic FHA philosophy.

Secondary Mortgage Markets

One problem with mortgage lending in general and especially with the long-term lending induced by FHA and VA policies is that the investment is not very liquid. If new investment opportunities come along, it is normally not very easy for a mortgage lender to convert his holdings into cash for the new investment. He certainly cannot call in the unpaid balance from the borrower since it was the borrower's own illiquid position that caused him to borrow in the first place. To overcome this difficulty of mortgage lending and to provide a means for lenders to pursue profitable opportunities as they appear, the state provided its third major structural addition in the housing sector—the national secondary mortgage market.

Prior to the 1930s there did exist some secondary markets for mortgages in which lenders would sell off their holdings to other investors. However, due to the great variation in mortgage characteristics and the great potential risk faced by such secondary investors, this market never became very large. One of the principal results of federal mortgage insurance was to provide the needed uniformity and security to make mortgages potentially more liquid.[31]

The standardization and insurance of mortgages did not, however, result in the creation (by private capital) of national mortgage associations to act as secondary trading posts for insured mortgages. Mortgage lenders wanted to be able to sell their holdings as desired, but they did not want to be bothered with having to peddle their mortgages themselves. They wanted a ready buyer always there to serve them.

In response to this desire by the powers of the mortgage business, in 1938 Congress created the Federal National Mortgage Association (FNMA), provided it with an initial capitalization of $10 million and ordered it to buy insured mortgages. In purchasing mortgages from approved lending institutions FNMA permitted the original lenders to continue to service the loans and to receive a fee of 0.25 percent to 1 percent for doing so. In addition, FNMA was authorized to raise additional capital for its operations by issuing notes backed by the federal government.[32]

FNMA thus made the housing sector more profitable in several ways. First, it gave mortgage lenders the liquidity they desired and still enabled them to make some profits on their mortgages even after the mortgages had been sold off. Second, by creating a large-scale, national pool of insured mortgages, FNMA was able to offer shares in this pool on a short-term basis in the securities markets, thereby making housing finance profitable for another whole group of investors.

Although initially the mortgage lenders had wanted the federal government to underwrite the costs and risks of establishing FNMA, by 1954 it had become so successful that there was great pressure for it to become privately owned and operated. The FNMA Charter Act of 1954 began the transfer process by authorizing the sale of stock to finance the secondary-market operations of FNMA.[33] the Housing Act of 1968 completed the process, and now FNMA is virtually private.

This sequence of events is one of the clearest examples of the intermeshing of the state and private business under modern capitalism. A national facility, greatly needed and desired by private business to reduce its risks and assure it of ready markets for its products, is first created and nurtured at public expense. Once it becomes established and begins to repay its costs, the facility is turned over to private interests so that its success can produce profits for them.

In the process of reorganizing FNMA in 1968, the secondary-market operations of FNMA were separated from more risky functions of special assistance, management, and liquidation of holdings, which were left with a new government-underwritten corporation known as the Government National Mortgage Association.[34] Thus the pattern of activity continues.

Finally, until 1970 FNMA was limited to purchasing government-insured mortgages. For a number of years after World War II a majority of new residential mortgages were either FHA or VA loans. In recent years the proportion has decreased to under one-fifth, mainly because the interest-rate ceiling on these loans remained somewhat below the market rate for long-term uninsured mortgage loans. This led to pressure for a secondary market for conventional mortgages. The Emergency Home Finance Act of 1970 provided for not one but two secondary-market structures for conventional

31. Leo Grebler, David M. Blank, and Louis Winnick, *Capital Formation in Residential Real Estate* (Princeton: Princeton University Press, 1956), pp. 252-53.

32. Henry E. Hoagland and Leo D. Stone, *Real Estate Finance* (Homewood, Ill.: Richard D. Irwin Inc., 1969), pp. 558-59.

33. Ibid., pp. 570-71.

34. *Savings and Loan Fact Book*, p. 129.

mortgages: first, FNMA was authorized to purchase conventional mortgages; and second, the new Federal Home Loan Mortgage Corporation, set up under the Home Loan Bank Board, can purchase both conventional and insured mortgages from any federally insured banking institution.[35]

Public Housing: The Exception?

The one apparent departure from the pattern of federal involvement in housing is the public-housing program. On closer examination, however, it turns out not to be so great a departure. Enacted in 1937 primarily as a job-creation program,[36] public housing was initially opposed by mortgage lenders because it is not financed by conventional mortgage loans. Nor, however, is it financed directly by public funds. Rather, local housing authorities raise funds by selling tax-exempt, federally secured bonds to private investors. In fact, the vast majority of such bonds are held by commercial banks.[37] The federal government then makes annual payments for interest and bond retirement. In financing terms the scheme is thus not so different from the FHA subsidy.

Public housing simply provides an additional way for private investors, most particularly commercial banks, to make profits in housing with the state assuming the risk. Additionally, in market terms public housing has offered very little competition to private housing, amounting to only about 1.5 percent of all housing in the country and serving families too poor to compete in the private market.[38] Finally, recent additions to the public-housing program (Turnkey and Leased Housing) have channeled funds to private developers and landlords and thereby indirectly to mortgage lenders.

Within the housing sector the crucial area of housing finance has very much participated in the transformation to a modern capitalist economy. The construction industry, which has only just begun the process of restructuring, is an important aspect of the housing sector but not the most important. Housing finance, in the shape of mortgage lending institutions, remains the dominant factor and will undoubtedly continue to be the central and focal point of power in American housing. This will be so, and millions of American families will continue to live in substandard homes and neighborhoods and continue to pay exorbitant sums for housing until and unless there are radical changes in the American political economy.

35. P. L. 91-351, 91st Cong., July 24, 1970.

36. *A Decent Home*, pp. 55-56.

37. Arthur P. Solomon, "The Cost Effectiveness of Subsidized Housing," Joint Center for Urban Studies, Working Paper no. 5, 1971 (rev. 1972), p. A-6; President of the United States, *Third Annual Report on National Housing Goals* (Washington, D.C.: Government Printing Office, 1971), p. 49.

38. *Statistical Abstract*, p. 672, table 1108; p. 673, table 1110.

37. *The Social Utility of Rent Control*

EMILY PARADISE ACHTENBERG

Rent control has been a mechanism cities have used periodically in the past to deal with the socioeconomic problems of housing costs. Extremely controversial because of its explicit control of individual property rights (profits, maintenance, evictions) and because of its involved administrative procedures, rent control recently has been again proposed and enacted in many cities. Emily Paradise Achtenberg presents an analysis of the public purposes that rent control serves, its effectiveness in terms of controlling housing costs, its impact on general housing objectives, and the degree to which it actually meets the needs of low income families. While she recognizes many of the inequities that may result from rent control and the need for a massive increase in the supply of low and moderate income housing, she finds that, given certain conditions, rent control can be the most expedient short-term response the legal system has to offer in providing decent housing that the poor can afford.

If you work and put aside a little for security, must it now go into an already well-to-do established landlord's pocket? . . . If rent control is not the answer, what is?

—A Cambridge, Massachusetts resident,
Boston Globe, June 1, 1969

Abandoned Buildings . . . Cancerous Slums . . . Unemployment . . . Tax Arrears . . . Neighborhoods Destroyed . . . *Rent Controls* . . . are the causes of these inequities and bring further decay and abandonment to our city every day . . .

—Metropolitan Fair Rent Committee, ad in the
The New York Times, March 27, 1969

In the perennial war between landlord and tenant, rent control has reemerged as a major battle front.

Outside of New York City, where rents in existing housing have been controlled for most of the past 50 years, recent efforts to revive rent control have encountered notable success. In the past year, three Massachusetts municipalities have adopted comprehensive rent control ordinances pursuant to recently enacted state enabling legislation. [1] Limited rent control measures are in effect in several Connecticut and

Copyright © 1971 by Emily Paradise Achtenberg. Reprinted by permission of the author. Emily Paradise Achtenberg is president of Urban Planning Aid, Inc., a private nonprofit organization that provides to community groups in the Boston area technical and organizing assistance on housing, transportation, health, and other issues.

I am grateful to Chester Hartman, Robert Schafer, and Michael Tietz for their comments on an earlier draft of this article.

1. The city of Cambridge passed a local rent control ordinance on September 17, 1970, followed by Brookline on September 29, 1970, and Somerville on December 1, 1970. A more limited complaint-initiated system of controls has been in effect in Boston since December 1969.

New Jersey cities, while rent grievance boards and other forms of voluntary controls are operating elsewhere. Increasing numbers of private developers are accepting governmental controls on rents as a *quid pro quo* for subsidized low interest mortgages. These trends have even prompted speculation that rent control will become a nationwide phenomenon within the next five years. [2]

Traditionally, rent control in the United States has been employed as a temporary stopgap against rapidly rising rents. Its use has been restricted to periods of general housing shortage—when a significant portion of the population is unable to secure housing of reasonable quality at a price commensurate with their ability to pay. In the past, shortages of this type have been closely associated with wartime and postwar construction slumps; hence rent control is commonly regarded as a temporary wartime emergency measure.

Thus, during World War I several states and cities permitted case-by-case rent regulation to establish "fair rents." In 1942, a federal regulatory system froze rents for most existing housing in urban areas, as part of wartime price controls. During the postwar years, as federal controls gradually expired, a number of states and cities set up their own rent control systems modeled after the federal one. Following a brief restoration of controls during the Korean conflict, rents were decontrolled in virtually all states but New York as the housing shortage eased. By the mid-sixties, New York City was the only major city to retain controls on its housing stock.[3]

The fact that rent controls significantly outlasted general price controls in many areas attests to some of. the peculiar aspects of housing which create the need for special consumer protection. While shortages in other sectors of the economy may lead to temporarily excessive price increases until the supply of goods can be expanded, the limited elasticity of the housing supply results in longer term imbalances. This situation allows landlords to sustain excess profits, which are passed on to tenants in the form of exploitative rent increases.

The current revival of demands for rent control has its roots in the severe housing shortage now existing in many urban areas. Rising rents are placing decent housing beyond the means of a large portion of the population, with the heaviest burden falling on low and moderate income families. While some view the present housing emergency as a temporary phenomenon, related to extraordinary but transitory events such as the Vietnam war, others see it as a more durable consequence of a permanently defense-oriented economy. In any case, there are few signs that the present crisis is significantly abating. Thus, considerations of the social utility of rent control would seem particularly appropriate at the present time.

While the details of rent control systems in this country have varied, most have followed a standard framework. Rents are "frozen" or "rolled back" to some previous date, with a variety of grounds prescribed for future adjustments upward or downward. Provisions may be made for general rental adjustments, covering all units or selected categories, and for individual adjustments on petition of the landlord or tenant. Rent control laws usually state that the landlord is entitled to earn a "fair return" on his

2. Dr. George Sternlieb of Rutgers University, in a speech at the University of Chicago, November 1970. See "Rent Control for all U. S. Seen Soon," *Boston Globe,* November 12, 1970, and "Rent Control Sought in Many Areas," *New York Times,* January 12, 1970.

3. See, generally, John W. Willis, "A Short History of Rent Control," *Cornell Law Quarterly* 36, no. 1 (Fall 1950); and "Residential Rent Control in New York City," *Columbia Journal of Law and Social Problems* 3, no. 5 (May 8, 1967). A number of other cities and towns in New York State have also retained rent control, including Albany, Buffalo, Yonkers, and White Plains.

investment and may include statutory standards for defining what a "fair return" should be.[4]

The range of housing covered by rent control is subject to considerable variation. At one extreme, all existing and future construction may be included. Commonly exempt, for both political and economic reasons, are such categories of housing as rental units in small owner-occupied dwellings, new construction, "luxury" housing, and publicly subsidized housing. The scope of controls may also extend beyond rent regulation *per se*, to include controls over eviction and, to some extent, over building conversions and demolition.

The relatively mild American version of rent control is worth contrasting with the more comprehensive European systems of control which have been in effect during the past 50 years. Western European countries such as England, France, and Germany have maintained systematic national controls on repairs, crowding, and lease terms as well as rents and evictions since World War I, with some modification in recent years. Some Scandinavian countries, including Norway and Denmark, also exercise strict controls over tenant selection to ensure that large families and other neglected groups are adequately housed.[5] In Eastern European Communist countries, where the state has effective control over most of the housing stock, rents are negligible and the capacity to pay virtually immaterial in the distribution of housing space. Housing is allocated largely according to one's needs or place in the productive system.[6]

Clearly, the limited form of rent control practiced in the United States cannot go very far toward alleviating the housing crisis—particularly in the absence of controls over prices in other sectors of the economy which affect housing costs. And most housing policy planners would agree that long-range solutions to the housing crisis must involve a vast expansion of the supply or a vast increase in purchasing power for some sectors of the population or both. Either approach would seem to require a level of government subsidization and control far beyond that which is presently

---

4. In the context of rent control, the "fair return" standard generally refers to some level of "net operating income" which the landlord is allowed to earn over and above normal operating expenses. If the landlord's income falls below this level, he is entitled to a rent increase.

"Net operating income" is most commonly measured in relation to property valuation: New York State's rent control statute defines "fair return" as 6 percent of equalized assessed valuation, while New York City's law, as amended in 1970, fixes "fair return" at 8.5 percent of equalized assessed valuation. In Massachusetts, where the definition of "fair return" is left to the local agency administering rent control, Cambridge uses the standard of 8-12 percent of present market value. Somerville allows 4-10 percent of present market value, depending on the owner's prerent-control profit level.

Other possible approaches to measuring "fair return" include net operating income as a percentage of gross rents, which begs the difficult question of determining property value, and net operating income as a percentage of the landlord's actual investment (equity) in the building. The latter formula has appealed to some tenants' groups as a more direct method of regulating profits.

5. See, generally, D. V. Donnison, *The Government of Housing* (Penguin Books, London, 1967). For a critical evaluation of rent control in Sweden, see Asar Lindbeck, "Rent Control as an Instrument of Housing Policy," in A. A. Nevitt, ed., *The Economic Problems of Housing* (Macmillan, New York, 1967).

6. Donnison, op. cit., pp. 142ff. The trend in these countries now is away from "free" housing, with cooperative housing—a form of publicly subsidized owner occupation—the most rapidly expanding sector of the new building industry. Coop owners usually pay some percentage of the capital cost, borrowing from the government at no or low interest. However, housing costs remain sufficiently low that ability to pay is a minor factor in the distribution of the housing stock. See also Adam Andrzejewski, "Housing Policy and Housing System Models in Some Socialist Countries," in Nevitt, op. cit.

available or contemplated. At the same time, there is a recognized need for some form of public intervention to protect tenants from the exploitation which occurs in a "landlords' market," until a more equitable balance of housing supply and demand can be achieved.

The real issue, then, is whether some form of controls makes sense under present circumstances as part of a broader housing policy. From this perspective, a number of important questions may be asked about the social utility of rent control. How effectively does it accomplish its primary purpose—that of reducing housing costs to levels more commensurate with tenants' ability to pay? How equitably and efficiently are the costs and benefits of rent control distributed? Finally, what is the potential impact of rent control on other housing policy goals, such as the equitable distribution of housing space, the expansion of housing supply, and the improvement of housing quality?

EFFECTIVENESS

The effectiveness of rent control in reducing rent, relative to "free market" levels, depends on two major variables: the degree to which rents prior to control are inflated above and beyond the level dictated by costs and reasonable profits, and the nature of rent increase mechanisms built into the rent control system.

It is important to recognize that rent control directly affects only the limited portion of rent which is attributable to the landlord's "cash flow"—the amount he actually "puts in his pocket" after all other expenses have been deducted. Tenants are often surprised to find that this is relatively small in relation to major components of the rent dollar such as taxes and debt service costs—even if the landlord is earning more than a "fair return" on investment.[7] (Generally speaking, the capital gains and "tax shelter" aspects of real estate investment are far more profitable to an owner than the cash flow potential—and neither of these forms of profit is directly reflected in the rent level.)

Any reasonable rent control system will permit rent increases to cover actual operating cost increases—such as a rise in the tax rate or an increase in fuel oil prices. Thus rents will most certainly continue to increase as long as local public services are financed from property tax revenues and prices in other sectors of the economy

---

7. The following breakdown of occupancy costs for a typical three-bedroom apartment in a recently constructed building is from the *Report of the President's Committee on Urban Housing, Technical Studies*, vol. 2 (U. S. Government Printing Office, Washington, D. C. 1968), p. 32.

	Percentage of Rent
Debt retirement	42%
Taxes	14%
Payroll, management, administration	11%
Utilities	9%
Maintenance, repairs	6%
Vacancies, bad debts	9%
Insurance	2%
Profit, reserve	7%
Total	100%

8. For example, the median contract rent in New York City's controlled housing increased 42 percent between 1950 and 1960. The bulk of these increases were granted through the "new lease increase" provision, allowing a 15 percent rise in rents for new lease agreements signed voluntarily by tenants. In effect, this was an awkward and arbitrary procedure for periodi-

(continued on p. 438)

remain subject to inflationary pressures.[8] Increases in the tax rate have a substantial impact on rent levels, since taxes constitute about 15 percent of rental occupancy costs nationally and considerably more in some areas.[9]

Rent control may have some impact on debt service costs, to the extent that it can discourage owners from choosing more expensive forms of financing. For instance, a "fair return" standard which allows only reasonable financing costs could reduce the extent of second and third mortgage financing at high interest rates, a major source of rent escalation in the uncontrolled market.[10] On the other hand, without provisions for rent increases to cover reasonable increases in financing costs on new or refinanced mortgages, the liquidity of investments in rent controlled buildings will be threatened. Generally speaking, then, rent levels in controlled housing will continue to follow the trend in interest rates over time.[11]

One important consequence of this limited nature of controls is that rents in controlled housing will continue to be higher than what most low and moderate income families can afford to pay. This has been true in New York City, where most families earning less than $3,000 pay more than 35 percent of their incomes for rent even in controlled units.[12] Obviously, broader solutions to the problem of housing cost are needed than those which merely limit the landlord's cash flow profits.

At the same time, the value to tenants of a control system which succeeds in keeping rents in line with costs should not be underestimated. In New York City, households occupying rent controlled units pay less rent, in proportion to income, than households occupying uncontrolled units, at all income levels.[13] While rent control has not reduced rents to levels that low and moderate income tenants would consider "fair," in terms

cally adjusting rents to rising operating costs. Since rent control creates a statutory tenancy for existing occupants of controlled units—thereby obviating their need for new leases—rent increases under this provision were virtually limited to circumstances where turnover occurred. An across-the-board 15 percent rent increase also occurred in 1953. See George Sternlieb, *The Urban Housing Dilemma: The Dynamics of New York City's Rent Controlled Housing,* preliminary draft, undated, pp. 81, 296.

Sternlieb's study also indicates that rent increases in many buildings have not kept pace with operating cost increases in the past few years. For example, while housing operating expenses rose by nearly 10 percent between 1965-1967, median contract rents in controlled apartments increased by only 4 percent (p. 318). As a result, another rent increase of up to 15 percent was approved in 1970 for selected building categories. This is the first phase of a major overhaul of New York City's rent control system, where, starting in 1972, "maximum base rents" will be established for each building category according to a computerized formula. The formula incorporates standard operating cost allowances for each type of building and is designed to bring controlled rents up to their economic levels. In the future, "maximum base rents" will be continually adjusted to reflect increases in operating costs. (See "Rent Plan Detailed," *New York Times,* May 24, 1970.) The important point here is that rents will now be permitted to catch up to operating expense increases, despite the temporary lag—and the considerable cost to low income tenants.

9. See note 7, *supra,* and Dick Netzer, *Impact of the Property Tax,* National Commission on Urban Problems, Research Report #1 (Washington, 1968). Netzer estimates that taxes average 15-17% of rental occupancy costs nationally.

10. Sternlieb, op. cit., estimates that about 17 percent of rent controlled buildings in New York City have second mortgages (p. 584).

11. Additionally, it is arguable that any reduction in the portion of building value that is financed will reduce the landlord's tax-sheltered return, thus creating the need for greater cash flow profits through increased rents or reduced maintenance. This would tend to offset any benefits to tenants that might accrue from limitations on financing costs.

12. New York City Rent and Rehabilitation Administration, *The Private Rental Housing Market in New York City,* by Chester Rapkin (New York, December 1966), p. 81.

13. Ibid.

of ability to pay, it has left them considerably better off than they would have been in an uncontrolled market.

Finally, the benefits of rent control to tenants may increase over time. In the uncontrolled market, the landlord's ability to capitalize excess profits into increased property values results in higher debt service, higher taxes, and once again, higher rents. By reducing and possibly stabilizing cash flow profits, rent control should also have a stabilizing effect on property values insofar as values reflect net income and expectations of future gain. To the extent that rent control succeeds in interrupting this circular process, there should be important secondary impacts on the more substantial components of the rent dollar, with cumulative cost savings to tenants over time.[14]

EQUITY AND EFFICIENCY

In one sense, rent control may be regarded as a means of redistributing the costs and benefits of housing that exist in the uncontrolled market. The redistribution operates not only between landlords and tenants of rent controlled housing but also between owners of controlled and exempt buildings and between protected tenants and other housing consumers. To the extent that the costs and benefits of rent control are arbitrarily distributed among various groups, it may be considered an inequitable and inefficient remedy for the problem of housing cost.

On the cost side, the primary burden rests with owners of controlled housing, who are deprived of some portion of the profits they might have earned in the "free" market. The assignment of these costs to landlords in a profiteering situation is not unreasonable, provided the rent control system allows a "fair return" on investment. To the extent that rent control meets this criterion, the burden imposed on landlords is merely that of a return to the *status quo ante* of reasonable—rather than excessive—profits.

Defining an equitable "fair return" standard is perhaps the most difficult aspect of rent control.[15] Apart from the need to satisfy judicial standards for due process in rate regulation,[16] the rate of return must be sufficiently attractive from an economic standpoint to permit continued investment in the housing market by reasonable investors and landlords. Presumably, a fair rate of return should therefore reflect the rate commanded by alternative investments with comparable risk elements. At the same time, a fair rate of return should reflect what landlords would earn in a "normal" or balanced housing market—a condition more abstract than real in this economy,

---

14. In some instances, however, temporary controls may only defer increases in property values and capital gains until after controls are lifted, with tenants eventually footing the bill. This occurred in some cities immediately after postwar decontrol. See Leo Grebler, "Implications of Rent Control Experience in the United States," *International Labour Review*, 65, no. 4 (April 1952, reprint), p. 20. According to some investors, rent controlled buildings in some areas of New York City are considered a good speculative investment because of the possibility of "luxury" decontrol in the near future. See "Residential Rent Control in New York City," op. cit., p. S-7.

15. See note 4, *supra*.

16. However, New York City's repeated justification of rent control as an emergency measure—rather than a form of public utility regulation—has permitted the ordinary due process principles of rate regulation to be circumvented. Several court rulings have suggested that landlords are not constitutionally entitled to *any* return on their investment, let alone a "fair" return. While interesting from a legal standpoint, this does not obviate the need to guarantee landlords a fair return for economic reasons. See "Residential Rent Control in New York City," op. cit., for a discussion of the legal aspects of "fair return" standards in New York City.

but which may be approximated by some point in time prior to the onset of rapid rent escalation.

However difficult, the need to arrive at a reasonable "fair return" standard, as well as equitable procedures for enforcing it, is fundamental to the utility of a rent control system. If the standard or its administration unduly penalizes landlords, tenants will pay the price in terms of gradual disinvestment by owners and lenders.[17] If the standard or its administration is overly generous to landlords, tenants will bear the burden of increased rents.[18]

Among landlords as a class, the problem of inequity arises with regard to owners of housing exempt from controls. Owners of sales housing or of rental units not covered by controls would be included in this category. With a disproportionate share of housing demand shifted to their units, owners of uncontrolled housing are potentially able to reap special benefits in the form of increased rents and capital gains beyond what they would have earned in the "free" market.[19] There is some evidence that this occurred in New York City, where exorbitant rent increases during the past few years in uncontrolled housing led to a program of rent stabilization for these units.

However, to the extent that owners exempt from rent control are those least likely to translate excess demand into rent increases, this form of inequity may be minimized. Resident owners, for example, may be less interested in maximizing returns than in securing a steady but limited stream of income to help defray amortization expenses. To the extent that such owners operate on the latter philosophy, the excess gains potential of their exempt status will not be realized.

Should substantial price increases occur in the uncontrolled stock, however, arbitrary inequities may also arise between tenants in controlled housing and other housing consumers. But if most families in need of special protection—e.g., the elderly, low income tenants, and others unable to keep pace with the general rise in living costs—live in controlled housing, the inequities should be minimized. For instance, even prior to the extension of controls to recently constructed housing in New York City, more than 90 percent of all households earning less than $4,000 lived in rent controlled units. At the same time, rent control also benefited 43 percent of all households earning more than $15,000, whose relative need for protection was considerably less.[20]

17. Sternlieb's study of New York City's housing market suggests that the pre-1970 fair return standard and the administrative procedures associated with its enforcement have contributed to housing deterioration. The allowed profit rate—then 6% of assessed valuation—is criticized for being too low, thereby discouraging adequate maintenance. At the same time, the cumbersome and expensive procedures required of landlords who apply for relief are said to discourage the filing of legitimate claims for rent increases. As a result, about half of the rent controlled buildings were operating at less than the "fair" profit rate in 1967. On the other hand, many landlords apparently did not seek hardship increases simply because the market would not support higher rents. See Sternlieb, op. cit., pp. 290 and 782ff.

18. Tenants in Cambridge, Massachusetts, have instituted a suit against the Rent Control Administration on the grounds that the city's fair return standard allows landlords to make higher profits than they were earning prior to the enactment of controls. See note 4, *supra*. Rent increases ranging from 7 to 40 percent were granted in the first group of rent adjustment cases, according to a report by the Cambridge City Council.

19. See John F. Kain, "An Alternative to Rent Control" (Department of Economics, Harvard University), unpublished mimeo, April 1, 1969, for a critical analysis of the redistributive aspects of rent control.

20. *The Private Rental Housing Market in New York City*, op. cit., pp. 3 and 4. The fact that rent control in New York City does benefit such a large proportion of relatively affluent families

The potential inequities of rent control are further compounded to the extent that households seeking entrance to the community from outside are equally as poor, elderly, or otherwise "deserving" of protection as existing occupants of controlled housing. Since rent controls place all existing occupants of controlled housing in a privileged position vis-à-vis other competitors for rent controlled space, regardless of need, "deserving" outsiders may be forced into the uncontrolled stock at higher prices, while relatively "undeserving" tenants continue to receive the benefits of controls. In fact, the "deserving" outsiders may be forced to pay higher rents than they would have in the absence of controls, if excess demand for available uncontrolled units drives prices up. Or, they may be economically barred from housing in the uncontrolled stock and thereby excluded from the community altogether. Of course, to the extent that outsiders bidding for rent controlled space are generally more advantaged than existing occupants of controlled housing—as in Cambridge and Brookline, Massachusetts, where controls are now in effect—this form of inequity will be minimized.

Another problem arising in this context relates to the issue of externality. What kinds of costs and benefits are imposed by the deflection of housing demand to surrounding communities, when a single community adopts rent control? Obviously, where one community is subject to excessive demand, the adoption of controls may be a reasonable means of effecting a more desirable distribution of demand throughout the region. In other cases, the equity argument provides a strong rationale for regional or statewide controls.

Alternatively, if demand is not deflected to surrounding communities or to uncontrolled portions of the city's housing stock, opportunities may arise for under-the-table payments to owners of rent controlled housing, or other forms of black-market-eering. Less reprehensible practices, such as the utilization of personal contacts to obtain apartments, serve to reduce the proportion of controlled units that come onto the market.[21] These tendencies clearly discriminate against less advantaged housing consumers, by increasing the significance of wealth and know-how as factors in the distribution of housing space. At the same time, black and gray markets are bound to arise in any tight housing situation, regardless of the existence of rent control, and adequate policing mechanisms should help reduce the more blatant aspects of control circumvention.

The basic shortcoming of rent control as a redistributive measure lies in its application to categories of housing, rather than to categories of housing occupants. A more equitable system of controls—for tenants—would key rents to tenants' ability to pay, as in federally subsidized public housing. However, this system of rent regulation would undoubtedly deprive landlords of a "fair return" when renting to low and moderate income tenants, in the absence of public subsidies.[22] Alternatively, maximum

---

has been important in maintaining local political support for controls over the years. Recently, the city has even assumed the burden of defending rent control through legal challenges to the state's new Vacancy Decontrol Act, which would remove controls from New York City's housing as units become vacant. See "Rent Decontrols Upheld by Court," *New York Times,* July 2, 1971.

21. It is estimated that possibly 50 percent of all controlled units in New York City never reach the market for this reason. See Ernest Fisher, "Twenty Years of Rent Control in New York City," in *Essays in Urban Land Economics,* University of California Real Estate Research Program (Los Angeles, 1966), p. 47. Similar problems in Sweden are noted by Lindbeck, op. cit., p. 68.

22. A recent amendment to New York City's rent control law marks a step in this direction, by temporarily exempting elderly tenants of limited income from rent increases mandated by

(continued on p. 442)

income limits could be established for controlled units that would correspond to the rents being charged, at a reasonable rent-income ratio. Since only tenants within the prescribed income limits would be eligible to occupy a given unit, however, this would constitute an equally threatening limitation on the landlord's freedom of tenant selection.

On equity and efficiency grounds, critics of rent control often contend that a program of direct rent subsidies for tenants in need of special protection would be a preferable approach to the problem of housing cost. Such a program, it is suggested, could even be financed through a tax on propertyowners equal to the unearned increment in value accruing from excess demand.[23] But while a rent subsidy program of this nature might appear to be a more effective redistributive measure, it hardly obviates the need for rent control in a market characterized by excess demand. Without controls, the cost of the tax might well be passed on to tenants in the form of increased rents. In any case, the political and economic feasibility of funding a massive rent subsidy program—either through an expanded local property tax or from federal revenue sources—seems unlikely at the present time.

SPACE UTILIZATION

A related concern, with regard to equity and efficiency, is the distribution of housing space effected by a rent control system. Critics charge that the increased demand for controlled units will generate pressures for overcrowding in the controlled stock. At the same time, rent control is said to induce underutilization of housing space, particularly as small families remain in large units after children have moved away.

In response to these claims, it is argued that rent control should decrease overcrowding by alleviating pressures which give rise to doubling up in order to meet "free market" housing costs. Additionally, if the rent control system allows a reasonable rate of return and contains increase provisions to cover rising costs, the gap between rents in the controlled and uncontrolled markets should not be so large as to inhibit upward mobility substantially.

In fact, studies of housing in New York City suggest that the inequities and inefficiencies in space distribution resulting from rent control are not significantly greater than those in the uncontrolled market, where space is allocated primarily according to ability to pay.[24] Much of the wasteful space utilization that does exist in New York City's controlled stock may well be attributable to the peculiar incentives for long-term occupancy provided by the city's former rent control law.[25]

---

the 1970 Rent Control Act. Specifically, elderly tenants earning less than $4,500 a year are exempt—for 1 year—from any portion of the rent increase that would make rents greater than one-third of income. Since no subsidies have been provided, this provision brings the conflict between "fair rents" for tenants and a "fair return" for landlords into sharp focus. Despite challenges to the law, the New York State Supreme Court has upheld its constitutionality. See New York City Housing and Development Administration, Department of Rent and Housing Maintenance, "The 1970 Rent Control Law: Implementation and Progress Report," February 10, 1971, p. 14; and "Exception to Rise in Rents Upheld," *New York Times,* May 6, 1971.

23. Kain, op. cit., p. 12.

24. See Fisher, op. cit., p. 58; Grebler, op. cit., p. 10; and New York City Rent and Rehabilitation Administration, *People, Housing, and Rent Control in New York City* (New York, June 1964), by Frank Kristof, p. 62, for a discussion of this issue.

25. See note 8, *supra.* Prior to the 1970 amendments, New York City's rent control law effectively ensured lower rents for long-term occupants by linking rent increases to turnover and thus discouraging mobility.

In this context, a more radical form of controls would establish minimum and maximum household size standards for rent controlled apartments. This would considerably enhance the efficiency and equity of controls as a space distribution mechanism—at the expense, once again, of the landlord's freedom of tenant selection.

NEW CONSTRUCTION

Perhaps the most substantive criticisms of rent control are concerned with the impact of controls on the climate of housing investment. Critics of rent control argue, first, that by reducing incentives for new housing construction, rent control intensifies the very housing shortage it was designed to alleviate. Even where new housing is exempt from control—as it has been generally in the United States—a substantial gap between rents in the controlled stock and the rents required for new housing may weaken the demand for new construction. Consequently, both owners and mortgage lenders may be induced to seek more profitable outlets for their investments.

But by the same token, a reasonable system of controls that allows rents to keep pace with cost increases and provides returns competitive with those from investments of comparable risk should not seriously inhibit construction activity on the part of reasonable investors. At worst, the gap between controlled and uncontrolled rents should be no greater than under "normal" supply and demand conditions. Additionally, it is arguable that the reduced turnover rate in the controlled portion of the housing stock will increase, rather than decrease, the demand for new housing.

Past experience offers little evidence that control of the existing stock has substantially deterred new housing construction. The volume of housing construction generally in the postwar period, and specifically in New York City during the past 25 years, has not been out of line with available resources.[26] In fact, New York City experienced a period of substantial overbuilding during the early 1960s, in reaction to builders' anticipations of a more restrictive zoning ordinance.[27] In general, it appears that broader economic factors—such as the availability and cost of land and mortgage money—are far more critical than rent control in determining the volume of new housing construction.

At the same time, the type of new housing built may be influenced by the existence of controls on older housing. For example, investors' fears about the extension of rent control to new construction may have contributed to the large volume of postwar sales housing and to the significant volume of condominium and cooperative housing built in New York City in recent years. However, other factors—such as the availability of FHA insurance for sales housing and the tax benefits of ownership available to housing consumers—undoubtedly provided more significant incentives.

Finally, it should be noted that an increased volume of new private construction would not substantially benefit the primary victims of the housing shortage—i.e., low and moderate income families. Without subsidies, new housing costs are far beyond what these groups can afford, and in periods of excess demand such housing is more likely to filter "up" than "down" the income scale. Rent control should have no effect on the rate of subsidized housing construction for low and moderate income families,

26. See Grebler, op. cit., p. 9, *The Private Rental Housing Market in New York City*, op. cit., p. 16. During the past few years new construction has fallen off considerably, but this is attributable more to the general shortage and high cost of mortgage money than to rent control.

27. Ira S. Lowry, ed., *Rental Housing in New York City*, vol. 1 (New York City Rand Institute, February 1970), p. 3.

since this type of construction is already subject to controls by public agencies.[28] The only effect of rent control in this regard might be to indirectly increase the number of sites available for such purposes.

HOUSING QUALITY

In addition to its impact on new construction, rent control may affect the scope and pattern of investment in existing buildings, by both owners and lenders. Critics charge that rent control inhibits the level of investment required for proper maintenance and improvement, thereby leading to deterioration and in the long run to abandonment.

On the one hand, it should be apparent that a system of controls which denies landlords reasonable profits may well have this effect. Under these conditions, any economically rational owner will be inclined to reduce discretionary expenditures on maintenance and housing improvement, particularly as lenders respond by tightening up credit terms. On the other hand, a system designed to reduce excess profits to a reasonable level should not result in a decline in housing services by reasonable landlords. Under these conditions reasonable lenders should continue to supply credit, thus preserving the liquidity of the owner's investment.

Moreover, while the job of enforcing housing quality standards properly belongs to the code enforcement agency, rent control may provide additional tools to encourage code compliance. Rent reductions for substandard housing may help to ensure that profits earned in excess of a reasonable rate are channeled into upkeep, rather than into the owner's pocket. This tactic is likely to be effective so long as the long-term costs of noncompliance to the owner—i.e., the loss of a significant portion of his income stream and capital gains potential—outweigh the costs of making the necessary repairs. By the same token, if the owner is not sanguine about the future profitability of his building or lacks the necessary resources for compliance, this form of punitive action may lead to further disinvestment.[29]

Provisions for linking rent increases to housing improvement may also complement code enforcement efforts. For instance, New York City's 1970 Rent Control Law mandates significant increases for some units, but stipulates that the increased income must be applied almost entirely toward improved building maintenance and operations. Future increases in rent controlled buildings are conditional upon the removal of all substantial "rent-impairing" violations, as well as most minor deficiencies.[30]

28. Rents in federally subsidized public housing, owned and operated by local housing authorities, are set by the local authority, usually according to family size and income. In moderate income housing owned by private developers who receive federally subsidized mortgages (under Sections 221d3 and 236 of the National Housing Act), rents are regulated by the Federal Housing Administration.

29. Lowry, op. cit., p. 14, notes that the mere threat of rent reduction was sufficient to compel code compliance in about 85 percent of all rent reduction cases in New York City in 1968. By contrast, the rate of complaince in cases where rents were actually reduced was minimal. Lowry concludes that the rent reduction sanction may work best as a threat, since those owners with the necessary resources and commitment for continued investment will comply before their income stream is cut off. On the other hand, little-exercised threats often lose their credibility.

30. New York City Housing and Development Administration, op. cit., p. 16. At present, the Department of Rent and Housing Maintenance relies primarily on landlord certification for enforcement of these provisions, but an inspection program to verify landlord reports will be instituted in the future.

Finally, some forms of incentive may be appropriate in encouraging continued investment in rent controlled buildings. For instance, owners of well-maintained structures might be allowed a higher rate of return than owners of poorly maintained buildings. An owner might be allowed to increase his profit level in return for making certain kinds of capital improvements. Of course, in the absence of subsidies, the goal of housing improvement soon comes into conflict with the goal of rent reduction, and the task of striking a proper balance between the two is one of the more difficult aspects of designing and administering a rent control system.[31]

In short, a rent control system containing a creative balance of economic rewards and penalties can facilitate the optimal level of maintenance and improvement that can be achieved, given other constraints. Beyond this, tighter controls over the level of discretion landlords have in maintaining their properties could be incorporated into the rent control system. For instance, it has been suggested that a special account should be established for rental properties, with each landlord obligated to pay a fixed percentage of rents annually—in the amount of his depreciation allowance—into a state fund. This would establish a continually enlarging reserve fund for housing rehabilitation and replacement, and would ensure that amounts now theoretically set aside for this purpose are appropriately channeled.[32]

In terms of the link between rent control and housing quality, recent studies of investment patterns in New York City's rent controlled housing market merit close examination. These studies indeed indicate a widespread policy of disinvestment by owners of rent controlled buildings. Between 1960 and 1968, the dilapidated housing inventory increased by 44 percent, and the deteriorated stock by 37 percent. In 1968, 29 percent of all rent controlled units were deteriorated, as compared to 8 percent of the uncontrolled stock. Even more strikingly, housing in New York City is being abandoned at the unprecedented rate of 38,000 units a year, exclusive of demolitions. Included in this figure are many structurally sound buildings which have apparently ceased to be of value to their owners.[33]

This phenomenon illustrates a pervasive "crisis in future expectations" on the part of owners and lenders, with regard to the future profitability of their structures. Even where the financial resources exist for adequate upkeep and improvement, continued investment is precluded by an overwhelmingly negative outlook on future earnings potential.

To what extent are these conditions attributable to rent control? On the one hand, the particular system of controls in effect in New York may be accelerating the process of private disinvestment by making it difficult for many owners to earn a reasonable return on investment.[34] But neighborhood factors and the structural obsolescence of most controlled buildings appear to be far more critical than rent control per se in promoting negative owner and lender expectations. The same problems are not prevalent with regard to rent controlled buildings in "good" areas, where owners retain a strong interest in the long-term future of their buildings.[35] Similarly, where

31. New York City attempts to deal with this dilemma by requiring the consent of at least a majority of tenants in the building before rent increases are granted for certain kinds of capital improvements.

32. Lawrence K. Frank, "To Control Slumlord Abuses—Private Housing Proposed to Become Public Utility," *Journal of Housing,* 20, no. 5 (July 1963), p. 271.

33. Lowry, op. cit., p. 6.

34. See notes 8 and 16, *supra.*

35. See Lowry, op. cit., p. 9., and Sternlieb, op. cit., p. 605ff and 620ff.

the neighborhood will not support future rent and capital value increments, the factor of control versus noncontrol status seems to have less and less significance for present and projected profitability.[36]

Finally, the problems of private disinvestment and abandonment are widespread in many cities where rent control does not exist. A recent survey of seven eastern and midwestern cities concludes that "entire neighborhoods, housing hundreds of thousands of central city dwellers, are in advanced stages of being abandoned by their owners."[37] In short, the withdrawal of private capital from urban areas is a complex and widespread phenomenon, which cannot be attributed in any significant respect to rent control.

CONCLUSION

In summary, rent control does appear to be an effective remedy for the problem of housing cost during a period of housing shortage. While a reasonable system of controls neither prevents rent increases nor reduces rents to levels that all low and moderate income tenants can afford, it does offer tenants some protection by keeping rents in line with costs.

By virtue of the fact that rent control focuses on the dwelling unit, rather than the occupant, its redistributive effects are far from perfect. Rent control arbitrarily taxes owners of controlled housing and tenants of noncontrolled housing, to benefit owners of noncontrolled units and tenants in the controlled stock. But these inequities may be offset if controlled housing occupants are in relatively greater need of protection and if owners of exempt housing are less apt to take advantage of market pressures. And while rent control may superimpose its own inefficiencies in the allocation of housing space upon those which exist in the "free" market, the resulting degree of over- or underutilization of space is probably no greater than in a market where ability to pay is the primary mechanism for space distribution.

Finally, a reasonable system of controls should not adversely affect the level of investment in new or existing housing by investors seeking a reasonable profit. The creative use of "carrots" and "sticks" within the rent control system can facilitate some degree of housing improvement, within the constraints established by market factors. But in general, other broad economic and social factors would seem to be much more critical determinants of how much new housing gets built and how well older housing is maintained.

If the present housing shortage persists as a relatively permanent feature of the economy—as seems likely—then the concept of a permanent and comprehensive regulatory system for housing may be worthy of serious consideration. Such a system, based on the public utility model, would go well beyond rent and eviction controls. State or local regulatory commissions might be fully empowered not only to set rents and rates of return but to enforce strict performance and service standards, to regulate

36. Sternlieb, op. cit., p. 410.

37. See National Urban League and the Center for Community Change, *National Survey of Housing Abandonment*, April 1971, p. 1. The study cities a number of basic social and economic factors underlying the abandonment process, including the changing economic functions of the central city, the exploitative response of realtors to racial and ethnic neighborhood transformations, and the precipitous withdrawal of municipal services and mortgage money from many urban areas.

the entry and withdrawal of owners from the market, and to supervise the operation of rental housing.[38]

Under a regulatory system of this nature, owners of rental property might be licensed, based on their qualifications, before entering the market; and they might be forced to withdraw for failure to meet performance standards. Housing distribution could be regulated according to family size and need. Housing quality standards could be enforced through the establishment of a sinking fund for replacement reserves, as described earlier. Formal expense and income accounting could be required annually, in order to provide the necessary information for rent setting.

A comparable degree of public regulation has long been accepted for other service-rendering operations—such as gas, electricity, and telephone—and already exists to some degree for privately owned housing receiving interest subsidies through FHA.[39] The arguments for classifying housing as a public utility are compelling—given its nature as an essential commodity, and the difficulties associated with increasing its supply which create opportunities for exploitation of consumers. However, given the constraints of rising prices in other sectors of the economy affecting housing costs, and the limited incomes of many housing consumers, it is clear that the basic problems underlying the housing shortage will not be resolved by a regulatory system alone.

In fact, the institution of controls on private housing operations for any significant length of time may well precipitate a crisis already in the making. The goals of adequate maintenance and housing production, reasonable rents for tenants, and reasonable profits for landlords seem increasingly incompatible under the present system of housing investment and ownership. If this is the case, then the society must be forced to confront the dilemma. If housing controls which are necessary to protect tenants serve to expedite the ongoing process of disinvestment by the private sector, then new forms of public subsidization, ownership, and financing must be created to take its place. To the extent that any system of housing controls can facilitate these needed changes in the housing system, its social utility is that much enhanced.

38. Frank, op. cit., and Leonard Rubinowitz, "Private Rental Housing as a Public Utility," unpublished paper, Yale University Department of City Planning, May 1968.

39. See note 28, *supra.*

38. *Public Housing and the Poor*

LAWRENCE M. FRIEDMAN

Public housing, the government's major effort to provide decent accommodations for the poor, in recent years has come under attack from both liberals and conservatives. In analyzing the evolving political support for public housing, Lawrence Friedman argues that the program was originally intended to serve the "submerged middleclass," the (white) temporary poor of the Depression years, but in the postwar period was increasingly called on to serve the "permanent poor" and those displaced by urban renewal, highways, and other public programs. That group is largely black, with a high proportion of broken, "multiproblem families" which has led to a decrease in political support for public housing as well as to problems in the administration and management of public housing. At present a gap apparently exists between the personnel who run the public housing program and the interests and life-styles of the program's clientele. Professor Friedman suggests the importance of shaping management procedures and styles to the needs of the various groups now housed under the program.

Public housing became a reality in the United States only in the days of the New Deal. There were some gingerly steps toward public housing during the First World War, and a few more in the states in the twenties, but a serious, living program had to wait for the days of the Great Depression.[1] The major piece of federal legislation on housing was the Wagner-Steagall Act of 1937[2] which, despite a gloss of amendments, remains on the statute books today, hardly altered in its basic design. . . . In the years since then, public housing has become a familiar aspect of the urban landscape. By the end of 1965 every state had some public housing units in planning or operation, and more than 2,100,000 people lived in low-rent public housing. In New York City more than half a million people lived in public housing units built with the aid of federal, state, or city money. The overwhelming majority of these units were products of the federal program. New York City had more public housing than any other city; but every major city and a host of minor ones ran more or less substantial programs of their own. . . .

Reprinted from *Law of the Poor,* edited by Jacobus ten Brock and the editors of the *California Law Review* (San Francisco: Chandler, 1966), pp. 318-32, 334-43 (edited), by permission of the publisher and author. Lawrence M. Friedman is a professor of law at Stanford University.

Some of the material on which this paper is based was gathered in the course of interviews. Some individuals who were interviewed would prefer not to be quoted directly. Some of the information supplied must be treated as confidential. Consequently, supporting authorities for some statements have been omitted.

1. On the forerunners of the Wagner-Steagall Act, see Fisher, *Twenty Years of Public Housing* (1959); a good short account is Riesenfeld & Eastlund, "Public Aid to Housing and Land Redevelopment," 34 *Minn. L. Rev.* 610 (1950). On the Wagner-Steagall Act itself, see McDonnell, *The Wagner Housing Act: A Case Study of the Legislative Process* (1957).

2. 50 Stat. 888 (1937), as amended, 42 U.S.C. §§ 1401-30 (1964), as amended, 42 U.S.C. §§ 1402-21b (Supp. I, 1965).

But to judge by some newspaper and magazine accounts—and even by the words of housing experts—the public housing program had betrayed its fond expectations. In 1937 Catherine Bauer, a highly respected expert on housing, praised the Wagner-Steagall Act as "progressive legislation"—a hopeful first step toward the goal of good housing for all.[3] Twenty years later, in 1957, Miss Bauer returned to the subject in an article in *Architectural Forum*. The title was significant: "The Dreary Deadlock of Public Housing."[4] She found little to praise in the program as it had evolved. Rather, she saw rigidity and paternalism in management, crudity and segregation in project design, and a deplorable fragmentation of overall housing policy. In the following issue of the magazine, 11 housing experts commented on her article and made suggestions for change.[5] Not one of the 11 disagreed with her general thesis: that the public housing movement was stagnant; that politically the program was at a standstill; that existing projects were badly conceived and perhaps did more harm than good; and that the whole program needed radical reformation. This was the twentieth anniversary of the Wagner-Steagall Act. . . .

Politically, the program has little appeal. Appropriations for additional units have been grudgingly voted in Congress; time and time again requests have been scaled down. What is perhaps more significant, authorizations have often gone begging because local government agencies have not been interested in applying for federal grants—authorized units have "washed away."[6] This is perhaps the darkest symptom of all: A program must be genuinely unpopular if free federal money is spurned. The unpopularity of public housing need not be left to oblique inference. In scores of cities and small towns, public housing has been put to the test by the voters. Where it is legally possible, opponents have demanded referenda on the question.[7] In a distressing number of cases, bond issues to finance the program have failed, or public housing has been voted out of town.

Where does the trouble lie? Is it in the conception, the shape of the public housing program? Is it in its mode of administration? Perhaps the problems lie in both. The indictment is clear: Public housing, ostensibly designed to clear the slums and to alleviate the sufferings of the poor, has failed to do either. We turn now to the facts.

THE PUBLIC HOUSING PROGRAM: CONCEPTION AND DESIGN

The public housing law is one of a vaguely defined group of statutes called "social" or "welfare" legislation.

It would be a mistake to suppose (if anyone did) that the Wagner-Steagall Act

3. "Now, at Last: Housing," *New Republic*, Sept. 8, 1937, pp. 119, 121.

4. Bauer, "The Dreary Deadlock of Public Housing," *Architectural Forum*, May 1957, p. 140.

5. "The Dreary Deadlock of Public Housing—How to Break It," *Architectural Forum*, June 1957, p. 139.

6. Seligman, "The Enduring Slums," in *The Exploding Metropolis* 92, 105 (1958).

7. Editors' note: In April, 1971 the U.S. Supreme Court upheld (5-3) a section of the California state constitution providing for mandatory local referenda on low-rent housing proposals, on the grounds that the provision did not on its face single out a racial minority and the record in the case did not show that a law seemingly neutral on its face was in fact aimed at a racial minority. *James* v. *Valtierra*, 91 S. Ct. 1331 (1971). With this decision the court refused to extend the equal protection clause of the U. S. Constitution to classifications based on income as well

(continued on p. 450)

arose solely out of a gradual persuasion of decent-minded people that the slums were odious, crowded, and evil, and that the federal government had a duty to relieve the sufferings of the poor. The social and economic conditions in the slums provided the opportunity, the background, and much of the emotive power of the law. Yet reformers had long dreamed in vain of public housing. And the slums were surely no worse than they had been in the 19th century, though possibly they were larger.

In 1937 the country was suffering from a deep and dangerous depression. Fully one-quarter of the work force was unemployed during the worst days of the Depression. In the spring of 1933, 13 to 15 million were unemployed. Millions of families were barely making a living. The number of "poor people" in the country had been vastly increased; indeed, many of the "poor people" were formerly members of the middle class, who had enjoyed prosperity in the twenties. They retained their middle class culture and their outlook, their articulateness, their habit of expressing their desires at the polls. There were, therefore, millions of candidates for public housing who did not belong (as later was true) to the class of the "problem poor"; rather they were members of what we might call the submerged middle class. The attractiveness of public housing was enormously enhanced because the potential clientele was itself enormous, composed of millions of relatively articulate citizens, angry and dispirited at their unjust descent into poverty. Public housing was not supported by the dregs of society; a discontented army of men and women of high demands and high expectations stood ready to insist on decent housing from government or at least stood ready to approve and defend it. The political climate was receptive to federal planning and federal housing—not so much as a matter of radical ideology, but out of a demand for positive programs to eliminate the "undeserved" privations of the unaccustomed poor.

Moreover, business was stagnant in the thirties. Programs of social welfare and relief were tested by their ability to create new jobs and prime the business pump as much as by their inherent welfare virtues. Public works programs were exceedingly popular for this reason. A vast federal program of housebuilding naturally received the enthusiastic support of manufacturers of building supplies and workers in the building trades. The normal opposition to "socialized" housing made its appearance in debate, but it was weak and somewhat muted. Nonetheless, business support for the act was conditioned upon the act being so structured as to avoid any actual government competition with business. Homes would be built only for those who could not possibly afford to buy them on their own. A clear wall must separate the public and the private sector. This too was only partly ideological. Government, it was felt, should not cut into the markets of private industry; it must stimulate fresh demand and make fresh jobs—otherwise the effect of the program on the economy would be wasted.

. . . If public construction increased the housing supply during a period in which many dwellings stood vacant, rents would decrease still more and vacancies would increase. In a decade willing to kill baby pigs and impose acreage controls on farmers, one could hardly expect to see government flooding the housing market with new units. And in fact, the Wagner-Steagall Act was careful to avoid the problem of oversupply. No units were to be built without destroying "dwellings . . . substantially equal in number to the number of newly constructed dwellings provided by the project."

---

as race. *But see Douglas* v. *California,* 372 U.S. 353 (1963). The federal district court had been willing to extend the coverage of the equal protection clause to the poor in this case. *Valtierra* v. *Housing Authority of the City of San Jose,* 313 F. Supp. 1 (D. Calif. 1970).

This provision—the so-called "equivalent elimination" provision—killed two birds with one stone. It neutralized potential opposition from landlords and the housing industry by removing the danger of oversupply; at the same time, by making slum clearance a part of the law, it appealed to those whose desire for public housing stemmed from their loathing of the slums and slum conditions. The Wagner-Steagall Act was thus shaped by the force of concrete social conditions; what emerged was a program geared to the needs of the submerged middle class, tied to slum clearance, and purged of any element of possible competition with business.[8]

Constitutional difficulties played a part in determining one of the most notable features of the program—its decentralization. From 1933 on, the Public Works Administration had run its own public housing program. In 1935 a federal district court case held that the federal government had no power under the constitution to clear land and build public housing. It was not proper, said the court, for the federal government "to construct buildings in a state for the purpose of selling or leasing them to private citizens for occupancy as homes."[9] The federal government never appealed this decision. In 1935 the government's prospect of sympathetic treatment by the United States Supreme Court seemed bleak; attempting to overturn the adverse housing decision might risk the whole program of public works. On the other hand, no important legal barriers stood in the way of a decentralized program. Washington could supply money and a certain amount of benign control; title to property and the motive force in condemnation could remain vested in local public agencies. A key New York State decision strengthened this view, distinguishing the federal cases as inapplicable to state power. Moreover, decentralization was politically attractive to those who dreaded further expansion of the "federal octopus."

Financial considerations had an important impact on the design of the housing law. If the federal government had made outright grants to local authorities to build houses, immense amounts of money would have been immediately required. Under the act, however, local authorities were invited to borrow money through bond issues; with the proceeds, they were to acquire sites, clear them, and put up houses. The federal government would enter into "contracts" with local housing authorities, under which the federal government would agree to make annual contributions for a long period of time. The federal government would pay (in essence) enough money for the interest on the bonds and the amortization of the principal. Operating expenses for the housing projects would come out of current rents. In this way, federal contributions would be kept relatively small; housing could be built on the installment plan, and paid for over a period of 50 or 60 years.

Note, too, that the tenants were only partially subsidized. They were not given "free" housing. Each tenant had to pay his rent. Project rents had to be sufficient to pay operating costs—maintenance, administration, and payments in lieu of taxes to local government for fire and police protection and other municipal services. Though the federal act was discreetly silent on the subject, the rent requirement meant that the unemployed and the paupers were not welcome in public housing. They could

---

8. The 1949 act, to make the point crystal clear, provided that no annual contribution contract be entered into unless the local agency demonstrates "that a gap of at least 20 per centum . . . has been left between the upper rental limits for admission to the proposed low-rent housing and the lowest rents at which private enterprise unaided by public subsidy is providing . . . decent . . . housing." 63 Stat. 422 (1949), as amended, 42 U.S.C. § 1415 (7) (b) (ii) (1964).

9. *United States* v. *Certain Lands*, 9 F. Supp. 137, 141 (W.D. Ky.), *aff'd*, 78 F.2d 684 (6th Cir.), *dismissed*, 294 U.S. 735 (1935), 297 U.S. 726 (1936). See also *United States* v. *Certain Lands*, 12 F. Supp. 345 (E.D. Mich. 1935).

not pay the rent, any more than in private housing. There are "some people," said Senator Wagner, "who we cannot possibly reach; I mean those who have no means to pay the rent. . . . [O]bviously this bill cannot provide housing for those who cannot pay the rent minus the subsidy allowed."[10] The projects were for poor but honest workers—the members of the submerged middle class, biding their time until the day when they regained their rightful income level. The tenants were not to receive any "charity." The difference between a dole and a subsidy is psychologically powerful, whether or not the distinction is good economics. The working-class residents of public housing were not to receive a gift from the government but their rightful due as citizens. Public housing, arguably, was no more "charitable" than the free land of the homestead act of 1862—an earlier form of middle class subsidy. Decent, sanitary apartments were a steppingstone to a fee simple cottage—the American dream. Perhaps a radical fringe of housing reformers looked on public housing as something more fundamentally "public"; but the core of support lay in an old and conservative tradition.

If this general analysis is correct, what would happen to public housing if a rising standard of living released the submerged middle class from dependence on government shelter? Public housing would be inherited by the permanent poor. The empty rooms would pass to those who had at first been disdained—the unemployed, "problem" families, those from broken homes. The program could adapt only with difficulty to its new conditions, because it had been originally designed for a different clientele. To suit the programs to the needs of the new tenant would require fresh legislation; and yet change would be difficult to enact and to implement precisely because the new clientele would be so poor, so powerless, so inarticulate. The political attractiveness of public housing would diminish. Maladaptations to reality in the program would disenchant housing reformers; they would declare the program a failure and abandon it to search out fresh cures for bad housing and slums.

All this is precisely what has happened, as a brief sketch of the history of public housing since 1937 will illustrate. The first public housing projects were, in general, low-rise rowhouses; they blended in fairly well with their surroundings. Some of them, outside the major cities, were "suburban" in location and design. The residents were members of the submerged middle class, and the projects were literally stepping-stones to middle-class life and a home of one's own. . . . During the war, conditions underlying the housing market were fundamentally altered. No longer was there a housing surplus, together with a surplus of the honorable poor. Private building completely halted during the war; defense factories soaked up all the employables and put high wages in peoples' pockets. The result was a stupendous housing shortage—the supply of housing remained constant while the demand multiplied inordinately. This demand would have driven rents to fabulous levels, except for stringent national controls on rents and evictions.

. . . The beneficiaries of the new [postwar] housing programs were the veterans and the middle class generally. Prosperity meant an end of concentrated political demand for minimum housing built in the city for the submerged middle class. The major need now was for veterans' houses, individually owned and detached from those of their neighbors. This was the only new program appealing both to homeowners and builders. To keep land costs down, any such mass development had to be outside of town. Thus began the suburban housing boom, financed by vast infusions of public money. The money was paid, however, in the form of subsidy, aid to private enterprise,

10. 81 Cong. Rec. 8099 (Aug. 3, 1937).

mortgage insurance, and tax breaks. It was never "charity." Moreover, a little public money went a very long way. Meanwhile, old-style public housing languished.

Worse than that: Public housing was now boxed in, in the core of the cities. Outlying sites, on the fringes of the metropolitan areas, where land was raw and cheap, were no longer available; this land was de facto reserved for veterans' subdivisions. Public housing was losing its best sites—and its best clientele. The submerged middle class moved out as fast as it reasonably could. Indeed, those who would have liked to stay were not given the option; they were simply thrown out. . . . Pressure built up to force people to give up subsidized apartments and buy subsidized homes instead. The economy (it was thought) depended on the health of the suburban building boom; the nation could not afford to let people with good incomes go on living with New Deal subsidies. The sharp, bitter struggle over evictions was not a struggle of rich against poor. It was a struggle between middle class veterans and defense workers, on the one hand, and business interests on the other. The scale tipped in favor of business presumably because of the strong general interest in a healthy level of construction. The dispossessed veterans were (in part) paid off by subsidized mortgages and a whole host of government programs which eased the journey to the suburbs. Public housing, meanwhile, was relegated to the permanent poor in the city, and to the new urban immigrants. In the big cities, these were chiefly Negroes from the South. The compromise of the late 1940s and early 1950s meant reinforcement of the notion that public housing was exclusively for those who were certainly, indisputably, and irreversibly poor.

But this development meant that the political strength of public housing had eroded and would continue to erode. The new tenants were precisely those who had the least power in our society, the least potent voice in the councils of city hall. The middle-class masses, moreover, were spending their sweat and treasure in a wild flight from the slums and their residents. Now that they had attained the status of suburban property owners, they had no intention of giving up their property values and their hard-won status by allowing their former neighbors (and even less desirable people) to move in. The slums were not to follow them into the suburbs. Race and income prejudice was by no means confined to the suburbs. It flourished in the city, too, particularly in the little enclaves of frame houses that formed ethnically homogeneous, proud, and self-contained neighborhoods. These subcities would also resist public housing in their midst. Public housing no longer meant homes for less fortunate friends and neighbors, but, rather, intrusions of "foreigners," the problem poor and those least welcome "forbidden neighbors," the lower class Negro. Public housing not only lost its political appeal but what was left of the program was confined to the core of the city. Public housing remained tied to slum clearance and rebuilding out of necessity. The suburbs and the middle-class areas of the city had shut their doors. Vacant land could not be used for sites unless the land happened to lie in skid row or a Negro neighborhood.[11]

Land in the core of the city was far more expensive than the raw land of the suburbs. City land had to be bought, cleared of commercial and residential properties, and then redeveloped. Labor and material costs were high and kept rising. So did the buildings. The cost squeeze meant the end of low-rise, "home-style" housing projects. The buildings turned into towers—6-story, 10-story, then 19, 20, or more in New York and Chicago. Costs and the enmity of the outside world squeezed the

---

11. See the now classic study of Chicago's site location problems, Meyerson and Banfield, *Politics, Planning and the Public Interest* (1955).

buildings into the heart of the slums. The ratio of Negroes to whites increased radically. The whites streamed out. By the early 1950s, project managers had to learn to cope with "problem" families. The texture of life in the projects changed for the worse; since more delinquent families lived in them, they were the locus for more and more delinquency. The attention of the public was now directed to public housing not as a hopeful program of reform but as the site of public folly and private decay—vandalism, crime, and unrest. The sordid facts of life in public housing merely reinforced the passionate resistance of the rest of the city to public housing projects. Who wanted such places in their neighborhood? It was a vicious circle. And when the intellectual community looked out of its own windows and saw the projects in the distance—drab, ugly blocks of cement standing like soldiers—when they observed that public housing built ghettos for Negroes and the despondent classes, they, too, called for a halt. Right and left wings, oddly enough, agreed that the program had outlived its utility; both called for a curtailment of fresh building. . . .

Ironically, the same forces that have crippled public housing have made possible the one bright exception to the "dreary deadlock": housing for the elderly. In many cities today the *only* public housing being built is housing for the elderly. The Wagner-Steagall Act of 1937 said nothing about old people; but in the last decade, the law has increasingly favored the elderly. The trend began modestly enough in 1956, when, for the first time, public housing was opened up to unmarried people (not members of a "family") who were 65 years of age or more. In the 1960s much more positive inducements have been offered. The 1961 act offered a subsidy of up to $120 per unit occupied by "senior citizens," where such assistance was necessary to operate these units in the black. In this regard, federal law has merely mirrored local opinion. Milwaukee, for example—a city notoriously hostile to public housing—has eagerly embraced housing for the elderly. In Chicago, 5,661 units were under construction as of June 30, 1964; 4,345 of these were reserved for the elderly. And Marin County, California, 3 years after defeating a public housing proposal, voted overwhelmingly to support a proposed 200-unit development for the elderly. In 1964, 52.6 percent of the new units placed under contract "were to be designed specifically for the elderly."

It is easy to see why housing for the elderly is succeeding where public housing in general has failed. Housing for the elderly taps the only remaining reservoir of poor people who are also white, orderly, and middle class in behavior. Neighborhoods which will not tolerate a 10-story tower packed with Negro mothers on AFDC might tolerate a tower of sweet but impoverished old folks. Old people are never vandals; they do not whore and carouse. Many of them are honest working-class people caught in a trap set by low retirement incomes, small pensions, inadequate savings, and high medical bills. Furthermore, housing for the elderly helps solve a problem all too common for middle-class people—what to do with aged, dependent parents. Subsidized housing for the grandparents is a solution to many people's troubles. Moreover, the old people are more likely than the problem poor to be grateful, docile, and unseen.[12]

ADMINISTRATION OF PUBLIC HOUSING

When public housing was conceived of as subsidized shelter for members of the submerged middle class, it did not call for modes of administration different from those

---

12. Similarly, special favors have been accorded in recent years to public housing for the handicapped. See, e.g., 73 Stat. 667 (1959), as amended, 12 U.S.C. § 1701(q) (1964), as amended, 12 U.S.C. § 1701(q) (Supp. I, 1965).

which any ordinary landlord would be called upon to use. Housing was run on a businesslike basis. Tenants were expected to pay their rent, and pay it promptly. . . .

In the early 1950s, housing officials began giving voice to uneasiness at the change in character of their tenants. Managers and housing officials worried out loud about the large number of "problem families" moving into their buildings. . . . The change in the clientele of public housing has continued until the present time, except insofar as housing for the elderly alters the picture. In many cities, it is not unusual if more than a third of the tenants derive all their income from welfare checks; and in individual projects the percentage may run higher. Naturally, under these circumstances public housing becomes more "institutional.". . .

Tenant Selection

Race discrimination was not unknown in the early days of public housing; indeed, the Public Housing Authority deliberately encouraged segregation in some cities.[14] Race discrimination has been abandoned as policy by the PHA; race is no longer officially a criterion for eligibility or assignment to a project. Many southern projects are still totally segregated. For example, there are seven projects in Anniston, Alabama—three all-white and four all-Negro.[15] And there is a great deal of de facto segregation in public housing in the North. It is as distasteful to Negroes as de facto school segregation. The remedies are if anything more elusive. In many cities, a majority of public tenants are Negroes. This is true in Chicago, for example. Chicago has virtually no all-white housing projects; but it has many all-Negro projects; and in some projects the percentage of white tenants is far greater than the percentage of whites in public housing in general. Spreading the few white tenants equally throughout the city would simply drive many of them out of public housing, without benefiting the Negro particularly. Yet the present pattern *is* one of de facto segregation. Public housing is, by and large, located in Negro areas and is inhabited by Negroes. Projects are so large in the major urban areas that a project would be impossible for a white, middle class community to digest, if some giant handpicked it up and transported it to the urban fringe. We have seen how political and social forces have transformed public housing into Negro ghetto housing. De facto segregation illustrates quite the opposite point from tenant selection. Here, the granting of formal rights to Negroes to demand desegregated projects would be meaningless in many cities, not because no real abuses exist, but because the problem is so basic that only a radical solution can remedy the matter; rights are not enough.

Tenure and Eviction

Once a family has moved into public housing, it becomes subject to rules regarding tenure and eviction. As is true of eligibility and selection, these rules are largely local. Since federal law, state statutes, and local rules all agree that only the poor may live in public housing, a tenant is liable to lose his right to stay if his income

13. Good general assessments can be found in Schorr, *Slums and Social Insecurity* 85-93 (1964); Mulvihill, "Problems in the Management of Public Housing," 35 *Temp. L.Q.* 163 (1962).

14. E.g., in San Diego, see Davis & McEntire, *Residence and Race* 320 (1960). In fairness to PHA, it ought to be pointed out that public housing accommodations were generally available to Negroes "in accordance with need . . . in striking contrast to the discriminatory distribution of local, state and Federal funds," and that it was white prejudice that defeated many attempts by housing officials to break out of the ghetto. Weaver, The Negro Ghetto 179 (1948).

15. Housing and Home Finance Agency, *Low Rent Project Directory,* June 30, 1965, p. 38.

exceeds the maximum set for the particular project.[16] In addition, however, his tenure is jeopardized if he misbehaves or breaches the terms of his lease. Misconduct may bring down upon him a variety of sanctions—fines, withholding of privileges, eviction. Eviction is the ultimate and major sanction of the authority, and the only one susceptible currently to any measurement. We shall, therefore, confine our discussion to the legal position of the tenant with regard to eviction.

The tenant has virtually no protection against eviction. His lease is rigged against him, and his tenancy is on a month-to-month basis. Leases for a year, or two years, which are common for tenants in private buildings, are unknown in public housing. Nothing in any state statute requires a short-term lease explicitly; yet there is probably no housing authority in the country which regularly grants more than a month-to-month lease to its tenants.[17] On 30 days' notice, then, any public housing tenant in the country can lose his rights to his home. . . .

Evictions are probably not common in any housing project,[18] even if we consider tenants as "evicted" if they are asked to leave and they comply without court order. The threat of eviction, however, may be a meaningful and potent sanction even if it rarely has to be carried out. The reported cases suggest that some authorities are anxious to rid themselves of troublemakers. In one case, the tenant's children were a nuisance. In another, a member of the family was alleged to be a dope addict. In another, the head of the family was in jail. There is a continued search for the submerged middle class, that lost legion whose ghost still haunts the program. And, to be sure, the safety and happiness of all may depend upon getting rid of the few. No one denies that management needs the right to protect the other tenants and the property by eliminating people who destroy the walls or the peace of their neighbors. But even the fragmentary evidence of the cases raises disquieting doubts whether management has restricted itself to clear-cut cases of gross misconduct.

There are similar doubts in regard to rulemaking powers. Authorities may evict without reason; in addition, and in consequence, they have very broad powers to impose rules and regulations upon the tenants—provided only that the rules are not illegal or so scandalous as to arouse rebellion. Again many rules and regulations are perfectly salutary and indeed necessary. But others are debatable. It would be a rare housing project, for example, which permitted dogs in high-rise buildings. Half a million people in New York City must choose between subsidy and pets.[19]. . .

C. Control of Management Behavior

How much can we expect from the tenants themselves? Tenants are "organized" in many projects, but for welfare or social purposes, not to run anything which manage-

16. In practice, there is considerable administrative leeway.

17. An examination of leases from more than 30 housing authorities, in big cities and little ones, and from every part of the country, confirms this.

18. In Minneapolis, with 2,462 dwelling units, 48 families were asked to leave in the fiscal year ending September 30, 1964. Twelve of these were "community problems" (misconduct). Letter from V. E. Dale, Director of Management, Housing and Redevelopment Authority, Minneapolis, Aug. 12, 1965. Public housing in Minneapolis is predominantly white, and more than half of the units are for the elderly. But in the same period St. Louis (largely Negro, nonelderly) had only 81 involuntary move-outs of "undersirable tenants," out of a low-rent population of more than 25,000. St. Louis Housing Authority, "Move-Out Study" (undated mimeo).

19. Editors'. See "Redesigning Landlord-Tenant Concepts For an Urban Society," note 15, Chap. 5 in this book.

ment considers important. Activist tenant organizations may have existed and flourished to a greater degree in some of the early projects. In those days, the projects were crowded with members of the submerged middle class; and among these were people who were politically active and anxious to form tenant organizations. Indeed, Harrison Salisbury claims that bureaucratic management helped stamp out tenant organizations, because left-wing activists among the tenants proved to be too much of an annoyance.[20] The passage of the Gwinn Amendment suggests that there might be some substance to this charge.[21] But in any event, the change in clientele of public housing, from the submerged middle class to the dependent poor, would in itself explain a decrease in group participation among tenants. The normal state of mind in public housing may be one of apathetic detachment.[22] And the officially approved state of mind for the dependent poor is a combination of shuffling servility and childish zest for arts and crafts.

Quite another sort of tenant organization has arisen recently. The Syracuse tenant organization can be taken as symptomatic of a latter-day unrest. This organizaton bitterly objects to certain of the rules imposed upon tenants by management. For example, they complain that management assesses unfair fines and penalties. Tenants have claimed that they must pay for broken windows, whether they themselves caused the breakage or not. And alongside their specific complaints goes a more general one: that they have no power or voice in the management. They demand "a voice and a vote."[23]

Is there sufficient evidence to judge whether the unrest at Syracuse arises because the housing administrators there are unusually harsh, or obtuse, or simply that the tenants are uncommonly restless? When residents of Chicago's Taylor homes call their project worse than the slums and use the nickname "Congo Hilton," are we hearing the voice of most tenants, a few tenants, or all tenants? Are we hearing a protest against a particular style of management, against management in general, or against conditions in society in general? Our lack of knowledge is itself,an important point. The tremendous leeway of management has the legal and social result of plunging management practices into the deepest obscurity. This lessens the extent to which the outside community can exert its influence. And the outside community has not been interested. As far as the public has been concerned, public housing projects (like mental hospitals and prisons) are warehouses where the poor can be stored and ignored. The literature on the management of public housing is nonexistent—a literature of silence. Managers write hints to each other in the trade journals; Washington advises and consents from above. An outside appraisal has been almost totally absent. The tremendous polemic literature over public housing has to do with the way projects look—the aesthetics of the projects, which means nothing or almost nothing to the residents—and with the misbehavior of the tenants, not with misbehavior toward them. The recent polemic literature tends to conclude, as one writer neatly

20. Salisbury, *The Shook-Up Generation* 81 (1958).

21. The Gwinn amendment made nonmembership in subversive organizations a condition of tenancy. 67 Stat. 307 (1953).

22. But at least one observer has analyzed a wide variety of "types" among slum and public housing dwellers. Salzman, "Redevelopment Effectiveness Contingent on Understanding Slum Occupants," 13 *J. of Housing* 289 (1956).

23. The Tenants' Report, "Public Housing Syracuse Style, This Is the Way It Is," 1967. Materials on the Syracuse movement were supplied to me by Professor Warren C. Haggstrom of Syracuse Univerity. For one study of attidues of tenants, see Hollingshead & Regler, "Attitudes Toward Slums and Public Housing in Puerto Rico," in *The Urban Condition* 229-45 (Duhl ed. 1963).

put it, that the tenants are the "same bunch of bastards".[24] they were before they moved in. It follows somehow that public housing is a failure and ought to be replaced. That the projects are misguided or mismanaged in operation rather than in conception is a possibility rarely considered. That meaningful reforms may be possible within present projects must at least be weighed as a chance before being rejected. Can society, or the tenants, control and improve public housing—as it is, not as it might be?

Management Styles

. . . [T]here is no one style of management.. The projects themselves are too different for one style of management. There are two polar types of project. One is the institutional, high-rise ghetto, largely inhabited by poor Negroes in the big city and characterized by a high number of "problem" families. Then there are communities of the submerged middle class—projects for the elderly, and low-rise, low-key projects in smaller communities or on the fringes of metropolitan areas (many of them built in the early days of public housing). Clearly, the two types call for—and must get—different styles of management. . . .

One source of difficulty is that the goals of public housing have never been agreed upon, even by those who strongly support the program—even perhaps within the minds of many housing officials or project managers. Is it the duty of public housing to provide a subsidized, sheltered home for the respectable, unfortunate poor? This is probably the predominant goal of housing for the elderly. Is it the duty of public housing to provide minimum facilities for the poor—to protect them from fire and rat bites, and incidentally, to protect the city from the spread of fire and infection? Or is it the duty of public housing to rehabilitate the dependent poor, by providing them with a total new environment and a massive infusion of social services?

These three goals are to a degree incompatible. They certainly cannot coexist in one project; they imply different rules, strategies, and modes of management. Housing for the submerged middle class can be and perhaps should be run in the same way that a major private landlord runs his apartment house. On the other hand, these projects are *not* private; they are run by government employees, and they are not subject to the discipline of a competitive market. There is no reason why "middleclass" public housing, including housing for the elderly, should not give its tenants a full battery of legal rights, long-term leases if anybody wants them, a strong tenant voice in project affairs, not as a matter of administrative grace, but of right, and tenure from eviction except for cause established by reasonable rules concurred in by tenants. We might even insist that internal procedures be judicialized to a degree. It is hard to think of any legitimate prerogative or duty of administration which would be harmed by adding some procedural and substantive restraints. On the other hand, it is precisely in these projects that abuse of discretion is least likely to occur and is least likely to endanger the prerogatives of tenants.

Projects inhabited by the dependent poor present much more difficult questions. The present state of affairs is certainly not ideal. The month-to-month lease is unnecessary and ought to be eliminated. Its value lies in the broad discretion it affords to housing administrators. Administrative discretion may be a good thing under many circumstances, but only if flexibility serves some real function; there is no reason to insulate managers completely from responsibility and embarrassment through the

24. Seligman, "The Enduring Slums," in *The Exploding Metropolis* 92, 106 (1958).

device of a short-term lease. And no device should be neglected that might increase the stake of the poor in their homes, their communities, and in their circle of neighbors.

Do we conceive of housing projects for the dependent poor as custodial? Or do we think of them as providing an environment within which society can attempt to rework wasted lives and untie the knots of decadence? These competing goals may imply competing rules of government. A custodial project may be as hard and orderly as a prison; but it might also be run on easy-going permissive terms. To create a total environment, however, a certain amount of discipline is essential—discipline to prevent tenants from living in terror, discipline to create a climate of order which is a prerequisite for rehabilitation. Those who wish to reform public housing—particularly those who complain that the projects are ugly, grim enclaves, shut off from the community—frequently suggest scattering pocket-size projects about town, and even insinuating a subsidized tenant or two into private housing. One can readily agree that in the long run the solution to the social ills of the Negro ghetto must include breaking down the walls that separate the poor Negro from his White neighbors. But in the short run, and within slum communities, a sheltered enclave is a vital prerequisite for the offering of massive social services to public housing tenants. Teachers and social workers should be able to walk unafraid on the grounds at least by daylight. There should be space for playgrounds and meeting rooms. If existing communities are destroyed by private building or by civic projects, public housing can at least provide a stable locale where the community could possibly be rebuilt. The isolation of the projects may be, in absolute terms, an evil; but the most radical causative factors producing that isolation arise out of political forces which condemn public housing to internal exile and high-rise life. These forces, at least in the short run, are not likely to be overcome.

39. Section 235 of the National Housing Act: Homeownership for Low-income Families?

ROBERT SCHAFER and CHARLES G. FIELD

A frequent proposal for assisting the poor by increasing their opportunities for homeownership was implemented in 1968 when Congress enacted legislation aimed at facilitating homeownership for families in the $3,000 to $5,000 annual income range. Robert Schafer and Charles G. Field ask whether this legislation can benefit the intended group, whether its benefits vary regionally, and whether it requires the buyer to spend too much of his income on housing. More generally the analysis suggests the reluctance of public programs to realistically face the high and increasing costs of providing low income families with decent housing. An editors' addendum describes some more recent difficulties uncovered in the operation of the Section 235 program and suggests some weaknesses inherent in supply-side subsidies of this type.

Section 101 of the Housing and Urban Development Act of 1968 added section 235 to the National Housing Act.[1] This new section was designed to assist low-income families in the purchase of their own homes. It provides payments by the Secretary of HUD to mortgagees on behalf of the mortgagors. Part of the rationale behind the selection of this mechanism was to encourage private money sources to extend the mortgage funds rather than have the government do so as it did under the below market interest programs.[2] The payments cannot exceed that amount which would reduce the mortgagor's contribution below that which he would pay on a mortgage at 1 percent interest. The payments are available to new or substantially rehabilitated housing and, to a limited extent, existing housing in standard condition. The program is restricted to one- and two-family houses and single units in a condominium. . . .

This homeownership provision provides lending institutions with mortgage insurance and reduces the homeowner's housing costs by making payments to the mortgagees on behalf of the owners. Mortgages are insured by FHA through a special risk insurance fund and qualify for special mortgage insurance assistance. Mortgage insurance is intended to protect the lending institutions (mortgagees) against foreclosures of mortgages held in portfolio. A family must contribute a prescribed amount of income toward debt service, and the government makes up the difference between the market costs and the contribution. . . .

Downpayment Limits

The minimum down payment requirement for families whose incomes are less than 135 percent of the maximum income limits for admission to public housing in the

Reprinted from the *Journal of Urban Law* 46 (1969): 667-85 (edited), by permission of the publisher and authors. Robert Schafer is an assistant professor of city and regional planning at Harvard University. Charles G. Field is with the Department of Housing and Urban Development.

1. 12 U.S.C.A. § 1715z (1969).

2. §§ 221 (d) (3) and 221 (h). 12 U.S.C. §§ 1715l (d)(3) & (h) (1964, Supp. II 1965-66).

area is $200. All other families must pay at least 3 percent of the cost of acquisition in cash or its equivalent. . . .

Mortgage Limits

Under section 235 the maximum mortgage amounts are: $15,000 ($17,500 in high cost areas) for single-family units and $17,500 ($20,000 in high cost areas) for single-family units where the mortgagor's family contains five or more members. The additional increment takes cognizance that required living space is, in part, a function of family size.

Income Limits

Section 235 sets definite owner-income restrictions on participation. At the time of initial occupancy no more than 20 percent of appropriated funds may be allocated to families with incomes exceeding 135 percent of the local maximum income allowable for admission to public housing. And no family shall have an income, at the time of initial occupancy, that exceeds 90 percent of the section 221(d)(3) BMIR [below market interest rates] maximum income limits. The condition "at time of initial occupancy" allows families to remain within the program as their incomes rise. Tables 39.1 and 39.2 illustrate these restrictions for Boston, Massachusetts.

TABLE 39.1 *The maximum income limits after exemptions for admission to public housing in Boston, Massachusetts*

Number of Persons in Family	General	Special Families (Displaced by Public Action)
1	$4,200	$5,040
2	4,600	5,520
3	5,200	6,240
4	5,700	6,840
5	5,900	7,080
6	6,100	7,320
7 or more	6,300	7,560

SOURCE: Boston Housing Authority, Interoffice Communication (November 30, 1967).

TABLE 39.2 *The maximum income limits for section 221(d) (3) BMIR occupants in Boston, Massachusetts*

Number of persons in family	Total family Income
1	$ 6,100
2	7,400
3 or 4	8,700
5 or 6	10,000
7 or more	11,300

SOURCE: Department of Housing and Urban Development. *Memorandum: Revised Section 221(d)(3) BMIR Income Limits, Massachusetts Localities* (June 19, 1968).

The section 235 program is intended to assist low- and moderate-income families specifically in the $3,000 to $5,000 income range. The major thrust of the program,

80 percent of appropriated funding, is directed at families earning less than 135 percent of the local maximum income limit for admission to public housing. Section 235 defines "income" as gross family income minus a deduction of $300 for each minor who is a member of the immediate family and is living with the family, and excluding the earnings of any such minors.[3] Unless otherwise stated, income will be used in this section 235 sense.

There is no attempt to penalize a family with a section 235 mortgage when its income rises. Instead the subsidy is gradually readjusted downward until the family assumes responsibility for the full mortgage and interest payments. When the family's income reaches the $7,200 level depending on family size, subsidy payments terminate. This mechanism is one of the ways the new housing provision seeks to gear its benefits to the individual owner's situation.

FINANCIAL ANALYSIS AND EVALUATION

The determination as to what a family *should* spend on shelter is crucial to the program and a basis for evaluation. Subsidies, mortgage limits, income limits, etc. are only important in terms of their effect upon the family expenditure for housing. Although not explicitly stated in section 235, it seems the intent of Congress as to what people under the program in question should pay for shelter ranges between 20 and 25 percent of gross income.[4] This is clear from section 236 of the National Housing Act, dealing with rental housing, which requires renters to pay 25 percent of their incomes toward housing.[5] The rent supplement program requires a 25 percent of adjusted income contribution by families.[6] Sections 23 and 10(c) of the Housing Act of 1937[7] require in effect a contribution of 23 percent of family income toward rent including utilities.[8] Logically, if Congress asks 20 to 25 percent of income to be contributed toward housing costs under these other programs, the same figures, without doubt, represent the congressional estimate of the proper percentage of income that the low and moderate income family should pay toward shelter costs.

Two questions must be raised. Does section 235 bring total shelter costs within the 20 to 25 percent range for low- and moderate-income families, thereby meeting the intent of Congress? Secondly, is it reasonable for Congress to assume a 20 to

---

3. 12 U.S.C.A. § 1715z(l) (1969). The HUD Handbook for section 235 also excludes "unusual or temporary income." According to the Handbook " 'unusual or temporary income' may include 5 percent of total family income (before deductions) for social security witholding and similar deductions, all or part of overtime pay which will be discontinued, departure of a secondary wage earner, unemployment compensation which does not occur regularly, or other income which will be discontinued." Department of Housing and Urban Development, *Homeownership for Lower Income Families* (Section 235): *A HUD Handbook*, FHA no. 4441.1, at 12 (October, 1968).

4. See S.R. No. 1123, 90th Cong., 2nd Sess., 9 (1968). (footnote number 2 to the table). See President's Committee on Urban Housing. *A Decent Home* 66 (1968).

5. 12 U.S.C.A. § 1715z-1 j(1969).

6. 12 U.S.C. § 1701s(d) (1964, Supp. I 1965).

7. 42 U.S.C. § 1410 (c) (1964, Supp. II 1965-66) (section 10 (c)); 42 U.S.C. § 142lb (1964, Supp. II 1965-66) (§ 23). Section 23 is a short-term leasing program while section 10(c) can be operated either as project owned by the local housing authority or as a long-term leasing program.

8. The effective rent is 23 percent of adjusted income. Boston Housing Authority, August, 1968.

25 percent rule as the basis for low-income family expenditure toward total shelter costs?

Under section 235 the Secretary of Housing and Urban Development pays the mortgagee the *lesser* of the following two amounts: (1) the difference between the sum of the monthly payment for principal, interest, taxes, insurance, and mortgage insurance premium, and 20 percent of the mortgagor's income; or (2) the difference between the sum of the monthly payment for principal, interest, and mortgage insurance premium, and the monthly payment for principal and interest which the mortgagor would be obligated to pay if the mortgage were to bear interest at the rate of 1 percent per annum.[9] Therefore, two calculations must be made before the subsidy and "effective" interest rate are known. Clause 2 sets the maximum amount of subsidy available. But clause 1 usually reduces the *actual* subsidy below this amount and consequently raises the "effective" interest rate above 1 percent.

The effect of these payments on the percentage of annual income paid by the mortgagor for housing costs is investigated for a 40-year mortgage bearing an interest rate of 6¾ percent plus the ½ percent FHA mortgage insurance premium.[10] The sale price of a single-family house is assumed to be $15,200. For persons with incomes less than 135 percent of the maximum income limits for admission to public housing in the area, the down payment can be $200 and the mortgage amount $15,000.

Table 39.3 itemizes all the costs associated with homeownership. The figures in Table 39.3 are typical costs on housing located in the Boston Model Cities Area.

TABLE 39.3 *Housing Costs (monthly)*

Payment for mortgage, interest, and mortgage insurance premium	$ 96
Heat	17
Gas and electricity	6
Mortgage insurance against death of mortgagor	4
Fire and hazard insurance	8
Maintenance and reserve	25
Sewer and Water	4
Real estate taxes	20
Total	$180

SOURCE: *A Homeownership Proposal for the Boston Model Cities Area*, vol. 2, Appendix J, table B, at J-5 (1968).

9. 12 U.S.C.A. § 1715z(c) (1969). The actual statutory language is: "The payment shall be in an amount not exceeding the lesser of

(1) the balance of the monthly payment for principal, interest, taxes, insurance, and mortgage insurance premium due under the mortgage remaining unpaid after applying 20 per centum of the mortgagor's income; or

(2) the difference between the amount of the monthly payment for principal, interest, and mortgage insurance premium which the mortgagor is obligated to pay under the mortgage and the monthly payment for principal and interest which the mortgagor would be obligated to pay if the mortgage were to bear interest at the rate of 1 per centum per annum."

10. The maximum mortgage term can vary from 30 to 40 years depending on the characteristics of the mortgagor. The maximum term was selected for this paper to give the mortgagor his lowest annual cost. Section 235(b)(l) incorporates the mortgage term restrictions of section 221(d)(2), 12 U.S.C. § 17151(d)(2) (1964, Supp. I 1965). Since the writing of this article HUD has raised its maximum allowable interest rate to 7½ percent per annum. *N.Y. Times*, Jan. 25, 1969, at 1, col. 7. The article uses an interest rate of 6¾ percent; the analysis would not differ under a higher interest rate.

Clause 1, the first of the two calculations in the section 235 payment formula, calls for the sum of payments for principal, interest, mortgage insurance premium, taxes, and insurance. For the situation depicted in Table 39.3 this sum is $128 per month. Consequently, $52 of monthly housing costs are excluded from the formula. These costs cover heat, gas, electricity, sewer, water, maintenance, and reserve. Consider the impact of the section 235 payment formula on a family with $6,000 annual income. Under clause 1 the difference between the sum of the monthly payment for principal, interest, taxes, insurance, and mortgage insurance premiums ($128/-month) and 20 percent of the mortgagor's income ($100/month) is $28 in the Boston Model Cities Area [Table 39.3]. Under clause 2 the difference between the sum of the monthly payments for principal, interest, and mortgage insurance premium ($96), and the monthly payment for principal and interest if the interest rate were 1 percent ($38) is $58. But since the subsidy is the *lesser* of $28 or $58, the $6,000 annual income family can only receive the $28 subsidy. It can be seen that the failure to include the $52 of monthly costs for heat, maintenance, gas, electricity, sewer, and water in clause 1 reduces the subsidy amount. If such items had been included in clause 1 the calculation under clause 1 would yield $180 minus $100 or $80 per month. Then the $6,000 annual income family would receive the maximum subsidy of clause 2, namely $58 per month. Areas of the country having warm, mild climates are not greatly affected by this exclusion because the climate reduces heating and maintenance costs to trivial amounts.

Tables 39.4 and 39.5 compare the percentage of annual gross income contributed toward total housing costs of $180 per month and $150 per month, with and without section 235 assistance, as a function of income. These two figures for monthly housing costs represent a high-cost area and a lower-cost warmer climate, respectively. The $180 per month figure is typical for the Boston Model Cities area.[11]

TABLE 39.4   *Percentage of Income toward Total Housing Costs without Section 235 Assistance*

Annual Gross Income after Statutory Deduction of $300/minor	Percentage of Income toward Total Housing Costs of	
	$180/mo.	$150/mo.
$3,000	72%	60%
3,600	60	50
4,200	52	43
4,800	45	38
5,400	40	33
6,000	36	30
6,600	33	27
7,200	30	25
7,800	28	23

Two conclusions can be drawn from Tables 39.4 and 39.5. First, in areas with higher housing costs ($180/month) section 235 does not reduce the homeowner's financial burden to 25 percent of annual gross income. Twenty-five percent has been selected because there is some indication that Congress excluded heat, maintenance, and the other items hoping that the percentage of income toward *total* housing costs would

11. Housing Innovations, Inc., *A Homeownership Proposal for the Boston Model Cities Area* (1968).

approach 25.[12] Second, for the $4,200 through $7,800 income group, section 235 payments bring the recipient's shelter payments down to approximately 25 percent in lower cost areas. Therefore, the payment formula inherently favors warm, mild climates. Because of the section 235 formula, it is improbable that much new or rehabilitated housing will be constructed with section 235 assistance in the northern sections of the country.

TABLE 39.5   *Percentage of Income toward Total Housing Costs with Section 235 Assistance*

Annual Gross Income after Statutory Deduction of $300/minor	Amount of Section 235 Payment	Percentage of Income toward Total Housing Costs of	
		$180/mo.	$150/mo.
$3,000	58	49%	37%
3,600	58	41	31
4,200	58	35	26
4,800	48	33	26
5,400	38	32	25
6,000	28	31	24
6,600	18	30	24
7,200	8	29	24
7,800	0	28	23

In addition, note that only families with incomes less than $4,200 receive the full benefits of a 1 percent mortgage. Yet this is not enough to make ownership a real possibility for them, especially in the higher cost areas.

Consider the import of a revision of clause 1 of the formula to include those housing cost items which it now excludes. Such a formula would be analogous to the one now in existence under section 115 of the Housing Act of 1949 rehabilitation grant program.[13] The section 115 test equates the family's contribution toward *total* housing expenses (including the items excluded by section 235) to 25 percent of its income. Table 39.6 presents the results of such a variation.

TABLE 39.6   *Percentage of Income toward Total Housing Costs with Revised Section 235 Assistance*

Annual Gross Income after Statutory Deduction of $300/minor	Amount of 235 Payment	$180/mo.	Amount of 235 Payment	$150/mo.
$3,000	58	49%	58	37
3,600	58	41	58	31
4,200	58	35	58	26
4,800	58	31	50	25
5,400	58	27	38	25
6,000	55	25	25	25
6,600	43	25	13	25
7,200	30	25	0	25
7,800	18	25	0	23

12. S.R. No. 1123, 90th Cong., 2nd Sess., 9 (1968) (footnote 2 to the table).
13. 42 U.S.C. § 1466 (b) (1964, Supp. II 1965-66).

The revision does not alter the basic impact in lower-cost areas, but it does make the statute a viable housing tool for families in the $5,400 through $7,800 income levels in high cost areas. The remaining difference between income levels served by section 235 in the two areas may be due to variations in the cost of living. At least the revised statute does not artificially accentuate such variations. In order to reach lower-income families, a payment that reaches to 0 percent interest or one that includes partial payment of principal would be needed. Congress has not yet indicated a willingness to give serious consideration to legislation along those lines.

So far this section has assumed that a 20 to 25 percent rule was a satisfactory criterion for Congress to adopt. Now we ask: Is it reasonable for Congress to accept a 20 to 25 percent rule?

A Department of Labor survey of consumer expenditures for 1960-61 indicated that the 20 to 25 percent gross income (before taxes) allocation for shelter was a high estimate of actual cash outlays.[14] The findings presented in Table 39.7 below indicate an inverse relationship between gross income and proportion spent on housing. Expenditures for shelter, by definition, were the sum of debt service, taxes, property insurance, maintenance, and utilities including heat. These costs of homeownership closely approximate the total shelter costs listed in Table 39.3.

TABLE 39.7   *Family Expenditures on Shelter, All Families in the Northeast, Urban and Rural, 1960-61*

Gross Income	Percentage of Gross Income (before tax)
Below $1,000	—
$1,000- 2,000	36
2,000- 3,000	26
3,000- 4,000	22
4,000- 5,000	17
5,000- 6,000	16
6,000- 7,500	15
7,500-10,000	13
10,000-15,000	11
15,000 +	8

What is the effect of section 235 upon the proportion of income spent on housing by lower-income families? To answer this question, estimates of housing expenditures by family size and gross income were tabulated. Using the shelter costs cited in Table 39.3 governmental subsidies were computed for families with 1 to 5 minors with gross incomes ranging from $3,000 to $9,000. The adjusted income for each family was based upon an exemption of $300 per qualifying minor. Once adjusted incomes and shelter costs were known, computation of subsidy and actual shelter costs (total shelter costs—subsidy) quickly followed. Table 39.8 lists actual shelter costs as a percentage of gross income for different family sizes and incomes.

The comparison of Tables 39.7 and 39.8 is striking. The expenditures required under the 1968 legislation far exceed actual consumer expenditures. At the $4,000 level, the 1968 act would require an expenditure equal to 37 percent of gross income

14. U.S. Bureau of Labor Statistics, Department of Labor, BLS Report #237-38, *Survey of Consumer Expenditures, 1960-61: Consumer Expenditures and Income, Urban United States, 1961* (1964), 76.

as compared to actual expenditures of 22 percent as reported by the Department of Labor survey. Most other comparisons reveal the same discrepancy. Another finding drawn from the comparison is that the 25 percent of gross income figure for total shelter costs does not hold up against empirical evidence. The proportion of income spent on housing is higher in metropolitan areas—the survey covers all Northeast families—but even a substantial increase in shelter expenditures at each income level would leave most income classes below the 25 percent level.

TABLE 39.8 *Expenditures of Owners for Housing as a Percentage of Gross Income by Family Size and Income under Section 235*

Gross Income (before Section 235 Adjustment)	Number of Qualifying Minors				
	1	*2*	*3*	*4*	*5*
$3,000	49	49	49	49	49
4,000	37	37	37	37	37
5,000	31	31	29	29	29
6,000	29	28	27	26	25
7,000	28	27	26	25	24
8,000		26	25	25	24
9,000					24

Housing is not an isolated expenditure and must be viewed in light of other family expenditures. The 1960-61 Survey of Consumer Expenditures does bring us closer to the actual budgets of low- and moderate-income families.[15] As illustrated in Table 39.9 when income decreases from the moderate living standard of $10,000,[16] the proportions of income spent on shelter (debt service, mortgage insurance, and taxes as defined in the survey), utilities and medicine increase. The proportion spent on food increases, but not as quickly. This reflects the importance of these basic necessities to the family regardless of income level. The decrease in proportions of consumption expenditures spent on transportation, clothing, and education clearly indicates the lower priority of these items for the lower-income family. Lower priority does not necessarily mean that they are not desired goods. Rather, it means that there is insufficient income to purchase them.

These trends are not indicative of the amount of expenditures that should be allocated to specific items; rather they reflect the pattern of observed expenditures. Low-income families are in greatest need of funds to spend on education, food, and transportation. Instead of decreasing the proportion spent for educational attainment or transportation (increased transportation costs may be necessary to reach better jobs), funds should be liberated for these purposes. Food, medicines, and utilities are basic needs, and expenditures for these items should not be curtailed.

Homeownership should be provided at a cost that does not discourage or distort a low-income family's opportunity for self-improvement. As shown, housing represents

15. Id.

16. A recent study by the Department of Labor concludes that a moderate income budget for a family of 4 (husband employed, age 38; wife unemployed; and 2 children, a girl age 8 and a boy age 13) living in Boston, Autumn 1966, needed a gross income of $10,505. The U.S. average budget for a metropolitan family was $9,588. The budgets of the lower income families discussed in this paper fall substantially below what was considered a moderate standard by the Department of Labor. U.S. Department of Labor, Bureau of Labor Statistics, *City Worker's Family Budget for a Moderate Living Standard Autumn 1966*, Bulletin no. 1570-1.

a significant portion of the budget. Upward social and economic mobility requires expenditures of funds. If we can reduce housing expenditures to 20 percent or less of total income, we can liberate funds for other family requirements such as education, food, and transportation.

TABLE 39.9   *Proportion of Total Consumption Spent on Selected Items, Northeast 1960-1961*

Gross Income	Food	Shelter	Utilities	Clothing	Medicine	Education	Transportation
Below $1,000	26.9	20.2	13.9	4.1	7.7	.0	7.4
$1,000- 2,000	29.8	15.7	13.8	4.7	9.7	.2	7.4
2,000- 3,000	29.3	12.9	10.6	5.9	9.1	.2	11.1
3,000- 4,000	25.6	11.8	10.1	7.4	9.3	.4	11.6
4,000- 5,000	27.1	10.8	7.5	8.8	6.1	.5	16.2
5,000- 6,000	26.7	11.7	7.0	8.6	6.7	.6	15.6
6,000- 7,500	26.1	11.7	6.3	11.0	6.1	1.2	14.3
7,500-10,000	25.3	10.9	5.5	10.7	5.6	1.4	17.3

SOURCE: U.S. Bureau of Labor Statistics, Department of Labor, BLS Report # 237-38, *Survey of Consumer Finances, 1960-61: Consumer Expenditures and Income, Urban United States, 1961* (1964).

The 20 to 25 percent rule, which tends to dominate our housing policies for low-income families, needs to be reviewed. To say a low-income family should spend 25 percent of its income on housing is playing a numbers game. If we are to play this game at all, the Department of Labor survey indicates that 15 percent of total income before taxes would be a more realistic figure. An optimum allocation of income might require an even smaller contribution for housing by the lowest-income family, if expenditures for food, clothing, and medical care are to be sustained at adequate levels. Poor families need free funds in their budgets. If they seek improvement by acquiring better educations or commuting longer distances to reach better jobs, these actions require money. Programs like section 235 restrict rather than liberalize the use of money for lower-income families by requiring a large portion of the budget to be used on shelter. . . .

EDITORS' ADDENDUM

The course of the section 235 homeownership program over its first two years illustrates some important aspects of the interplay between government subsidies and the private sector. The program has proved exceedingly popular: through March 1971, an estimated 160,000 families became homeowners under the section 235 program[1] and 221,100 section 235 units are projected for fiscal year 1972.[2] At the same time many abuses have been uncovered as private developers and realtors seek to maximize their profits and exploit low- and moderate-income consumers with little or no experience in owning or purchasing a house.

1. See U.S., Congress, House, Committee on Banking and Currency, *Interim Report on HUD Investigation of Low and Moderate Income Housing Programs*, Hearings before the Committee on Banking and Currency, 92d Cong., 1st sess., March 31, 1971 (testimony of HUD Secretary George Romney), p. 5.

2. U.S., Congress, House, Committee on Banking and Currency, *Third Annual Report on National Housing Goals, Message from the President of the United States*, 92d Cong., 1st sess., House Doc. 92-136, June 29, 1971, table 2, p. 8.

TABLE 39A-1. *Dwelling Units Insured under Section 235 of the National Housing Act by Census Region and Character of the Neighborhood, December 31, 1970*

| | 1970 | Units with Section 235 Insurance | | | | | | | | |
| | Households* (1,000's) | Located in nonblighted areas | | | Located in blighted areas | | | All areas | | |
Region		existing units	new units	total	existing units	new units	total	existing units	new units	total
Number										
U.S.	68,631	37,202	87,001	124,203	5,066	1,946	7,012	42,268	88,947	131,215
Northeast	16,621	3,358	2,627	5,985	563	3	566	3,921	2,630	6,551
North Central	18,974	9,217	17,693	26,910	2,835	721	3,556	12,052	18,414	30,466
South	21,003	14,659	46,423	61,082	954	1,019	1,973	15,613	47,442	63,055
West	12,033	9,956	18,900	28,856	714	203	917	10,670	19,103	29,773
Puerto Rico	†	12	1,358	1,370	—	—	—	12	1,358	1,370
Percentage distribution										
U.S.	100%	100%	100%	100%	100%	100%	100%	100%	100%	100%
Northeast	24.2	9.0	3.2	4.8	11.1	0.2	8.1	9.3	2.9	5.0
North Central	27.6	24.8	20.3	21.7	56.0	37.0	50.7	28.5	20.7	23.2
South	30.6	39.5	53.3	49.2	18.9	52.3	28.2	38.0	53.3	48.1
West	17.5	26.8	21.7	23.2	14.1	10.4	13.1	25.2	21.4	22.6
Puerto Rico	†	‡	1.5	1.1	—	—	—	‡	1.5	1.0

*Approximated by housing units.
†Not available.
‡Less than 0.1 percent.

SOURCES: U.S. Commission on Civil Rights, *Home Ownership for Lower Income Families: A Report on the Racial and Ethnic Impact of the Section 235 Program* (Washington, D.C.: Government Printing Office, June 1971), Appendixes A and B; U.S. Bureau of the Census, *1970 Census of Housing: General Housing Characteristics, United States,* HC (V1)-1 (Advanced Report) (February 1971), table 1.

A House Committee on Banking and Currency[3] study documented widespread inflation of prices on houses being built and sold under the section 235 program, as well as sales of houses with serious defects. Realtors purchase homes in "soft" housing markets, frequently areas undergoing racial transition, and sell them within a short time at substantial markups. Among the examples cited in the congressional report were a house bought for $8,500 and sold 4 months later for $14,500, and a house bought for $10,000 and sold 3 months later for $17,500. Any interim repairs are at best cosmetic in nature.

Serious housing code violations also were found in section 235 houses, including some that had been newly constructed. "The construction of these [new] homes," the report notes, "is of the cheapest type of building materials; and, instead of buying a home, people purchasing these houses are buying a disaster."[4] The houses noted above, for example, had 25 and 30 code violations, respectively, including holes in walls, leaking roof, obstructed plumbing, and defective kitchen equipment.[5]

The report concludes that "FHA has allowed real estate speculation of the worst type to go on in the 235 program and has virtually turned its back to these practices."[6] According to the House report, "The Federal Housing Administration is insuring existing homes that are of such poor quality that there is little or no possibility that they can survive the life of the mortgage. . . ;"[7] and low- and moderate-income owners are being saddled with large repair bills, sometimes within months after making their purchases, bills they cannot afford, given the tenuous financial positions that Schafer and Field outline. "Such houses," the House report states, "have no resale value, and even minimal repairs will place such a burden on the homeowner's income that the congressional purpose of affording decent, safe, and sanitary housing for low- and moderate-income individuals not only has been thwarted but amounts to sheer fraud."[8]

After release of the House report, HUD suspended the 235 program for existing housing—which has accounted for 30 percent of all 235 mortgages—and reinstated it selectively in areas where the department was satisfied that abuses were not occurring. In addition, a provision of the 1970 Housing Act authorizes HUD to compensate 235 owners for serious defects that existed at the time of sale, and those who sell 235 houses must agree to reimburse HUD for any such payments to owners and to certify that no serious defects exist. These are partial remedies, and it remains to be seen how well they will work. (One clear weakness is that owners must request such assistance no later than one year after receipt of mortgage insurance, and many basic defects may not appear until after that time.)

The conflict is inherent and the problems basic to the nature of public-private interaction not only in the housing field but in other areas of the economy as well.

3. U.S., Congress, House, Committee on Banking and Currency, *Investigation and Hearings of Abuses in Federal Low and Moderate Income Housing Programs—Staff Report and Recommendations*, 91st Cong., 2d sess., December 1970. [Hereinafter cited as *1970 House Report*.] See also the March 31, 1971, follow-up report "Interim Report on HUD Investigation of Low and Moderate Income Housing Programs," *supra* note 1.

4. See *1970 House Report*, p. 1.

5. The report is replete with shocking case studies and photographs. In the "Introduction" it is asserted that "FHA has approved housing for the 235 program which within months after purchase has been condemned by municipal authorities." Ibid.

6. Ibid.

7. Ibid.

8. Ibid., p. 4.

(Similar scandals may be anticipated in the near future with respect to the section 236 program of interest subsidization for moderate-income rental housing.) Real estate brokers, housing developers, and lending institutions are interested in maximizing their profits. The federal regulatory agency is, by virtue of its history, orientation, personnel, and operating style, unsuited to, and apparently unwilling to undertake, the task of controlling private profit-making instincts.

The housing consumer whom these subsidy programs aid has neither the power nor the experience to negotiate effectively in the private market,[9] and, indeed, the nature of the 235 program fails to maximize whatever consumer sovereignty might be developed as a countervailing force. The consumer is satisfied with any level of housing quality above his present one, and since under the subsidy program he pays no more of his own funds, his bargaining power for additional housing quality is not enhanced. In addition the number of eligible households in the vicinity of any subsidized project far exceeds the number of available units. Minimization of the number of subsidized developments in local market areas—the result of insufficient appropriations and HUD policies—limits competition for tenants among housing suppliers. Experience with the 235 program (as well as previous experience with the infamous FHA section 608 program of the postwar period) shows clearly the inefficiency of supply-side subsidies such as the 235 and 236 programs, as compared with transfer payments to the consumer in the form of housing allowances or rent certificates, which would permit the market to perform the function of insuring quality performance. These issues are discussed further in the Welfeld, Hartman, and Netzer selections below.

9. The 235 program and FHA have been receiving their lumps from other parts of the federal government as well. A recent report of the United States Commission on Civil Rights concluded that the 235 program was acquiescing in existing patterns of residential segregation and doing virtually nothing to foster racially integrated living. Many of the same explanations for the defects uncovered by the House Banking and Currency Committee underlie the Civil Rights Commission's criticisms as well. See U.S. Commission on Civil Rights, *Home Ownership for Lower Income Families: A Report on the Racial and Ethnic Impact of the Section 235 Program* (Washington, D.C.: Government Printing Office, June 1971).

40. *The Boston Rehabilitation Program*

LANGLEY C. KEYES, JR.

In 1967-68 the Department of Housing and Urban Development conducted an experiment to demonstrate its ability to process and complete a large number of units for rehabilitation within the shortest possible time period. In less than a year 2,000 units were purchased and renovated for low and moderate income occupancy in the Roxbury area of Boston, a largely black community. Because the experiment was well documented and illustrates many of the important elements that must be considered in attempting to salvage a large portion of the nation's stock of substandard housing, we have chosen it for extensive treatment. In a report done under the auspices of the MIT-Harvard Joint Center for Urban Studies, Langley Keyes describes the political background of HUD's decision to undertake this project, some of the traditional bureaucratic barriers to inner-city rehabilitation work of this sort, and the basic elements of the BURP (Boston Urban Rehabilitation Program) model.

Immediately on its announcement the project was embroiled in controversy that was to continue unabated throughout its life. The buildings' residents, pre- and postrehabilitation, and the larger Roxbury community objected to the lack of community participation in the project, the quality of rehabilitation work, inadequate relocation provisions, absence of opportunity for black workers and entrepreneurs, known slumlords' participation in the project, and many other features. A report commissioned by the community and carried out by Urban Planning Aid, a local advocacy planning organization, extensively documents some of the project's shortcomings and suggests that HUD's criteria of speed and efficiency were inadequate in both concept and execution.

Finally, from the corporate investor's viewpoint, a key actor in the project, Eli Goldston, describes the profit potentials in BURP and, more generally, under various government incentive programs. The complex profitability calculations of real estate investors are a key to understanding the impact of government intervention and how the housing market functions. Mr. Goldston's candid description of how his company benefited from its involvement in the BURP program, particularly through astute use of income tax laws, indicates that investment of this sort can produce an annual rate of return slightly greater than 40 percent (in addition to the benefits that his Boston Gas Company received from the added gas load from 2,000 units.)

In 1970 HUD announced its Project Rehab, involving the rapid rehabilitation of 2,000 to 2,500 units in each of about a dozen large cities. It is unclear at this point whether the lessons learned in Boston will be heeded in this larger effort.

Reprinted from *The Boston Rehabilitation Program: An Independent Analysis* (Cambridge, Mass.: The Joint Center for Urban Studies of M.I.T. and Harvard, 1970), pp. 14-19, 31-47 (edited), by permission of the publisher and author. Langley C. Keyes, Jr. was director of Housing development for the Boston Model City Administration and is a member of the faculty of the Department of Urban Studies and Planning at M.I.T.

THE ORIGINS OF BURP

The Political Background

The Boston Rehabilitation Program (BURP) emerged in response to a series of complex political pressures which came to a head during the summer of 1967. The Department of Housing and Urban Development (HUD) had, by 1967, come to place an increased reliance on rehabilitation as a prime means of revitalizing urban neighborhoods. Secretary Weaver's lengthy statement before the Senate Subcommittee on Urban Affairs outlines HUD's position at that time. While recognizing the "difficulties and complications that are inherent in rehabilitation," Weaver stated that he "had some real achievements to report,"[1] and pointed out that "since we began a series of experiments and studies in 1961 to improve our techniques, rehabilitation has become a far more important tool in local urban renewal activities."[2] The Secretary made it clear that he was aware of the problems involved in the rehabilitation process but was prepared to go on experimenting in a number of cities and in a number of ways "to accomplish massive rehabilitation."[3] Just prior to Secretary Weaver's testimony President Johnson had established the Kaiser Committee "to develop a plan for mobilizing the resources of private industry and labor for a broad attack on city slums, with particular emphasis on rehabilitation";[4] and Weaver saw the Committee "as a means of building on the rehabilitation momentum which has been achieved in a number of places. . . ."[5]

During the same Senate hearings, the Federal Housing Administration (FHA), the office responsible for most of HUD's involvement in rehabilitation, was being criticized for its lengthy processing of a new construction project in Malden, Massachusetts. Malden's Mayor Kelliher asserted

. . . that FHA has been accustomed to operating in a vacuum, and they are not fulfilling the function they should fulfill in the matter of coordinating with the other members of the HUD family.[6]

Mayor Kelliher's complaint was representative of an always large but now expanding body of opinion which held that the FHA was basically an insuring agency and that it was unable to adapt to the demands of the special assistance programs which were in its charge.[7] Secretary Weaver might see rehabilitation as a major thrust of his administration, but the FHA had never been in the vanguard of that movement. Yet FHA special assistance programs constitute the backbone of any HUD effort in the rehabilitation field.

The record did show that for all Secretary Weaver's hopes for the rehabilitation of the nation's central cities, the FHA 221(d) (3) program, the agency's major moderate income rehabilitation program, has not made a significant contribution to the rehabilitation program that has so far been accomplished. As of the summer of 1967, less

1. "Housing Legislation of 1967: Hearings before the Subcommittee on Housing and Urban Affairs," United States Senate, 90th Cong., I, p. 96.

2. Ibid.

3. Ibid., p. 106.

4. Ibid.

5. Ibid.

6. Ibid., p. 545.

7. See Charles M. Haar, *Federal Credit and Private Housing* (McGraw-Hill, New York, 1960), for a detailed exposition of the FHA's problem of identity.

than 5,000 units had been rehabilitated across the nation under this program.[8] At the end of 1966 only 68,000 units had been rehabilitated under federal urban renewal programs of any kind.[9]

No one was more critical of the cautious FHA than the newly elected Senator from Massachusetts, Edward Brooke. He maintained with increasing force that the FHA was not attuned to the demands for low and moderate income housing in the central city.

> The criteria are different. The procedures are different. And even though Commissioner Brownstein [FHA Commissioner] has attempted, and I think unquestionably in good faith, to move low and moderate income housing, the personnel that he has just are not attuned to doing it. And I think the record speaks for itself.[10]

Thus in the summer of 1967 Secretary Weaver was in the position of strongly supporting the rehabilitation process and yet by his own admission had few demonstrations to indicate that rehabilitation could be carried out on a massive scale. With Senator Brooke acting as constant critic of the FHA's performance in the old neighborhoods of the nation's central cities, the interesting situation arose in which the highest appointed black in the executive branch of the Democratic administration was under fire from the highest elected black in the Republican Party. A national election was slightly more than a year away; in it the "urban crisis" would figure as a major issue, and Senator Brooke had found a point at which the Democratic administration seemed particularly vulnerable. In highlighting Secretary Weaver's aspirations for central-city rehabilitation and the FHA's problems in providing it, the 1967 Senate hearings touched obliquely on one of the major power issues within the newly formed Department of Housing and Urban Development. For one of Secretary Weaver's major tasks at HUD was to bring the semiautonomous Federal Housing Administration under his control. A significant aspect of that control was the degree to which FHA was going to direct its programs to the needs of the inner city and the black ghetto. During the long summer of 1967, punctuated with the fires of Detroit and Newark, the struggle over the role of the FHA reached a peak.

It is important to point out that the FHA was being severely attacked from different sides during this period. On the one hand it was criticized by Senators Brooke and Percy for failing to meet the needs of moderate- and low-income city dwellers. On the other hand it was lashed by Senator John Williams—a traditional critic of the FHA's role in social welfare programs—for allowing windfall profits to an FHA-insured project in Los Angeles. Secretary Weaver and Undersecretary Wood were put in the complex position of trying to use Percy's and Brooke's criticism as leverage on the FHA at the same time that they were supporting that agency in standing up to its other critics.

The direction of the FHA's response to the pressures put upon it was still unresolved in August 1967. And the individual on whom the decision hung most heavily was Philip Brownstein; as assistant secretary for mortgage credit he was charged with

8. Extrapolated from a Memorandum from Edwin H. Callahan to Robert Tracy, January 13, 1969.

9. "Housing Legislation of 1967," op. cit., p. 96.

10. "Housing and Urban Development Legislation of 1968: Hearings before the Subcommittee on Housing and Urban Affairs," United States Senate, 90th Cong., Pt. I, p. 131. In defense of the FHA's position in the celebrated Malden case it must be recognized that one of the factors slowing the project down was the involvement of a "packager" who was on the FHA blacklist.

the leadership of the FHA. Whether Brownstein was going to be the last of the "old" or the first of the "new" secretaries would depend very much on the degree of support he could muster within the FHA itself. Given the large and well-established bureaucracy with which he had to work, Brownstein could not make any unilateral decision to plunge full force into the central city. The 74 individual insuring offices were as autonomous in their own right as was the FHA within HUD. Moreover, any decision would require the support of other key figures within the organization.

None of Brownstein's lieutenants was more important than Edwin G. Callahan, the FHA's executive assistant commissioner. He was a lawyer with 33 years of service to the FHA and had a reputation as a no-nonsense, tough-minded individual who could "get things done."[11] Callahan was also a believer in the traditional FHA approach. He had little sympathy for rehabilitation and the suggested thrust of the FHA into the ghetto, and he was not in agreement with the new role that the agency was being asked to play. As the "number-two" man in the FHA, his opinions were of great significance.

It is important to consider the complex relationships within HUD, as well as between HUD and its critics on Capitol Hill, during the summer of 1967. HUD's pressure on the FHA, and also the need for Weaver and Wood to find allies within it, were as critical in producing BURP as were the external pressures generated by Brooke's criticism and the fires of Detroit and Newark. BURP emerged in response to manifest need and political pressure; but the particular form it took was the result of the internal political demands of the HUD-FHA confrontation. BURP was a means of luring the FHA into central-city rehabilitation. The external pressures on HUD coincided with the internal pressures in the FHA to focus on a single massive program of slum rehabilitation in Boston. And this program was conceived, and executed, by the FHA's own Edwin G. Callahan.

For Callahan, after much thought, analysis, and change of heart, had become convinced of the viability of a rehabilitation project in Boston. He took his concept to Brownstein and Weaver. For both of them the project symbolized Callahan's willingness to establish a new direction for the FHA. His desire to sponsor the program was enormously significant, because it led him to support not only rehabilitation as such but rehabilitation in the black ghetto. He was welcomed, therefore, with open arms and all the support that Weaver and Wood could muster.

THE BURP MODEL

Streamlining the FHA Rehabilitation Process

To understand the bewilderment, confusion, and anger that followed the announcement of BURP, it is necessary to look more analytically at the assumptions under which Callahan and the FHA had orchestrated their rehabilitation effort and to examine the characteristics of the rehabilitation system emerging from those assumptions.

To lapse for the moment into the language of the social scientists, it is useful to characterize the BURP model as one of major innovation within a closed system. Basically, what Ed Callahan did was to throw away the controlled caution with which the FHA had traditionally handled rehabilitation, and to introduce speed, flexibility, and a minimum of paper work as the agency's overriding goal. Innovation was directed

11. Interview with Don Patch, Washington, March 21, 1969.

at those people with whom FHA had always done business; and there was little recognition of the fact that a massive rehabilitation project in the black ghetto was "just another rehabilitation project" only in the same limited sense that Alfonso's first evening with Lucrezia Borgia was "just another blind date."[12] The great innovation of the BURP model was the way the FHA streamlined the process for insuring mortgages. Its weakness was the degree to which it failed to recognize the necessity of opening up FHA's network of traditional relationships.

Two significant innovations were made during the processing period: first, simplification of the architectural exhibits and rehabilitation specifications and, second, a coordinated FHA team approach to the project.

Simplification of Exhibits and Specifications. In the FHA's "Multi-Family Rehabilitation: Information Guide and Instruction Handbook," it states:

> Because the nature and extent of rehabilitation varies widely among individual projects, the particular exhibits essential for each case cannot be definitely identified until . . . joint examination and write-up.[13]

The sole architectural exhibits required for BURP were the feasibility drawings, consisting of a site plan, a basement layout, a first-floor layout and a typical floor plan. On the conventional FHA project these four items would comprise merely two preliminary sets of drawings for purposes of the initial FHA inspection. In BURP's case they constituted the sum total of architectural drawings. In most FHA rehabilitation jobs there is an extended period during which the developer's architect and the FHA architect bounce drawings back and forth to each other. It is this process which has typically been a major source of delay, and also of cost since architects want money and they do not like to wait for the deal to be closed before they are paid. Developers tend to blame the FHA for the tie-up and also for the agency's inability to make architectural changes in a reasonable time period. The FHA architects, on the other hand, feel that the delays are equally the fault of the developer's architect, who generally moonlights on rehabilitation work and thus often takes months to make recommended revisions. Wherever the fault has lain in the past, this issue was avoided entirely by BURP. Between the time of initial submission of plans and commitment by the FHA, the latter worked in the field directly with the sponsors' architects, making whatever changes were necessary on the basis of on-the-spot decisions.

Because the buildings were chosen specifically to avoid structural changes, the architectural issues that did have to be discussed were not complex or subject to significant debate. And because decisions were negotiated in the field there was no time lag between the FHA's formulation of recommendations and the developers' response. The main architectural issues involved closets (which had to be 18 inches deep), kitchens, and bathrooms, where major changes of layout were often necessary. Other issues were worked out on an individual basis.

A second general area of simplification involved the specifications for the rehabilitation work to be done. Worked out jointly between the FHA office and Schuster and Polishook,[14] the specifications emphasized performance standards rather than specific

12. Variation on a statement in "Urban Redevelopment—the Viewpoint of Counsel for a Private Redeveloper," by Eli Goldston, Allan O. Hunter, and Guido Rothrauff, *Law and Contemporary Problems* 26, no. 1 (1961): 119.

13. "Multi-family Rehabilitation: Information Guide and Instruction Handbook," Federal Housing Administration, 1967, p. 16.

14. Editors' note: Gerald Schuster and Benjamin Polishook were the second largest BURP developers (468 units).

work items. The scope and intent of the program are stated in the introduction
to the "Boston Rehabilitation Plan: Specifications."

To provide rehabilitated housing that is structurally durable with reasonably low
future maintenance, and contains the highest degree of liveability abtainable.
*These levels of acceptability represent a departure from our standard procedures in that
specific items are minimized and emphasis is directed to general overall conditions as they
relate to the finished dwelling.*[15]

"Component Rehabilitation" was the approach utilized. The general requirements
for the buildings included a

. . . new roof, plumbing and fixtures, new street water connections as required,
new or completely revamped heating systems . . . revamp (sic) wiring and new
service, new or reconditioned windows, sash and trim, new kitchen cabinets and
floor, sanded floors, ceramic tile bath, new or completely reconditioned doors,
painting of brickwork as required, public areas completely done over with new
or reconditioned floors. Repair plaster all ceilings, new lobbies, clean cellar and
outside, landscape and provide walks as needed, and provide structural soundness
to buildings.[16]

The simplification of exhibits and specifications that was an integral part of the BURP
model constituted a major revolution in FHA's approach to the rehabilitation process.
Only those like Schuster, Polishook, and Brown[17] who had fought through the red
tape of requirements on previous occasions could appreciate the breakthrough.[18]

Historically, the FHA has been significant as an insurer of new buildings; the Section
207 insurance program has been the lifeblood of FHA's approach to multifamily
structures. Previously geared to new construction, the "207 mentality," as some have
come to call it, has never been suited to the very dissimilar demands of central-city
rehabilitation.[19] Prior to BURP some steps had been taken, certainly, to bridge the
gap between the demands of new construction and the constraints of rehabilitation,
but in relative terms the flexibility provided by BURP constituted a quantum leap.

The payoff for the simplifications allowed during the processing and project feasibility period was a vast shortening of the negotiations prior to FHA commitment. During
the actual rehabilitation period, the increased flexibility provided by the simplified
architectural exhibits would minimize the need for change orders and facilitate onsite
decisions.

15. "Boston Rehabilitation Plan: Specifications," Federal Housing Administration, 1967, p. 1.

16. Federal Housing Administration Form #2432.

17. Editors' note: Harold Brown was a BURP developer-contractor with 199 units.

18. As Gerald Schuster pointed out at a conference on rehabilitation several years ago:

At present FHA is using the same method of processing for a 207 high-rise building as
they are using for 221(d) (3) rehabilitation. The average 221 will run somewhere from
$150,000 to $600,000. A 207 usually is not conceived unless they hit pretty close to the
100 apartment mark. So you're talking somewhere around $24,000, $26,000 a unit, a total
of $2,500,000. The fellow who processes a 207 has a tremendous advantage over the processor
of a D3 because his overhead costs except for architectural costs are no more than ours.
(Conference on Rehabilitation, Citizens Housing and Planning Association of Greater Boston,
1968, p. 16.)

19. Five years ago the FHA had no specific standards for rehabilitation. Critics of Edward
Logue's strategy as Development Administrator of the Boston Redevelopment Authority point
to his failure to force the specification issue with the FHA as one of the main flaws of his
administration. (Interview with Jay Berger, August 12, 1968.)

Local Decision-making and the Project Team Approach. BURP had the highest possible priority and thus received maximum attention in the Boston FHA office, but organizational changes within the FHA system also helped to make rapid processing possible. As has been pointed out, Ed Callahan came to Boston with $24.5 million already allocated to the project. Thus there was no need to involve the New York regional office in negotiations for an allocation, a traditionally time-consuming task. Second, the usual regional review of project feasibility was cut out entirely. The New York office sent its man to Boston to pass on the papers on the spot; thus, decisions that were made in Boston did not have to wait upon the usual round of negotiations with New York.

Within the Boston FHA office itself, a team was set up to deal specifically with BURP. The FHA "Information Guide and Instruction Handbook" makes clear that "coordination of individual FHA underwriting functions into a simultaneous processing effort is particularly essential."[20] Traditionally a major bottleneck in FHA processing has been the degree to which packages under review get lost in the FHA among the architect, the appraiser, and the underwriter. The BURP team approach eliminated the traditional lags between these functions because the group's focus was on the total project rather than on a series of independent operations.

The most obvious result of these organizational changes, together with the simplification of exhibits, was, of course, the extraordinarily short time necessary to reach an FHA commitment. In terms of dollars and cents the accelerated application process also has a real payoff for the developer-sponsor: the overhead expenses involved in precommitment negotiations are dramatically cut back. One BURP developer estimated that for a previous rehabilitation effort his office overhead prior to getting an FHA commitment ran to $13,000 per mortgage. Under BURP processing he figures his precommitment overhead at $1,000 per mortgage.[21] Robert Whittlesey's detailed account of rehabilitation efforts in Boston's South End gives a vivid picture of the complex negotiations, time delays, and lengthy paper work involved in getting a traditional FHA rehabilitation project off the ground. He estimated, for his own negotiations, that "administrative costs to obtain a $50,000 mortgage have run as high as $10,000—the allowed FHA fee was $235."[22]

The BURP model broke ground in other areas as well. Two of the most significant were the FHA willingness to give BURP buildings a 55-year economic life (and thus a 40-year mortgage) and to place noncontiguous properties in the same mortgage.

The 55-Year Economic Life. The concept of "economic life" has been under attack for years by many of those concerned with the future of old neighborhoods. Most observers feel that it is unlikely, even under the best of circumstances, that central-city rehabilitation will last the life of the mortgage. Critics have asked "whether the publicly aided renovations should be mortgaged for 40 years; is that a sensible thing to do?"[23]

The conflict here is between a realistic view of economic life and the desire to stretch out a mortgage so as to reduce the monthly debt service. Prior to BURP the Boston FHA had never given the maximum 55-year economic life to any properties

20. "Multi-family Rehabilitation," op. cit., p. 15.

21. Interview with Gerald Schuster, October 15, 1968.

22. Robert Whittlesey, *The South End Row House and Its Rehabilitation for Low Income Residents* (Low Income Housing Demonstration Grant, Boston, 1969), p. 16.

23. *Conference on Rehabilitation,* Citizens Housing and Planning Association of Greater Boston, 1968, p. 17.

rehabilitated under the 221(d) (3) program. The monthly debt service difference between a 40-year and a 30-year mortgage (the usual mortgage length for rehabilitated housing in Boston) is $8.40 when $12,000 is taken as the average per-unit mortgage amount. By granting 40-year mortgages for the BURP buildings, the FHA was saying essentially: "The mortgage probably isn't going to last more than 20 years anyway, at best. So why not maximize the current benefits to be gained by low rental levels and worry about the life of the mortgage sometime in the future?"

What is important here is that the myth of economic life gave way before an overriding desire to keep rents down, a significant rechanneling of traditional FHA thinking.[24]

Clustering. A major complaint about the processing of FHA rehabilitation mortgages in the past had been the unwillingness of the agency to "package" buildings that were not contiguous or located within a block of each other. Yet structures under consideration for rehabilitation by a developer were often scattered; and when they had to be processed in separate mortgages this led to additional overhead expenses and paper work. The basic administrative overhead for the developer-sponsor is essentially the same whether he is processing 20 or 200 units in one package. Thus, the degree to which the FHA allows him to package noncontiguous units together largely determines his overhead expenses.

In BURP, not only were large numbers of buildings packaged together—42 in one of the Simon[25] mortgages—but such packages included buildings that were neither contiguous nor within a block of each other. This elimination of the contiguity requirement was important in allowing for the creation of packages of sufficient size to enable the developer to mix good and bad buildings (what Ben Polishook has called headache and cancer cases). The construction allowance for each mortgage was based on the average cost of rehabilitating the units in the package, and the FHA cost certification was made for the entire package rather than for the individual buildings included; together these factors allowed far greater flexibility to meet unforeseen expenditures and overruns. Thus, the packaging of several noncontiguous buildings provided not only savings in paper work but also a flexible framework within which to balance out unforeseen costs.

FHA Constraints and Their Impact on the BURP Model

The BURP experiment was put together with two very specific goals in mind: "speedy processing techniques and a short construction period"[26] for a massive number of units. The innovations introduced into the processing phase were extensive and very significant for the FHA's approach to rehabilitation. Equally important, in light of subsequent events, were the constraints that those goals put on the FHA's perception of how the program should be carried out.

24. Roscoe Pound describes this type of bending of economic principles to needs in a somewhat different context when he says: "When legislation or tradition prescribed case-knives for tasks for which pick-axes were better adapted, it seemed better to our forefathers, after a little vain effort with case-knives, to adhere to the principle—but use the pick-ax. They granted that law ought not to change. Changes in law were full of danger. But, on the other hand, it was highly inconvenient to use case-knives. And so the law has always managed to get a pick-ax in its hands, though it steadfastly demanded a case-knife and to wield it in the virtuous belief that it was using the approved instrument." (*The Spirit of the Common Law,* Boston, 1921, p. 167.)

25. Editor's note: Maurice Simon was the largest BURP developer with 1,030 units.

26. Letter from Jack Flynn to Daniel Richardson, December 19, 1967.

The Costs of Secrecy. Public knowledge of the enormous number of units to be included in BURP could have had a considerable impact on Roxbury real-estate prices, and because of this Ed Callahan thought it most important to keep the project under cover. This secrecy meant that the residents of Roxbury were not the only ones surprised by the announcement of the program; so were the city departments—the fire and building departments and the Boston Redevelopment Authority—upon whom the ultimate success of BURP depended. During the formulation period, from August to November 1967, such news as the city agencies did receive about BURP was fragmented and presented in a way that was not aimed at soliciting their advice or involvement.

During the period that BURP was being mobilized, the city of Boston was virtually in a state of interregnum. John Collins was about to retire from the mayor's office. The new mayor, Kevin White, was not elected until early November and did not take office until January. The Boston Redevelopment Authority (BRA) would have been the most logical point of relationship, but the director, Edward J. Logue, had resigned early in the summer to run for mayor. And it was clear that the newly appointed BRA Administrator, Francis Cuddy, was an interim appointment. Walter Smart, the BRA's director of relocation, had been involved in some earlier discussions with the FHA, but no definite plan for relocation had been worked out prior to the public announcement of BURP. The information that did filter out about BURP was generally couched in uncertainties, and there was the implication that some kind of big deal was being hatched in the back rooms of the FHA.

The FHA has no history of working closely with mayors and city governments. Its clients have always been the banking and construction community; and its failure to involve Boston officials actively was nothing extraordinary but rather consistent with its traditional methods of doing business.

There is no question that secrecy helped to keep acquisition costs down in some instances. One landlord who sold to a BURP developer freely admitted, "I would have asked at least another 600 a unit if I'd known what was going on."[27] In other cases, it is doubtful how successful this technique was either in preventing the magnitude of the operation from being known or in holding down acquisition prices. It must be remembered that there were five developers in the field, four of whom were trying to pick up units as rapidly as possible. The grapevine being what it is in the real-estate market, it would have been hard to keep such heightened activity from general notice. Some indication of the degree to which BURP raised sales prices despite the secrecy is given by the fact that the average acquisition price of all BURP units was $4,867, whereas 6 months previously the average acquisition price on 400 of the units included in Maurice Simon's rent-supplement program had been somewhat less than $4,100. Given the similarity of units involved in the two programs, it seems valid to estimate that BURP drove the market price up by more than $600 a unit. The extent to which publicity would have driven prices up still further has to be measured against the high costs of the negative community response generated by that secrecy.

Lack of Participation of Black Sponsors and Black Labor. One of the aspects of the Boston situation that made it attractive to Ed Callahan was the inclusion of knowledgeable developers, "savvy, sharp and experienced in rehabilitation."[28] However, this

---

27. Interview with Daniel Weisberg, June 27, 1968.
28. "Housing," *City,* March 1968, p. 14.

demand for previous experience, ability to move fast, and capacity to handle large numbers of units precluded black contractors and developers, because there were none in Roxbury who had experience either in large-scale rehabilitation, new construction, or FHA processing and finance. Without experience in major construction jobs, no black builder had ever previously been bonded for a major construction job, and thus none could anticipate eligibility for bonding at a level that would enable him to take on more than a dozen or so units. Given the mandate for size and speed, there seemed little latitude in the program for the kind of black developer-builders who did exist in Roxbury.

The rehabilitation of 2,000 units would clearly generate hundreds of jobs for laborers, carpenters, and all the trades associated with the building process. Yet it is clear that BURP was not conceived as a means of utilizing either the small cadre of skilled Black contractors which already existed in Roxbury or as a means of training more workers or subcontractors. Unskilled workers and training programs would cut down on productivity and thus on speed: given the basic goals of BURP, there was no incentive to use the project as a means of teaching the skills required in the rehabilitation process.

Minimal Options for Building Type and Quality. A basic requirement set by Ed Callahan for the BURP developers was that the total mortgage per unit should be $12,000 or under. This figure became the criterion around which the eligibility for the program of a particular building was evaluated rather than the degree to which the building actually needed rehabilitation or the size of its apartments and their bedroom count.

How the $12,000 was split among the acquisition price, cost of rehabilitation, and the relatively fixed percentage for financing was left up to the individual developer. In theory, he could buy higher priced units which would need comparatively little rehabilitation or go after the more run-down, therefore less expensive, units and put the bulk of his $12,000 into the rehabilitation. Such freedom did not mean that a sponsor could buy a $10,000 unit in Roxbury—on the unlikely assumption that he could find one—and do $1,000 worth of work on it. Given the BURP rehabilitation specifications, any unit would absorb a minimum of $3,500 in labor and materials.

Within the requirements, however, the real areas of differential among units lay in expenditures on room layout, wiring, masonry, walls, and ceilings. For example, on a 1,000-square-foot apartment (the average size of 4-bedroom units in the program), the difference between rehabilitating a "creampuff" and a "dog," to use local jargon (using $5.80 per square foot as the cost for a "creampuff" and $7.50 for a "dog"), could be about $1,700. Or to look at it from another point of view: the possible cost range between a structure with 1-bedroom units which required minimal work and a structure with 4-bedroom units which demanded a maximum dollar outlay would be over $5,300. In reality no BURP building was all four-bedroom units in terrible condition or all singles in good shape, but still the range in rehabilitation costs among the various buildings was potentially tremendous. The practice of packaging the good units with the bad provided a way of covering for this possible variation, yet the $12,000 maximum tended to obscure the very real differences among the buildings, their bedroom count, and general physical condition.

The greatest area of cost uncertainty in the rehabilitation process is in the construction phase; so a developer who wanted to hedge his bets would have acquired only units that were priced at the upper end of the scale—around $6,000—and thus have minimized his exposure to uncertainties. Given the speed with which the BURP packages were put together and the limitations of such opportunities in the market itself, it was in fact impossible for all developers to carry out this principle. But there was clearly little incentive for the developers to acquire those buildings that most needed rehabilitation. The effect of this incentive system was to bring into the program many structures that in fact were not desperately in need of rehabilitation. Of course the units in these buildings would benefit from new bathrooms, new walls, and all the other improvements that BURP could bring. Considering that they were being refinanced for a 40-year mortgage, there is no question that they required extensive rehabilitation. But the real issue was the absence in the BURP structure of selection criteria, with the result that each dollar spent acquiring property did not necessarily introduce into the program buildings that could most benefit from rehabilitation dollars. It is interesting to note that a number of buildings were proposed by the developers which were not acceptable to the FHA for inclusion in BURP because they would not, given their unit size and structural condition, cost less than $12,000. But there seems to have been no instance where a building was excluded from consideration because it was judged to be in sufficiently good condition not to warrant inclusion.

Relocation. Relocation was one of the first issues that Secretary Weaver raised with Callahan when he was presented with the concept of BURP. The Secretary was assured that relocation would not be a problem.[29] But the FHA never really followed through on Weaver's order that it should communicate with the various other HUD agencies that could help out. And the failure to do so resulted in one of the major problems of the program. However, the original BURP model did make certain specific assumptions about the handling of relocation for the inhabitants of the 1,694 occupied units (380 of the 2,074 were vacant at the time of the initial commitment).

1. Relocation would be phased so as to cycle people from one building, or one entry, to the next, using the vacant buildings as the first relocation resource.

2. Each developer would take tenants from other developers, thus creating a general pool of units.

3. The first phase of the rent-supplement program—which included over 300 units —would be ready just as the BURP program was getting under way and would serve as a resource for low income tenants who could not afford to go back into the 221(d) (3) units.

4. The Boston Redevelopment Authority would help out in those buildings in the Washington Park urban renewal area where they were already doing relocation work and where, therefore, tenants were eligible for such assistance.[30]

In retrospect, the FHA's plans for relocation were optimistic, naïve, incomplete, and based on little more than a statement from the five developers that relocation would not be a problem. But those who maintain that the FHA had no relocation plan at all, and that the agency was prepared to dump 1,700 families out in the street, are oversimplifying the case.

The relocation model was predicated on the most optimistic assumptions about the degree of coordination that could be maintained between the five developers and about the staging of the rent-supplement program and BURP. It also assumed a working relationship with the Boston Redevelopment Authority, which was anything but clarified at the time of the FHA commitment.

One of the murkiest aspects of BURP has been the lack of understanding between

29. Interview with Robert Wood, June 27, 1969.
30. Interview with John Makinen, December 26, 1968.

the BRA and the FHA over the issue of relocation. To this day each agency feels that the other operated in bad faith. From the FHA's point of view, the BRA (1) was guilty of not following through on commitments that it had made to occupants of the BURP buildings in the Washington Park urban renewal area some eight weeks prior to the public announcement of BURP, and (2) in general dragged its feet so as to get more money from HUD for relocation work that it was perfectly capable of handling with existing funds. The BRA, on the other hand, claimed that the FHA was unwilling to involve it as a partner in the program. Walter Smart, the director of relocation for the BRA, allegedly found out about the program by chance, went to the FHA to get the complete story, and was made to understand that he had best mind his own business.

If judged solely in terms of its innovative approach to traditional FHA processing, the Boston Rehabilitation Program constitutes a creative and seminal breakthrough. Yet as this analysis points out, other aspects of the rehabilitation process failed to receive the same innovative attention. It was as a result of these omissions that BURP was to become enveloped in round after round of confrontation and controversy.

41. *An Evaluation of the Boston Rehabilitation Program*

URBAN PLANNING AID, INC.

As BURP became operational, the presumptions about the program's ability to function in the interest of its intended beneficiaries were challenged by events. As problem after problem arose, only the initiatives of community organizations, Roxbury agencies, and the BURP tenants themselves forced modifications in the BURP concept which enabled the program to meet some of the community's needs. But these positive changes were necessarily limited, for developers and FHA continued to control the resolution of major issues.

SELECTION OF BUILDINGS FOR REHABILITATION

The stock of low-income housing, which is inadequate to meet present needs, is continually losing habitable buildings through a process of deterioration. In order to add to the total housing stock, rehabilitation programs should deal with buildings which have deteriorated off of the housing market or which are about to do so.

A random sample of 646 of BURP's initial 2,074 apartments disclosed that 97.6 percent were found to be standard with all facilities in the housing census of 1960.[1] BURP buildings undoubtedly underwent some deterioration between the 1960 census and their selection for rehabilitation in 1967. It is also true that a housing census classification of "standard" does not necessarily imply that a building needs no repairs or redecoration. Yet the same 1960 census showed 20 percent of Boston's housing stock to be substandard, and a good deal of that substandard housing was located in and around the BURP area.[2]

Thus the buildings selected for rehabilitation under BURP included many which, from the perspective of the total low-income housing stock, were least in need of rehabilitation. This selection of buildings can only be explained by FHA's desire that the program "succeed," and by the developers' desire to avoid the financial uncertainties of extensive rehabilitation. These imperatives precluded community involvement in the first major decision affecting it: the selection of buildings for rehabilitation.

SELECTION OF DEVELOPERS

BURP's goal of speed and large-scale production also precluded participation by developers primarily concerned with the interests of the community. FHA's criteria

Reprinted from *An Evaluation of the Boston Rehabilitation Program* (Cambridge, Mass.: Urban Planning Aid, Inc., September 1969), pp. 11-23 (edited), by permission of the publisher. Urban Planning Aid, Inc., is a private nonprofit organization that provides to community groups in the Boston area technical and organizing assistance on housing, transportation, health, and other issues.

1. Keyes, "BRP—An Independent Evaluation of Its Costs and Benefits," unpublished text of a speech delivered to the Institute on Innovative Technology in Housing Rehabilitation at Boston University, 1/23/69, pp. 17-18.

2. *Housing in Boston,* Boston Redevelopment Authority, 1967.

for sponsors—expertise, past experience with volume housing production, and the capacity to move fast on a large scale—could not be met by existing Roxbury developers, especially not by fledgling community-based, nonprofit corporations. Some of the developers who met these criteria and were chosen by FHA to participate in BURP were regarded by Roxbury residents as slum landlords. The fact that these individuals had become the beneficiaries of federal subsidies was viewed as an insult to the community. Moreover, the favorable treatment of BURP developers appeared in sharp contrast to the frustrating experience of local sponsors in their dealings with FHA. As one local leader charged at BURP's public announcement:

> The program being dedicated has given no consideration to local developers, non-profit developers. . . . The FHA has shown that it can move with unprecedented speed . . . to give high profits to developers from outside the community and to establish a huge preserve for exploitation by absentee landlords. . . . Apparently Secretary Weaver's department can move quickly only when it is operating against community interest.[3]

In a letter to HUD Secretary Robert Weaver, another black leader, Melvin King of the New Urban League, also condemned the announcement of BURP. Pointing to the ways in which the American economic system acted to inhibit the development of black people, King charged:

> One of the ways in which this happens is for the Department of Housing and Urban Development to devise a program in Washington and to bring it into the community in the hands of Eastern Gas and Fuel Association and Penn Simon Corporation. In this manner, you have ignored resources within the community, undercut institutions and programs we are attempting to develop and supported those outside interests that so long have kept us oppressed and subjugated. This is neo-colonialism in its most subtle form. A program ostensibly designed to "help" us operates in such a way as to continue to deprive us and keep us powerless, and therefore, "in our place."

King continued to outline steps which HUD could take to involve the black community in the program, including the transfer of 1,000 BURP units to community-based rehabilitation sponsors.

In response to these and other pressures from the black community, FHA, at the urging of Eastern Gas and Fuel, designated two black developers, Sanders Associates and State Enterprises. These developers were chosen without community participation in the decision making. Neither nonprofit sponsors nor community organizations were considered. Instead, FHA and Eastern picked black businessmen who could provide well-known names, properties, or limited partnership equity contributions. As Eastern's Goldston recounts, "Most of the fellows talked entirely about the glory of doing something for the black community. But, when one fellow came in and asked, 'What's in it for me?', I knew we could understand each other, and might really get something done."[4]

However, Sanders Associates' construction work has been as substandard and its treatment of tenants as highhanded as that of the white developers. State Enterprises, which appears to have been preoccupied throughout BURP with its other financial interests, has, at this writing, failed to complete any of its units. Preliminary inspection

3. Speech by Bryant Rollins at Freedom House, Boston, 12/4/67.
4. Eli Goldston, quoted in *Fortune*, February 1969, p. 124.

of some of its nearly complete units suggests that State's rehabilitation work is also inadequate.[5]

RELOCATION

Initial Assumptions

The 221 (d) (3) program under which BURP was financed could not meet the needs of low income families without additional rent supplements or leased housing subsidies. These subsidies were not included in the original BURP plan. BURP units were designed for families in the $5,000-$8,000 income group, and FHA *assumed* that the low income families displaced from BURP could be rehoused in a separate rent supplement project planned for completion prior to BURP.

FHA also refused to accept any formal responsibility for the relocation of displaced BURP tenants who could afford to move back into rehabilitated units. Despite the fact that BURP had been initiated by a public agency and made possible by the commitment of $27 million in public funds, FHA maintained that it had no responsibility for eviction of tenants by private owners. Seven hundred and fifty of the families to be relocated would be moving from units inside the Washington Park renewal area. Since the Boston Redevelopment Authority (BRA) had overall responsibility for relocation within this area, FHA concluded that BRA would take care of it. BRA pointed out, however, that it had only learned of BURP at the advanced stages of project formulation, and that it had been given neither time nor funds for the surveys, relocation payments, and services which were needed.

For the 1,200 families to be displaced from units outside of the urban renewal area, no formal relocation arrangements of any kind were made. No information on the size, income, housing, or social needs of the families to be displaced was available. FHA assumed that the developers themselves would handle whatever relocation was necessary, by carefully staging displacement to take advantage of vacancies within the BURP buildings.

FHA's reluctance to recognize the public responsibility involved in BURP displacement and its failure to involve other agencies as effective partners in relocation planning suggest that concern for the human needs of the BURP tenants was clearly overridden by other priorities. As Boston FHA Director John Flynn said, "We want to get the dumps these people are living in fixed up as soon as possible. Somebody will have to be inconvenienced along the way."[6]

Problems

In fact, more than a few families were "inconvenienced." The first stage of BURP began long before the program was announced with the eviction of families from the units slated for rehabilitation.[7] Some of these evictions were accomplished informally through utility shutoffs or general deterioration during this period.[8]

---

5. Documentation of the statements concerning Sanders Associates and State Enterprises is . . . [contained in pp. 24-49 of the Urban Planning Aid, Inc. Report.]

6. *Boston Globe,* 12/24/67.

7. Sadelle Sacks, Director of Fair Housing, Inc., speech to the Institute on Innovative Technology in Housing Rehabilitation at Boston University, 1/23/69.

8. "'The landlord just let the building run down and run down . . . and then there was no heat for five days,'" said one mother of five forced out of a building on Walnut Avenue along with nine other families (*Boston Globe,* 12/24/67). Among the most notorious cases were those involving Insoft, manager for Simon, and Cantor, who failed to provide heat in some

Since neither the tenants nor community and city agencies had been informed of the BURP program, few were able to determine where to turn for help. Inside the Washington Park urban renewal area, many families were not told of their right to relocation assistance, or of the priority for public housing and home purchase assistance which accompany public displacement. The developers frequently failed to notify the BRA when apartments were available or when they were about to evict tenants; in other cases they notified the BRA only at the last minute.[9]

Outside Washington Park, where the majority of units were located, many families were simply thrown on the market, with little assistance from the developers. Only tenants considered "desirable" by developers were allowed to return, and, in any case, many families were unable to afford the rents of BURP units. The rent supplement units which FHA assumed would house BURP's low income displacees had not been completed.

Since no relocation surveys had been conducted, it is impossible to know exactly how many families were evicted during this period. But the overriding picture for community groups and agencies working in Roxbury was that of "scores of families being moved from house to house and from agency to agency with no assurance that they will be able to return to the rehabilitated apartment."[10]

Community Response

The outcry raised against evictions at the announcement of the program in December 1967 generated demands in the community concerning relocation. These demands included establishing the right of displaced persons to return to the rehabilitated units, the formulation of a humane relocation plan, and the involvement of the community in tenant selection through a formal appeals panel for rejected tenants.[11] A factfinding committee on BURP of the Citizens Housing and Planning Association of Metropolitan Boston, Inc. published similar recommendations and also urged an immediate relocation survey.

As a result, a HUD grant for a relocation survey was awarded to BRA, and additional funds were secured to cover moving expenses and relocation payments for displaced BURP tenants.[12] Relocatees were guaranteed the right to return to rehabilitated units, and the developers committed themselves to offer no units on the private market until the needs of displaced families were met. The Boston Housing Authority, which had already been criticized by Washington for failing to use its available fund allocations for federally subsidized leased housing apartments, committed itself to lease as many units as would be necessary to house displaced tenants whose incomes were low enough to qualify them for public housing. All in all, over 600 low-income families displaced from their apartments returned to BURP as BHA leased housing tenants.[13] But had

---

of their buildings during the height of a cold wave. Because there was no adequate BURP procedure for remedying this situation, the tenants took the case to court. Insoft and Cantor were fined $2,100 and $3,000 respectively, and the tenants were allowed one month's free rent. This marked the first time that the Roxbury District Court awarded tenants relief in the form of rent abatement for a landlord's negligence in providing services. (*Boston Globe*, 1/20/68).

9. Interview with Sadelle Sacks, June 1969.

10. *Boston Globe*, 12/24/67.

11. *Bay State Banner*, 4/25/68.

12. *Boston Globe*, 1/16/68.

13. Background on the BHA's leased housing allocation and its role in BURP was obtained from an interview with Keyes, 6/69.

the BHA's leased housing subsidy not been so luckily available, these 600 low-income families would have been displaced in a city in which the waiting list for public housing is in the thousands.

Thus, community pressure ultimately forced federal agencies to accept some responsibility for the relocation problems caused by BURP. But the resolution of one of the program's major relocation problems, the provision for displaced low-income families, was made possible by chance.

JOBS AND TRAINING

The BURP program contained no provisions to ensure that community residents would obtain jobs or training in the project, even though it is located in an area of low income and high unemployment. Even before BURP was announced, the failure of private developers to hire a significant number of local residents in rehabilitation jobs had become an issue of intense concern to the Roxbury community.

Maurice Simon, who was to become the largest BURP developer, was rehabilitating a rent supplement project in the Grove Hall section of Roxbury. When, a month before the BURP program was announced, his general contractor laid off 54 black workers, a walkout and picketing by the remaining black employees shut down 13 construction sites.[14] Subsequent pressure and emergency negotiations resulted in the rehiring of most, though not all, of the black workers.

The announcement of Simon's lucrative BURP contract angered the groups involved in the Grove Hall conflict, and a loose coalition of groups and individuals in Roxbury began to form around the job issue.[15] In February 1968, after a ruling by the Massachusetts Commission Against Discrimination that the remaining Grove Hall workers be rehired was totally ignored, community leaders and a group of workers still laid off from Grove Hall went to Simon's office and demanded immediate rehiring. Simon capitulated and also agreed to institute a $30,000 training program in his BURP project for 300 largely unskilled black workers. The United Community Construction Workers (UCCW) demanded and won Simon's agreement to finance the program out of his BURP profits, but the continued refusal of both developers and the FHA to make financial figures public made this agreement impossible to monitor.

No governmental agency was willing to assume the cost of this training program. Furthermore, neither FHA, the Department of Labor, nor any other government agency recognized its responsibility to link a major housing rehabilitation effort to the employment needs of the community.[16] Nor did any of these agencies seem concerned with the fact that BURP tenants might have to pay for the costs of the training program forced on Simon.[17]

14. *Boston Globe,* 11/21/67.

15. Including Bryant Rollins of the New Urban League, Boston City Councillor Thomas I. Atkins, Melvin King and Martin Gopin of the New Urban League, and Leo Fletcher of the United Community Construction Workers Association, a black union formed during the Grove Hall shutdown.

16. A letter from Melvin King to HUD Secretary Weaver explicitly requested "training programs for journeymen, apprentices and rehab specialists." The letter was ignored.

17. Simon claimed that construction inefficiencies resulting from the training program cost him $600,000 (Keyes' interview with Simon, July 1969). FHA subsequently granted Simon a mortgage increase of about $1 million. The carrying charges on this mortgage increase allow Simon to charge his 1,030 BURP families higher rents.

LANDLORD-TENANT RELATIONS

The initial design for BURP ignored the possibility of community or tenant participation in any aspect of decision making in the program. Immediately following the public announcement of BURP in December 1967, the Roxbury community raised several demands, including community participation in a formal appeals panel to protect tenants against arbitrary exclusion from rehabilitated apartments. By January 1968, tenants in the BURP buildings formed the Tenants Association of Boston to unite their efforts in dealing with the BURP developers. And in April the pressure of community and tenant organization resulted in the establishment of the Tenants' Review Panel, including representatives from TAB, several other Roxbury groups, public agencies, and developers. The Panel was created as an *advisory* body which would oversee the developers' agreements to guarantee the return of former tenants, and would mediate landlord-tenant disputes.

The attitude of the developers and FHA toward the Review Panel was, from the outset, unenthusiastic. Only one developer—Brown—agreed to the procedure initially, although the others eventually joined. FHA's representative was an "observer" who lacked the authority to commit FHA to Panel decisions and who was often absent when crucial matters concerning FHA policy were discussed.[18]

Despite these constraints, the Tenants' Review Panel was able to provide some constructive solutions to landlord-tenant conflicts. However, it was seriously hampered by its lack of formal authority and by the frequent lack of cooperaton from developers and the FHA. Often, proposed arrangements and recommendations were later undermined or ignored, and frequently tenants were forced to resort to other methods of dealing with the developers and FHA.

The following discussion illustrates problems facing the Tenants' Review Panel, the means by which resolution was attempted, and the limitations imposed on effective solutions by the role of private developers and federal agencies.

Discrimination

The issue of discrimination arose when a black tenant displaced from one of the BURP buildings was refused an apartment in Irwin Cantor's rehabilitated Adams Street complex, which was predominantly white. Although TAB was able to document through subsequent testing that Cantor was discriminating in his rental practices, the Tenants' Review Panel could not force Cantor to accept the tenant in question. The FHA repeatedly refused to intervene despite the prohibition against discrimination in federally assisted housing contained in its own contracts with the developers.

The Massachusetts Commission Against Discrimination found "probable cause" for action against Cantor in October 1968 and ordered him to comply with antidiscrimination laws and to take corrective measures. Cantor refused to accept the tenant. The issue is now being continued through a suit against Cantor.[19]

The federal government, through FHA or HUD, took no action on this matter.[20]

18. Tenants' Review Panel minutes, 7/11/68, 8/1/68, 9/26/68.

19. *Boston Globe*, 8/12/69, Tenants' Review Panel minutes, 7/11/68, 7/25/68, 8/1/68, 7/18/69.

20. FHA's recent approval of Cantor for another development infuriated TAB and demonstrates FHA's failure to respond to the social consequences of its actions.

Failure to Provide Essential Services During Rehabilitation

A common complaint among BURP tenants has been the failure of owners to provide essential services, particularly during rehabilitation, while charging tenants full rent under threat of eviction. In a number of instances brought to the attention of the Tenants' Review Panel, tenants had no water or heat for periods ranging from several days to several weeks. The Panel agreed that tenants forced to live temporarily under such conditions should receive substantial rent reductions.

In some cases, the developers have appeared to abide by this decision. But the Panel continued to learn of new cases involving tenants living in units under rehabilitation who are being asked to pay full rents.[21]

Model Lease and Arbitration Procedures

After its experience with the limitations of the Tenants' Review Panel, TAB attempted to strengthen its bargaining position with FHA and the developers. In January 1969, a new series of agreements was drawn up with the developers. These included:

(a) Developer participation in a formal Community Advisory Board (CAB) along with representatives of the tenants, community agencies, FHA, and several other public agencies. The CAB was set up as a major forum for discussion and resolution of BURP-related problems.

(b) A formal system of collective bargaining and arbitration to resolve particular landlord-tenant grievances.

(c) A model lease to replace the standard lease form, which is heavily weighted in favor of the landlord. The landlord is obligated to provide decent living conditions and adequate services to the tenants. If he fails to do so, the tenants are entitled to pay rent into an escrow account and submit the issue for arbitration. The arbitrator may order repairs or rent abatement. Or the tenants may choose to finance repairs out of the withheld rent, after a finding by the arbitrator that the landlord has failed to meet his obligation.

Another important clause of the model lease limits the grounds for eviction to nonpayment of rent (except when nonpayment is justified by the landlord's failure to meet his obligations) and misrepresentation of income. Any other grievances raised by the developer must be resolved through the formal arbitration system.

The initial attitude of FHA toward these agreements is worth noting. When TAB submitted its original proposals for a Community Advisory Board, an arbitration system, and a model lease to FHA official Callahan, he replied:

> . . . it would seem that it is somewhat premature to anticipate abuse and exploitation. The buildings have not yet been rehabilitated in sufficient quantity, nor occupied long enough since rehabilitation to provide substantial evidence that abuse and exploitation have been committed on the part of the developers. Without disagreeing with the general objectives of the Tenants Association, we do not believe at this time that it is necessary or desirable to create the proposed procedure.
>
> FHA Section 221(d) (3) owners are controlled as to the rents they may charge and with respect to matters such as nondiscrimination in tenant selection because of race, color or creed. Also, the amount of dividends or profits is restricted and the projects are subject to inspection by a federal agency with respect to maintenance and operation. These controls are encompassed within the provisions of the National Housing Act, the FHA Regulations, the mortgage documents and a Regulatory Agreement entered into between each owner and the FHA. We believe that these controls will prevent the abuse and exploitation which you anticipate.[22]

21. Tenants' Review Panel minutes, 10/3/68, 10/17/68, 12/12/68, 1/18/69.
22. Letter from Edwin Callahan to the Tenants Association, 6/21/68.

Coming after BURP's tumultuous first half-year of operation, Callahan's response displayed a remarkable optimism concerning his agency's willingness to enforce the requirements of federal legislation, a willingness for which there had been very little evidence.

The model agreements, which FHA did eventually agree to accept, were designed to create a formal system through which the accountability of developers to tenants could be guaranteed. In practice, the agreements have failed to function effectively to this end. The grievance procedure deals with individual cases and is ineffectual in handling the widespread, recurring problems of BURP. The body set up to handle these procedures, the Community Advisory Board, appears to function in essentially the same manner as the earlier Review Panel, resolving issues on a case-by-case basis and frequently finding its decisions circumvented by developers and the FHA. In addition, the arbitration system has proved cumbersome to handle for the community organizations, such as the Tenants Association, which have limited financial resources and technical assistance. Only one case has reached the intermediary level, and no cases have been submitted for final arbitration.

The experience with the model agreements has been a frustrating lesson for the BURP tenants—that formal agreements and mediation machinery are inadequate to deal with the program's recurrent and widespread deficiencies.

Incomplete Rehabilitation

Because of the relocation problems created by BURP, federal and city agencies agreed to approve apartments for occupancy even though "minor" items might be incomplete.

In the BHA leased units, the agreement was that the Authority would not pay rents to the developer until the apartment was completed and approved, but, at that time, it would pay all back rent to the developer. It was also agreed that developers would complete the occupied apartments with no delay.

In fact, what appears to have happened is that as soon as tenants moved in (assuring the developer in the case of leased housing units of eventual rent payment by BHA) the developers pulled their work force out and focused on getting other apartments on the rent roll. Many apartments remain incomplete after more than a year of occupancy. Conditions in some of these apartments expose the tenants to serious health and safety hazards.

Even though the work was incomplete, some developers demanded full rent for such apartments. Sanders Associates threatened to evict 14 tenants because the Boston Housing Authority withheld its share of the leased housing rents due to serious deficiencies—even though the tenants had paid their share regularly.[23]

FHA would not take responsibility for living conditions until they had finally approved the building. In many cases buildings which have been occupied for a year and which contain serious hazards have not yet been submitted by the developer to FHA for final approval.[24]

Dissatisfied with the inability of the Tenants' Review Panel and the FHA to resolve matters of incomplete rehabilitation, tenants on Wyoming Street decided to conduct a rent strike to force Kavita Realty (Kelly) to bring their buildings up to standard.

23. Community Advisory Board minutes, 7/14/69, 8/7/69.

24. In a particular case which arose concerning a Simon building on Devon Street, the Tenants' Review Panel requested copies of the contracts and specifications for these buildings to determine whether the required standards had been met (minutes, 7/25/68). After a lapse when no information was made available to the Panel, FHA asserted that it had no jurisdiction over complaints concerning these and other buildings because they had not been "closed out" (minutes, 9/19/68). In other words, the FHA refused to assume responsibility for the condition of the unit until at least a month after it had been designated "completed" by FHA.

The tenants were able to report to the Panel in January that the deficiencies were being remedied, and $12,500 in escrowed rent was released to Kavita.[25]

Thus, BURP tenants, unable to get FHA to take action to ensure safe and completed housing, were forced to resort to economic coercion in order to gain even limited improvements in their living conditions.

CONCLUSION

A pattern emerges from the examination of each of the procedural problems involved in the implementation of the BURP program. Repeatedly, the community and/or the tenants attempted to improve the program and to alleviate the condition of damaged individuals. Again and again, these efforts were met with developer and FHA recalcitrance and, on occasion, grudging concession. The selection of buildings for rehabilitation was done in secrecy and harmed the overall interests of the community. The initial selection of developers was done in secrecy, but because of incipient community mobilization, FHA and Eastern Gas chose without community participation two black entrepreneurs who subsequently performed poorly. When displacement of tenants became a widespread problem, pressure from the Tenants Association of Boston and other groups finally brought forth governmental action—helpful to some, but too late for many. When pressure from the United Community Construction Workers forced one developer to institute a training program for black workers, no governmental agency was sufficiently concerned to finance it, *nor* was FHA willing to provide information so that the cost effects of the agreement could be monitored. Finally, when FHA and the developers conceded the necessity of establishing a mechanism for handling tenant grievances, they were unwilling to give it real decision-making power. Reforms in the process which were won by tenant pressure were accepted by FHA and the developers only if they were consistent with their prior political and economic needs. The result was minimal adjustment in the BURP process —inadequate to deal with the gross inequities visited upon tenants and the community.

25. Tenants' Review Panel minutes, 1/16/69.

42. *BURP and Make Money*

ELI GOLDSTON

The typical BURP project involved the acquisition of existing buildings at an average cost of nearly $4,000 per unit and rehabilitation at an average cost of about $8,000 per unit, or a total of $12,000 per unit. Hence the acquisition and rehabilitation of about 80 units could be accomplished in a $1-million project. Table 42.1 summarizes the cost and financing of such a project.

The National Housing Act provides, among other things, that under specified conditions (which are generally easily met) the developer-sponsor is entitled to add to the cost of rehabilitation a 10 percent builders' and sponsors' profit-and-risk allowance. This and certain other costs are included in the $682,000 total rehabilitation cost shown in Table 42.1. In reference to this exhibit, note that:

If the sponsor leaves his allowance in the project rather than taking it out in cash, he may include it in calculating the cost of the project eligible for 90 percent mortgage financing. So in the case shown he would be able to obtain a $900,000 mortgage.

On the books, equity totals $100,000. But $62,000 of this amount (10 percent of the cost of rehabilitation) is represented by the profit-and-risk allowance, leaving only $38,000 required as cash investment. This approximates the amount of "front money" necessary at the time the FHA mortgage commitment becomes effective. By comparison, a conventionally financed project would probably require an equity investment of up to $300,000, depending on the location of the buildings. (FHA financing affords a great deal of leverage—an important incentive in itself for a developer.)

TABLE 42.1   *Financing of typical 80-unit BURP project*

Cost:		
Acquisition (80 dwelling units)		$318,000
Rehabilitation		
Cost	$620,000	
10 percent profit-and-risk allowance	62,000	682,000
		$1,000,000
Financing:		
90 percent FHA mortgage		$ 900,000
Equity		
Waived profit-and-risk allowance	$62,000	
Cash front money	38,000	100,000
		$1,000,000

Reprinted from *Harvard Business Review*, September-October 1969, pp. 96-99 (the Appendix), by permission of the publisher and author. Copyright © 1969 by the President and Fellows of Harvard College; all rights reserved. Eli Goldston is the President of Eastern Gas and Fuel Associates.

In a low-income housing project it is of course essential to establish the lowest possible rent structure. If too few people in the ghetto area can afford the rehabilitated apartment units, the developer will be unable to maintain high occupancy rates, and the result will be financial disaster.

In my $1-million rehabilitation example, monthly rentals are comparatively low, ranging from $105 for a 1-bedroom unit to $140 for a 5-bedroom apartment. Total annual rental income from the project amounts to $108,000 after deducting a 7 percent vacancy and bad debt allowance, as permitted by the FHA in computing project feasibility.

It is essential also to keep a tight rein on expenses to avoid the necessity of raising rents. In a typical project, the direct expense (management, maintenance, heat, utilities, and so on) averages about 35 percent of net rental income. In Boston, by agreement with the city, real estate taxes amount to about 15 percent of net rental income, leaving roughly half of project rentals to meet debt service, provide for replacements and renewals, and allow for a cash distribution to the limited partners. The cash distribution is limited by law to 6 percent of book equity. Based on these guidelines, the project has a pro forma income statement for the first year as shown in Table 42.2.

Debt service absorbs a significant portion of rental income. Today, conventional financing, even if available for this type of project, would bear interest at 8 percent or more and probably could not be obtained for a term of more than 25 years. Annual debt service for such a loan would total $83,300 (instead of the $38,600 shown), thus forcing the owners to increase the average monthly rent from about $110 to about $160. Obviously, low-cost long-term financing is important in keeping the rent structures of rehabilitation projects within reach of ghetto residents.

TABLE 42.2   *First-year operating results and cash flow of typical 80-unit BURP project*

		Total		Per unit
1.	Rental (after deducting 7 percent of potential rent roll for vacancies and bad debt allowance)		$108,000	$1,350
	Cash expense:			
2.	Direct (management, maintenance, heat, utilities, and so forth)	$40,000		$500
3.	Real estate taxes (15 percent of rental income)	16,200	56,200	203
				703
4.	Cash income available for debt service		$ 51,800	$ 648
	Debt service (level payments, 40 years, 3 percent interest):			
5.	Interest	$26,800		$335
6.	Amortization of principal	11,800	38,600	148
				483
7.	New cash flow		$ 13,200	$ 165
8.	Replacement fund (3 percent of net rental income)		3,200	40
9.	Balance available for owners		$ 10,000	$ 125
10.	Distribution to owners (6 percent of equity)		6,000	75
11.	Excess cash to replacement fund		$ 4,000	$ 50

I might add that this points up again the importance of the financing subsidy. With 3 percent, 40-year FHA financing the project could cost more than twice as much to acquire and rehabilitate before the $83,300 level of debt service would result. So low rents are much more easily achieved in the financial than in the physical structure.

A relatively small drop in rental income or increase in expenses will wipe out the cash available for distribution to the partners. Such distributions are unimportant, however, compared to the attractions of the project's tax benefits, which increase if it does not earn enough cash for distributions.

Assuming a depreciable base of $888,000 ($1 million less a $50,000 assumed value of land and the waived $62,000 profit and risk fee), straight-line book depreciation over 30 years averages $29,600 annually. Under the Internal Revenue Code, however, investors are allowed to take liberalized depreciation (200 percent declining balance on the cost of rehabilitation and 150 percent declining balance on the cost of buildings originally acquired), with the result that during the first year the owners may take $53,800 of tax depreciation. This, incidentally, compares with a mortgage amortization during the first year of $11,800.

Table 42.2 shows that $51,800 of cash income is available for debt service, the replacement fund, and distribution to investors. Table 42.3 compares what happens to this $51,800 on the "book" books of the partnership with what happens on the tax books.

On the "book" books for the first year of operation, the partnership pays $26,800 in interest and $11,800 for principal, leaving $13,200, part of which must be credited to the replacement fund. The balance may be distributed to the limited partners, within the 6 percent limit.

TABLE 42.3 *Disposition of cash income from first year's operation of typical 80-unit BURP project (before debt service and allocation for replacement fund) on "book" books and tax books*

"Book" books:			
Cash income			$51,800
Interest	$26,800		
Principal	11,800		38,600
Cash balance			$13,200
Tax books:			
Interest	$26,800		
Depreciation	53,800		$80,600
Cash income			51,800
Tax loss			$28,800
Tax saving = 50 percent of $28,800		$14,400	
Plus cash distribution		6,000	
Total cash benefit		$20,400	

On the tax books, only the $26,800 of interest is deductible. In addition, however, the investors may take $53,800 of depreciation, resulting in total deductions from the $51,800 of $80,600, and leaving a tax loss of $28,800. For a taxpayer in the 50 percent bracket, such as a corporation, this tax loss becomes a cash saving of

$14,400, which, when added to the cash distribution of $6,000, results in net proceeds to the corporate partner of $20,400.

Tax deductions for interest and depreciation decline gradually, of course, after the first year. Nevertheless, they are sufficiently large during the early years of the project for the tax shelter to provide an attractive return to investors. Table 42.4 summarizes the tax losses, cash tax savings, and direct cash distributions created during the first 10 years of the project's operation. This projection assumes the rental income and expense outlined in Table 42.2.

It is apparent that the initial $38,000 investment is recovered in the second year; the investor's net gain over the entire 10-year period is almost $100,000. Of course, there would be capital gains taxes on the sale of the partnership interest. If this is assumed to occur in the 11th year, since at about this time the tax benefits begin to run out, the net gain would still be about $70,000.

TABLE 42.4   *Annual tax loss, annual tax saving, and cumulative cash gain for first 10 years of operation of typical 80-unit BURP project*

Year	Annual tax loss	Annual tax saving (50% rate)	Direct cash distributions	Cumulative cash gain
*				$(38,000)
1	$28,800	$14,400	$6,000	(17,600)
2	25,500	12,750	6,000	1,150
3	22,600	11,300	6,000	18,450
4	19,100	9,550	6,000	34,000
5	16,200	8,100	6,000	48,100
6	13,400	6,700	6,000	60,800
7	10,700	5,350	6,000	72,150
8	8,100	4,050	6,000	82,200
9	5,600	2,800	6,000	91,000
10	3,300	1,650	6,000	98,650

*Original investment.

Assume that because either expenses were up or rental income was down, the project earned only $26,800, instead of $51,800, of cash income (line 4) before debt service. At its discretion, the FHA may waive the repayment of principal (line 6), so that the project can remain solvent simply by meeting interest payments (having line 4 equal line 5). Since the interest and depreciation deductions in Table 42.3 remain the same (a total of $80,600), the tax loss resulting after deducting $26,800 of cash income is $53,800. For a 50 percent tax-bracket investor this means a $26,900 cash tax saving, or $6,500 more than if enough cash had been available to make a distribution up to the 6 percent limit.

43. *Housing Codes*

NATIONAL COMMISSION ON URBAN PROBLEMS

Housing codes regulate occupancy conditions for existing housing (unlike building codes, analyzed in Chapter 30, which regulate new construction and major remodeling.) This selection from the final report of the National Commission on Urban Problems (the Douglas Commission) raises some fundamental questions about the various purposes of housing code enforcement and the realistic possibilities of achieving some of the ends that proponents of code enforcement advocate. The Commission's findings are that few standards for minimum habitability actually are enforced, and many are not easily enforceable. In addition, a great many communities do not even have housing codes. The Commission's report itemizes the defects of current code administration and suggests that adequate code enforcement is possible only within the broader context of an increased supply of low- and moderate-income housing and large-scale rehabilitation aids.

The Commission was charged with examining housing codes to see if local property-owners and private enterprise could be encouraged to meet a larger part of total housing needs; to consider the impact of housing codes on housing costs; and to determine how housing codes might be simplified, improved, and enforced at the local level. . . .

Is their purpose to upgrade housing in the slums or only to prevent deterioration in the "gray" areas? Are they to establish "minimum" standards of health and safety or do they have a larger role to play in providing decent housing in a suitable living environment? Are they to be enforced only in special areas or should they apply to all housing, urban and rural, central city and suburb, in affluent neighborhoods as well as in the slum? Are they to be enforced in areas awaiting urban renewal or only in concentrated areas not yet ready to be put under the bulldozer?

Can they be enforced effectively or does that action merely result in putting people "out in the street" or into already overcrowded housing?

Where repairs are made and housing upgraded, does such action result in increased rents and thus place minimum housing beyond the reach of those whom good code enforcement was designed to help?

Do present codes, even when adequately enforced, bring about a level of housing which meets even the minimum conditions of health, safety and welfare?

Can every family in every city be guaranteed that the local code will be enforced and that the result will be a "minimum" level of housing which is fit to live in?

Should there be different codes for different problems? Should the old-law tenements, built under ancient standards, have to meet the latest housing code provisions? Should the same standards apply to rehabilitated housing as to existing or new structures? . . .

Reprinted from National Commission on Urban Problems, *Building the American City* (Washington, D.C.: Government Printing Office, 1968), pt. III, chap. 4 (edited).

These are some of the questions which confront any study of housing codes in urban centers.[1] . . .

WHAT IS A HOUSING CODE?

A housing code is an application of state police power put into effect by a local ordinance setting the minimum standards for safety, health, and welfare of the occupants of housing.[2] It covers three main areas: (1) the supplied facilities in the structure—that is, toilet, bath, sink, etc., supplied by the owner; (2) the level of maintenance, which includes both structural and sanitary maintenance, leaks in the roof, broken banisters, cracks in the walls, etc.; (3) occupancy, which concerns the size of dwelling units and of rooms of different types, the number of people who can occupy them, and other issues concerned on the whole with the usability and amenity of interior space. . . .

SUMMARY OF GENERAL FINDINGS

A host of problems and questions arise concerning housing codes. Wide divergences of opinion exist among code groups and governments at all levels with respect to the purpose of housing codes, how they should be enforced, and the standards they should provide.

Existing housing codes

The provisions established in the codes for "minimum" standards of health, safety, and welfare are often inadequate to provide even a "minimum" level of performance for the bulk of the population. A house can meet the legal standards set in a local code, pass a housing code inspection, and still be unfit for human habitation by the personal standards of most middle class Americans.

There is an obvious and urgent need for action to bring the provisions of housing codes up to an actual minimum level of health (including physical, mental, and social well-being), safety, and welfare.

1. A carefully organized and integrated series of research led to the following [Commission] studies: "The Present State of Housing Code Enforcement," Robert L. Hale, Program Coordinator, National Association of Housing and Redevelopment Officials; "The Development, Objective and Adequacy of Current Housing Code Standards," Eric W. Mood, Associate Professor of Public Health, Yale University; "A Comparative Analysis of the Administrative Section of Substandard Housing," Oscar Sutermeister, Assistant Director of the Commission staff; "Housing Code Administration," Joseph S. Slavet, Lecturer in Urban Affairs, and Melvin F. Levin, Director of Research, Area Development Center, both of Boston University; "Legal Remedies for Housing Code Violations," Frank P. Grad, Associate Director, Legislative Drafting Research Fund, Columbia University; "Costs and Other Effects on Owners and Tenants of Repairs Required Under Housing Code Enforcement Programs," Joseph R. Barresi, Secretary, Boston Municipal Research Bureau.

The chapter on housing codes in the Commission's report is in large measure built upon and contains passages taken from the reports by these experts, generally without specific attribution. Their expert contributions are gratefully acknowledged and most are being published separately.

2. However, relevant legislation also includes state enabling acts for local housing code adoption, state housing legislation, general state legislative provisions relating to the criminal process and other enforcement sanctions, state legislation granting power to use equitable remedies, including injunctions and receiverships, and power to make repairs and impose the cost as a lien, and state laws on real property as related to tenant rent strike remedies. See note 1, Grad, chap. 1, "Housing Codes as a Function of State and Local Lawmaking." For a technically more adequate definition and description of a housing code, see note 1, Grad and Mood.

Our most important single finding, however, is that minimum standards, while enforceable, are often unenforced. Although intended to apply citywide, the inspection of housing and the enforcement of housing codes are frequently carried out only in limited areas, generally excluding both the worst and the most affluent neighborhoods.

This is due, in part, to various federal policies. For example, code enforcement funds have been available mainly in those areas where blight can be arrested and dwellings upgraded. Areas which have hit bottom or where blight has not yet set in have been largely ignored.

The primary need, therefore, is for vigorous enforcement of housing codes over the entire geographic area of adoption. Such enforcement is a never-ending task.

Furthermore, as can be seen from our census survey figure of only 5,000 housing codes in the country, hundreds of cities and counties, most states, and virtually all rural areas do not have housing codes. Thus, a third need is to extend the coverage or application of housing codes to those jurisdictions whose residents do not now enjoy this type of environmental health protection.

These three steps could greatly improve and upgrade the present housing inventory. But it is almost impossible to say, even in those areas where a code is actively enforced, that because of code enforcement all residents will live in housing which meets a minimum standard of health and safety. Housing codes alone cannot do that job.

To reach the three stated goals, a number of additional steps must be taken along with code enforcement. Among these are:

1. An adequate supply of temporary or relocation housing must be available so that the occupants of below-minimum housing do not have to be put out in the street or moved into worse conditions of deterioration or overcrowding when the code is enforced.

2. The total amount of housing built for low-income groups and for society in general must be substantially increased. In the long run, effective housing code programs will depend on the existence of an abundance of new housing, the demolition of dilapidated and deteriorated housing, and the natural working of the filter-down process.

3. Adequate loans, grants, and other incentives and aids to low-income homeowners, landlords, and tenants must be provided to promote repair to code standards, in order that the enforcement of housing codes does not merely increase housing costs and thus make standard housing economically inaccessible. Since the provision of at least a part of new and rehabilitated housing for the poor by society is a long acknowledged responsibility—through public housing, moderate-income housing, rent supplements, welfare payments, and so forth—the provision of adequate aid for housing code administration nationwide is clearly within this recognized duty of society.

In summary, we must enforce the codes, extend their coverage, and improve them, and in order to do these three things we must also build an abundance of new housing, create additional standard relocation housing through repair, and provide the funds for at least the needy owner or occupant to meet minimum code requirements without an undue burden.

Even this, however, while it would vastly improve the existing situation, would be wholly inadequate. Much more should be done. . . .

Local codes

. . . As late as 1956, 100 or fewer of the larger cities had housing codes. The number has increased rapidly since then, and the Commission's detailed census survey indicates that in 1968, 4,904 local governments out of 17,993 surveyed had housing codes. Of these, HUD has estimated that some 3,000 now have or once had or were committed to have housing codes under the workable program provisions. The total of close to 5,000 is still only about 1 out of 4 (27.3 percent) urban communities in the United States.

Within SMSA's 85 percent of the cities of 50,000 or more have codes, as do 53 percent of those between 5,000 and 50,000. A special sample survey of governments of 5,000 or more both within and outside SMSA's indicated that almost half (47 percent) of them, in about the same proportions inside and outside SMSA's, had housing codes.

The 4,904 local governments with housing codes are classified in Table 43.1. . . .

TABLE 43.1   *Local Governments with Housing Codes*

	Number of governments with housing code, 1968
Type of government:	
Counties	211
Cities	3,976
Townships (New England type)	717
Total	4,904

SOURCE: National Commission on Urban Problems, *Local Land and Building Regulation*, table 1, Research Report no. 6, 1968. Municipalities and townships of less than 1,000 population outside of SMSA's were not surveyed.

It is clear that, except in a few score municipalities, the history of housing code administration as a national development is barely 12 years old. In reviewing the failures and shortcomings, as well as the successes of code administration, including enforcement, it must be kept in mind that we are examining what is in some respects and in most municipalities a very recent legal and administrative development. Patterns of organization and techniques of performance have not, in most instances, had an opportunity to stabilize. Many aspects of the new field remain fluid. Much of the administrative organization of the code compliance effort still seems to be on an experimental trial-and-error basis, and many questions with respect to personnel and performance have never been asked, let alone answered. . . .

Conclusions on administrative provisions

From the comparative statistical analysis of existing housing codes, the following conclusions are drawn.

1. Except for a few "traditional" provisions, very few of the ordinances or codes have similar administrative powers, and the powers actually set out have been shown to be too weak and ineffective to prevent deterioration or to improve the quality of housing.

2. Despite the great increase in the number of municipalities and states adopting housing ordinances and codes and the slow but steady progress in raising the minimum housing standards in these laws, little has been done to improve the provisions dealing with administrative powers, procedures, and sanctions.

3. The factors involved in this situation have been (*a*) political fear and reluctance on the part of local officials; (*b*) the position of HUD that administration is purely

a local matter, and therefore beyond HUD's concern; *(c)* the strong resistance of. HUD, until recently, to federal financial assistance for local code enforcement; and *(d)* the HUD "pressure" on local communities to adopt one of the national model codes without apparent recognition of the fact that these codes differ in some important administrative matters and fail to provide for many new approaches, procedures, and sanctions found effective over the past five years.

For instance, all the ordinances and codes reviewed still call only for criminal penalties. None specifically provides for civil monetary penalties, injunctions, and receivership, for stronger power to the code agency to do the necessary repair work, for proceeding under "the abatement of nuisance" theory, for preventing retaliatory evictions, or for giving tenants any rights against a violating landlord.

4. Many of the deficiencies mentioned can be corrected only by state enabling legislation. HUD must begin promptly to convince state and municipal governments to pass the necessary legislation. . . .

PRESENT EFFECTIVENESS OF HOUSING CODES[3]

Although housing codes generally say "No person shall occupy as owner-occupant, or let to another for occupancy, any dwelling unit which does not comply with the following requirements," etc., it is readily apparent that most housing codes are not administered effectively enough to achieve full compliance even with minimum requirements for health and safety. The continued existence of slums and blighted areas in many cities which have housing codes provides inescapable evidence of this fact.

The most widely available generalized data are those published by the U.S. Bureau. of the Census in the decennial census of housing for the categories of housing quality identified as "dilapidated," "deteriorating," and "sound but lacking certain plumbing facilities." Any dwelling unit falling into one of these three categories is almost certain to be in violation of the local housing code, if one exists. Since national census data cover urban and rural areas which lack housing codes as well as those which have them, national census totals cannot be equated generally with figures (if they are available) for dwelling units not in compliance with existing housing codes. However, it is fair to say that if housing codes were adopted throughout the land, all the dwelling units falling into these three census categories would most probably be in violation of the housing code applicable to them.[4] The housing units which in 1960 were dilapidated, deteriorating, or lacking in certain plumbing facilities constituted the percentage of the total U.S. housing stock shown in Table 43.2. . . .

As part of this Commission's studies, data were collected . . . which give an accurate though fragmentary picture of the extent of incomplete compliance prior to use of federal aid for housing code enforcement. These data report on the progress of the initial inspection stage of federally aided concentrated code enforcement programs in 12 cities across the country. By definition, none of these areas was a severely blighted area or a slum. Under current regulations for federal aid for concentrated housing code enforcement, the areas in which code enforcement work was undertaken

3. For discussion and analysis of responsibilities falling on local, state, and federal governments and the private sector for effectiveness of housing code administration, see *supra*, note 1, Hale, chaps. iv, v, and vi.

4. The question of differences between census data and housing code violation data is dealt with in the Commission's research study on housing code standards. See note 1, *supra*.

were (by statutory limitation) of sufficiently good quality that housing code enforcement together with certain improvements in community facilities would "prevent further decline of the area." The percentage of buildings which would be found in violation of the housing code, or the number and severity of code violations, or both, would be much higher in the poorer sections of these cities than in the sections inspected and reported upon in Table 43.3.

TABLE 43.2 *Percentage of Housing Units in the Census Categories* of Dilapidated, Deteriorating, and Sound but Lacking Certain Plumbing Facilities, United States, 1960*

	Percent
Total United States	18
Total SMSA's	11
Central cities inside SMSA's	11
Other than central cities inside SMSA's	10
Outside SMSA	31
Urban	10
Rural	36

*These categories do not cover all housing code violations, but it is presumed that every housing unit falling in any one of these categories would contain one or more housing code violations, if the unit were covered by a housing code.

SOURCE: *U.S. Census of Housing: 1960*, vol. I, U.S. Summary, tables 9 and 12.

TABLE 43.3 *Residential Buildings with Housing Code Violations in Concentrated Code Enforcement Program* Areas of Selected U.S. Cities, 1968, Together with Years of Workable Program Certification*

City	Residential buildings inspected in concentrated code enforcement area		Years certified workable program in effect†
	Number inspected (1)	Percent found in violation of housing code (2)	(3)
San Francisco, Calif.	2,210	85	13
Baltimore, Md.	9,063	70	13
Malden, Mass.	1,181	51	9
Cincinnati, Ohio	3,499	82	13
Mansfield, Ohio	580	90	5
Salem, Ore.	201	98	6
Lancaster, Pa.	505	90	10
Philadelphia, Pa.	6,554	81	13
Providence, R.I.	2,691	49	10
Chattanooga, Tenn.	1,536	88	12
Fort Worth, Tex.	1,640	54	12
Grand Prairie, Tex.	1,337	35	11

*Federally aided under sec. 117 of the Housing Act of 1949, as amended.

†Counted from year of original certification. Mansfield is only city reported by HUD to have had significant gaps between annual recertifications.

SOURCES: Cols. 1 and 2 "Costs and Other Effects on Owners and Tenants of Repairs Required under Housing Code Enforcement Programs." Prepared for National Commission on Urban Problems by the Boston Municipal Research Bureau, 1968; col. 3, HUD Workable Program Office.

The data on concentrated code enforcement areas show a disappointingly small degree of full housing code compliance accomplished prior to the start of the federally aided programs, even though certified workable programs had been in effect for up to 13 years. However, this record should not be taken to indicate that there is no hope for the future. While the past has been disappointing, a study conducted for the Commission as a survey of the present state of housing code enforcement in the United States concluded among its findings that "housing code enforcement is on the threshold of constituting a far more significant element of a community's overall community development activities than it has been in the past."[5]

Among the major reasons for this hope is that many communities have only recently adopted codes for the first time. The new codes, if enforced, can gradually make a major change in the quality of housing and in the degree of protection of health and safety provided to occupants. But to do this, the nation must produce an abundance of new housing for low-income families, vigorously enforce housing codes, and provide enough temporary and relocation housing to make the system work. . . .

ISSUES IN HOUSING CODE ADMINISTRATION

Why have housing codes been administered so ineffectively that we still have slums, blighted areas, and widespread noncompliance with code provisions? Nineteen years after establishment of a national goal of a decent home and a suitable living environment for every American, why have housing codes been unable to bring the housing inventory up even to minimum health and safety standards?

For housing codes to be administered with full effectiveness, society must address itself to a wide variety of social, economic, and political factors underlying the existence of slums and blight.

Some of the factors which presently limit the effectiveness of housing code administration are [the following].

Private sector factors

Poverty. In contrast to the large slum landlord, many owner-occupants are simply too poor to pay the cost of removing housing code violations. Some live in slums, others in deteriorating neighborhoods where the occupants have grown old with the houses.

Experience with a test program of massive code enforcement in the slums of Providence, R.I., showed that 35 percent of the violations were never corrected.

The Commission's study of code enforcement costs has revealed that in the better areas of a city where federal aid for code enforcement is now being used,

> . . . the typical recipient of a [section] 115 rehabilitation grant is likely to be, literally, a little old lady, probably living on social security with almost no other resources. In fact, many of the [section] 117 areas seem to be characterized by an aging—middle-aged and up—population. The numbers of elderly and moderate-income recipients of grant and loan funds make one wonder whether some sort of medicare-medicaid program for sick houses could be devised.[6]

Preference for nonhousing expenditures. Educational level, class status, social background, neighborhood environment—factors such as these influence the decisions owners make

5. *Supra*, note 1, Hale.

6. *Supra*, note 1, Barresi. This research report constitutes the principal work of the Commission on code enforcement costs.

as to how to spend their income. Should it go for needed housing repairs or for repairs to the car in order to get to work, children's education, TV repair or a new set, or other consumer goods that may yield a greater satisfaction than housing repair? Similarly, in the case of tenants, all other uses of time may be considered personally more re·varding than trash removal, yard maintenance, or the making of minor building repairs. This may be especially true if a city has allowed a neighborhood to deteriorate and the effort of any one individual seems ineffective in fighting general neighborhood conditions. Low-income tenants frequently have many personal and family problems which take precedence in their minds over structural and sanitary maintenance. Homemaker training and other types of tenant education seek to treat the basic problem in such cases. But the community and the local government must be involved as well.

Profit motive. Some absentee owners, whether major slum landlords or local small-businessmen investors, own code-violating properties for the major purpose of maximizing income. Money spent on repairs reduces profit and is likely to be spent grudgingly. The main purpose of owne·rship may be to obtain accelerated depreciation which offsets the income derived from the property or other sources, thus reducing net taxable income and the income tax paid, and increasing the net retained income and cash flow.[7]

Where a tax *shelter* is not the primary goal, needed repairs may simply reduce net income so sharply that the owner will resort to court delays and other legal maneuvers to spend the absolute minimum for upkeep.

Local government factors

Governmental reluctance at the local level. A major factor in poor code compliance may be the reluctance of a local government to support a strong program of housing code administration. This is generally seen in a failure to budget for an adequate inspection staff and for those housing services which are essential to the effective administration of a code before moving to legal enforcement.

Budgetary inadequacies may, in turn, be based on a variety of reasons, many related to political acceptability of alternative local government expenditures. In the past, the poor have been relatively silent and unseen; underfunding of housing code enforcement may not have produced an outcry significant enough to bring change.[8]

Governmental reluctance to act may appear in the office of the corporation counsel (city attorney) as well as in the council chamber. The best compliance program can be undone by ineffective prosecution or by absence of prosecution.

Finally, the deliberate *refusal to adopt a workable program*, in order to stymie federally aided housing for the poor or near-poor, has been the reason for the lack of a housing code in some localities.

Loss of housing. Assuming the best intent, funding, and prosecution, code enforcement may be purposely blunted by the local government in a situation of short housing supply in order to avoid the loss of dwelling units that might be vacated on court order and then held vacant by the owner to avoid the cost of repairs. Commission studies on this point have led to the conclusion (at least in Boston, and the Boston

---

7. See National Commission on Urban Problems, *The Federal Income Tax in Relation to Housing*, Research Report no. 5, 1968.

8. For a discussion of problems of staffing and financing, see the Commission's research report on Housing Code Administration. (*Supra*, note 1, Slavet).

housing code is less stringent than many) that strict enforcement on a mass basis would lead to mass abandonment of properties by their owners and/or higher rents with resultant occupant displacement.[9] When mass enforcement is applied to properties that have been heavily milked and are under rent control, as in the Brownsville section of Brooklyn, N.Y., mass abandonment will occur if alternative housing is *not* in short supply. In Philadelphia, without rent control, strict code enforcement has developed thousands of vacant, dilapidated houses, most of which are tax delinquent. In this case, the city's acquisition of these properties at tax sale has given it a valuable large inventory of structures which are now being fed into the city's scattered housing rehabilitation program. This program is conducted jointly by the local public housing authority and the Philadelphia Housing Development Corp., a nonprofit corporation.

Thus, it is essential that there be an abundance of housing for the low income population in order to enhance the feasibility of strict housing code enforcement.

Blight from vandalized vacancies. Buildings left vacant, especially in poorer areas of a city, are vulnerable to vandalism and arson. If a city's powers are weak or its procedures cumbersome for demolishing vacant structures, it faces the threat of creating new blighting influences by housing code enforcement action that produces as an end product a vacant, vandalized structure. The end result should be, instead, either demolition with a neat cleared lot or a building repaired to meet code standards. As a step in this direction, the 1967 revised model housing code developed by the American Public Health Association and the Public Health Service provides that a city may *(a)* repair at a cost up to 50 percent of market value, if the owner has refused to do so; and *(b)* demolish a structure declared unfit for human habitation, if the owner does not do so. The program of federal aid for demolition . . . is very helpful with this problem.[10]

Relocation. One problem with strict code enforcement is the possibility of leaving a poor family on the sidewalk with no place to go, if local relocation or welfare agencies do not or will not provide relocation housing. Several federal aid programs (starting with urban renewal) have in recent years made it mandatory that relocation housing be found, meeting specified requirements for quality, price, and location. Though this effort may have been less than fully effective, existing local housing codes do not even contain such a requirement. As a result, there is variation from city to city in the level of enforcement. Some cities believe they must proceed with vacating action within the strict time limits set by the code. Others use the real or claimed lack of relocation housing as an excuse for nonenforcement.

Narrow range of remedies. Several of the model codes and many individual local codes have a limited number of enforcement remedies, usually a fine and jail sentence for lesser violations and placarding (vacating) for major ones. None of these by itself accomplishes the job of correcting the violation and returning the house to the usable housing inventory. Most housing codes need modernization to provide an arsenal of alternative compliance tools to increase the possibility of accomplishing repair.[11]

Environmental degradation. The legal theory underlying a housing code states that the specified minimum level of housing quality must be maintained on each privately

9. *Supra*, note 1, Barresi.
10. *Supra*, note 1, Hale.
11. *Supra*, note 1, Grad.

owned residential property for the principal structure, outbuildings, fences, and premises. Nothing is said, in the typical housing code, about private nonresidential properties, such as stores and factories—how they are mixed in with homes; how much noise, smoke, dust, or glare they make; how many signs they put up; how well they are maintained and landscaped. Nothing is said in the typical housing code about the adequacy of public lands such as parks and playgrounds; public structures such as schools, libraries, fire and police stations; or even public facilities such as rights-of-way for access, paving for streets, exclusion of nonneighborhood traffic, sidewalks, storm sewers, street lights, street trees, and street signs. All these are important to the quality of housing, because they are or could be part of the immediate neighborhood and the residential environment. The more degraded the environment, the more difficult it is to preserve housing quality. The incentives for private maintenance and pride in one's surroundings can be dealt crushing blows by lack of public maintenance, by lack of courageously and sensitively exercised public control over the intermixtures of incompatible land uses, and by simple failure to provide necessary public facilities. For these reasons, effective housing code administration must be accompanied by aggressive, thoughtful consideration of the residential environment and of remedies appropriate to its deficiencies. Environmental deficiencies breed housing code violations. Hard-won code compliance, once achieved, is likely to evaporate in such an atmosphere.

Court weaknesses. Enforcement of housing codes has, for the most part, been entrusted to preexisting legal machinery. But courts which may have served well in private litigations of torts and contracts or in preserving the public order have not been as well equipped for the enforcement of housing codes.

As in all criminal prosecutions, a violator of a housing code must be physically before the court in order for it to exercise jurisdiction. The personal serving of process on an all too often will-o'-the-wisp landlord can result in months of delay.

In most communities criminal prosecutions of housing violations are tried before a magistrate or other judge of the lower judiciary, together with disorderly conduct, assault, and petit larceny cases. As a result of the usually overcrowded dockets, long delays and minimal amounts of time spent on each case are usually the rule.

The harried judge usually finds such housing cases nuisance litigations. Lacking expertise in housing law, the typical judge exhibits a deep-seated reluctance to consider housing code violators as criminals. This hesitancy is partially due to the nature of a violation; in a social welfare crime, an evil intent or *mens rea* is not required for conviction. Jail sentences, although authorized in most codes, are almost unheard of in actual practice.

Judicial permissiveness toward recalcitrant landlords is further reflected in the imposition of low or nominal fines. In most instances, a defendant will plead guilty and engage in repairs just before sentencing. In appreciation of this "cooperativeness," the courts will not treat this owner much more harshly than the owner who does extensive work without legal delays.

Prosecutions for code violations usually are brought by the local corporation counsel. To the municipal law department, housing cases are just another variety of minor ordinance violation that is dealt with in perfunctory manner.

Although courts are more willing to utilize civil remedies provided for in a number of codes, the use of such remedies by the local prosecuting authority usually has been minimal. Municipal authorities rarely use the mechanism of civil suit. Civil litigation involves detailed pleadings with much paper work, as compared to the relative ease of criminal prosecution. Furthermore, in many jurisdictions there can be years of delay, due to heavy backlogs, before a trial date is at hand. Finally, a municipality must follow the same procedures as a private party in collecting a judgment placed on the docket with all private judgments. The judgment must await collection by traditional mechanisms of execution upon property of the defendant. However, new approaches to civil remedies suggest that this entire area needs reexamination.[12]

State Government factors–Lack of State support

Part of the reason for incomplete geographical coverage by housing codes and less than full compliance with those that exist is lack of support from most state governments. The police power resides in the state and is delegated by the state to the city. After such delegation, the state often shows little concern as to whether or how the power is used. The state seldom monitors the adequacy of local use of the police power.

Many states have shown no interest in housing quality. Few states have a housing program or a department of state government devoted to housing. California, New York, Georgia, New Jersey, Pennsylvania, Connecticut, and Kentucky are perhaps the most active. Where state assistance is available with respect to housing codes and their administration, it is likely to be through an environmental health activity of the state health department or an agency devoted to community affairs or community development in general. More widespread involvement of state governments is needed.[13]

Federal Government factors–Inadequacies of support

While the federal government does not exercise the police power and thus participate directly in enforcing local housing codes, the financial assistance it is now giving to local housing code enforcement efforts through the section 117 concentrated code enforcement program is the most important boost to code enforcement since the passage of the Widnall amendment[14] in 1964 and the establishment of the Workable Program in 1954.[15]

On the other hand, conflicting standards and inadequate support from the federal government in critical policy and program areas are most serious handicaps to really effective housing code administration, as is summarized below and detailed in the Commission's research study on housing code standards.

Many specific areas of inadequate federal support and conflicting federal standards, even as to the meaning of the term substandard housing, have been identified and analyzed. We find that there is pervasive federal neglect of and even opposition to the effective use of housing codes, although this does not excuse those state and local governments which fail to provide any program at all.[16]

Inadequate and inconsistent definitions. The accomplishments of many specific federal housing programs, and indeed the thrust of the total federal housing program, are

12. *Supra*, note 1, Grad.

13. *Supra*, note 1, Hale.

14. The Widnall amendment requires adoption and six months' effective administration of a housing code as prerequisites for Workable Program approval.

15. For a description of federal assistance programs related to housing code administration, with an evaluation of their contributions, see note 1, Hale, chaps. ivb and vi, and Robert P. Groberg, *Urban Renewal Programs*, report to the Commission, 1968.

16. *Supra*, note 1, Hale, Grad.

vitally affected by the standards used to determine what is "standard" housing and what is "substandard" housing. A related and equally significant question is whether "standard" housing is the same as "decent, safe, and sanitary" housing and a "decent home."

The Commission made a careful analysis of the various definitions of substandard housing as the phrase is currently used. Details of the analysis are reported in the research study on housing code standards.

We found there is no single definition of substandard housing. Many conflicting definitions are used by different groups in connection with various programs.

The following examples of conflicting definitions may serve to make the point.[17]

1. *HUD's Office of General Counsel* approved for general public distribution through the Consumer Relations Office a definition of substandard housing limited to those dilapidated dwelling units which endanger health and safety or lack private toilet, bath, or hot running water.

2. *The Senate Subcommittee on Housing and Urban Affairs* of the Committee on Banking and Currency printed for members of Congress and the public a list of three census of housing categories making up substandard housing: sound lacking plumbing, deteriorating lacking plumbing, and dilapidated.

3. *The ICBO model housing code* lists 39 deficiencies, any one of which makes a residential building substandard.

4. *The St. Louis Housing Code* defines as substandard all buildings used for purposes of human habitation which do not conform to the minimum standards established by the "Minimum Housing Standards Law."

There should be a single, widely used definition, and we so recommend in this report.

The Commission also finds that both definitions and data for substandard housing used in most federal housing activities are *inadequate* (in addition to being inconsistent with one another), because they are arrived at by combining sets of data from the U.S. Census of Housing which correspond in no more than a *fragmentary* manner with the standards set forth in accepted minimum standard housing codes.

Standard housing is generally considered to be that which meets minimum code standards.

Housing which is above the substandard level (as that level is often defined by units of the federal government) is not necessarily standard housing (as that level is usually defined by both federal and local interests). There is a nameless gap for housing that falls between the standard and substandard levels.

Into this gap fall dwelling units having no kitchen sink, no required window in a habitable room, undersized rooms, overcrowding, [and] dozens of other conditions prohibited by the housing code but not making the unit substandard according to HUD.

Failure to clarify the definition of substandard housing and to use it consistently creates a built-in element of predictable failure in many federal housing programs. Congressional decisions on authorizing and funding specific programs are consistently and repeatedly based on housing needs data which are inadequate because of this use of an inadequate definition of substandard housing. A new type of housing quality

17. A detailed analysis of 12 different definitions and a brief account of how the Commission arrived at its own definition are included in the Commission's study on housing code standards under the heading Inadequacies and Inconsistencies in the Definition of Substandard Housing by Sutermeister.

survey should be added to the census of housing, to report on housing needs in terms of housing that is substandard according to code requirements. . . .

Public assistance payments for substandard housing[18]

While the provision of federal aid to increase the construction and supply of decent housing for low income individuals and families is the responsibility of the Department of Housing and Urban Development, the Social and Rehabilitation Service in the Department of Health, Education and Welfare, with its widespread system of grants to states for public assistance and welfare services for the poor, administers the federal portion of the *largest single housing assistance program in government*. It has been estimated that between $750 and $850 million in federal funds is used annually to pay for substandard housing. Those who must depend upon public assistance have a right to expect government policies of financial aid and services that will help them improve their living conditions and move out of the slums, instead of consigning them permanently to substandard housing.

Public welfare is today a federal-state partnership which reaches into more than 3,100 counties and political jurisdictions of the nation to assure that individuals and families receive the recognized basic essentials of living within a framework of related governmental and voluntary measures. At the present time, the public welfare program is hobbled by its legislative mandate and the financial resources with which it must operate. Because of such limitations, only about a fourth of those persons considered to be "poor" are receiving financial assistance or services under the categorical system.

The *states* are responsible for determining *eligibility*, within specified categories of the needy—the aged, disabled, blind, and families with dependent children. The states also set the *items* and *levels* of assistance to be included in the relief check. The federal government matches the states' contributions in accordance with various provisions of the law.

Although information about the quality and costs of recipients' housing has not been systematically collected, it is clear that by and large the quality is poor and the cost excessive for value received. In many states, the amount of the recipients' money payment is not sufficient to meet living costs, nor does it include a shelter allowance that is sufficient to meet the cost of standard shelter.

More than 8.6 million recipients of public aid in the categorical assistance programs —including more than 2 million of the aged—pay for shelter out of their monthly assistance checks. Though shelter is included as a basic item in each state assistance plan, only a few states have established housing standards or have, as yet, developed the funds and services or initiated community action to assure adequate shelter in return for rent paid or to increase the available supply of proper housing.

We have, as yet, only meager statistical information as to the detailed extent of housing need experienced by recipients of public assistance in the various States. . . .

In 1961, a national study of characteristics of AFDC families showed 60 percent, or 716,400 families, living in substandard housing that was grossly overcrowded. This included rented and owned, rural and urban dwellings.

18. Material for this section was furnished to the Commission by the Social and Rehabilitation Service, Department of HEW (Mrs. Olive Swinney).

44. Effects of the Property Tax in Urban Areas

DICK NETZER

Dick Netzer's analysis of the property tax, the largest single source of local government revenue, shows that it is essentially a very high rate and extremely regressive consumption tax, which as presently administered discourages consumption of housing services and deters improvements. Netzer suggests several remedies, ranging from increased state and federal responsibility for the fiscal burdens of cities and greater reliance on user charges and local income tax to more radical schemes for public recapture of the increased value of land.

HOUSING AND THE TAX BURDEN

. . . [T]he property tax on housing is analogous to taxes commonly known as consumption taxes—that is, general sales and selective excise taxes. Like the ordinary consumption taxes, the great bulk of the burden of the housing property tax appears to rest upon housing consumers, whether they are owner-occupants or tenants. There are some exceptions; the chief one is that owners of rental property cannot shift the burden of that portion of the tax which falls on the land underlying their buildings. But, for the country as a whole, probably well over 90 percent of all property taxes on housing are borne by housing occupants.

Since this is so, it is useful to view property taxes in relation to consumer expenditures for housing. This expresses the relationship in a form similar to that with which we are familiar in connection with other consumption taxes—a sales tax of 4 percent of taxable purchases, for example. There are two sets of data available to illustrate this relationship. The first expresses property taxes as percentages of the estimated rental value of housing (as found in the national income accounts).

As Table 44.1 shows, property taxes average about 19 percent of the rental value of nonfarm housing in the United States currently, equivalent to an excise tax of nearly 24 percent on rental value, excluding property taxes (parallel to the way in which sales tax rates are stated, as percentages of sales before sales tax is added).

The second set of relationships, also shown in Table 44.1, is perhaps a more realistic one, from the standpoint of housing consumers themselves. . . . It expresses taxes as percentages of actual cash outlays for housing—expenses of owner-occupants or rental payments of tenants. The percentages are very high expressed in this way, too, especially outside the South. Converted to a before-tax form, they range—excluding the South—from sales-tax-equivalent rates of 18 percent for large apartment houses outside New York City to 30 percent or more for single-family houses in the Northeast

Reprinted from *Impact of the Property Tax: Effect on Housing, Urban Land Use, Local Government Finance*, Research Report no. 1 to the National Commission on Urban Problems (Washington, D.C.: Government Printing Office, 1968), pp. 16-22, 36-47 (edited), by permission of the author. Dick Netzer is a member of the faculty of the Graduate School of Public Administration at New York University.

and multifamily properties in New York City. In general, the upper end of this range applies to most of the nation's large cities outside the South.

TABLE 44.1 *Property taxes on housing as percent of housing expenditure*

	1960	1965
I. In relation to rental value of nonfarm housing (national income data)*		
Owner-occupied housing.........................	18.1	18.9
Rental housing....................................	19.3	19.4
All nonfarm housing	18.5	19.1
II. In relation to actual housing expenditure or rents (census data)†		
Owner-occupied single-family houses		
All United States	17	....
In standard metropolitan statistical areas	19	....
Northeast region..............................	24	....
North central.................................	20	....
South	10	....
West	18	....
Rental properties		
1-4 unit properties............................	17	....
5-49 unit properties...........................	17	....
New York City	23	....
Elsewhere	16	....
50-or-more unit properties	20	....
New York City	23	....
Elsewhere	15	....

*Includes the imputed rental value of owner-occupied houses. Based on data in U.S. Department of Commerce. *The National Income and Product Accounts of the United States, 1929-65,* A Supplement to the Survey of Current Business (1966). Taxes on rental property estimated by the author.

†Based on 1960 Census of Housing data, including special tabulations for New York City. The data, except for the New York figures, appear in Netzer, *Economics of the Property Tax* (Brookings Institution, 1966), tables 2-8 and 5-6. For owner-occupied houses, taxes are expressed as percentages of annual cash housing outlays by owners; for rental properties, taxes are expressed as percentages of rental receipts for mortgaged properties.

Share Paid Through Rents

What this means is that very large numbers of urban families pay, via their rents, or directly if owner-occupants, taxes which amount to very sizable increments to their housing costs. This is shown more directly in Table 44.2, which contains a distribution of housing units in multifamily rental housing subject to property taxes amounting to a sales tax equivalent of 20 percent or more. New York City is broken out, because it accounts for so large a fraction of the multifamily housing stock (about one-fourth), because its property tax rates are high (though no higher than in most other cities in the Northeast and a few elsewhere), and because its sales-tax-equivalent tax rates are so high (in part because rent control keeps rents, the denominator of the fraction, down). For the country as a whole, as of 1960, 3.6 million households—more than half the total in this type of housing—were subject to rates of 20 percent or more, and 1.2 million were subject to rates in excess of 33.3 percent.

These very high tax rates are greatly in excess of the rates applicable to other forms of consumer expenditure, with the exception of taxes on liquor, tobacco, and gasoline. The highest retail sales tax rate currently is 5 percent, and this rate applies only in places which exempt food from the tax; the typical sales tax rate is closer to 4 percent. If we exclude liquor, tobacco, and gasoline, all the indirect taxes which fall upon consumers—including shifted business taxes as well as ordinary sales and excise taxes—probably amount to less than 10 percent of nonhousing consumer expenditure—less than half the level of housing taxation. It is simply inconceivable that, if we were starting to develop a tax system from scratch, we would single out housing for extraordinarily high levels of consumption taxation. More likely, we would exempt housing entirely from taxation, just as many states exempt food from the sales tax.

TABLE 44.2   *Estimated number of households living in rental housing subject to high property tax rates, 1960**

[*In thousands*]

Real estate tax relative to rental receipts, stated as a sales tax equivalent†	New York City	Elsewhere in United States	U.S. total
33.3 percent or more	541	676	1,217
25 to 33.3 percent	568	513	1,081
20 to 25 percent	293	1,021	1,314
Total, 20 percent or more	1,402	2,210	3,612

*Adapted from U.S. Census Bureau, *1960 Census of Housing*, vol. V, *Residential Finance*, pt. 2, *Rental and Vacant Properties* and from special tabulations for New York City. The census data for this purpose cover only mortgaged properties acquired before 1959; the estimates shown here have been adjusted to cover all rental properties. These data cover only properties with five units or more.

†Real estate tax as a percent of rental receipts *less* real estate tax.

Special Burden on the Poor

The situation is even worse than the preceding discussion implies with respect to the low income population. We have not discussed income heretofore. But the housing property tax is heavily regressive, absorbing a much higher fraction of the incomes of the poor than of the rich. This is largely because housing expenditure looms so large in the budgets of poorer families; in addition, the poor tend to be concentrated in the high property tax rate central cities.

Table 44.3 indicates how heavily the property tax does burden poorer renters in the country as a whole, and for New York City, the only individual city for which good evidence exists.[1] The burden on the poor in the latter case is even heavier than in the country as a whole. However, because rent control in New York City moderately reduces ratios of rent to income for poorer families in the city, the housing property tax is probably more severe for poor families in other large northern cities than it is in New York, on balance.

This regressivity, illustrated in Figure 44.1, is of concern, and not just from the standpoint of equity pure and simple. High taxes on housing, relative to taxes on other uses of the consumer's dollar, are likely to discourage expenditure for housing. But they are likely to be an especially severe deterrent to the poor, since they have so little leeway in family budgeting—there is little else that they can forego in order to rent better housing. This amounts to saying that the poor probably are more

1. The New York City figures apply to homeowners as well as renters, but are dominated by the latter, who occupy 79 percent of the city's housing units.

sensitive to price (rent) differentials than are the rich, out of necessity rather than choice.

TABLE 44.3 *Estimates of housing property taxes as a percent of income, by income class*

Income class	All renters, United States, 1959-60*	New York City 1960-61†
Less than $2,000	8.5	8.6
$2,000 to $3,000	3.9	5.6
$3,000 to $4,000	3.0	4.1
$4,000 to $5,000	2.5	3.4
$5,000 to $7,000	2.1	2.8
$7,000 to $10,000	1.8	2.4
$10,000 to $25,000	1.6	2.2
Over $15,000	1.4	2.7

*From Netzer, op. cit., table 3-8.
†Adapted from Alan D. Donheiser, "The Incidence of the New York City Tax System," in Graduate School of Public Administration, New York University, *Financing Government in New York City* (1966), p. 177.

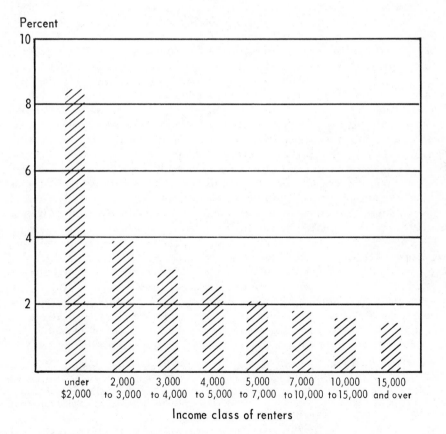

FIGURE 44.1 *Housing Taxes Paid on Rented Nonfarm Housing as a Percent of Family Income of Renters By Income Class, 1959-60*

The general effect of these very high property taxes on the supply of housing to the low-income population has two components. First, taxes raise the cost of housing to the occupants and simply put a significant part of the existing housing stock beyond the reach of many in the low-income population. For example, take a large urban family with an income of $4,000. The maximum tolerable rent for such a family (if the rent is not paid by public assistance) might be said to be 30 percent of income, or $100 a month. Assume that the prevailing level of property taxes is 25 percent of rents in that city. Were property taxes on housing eliminated, this family could afford to rent an apartment now renting for $133 a month, without exceeding the 30 percent rent/income ratio, an apartment which is now out of reach.

Second, high property taxes discourage consumption of and investment in housing in general by the entire population.[2] There is ample evidence that consumers will buy more and better housing if its price is lower, just as they do with regard to most other objects of consumption. It can be and has been argued persuasively that one of the most effective ways of helping the low-income population (with respect to housing) is to rapidly increase the total supply of housing in a particular city and metropolitan area; a decrease in prices (rents), while having no immediate effect on total housing supply, does create a larger effective housing market for those who now suddenly can afford more of the existing housing. The evidence from the 1950s strongly suggests that the housing conditions of the poor improved most radically in those areas in which the total supply of housing rose most rapidly. The process by which this occurs is related to the rate of turnover of housing; this argument has been carefully developed in a recent article, using New York City evidence.[3]

There is yet another aspect to all this. Most low-income families do spend large proportions of their incomes for housing, but not all of them do so. In the 1960 census, there were 3.8 million renter households with incomes below $3,000 for whom rent/income ratios were computed. Roughly 600,000 of these spent less than 25 percent of their incomes for housing. Now it is a worthy objective to attempt to persuade some of these families to moderately increase the proportions of income spent for housing, by offering them greatly improved housing conditions at small increases in rent. A reduction in the property tax burden could do just that, by reducing the prices of housing across the board. To return to the $4,000 urban family, assume a present rent/income ratio of 20 percent, which means a monthly rent of $67. A 50 percent reduction in property taxes, combined with an increase in the rent/income ratio to 25 percent, would permit this family to rent an apartment which now rents for $97 a month, a 45 percent improvement in housing conditions (presumably) with a one-fourth increase in actual rental payments.

Property Tax Deters Improvements

This line of argument applies not only to the central city poor. It can be generalized to apply to be the broader problem of improving the future prospects of the large, old central cities as attractive residential locations for families of all income levels. An essential ingredient of such an improvement program must include offering a

2. It should be noted here that *any* tax tends to reduce income available for expenditure by consumers, and that a reduction in disposable income will reduce demand for housing as well as demand for other consumption goods and services. But in general, this reduced-income effect will depress demand for housing much less than will the increased price effect of a tax which, like the property tax, specifically applies to housing as such.

3. See Frank S. Kristof, "Housing Policy Goals and the Turnover of Housing," *Journal of the American Institute of Planners*, August 1965, pp. 232-45.

stock of housing which affords a reasonable alternative to the housing available in suburban locations. This means modernizing of that portion of the central city housing stock which is amenable to modernization,[4] replacing other parts of the old housing stock with new housing, and building housing on the limited amount of available central city land.

High property taxes effectively shrink the market for all these types of improvement in the central city housing supply. This is perhaps most obvious for owner-occupants of unmodernized older housing considering rehabilitation; the rehabilitation is not only costly and difficult to finance, but in most cities it also will result in some increases in assessment. In some cases, the assessor will heavily discount the improvements, but in other places where the old housing is assessed at levels which are low for that city, the rehabilitation may trigger a very large increase in the assessment and in tax liability. In any event, one of the few case studies of this subject suggests that *fear* of potential property tax increases can be a potent deterrent to improvements of central city residential properties.[5]

The effects of high property taxes in shrinking the market for *new* central city housing seem to be obvious to policymakers, for they are increasingly attracted to tax exemption or abatement schemes for specified types of new housing, of types similar to the New York arrangements under which 70,000 middle-income housing units have been built. It should be noted that the issue here is *not* the height of central city tax rates compared to those in the suburbs, for middle-income families. Indeed, frequently the central city tax bills, for the housing which could be an alternative to suburban housing, will be lower than the taxes in the suburbs.

In suburban communities, particularly bedroom suburbs, the public services that a family receives or has access to are very closely tied to the local taxes that the same family pays. Therefore, in a sense, the property tax in many suburbs is analogous to a general charge for the use of public services, or perhaps even to a local income tax. It is unlikely to be a deterrent to consumption of housing—that is, to the expenditure of consumer income for housing.

For the central cities, this is not the case. Central cities provide a wide variety of services and tax a wide variety of property types. Individuals cannot reasonably assume that the prices of housing confronting them include an identifiable tax component which is in effect a charge for a preferred package of public services. What they do observe is that housing is expensive in the central city. It may *not* be any more expensive in the central city than in the suburbs. But an effective city-rebuilding strategy requires that the central cities encourage more private expenditure for housing, and this may in turn require that housing be much cheaper in the central city than in the suburbs.

Moreover, the suburban nexus between taxes and public services is likely not to be present in the central city for yet another reason—inevitably more of the new central city housing will be rental housing, rather than owner occupied. Therefore, the taxes per se will not be apparent to the central city housing consumer—only the rentals, which reflect a tax component. And, making the comparison still worse, property taxes paid through rents are not deductible in computing federal income tax liability, as are taxes on owner-occupied properties. . . .

4. Experience in a number of cities suggests that there is very little old housing which is not amenable to modernization, although some of it is very costly.

5. George Sternlieb, *The Tenement Landlord* (Urban Studies Center, Rutgers—The State University, 1966), chap. 11.

POSSIBLE REMEDIES

To the extent that the defects of the property tax are inherent ones, the principal remedies must take the form of some reduction in the reliance on the property tax for the financing of urban public services.[6] The alternative financing is by higher levels of government which do not use the property tax, or by other local government revenue sources. Reduced reliance on the property tax will also diminish the importance of the other types of defects, mainly related to the fragmented local government patterns. But these latter defects can also be remedied in part by reforms within the institution of the property tax itself.

Increase State-Federal Responsibilities

The increase of state and federal government responsibilities is an obvious route toward reduced reliance on the property tax, and one which is in keeping with developments in fiscal federalism since the 1920s.

These developments include both the transfer of direct responsibility for the actual performance of some functions from the local to state and federal levels of government, and increased state and federal financing of functions still performed at the local level.

Consider four of the major functional classes of civilian public expenditure: education, highways, public welfare, and health and hospitals. In each case, the local government share of total direct public expenditure by all three levels of government declined appreciably from 1927 to 1965-66; for example, from 71 to 32 percent for highways and from 69 to 52 percent for welfare. But there were even larger declines in the proportions of local government expenditure financed from local, rather than state and federal, revenue sources. As a result of this (and of another much less important factor, the expansion of local nonproperty revenue sources), the property tax now finances half or less of *local* expenditure for these functions, compared to 75 percent or more in 1927. . . .

. . . [A] strong argument can be made for further upward shifts in two functional areas. One is education; very small portions of the eventual benefits from education are recaptured within the confines of individual school districts, since our population is so mobile—perhaps no more than 20 percent on the average. This argues for a much increased role for external financing, especially at the federal level. Since education now absorbs slightly over half of current property tax revenues, such shifts could greatly reduce reliance on the property tax.

A second area is that of poverty-linked services, notably welfare and health services, which now absorb roughly 10 percent of total property tax revenues, but substantially more for the large central cities. A good case can be made for relieving the property tax of the job of financing *all* public services linked to the existence of poverty. Since this burden is concentrated in central cities, it would alleviate the central city-suburban disparities and the property tax problems these create; it would also alleviate the regressivity problem in the sense of taxing the poor for services to the poor.

This is very much in keeping with the historic trends. During the last 30 years, each of the important institutional changes which reduced pressures on the property tax has been associated with redistributive services. These include the federal and state assumption of most public welfare costs in the thirties, via grants-in-aid, transfers

6. This does not necessarily mean a rollback in property tax levies or rates. In practice it will mean a reduction in the *relative* role of the property tax—that is, financing increased expenditures in future years from revenue sources other than the property tax.

of functional responsibilities, or direct federal social insurance programs; the steady expansion of the state government role in financing education in the past 20 years; the gradual increase in federal financing of health services (either directly or through grants-in-aid), culminating in medicare and the 1965 social security amendments; the federal role in the provision of housing for low income people; and most recently, the new federal participation in antipoverty programs and in the costs of education where there are extensive pockets of poverty. All of these federal-state aids combined have not been sufficient to keep effective property tax rates from rising at a fairly rapid rate. But without external aid to urban-area local governments, the rise might have been far more rapid. . . .

Other Local Revenue Sources

. . . [To the extent that] the central city accommodates the surrounding suburban population with places of employment, shopping, and cultural facilities and, presumably, the public services supportive of these activities . . . , it strengthens the argument for greater reliance on other governmental revenue sources, notably direct charges for the use of public services and facilities (paid by actual users wherever they may live) and local income taxes paid by residents and commuters alike.

1. *User Charges for Public Services.*

Local governments do currently employ user charges; they obtain roughly 18 percent of their locally raised general revenue from charges for services (other than utility services) and from special assessments. About half of this amount comes from school lunch and similar charges, hospital charges, and public housing rental payments, but charges apply to a wide range of other services. Despite this, there is considerable potential for greater exploitation of user charges, in connection with activities which do *not* have significant income redistribution objectives. The case for this has been put as follows:

> . . . many of the public services provided by local governments are in many ways like those provided by public utility companies. That is, they are not provided uniformly to the entire population, but rather in distinguishable quantities and qualities to individual families in the population, who consume them in accord with their personal preferences. For example, not all families use the same amount of water, not all use the same amount of highway transportation, and so on. There is a strong case for financing such services in the same way public utility services are financed—that is, via user charges which are like prices, rather than through general taxes.
> If the purpose of providing the public service is to offer different consumers the services they want, and place some value on, then they ought to pay for such services in proportion to the costs. Otherwise, governments will be called upon to provide a great deal more of the service than people would be willing to consume if they did have to pay for it, which is a wasteful use of resources; or the service will be in such short supply that a form of nonprice rationing will be employed to allocate the service among consumers. The outstanding example of this is street congestion in cities: users pay for highways in the aggregate but not for specific individual uses of the streets, and therefore, not surprisingly, treat highways as a free good. The only deterrent to use of the streets at the most crowded times and in the most crowded places is the value one places on time; the rationing in effect then results in those who place a low value on time pre-empting the street space from those who place a high value on time. Ordinarily, in our society, rationing is on the basis of price. Somebody who values a service highly bids it

away from someone who places a lower value on that service and would rather use his income for alternative kinds of consumption.[7]

The most striking opportunities for greater utilization of user charges, as this would suggest, are in connection with financing of urban highway and parking facilities and services, waste collection and disposal, and recreational activities; the potential revenue in these areas alone equals roughly one-tenth of property tax revenue on a nationwide basis. The potential is relatively larger in urban areas, especially the larger ones, which provide more of these services and are generally less effective exploiters of user charges.

2. *Local Income Taxes*

The case for local income taxation does not rest on the argument that it is a good device for central city taxation of commuters. To be sure, the potential here is a large one. The municipal governments of the 43 largest cities collected $3.3 billion in property tax revenue in 1965-66. Excluding Washington, D.C., their local income tax revenue was $242 million, largely made up of the collections in Detroit, Louisville, and the larger cities in Pennsylvania, Ohio, and Missouri. But if all 43 cities had a flat 1-percent tax on income earned within the central cities, revenue would have amounted to perhaps $1.3 billion, probably $300 million of this from commuters. This is a substantial fraction of property tax revenue for these units of government.

The more general case for income taxation is that it does *not* have an especially adverse effect on housing, as does the property tax. It escapes the regressivity charge. Moreover, for central cities, it is superior to local sales taxes and other local business taxes, since unlike the latter, it is highly unlikely to encourage migration of economic activity away from the central cities. . . .

3. *Land Value Taxation*

An entirely different type of alternative revenue source would be a heavy tax on land values in urban areas as a partial substitute for currently collected property tax revenues.

As the name implies, land value taxation is a tax on the value of land alone, irrespective of the value of buildings or the lack of buildings on a site. A step in this direction is the graded or differential tax—the application of a higher tax rate to the land portion than to the improvement portion of property valuations.

The argument for exclusive taxation of site values, or for substantially heavier taxation of land than of buildings, is an old one, and differential site value taxation is widely practiced—in western Canada, Australia, New Zealand, and South Africa, for example. The merits of the case have been submerged for many years by the extravagant claims of the proponents of site value taxation. Moreover, skepticism has been bolstered by the apparent absence of discernible effects in the places where site valuation is utilized.

However, the case for site value taxation is a good one. The argument, on equity grounds, is that most of the value of land is a consequence, not of actions by individual owners, but of collective investment, community development, and population growth. Individual landowners therefore can realize large "unearned increments" over time. It is entirely appropriate for the community to recapture these unearned increments

7. Netzer, "Financing Urban Government," in James Q. Wilson, ed., *The Metropolitan Enigma* (Chamber of Commerce of the United States, 1967), p. 65.

by taxation, and use them for community purposes. There are complications in this equity argument, related to the fact that most landowners have already paid, in their purchase prices, for at least some of the unearned increment, but by and large the equity argument makes sense.

The economic argument is even more compelling. A tax on site value which is independent of the improvements on the site will not affect entrepreneurial decisions as to the use of the site; the best (most profitable) use before tax remains the best use after the tax is imposed. In other words, the tax is neutral with regard to land use decisions. Since the present property tax, on both land and improvements, is *not* neutral but tends to discourage investment in buildings, a switch from the present tax to exclusive site value taxation (or to a tax heavily weighted on the land portion) would tend to have strong land use effects.

Provided that demand permits, it would encourage owners to develop their sites more intensively, in an effort to minimize tax liability as a percentage of current receipts, since additional investment in buildings would not increase tax liability. Within individual urban jurisdictions, taxes on vacant land would tend to rise, thereby increasing the holding costs of vacant land and making the speculative withholding of land from development a less attractive proposition. Thus, a switch to site value taxation is likely to have its maximum impact in two parts of a metropolitan area—in the central areas, where it would encourage more investment in buildings, and in the outlying sections, where it would tend to discourage land speculation and the resulting patchy patterns of land development (less "leapfrogging" over sites withheld from the market).

In theory, there are few if any legitimate economic arguments against site value taxation. On an operational level, there are grounds for hesitation.

First of all, one may doubt the actual strength of the positive tendencies associated with a switch to site value taxation. It is, after all, a major institutional change, and major institutional changes should not be pressed unless their positive effects are also expected to be major in extent. However, it should be noted that effective property tax rates in most American metropolitan areas are high and rising. The negative land use effects of the present tax are likely to become increasingly apparent in time, and the likely benefits from a change in the basis of taxation will correspondingly increase.

Second, there is some question about the revenue adequacy of site value taxation. Some calculations suggest that the present yield of property taxes on nonfarm realty substantially exceeds the total rental value of privately owned nonfarm land. Thus, even a 100 percent site value tax might not yield enough to fully replace the existing property tax (on real property, exclusive of personalty). This suggests that only a partial, rather than a complete, shift is possible, diluting the possible advantageous land use effects.

Third, there are administrative problems if both land and buildings are taxed, but at differential rates—the "graded tax" concept applying in Pittsburgh, Hawaii, and western Canada, for example. This makes it very important to accurately value land and buildings *separately*. Under a pure system of site value taxation, the building value is irrelevant. Under the conventional property tax, the distinction between land and building for any individual site is also irrelevant, although the statutes may require the assessor to make some statement about the notional separation. It seems likely that joint administration of the two different types of taxes will produce bad administration of the site value tax, in that assessors will tend to relate land and building valuations as they often do at present. Therefore, the proposal here is for a *separate* system of land value taxation, levied and administered, if possible, over a wide geographic area—a whole state or SMSA.

4. *Taxation of Land Value Increments*

The equity argument for taxation of *increases* in land values is at least as strong as that for annual taxes on total land values. This kind of tax is aimed at recapturing for the government a higher proportion of what economists call the unearned increment—the rise of land value that occurs, not through efforts of an owner but through governmental action (new highways, subway lines, zoning changes, etc.) and through growth of the population and industry of the community.

Land value increment taxes strike directly at the unearned increments realized by specific individual owners, and do not penalize present owners who have *not* realized substantial land value increments. The claim in this case is not that community improvements *tend* to enrich landowners in general; tax liability occurs only when enrichment is demonstrated by the realization of capital gains on land. . . .

Like annual land value taxation, this form of taxation would be largely neutral with respect to the use of land and would not discourage new construction. However, its economic impact and revenue potential would be somewhat less. Presumably, the land value increment tax would apply only to gains actually realized (including constructive realization at the death of the owner). Very high tax rates would tend to postpone realization of gains, although closing the transfer-by-death loophole would reduce this. Nevertheless, the economic impact would be in the right direction and the equity effects appropriate. Therefore, this seems good policy, especially if straightforward annual land value taxation does not prove acceptable.

Improvement of the Existing Institution

Since some of the major defects in the existing institution relate to the fragmented structure of local government in urban areas, an obvious direction for reform is application of the property tax over wider geographic areas, thereby reducing tax rate disparities by evening out the differences in tax base per capita or per pupil. There are two approaches to this.

1. *Tax Base Consolidation*

One would be to regionalize a segment of the tax base—eliminate local taxes on some types of property and levy property taxes on these types over a broader area, with either use of the proceeds for regionwide (or statewide) functions or distribution of the proceeds to local government units on the basis of some measure of need. A frequent suggestion along these lines is for regional or statewide taxation of business property, to eliminate local competition for economic activity and attendant pressures on land use planning.[8]

2. *Fiscal Federation*

A second approach is to regionalize the financing (and perhaps administration) of part or all of selected local government functions, but still utilize the property tax to the extent it is now used. . . .

---

8. It should be noted that the planning difficulties could be accommodated in another way—by regionalizing *land use controls* rather than taxation. There is much to be said for this course of action; indeed, there is hardly anything to be said in defense of land use planning by a huge number of small jurisdictions. But this is an entirely separate subject.

3. Better Administration

The position in this report is that improved assessment of most types of complex business property is a utopian goal, but that it is possible to do a much better job with respect to housing, vacant lots and the simpler, more common types of business property, like small store buildings. The basis for this argument is that there are fairly frequent sales of such property to provide a basis for assessment. The requirements for realization of such improvements as are achievable are professionalization and adoption of truly systematic procedures—indeed, full computerization of the primary assessment process.[9] These in turn imply large-scale assessment organizations.

Except in the very largest states, this may very well imply statewide assessment; it surely is not consistent with assessment districts having populations of very much less than 500,000. The general rule seems to be, if full use is to be made of the possibilities for computerization, the bigger, the better. This, then, is no less radical a proposal than the others advanced in this report, since this country hss been firmly wedded over many decades to the notion that small local assessment districts are an essential component of local self-government.

4. Hardship Adjustments

One way in which the burdensomeness of the property tax, including its regressivity, has been attacked has been through the device of special exemptions and abatements for various kinds of "hardship" cases. The homestead exemptions which became popular in the 1930s were one manifestation of this. More recently, there have been adoptions of devices to relieve property tax burdens for older people. Almost without exception, exemptions and abatements have proven to be clumsy and inefficient methods of relieving hardship. If a partial tax exemption is offered to a whole class of property owners—such as the aged—it is likely to relieve the real hardship cases only if it is very generous, and hence very costly in foregone tax revenue. Meanwhile, many property owners who are not hardship cases benefit. If the generosity of the provision is tempered by revenue-loss considerations, it may be of trivial value for those really hard hit, and administratively complex as well. Moreover, tax relief for homeowners, whether aged or not, tends to ignore the frequently worse-off cases among renters.

One way out of this is to offer carefully tailored credits for very burdensome property tax payments under state income tax laws. Such credits can be restricted to those whose income status makes it clear that the burdens are real ones. An example of this is the provision in Wisconsin, adopted in 1963, for income tax credits for the aged, both homeowners and tenants, who *both* have low incomes *and* pay high proportions of their incomes in property taxes, directly or through rents.[10] This kind of provision parallels the spreading use of income tax credits to offset the regressivity of state sales taxes, and could be usefully employed on a widespread basis.

5. Housing Tax Incentives

The obvious deterrent effects of high property taxes on housing have led to the use of tax exemptions and abatements for specific kinds of new housing construction and rehabilitation, most notably in New York State. The New York programs have

9. This has been done on an experimental basis with extraordinarily good results in California.

10. Billy Dee Cook, Kenneth E. Quindry, and Harold M. Groves, "Old Aged Homestead Relief—The Wisconsin Experience," *National Tax Journal* 19 (September 1966): pp. 319-24.

had some success in stimulating construction of middle income housing, with real though indirect effects on the housing status of poorer families.

Even from the standpoint of an exclusive emphasis on increasing the supply of housing, the tax abatement programs now being used have a serious drawback—they are administratively very cumbersome and therefore slow-moving. When governments single out particular groups in the population for extraordinarily favorable treatment, they are likely to try very hard to insure that the benefits do in fact accrue to the worthy target population, rather than to unintended freeloaders with no special claim on the public purse. The attendant restrictions can greatly complicate matters.

New York's most generous tax abatement scheme is a good example of this. Under this plan, designed to encourage rehabilitation of older housing occupied by lower income people, an owner can recover 75 percent of the cost of the improvements through tax reductions over 9 years. However, the improved property is subject to rent control, and the owner typically must forego rent increases he might otherwise be entitled to. As a result of this and other complications, the program is little used.

The administrative difficulties could be overcome by a general tax abatement or exemption for *all* new housing investment, not just that which satisfies complex administrative requirements. The selective tax abatement programs are moderate in size,[11] and therefore the reduction in taxes has a negligible effect in increasing property taxes on other types of housing. But an effective across-the-board exemption program for all new investment would be a different matter. It could result in a significant shift in the tax burden to older properties, including older properties occupied by relatively low income households. Therefore, such a program is a questionable one unless it is linked to steps to reduce the reliance on the property tax in general, such as those suggested in the preceding section of this study. And if there is a substantial reduction in reliance on the property tax in general, the need for special housing exemptions will be greatly reduced.

Deemphasis

In summary, the highest priority would seem to attach to deemphasis of the property tax per se. It is a generally inferior tax instrument, although not the worst of all possible taxes. But an inferior tax becomes a monstrous one if applied at high enough rates.

There *are* alternatives to ever-increasing property tax rates in urban areas, alternatives which require a willingness to accept real change in that most conservative of all institutions, local government.

11. The various New York City programs as of the end of 1965 covered 75,000 units, 2.5 percent of the city's housing inventory. City of New York, Committee on Housing Statistics, *Housing Statistics Handbook* (August 1966), table 1-3.

45. *New Communities*

EDWARD EICHLER and MARSHALL KAPLAN

New towns are supposed to do many things: reduce the journey to work, provide better housing and site planning, minimize public costs for schools and other services, and produce socioeconomic integration. Edward Eichler and Marshall Kaplan offer a critical analysis of these expectations and suggest that new towns may, in fact, increase social and economic segregation.

The general consensus on new communities has been that they can contribute greatly to the public good but that they require (1) financial aid, with certain strings attached, from the federal government; and (2) some added regulation by state and local government.

. . . Junior governments have the necessary power to provide such regulation if they care to do so. But the question is to what purpose such power should be put at any level of government.

Since the Johnson Administration is a strong supporter of a loan program to aid new communities, it is not surprising that one can find articulate justification for the program in the statements of the government's representatives in HHFA [Housing and Home Finance Agency, HUD's predecessor], even though these ideas did not originate primarily from within HHFA but represent the thinking of many experts. Its most comprehensive defense is to be found in a speech given at the University of Illinois by Dr. Robert Weaver, the director of HHFA. Because of its comprehensiveness, Dr. Weaver's speech (now published in book form)[1] serves as a useful basis for discussion. We wish to emphasize here that we respect Dr. Weaver as a dedicated public servant, and to state that he is presenting a position developed only after consultation with a great many city planners and developers. It is this position, and not Dr. Weaver as an individual, with which the following discussion is meant to take issue.

SCATTERATION, EFFICIENCY, AND THE JOURNEY TO WORK

Many contend that new communities will decrease the journey to work as well as to other activities. It is argued that this would save public costs for transportation, utility lines, school busing, etc. In addition, the residents of new communities would have the advantage of being close to a variety of facilities and services. As Weaver

Reprinted from Edward Eichler and Marshall Kaplan, *The Community Builders* (Berkeley: University of California Press, 1967), pp. 166-79, by permission of the publisher and authors. Originally published by the University of California Press; reprinted by permission of the Regents of The University of California. Edward Eichler is executive vice-president of the Klingbeil Company. Marshall Kaplan is a principal in Marshall Kaplan, Gans and Kahn, a firm specializing in economic and social planning and evaluation.

1. Robert C. Weaver, *Urbanization in the Middle and Late 1960's; The Lorado Taft Lecture* (Evanston: University of Illinois, March 18, 1964).

put it in his speech: "More rational development of the surburban areas would minimize transportation needs and utility line extensions. And, too, the development of satellite communities affording employment opportunities, as well as educational, recreational and commercial facilities, would serve the same purpose."

How are these advantages to come about? First, the supporters of new communities argue, such developments would contain higher densities than those of conventional suburbia. But the projected density for most new communities is 3 to 3.5 dwelling units per acre, which hardly indicates great compaction. Indeed, it would require density of at least triple this figure to make any major difference in utility or transportation needs than now exists. Since the 3 to 3.5 figure appears to reflect the mutual desires of house consumers, retailers, and industry, it is unlikely that a governmental agency could establish significantly higher densities, except by adopting extremely restrictive measures.

The supporters of new communities also argue that the communities offer greater opportunities for local employment, recreation, culture, and commercial activities than do other types of development. However, while such opportunities are brought about in new communities with a marginally higher degree of speed than normally, it is nonetheless the case that the development of surburban housing on fragmented parcels has consistently been followed by the appearance of industry, recreation, and commerce. In fact, one aspect of the urban-development critique, and a cause also of federally financed urban renewal, is the accurate contention that central cities are losing their industry and commerce. The point is, stores and plants *are* relocating in the suburbs. Moreover, there is little a community builder could do to attract such facilities to his particular project, even with the aid of any of the powers now available to government.

In Great Britain, the publicly initiated new towns do serve as industrial sites, but only because there are a host of formal and informal controls regulating industrial location. Theoretically a national policy to regulate industrial settlement could be enacted in the United States (in combination with a new community, new towns, or even a new metropolis policy), but this is far more drastic action than the advocates of new communities propose or, apparently, desire. Without such an effort, however, new communities will follow the regular pattern of development. Residents will arrive first, and the growth of local commerce and industry will follow. Moreover, as in Janss/Conejo[2] most new residents will be traveling farther to work, and to many other places, than they did before they moved. It is true that some recreation facilities are built very much earlier in new communities than they would be in other developments, but, as noted, the lakes, golf courses, and parks are more for providing symbolic investment protection for the residents than great opportunities for their enjoyment.

Finally, it has been argued that new communities would reduce utility extensions and transportation needs because the communities would develop more rapidly than do areas under fragmented ownership. At the moment, there is little evidence that this is so, but here government action *could* make some difference. State and local governments could give zoning and other advantages to selected new communities (by constructing a freeway to them, for example, or a university campus within them). If federal aids of this kind were passed along to the consumer in the form of lower prices, better houses, or more amenities, sales would obviously be spurred.

Still, if densities are not likely to be raised, the *total* amount of land consumed by a new development, whether it is in a new community or not, will remain the

2. Editors' note: A new community in Southern California.

same. Thus, those who are staggered by the fact that "the process of urbanization consumes a million acres a year,"[3] can find no consolation in the advent of new communities, with or without government aid or control.

But what about the prevention of "scatteration" which leaves holes of undeveloped parcels of land all over the place? Isn't this a beneficial consequence of new communities? Wouldn't it reduce the cost of public facilities and services and increase services? In the short run it might, but no reliable evidence has yet turned up which projects savings of sufficient magnitude to warrant the necessary rationing of land use and selection of some landowners for such gigantic favors.

Since the prevention of scatteration or, as it sometimes is called, sprawl, is emphasized so strongly by the supporters of new communities, it might be well to consider in more detail what the terms mean, what evils come with them, and what new communities might do about them. Harvey and Clark give the following definition:

> Sprawl, measured as a moment of time, is composed of areas of essentially urban character at the urban fringe but which are scattered or strung out, or surrounded by, or adjacent to underdeveloped sites or agricultural uses. A sprawled area has a heterogeneous pattern, with an overall density less than that found in mature compact segments of the city. Sprawl areas are less dense than would be found if the areas developed for housing would be developed with discipline exercised in the assembling of jig-saw puzzles by adding pieces from the bottom up.[4]

The authors go on to cite the causes of sprawl, among them tax laws, zoning regulations, mortgage policies, fragmented ownership of land, and the character of land developers. Clearly community building, as it has been discussed here, eliminates some of these factors. But to what extent are such defects critical? Harvey and Clark go on to identify two fundamental aspects of sprawl which most commentators have failed to recognize.

The first is time. Sprawl usually occurs at the fringe of a rapidly growing area. It is costly to the degree to which capital must be used to install sewer and water lines, roads, and so forth earlier than if development had proceeded in a more compact manner. However, since the area is growing rapidly, the gaps will be filled in quickly and the extra costs will be minimal. As Harvey and Clark argue: "A static or very short-run view on urban development permits an exaggeration of development cost per unit, which cost may in fact be modest on a unit basis once the development is viewed as a complete entity."[5]

Even more important is the second issue they raise—of who bears the extra cost, if any, of sprawl. Freeways are usually installed without regard to the specific character of urban development. Thus the capital cost of freeways is probably unaffected by sprawl. Sprawl may increase driving time and cost, but these burdens are borne by the resident not society. Again, most scattered projects (at least in California) must pay for the cost of longer runs for sewer and water mains. But here, too, it is the resident—not society—who pays the price.

However, in some cases this situation does not obtain. Electricity and gas, for instance, are supplied to almost any site, and the costs of their distribution are reflected in *general* rates. Thus, all users share the burden of capital outlay. In such circumstances,

---

3. President Johnson's message to Congress, March 12, 1965.

4. Robert O. Harvey, and W. A. V. Clark, "The Nature and Economics of Urban Sprawl," *Land Economics*, 41, 1 (February 1965): 1-9. Harvey is an economist, Clark a geographer.

5. Harvey and Clark, *op. cit.*

a change in laws and regulations is required so that the specific users pay the cost of their locational choice without subsidy from society as a whole.

It cannot be said that new communities necessarily reduce the extra costs which supposedly come from sprawl or scatteration, for usually communities leapfrog open land and so require extensions of utility lines. From society's viewpoint, however, their value is that these burdens accrue to the land itself, in the form of lower receipts to the landowner or higher costs to the new user. In any event, if one keeps in mind the concept of time, sprawl does not seem to result in additional economic cost of great magnitude. The same can be said about esthetics, for the unsightliness of scattered development is only temporary.[6] If one is concerned not just with scatteration but also with the visual quality of developed suburbia, one really is objecting to the taste of America's middle class. We find it difficult to believe that market-oriented new communities, aided by federal loans, will drastically alter such esthetic values.

Supporters of new communities are on fairly strong grounds when they cite greater open space as a likely consequence of new communities. To be more precise one might say that when community builders dedicate open land to a public agency or a homeowners association, the land is likely to remain largely undeveloped for a long time. When ownership is fragmented and open space is desired, the local government must purchase the land to prevent it from being used. If the government waits until surrounding land is developed, then the price it must pay becomes very high.

With community builders, however, the cost of the open land is added onto the price of the developed land. Thus, in effect new communities offer consumers the opportunity to pay for open space and amenities as part of their house purchase. Since there is no evidence in California that consumers will buy these benefits by trading off smaller lots, they necessarily must pay in some other fashion—a longer journey to work, higher prices, smaller houses, or a combination thereof. In any case, it should be noted that whatever the consumers decide, more permanent open space within a new community will mean more scatteration, an evil supposedly avoided by community building.

HOUSING MIX

The most persistent argument for aid to, and control of, community building is that it does not provide housing for lower-income families under present circumstances. It is argued that large enclaves of middle- and upper middle-class residents are in themselves inequitable and otherwise undesirable. This was the principal reason for the program proposed in the California Housing Report. Weaver puts the case simply when he writes: "There can be, and there should be, an economic mix in the population of new communities in a democracy."

But this represents a vast oversimplification of the situation. . . . [T]he very thing buyers in new communities hope to avoid is the inclusion of lower-income families. One can recognize this without approving of it. Further, it also appears that lower-income families are improving their residential status precisely by occupying the housing left vacant by the more affluent, and that most of the housing is closer to blue-collar employment than are the new communities. There is, no doubt, some amount of

6. There is a growing body of opinion questioning the supposed ill effects of sprawl. Indeed economist Jack Lessinger sees positive benefits in it.

"In general we hypothesize that scatter suits an economy where growth and technological change predominate. Compaction may suit a stabilized economy, without inequalities in the distribution of income, seeking optimization of its resources." Lessinger, *AIP Journal*, 28, 3 (August 1962).

subsidy which would induce lower-income families to move to new communities, and also to get higher-income residents to tolerate this. But such subsidies would certainly have to be far larger and more direct than a loan to the developer.

An increasing amount of economic separation seems more or less inevitable then. However, there are certain problems which might follow from this development that can, to an extent, be controlled. The first is the possibility that the wealthier members of society may use their spatial homogeneity to create local governments which would insulate them from contributing to the costs of the services provided for the less advantaged in the country's urban centers. However, the more taxes collected at the state and federal levels and then returned to local governments on the basis of population and/or need, the less meaning tax enclaves have. The country increasingly is operating in just such a manner. In California almost half the cost of primary and secondary education is borne by the state. The newly passed bill providing federal aid to education further contributes to the trend. . . .

The other serious problem that stems from separation on the basis of income is that it is also likely to mean racial separation. Yet how much can be done about this through any policy of controlling or aiding privately sponsored new communities? In regard to housing policy, it seems crucially important that a single, simple principle ought to be followed wherever possible. To improve the housing of those with low incomes, one should give direct aid and let the recipients make their own choice as to where they want to live. In 1965 Congress enacted a program of rental supplements which points in this direction. Direct loans at low interest rates and grants for homeownership would also be appropriate.[7]

Most other attempts to use more devious, although perhaps politically more palatable, devices have largely failed to get assistance to those who most needed it. Further, despite the good intentions of the proponents of federal aid to new communities, there is not much chance, for the reasons already outlined, that many families with low incomes would become residents of these developments. Once the loans were made, the FHA would be strongly interested in the financial security of the project. What would an administrator do when confronted with the quite plausible assertion that the market for low-priced houses is not big enough to support a new community and that, indeed, the few such houses that could be sold might severely decrease total sales?

SITE PLANNING, DESIGN, AND INNOVATION

Weaver, along with many other supporters of new communities, believes that in addition to attacking the broad social questions of public costs and the relationship of classes and races, new communities also will offer more efficient use of specific sites, more creative design, and even outright innovation. Commenting on the possibilities of efficient site planning, Weaver writes:

> Even if the cost of acreage increases, the price of a developed site to the homebuyer need not advance to the same degree. Indeed, good planning can produce improved lots at a lower cost to the home owner or renter. This has been, and can be, accomplished by greater clustering of dwelling units and inclusion of town houses and apartments on a portion of the available land in the development areas, so that the amount of land that has to be graded and improved is reduced. Streets and

7. State of California 4 percent loans to veterans are an example of such a form of direct subsidy. But such loans should be made on the basis of need rather than military service.

utility lines are shortened, cost of construction per dwelling unit is sometimes reduced at the same time that the number of housing units in the site is increased. In addition such site planning requires less bulldozing of trees, greater preservation of other scenic attributes, and wider possibilities of open space.[8]

Most of this argument is fallacious insofar as it implies that all these accomplishments are more likely to come about in new communities than in an amalgamation of subdivisions. The key word in the argument is one which has gained an almost mystical quality in the lexicon of land development—clustering. Clustering means the concentration of buildings on less land than would otherwise be used. The land that is thereby saved can be put to some public (or at least pleasing) use—a lake, golf course, a park—or it can merely be left untouched.

In some parts of the United States, local jurisdictions have restricted housing development to very large lots—one-half to four acres. Under such conditions, land can be better used in terms of economy, esthetics, and, ultimately, market response if houses are clustered on smaller lots (7,000 to 15,000 square feet). This is precisely what Rouse has proposed for Columbia.[9] . . .

Clustering can be accomplished even when ownership is fragmented. The kind of land ordinarily left unused is a mixture of hills, valley streams, rock outcroppings, etc. In other words, it is the land most difficult to develop and therefore least valuable in money terms. A county could make a master plan identifying such areas for open space and recreation, and then purchase them. The price would be nominal, especially if the land is bought before there is much surrounding development. Minimum lot sizes for the remaining land could then be reduced. The net effect would be exactly the same as clustering.

Government purchase of land for open space would raise the value of the land not purchased, but this is also what happens with a community builder. If a county felt that the benefits from such expenditures did not accrue to all its citizens, it could establish an assessment on the area affected. As residents and other land consumers took title, they would pay for the amenities, which again is what happens in a new community. The higher tax on the land, due to its increased value as well as the county's special assessment, would increase the probability of its sale for development. Holdouts might still occur, producing greater scatteration than in a new community. Since scatteration is not an unmitigated evil, this is not a serious drawback. Because landownership usually is not concentrated, and because its assembly is extremely difficult, government should devise methods for reaching its objectives with or without single ownership.

A different kind of clustering occurs when the maximum lot is already as small as 6,000 square feet (the case in most parts of California). In this situation, land can be freed for other uses, or higher densities can be obtained, only by attaching houses. This results in what is now called the "suburban town house." . . . Weaver seems to be promoting such a concept when he says: "This type of land planning runs counter to the tradition of a free standing house in the 'country' surrounded by a large lot; however, where it has been well done, the consumer response has been favorable."

Of course people differ on their definition of what is "well done," but most suburban

---

8. Weaver, *op. cit.*
9. Editors' note: A new community in Maryland being developed by James Rouse.

town house developments have not been favorably received by buyers. (. . . [T]he early evidence at Reston[10] does not in market terms justify Simon's decision to base his whole plan on this concept.) On the other hand, it can be argued that suburban town houses offer some people a physical arrangement not otherwise attainable and that sales will improve as time goes on. But the key point here is that whatever the demand for the type of house now or in the future, its development does not depend upon large-scale ownership. In 1964, over 100 townhouse projects were started in Orange County, California, none of which were in a new community.

A third way to produce clustering is to build more apartments on any given piece of land than might otherwise have been erected and then to transfer the land saved (assuming constant overall density) to open space or public use. Again, there is nothing intrinsic to new communities that would prevent this from happening elsewhere. If a county wants a higher density of apartments, it can achieve this by zoning regulations. It then can either purchase the unused land for open space or require that developers hold it, as a part of a quid pro quo for the apartments.

In predicting that new communities will bring a tide of new creative design and innovation, its supporters are on even more tenuous grounds. In the process of development, the community builder necessarily becomes a land manager trying to maximize the value of unused holdings. His essential job is to conserve, to make sure that nothing goes on the land which will have a harmful effect in the future. This is hardly a climate from which unusual physical forms are likely to emerge. In fact, one may well find community builders rejecting novel proposals of merchant builders because of the uncertain effect they will have on the value of the land. Simon, who is trying to make of Reston a "laboratory" for one new approach to suburban design, is an exception, who only proves the rule.

Problems of Federal Aid

New communities *do* offer some improvements in the physical environment and some choices which consumers have not often had. A new community offers a consumer the opportunity of paying either through a longer commuting time or a higher price for a house (or both) for parks, lakes, golf courses, and underground utilities. Whether he makes this choice for esthetic or status or investment reasons or to use the recreational facilities, is not relevant.

However, it is one thing to recognize a few product improvements and another to argue that public funds, through tax-exempt bonds or direct federal aid, should be used to aid in their creation. To whom would the benefits of such aid flow but either to present landowners or to the middle- and upper-income families who avail themselves of the opportunity to live in a new community? Thus, such aid would represent government's commitment to confer minor benfits upon the least needy families.

Moreover, a program of loans to community builders is fraught with paradoxes and pitfalls. In the first place, the developers most likely to apply for help are those with the least desirable and riskiest sites. An entrepreneur convinced he can do well without federal aid is not apt to subject himself to the myriad of controls that such aid would no doubt entail. Since the state of the art of market analysis is so low and since the terms of a loan can so markedly affect the rate of return, FHA would almost be bound to set conditions to try and insure success.

10. Editors' note: A new community in Virginia initiated by Robert E. Simon.

Again, what would constitute an acceptable rate of return on a loan and how is it to be calculated? These are questions FHA has not had to face because in all its dealings it could rely on past market transactions. But no history of the sales of 10,000-acre holdings is available to help determine questions of market value in the case of new communities. A vicious circle would be created. The value of land and of improvements can only be determined by sophisticated investment analysis which depends on one's ability to predict the capital costs and also demand, a highly unscientific affair. If the loan is favorable enough, almost any project will succeed because it will be able to withstand high early costs and slow sales. The effect of such favorable terms would be to increase artificially the value of the land.

Still another difficulty of providing community builders with the federal loans concerns the methods FHA would use to see that a builder's original plan is carried out. A FHA loan normally is based on a study of detailed plans and specifications, which the builder promises to follow. But is it possible or even desirable that the same method be adopted in regard to a 15-year project? How detailed can the plan of such a project be? To what degree can a builder adhere to it? With as much as $25 million committed to a single project, FHA in fact would have to permit changes to protect its insurance. Yet these changes might well be in conflict with the very purposes of the original program.

There is no need to go on endlessly describing the difficult decisions facing the government and the financial uncertainties involved in a program of such loans. Our case must rest on the claim that the risks are high and the potential benefits minimal.

Public Sponsorship

The second part of the new-communities section of the 1965 housing bill is a program of low interest rate loans to state land development agencies. This program is designed to achieve the same results as the program of direct loans to builders, with the difference that here the benefits of increases in land value at least would go to the government. But in so far as the results are the same, the program, in our opinion, is essentially no more valid.

There is one condition, however, under which public sponsorship might be useful: if it were made part of a program of research and demonstration. The building and development industry does not have firms large enough to engage in serious technological research. On the other hand, basic science and technology probably hold much that could be applied to make great improvements in local transportation, communication, air temperature control, illumination, more flexible houses, etc. The government would be spending its money wisely if it used it to ferret out these applications and then sought to test them in a development like a new community. Obviously, this is not the sort of research or the sort of risks a private sponsor would be willing to undertake.

A second kind of experimental program might involve racial integration. Very little is known about Negro demand for housing, but it is possible that Negroes are extremely reluctant to buy new housing. They may fear difficulties in the buying process itself or hostility from the other residents, and they may want to be assured that there will be enough Negroes in the project for a reasonable social life. (Such fears are probably strongest in working and lower middle-class Negroes.) A public or publicly funded nonprofit sponsor could be committed to maximizing opportunities in such a way that 10 to 30 percent of the residents would be Negro. The demonstration of what it would take to make such a project viable could provide sorely needed information on how to open up the suburbs to Negroes as they rise financially.

It cannot be stressed too strongly that such programs should be public efforts directed to the provision of *information,* and not the first step in a statewide or national program of public landownership. They should be part of an overall effort at the state and federal levels to improve the flow of information to local agencies, public and private.

46. *Private Participation in Low Income Housing*

MICHAEL A. STEGMAN

Of the several proposals for making investment in poverty areas attractive to private capital—the alternative approach to direct government action—the two most prominent recent ones have been the late Senator Robert F. Kennedy's bill to provide massive tax incentives and the National Housing Partnerships. Congress enacted and the President signed into law (1968) the National Housing Partnerships, and by 1970 it was just getting underway. Michael Stegman compares the two proposals and concludes that they are quite similar. It is important to recognize that the various programs discussed here that make use of tax credits and subsidize interest rates to builders and investors do not reduce housing costs to what is usually termed the "low income" level but are essentially programs that can assist families in the $5,000-7,000 income range.

In July 1967, the late Senator Robert F. Kennedy introduced Senate bill S.2100, designed to stimulate investment in low income housing in poverty areas of major urban centers.[1] Relying on the use of massive incentives to attract private capital, Kennedy pragmatically justified this approach on the basis of a history of similar means of tax incentives to achieve such diverse goals as encouraging the exploration of natural resources, constructing grain facilities, increasing the purchase of heavy machinery, developing U.S. rural farmlands, and increasing Puerto Rico's economic growth rate.[2] Yet, he was fought by those who deplored the use of federal income tax laws as an instrument of social policy and was subjected to blistering attacks by members of the Johnson administration, particularly Secretary Robert Weaver who called the bill a cruel hoax. Because the Kennedy Bill proposed a veritable arsenal of tax aids and outright cash subsidies to private investors willing to construct housing developments in ghetto communities, it might be worthwhile to use S.2100 as a yardstick to measure the extent and nature of federal commitments to the private sector recommended by each of the three study groups.[3]

Senator Kennedy suggested piggybacking a sufficient number of tax and other incentives to ensure after-tax returns to equity commensurate with the returns that might be expected in alternative investment outlets. This would be accomplished with a sliding scale of tax benefits that increased with the equity proportion of the investment,

Reprinted by permission of the *Journal of The American Institute of Planners*, 35, no. 3 (November 1969): 424-25, and of the author. Michael A. Stegman is an associate professor of city and regional planning at the University of North Carolina, Chapel Hill.

1. U.S., Congress, Senate, Committee on Finance, "Tax Incentives to Encourage Housing in Urban Poverty Areas," *Hearings on S.2100*, 90th Cong., 2d sess., 1967.

2. Ibid., p. 56.

3. Editors' note: The three groups are: National Advisory Commission on Civil Disorders (Kerner), National Commission on Urban Problems (Douglas), and President's Committee on Urban Housing (Kaiser).

with a minimum equity contribution of 20 percent required to participate in the program. To reduce the economic rents of project units, it was proposed to provide 50-year mortgages at 2 percent interest rates. For local communities willing to exempt such projects from property tax liability, the bill provided for federal subsidies to the communities in an amount equal to one-half of tax revenues lost. Project rents would then be pegged to return sponsors 3 percent on their equity investments, before taxes and depreciation.

To sweeten the after-tax returns to the developer who is probably used to seeking and securing somewhere around 15 percent on equity, S.2100 proposed the following sequence of incentives.

1. Tax credits to be allocated to investors in the year in which projects are completed. The sliding scale set a credit equal to 3 percent of project cost on a 20 percent equity investment and progressively greater credits up to a maximum of 30 percent of project cost for a 100 percent cash investment.

2. The use of a sliding scale depreciable life of projects, with a 20 year depreciable life for a 20 percent equity contribution all the way down to one of 7 years for a 100 percent cash investment.

3. Finally, to encourage the rapid turnover of capital, maintain after-tax returns at a satisfactory level, and increase community control over residential stock, the bill provided for capital gains tax forgiveness if projects were sold in the early years of ownership to tenant management councils, and the proceeds reinvested in similar ventures. The tax forgiveness benefit becomes highly significant in light of the accelerated depreciation allowances that would wear the tax shelter quite thin in a couple of years.

In short, S.2100 combined the use of extended mortgage terms, interest rate subsidies, property tax abatement incentives, tax credits, accelerated depreciation allowances, and tax forgiveness benefits to attract large-scale investors to the development of low and moderate income housing projects.

While none of the present studies recommended such comprehensive packages to assist the private sector, significant elements of the Kennedy proposal were suggested by each. This is so in spite of a Douglas Commission study that cautioned against the widespread use of the back-door spending route to housing subsidies. The solution most strongly pressed by the Kaiser Committee, and one written into law as Title IX of the 1968 Housing Act, moves strongly counter to the Kennedy bill and other similar proposals.

Title IX, known as the National Housing Partnerships (NHP) section of the Housing Act, pertains to the formation of broadly based national partnerships that would bring otherwise unrelated, private, profit-motivated investors together for the purpose of investing in low and moderate income housing developments. The NHP will consist of a general partner, a profitmaking corporation whose officers are appointed by the President, and as many limited partners as can be attracted from the private sector. The general partner will raise revenues through the sale of stock and contribute as much as 25 percent of needed equity for local housing projects throughout the country. Members of the partnerships will share in book losses to offset otherwise taxable income. While the partnership form is an accepted organizational framework and no new legislation was needed to legitimize the NHP, the Kaiser Committee suggested that putting it into legislation would serve as an open invitation to private industry to participate in low income housing.

It is important to note that the committee believes that the partnership notion will attract investors for two reasons, even without such additional incentives as are called for in the Kennedy Bill.

1. Since investments in low- and moderate-income housing projects are risky, the partnership approach will permit the spreading out of risk over a large number of projects.
2. The reasons why major corporations have not reacted positively to existing programs are that their management personnel are not familiar with the low-income housing investment area. The NHP, having long-range investment objectives and commitments, would be able to attract topflight management personnel who can competently manage investment portfolios.

Thus, while Kennedy and others have suggested that insufficient incentives exist, regardless of the organizational format adopted, to attract large-scale investors into the low income, inner-city market, Kaiser suggests that professional management of portfolios, sharing of book losses on the basis of existing federal income tax structure, and safety of numbers can act in concert to turn the tide. However, the Kaiser Committee does, in other sections of its report, suggest the need for substantial alterations in current financial and federal income tax arrangements surrounding limited-dividend housing programs.

Under the existing 221(d) (3) Below Market Interest Rate Program (BMIR), profit motivated sponsors are eligible to receive 90 percent, 40-year mortgages at 3 percent interest rates in order to develop moderate income housing projects, if they agree to limit themselves to 6 percent cash returns on their 10 percent equity investments. Assuming high levels of occupancy along with no unusual management and maintenance problems, the 6 percent cash return can be increased to satisfactory levels approaching 15 percent on equity as a result of tax savings available from taking normal depreciation on the buildings during the first 5 years or so of operation.

In relatively short order, however, the depreciation cover begins to wear thin, and it becomes economically rational to sell the project. Here is where the problems arise. If FHA permits the sale, then in the year in which the buildings are sold, the seller must pay off the unamortized portion of his mortgage and also pay a capital gains tax on the difference between the sales price and the depreciated basis of the property. The tax liability would, of course, have a substantial effect on the average yield on the investment. The Kaiser report estimates that if a project is sold for the amount of the unamortized mortgage (assuming 100 percent financing), thereby permitting the investor to recover his equity, the average yield on the property would be reduced to between 3 and 5 percent, depending upon when it is sold. Again, since many investors seek around 15 percent on equity, after taxes, the tax implications of such investments are quite serious.

In the private market, generally increasing real estate values minimize the significance of capital gains taxes since the taxes due can be paid out of profits from the sale. As the Kaiser Committee indicates, however, inflated sales prices on moderate income developments would force up rents and cannot be permitted. Therefore, some means of permitting the sale of such projects to, say, nonprofit sponsors are needed. These would have to allow investors to recover their equity and pay the tax liability while maintaining a satisfactory average overall rate of return on their investments. To accomplish this end, the Kaiser Committee recommends the consideration of three possible avenues. First, permit the transfer of limited-dividend housing to nonprofit sponsors at prices sufficient to recover equity and taxes due upon sale. Second, provide a 3 percent tax credit to limited-dividend sponsors in the year in which the projects are completed. This would balance out the tax liability due upon sale. Finally, the committee suggests tax forgiveness as another route to the same end.

Thus, the net result of the committee's recommendations is not, in principle, unlike that underlying S.2100. While the Kennedy bill did provide for larger depreciation allowances and tax credits, existing programs permit investors to earn greater returns before taxes. In fact, each of the three studies suggests increasing maximum permissible returns from 6 to 8 percent which, it is estimated, would necessitate a unit increase in monthly rentals of $2.50.

By providing increased cash returns and a mechanism for transferring limited-dividend projects to nonprofit sponsors, we would no doubt speed up the construction of low and moderate income housing developments. Professional investors are much more knowledgeable and efficient producers of housing than are nonprofit institutions such as churches. Thus, if projects are initially developed by professionals, managed by them for a few years until the kinks are out, and then spun off to nonprofit sponsors for the remainder of their economic lives, both the limited-dividend and nonprofit programs would operate more efficiently.

47.   The Private Sector and Community Development: A Cautious Proposal

CHESTER W. HARTMAN

A key housing policy issue is whether the government or private enterprise should develop, own, and operate subsidized housing. Chester Hartman reviews the potential benefits of private sector involvement as he raises the question of how much and what kind of government regulation, particularly in such areas as housing choice, tenant selection, location of developments, and population mix. He offers a model for a specific program to maximize the contribution of the private sector while retaining necessary public controls and maximum consumer sovereignty.

It is obvious that the private sector plays an enormous role in urban development and that the aggregate of individual private investment and location decisions has a profound impact on the shape of our urban areas and on the quality of urban life. This paper will confine itself, however, to the issue of participation of the private sector in publicly directed programs to solve pressing urban problems. More specifically, the paper will focus on the area of housing and community development, although the issues raised will, to a greater or lesser degree, be relevant to other urban problems as well. The underlying assumption of this paper is that attainment of certain public welfare goals for our cities and their inhabitants is the overriding issue; means, then, are determined according to the most efficient and efficacious way of achieving this end, not according to any preconceived social and economic philosophies or set of interests and allegiances.

The major questions to be asked are:

1. In what ways does the public mechanism fail to perform adequately in solving existing problems?

2. What advantages are there in placing greater reliance on the private sector?

3. What sorts of motivations and operative styles might lead to inherent conflict between public and private goals?

4. What forms of public control are needed to insure the congruence of private performance to public goals, and in what way might these controls reduce the level of public-private cooperation?

[A discussion of the first question is contained in Chester Hartman's "Politics of Housing" reproduced in Chap. 10 of this book.]

One of the distinct advantages to greater involvement of the private sector is the opportunity thereby presented to solve the dilemmas of insufficient motivation and inadequate jurisdiction. Regarding the issue of incentives, it is axiomatic that if these are made sufficiently attractive, the private sector will produce. . . . The obvious

Reprinted from U.S. Congress, Joint Economic Committee, *Urban America: Goals and Problems*, 90th Cong., 1st sess. (Washington, D.C. Government Printing Office, 1967), pp. 272-82 (edited), by permission of the author. Chester W. Hartman is senior planning associate, National Housing and Economic Development Law Project, University of California at Berkeley.

question that must be asked about utilizing the private sector to achieve a public welfare goal is: at what price? To allow for an increase in the rate of profit (either through tax credits or a higher rate of return on investment) results in higher housing costs to the consumer (and hence a need for greater subsidy if all income groups are to be served—or, barring that, a raising of the effective lower income limit served by the program) or in a shifting of costs to some other part of the public sector (i.e., in the form of foregone tax revenue). . . .

In the opinion of this writer, higher profits rates and/or tax breaks are an unnecessary, as well as unwise, feature of a low-rent housing program. The limited-profit approach (in most instances stipulated as 6 percent maximum, although with only a moderate amount of ingenuity the effective rate can be somewhat higher) would seem to offer sufficient incentive, if unnecessary red tape is eliminated and if builders have the opportunity to work rapidly and at a sufficient volume. Incentives can and should be offered to developers who demonstrate the ability to produce well and efficiently, but these incentives should be in the form of reduced capital requirements, which will permit the developer to operate on a large scale while tying up a minimum of his own capital. Considerable direct assistance can be given to private developers in the two areas where they find the greatest difficulties: financing and land acquisition. The direct low-interest loan reduces the cost of capital, one of the major components of high housing costs; and government assistance in assembling buildable sites (through eminent domain, use of land banks, and conveyance of tax-title property) and in reducing the cost of land through write-down subsidies (as is presently done under the urban renewal program) offers help in another critical area. This kind of aid, plus the creation of an operating climate in which private developers are allowed to make maximum use of their entrepreneurial skills, can effectively tie the private sector into a comprehensive program of housing and community development whose overall goals and strategies are determined by considerations of public policy.

Once set into motion, the private sector would be able to reproduce for families of low and modest income the variety and freedom of operation which it presently offers to families able on their own to pay the going costs for housing. Thus, the private developer can build anywhere within the metropolitan area (or outside of it), unhampered by narrow jurisdictional limitations and the continual political constraints imposed on a public agency. A loosening of the "suburban noose" around the central cities might then be facilitated, all the more so if progress can be made in modifying some of the restrictive zoning and subdivision regulations that presently characterize the suburban scene. . . .

It is clearly advantageous, then, to involve the private sector in community development programs, and incentives to greater private participation are not difficult to design. The key issue is to design a set of public policy controls that will at once be acceptable to the private sector and effective in keeping private participation within the confines of publicly established goals and strategies. Adherence to a general set of public policy controls becomes a quid pro quo for receipt of government aids. In effect, what is called for is a modification in the traditional absolute control over property exerted by landlords, in favor of a degree of public control over the tenancy of publicly assisted projects. To an extent, the present FHA 221 (d) (3) program provides precedent for this, as do some of the analogous state programs (such as New York's Mitchell-Lama program). In programs such as these, the private developer, in exchange for benefits received in the form of direct low-interest government loans, agrees to limit his profits and to place a ceiling on rents, as well as certifying that the annual income of prospective tenants falls below a stipulated maximum. These programs work well (apart from their limited volume), attributable in part to their concentration on middle income families. Once these programs begin to reach down into the low income group (all segments of this group, down to those with no income), new problems arise, which require even greater public supervision and control. In the first place, the kinds of government assistance to the private sector being discussed here—low-interest loans (approximately a 3 percent interest rate) and/or land acquisition assistance—are not in themselves sufficient to bring housing costs within the reach of very poor families, those earning under $4,000 per year. In order to permit families at these income levels to live in housing of this type, additional subsidies are needed, which ideally should be given to each individual family, adjusted according to the family's actual income. Supplementary individual family housing subsidies would permit the family to become a "sovereign consumer" in the housing market, with all the advantages this implies in terms of freedom of choice, more dignified treatment, and absence of invidious distinctions. A family would be eligible for this subsidy if its income (relative to household size) was inadequate to obtain decent housing on the private market. The family would apply to a public agency, with jurisdiction over an entire metropolitan area, which would establish the family's eligibility for a housing subsidy, and the amount of subsidy to be given, and would then issue a rental certificate to cover the gap between the family's paying ability (computed at roughly 20 percent of income) and the cost of obtaining decent housing on the private market. Under one system which has been suggested, these rental certificates would be tied into the program of inducements to private developers (which might be administered by the same metropolitan agency, to facilitate integrated planning), so that the rental certificates are usable only for housing that has been constructed or rehabilitated under the program of inducements to the private sector; correspondingly, a certain proportion of the units stimulated by this program of aids to the private sector must be made available to certificate holders.

There are a great many advantages to a program of this sort, including the provision of a "built-in market" for a portion of the privately produced housing and an enhanced freedom of choice for the housing consumer. The key issue here, however, is the requirement that a certain proportion of low-income families be accepted as tenants and the conditions under which this provision is implemented. Because it is in itself the critical feature of any program of public housing subsidies, and because it represents so well the kind of issue that is the source of potential public-private conflict and friction, this question of public control over tenant placement will be treated in some detail.

It is obvious to anyone familiar with the current housing picture that there is an enormous amount of prejudice toward, discrimination against, and maltreatment of low-income families on the part of private landlords. These families have severely limited housing choice, and little ability to cope with prevailing economic and political forces and hence are forced to endure a great deal of arbitrary and unjust treatment at the hands of the owners and managers of the housing they live in. Private landlords do not consider low-income families as desirable tenants, a sentiment traceable to a multitude of attributes, including race, family size, receipt of public welfare assistance, irregular family composition, life-style, personal behavior—to name just the more common sources of these attitudes and conflicts. Many issues are involved: To what extent is this prejudice based on real behavioral attributes which landlords find objectionable, as opposed to contemptuous preconceptions? To the extent that objectionable (destructive of property, antisocial) behavior exists, is it due to inherently different values and life-styles, to lack of necessary training and services, to general resentment against poverty and discrimination and/or specific resentment against the landlord? Is a really good enviroment (i.e., one which offers amenities, dignity, and control, in addition to safe and hygienic conditions) capable of altering people's behavior and outlook on life? But despite the complexity of the issue, one point stands out clearly: these families—who number in the millions—desperately need decent homes and environments, and if a program is developed for the maximum feasible participation of the private sector in attaining the national housing goal, then there must be complete assurance that families of low income will be full beneficiaries of the program and will benefit in a way commensurate with their needs for a healthy social environment and dignified treatment.

In summary, what is required is sufficient public supervision to insure that publicly assisted private developers accept a certain, mutually agreed upon proportion of low-income families at rents commensurate with their ability to pay, with the remaining units available at "normal" rents (i.e., rents established in accord with actual costs, including limited profit, and taking into account the subsidy that has been received in the form of low-interest loans and/or land write-downs). Low-income families who are eligible for and have received further subsidies in the form of rent certificates would apply for admission directly to the private developers, and developers would be required to accept these families (with consideration given, of course, to appropriate family size for the available units) on a first-come, first-served basis. In other words, no family could be rejected (once declared eligible by the public agency) on the basis of the traditional prejudices held by landlords against low-income tenants (incomplete household, receipt of welfare assistance, race, etc.). Naturally, once accepted, the family would be subject to eviction through normal legal procedures, for any of the causes that are the grounds for eviction of unsubsidized families: nonpayment of rent, willful destruction of property, severely antisocial behavior, etc.

The plan being described here (the basic outline of which was first introduced at a 1960 conference of the Metropolitan Housing and Planning Council of Chicago) requires resolution of two important, and related, issues of public policy: (1) what sorts of noneconomic criteria, if any, are to be used by the public agency in establishing the eligibility of low-income families for subsidization on the private market in the form of rental certificates? and (2) what is public policy to be regarding socioeconomic and racial "mix"?

At present, housing subsidization programs for low income families are characterized by a definite screening process, which serves to eliminate families with severe social problems. The rent-supplement program does this by giving the private developer complete control over tenant selection, the public housing program through an elaborate set of locally determined standards for tenan5 selection (the New York City Housing Authority, for example, has a list of 30 problem indicators, any one of which can serve to exclude a potential applicant). . . . This procedure does not emerge as grossly unjust in a situation where there is so great a discrepancy between the number of families who need assistance and the number of families to whom assistance can be given. But if and when we embark on a program of sufficient magnitude to provide all families with decent housing, then the question of social exclusion becomes of very great importance, since establishment of a strict set of criteria would exclude a very large proportion of needy families from the benefits of the program. The exact answer to this question must be worked out on the basis of further discussion and debate among those who make public policy and further investigation into the nature of these social problems and how amenable they are to social services and the influence of an improved social environment. If the program is to have any real impact, however, it must be as inclusive as possible; if families are to be excluded at all from the benefits of this program, it must be only on the basis of narrowly defined, clearly pathological patterns that make the family demonstrably unsuited for the kind of social and physical environment being developed under this program. An approach of this sort will necessitate: (1) a comprehensive program of social services for all families who are aided by the program and are in need of this assistance; (2) development of a specific alternative program to assist those families judged to be unsuited for general community living (along the lines of the special services and projects which some European countries have initiated to aid "hard-core" problem families). The program's inclusiveness will, of course, tend to clash with inherent tendencies toward exclusiveness on the part of the private sector, and it is clear that public regulation and control will be most needed in this area. To the extent that truly healthy environments can serve to reduce various forms of social pathology (particularly those aspects which are of most concern to landlords and neighbors: property destruction and antisocial behavior)—and this writer firmly believes that this effect will occur, if we will only design the proper kinds of housing and environments—then initial resistance to inclusion of low-income families may, over time, be sharply reduced. But unless the attempt is made, and unless the program can serve those most in need of help, extensive private participation cannot be recommended.

The issue of what sort of population mix to have in these publicly assisted, privately developed units is another matter which must be guided by public policy. If we are to insure that low-income families will be served by this program, it will be necessary to establish for each development a certain percentage (or range) of low-rent and "market"-rent units. This will require some overall conception as to whether residential heterogeneity or homogeneity is the more appropriate goal for the community and conformance of the private sector's operations to this goal. It is, of course, possible to produce homogeneous low income developments under this program, merely by establishing that all of the units should be made available to holders of rental certificates. (This, in fact, is what is happening in many of the present developments which are making use of the rent supplement program.) On the one hand, this will insure that a larger number of the units produced will go to low-income families. On the other hand, it will reproduce one of the more objectionable features of present public housing projects—the concentration of low income families in a single location, easily identified (and hence stigmatized), isolated from diverse (and presumedly healthier) influences. We haven't sufficient knowledge yet to make a judgment about this specific issue, and some amount of experimentation is called for to answer the following question: To what extent are current public housing projects unhealthy places to live in simply because of this population concentration, and to what extent are they objectionable on other grounds (public ownership and management, oppressive design, lack of amenities, excessive regulations, etc.) which might be eliminated through a market-oriented, privately operated program, thereby making the issue of population concentration irrelevant? We must also have some concrete evidence regarding the question of whether a residential mixture of different socioeconomic groups is inherently more democratic and healthy, or whether, as some persons maintain, this kind of mixing can only exacerbate conflict, cause resentment, and destroy incentive, as well as destroying some valuable forms of cultural vitality and cohesion. We must also know more about what kinds of "mix" people will accept, and under what conditions, so that the market component of the program can be adequately planned for. Thus, the proportion of low-income to moderate-income families might run anywhere from 10:90 to 70:30, depending on different conditions and demands, and middle-income families may find living next to low-income families more acceptable, if they have the assurance that the proportion will not exceed a stipulated maximum.

The question of racial mix must also be determined by public policy, rather than left to private entrepreneurs. Although it goes without saying that discriminatory tenant selection policies would not be permitted in these government-assisted developments, the more realistic issue has to do with location and site selection, which will to a large extent determine the clientele for the program and the racial composition of the development. Obviously, projects built in nonwhite sections of the city will find few white applicants, while nonwhites may, for a variety of reasons, be reluctant to move into developments located in white areas. The program should plan for a wide range of locational choices and should insure that a sufficient number of private developments are planned for all areas of the metropolis, in order to reflect the full spectrum of residential demands and options. As the program develops and as the housing demand pattern for moderate- and low-income families manifests itself, the public agency can adjust the location and site selection decisions of private developers accordingly.

The advantages of the program that has been developed in this paper are manifold.

1. Through widespread use (limited only by the total potential demand) of low-interest loans and other inducements to private developers, the private sector is given the tools and incentives needed to participate fully in this newly opened housing market, making maximum use of its own capabilities and motivations.

2. Insofar as possible, this program reproduces for low income subsidized families the variety, choice, and conditions of occupancy that prevail in the private housing market. A variety of locations, housing types, tenure options, and neighborhood patterns become available for the first time to a segment of the population which has traditionally been excluded from exercising any meaningful options in the market. To the extent that free choice results in more satisfactory living conditions and a greater commitment to the home and community, a critical new element has been introduced into the government's program of housing subsidization.

3. Public controls are kept to a minimum and are exercised only at key points of intervention, as opposed to the all-encompassing system of controls that characterize the present public housing program.

4. A metropolitan approach to solving the nation's housing problems is possible for the first time.

Clearly, the costs of a program of this scale represent a new concept for public intervention.[1] But at the same time it offers a vast array of new opportunities for the private sector, for the development of new forms of public-private cooperation,

---

1. An estimated annual expenditure of $7 to $8 billion is based on calculations derived from 1960 census figures on the incomes of families living in substandard housing and 1959 Bureau of Labor Statistics figures on the costs of obtaining "decent but modest" housing in our metropolitan areas. It is a figure that will be reached incrementally, over the course of a few years; it is an expenditure which is of unknown duration, since we cannot predict when present income distribution patterns will be sufficiently altered so that a greater number of families presently in need of housing subsidies will be able, without assistance, to afford housing on the private market; and it does not assume that housing costs will significantly decrease in the near future due to a technological revolution in the housing industry, brought about by a vast increase in the volume of production (an assumption made by many that this writer, at least, finds highly questionable). In short, it is a rough estimate, but one which in all probability will not be too far off the mark once the detailed investigations necessary for a precise estimate are made.

and, most important, for the increased satisfaction of the needs and desires of the housing consumer. This single concrete proposal has been developed in such great detail, in part because it seems to offer the most promising solution to one of the two or three most pressing current urban problems, and in part because it illustrates so well the necessary interplay of the public and private sectors, the critical "pressure points" for government intervention, and the modifications needed in the private sector's usual modus operandi, if it is to play a role in meeting the society's most urgent obligations.

48. *Toward a New Federal Housing Policy*

IRVING H. WELFELD

A currently popular idea for housing the poor is to provide each household with sufficient funds to buy a standard dwelling unit—the housing allowance plan—rather than using rent supplements, subsidized interest rates, or other means to reduce the price of dwelling units. Irving Welfeld reviews the economic inefficiency and political palpability of present and past programs, and recommends using housing allowances to house the poor in existing stock and subsidizing middle income families into new housing to fulfill the nation's production goal.

For some time now, it has been generally accepted that the federal government has a duty to ensure adequate housing for all its citizens. Accordingly, Congress has enacted a long series of housing subsidy programs that include public-private partnership and many sophisticated financial devices. Yet despite all these efforts extending over several decades, the results have been meager. . . .

Why have we done so badly? The fault lies with the basic approach we have taken. The key components of the present subsidy system—public housing, below market rate interest, rent supplements, and the interest subsidy programs—all aim at solving the problem by providing new dwelling units for the poor. Because there is a shortage of standard units and many of the poor live in substandard units, the production of new units for the poor has the virtue of conceptual simplicity and goodness of intention. Unfortunately, the strategy does not work.

As a matter of elementary logic the strategy of providing new housing for our poorest citizens is an expensive way of approaching volume production. Let us assume that the total amount of government assistance and the cost per housing unit are constant. It follows that the number of units that can be subsidized varies inversely with the rental paid by the occupant of the average unit. And as the income of the potential occupant declines, the amount of the necessary per-unit subsidy increases—and the total number of units that can be subsidized declines. *Thus, by choosing to provide new housing for our poorest citizens, the federal government has adopted a most expensive strategy for increasing the nation's housing supply.*

What we mean by expensive can be seen by briefly examining the subsidy needed for public housing. The development of projects is financed through the sale by local housing authorities of bonds to private investors. The federal government guarantees the full cost of the principal and interest on the bonds. In recent years the actual payment has equaled 95 percent of the debt service. The estimated total development cost of a unit of public housing in early 1969 was $17,250. Assuming

Reprinted from *The Public Interest*, Spring 1970, pp. 31-43 (edited), by permission of the publisher and author. Copyright © 1970, by National Affairs, Inc. Irving H. Welfeld is in the Office of the Undersecretary of the Department of Housing and Urban Development.

a 40-year amortization and an interest rate of 5.55 percent, the annual federal payment for each new unit of public housing comes out to $1,018.

Moreover, interest on these bonds is exempt from federal taxes. The resulting revenues loss to the federal government is estimated to be 40 percent of the interest rate. For a $17,250 unit, this comes to another $283 per year.

These two amounts, which total over $1,300 annually, may be considered the minimum federal subsidy for a unit of public housing. But there are additional subsidies as well. A federal contribution of $120 per unit per year is available for housing units occupied by an elderly family, a large family, a family of unusually low income, or a family displaced by urban renewal or a low-rent housing project. If the public housing development is located on an urban renewal site, there usually is a substantial write-down on land costs, a large fraction of which are paid for by the federal government.

Nor is the federal government the only source of subsidies. The exemption of the bonds from local income taxation results in a revenue loss at the local level. Moreover, the projects are exempt from local real estate taxation. It is true that the local housing authority makes "payment in lieu of taxes," but such payment rarely exceeds 10 percent of the shelter rents of the projects and is considerably smaller than expected tax revenues from new commercial, industrial, or residential development.

In light of these many subsidies, a conservative estimate of the total subsidy for a unit of public housing would be $1,500. This is a rather startling figure especially if compared to the market cost of decent housing in a suitable living environment. The most recent government statistics on standards of living tell us that a 5-room unit in sound condition—with complete private bath, fully equipped kitchen, hot and cold running water, electricity, central or other installed heating, in a neighborhood free of hazards and nuisances, and with access to public transportation, schools, grocery stores, and play space for the children—could be obtained in metropolitan areas for approximately $1,400.

Assuming a rent-to-income ratio of 20 percent, such a unit costs approximately $800 more than a family with an annual income of $3,000 can afford. But the public housing subsidy is approximately double that amount! When that subsidy is added to the rent paid by such a family, *the total cost of the new public housing unit would be about $2,000, or approximately 150 percent of the amount that a decent secondhand unit rents for on the open market. . . .*

The slow pace of present programs is explained not only by the economic inefficiency of the approach, but also by its political unpalatability. There is a basic inequity built into the "new housing for low income families" approach. A policy of taxing Peter to provide housing for Paul, who would otherwise live in squalor, has a simple appeal to human generosity. But a policy of taxing Peter to provide better housing than his own for Paul requires an almost saintly degree of altruism.

Congress in order to avoid the charge that the program will build "penthouses for the poor" has attempted to resolve the problem by limiting the amenities (both structural and environmental) of the new unit, thereby avoiding both the need for large subsidies and the possibility that those who don't have it will nevertheless be able to flaunt it. Accordingly, every housing subsidy program requires that the unit not be of "elaborate or extravagant design.". . .

Other ways of limiting expenses have had equally unfortunate consequences. For instance, Congress has set various upper limits on permissible pre-unit rents, construction costs, and mortgage amounts which have made it impossible to build new units in the major cities and suburbs of the North and West.

Attempts have also been made to channel the location of the housing so as to limit environmental amenity. A building, even of superior quality, to house the poor may not offend one's sense of equity if it is placed in an inferior neighborhood. If Peter has to pay for Paul's housing, he need not be forced to live next to Paul. . . .

The present federal housing approach is impaled on the horns of interlocking political and economic dilemmas. New housing for the poor must be of sufficient quality to serve a market for at least the life of the mortgage (usually 40 years). It must, therefore, if it is not to be functionally obsolete many years prior to its attaining physical obsolescence, include certain facilities which were yesterday's (and possibly today's) luxuries. The dangers of false economy go beyond the structure itself. If the model tenements of the 19th and early 20th centuries are the building blocks of today's slums, the overly modest projects of today may be the cornerstones of the slums of tomorrow. Yet plain political reality makes it improvident to ignore the taxpayer argument that the necessity to provide decent housing for all is no reason to provide better housing than the unit in which he, the taxpayer, lives. . . .

The obvious question at this juncture is why has federal housing policy continued to receive support in Congress. Part of the answer is to be found in a law of political physics—that a program in being tends to stay in being. But there is an additional explanation that has to do with the peculiar dynamics of liberal and conservative opinion in Congress. Faced with the need to do *something* about poor housing, liberals seem willing to accept a policy that produces only tiny numbers of housing units in the hope that, someday, the American people will rise up en masse and remove the constraints that vitiate that policy. Meantime, these liberals are content to wage a slow and ineffective struggle that aims at the merest marginal improvements. The conservatives also acknowledge the need for more housing but are deeply uneasy about the political principles implicit in the subsidy program. Yet as long as only a token number of units are built—usually in someone else's district—they are willing to go along with existing policy.

Federal housing policy is thus a classic instance of the art of muddling through. Neither conservatives nor liberals are satisfied with the results of that policy, but both groups continue to accept it because there are seemingly no alternatives. Given that failure to perceive alternatives, the most remarkable thing about federal housing programs is not that they are hampered by limitations, but rather that they exist at all.

SOME POPULAR ALTERNATIVES

. . . If housing subsidies are needed, then perhaps they should be limited to *existing* units. Certainly this is a logical extension of the previous analysis. One virtue of this strategy is that the required federal payment per-unit would be smaller. The cost of the previously used, secondhand, 3-bedroom unit on the private market was approximately $1,400 per year. Even assuming no contribution by the tenant, this is $100 less than the minimum subsidy for an average unit of new public housing. Given the same total amount of subsidy, the smaller unit subsidies would increase the number of families which could benefit from a housing subsidy program.

Such an approach is also attractive on political grounds. The provision of standard used housing is a response that seems more nearly commensurate with the problem. Given the fact that the commandment requires only that we love our neighbors as ourselves, but not more so, it is far more likely that American voters, 98 percent of whom are living in existing units, will find such a program a more palatable way of moving toward the Golden Rule.

There are two basic ways to provide a subsidy which bridges the gap between the rent the poor can afford and the rent the market demands for existing units. The government could subsidize a particular dwelling unit, thereby reducing the required rent, or it could subsidize a particular individual, thereby increasing the amount he has available for housing. In the former approach, the occupant loses the subsidy if he moves; in the latter approach, the subsidy moves with the occupant. Both these approaches are now used on a small scale. . . .

In the past few years the latter housing allowance approach has acquired a considerable popularity among liberals. . . .

. . . [E]ven if programs restrict use of the subsidy to standard units, a used housing subsidy is of value only in areas in which there are vacancies in standard units—but that is not the typical situation we face today.

Thus even the housing allowance program shares many of the weaknesses of the project subsidy system and has some of its own as well. Unless one envisions that rental allowances will be raised to the level of public housing subsidies, or that the subsidy will be extended to those who are not poor, the expectation of upgrading slum properties or stimulating new construction through the housing allowance program is nothing more than a pipe dream. Indeed, as even the Kaiser Committee conceded, the most likely result of such a program would be, not the production of new housing, but the raising of rents on existing units. As long as it is directed exclusively at the low income segment of the housing market, a housing allowance program is no more effective an alternative to the current system of federal policy than Tweedledum was to Tweedledee.

A CONSTRUCTIVE ALTERNATIVE

It is clear that there are direct linkages between the production of new housing and the improvement of the lot of those who are housing poor. But if we are to achieve our national housing goal, *the question of housing production must be divorced from the question of housing assistance to low income families.* It seems reasonable to join these objectives because many of the poor are ill-housed. But the history of federal housing policy demonstrates that the result of this connection is more like a short circuit than a shortcut.

There *is* an alternative. If we must simultaneously achieve large-volume production and provide the poor with decent housing, there is no reason why we have to follow a single path to achieve these two objectives. And my suggestion is that the federal government should actually begin to follow a double path. It should pursue the objective of increasing housing supply by *subsidizing middle income households;* and it should alleviate the housing problem of the poor by *subsidizing low income families.* The effect, hopefully, would be to increase housing turnover and thereby free a sizable portion of the existing housing stock for (subsidized) poor families.

Such a strategy would do away with the need for building further public housing projects; it will not, however, negate the need for providing housing assistance to low-income families in order that they may afford to move into vacated housing. For this purpose either a variant of an existing used housing program or a new housing allowance program seems to be a perfectly adequate device.

What is required, above all, then, is a new program that will stimulate the construction of new housing for those who are not poor, and especially for those in the middle ranges of the income spectrum. . . .

[The author here offers a detailed program for the production of housing for middle-income families.]

By attempting too much, each of our present housing programs produces too little. By attempting in one fell swoop to produce large numbers of new housing units for the poor, each program has managed to antagonize a substantial part of the population. In order to redress their grievances, Congress has imposed restrictions that cripple the program's capacity either to produce very many units or to help very many of the poor. This in turn dashes the expectations of the poor and raises the need for new legislation, which starts the vicious cycle in motion again.

The alternative approach set forth here dissolves the bond between the production problem and the poverty problem. The new framework separates subsidies to facilitate new housing production from subsidies to alleviate the housing problems of the poor. Through these means it is possible to create a harmony of political interests and an economically efficient system. It might even be deemed a virtuous circle. Serving the needs of middle-income families has obvious appeal in a predominantly middle-class society. It also provides substantial benefits to poor families by allowing existing standard units to "flow down" to lower-income families. This in turn makes the more politically acceptable forms of assistance to the poor economically viable, thereby resulting in the achievement of both goals—the elimination of poor housing and of housing poverty.

49. *The Lessons of Pruitt-Igoe*

LEE RAINWATER

In many ways Pruitt-Igoe is a symbol of all that is wrong with our approach
to the housing problems of the poor. In this 12,000-person public housing
project, hailed by the architectural magazines when it was built in 1955-56,
many of the 11-story buildings have been demolished. Against the background
of this social, financial, and architectural disaster Lee Rainwater looks at
the living patterns and adaptive styles of the project's lower class Negro
inhabitants and concludes that more than a housing strategy is needed. In
order for the slum poor to achieve their aspirations the condition of poverty
itself must be eliminated, and this can be done only through an income
strategy as opposed to an approach that stresses provision of special remedial
services.

The Pruitt-Igoe Housing Project is in St. Louis. Built in 1954, the project was the
first high-rise public housing in the city. It consists of 33 11-story slab-shaped buildings
designed to provide housing for about 2,800 families. At present, it houses about
10,000 Negroes in 2,000 households. What started out as a precedent-breaking project
to improve the lives of the poor in St. Louis, a project hailed not only by the local
newspapers but by *Architectural Forum*, has become an embarrassment to all concerned.
In the last few years the project has at all times had a vacancy rate of over 20 percent.
News of crime and accidents in the project makes a regular appearance in the newspapers, and the words "Pruitt-Igoe" have become a household term—in lower class
Negro homes as well as in the larger community—for the worst in ghetto living.

The description of Pruitt-Igoe which follows and the implications drawn are based
on a three-year study which I, together with a dozen colleagues, have been conducting.
Pruitt-Igoe is not offered as typical of slum conditions in the ghetto—no other public
housing project in the country approaches it in terms of vacancies, tenant concerns
and anxieties, physical deterioration. Rather, Pruitt-Igoe is interesting precisely because
it condenses into one 57-acre tract all of the problems and difficulties that arise from
race and poverty, and all of the impotence, indifference, and hostility with which
our society has so far dealt with these problems. Processes that are sometimes beneath
the surface in less virulent slums are readily apparent in Pruitt-Igoe. And because
Pruitt-Igoe exists as one kind of federal government response to the problems of
poverty, the failure of that response is worth contemplating.

THE DUMPING GROUND

Pruitt-Igoe houses families for which our society seems to have no other place. The
original tenants were drawn very heavily from several land-clearance areas in the

Reprinted from *The Public Interest*, Summer 1967, pp. 116-26, by permission of the publisher
and author. Copyright © 1967, by National Affairs, Inc. Lee Rainwater is a professor of sociology
at Harvard University.

inner city. Although there were originally some white tenants (Igoe was built for whites, Pruitt for Negroes, but a Supreme Court decision outlawing segregated public housing resulted in an "integrated" project in its earlier years), all of the whites have moved out and the population is now all Negro. Only those Negroes who are desperate for housing are willing to live in Pruitt-Igoe—over half of the households are headed by women and over half derive their principal income from public assistance of one kind or another. The project has proved particularly unappealing to "average" families, that is, families in which there is both a mother and father and a small number of children. Thus, while the overall vacancy rate has run between 20 and 25 percent for several years, the vacancy rate in 2-bedroom apartments has been in the 35-40 percent range.

Life in Pruitt-Igoe, and in the St. Louis ghetto generally, is not quite as flamboyant as in Harlem, but it has the same essential characteristics. As sociologists have discovered each time they have examined a particular lower-class community in detail, the lower class lives in "a world of trouble."

In the slum, people are continually confronted with dangers from both human and nonhuman sources. Public housing removes some of the nonhuman sources of danger (like rats, or faulty electrical wiring), but can replace them by others, as when children fall out of windows or into elevator shafts in Pruitt-Igoe's high-rise buildings, or burn themselves on exposed steam pipes, or cut themselves on the broken glass outside. After about two years of intensive field observation in the Pruitt-Igoe project, our research team administered a questionnaire to a representative sample of tenants to discover how extensive were some of the difficulties we had noticed. Let me list some of the troubles which over half of this representative sample of tenants characterized as "a very big problem" in the project.

A few of these problems had to do with the design and maintenance of the project.

> There's too much broken glass and trash around outside.
> The elevators are dangerous.
> The elevators don't stop on every floor, so many people have to walk up or down to get to their apartments.
> There are mice and cockroaches in the buildings.
> People use the elevators and halls to go to the bathroom.

However, by far the greatest number of troubles that people complained about had as much to do with the behavior of their fellow tenants as it did with design and maintenance problems per se.

> Bottles and other dangerous things get thrown out of windows and hurt people.
> People who don't live in the project come in and make a lot of trouble with fights, stealing, drinking, and the like.
> People don't keep the area around the incinerator clean.
> The laundry rooms aren't safe: clothes get stolen and people get attacked.
> The children run wild and cause all kinds of damage.
> People use the stairwells and laundry rooms for drinking and things like that.
> A woman isn't safe in the halls, stairways or elevators.

Given these kinds of experiences it's hardly surprising that, although the great majority of the tenants feel that their *apartments* are better than their previous dwelling units, only a minority demonstrate any real attachment to the project community, and most would very much like to move out to a neighborhood that would be nicer and safer.

It is also understandable that a good many of them develop a rather jaundiced view of the public housing program. Thus, when we asked tenants what the government was trying to accomplish by building public housing and how well this had in fact been accomplished, we got answers like these.

> "They were trying to put a whole bunch of people in a little bitty space. They did a pretty good job—there's a lot of people here."
> "They were trying to better poor people (but) they tore down one slum and built another; put all kinds of people together; made a filthy place and so on."
> "They were trying to get rid of the slum, but they didn't accomplish too much. Inside the apartment they did, but not outside."

Other troubles also make life difficult for the project tenants. For example, we asked our sample to indicate from a list of various kinds of aggressive and deviant behaviors how serious and how frequent they felt such behavior to be. One cluster of items turned out to be judged by the tenants as both highly serious and very frequent (over half of the people characterizing these behaviors as very frequent).

> Holding somebody up and robbing them.
> Being a wino or alcoholic.
> Stealing from somebody.
> Teenagers yelling curse words at adults.
> Breaking windows.
> Drinking a lot and fooling around on the streets.
> Teenagers getting in fights.
> Boys or girls having sexual relations with a lot of different boys or girls.

In short, though some social scientists have quarreled with Kenneth Clark's emphasis on the "tangle of pathology" in the ghetto, it would seem that at least this sample from one federally supported ghetto shares his views.

THE LOWER-CLASS ADAPTATION

The observer who examines the lower-class community in any detail perceives an almost bewildering variety of difficulties that confront its inhabitants. But if one wishes to move from simple observation to understanding and on to practical action, it is necessary to bring some order into this chaos of troubles, problems, pains, and failure. That is, one must move from a description of *what* lower class life is like to an understanding of *why* it is that way.

Let us start with an inventory of behavior in the lower-class community that middle-class people think of as hallmarks of the "tangle of pathology" of slum and ghetto worlds:

> High rates of school dropouts.
> Poor school accomplishment for those who do stay in.
> Difficulties in establishing stable work habits on the part of those who get jobs.
> High rates of dropping out of the labor force.
> Apathy and passive resistance in contacts with people who are "trying to help" (social workers, teachers, etc.).
> Hostility and distrust toward neighbors.
> Poor consumer skills—carelessness or ignorance in the use of money.
> High rates of mental illness.
> Marital disruptions and female-headed homes.
> Illegitimacy.
> Child abuse or indifference to children's welfare.
> Property and personal crimes.
> Dope addiction, alcoholism.
> Destructiveness and carelessness toward property, one's own and other people's.

All of this behavior is highly disturbing to middle-class people—and most of it is even more disturbing to the lower-class people who must live with it. It is not necessary to assume that all lower-class families engage in even some of these practices to regard such practices as hallmarks of the pathology of the lower-class world. Lower-class people are forced to live in an environment in which the probability of either becoming involved in such behavior, or being the victim of it, is much higher than it is in other kinds of neighborhoods. From the point of view of social epidemiology, then, this is a high-risk population.

Behavior of this kind is very difficult for most middle-class observers to understand. If, however, this behavior is seen in the context of the ways of life lower-class people develop in order to cope with their punishing and depriving milieu, then it becomes much easier to understand. Much of the social science research dealing with lower-class life in general, or with particular forms of deviant behavior such as juvenile delinquency, has sought to place these kinds of behavior in their contexts. As a result of these studies, we now understand that the "unreasonable" behavior which so often perplexes outsiders generally arises as a logical extension of the styles of life that are available to lower-class people in their efforts to adapt to their world.

The ways people live represent their efforts to cope with the predicaments and opportunities that they find in the world as they experience it. The immediately experienced world of lower-class adults presents them with two kinds of problems.

1. They are not able to find enough money to live in what they, and everyone else, would regard as the average American way. Because of inability to find work or only work at very low pay, they learn that the best they can hope for if they are "sensible" is despised housing, an inferior diet, a very few pleasures.

2. Because of their poverty, they are constrained to live among other individuals similarly situated—individuals who, the experience of their daily lives teaches them, are dangerous, difficult, out to exploit or hurt them in petty or significant ways. And they learn that in their communities they can expect only poor and inferior service and protection from such institutions as the police, the courts, the schools, the sanitation department, the landlords, and the merchants.

It is to this world that they must adapt. Further, as they grow up, they learn from their experiences with those around them that persons such as they can expect nothing better. From infancy on, they begin to adapt to that world in ways that allow them to sustain themselves—but at the same time often interfere with the possibility of adapting to a different world, should such a different world become available to them. Thus, in Pruitt-Igoe, eight-year-old girls are quite competent to inform the field worker that boys and men are no damn good, are not to be trusted, and that it isn't necessary to listen to or obey your mother because she's made such a mess of her life.

We know from sociological studies of unemployment that even stable middle- or working-class persons are likely to begin to show some of these lower-class adaptive techniques under the stress of long-term unemployment. In the lower class itself, there is never a question of responding to the stress of sudden deprivation, since a depriving world is often all that the individual ever experiences in his life, and his whole lifetime is taken up in perfecting his adaptation to it, in striving to protect himself in that world and to squeeze out of it whatever gratification he can.

STRATEGIES FOR SURVIVAL

It is in terms of these two cardinal characteristics of lower-class life—poverty and a potentially destructive community—that lower-class individuals work out their strategies for living.

In most of American society two grand strategies seem to attract the allegiance of its members and guide their day-to-day actions. These are the strategies of the good life and of career success. A good-life strategy involves efforts to get along with others and not to rock the boat; it rests on a comfortable family environment with a stable vocation for husbands which enables them to be good providers. The strategy of career success is the choice of ambitious men and women who see life as providing opportunities to move from a lower to a higher status, to "accomplish something," to achieve greater than ordinary material well-being, prestige, and social recognition. Both of these strategies are predicated on the assumption that the world is inherently rewarding if one behaves properly and does his part. The rewards of the world may come easily or only at the cost of great effort, but at least they are there for the individual who tries.

In slum worlds, little in the experience that individuals have as they grow up sustains a belief in a rewarding world. The strategies that seem appropriate are *strategies for survival*.

Three broad categories of lower-class survival strategies can be observed. One is the strategy of the *expressive life style*. In response to the fact that the individual derives little security and reward from his membership in a family which can provide for and protect him, or from his experiences in the institutions in which he is expected to achieve (the school, later the job), individuals develop an exploitative strategy toward others. This strategy seeks to elicit rewards by making oneself interesting and attractive. In its benign forms, the expressive style is what attracts so many middle-class people to the lower class—the fun, the singing, the dancing, the lively slang, the spontaneous gratification of impulse. But underneath the apparent spontaneity, the expressive style of lower-class people is deadly serious business. It is by virtue of his ability to manipulate others by making himself interesting and dramatic that the individual has an opportunity to get some of the few rewards that are available to him—whether these be gifts of money, a gambling bet won, the affections of a girl, or the right to participate in a community of peers, to drink with them, bum around with them, gain status in their eyes. The individual learns by his expressive ability to "work game" on his peers, to "sound" on them, to "put them in a trick" (thereby raising his status by lowering the other fellow's). While the expressive style is central to preserving the stability and sanity of many (particularly younger) members of the lower class, the pursuit of expressive and self-dramatizing goals often results in behavior which makes trouble for the individual both from his own community and from representatives of conventional society. Dope addiction, drunkenness, illegitimacy, "spendthrift behavior," lack of interest in school on the part of adolescents—all can arise in part as a result of commitment to a strategy of "cool." For example, in Pruitt-Igoe teen-age boys drink, and some smoke marijuana, in order to be able to loosen up enough to develop a "strong game" (i.e., a really persuasive line with peers or girls).

When the expressive strategy fails—because the individual cannot develop the required skills or because the audience is unappreciative—there is a great temptation to adopt a *violent strategy* in which you force others to give you what you need. The violent strategy is not a very popular one among lower-class people. There is little really cold-blooded violence toward either persons or property in the slum world; most of it is undertaken out of a sense of desperation, a sense of deep insult to the self. Yet this strategy does not seem as distant and impossible to them as it does to the most prosperous.

Finally, there is the *depressive strategy* in which goals are increasingly constricted to the bare necessities for survival (not as a social being, but simply as an organism).

This is the strategy of "I don't bother anybody and I hope nobody's gonna bother me; I'm simply going through the motions of keeping body (but not soul) together." Apparently this strategy of retreat and self-isolation is one that is adopted by more and more lower class men and women as they grow older, as the payoffs from more expressive strategies begin to decline.

HOPES AND ASPIRATIONS

And along with these survival strategies, lower-class people make efforts to move in the direction of the more conventional strategies of the good life or (occasionally) of career success. One can observe in the lives of individual families (or in whole groups, during times of extraordinary demand for lower-class labor) a gradual shift away from the more destructive components of these survival strategies. It is from observations such as these, as well as from interviews about the lower-class people's hopes and aspirations, that one learns that lower-class styles of life are pursued, not because they are viewed as intrinsically desirable, but because the people involved feel constrained to act in those ways given the deprivations and threats to which they find themselves subject. *The lower class does not have a separate system of basic values. Lower-class people do not really "reject middle-class values." It is simply that their whole experience of life teaches them that it is impossible to achieve a viable sense of self-esteem in terms of those values.*

But lower-class people are also intimately alive to how things might be different. They know what they would like if only they had the resources of the average working-class man—they would want a quiet, rather "square" life in a quiet neighborhood far from the dangers, seductions, and insults of the world in which they live. In the slums, there is no personal preference for—or sociological value attached to—matrilocal families, or a high incidence of premarital sexual relations resulting in unwanted pregnancies, or living alone as a deserted or divorced wife and having a boyfriend because you're afraid that if you remarry your welfare will be cut off or your new husband will not prove a stable provider. Lower-class people are not easily confused between how they must live and how they would like to live. What they might wish to preserve from the expressive heritage of lower-class ways (particularly when, as among Negroes, those ways provide a kind of ethnic identity and not just a class identity) they feel that they can preserve while living a more stable kind of life. Lower-class people would not find it nearly as agonizing as some intellectuals seem to feel they would to try to reconcile their traditions and their aspirations.

SERVICES OR INCOME?

How can we help the slum poor achieve their aspirations? Whatever our precise answer to this question, it obviously must involve eliminating these people's poverty.

The elimination of poverty has a very simple referent. Since poverty is a relative matter—that is, relative to the total resources of the society to provide a life of particular material quality—the elimination of poverty means that the present income distribution of the nation, in which a small group of the population earns a great deal of money, a large proportion earns a more moderate amount of money, and a small proportion earns very little money, must be changed by moving that bottom portion up into the middle category. In short, the current diamond-shaped income distribution must be changed into one which has the shape of a pyramid. (I am speaking here about *family income* rather than individual income. There is certainly nothing wrong about a teen-age boy earning $1.50 an hour while he goes to school, or while he learns a trade. But there is something very wrong about that kind of an income for a head of the family with two or three children, or for a man who would like to be the head of the family but cannot afford to be.)

But there is disagreement—among experts and ordinary citizens alike—about the best way to achieve this. That is to say, there are basically two competing approaches implicit in the various programs for doing something about poverty. One, by far the most entrenched at present, might be called the *services strategy;* the other is the *income strategy*.

The services approach involves the design of special services for the poor. Some of these services have as their goal enabling the poor to earn an income which would make them no longer poor (as in the Job Corps and other job training programs, or over a generation's time as in Project Head Start). Other services are designed to help poor people more directly—as in special health programs, community action programs, consumer education programs, etc.

The problem with the services approach is that to a considerable extent it carries the latent assumptions either (*a*) that the poor are going to be permanently poor and therefore must have a vast network of special services, or (*b*) that the poor can be changed—by learning productive skills, by learning how to use their money more wisely, by developing better attitudes, etc.—*while they are still poor*, and that once they have changed they will then be able to get rid of their poverty.

I think these assumptions are extremely pernicious ones. Whatever characteristics the poor have which interfere with their upward mobility, they have by virtue of the fact that they *are poor*. To persuade a housewife harassed by the problems of supporting a family of 4 on $125 a month that she would be better off if she learned better consumer skills, or even to participate in a job training program for a relatively low-paying and insecure job, is to bring to bear a very weak intervention against the massive problems to which she has to adapt. It may be better than nothing, but it's certainly not much better than nothing.

A second problem with the services approach is that the priority of needs of the poor is categorically established when the service programs are set up. Even if these service programs are decided with "the maximum participation of the poor," it is nevertheless true that many poor families might have their own individual priorities. For example, the federal public housing program provides a service to each household in Pruitt-Igoe in the form of a subsidized apartment that costs about $545 a year. This amounts to one-fifth of the mean family income of the tenants in the project. It is very likely that, from the point of view of the needs of many of the families who live in Pruitt-Igoe, this $545 could be put to better use.

It seems to me that one should ask of any comprehensive poverty program what dollar expenditure per poor family served that program represents, and then one should ask further whether the package of services this money represents will accomplish more than would the income itself.

For example, the Council of the White House Conference on "To Fulfill These Rights" recommended that one program to help do away with Negro disadvantage could be to increase the average school expenditure per child by $500 per year. Consider a poor family with three or four school children. Such an increase would mean devoting $1,500 to $2,000 a year to better educational facilities for that family's children. Yet might it not be that an increase of $1,500 to $2,000 in that family's income would have as much or more educational effect on those children because of its effect on the family environment?

One final problem with the services approach needs to be considered. All that we know so far of our ability to provide services to the poor suggests that it is extremely difficult to design them so that they do not have the effect of emphasizing the stigma of poverty. To provide efficient service which does not stigmatize seems a political and administrative enterprise that is beyond our capabilities. Most current federal thinking in the labor and welfare area seems much too blandly to assume that we have the skills to develop really effective services for such a special population as the poor. (Again, see the report of the Council of the White House Conference "To Fulfill These Rights," with its proposed "Metropolitan Jobs Councils," "Rural Jobs Task Force," "Comprehensive Year-Round Employment, Training and Counseling Programs," etc.) Yet most of those who have studied the actual operation of service programs for the poor find these programs lacking in both efficiency and humanity.

In contrast, the income approach goes a long way toward avoiding the difficulties that past experience suggests are inherent in the services strategy. Here the task is to develop a set of economic programs that have the direct result of providing poor families and individuals with an adequate income. There are good reasons, from the social science information now available to us, for believing that the most powerful and immediate resource to assist the poor to cope with their problems is money. We know that when a man has a job and an adequate income he is more respected in his home, and he is less likely to desert or divorce his wife. We know that, under these circumstances, parents are more optimistic about their children and more likely to teach the children, by example as well as by words, that they have much to gain from pursuing their educations through high school or beyond. In short, if one wishes to reverse those effects of lower-class adaptations that are unconstructive, the most direct way of doing it is to strike at the root of the problem—at the lack of an income sufficient to live out a stable, "good American life."

Those economists who have pursued this line of thinking have suggested various ways in which the poor can be both given money and encouraged to earn money. I am not an economist and though I have my own preferences in this area, I see no need to express them here. What I do wish to stress, rather, is that a genuine attack on income inequality is a precondition for any serious urban program—whether it be in housing, education, or health. In a good deal of the social planning going on today, the question of providing income for the poor is regarded as subsidiary to the provision of urban services. I would turn the priorities around the other way. It is only when the poor are disentangled from hopeless poverty that we can think creatively about providing services for urban Americans—one kind of service, for all urban Americans.

50. *Income Strategy and Housing Supply*

DICK NETZER

> According to Dick Netzer's analysis, an "income strategy"—giving the poor additional income—would produce, in the short run, a demand for housing services greatly in excess of the supply. This demand, in turn, would lead merely to increased prices, with little improvement in housing quality. Netzer concludes that an income strategy must be accompanied by government measures to speed the response of the housing supply.

Clearly, the policies used during the past 20 years have been inadequate or inappropriate, especially for low-income urban families. Postmortems on past policies are seldom interesting or useful, but it is worthwhile considering whether past as well as present policies may not involve an error of a fundamental nature.

In nearly all American cities, building and housing codes define the physical characteristics of the lowest quality housing units that it is permissible to build. Construction technology, work practices and wage rates, land prices, building materials costs, and interest rates determine the prices at which such minimum quality housing units must sell or rent. It turns out, of course, that these prices are higher than can be afforded by families in the lower half of the income distribution. As has been pointed out,

> . . . the income which any household must attain to rent or buy adequate quality housing without spending too high a proportion of its total income on housing is significantly higher than the official "poverty level" as defined by the Social Security Administration, which is based on costs of an adequate diet rather than on costs of adequate housing. There are millions more "housing poor" households in the United States than "food poor" households.[1]

This, too, is not a recent development. Lower-income families seldom have been able to afford *new* unsubsidized housing in cities. Instead, they occupy older housing that is less attractive to its earlier occupants and therefore commands lower prices or rents. But the prices or rents for older housing units are too high for the urban poor unless the housing units are grossly overcrowded by poor families or unless the old housing has greatly deteriorated in physical terms. Here, too, building and housing codes and the community's determination of acceptable minimum housing standards are at work: we are unwilling, as a nation and as individual cities, to tolerate gross overcrowding and physical deterioration.

The set of housing policies prevalent in the United States works on the cost side of the imbalance between the costs of minimum standard acceptable housing and

Excerpted from Dick Netzer, *Economics and Urban Problems* (New York: Basic Books, 1970), pp. 73-75, 77-79, by permission of the publisher and author. Copyright © 1970 by Basic Books, Inc. Publishers, New York. Dick Netzer is a member of the faculty of the Graduate School of Public Administration at New York University.

1. Anthony Downs, "Moving Toward Realistic Housing Goals," in Kermit Gordon, ed., *Agenda for the Nation* (Washington, D.C.: Brookings Institution, 1968), p. 147.

the income necessary to pay for these costs. We subsidize rents (in public housing); we subsidize land costs; we provide interest rates on mortgages far below the market; and we worry about means to reduce actual construction costs. A wholly different approach would be to concern ourselves largely with the income side: raise incomes of the urban poor . . . and let the private housing industry satisfy the greatly expanded effective demand for housing. Clearly, this would be administratively much easier, for a wide range of governmental housing programs could be dismantled, but would it work? . . .

If . . . the demand for housing is today reasonably sensitive to income, as people become better off they will abandon low-quality housing and slum neighborhoods. This would seem to argue that income transfers would be as efficacious as housing subsidies in improving the housing conditions of the poor. But there are some further difficulties in the income transfer strategy.

One is a short-term difficulty. If the incomes of the central-city poor were rapidly increased, the immediate effect would be a sharp rise in the price of existing housing stock. Few central cities have any supply of unoccupied decent housing into which people could move now that their higher incomes permitted them to pay higher rents or prices. More generally, the addition to the supply of housing that can be provided by the construction industry within a short period is only a small fraction of the existing housing supply. If 5 million poor families suddenly had the income to command better housing, house prices and rents would rise sharply during the three, four, or more years it would take, under the most favorable conditions, to expand the nation's housing stock by 5 million units above and beyond that necessary to accommodate the normal increase in new families being formed. Since central cities have relatively little vacant land on which to build and since the minority-group poor are concentrated there, the price and rent increases would be especially severe in the central cities.

In addition, the income transfer strategy may not help in changing the character of whole neighborhoods. Our national housing policy is not concerned solely with the physical characteristics of an individual housing unit but more generally with the quality of the physical environment in which children in poor families grew up: the housing unit itself, the building, the block, the neighborhood. This larger environment cannot be transformed by improving a single building in a slum neighborhood.

Moreover, it is doubtful whether it is really sensible to expect that greatly increased incomes will result in improvement or replacement of individual buildings. Both the individual households that might buy housing units (with the higher incomes) and the investors that might be attracted by increased housing demand are unlikely to put much money into scattered buildings in a generally squalid neighborhood. The ownership of slum housing typically is highly fragmented and therefore the potential private housing investor does confront exactly this situation. Thus, the response to a pure income transfer strategy is likely to be an effort to leave the old neighborhoods, rather than their reconstruction under private auspices.

In short, a housing strategy as well as an income strategy seems essential, if the housing problems of the urban poor are to be successfully attacked. That strategy must provide rapid increases in the total supply of housing available, so that higher incomes are not dissipated in higher prices with little improvement in quality. It must also include governmental action to deal with the needed upgrading of whole neighborhoods. Public intervention usually means subsidy, in direct money terms or indirectly in the form of lowered interest rates, the use of public powers to condemn property, and the application of managerial energy and administrative talent.

51. *Housing and Public Policy Analysis*

ARTHUR P. SOLOMON

Rational housing policy requires explicit economic, social, and environmental objectives on which to base program choices. However, public policy objectives usually are not formulated with clarity, and the costs and benefits of programs designed to meet these objectives have seldom been measured. In this paper Arthur Solomon measures and compares the performance of three major low income housing programs with respect to the social and economic criteria of maximizing aggregate housing consumption, promoting equal residential opportunities, closing the housing gap in the most cost effective manner, and equitably redistributing housing consumption. Solomon indicates that opposite conclusions can be drawn by using different evaluative standards, but he concludes, overall, that consumer-oriented strategies such as leased public housing, housing allowances, and income maintenance will be less costly and more equitable. He suggests that national housing policy should be redirected toward these more consumer-oriented strategies, although it is likely that this approach will meet great resistance from powerful production-oriented lobby groups.

In recent years the debate over national housing policy has intensified. Growing federal involvement in the housing market, dissatisfaction with existing subsidy approaches, and stepped-up efforts to evaluate social welfare programs have generated interest in the formulation of a more effective federal housing strategy. Essentially, policymakers have been faced with a choice between supply and demand strategies for improving the housing conditions of the poor. To pursue a supply strategy, the federal government can either directly subsidize the construction or rehabilitation of dwellings for the poor or assist in the production of housing for higher income households, hoping thereby to set off a chain of moves in which vacated units eventually "filter down" to the poor. To enhance the purchasing power of the poor—the demand-side approach—the government can subsidize the actual rents paid by low income tenants (as in the leased public housing program), provide a general income maintenance subsidy (an unrestricted cash transfer), or earmark income transfers for housing (a restricted cash transfer through housing allowances or rent certificates). In other words, the federal government has the choice of subsidizing housing production or of directly enhancing the effective demand of poor consumers.

Historically, housing assistance programs have been supply-oriented, involving the redistribution of housing through the transfer of goods-in-kind (e.g., provision of specific housing goods and services as in public housing). Some proposed strategies, however, would provide for the redistribution of housing through money transfers, restricted to housing consumption or in the more general form of an income supple-

Copyright © 1972 by Arthur P. Solomon. Reprinted by permission of the author. Arthur P. Solomon is assistant professor of urban studies and planning at the Massachusetts Institute of Technology and associate director of the M.I.T.-Harvard Joint Center for Urban Studies.

The author wishes to acknowledge the assistance of Kate Gardner in preparing this paper. In addition he would like to thank Robert Schafer, Chester Hartman, Jon Pynoos, and John Kain for their helpful comments on earlier drafts.

ment. The indirect expansion of consumption opportunities through manpower training, compensatory education, and other programs aimed at increasing the productive
capacity and earning power of disadvantaged groups is also designed to redistribute
income and thereby housing consumption as well.

Those who favor demand- or consumer-oriented strategies argue that cash transfers
would be the most effective means of income redistribution.[1] They maintain that
a negative income tax or housing allowance would be less costly to federal and local
governments since there would be no tax shelters, developer profits, or increases
in municipal service requirements. Without administrative intermediaries, more of
the subsidy appropriations would reach target groups.[2] Moreover, since income maintenance and housing allowance schemes would rely on the existing housing stock, they
would overcome some of the major objections of suburban communities to the construction of low- and moderate-income housing: incompatible land uses, overcrowding
of schools, creation of traffic congestion. Consumer subsidies would leave the choice
of housing type, structural quality, and location with individual families, avoid concentrations of subsidized units, and thus make it easier for low income households to
gain access to suburbia. To the extent that households wished to remain in central
cities, their increased rent-paying ability would provide inducements to landlords to
improve their structures, thereby reducing housing deterioration and abandonment.

The arguments for consumer-oriented strategies are intuitively convincing but
inadequate as a basis for decision making. Past experience has shown that intuitive
solutions to urban problems are not always effective and occasionally produce results
opposite to those intended. The complexity of the decision-making process, and the
importance of political considerations have made rational policymaking difficult.
Professional judgments about the relative performance of the major strategy alternatives have been largely inconclusive. Most evaluations of housing programs have
emphasized administrative, ideological, and design features.[3] But there has been little
effort made to compare strategies in a systematic and informed manner.

Yet as the nation approaches the last quarter of the 20th century, there is need
for a more open and explicit approach to national housing policy formation. Federal
budgetary appropriations for housing assistance are close to $2 billion per annum,
about 7.8 million households are unable to afford "standard" housing, and there
are myriad proposed or existing schemes for providing decent shelter. Under such
circumstances—limited federal resources, a serious housing problem, and a variety
of program options—choices are unavoidable. Obviously, political considerations will

1. See, for example, Ira S. Lowry, "Housing Assistance for Low-Income Urban Families:
A Fresh Approach"; and Frank deLeeuw, "The Housing Allowance Approach," U.S., Congress,
House, Committee on Banking and Currency, *Papers submitted to Subcommittee on Housing Panels*,
92d Cong., 1st sess., 1971.

2. Frieden estimates that between one-fifth and one-half of current total federal housing
subsidy dollars goes for federal and local administrative expenses and for tax benefits to investors.
See Bernard J. Frieden, "Improving Federal Housing Subsidies," U.S., Congress, House, Committee on Banking and Currency, *Papers submitted to Subcommittee on Housing Panels*, 92d Cong.,
1st sess., 1971.

3. Exceptions are the recent studies of conventional and leased public housing by Frank
deLeeuw, "The Cost of Leased Public Housing," Urban Institute Working Paper S8-112-5, 1971;
the analysis of the efficiency and equity effects of public housing by Eugene Smolensky, "Efficiency
and Equity Effects in the Benefits from Federal Public Housing Programs in 1965," U.S., Congress,
Joint Economic Committee, 93d Cong., 1st sess., 1972; and the Rand Corporation studies of
housing in New York City, Ira S. Lowry et al., *The Demand for Shelter* (The New York City
Rand Institute, 1971).

always influence such choices; yet, a more rational decision-making process can yield more social benefits for the same expenditures. Underlying this essay, then, is the belief that evaluating and comparing policy alternatives on the basis of objective criteria can sharpen policy choices and reduce reliance upon ideological assertions, political horse trading, and undocumented rhetoric.

While the nation lacks a consensus on national housing goals and therefore on criteria for comparing the performance of policy alternatives to achieve such goals, there are a number of standards or criteria for measuring the efficiency and equity effects of national housing programs. The following list, although by no means exhaustive, should command wide support as a basis for policy choices.

1. *Maximize aggregate housing consumption*.   The most explicit national housing goal is to improve aggregate housing consumption, especially for low income households. Thus, one objective criterion for our analysis is to determine which housing program contributes most to overall economic consumption.

2. *Promote equal residential opportunities (freedom of choice)*.   The availability of unrestricted access to a variety of housing types, tenure arrangements, and geographic areas is an essential element of social welfare since unimpeded economic and racial mobility provides access to jobs, educational opportunities, environmental amenities, and other consumer preferences. It is necessary, therefore, to establish the relative performance of each program with respect to fostering economic and racial integration.

3. *Close the housing gap in the most cost effective manner*.   The housing subsidy program which most effectively closes the housing gap is the one which moves the largest number of households from substandard to standard housing for a given resource expenditure. This standard provides an estimate of the least costly approach for providing low income families with decent shelter.

4. *Redistribute housing consumption equitably*.   The efficiency with which each strategy redistributes housing consumption is measured by determining the proportion of the total subsidy dollars which actually reaches the target population (vertical efficiency) and the comprehensiveness of the program in assisting all of the eligible target population (horizontal efficiency).

In this essay, the performance of the federal government's three major low-income housing programs—conventional public housing, leased public housing, and rent supplements—is compared with respect to each of the foregoing social objectives. For illustrative purposes, empirical estimates are made using data obtained from these federal programs as they operate in the City of Boston.

Since in the conventional public housing and rent supplement programs the federal government subsidizes housing production while in the public housing leasing program the demand of poor tenants is directly enhanced, our analysis provides a basis for drawing some inferences about the choice of a national housing policy. In the conventional public housing program the federal government assumes the full capital costs of each development by retiring the local housing authority's (LHA) 40-year serial bonds. By paying the full production costs, the federal government is able to provide new housing at below market rents. On the other hand, the rent supplement program relies on private developers who are encouraged through federally insured and subsidized mortgages to increase the supply of low-rent housing. Under contract with the Federal Housing Administration (FHA) a private sponsor constructs or substantially rehabilitates dwelling units. The rents of some or all of these dwellings are brought within the reach of the poor through mortgage interest rate subsidies and direct rental assistance paid to the owners on behalf of qualified tenants.

Unlike the foregoing production programs, the public housing leasing program tends to operate by increasing consumer demand. Under this program authorized LHA's provide accommodations for the poor in dwellings leased from private owners. To enhance the ability of low income households to occupy standard housing, the government pays to the private owner the difference between the rent which the poor tenant can afford and the fair market rent of the unit. Although the public housing leasing program is not a "pure" demand-side strategy, since the subsidy is linked to a particular dwelling and cannot move with the tenant, it still is the only existing categorical housing assistance program which resembles a demand-oriented approach.[4] In the following sections, then, we are able to measure and compare the performance of supply and demand strategies for housing the poor, according to the four criteria outlined above.

MAXIMIZING AGGREGATE HOUSING CONSUMPTION[5]

Federal housing programs have both direct and indirect effects on housing consumption. For the program participants there is an opportunity to live in standard housing at below market rents. At the same time, subsidized housing creates benefits for nontenants who value a reduction in slum conditions or receive satisfaction from assisting poor households. These program effects are referred to as tenant and nontenant housing consumption benefits, respectively.

To measure the aggregate (tenant and nontenant) effect of federally assisted programs on housing consumption, it is necessary to trace the adjustments of the existing stock which result from the addition of subsidized units through new construction, extensive rehabilitation, and the leasing of existing housing. By estimating the adjustments in supply and demand generated by housing programs, the change in the equilibrium price and quantity of housing services consumed can be determined. This gives an aggregate measure of housing consumption added. The calculation of supply and demand adjustments, however, is a complex task. Without a complete model of the urban housing market, assumptions about the behavior of that market are necessary. This essay assumes, therefore, a competitive housing market with a supply schedule that is almost perfectly elastic.[6] A perfectly elastic supply schedule means that the amount of housing services available for consumption changes as soon as there is a change in demand, and by an equivalent amount. Thus, a 10 percent increase in housing expenditures will result in a 10 percent increase in the housing services available for consumption. Undoubtedly, the supply of low-rent hous-

---

4. A small-scale experimental housing allowance program was incorporated into the Omnibus Housing Bill of 1970. The housing allowance is a direct subsidy to low income households designed to improve their housing condition. The experiment is being conducted jointly by the Department of Housing and Urban Development's Research and Technology Division and the Urban Institute.

5. We define housing consumption in terms of the housing goods and services which a household receives when it rents or purchases a home: a particular location, neighborhood, environment, quality of schooling and other municipal services, as well as the specific physic l structure. One unit of housing service is that quantity of service yielded by one unit of housing stock per unit of time. See Edgar Olsen, "A Competitive Theory of the Housing Market," Chap. 19 in this book.

6. For a detailed analysis of the full implications of this assumption, see Arthur P. Solomon, *Housing the Urban Poor: A Critical Analysis of Federal Housing Policy* (forthcoming), chap. 3.

ing is less than perfectly elastic due to differences among structures in their conversion costs, the existence of specialized markets (for poor or minority households), institutional barriers, and other factors such as union practices and building codes. There is, however, some evidence that housing supply is relatively elastic with respect to both income and price.[7] Moreover, the scale of current subsidy programs is quite small, and therefore the increased demand results in little price inflation. Hence, our assumption that an increase in housing expenditures would result primarily in an increase in housing services (through maintenance and repairs) rather than an escalation of prices seems appropriate.[8]

The effect of different supply elasticity assumptions on the measure of housing consumption added is critical to our analysis and can be illustrated by contrasting the change which results from the construction of new public housing, a supply-oriented strategy, with the leasing of existing units, a demand-oriented strategy. For the purpose of this illustration we make the extreme assumption that the supply schedule is either perfectly elastic or perfectly inelastic.

With a perfectly inelastic supply of housing services, the market does not respond to a shift in housing demand, and the leasing of existing units causes rent increases without commensurate improvements in housing quality. For example, subsidies which raise poor families' housing expenditures by 25 percent will result in an average rent increase of 25 percent, while the quantity of housing services available for consumption remains the same. There would be no consumption benefit. Therefore, a perfectly inelastic supply implies the need for government assisted construction programs which directly increase the supply of housing to meet market demand (e.g., conventional public housing). On the other hand, with a perfectly elastic supply every additional dollar of housing expenditure results in the provision of an additional dollar of housing consumption. The total quantity of housing services increases since the owners of smaller bundles of housing services increase their maintenance expenditures while owners of larger bundles allow their dwellings to filter down to a more profitable submarket, eventually meeting shortages through new construction.[9]

With a perfectly elastic supply schedule, housing programs which directly increase the supply (new construction or upgrading of existing dwelling units) have no effect on the equilibrium price or the quantity of housing services. The government's action merely replaces a similar response by the private sector, and there will be no change in aggregate housing consumption. Thus, if government agencies charge the market price for the housing services provided through government-assisted construction programs there will be no consumption benefit. The existence of a perfectly elastic supply, then, favors housing allowances or income maintenance strategies. In order to provide an empirical measure of the actual consumption benefit, several additional assumptions are necessary: (1) that on an aggregate basis, subsidized tenants do not reduce their own housing expenditures; (2) that the value which tenants place on direct consumption benefits plus the value which nontenants place on indirect con-

---

7. See, for example, Frank de Leeuw, "The Demand for Housing: A Review of Cross-Section Evidence," *Review of Economics and Statistics*, February 1971, pp. 1-10; and Richard F. Muth, "The Demand for Non-Farm Housing," in *The Demand for Durable Goods*, ed. Arnold C. Harberger (Chicago: University of Chicago Press, 1960), pp. 29-96.

8. This assumption overstates slightly the relative advantage of leasing existing units with respect to the measure of housing consumption added since there will be some price inflation, especially in the short run.

9. For a more thorough discussion of the behavior of a competitive housing market see Edgar O. Olsen, op. cit.

sumption benefits equal the cost of producing the additional housing services; (3) that the local housing market is in equilibrium—that is, that market rents reflect differences in housing structures, neighborhood environments, municipal services, etc. Under these conditions, the assumption of a nearly perfect supply elasticity means that the demand strategies create a significant consumption benefit, whereas the supply or production strategies create a minimal benefit. Since the tenants in the production programs such as conventional public housing are, however, charged less than the market price for the housing services they receive, there is a housing consumption benefit. The appropriate measure of the housing consumption benefit of each program, then, is the dollar amount of the government's subsidy. The method for calculating the dollar value of the subsidy is set forth below.

Conventional public housing is intended for low-income families, generally for those with annual incomes of $6,500 or less for a family of 4. Because most tenants previously occupied substandard units, public housing undoubtedly provides an improvement in housing quality. The housing consumption benefit (the dollar amount of government assistance) for public housing is the difference between the tenant's rental payment and the estimated rent for comparable housing on the private market. The private market rents for comparable units are taken from the Boston Area Survey.[10] In the Boston *public housing leasing* program, standard private units which conform to local housing codes are leased for low income families at prevailing market rents. Since the majority of leased housing tenants also previously lived in substandard housing, their participation in the subsidy program also involves an improvement in housing and environmental conditions. Tenants pay a fixed proportion of their income (usually 20 to 25 percent of net family income) toward rent rather than the full market rent of the leased unit. The portion of the market rental paid by the local housing authority is the value of the consumption benefit. The *rent supplement* program enables poor families to occupy new or substantially rehabilitated housing at below market rents. The federal rent supplement payment is the difference between the private market rent for the housing and the tenant's rental share computed at 25 percent of adjusted income.

Since we have assumed that the local housing market is in equilibrium, the differences in market rent for similar bedroom size units reflect differences in housing quality and neighborhood environment. Table 51.1 compares market and tenant rents and the housing consumption added by each low income housing program. When applicable, program benefits are broken down by type of housing stock in use (existing, rehabilitated, new) to reflect substantial benefit differences which exist within a single program.

The consistently higher average market rent for the rent supplement units reflects their higher level of housing services compared to other programs. The rent supplement program and the leased housing program with new construction offer the greatest consumption benefits. Thus, if the goal of national housing policy were to provide the maximum improvement in the living condition of assisted households without

10. In 1969, the Survey Research Program of the Joint Center for Urban Studies of M.I.T. and Harvard conducted the first of a series of annual surveys planned to provide information on basic characteristics of the population and various neighborhoods in metropolitan Boston. The sample of Boston households was a carefully selected sample of 552 respondents designed to give information close to what would be obtained by interviewing the total population. For a more detailed explanation of the sampling technique and reliability of the data, see M.I.T.-Harvard Joint Center for Urban Studies, *Boston Area Survey: How the People See Their City, Boston 1969* (Cambridge: M.I.T.-Harvard Joint Center for Urban Studies, 1970).

regard to cost, rent supplements or the leasing of new housing would be ranked first among policy choices. However, since federal resources are scarce, the cost effectiveness of each program must also be considered.

PROMOTING EQUAL RESIDENTIAL OPPORTUNITIES

The provision of housing assistance has important socioenvironmental as well as economic effects. When a housing consumer rents a dwelling unit, he purchases a specific location, neighborhood environment, landlord relationship, and municipal service package along with the physical space. While we have limited knowledge about how these factors affect a particular household's social relationships or psychological health, most national housing legislation assumes that free residential mobility contributes to social and economic welfare. Therefore, in a preliminary manner, each low-rent housing program is evaluated in terms of its ability to foster consumer choice (sovereignty), residential racial desegregation, and economic integration.

Consumer sovereignty with respect to housing subsidy programs involves three separate aspects: (1) a choice of the neighborhood, type of structure, and location of the dwelling; (2) an opportunity to remain in the same apartment unit at full market rent when family income rises above program limits; and (3) a chance to achieve a normal landlord-tenant relationship, independent of public supervision and scrutiny. Conventional public housing has the lowest rank in terms of all three criteria because prospective tenants have little or no choice of physical design or location, families over the administrative income limit are supposed to be evicted, and tenant-management relations are somewhat institutionalized. The rent supplement program also ranks low in consumer sovereignty. Restrictive design requirements and severe construction cost limits have resulted in commonplace structures, although less institutionalized than public housing. Of even greater consequence is the serious restriction on consumer choice imposed by administrative regulations that limit rent supplements to specific buildings under contract with the FHA. Furthermore, rent assistance payments go directly to private owners, on behalf of qualified tenants, instead of to the beneficiaries and thus detract from normal landlord-tenant relations. In contrast, with the leasing of existing units there is a wider range of choice with respect to structural type and location, and relatively little public intervention in landlord-tenant relations.

The amount of racial and economic integration fostered by the subsidy programs is disappointing. The economic, racial, and physical isolation of public housing tenants has been severe. Leased housing and rent supplement tenants[11] have not experienced the consummate isolation of public housing tenants, and both programs have avoided the economic and social stigma attached to public housing projects; but leased housing and rent supplements have been concentrated in blighted, low income neighborhoods. Tight housing market conditions, expedience, and neighborhood resistance have undermined legislative provisions for scattered sites and have limited the percentage of units in any structure occupied by nonsubsidized tenants. Within the central city itself are substantial political pressures against building rent supplement or leased

11. Occupancy of rent supplement units in Boston is 100 percent black, but according to the local rent supplement coordinator for FHA this is because of the exceptional circumstances surrounding the FHA-sponsored Boston Urban Rehabilitation Program. For a discussion of BURP see Langley Keyes, *The Boston Rehabilitation Program* (Cambridge: M.I.T.-Harvard Joint Center for Urban Studies, 1970).

housing developments in middle-income neighborhoods, and the congressional requirement that local governments consent to the construction of rent supplement projects has severely curtailed their development in the suburbs.

TABLE 51.1 *Housing Consumption Benefits*
Boston, Massachusetts
(Dollars per 2-Bedroom Unit per Month in 1970)

	(a) Private Average Monthly Rent‡	(b) Tenant Monthly Rent Payment	(a) − (b) Monthly Consumption Benefit
Conventional public housing*	$129	$69	$60
Leased public housing			
Existing units	124	69	55
Rehabilitation	148	69	79
New construction	167	69	98
Rent supplements†			
Rehabilitation	167	73	94
New construction	184	77	107

*Conventional public housing refers to new construction.

†Since the political process is assumed to work in a reasonable Pareto optimal fashion—that is, public investments will continue until the point where no individual can benefit without some other individual's incurring costs—indirect beneficiaries are not expected to value increments in subsidized housing services beyond a certain amount. For example, nontenants do not receive psychic satisfaction if subsidized tenants are provided luxurious penthouses. In this case Pareto optimality is not achieved since the indirect benefit to nontenants is less than the amount by which the direct tenant benefit falls short of the government subsidy cost. The rent supplement program may be a less extreme example of this situation.

‡With the leased public housing and rent supplement programs the private average monthly rent is for the units actually occupied, whereas for conventional public housing the monthly rent is for "equivalent" private units (the actual rent computed from the Boston Area Survey for standard units occupied by households with less than $6,500 annual income).

Rent supplement developments generally have been more attractive than public housing projects, but strict cost limitations and the absence of amenities (e.g., air conditioning, more than one bathroom per unit) and attractive design features have limited the appeal of rent supplement projects for nonsubsidized tenants. Consequently, the program's ability to promote economic integration within structures is restricted, and most apartments in FHA mortgage-insured developments are occupied by subsidized tenants. In Boston, over 90 percent of the apartments in structures with rent supplements are occupied by government-assisted tenants. To a certain extent, leased public housing also reinforces segregated living patterns, since the major economic incentive for a landlord to lease an existing unit to a local housing authority is the opportunity to secure a stable rent roll. Landlords with stable rent rolls and high occupancy rates are unlikely to be attracted to the leased housing program, while those with high vacancy rates and high rates of turnover and debt collection problems would be attracted to the guaranteed rent payments. In Boston, for example, it was found that 70 percent of the units under lease with the Housing Authority were located in the Roxbury-North Dorchester area, where economic and racial segregation are severe and where problems of debt collection, high turnover rates, and high vacancy rates are concentrated.

In order to compare the performance of conventional public housing, leased public housing, and rent supplements in terms of promoting equal residential opportunities, an ordinal ranking system has been devised. (see Table 51.2). The range of the ordinal system is from 0 to 5, with 0 the least and 5 the most positive. Thus, a ranking of 5 would mean that a program fostered complete consumer sovereignty and racial and economic integration, while a ranking of 0 would mean that a program did not offer equal residential opportunity. As anticipated, the highest overall ranking goes to the leasing of existing units. As the only program under investigation which directly subsidizes the tenant, the public housing leasing program offers more oppor tunity for residential mobility than the production programs where the choice of location is made by a governmental agency or private developer.

Patterns of residential segregation and consumer sovereignty vary considerably across the country. Therefore, since the ordinal rankings are based on findings from one city, it is necessary to undertake more cross-sectional and historical comparisons before reaching definitive conclusions. Because some of the social and market effects are inherent in the structure of the respective programs, however, the ranks shown in Table 51.2 probably would remain intact, providing policymakers with an explicit basis for assessing trade-offs.

TABLE 51.2   *Ordinal Rankings* of Social Effects*
Public Housing, Leased Housing, and Rent Supplements
Boston, Massachusetts

	Consumer Sovereignty	Racial Desegregation	Economic Integration
Conventional public housing	1	0	0
Leased public housing			
Existing units	4	2	2
Rehabilitation	3	1	1
New construction	3	1	1
Rent supplements			
Rehabilitation	3	0	1
New construction	2	0	0

*The basis for the ordinal rankings is set forth in the preceding pages. Although the criteria are objective, some subjective considerations have undoubtedly influenced our scoring system.

CLOSING THE HOUSING GAP IN THE MOST COST EFFECTIVE MANNER

The efficiency of each program in providing decent shelter and a suitable living environment for every American can be measured by estimating the number of families moved from substandard to standard housing for a given expenditure. In order to compare the alternative programs, it is necessary to estimate the full economic costs of each subsidy program (the overall value of the resource inputs—land, labor, and capital—to the economy). This involves calculating the capital, operating, and adminis-trative costs of each program for a standardized dwelling unit (a two-bedroom unit).

The real capital cost of a newly constructed unit of conventional public housing is computed by making two separate adjustments to the original Boston Housing Authority (BHA) development costs. First, the historical development cost data are standardized in terms of the prices of a single base year, 1970. Second, the housing units themselves have to be made comparable, since public housing construction requirements have become more demanding over the years. The capital costs are adjusted to equivalent 1970 dollars by applying Gordon's Final Price of Structures

TABLE 51.3   *Gross Economic Costs per Unit per Month* (1970)
Boston, Massachusetts

	Conventional Public Housing		Leased Public Housing		Rent Supplements	
	New Construction	Existing Units	Rehabilitation	New Construction	Rehabilitation	New Construction
Capital costs						
Capital cost	$123.00	$ 42.00†	$ 65.00	$108.00	$ 65.00	$108.00
Foregone federal revenue	—	—	7.50	4.50	7.50	4.50
Operating and administrative costs						
Operating cost	69.50	82.00	89.00	65.00	102.00	72.00
Foregone local revenue	15.00	—	—	16.50	—‡	—‡
Local administrative cost		10.50	10.50	10.50	3.00	3.00
Federal administrative cost	8.00	2.50	2.50	2.50	2.50	2.50
Total per Unit per Month	$215.50*	$137.00	$174.50	$207.00	$180.00	$190.00

*Because of lower capital costs ($110 per unit per month) the total cost for turnkey public housing is $202.50.
†This figure includes both the average monthly capital on outstanding mortgages and the additional capital cost incurred in removing code violations. For Boston the average amount of debt associated with upgrading units with code violations was $9 per unit per month. The basis for this calculation is an estimate of the cost incurred in removing code violations listed on Housing Authority inspection reports.
‡In those municipalities which provide a property tax exemption for FHA mortgage-insured developments in which rent supplement units are located, there will be an additional cost in the form of foregone local revenue. In most instances, the value of this local property tax subsidy, however, is less than the public housing exemption.

Index to the original construction costs.[12] The adjusted mean development cost per unit in 1970 dollars is $17,070. To take account of the additional capital cost of higher standards of construction, site improvement, and equipment requirements, we use the average of two different estimates—the foregoing adjusted mean development cost and the development cost of a two-bedroom public housing unit in a metropolitan area of average construction cost. The first estimate is $17,070 and the second is $18,200.[13] Therefore, the average development cost is $17,635. The development or capital cost is converted to a monthly basis by using the prevailing interest rate (8 percent in 1970) and public housing's normal mortgage term of 40 years. Although public housing capital carries an interest rate below 8 percent, it cannot be used because of the tax-exempt feature on the bonds which finance the capital costs. The monthly payment necessary to amortize a 40-year, 8 percent mortgage of $17,635 is $123.

According to BHA records, the average public housing operating cost for 1970 was $69.50 per dwelling unit per month. However, these records underestimate the real operating costs because they are computed on the basis of a property tax exemption. Instead of paying full property taxes, as is required of private owners of short-term leased public housing and rent supplement units, conventional public housing makes a payment in lieu of taxes (PILOT). This PILOT is equivalent to 10 percent of shelter rent (gross tenant rental payments minus utility costs). The actual PILOT per unit in 1970 was $5.40 per month, significantly below the amount required for full property taxes. Foregone property taxes are equal to the difference between the full tax and the PILOT. The full property taxes for public housing are estimated to be $20 per unit per month.[14] Consequently, the foregone property taxes are approximately $15 per unit per month. The value of this foregone local revenue is added to the operating costs. Finally, a direct expenditure for federal administrative costs is included in calculating the real monthly cost of providing public housing in Boston. In 1967 the average federal administrative cost was $7.10 per dwelling unit per month for all public housing projects.[15] Assuming an average increase in personnel and material costs of 4 percent per annum, the average federal administrative cost for 1970 would be approximately $8.00 per unit per month. The full economic cost of public housing is set forth in Table 51.3.

In recent years, some public housing units have been constructed by private firms and then sold to local housing authorities; this program is known as turnkey public housing. For this program one might expect that the gross economic cost would be lower because of more efficient development practices on the part of private sponsors. The members of the BHA Planning and Development staff estimate that the

---

12. For the purpose of this essay the Gordon Price Index was updated to 1970. A detailed explanation of the composition of the index is set forth in Robert J. Gordon, "A New View of Real Investment in Structures, 1919-1965," *Proceedings of the Econometric Society*, Washington, D.C., 1967.

13. The development cost of a two-bedroom unit of conventional public housing in an area of average housing cost was approximately $18,200. See Frank de Leeuw, "The Cost of Leased Public Housing," op. cit., p. 26 and appendix B.

14. The full property taxes are computed first by capitalizing the adjusted rent receipts in order to determine the aggregate property value and then by applying the prevailing property tax rate to the state equalized assessed value of the property. For a full description of the capitalization approach, see Arthur P. Solomon, *Housing the Urban Poor*, op. cit., chap. 5.

15. See B. T. Fitzpatrick, "FHA and FNMA Assistance for Multifamily Housing," *Law and Contemporary Problems* (Duke University Law School, 1968), p. 457.

turnkey approach results in a 10 percent saving in development cost.[16] Therefore, the average development cost would be approximately $15,872 per unit, instead of $17,635. With a 40-year, 8 percent mortgage, the monthly capital payments would be $110.

When the local housing authority leases existing private units, there are operating and administrative costs but only minimal capital costs.[17] However, there are capital costs in those instances when private developers and real estate owners construct new units, reconstruct vacant units or eliminate housing code violations in response to program incentives. Whenever these private investments are undertaken, moreover, there are federal revenue losses associated with accelerated depreciation provisions. Because the magnitude of these private costs and tax losses varies with the amount of construction or rehabilitation involved, the cost calculations for leased public housing must be divided into three program subcategories: leasing with existing, rehabilitated, and newly constructed units.

The cost of leasing an existing dwelling unit consists of the expenses incurred in managing, maintaining, and operating the unit, the government's administrative overhead, the capital cost on outstanding mortgages, and the average debt incurred in removing code violations (See Table 51.3). Unlike public housing, it is not necessary to make an adjustment for property tax subsidies since private owners pay full property taxes under the short-term Section 23 program. The federal and local administrative costs are prorated among the program subcategories in accordance with their respective share of the total number of leased housing units.[18] As government administrators gain more experience with the leasing program and more units are added to the leased housing stock, there may be some greater efficiencies as well as economies of scale which would lower the per unit administrative costs.

For leased housing units involving either rehabilitation or new construction, substantially higher capital costs are involved. In addition, the foregone federal revenue from "accelerated" depreciation must be included since this federal income tax provision involves real costs to the economy. The average capital cost for the substantial rehabilitation of multifamily housing accomplished under agreement with the BHA is $8,412 per unit, in 1970 prices. Assuming a 25-year, 8 percent mortgage, this translates into a monthly capital cost of $65 per unit. The average capital cost of new construction under BHA long-term leasing is $15,512 per unit, in 1970 prices, or $108 per unit per month at an interest rate of 8 percent and a 40-year term.

Since the 1969 Tax Reform Act provides a special five-year write-off of expenditures incurred in rehabilitating rental housing for low income occupancy, thus reducing the capital cost to the investor, the cost of this tax subsidy must be taken into account. The value of this foregone federal revenue is computed by establishing the depreciation schedules for both the accelerated (5-year) and conventional straight line (25-year)

16. Interviews with Andrew Olins, director, and Daniel Smith, special assistant, Boston Housing Authority Planning and Development Division, November 11, 1970.

17. Although there are minimal capital costs, the actual amount of the annual federal contribution still is determined by estimating the development cost of a newly constructed project for comparable occupancy and then establishing the level debt service which would apply to a 40-year, tax-exempt LHA serial bond.

18. Congress allocates federal administrative funds for low-rent public housing and does not prorate the funds among conventional public housing, turnkey, and leased housing. However, the Budget Office in the Office of the Secretary, U.S. Department of Housing and Urban Development, estimates that the federal administrative cost for leased housing is approximately one-third of the amount for conventional public housing. Telephone interview with William Rhodes, U.S. Department of Housing and Urban Development, March 1971.

depreciation methods, calculating the annual differential, and multiplying this differential by the marginal tax rate of real estate investors.[19] The amount of the depreciation is valued more highly in the early years; thus, to avoid the bias entailed in using the value of the tax loss for any single year, the average of the annualized discounted present values is employed. In calculating the present value of the tax shelter (or foregone federal revenue), the deductions for interest payments, real estate taxes and other expenses incurred during the construction period are also included. It is assumed that these deductions are equal to 10 percent of the total construction cost. Also, tax revenue from the sale of the property offsets some of the earlier tax losses. To calculate this offset it is assumed that the property is sold at the end of the 20th year for the amount of the remaining mortgage balance. Applying this methodology, the average annual discounted present value—using a 10 percent discount rate—is $88, and the monthly value is approximately $7.50.

The same approach is used to calculate the monthly economic cost of the leased housing program with new construction, with two modifications. First, the city makes a property tax exemption available to the long-term leasing program. Thus, we have to add the value of the foregone property taxes to the operating and capital costs in order to determine the full economic cost of the program.[20] The local property tax exemption is $16.50 per unit, which is added to the $6.10 per unit paid in lieu of taxes by the owners of the leased housing dwellings. This additional $16.50 is included as part of the total monthly cost, since the actual in lieu payments are already accounted for in the operating costs.

Second, the mortgage term and capital costs of the rehabilitation and new construction programs are different. The monthly capital costs of new construction are calculated on the basis of the amortization and interest payments on a 40-year, 8 percent mortgage for $15,512. This amount is also used as the depreciable base for the computation of the tax loss (see Table 51.3).

Finally, it is necessary to estimate the cost of providing adequate shelter under the rent supplement program. Since the number of newly constructed rent supplement units in Boston is small, the use of their actual development costs may bias our comparison with the other programs. Moreover, since there is no *a priori* reason to expect the new construction or rehabilitation costs of rent supplements and leased public housing programs to differ, it is assumed that their development costs are equal. This assumption allows a general comparison of program costs rather than an idiosyncratic comparison of particular projects in one city. In other words, the respective costs of providing similar housing can be contrasted. If the capital costs are equal, then any differences in total monthly costs are attributable to administrative and operating costs.

Because federal subsidies are used to supplement the rents of tenants occupying designated dwellings bearing FHA-insured mortgages, it is assumed that the federal administrative costs approximate those of the leased public housing program. The federal administrators of rent supplement and leased housing programs, in contrast

19. It is assumed that the marginal tax rate of real estate investors is 50 percent and that the taxable portion of rental income applied toward amortization is offset by the depreciation deductible under the straight line method.

20. The method for calculating the full and foregone property taxes is set forth in the discussion of the public housing program. The reason the leased housing new construction units result in a higher municipal cost (foregone property tax revenue) than the conventional public housing units is because the former have higher market value and have the potential of paying full property taxes.

to conventional public housing programs, do not have to review architectural drawings, development plans, and other construction-related activities. Under both programs responsibility for ownership and development is shifted from the public to the private sector. Reliance on the private sector rather than the government results in lower federal administrative costs for leased housing and rent supplements than for the conventional public housing program.

While the federal administrative costs for the leasing and rent supplement programs are similar, there are differences in the local administrative and operating costs. The leasing program has higher local administrative costs due to the administrative responsibilities assumed by the local housing authority. Housing authority staff are responsible for locating and inspecting individual dwelling units, determining market rents, negotiating lease arrangements, and monitoring landlord-tenant relations. By contrast, the local FHA office in Boston, which is responsible for administering the rent supplement program, assigns only one staff specialist to approve tenant eligibility and oversee program operations. On the other hand, the rent supplement program has higher operating costs. This difference results, in part, from the relative locational and qualitative advantages of the rent supplement units.[21] These units, located in federally subsidized multifamily apartments, are found in neighborhoods where public services, amenities, and environmental conditions are qualitatively better than in the case of public housing units. Moreover, any program that pays the owner the difference between a fixed percentage of tenant income and the fair market rent of the occupied unit encourages the participating households to occupy as expensive a housing unit as the government agencies have available. Thus, assuming the same capital costs and foregone tax revenue as with leased housing, the monthly cost of rent supplement rehabilitated units is $180. (Table 51.3).

The monthly cost of providing newly constructed units with rent supplements is computed in the same manner. The total monthly costs for newly constructed units are higher than for rehabilitated units due to differences in development costs. These higher capital costs are sufficient to offset the lower cost associated with the less accelerated depreciation schedule.

On the assumption that families residing in conventional public, leased public, and rent supplement housing units have been moved from substandard to standard housing conditions, the estimated resource cost of each program can be utilized to measure the extent to which each program closes the housing gap. This is done by dividing a fixed amount of resource expenditures by the resource cost per unit per annum under each program. The results are summarized in Table 51.4.

Although specific costs in other cities might differ from those in the table, because of differing input costs and supply and demand conditions, the advantage of leased housing with existing units is overwhelming. Leasing existing units provides the highest number of families with standard housing per fixed dollar amount and thus is the most cost effective approach to closing the housing gap.[22]

21. Most of the rehabilitated units were part of the Boston Urban Rehabilitation Program (BURP). There is some evidence that some of these units were inadequately renovated, and this may have contributed to higher maintenance costs. See Urban Planning Aid, Inc., *An Evaluation of the Boston Rehabilitation Program* (Cambridge: Urban Planning Aid, Inc., 1969).

22. This type of gross performance measure, analogous to a poverty gap study, assumes that standard and substandard housing are dichotomous bundles. Thus, implicit in this type of measure is the assumption that there is a significant improvement in living conditions associated with moving into standard housing. Obviously, the limitation of the housing gap measure is that it fails to make any distinction between differential housing conditions above or below

Continued on p. 572

TABLE 51.4   *Closing the Housing Gap: Federally Assisted Rental Housing per Two-Bedroom Unit per Annum*

Boston, Massachusetts 1970

	Annual Resource Cost	No. of Families Moved Substandard to Standard Housing per $1 million Resource Cost
Conventional public housing	$2,586	387
Leased public housing		
Existing units	1,644	608
Rehabilitation	2,094	478
New construction	2,484	403
Rent supplements		
Rehabilitation	2,060	485
New construction	2,280	439

REDISTRIBUTING HOUSING CONSUMPTION EQUITABLY

Policymakers, housing administrators, and potential beneficiaries alike are concerned with the means by which income is redistributed as well as with the actual amount of redistribution. Conceptually, there are two distinct measures of the efficiency of redistribution programs. One computes the proportion of the total benefits which actually reach the target population, while the other estimates the extent to which members of the target population are treated equally (the distribution of benefits among the target population). These concepts are termed vertical and horizontal equity, respectively. Federal housing assistance may be considered inefficient to the extent that it benefits the nonpoor as well as the poor. Similarly, federal housing programs are inefficient if they provide some low-income households with more assistance than others who are equally situated.

One of the major arguments made for housing allowance, rent certificate, and income maintenance schemes is that virtually every dollar of housing aid reaches the target group. Although these demand- or consumer-oriented strategies require some degree of administrative support and program monitoring, the amount of resources deflected to the nonpoor should be minimal. The analysis of the allocation of benefits under existing in-kind or supply-side programs provides some basis for comparison. Under current federal subsidy programs a significant portion of housing aid is diverted to governmental intermediaries and to high income investors, financial syndicators, and developers. Before federal housing aid reaches the consumer it must pass through several intermediaries. In the case of conventional public housing, for example, the local housing authorities actually develop, administer, and operate the housing units. Under the leased public housing program, the same housing authority negotiates with landlords for the lease of private dwellings. Rent supplement aid passes through the hands of FHA administrators and local sponsors.

Diversion of federal funds to nonpoor beneficiaries also results from the use of high income investors as a conduit for raising capital for housing developments. In

the minimum standard level. But since data are generally available in dichotomous form, the programs are compared on this basis.

the case of conventional or turnkey public housing the federal government raises capital through the sale of housing authority 40-year serial bonds. In order to lower the capital costs the federal government exempts the interest payments of these bonds from federal income taxation. The net cost of issuing these tax-exempt bonds is the difference between the loss of federal tax revenue on the tax-exempt interest payments and the interest cost saving that results because the payments for retiring the bonds are less than those for retiring fully taxable bonds.[23] For privately owned new construction and rehabilitation units in the leased housing and rent supplement programs, accelerated depreciation provisions provide high income investors with a means of sheltering income from the federal income tax. The syndication of these tax shelters is a costly method of raising development capital and results in additional foregone federal revenue. Thus, as the data in Table 51.5 indicate, the share of the total direct benefits received by the poor varies significantly among the alternative housing strategies, from a low of 65 percent in conventional public housing to a high of 91 percent in rent supplement new construction units.[24]

TABLE 51.5 *Allocation of Total Housing Benefits to Tenants, Intermediaries, and Investors* Boston, Massachusetts 1970*

Program	Tenant Consumption Benefit (2 Br.)		Government Intermediaries†		Investors and Syndicators‡	
Conventional public housing	64%	($ 60)	24%	($22)	12%	($11)
Leased public housing						
Existing units	81	(55)	19	(13)	0§	(0)§
Rehabilitation	79	(79)	13	(13)	7	(7.50)
New construction	84	(98)	12	(13)	4	(4.50)
Rent supplements						
Rehabilitation	88	(94)	5	(5.50)	7	(7.50)
New construction	91	(107)	5	(5.50)	4	(4.50)

*The allocation of benefits is derived from Tables 51.1 and 51.3.
†The amount diverted to federal and local intermediaries is based on the program's respective administrative costs.
‡The share of the total costs diverted to high income investors and financial syndicators is based on estimates of foregone federal revenue from accelerated depreciation and tax-exempt bonds.
§Because many structures containing existing units have been under the same ownership for at least 5-10 years it is assumed that the cost of any tax shelter from an earlier syndication is no longer incurred.

The second measure of redistributive efficiency concerns the horizontal equity of providing equal assistance to households in equal need. In the case of federal housing

23. For a detailed explanation of this cost estimate see Arthur P. Solomon, "The Cost Effectiveness of Subsidized Housing," Working Paper no. 5 (Cambridge: M.I.T.-Harvard Joint Center for Urban Studies, 1972), appendix A.

24. In a study of the distribution of direct benefits of public housing Bish found that the poor and near-poor received nearly 80 percent of the subsidy. See R. L. Bish, "Public Housing: The Magnitude and Distribution of Direct Benefits and Effects on Housing Consumption," *Journal of Regional Science* 9 (December 1969): 27-39. This is an overestimate, however, since

(continued on p. 574)

programs not only do the programs reach a small fraction of those in need,[25] but even those assisted receive differential levels of benefit. Since the amount of tenant rental payments is based on the ability to pay, not the market rent of the occupied unit, participants in the several programs pay roughly the same dollar amount for their housing. However, for these comparable payments participants occupy units and live in neighborhoods of markedly different quality. Differences in the quality of housing and neighborhood environments provided under the alternative housing redistribution schemes, as measured by differences in resource costs, reflect inefficiencies in the design of the subsidy programs. One way to measure the extent of·this inefficiency is to compare the market rental of units occupied by subsidized tenants with the mean rent for "standard" private dwellings paid by other low income households in the same Boston housing market. Instead of assisting the maximum number of poor households possible with a given budgetary or resource expenditure through the provision of minimal standard housing, the rent supplement and leased public housing programs involving new construction provide housing services far in excess of the minimum acceptable quality. As Table 51.6 indicates, only the leasing of existing dwellings provides standard housing under federal programs at resource costs comparable to rents of low-income standard units in the private market (or to the Bureau of Labor Statistics' lower family budget for housing in Boston).

THE DIRECTION OF HOUSING REFORM

As the foregoing discussion has indicated, national housing policy encompasses multiple economic, social, and environmental objectives. Making explicit the objectives against which program performance can be measured is the first step in effective policymaking. However, the identification of these objectives in itself does not provide adequate guidance to decision makers who must choose among alternatives, because no single program or set of programs can meet all these goals. Program outputs· may even conflict. Further, program resources available to the federal government are not unlimited, so choices must be made among many public objectives.

If the costs and benefits of all housing programs could be valued in terms of a single unit of value (e.g., dollars) it would be possible to make objective decisions on the basis of a public expenditure efficiency criterion. By this criterion programs are evaluated on the basis of the difference between the money values of their costs and benefits. But many of the objectives are not susceptible to market valuation; program outputs may manifest externalities, may be indivisible by discrete units, or in some other way may be immeasurable in quantifiable terms. Even objectives which are quantifiable may not be commensurable. Hence the problem of multiple objectives is one of providing weights or values for these objectives—e.g., how much racial integration can be traded off for every additional dollar of housing consumption.

In a review of techniques for evaluating programs with multiple objectives, Freeman notes three alternatives for dealing with the valuation problem.[26] One suggests that

---

the cost of the income tax subsidy associated with the interest payment exemption on the public housing serial bonds is not included in the Bish analysis.

25. Smolensky and Gomery have estimated that actual public housing tenants constitute only 2.9 percent of those eligible for the program. Eugene Smolensky and J. Douglas Gomery, "Efficiency and Equity Effects in the Benefits from Federal Public Housing Programs in 1965," Working Paper no. 2 (Madison, Wis.: Institute of Poverty, 1971), p. 24.

26. A. Myrick Freeman III, "Project Design and Evaluation with Multiple Objectives," U.S., Congress, Joint Economic Committee, *The Analysis and Evaluation of Public Expenditures: The PPB System*, 90th Cong., 2d sess., 1969, pp. 565-91.

decision makers be provided with a schedule showing net money benefits for goals susceptible to market valuation and qualitative descriptions of other benefits and costs. The policymaker can then choose the program which best conforms to his subjective valuations, his interpretation of society's preferences, or his valuation of money valued benefits. Another technique establishes a minimum level of one benefit and seeks to maximize other benefits subject to that constraint. There is no established criterion, however, for selecting benefits to be constrained or maximized in the analysis. The third method for dealing with multiple objectives attempts to formulate an explicit objective function by assigning weights to each benefit. The decision-maker can then seek to maximize the sum of the valued benefits. Implicit in the first two methods is the need to establish values for noncomparable benefits. Since incommensurable benefits cannot be compared or traded off on an objective basis, however, each type of benefit—whether susceptible to a dollar valuation or not—should be displayed for policymakers.

TABLE 51.6 *Comparative Monthly Costs*
Federally Assisted Rental Housing (Two-Bedroom Units)
Boston, Massachusetts 1970

Program	Monthly Resource Cost	Monthly Resource Cost Divided by Boston Survey Low-Rent Standard Housing Cost ($129)
Conventional public housing	$215.50	1.7
Conventional turnkey housing	202.50	1.6
Leased public housing		
Existing units	137.00	1.1
Rehabilitation	174.50	1.4
New construction	207.00	1.6
Rent supplements		
Rehabilitation	180.00	1.4
New construction	190.00	1.5
Private market low-rent		
Standard housing*	129.00	
BLS lower family budget†	136.00	

*Derived from Boston Survey data, Joint Center for Urban Studies of M.I.T. and Harvard, Survey Research Program.
†U.S. Department of Labor, Bureau of Labor Statistics, "Three Budgets for an Urban Family of Four Persons, 1969-1970," Supplement to Bulletin 1570-5, table A-1. Housing includes shelter, household operations, and house furnishings. All families with the lower budget are assumed to be renters. In Spring 1970, the average cost of a lower budget for a family of 4 persons living in urban areas of the United States was $6,960.

If weights are assigned to all benefits and an explicit function formulated, tradeoffs are clear and policymakers can make choices on an intelligent and informed basis. Decisions are then reflective of general social preferences, consistent over time and founded on the basis of explicit choice. Administrators can choose alternatives most appropriate to local housing market conditions. For example, a mayor confronted with severe fluctuations in the local housing market might value a program's adaptability more than its benefit-cost ranking. Under such conditions the mayor is willing to trade more market flexibility for less economic efficiency. Policymakers have attempted to realize many objectives through federal housing programs. If there were a consensus about these objectives, the task of evaluating program performance would be relatively straightforward. Since such a consensus does not exist, however, we have chosen four separate criteria for assessing and comparing alternative strategies for achieving redistributive goals. This approach seems reasonable since, in the absence of a consensus, each decision maker has to establish his own priorities and subjective weighting scheme. Using Table 51.7, comparisons of explicit trade-offs can be made more systematically.

This analysis illustrates that opposite conclusions can be drawn from the use of different evaluative standards. Using the criterion of maximizing aggregate housing consumption added, for example, the new construction programs are preferable since they make the largest contribution. In other words, in the absence of any cost considerations the housing production programs provide assisted families with the best quality units (most housing services). In terms of the ability to close the housing gap or to foster racial and economic integration, however, these programs are the least preferable. Tenants in the rent supplement units receive more housing than participants in the public housing or leasing programs since the rent supplement units are located in FHA-insured developments designed primarily for moderate income households. On the other hand, providing newly constructed housing is considerably more expensive. Fewer households can be assisted for a given budgetary appropriation. Thus, the inequitable distribution of benefits between the small number of low income families receiving federal housing assistance and the vast majority excluded from such assistance becomes more pronounced.

Since federal housing policies embrace such a wide range of objectives it is unrealistic to assume that any single housing strategy would be preferable for different phases of the economic cycle, housing market conditions, or geographic and social situations. One can conclude, therefore, that is is important to maintain a variety of housing strategies.

The present analysis, however, suggests that the existing dominance of production or income in-kind strategies is inappropriate. While such programs should be continued, national housing policy should create more of a balance between production- and consumer-oriented strategies. The latter approach—which includes leased public housing in existing units, housing allowances, and income maintenance schemes—is less costly, more equitable, and more responsive to consumer choice. There is need for more emphasis on redistributive housing stragegies which rely on direct cash transfers. In order for these strategies to function in an optimal manner, however, it is necessary for all levels of government to work toward the elimination of existing housing market barriers such as racial discrimination, restrictive zoning, and collusive real estate practices, which impede full utilization of increments in rent-paying ability.

TABLE 51.7 *A Comparative Analysis*

Federal Housing Redistributive Programs

Programs	Monthly Consumption Benefit (Aggregate Income)	Consumer Sovereignty*	Racial and Economic Integration*	Number of Households Moved Substandard Standard per $1 million	Tenant Share of Total Benefits (Vertical Equity)	Resource Cost Divided by Private Market Low-Rent Standard Unit Cost (Horizontal Equity)†
Conventional public housing	$ 60	1	0	387	64%	1.7
Leased public housing						
Existing units	55	4	2	608	81	1.1
Rehabilitation	79	3	1	478	79	1.4
New construction	98	3	1	403	84	1.6
Rent supplements						
Rehabilitation	94	3	1	485	88	1.4
New construction	107	2	0	439	91	1.5

*The range of the ordinal system is from 0 to 5, with 0 the least and 5 the most positive; e.g., 5 means foster complete economic integration, while 0 means complete segregation.

†A unitary score (1.0) on the horizontal equity measure means that the tenant beneficiaries are consuming minimal standard housing. Values above 1.0 indicate overconsumption and an inefficient use of federal subsidy dollars. Above the unitary score, the higher the ratio, the more inefficient the federal program.

Bibliography

Citations to current housing materials may be found in the *Journal of the American Institute of Planners, Land-Use Controls Quarterly, Housing and Planning References* (Department of Housing and Urban Development), *Today's Housing Briefs*, and the *Journal of Economic Literature*. The bibliography in William L. C. Wheaton et al., eds., *Urban Housing* (New York: The Free Press, 1966), is an excellent source of earlier material. Another useful source is Byrl N. Boyce and Sidney Turoff, *Minority Groups and Housing: A Bibliography 1950-1970* (n.a.: General Learning Press, 1972). In addition, Doris B. Holleb, *Social and Economic Information for Urban Planning*, vol. 2 (Chicago: University of Chicago Center for Urban Studies, 1969), contains a comprehensive summary of data sources relevant to housing analysis, and the *Statistical Reporter*, published by the United States Bureau of the Budget, describes the availability of federally gathered statistics.

I. POLITICS

Aiken, Michael, and Alford, Robert. "Community Structure and Innovation: The Case of Public Housing." *American Political Science Review* 64 (September 1970): 843-64. For a critique see Stephen Stephens, "Communication," *American Political Science Review* 65 (June 1971): 499-501.

Altshuler, Alan A. *Community Control*. New York: Western Publishing Co., 1970.

Altshuler, Alan A. *The City Planning Process: A Political Analysis*. Ithaca, N.Y.: Cornell University Press, 1965.

Bachrach, Peter, and Baratz, Morton S. *Power and Poverty: Theory and Practice*. New York: Oxford University Press, 1970.

Banfield, Edward. *Political Influence*. New York: The Free Press, 1961.

Banfield, Edward, ed. *Urban Government: A Reader in Administration and Politics*. Rev. ed. New York: The Free Press, 1969.

Banfield, Edward, and Wilson, James Q. *City Politics*. Cambridge, Mass.: Harvard University Press, 1963.

Burghardt, Stephen, ed. *Tenants and the Urban Housing Crisis*. Dexter, Mich.: The New Press, 1972.

Carmichael, Stokely, and Hamilton, Charles V. *Black Power: The Politics of Liberation in America*. New York: Vintage Books, 1967.

Dahl, Barding. "A White Slumlord Confesses." *Esquire* 66 (July 1966): 92-94.

Dahl, Robert A. *Who Governs? Democracy and Power in an American City*. New Haven, Conn.: Yale University Press, 1961.

Domhoff, G. William. *Who Rules America?* Englewood Cliffs, N.J.: Prentice-Hall, Inc., 1967.

Donnison, D. V. *The Government of Housing*. Baltimore: Penguin Books, 1967.

Downs, Anthony. "Alternative Futures for the American Ghetto." *Urban Problems and Prospects*, chap. 2. Chicago: Markham Publishing Co., 1970.

Eley, Lynn W., and Casstevens, Thomas W., eds. *The Politics of Fair-Housing Legislation: State and Local Case Studies*. San Francisco: Chandler Publishing Co., 1968.

Farkas, Suzanne. *Urban Lobbying: Mayors in the Federal Arena*. New York: New York University, 1971.

Fenno, Richard. *The Power of the Purse*. Boston: Little, Brown & Co., 1966.

Flaum, Thea, and Salzman, Elizabeth C. *The Tenants' Rights Movement*. Chicago: Urban Research Corp., 1969.

Frank, Lawrence K. "To Control 'Slumlord' Abuses—Private Rental Housing Proposed to Become Public Utility." *Journal of Housing* 20 (July 8, 1963): 271-72.

Freedman, Leonard. *Public Housing: The Politics of Poverty*. New York: Holt, Rinehart & Winston, 1969.

Goldblatt, Harold, and Cromien, Florence. "The Effective Social Reach of the Fair Housing Practices Law of the City of New York." *Social Problems* 9 (Spring 1962): 365-70.

Grayson, George W., Jr., and Wedel, Cindy L. "Open Housing: How to Get Around the Law." *The New Republic*, June 22, 1968, pp. 15-16.

Hawley, Willis D., and Wirt, Frederick M., eds. *The Search for Community Power*. Englewood Cliffs, N.J.: Prentice-Hall, Inc., 1968.

Hirshen, Al, and Brown, Vivian. "Too Poor for Public Housing: Roger Starr's Poverty Preferences." *Social Policy* 3 (May/June 1972): 28-32.

Hollister, Rob. "The Politics of Housing: Squatters." *Society* 9 (July/August 1972): 46-52.

Indritz, Tova. "The Tenants' Rights Movement." *New Mexico Law Review* 1 (January 1971), 1-145.

Kain, John F., and Persky, Joseph J. "Alternatives to the Gilded Ghetto." *The Public Interest*, no. 14 (Winter 1969), pp. 74-87.

Kotler, Milton. *Neighborhood Government: The Local Foundations of Political Life*. Indianapolis: The Bobbs-Merrill Co., 1969.

LeGates, Richard T. "Can the Social Welfare Bureaucracies Control Their Programs: The Case of HUD and Urban Renewal." Working paper no. 176. Berkeley: Institute of Urban and Regional Development, University of California, 1972.

Lipsky, Michael. *Protest in City Politics: Rent Strikes, Housing, and the Power of the Poor*. Chicago: Rand McNally & Co., 1969.

———. "Rent Strikes: Poor Man's Weapon." *Trans-Action* 6 (February 1969): 10-15.

———. "Street-level Bureaucracy and the Analysis of Urban Reform." *Urban Affairs Quarterly* 7 (June 1971): 391-409.

Lipsky, Michael, and Levi, Margaret. "Community Organization as a Political Resource." In *People and Politics in Urban Society*, edited by H. Harlan. Beverly Hills, Calif.: Sage Publications, 1972.

Lowi, Theodore. *The End of Liberalism: Ideology, Policy, and the Crisis of Public Authority*. New York: W. W. Norton & Co., 1969.

Makielski, S. J., Jr. *The Politics of Zoning: The New York Experience*. New York: Columbia University Press, 1966.

Martin, Roscoe. *The Cities and the Federal System*. New York: Atherton Press, 1965.

Mayhew, Leon H. *Law and Equal Opportunity: A Study of the Massachusetts Commission Against Discrimination*. Cambridge, Mass.: Harvard University Press, 1968.

Meyerson, Martin, and Banfield, Edward. *Politics, Planning and the Public Interest: The Case of Public Housing in Chicago*. New York: The Free Press, 1955.

Meyerson, Martin; Terrett, Barbara; and Wheaton, William L. C. *Housing, People and Cities*. New York: McGraw-Hill, 1962.

Michelman, Frank I. "The Advent of a Right to Housing: A Current Appraisal." *Harvard Civil Rights–Civil Liberties Law Review* 5 (April 1970): 207-26.

National Clearing House for Legal Services (National Institute for Education in Law and Poverty) *Clearinghouse Review*. Washington, D.C. First issued September 1967.

Organization for Social and Technical Innovation. *Housing Action: A Guide for Doing Something about Housing Problems in your Community*. Cambridge, Mass.: OSTI Press, 1969.

Piven, Frances, and Cloward, Richard. "Desegregated Housing: Who Pays for the Reformers' Ideals?" *The New Republic*, December 17, 1966, pp. 17-22.

————. "Rent Strike: Disrupting the Slum System." *The New Republic*, (December 7, 1967), pp. 11-15.

Polsby, Nelson W. *Community Power and Political Theory*. New Haven, Conn.: Yale University Press, 1963.

Rabinowitz, Francine F. *City Politics and Planning*. New York: Atherton Press, 1969.

"Racial Discrimination in Public Housing Site Selection." *Stanford Law Review* 23 (1970): 63-147.

Rossi, Peter H., and Dentler, Robert A. *The Politics of Urban Renewal: The Chicago Findings*. New York: The Free Press, 1961.

Ryan, William. *Blaming the Victim*. New York: Pantheon Books, 1971.

Saltman, Juliet Z. *Open Housing As a Social Movement*. Lexington, Mass.: Heath Lexington Books, 1971.

Sax, Joseph L., and Hiestand, Fred J. "Slumlordism as a Tort." *Michigan Law Review* 65 (1967): 869-77.

Schier, Carl. "Protecting the Interests of the Indigent Tenant." *California Law Review* 54 (May 1966): 670-93.

Schoshinski, Robert S. "Remedies of the Indigent Tenant: Proposal for Change." *Georgetown Law Journal* 54 (1966): 519-58.

Shuman, Howard E. "Behind the Scenes . . . And Under the Rug." *The Washington Monthly* 1 (July 1969): 14-22.

"Slum Renewal Through Landlord-Tenant Law." *Harvard Civil Rights–Civil Liberties Law Review* 2 (Spring 1967): 177-258.

Straayer, John Adrian. "The American Policy Process and the Problems of Poverty and the Ghetto." *Western Political Quarterly*, March 1971, pp. 45-51.

U.S. Department of Housing and Urban Development, Department of Justice, Office of Economic Opportunity. *Legal Tools for Better Housing*. Report on a National Conference on Legal Rights of Tenants. Washington, 1967.

U.S. National Advisory Commisson on Civil Disorders. *Report*. Washington, D.C.: Government Printing Office, 1968.

Vaughan, Ted R. "The Landlord-Tenant Relation in a Low-Income Area." *Social Problems* 14 (Fall 1968): 208-18.

Wolman, Harold. *Politics of Federal Housing*. New York: Dodd, Mead & Co., 1971.

Wood, Robert C. *Suburbia: Its People and Their Politics*. Boston: Houghton Mifflin, 1958.

Zelder, Raymond E. "Residential Desegration: Can Nothing Be Accomplished?" *Urban Affairs Quarterly* 5 (March 1970), 265-77.

II. SOCIAL ASPECTS

Abrams, Charles. "Housing in the Year 2000." In *Environment and Policy: The Next Fifty Years*, edited by William R. Ewald, Jr. Bloomington: Indiana University Press, 1968.

Bressler, Marvin. "The Myers' Case: An Instance of Successful Racial Invasion." *Social Problems* 8 (Fall 1960): 126-42.

Chapman, Dennis. *The Home and Social Status*. London: Routledge & Kegan Paul, 1955.

Chermayeff, Serge, and Alexander, Christopher. *Community and Privacy*. Garden City, N.Y.: Doubleday, 1963.

Clark, Kenneth. *Dark Ghetto: Dilemmas of Social Power*. New York: Harper & Row, 1965.

Clinard, Marshall B. *Slums and Community Development: Experiments in Self-Help*. New York: The Free Press, 1966.

de Lauwe, P. Chombart. *Survey of the Desires and Needs of Men in Terms of Housing: Social Implications of Housing Conditions*. Paris: International Council for Building Research Studies and Documentation, February 1956.

Foote, Nelson N. et al. *Housing Choices and Housing Constraints*. New York: McGraw-Hill, 1960.

French, Robert Mills, and Hadden, Jeffrey K. "Mobile Homes: Instant Suburbia or Transportable Slums?" *Social Problems* 16 (Fall 1968): 219-26.

Fried, Marc. "Functions of the Working-Class Community in Modern Urban Society." *Journal of the American Institute of Planners* 33 (March 1967): 90-103.

————. "Grieving for a Lost Home." In *The Urban Condition*, edited by Leonard Duhl. New York: Basic Books, 1963.

Fried, Marc, and Gleicher, Peggy. "Some Sources of Residential Satisfaction in an Urban Slum." *Journal of the American Institute of Planners* 27 (November 1961): 305-15.

Gans, Herbert. "Effects of the Move from the City to the Suburb." *The Urban Condition*. Edited by Leonard Duhl. New York: Basic Books, 1963.

————. *The Levittowners: Ways of Life and Politics in a New Suburban Community*. New York: Pantheon, 1967.

————. *People and Plans: Essays on Urban Problems and Solutions*. New York: Basic Books, 1968.

————. *The Urban Villagers: Group and Class in the Life of Italian-Americans*. Glencoe, Ill.: The Free Press, 1962.

Glazer, Nathan. "Housing Problems and Housing Policies." *The Public Interest*, no. 7 (Spring 1967), pp. 21-51.

————. "Slum Dwellings Do Not Make a Slum." *New York Times Magazine*, November 21, 1965, pp. 55-56.

Glazer, Nathan, and McEntire, Davis, eds. *Studies in Housing and Minority Groups*. Berkeley: University of California Press, 1960.

Glazer, Nathan, and Moynihan, Daniel P. *Beyond the Melting Pot*. 2d ed. Cambridge, Mass.: M.I.T. Press, 1970.

Gordon, Milton M. *Assimilation in American Life*. New York: Oxford University Press, 1964.

————. *Social Class in American Sociology*. New York: McGraw-Hill, 1963.

Greenbie, Barrie Barston. "New House or New Neighborhood? A Survey of Priorities Among Home Owners in Madison, Wisconsin." *Land Economics* 45 (August 1969): 359-65.

Grier, Eunice, and Grier, George. "Equality and Beyond: Housing Segregation in the Great Society." In *Urban Planning and Social Policy*, edited by Bernard J. Frieden and Robert Morris. New York: Basic Books, 1968.

————. *Privately Developed Interracial Housing: An Analysis of Experience*. Berkeley: University of California Press, 1960.

Gutman, Robert, ed. *People and Buildings*. New York: Basic Books, 1972.

Hartman, Chester. "Social Values and Housing Orientations." *Journal of Social Issues* 19 (April 1963): 113-31.

Hatt, Paul K., and Reiss, Albert J., Jr., eds. *Cities and Society*. 2d ed. Glencoe, Ill.: The Free Press, 1957.

Hunt, Chester. "Research Report on Integrated Housing in a Small Northern City." *Journal of Intergroup Relations* 3 (Winter 1961-62): 65-79.

Hunter, David R. *The Slums*. New York: The Free Press, 1964.

Isler, Morton; Drury, Margaret; and Wellborn, Clay. *Housing Management: A Progress Report*. Working paper 112-27. Washington, D.C.: The Urban Institute, September 18, 1970.

Jacobs, Jane. *The Death and Life of Great American Cities*. New York: Random House, 1961.

Jiobu, Robert M., and Marshall, Harvey H., Jr. "Urban Structure and the Differentiation Between Blacks and Whites." *American Sociological Review* 36 (August 1971): 638-49.

Keller, Suzanne. *The Urban Neighborhood*. New York: Random House, 1968.

Klein, Woody. *Let in the Sun*. New York: MacMillan, 1964.

Ladd, Florence C. "Black Youths View Their Environments: Some Views of Housing." *Journal of the American Institute of Planners* 38 (March 1972): 108-15.

Lansing, John B.; Clifton, C. W.; and Morgan, J. N. *New Homes and Poor People*. Ann Arbor: Institute for Social Research, Survey Research Center, University of Michigan, 1969.

Lansing, John, and Mueller, Eva. *Residential Location and Urban Mobility*. Ann Arbor: Institute for Social Research, Survey Research Center, University of Michigan, 1964.

Liebow, Elliot. *Tally's Corner: A Study of Negro Streetcorner Men*. Boston: Little, Brown & Co., 1967.

Lubove, Roy. *The Urban Community: Housing and Planning in the Progressive Era*. Englewood Cliffs, N.J.: Prentice-Hall, Inc., 1967.

Lyford, Joseph. *The Airtight Cage: A Study of New York's West Side*. New York: Harper & Row, 1966.

McEntire, Davis. *Residence and Race: Final and Comprehensive Report to the Commission on Race and Housing*. Berkeley: University of California Press, 1960.

Marcuse, Peter. "Benign Quotas Reexamined." *Journal of Intergroup Relations* 3 (Spring 1962): 101-16.

Metzger, L. Paul. "American Sociology and Black Assimilation—Conflicting Perspectives." *American Journal of Sociology* 76 (January 1971): 627-47.

Michelson, William. "Potential Candidates for the Designers' Paradise: A Social Analysis From a Nationwide Survey." *Social Forces* 46 (December 1967): 190-96.

Mitchell, Robert Edward. "Some Social Implications of High Density Housing." *American Sociological Review* 36 (February 1971): 18-29.

Molotch, Harvey. "Racial Change in a Stable Community." *American Journal of Sociology* 75 (September 1969): 226-38.

———. "Racial Integration in a Transition Community." *American Sociological Review* 34 (December 1969): 878-93.

Moore, William, Jr. *The Vertical Ghetto: Everyday Life in an Urban Project*. New York: Random House, 1969.

Morrison, Denton E. "Some Notes Toward Theory On Relative Deprivation, Social Movements, and Social Change." *American Behavioral Scientist* 14 (May/June 1971): 675-90.

Moynihan, Daniel P., ed. *On Understanding Poverty: Perspectives from the Social Sciences*. New York: Basic Books, Inc., 1969.

Peattie, Lisa. "Social Issues in Housing." In *Shaping an Urban Future*, edited by Bernard Frieden and William W. Nash, Jr. Cambridge, Mass.: M.I.T. Press, 1969.

Rainwater, Lee. *Behind Ghetto Walls: Black Family Life in a Federal Slum*. Chicago: Aldine Publishing Co., 1970.

———. "Crucible of Identity: The Negro Lower-Class Family." *Daedalus* 95 (Winter 1966): 172-216.

Rosow, Irving. "Old People: Their Friends and Neighbors." *American Behavioral Scientist* 14 (September/October 1970): 59-69.

———. "Retirement Housing and Social Integration." In *Social and Psychological Aspects of Aging*, edited by Clark Tibbits and Wilma Donahue. New York: Columbia University Press, 1962.

———. "The Social Effects of the Physical Environment." *Journal of the American Institute of Planners* 27 (May 1961): 127-33.

———. *Social Integration of the Aged*. New York: The Free Press, 1967.

Rossi, Peter. *Why Families Move*. Glencoe, Ill.: The Free Press, 1955.

Schorr, Alvin. *Slums and Social Insecurity*. Washington, D.C.: Government Printing Office, 1963.

Scobie, Richard. "Family Interaction as a Factor in Problem-Tenant Identification in Public Housing." Ph.D. dissertation, Florence Heller School, Brandeis, April 1972.

Seeley, John. "The Slum: Its Nature, Use, and Users." In *Urban Housing*, edited by William L. C. Wheaton et al. New York: The Free Press, 1966.

Shanas, Ethel. "Living Arrangements and Housing of Old People." In *Behavior and Adaption in Late Life*, edited by Ewald W. Busse and Eric Pfeiffer. Boston: Little, Brown & Co., 1969.

Starr, Roger. *The Living End: The City and Its Critics*. New York: Coward-McCann, 1966.

Stokols, Daniel. "A Social-Psychological Model of Human Crowding." *Journal of the American Institute of Planners* 38 (March 1972): 72-83.

Suttles, Gerald D. *The Social Order of the Slum: Ethnicity and Territory in the Inner City*. Chicago: University of Chicago Press, 1968.

Taeuber, Karl E., and Taeuber, Alma F. "The Negro As An Immigrant Group: Recent Trends in Racial and Ethnic Segregation in Chicago." *American Journal of Sociology* 69 (January 1964): 374-82.

———. *Negroes In Cities: Residential Segregation and Neighborhood Change*. Chicago: Aldine Publishing Co., 1965.

Taube, Gerald, and Levin, Jack. "Public Housing As A Neighborhood: The Effect of Local and Non-Local Participation." *Social Science Quarterly* 52 (December 1971): .534-42.

Wallace, Anthony F. C. "Housing and Social Structure: A Preliminary Survey with Particular Reference to Multi-Story, Low Rent Public Housing Projects." Mimeographed. Philadelphia: Philadelphia Housing Authority, 1952.

Warren, Donald I. "Suburban Isolation and Race Tension." *Social Problems* 17 (Winter 1970): 324-39.

Williams, J. Allen, Jr. "The Multifamily Housing Solution and Housing Type Preferences." *Social Science Quarterly* 52 (December 1971): 543-59.

Wilner, Daniel et al. *The Housing Environment and Family Life*. Baltimore: Johns Hopkins Press, 1962.

Wolf, Eleanor P. "The Tipping Point in Racially Changing Neighborhoods." In *Urban Planning and Social Policy*, edited by Bernard Frieden and Robert Morris. New York: Basic Books, 1968.

Yancey, William L. "Architecture, Interaction, and Social Control: The Case of a Large-Scale Public Housing Project." *Environment and Behavior* 3 (March 1971): 3-21.

III. ECONOMICS

Abrams, Charles. *Forbidden Neighbors: A Study of Prejudice in Housing*. New York: Harper & Bros., 1955.

Adams, F. Gerard; Milgram, Grace; Green, Edward W.; and Mansfield, Christine. "Undeveloped Land Prices During Urbanization: A Micro-Empirical Study over Time." *Review of Economics and Statistics* 50 (May 1968): 248-58.

Alonso, William. *Location and Land Use: Toward a General Theory of Land Use*. Cambridge, Mass.: Harvard University Press, 1964.

Babcock, R. F. *The Zoning Game: Municipal Practices and Policies*. Madison: University of Wisconsin Press, 1966.

Bailey, Martin J. "Effects of Race and of Other Demographic Factors on the Values of Single-Family Homes." *Land Economics* 42 (May 1966): 215-20.

Becker, Gary S. *The Economics of Discrimination*. Chicago: University of Chicago Press, 1957.

Benson, Robert S., and Wolman, Harold, eds. *Counterbudget: A Blueprint for Changing National Priorities 1971-1976*. New York: Praeger, 1971.

Blank, David M., and Winnick, Louis. "The Structure of the Housing Market." *Quarterly Journal of Economics* 67 (May 1953): 181-208.

Bouma, Donald H. "Analysis of the Social Power Position of a Real Estate Board." *Social Problems* 10 (Fall 1962): 121-32.

Brigham, Eugene F. "The Determinants of Residential Land Values." *Land Economics* 41 (November 1965): 325-34.

Crecine, John P.; Davis, Otto A.; and Jackson, John E. "Urban Property Markets: Some Empirical Results and Their Implications for Municipal Zoning." *Journal of Law and Economics* 10 (October 1967): 79-99.

David, Martin H. *Family Composition and Consumption*. Amsterdam: North Holland Publishing Co., 1962.

Delafons, John. *Land Use Controls in the United States*. 2d ed. Cambridge, Mass.: M.I.T. Press, 1969.

deLeeuw, Frank. "The Demand for Housing: A Review of Cross-Section Evidence." *Review of Economics and Statistics* 53 (February 1971): 1-10.

deLeeuw, Frank, and Ekanem, Nkanta F. "The Supply of Rental Housing." *American Economic Review* 59 (December 1971): 806-17.

Edel, Matthew, and Rothenberg, Jerome, eds. *Readings in Urban Economics*. New York: Macmillan, 1972.

Engels, Friedrich. *The Housing Question*. New York: International Publishers, 1935.

Farley, Reynolds. "The Changing Distribution of Negroes Within Metropolitan Areas: The Emergence of Black Suburbs." *American Journal of Sociology* 75 (January 1970): 512-29.

Forrester, Jay W. *Urban Dynamics*. Cambridge, Mass.: M.I.T. Press, 1968.

Frieden, Bernard. "Housing and National Urban Goals: Old Policies and New Realities." In *The Metropolitan Enigma*, edited by James Q. Wilson. New York: Doubleday, 1970.

Funnye, Clarence. "Zoning: The New Battleground." *Architectural Forum* 132 (May 1970): 62-65.

Grigsby, W. G. *Housing Markets and Public Policy*. Philadelphia: University of Pennsylvania Press, 1963.

Harris, R. N. S.; Tolley, G. S.; and Harrell, C. "The Residential Site Choice." *Review of Economics and Statistics* 50 (May 1968): 241-47.

Haugen, Robert A., and Heins, James. "A Market Separation Theory of Rent Differentials in Metropolitan Areas." *Quarterly Journal of Economics* 83 (November 1969): 660-72.

Helper, Rose. *Racial Policies and Practices of Real Estate Brokers*. Minneapolis: University of Minnesota Press, 1969.

Herbert, John D., and Stevens, Benjamin. "A Model for the Distribution of Residential Activity in Urban Areas." *Journal of Regional Science* 2 (Fall 1960): 21-36.

Hester, James, Jr. "Systems Analysis for Social Policies." Review of *Urban Dynamics*, by J. Forrester. *Science* 168 (May 8, 1970): 693-94.

Hoover, Edgar M., and Vernon, Raymond. *Anatomy of a Metropolis*. New York: Doubleday-Anchor, 1959.

Ingram, Gregory K. Review of *Urban Dynamics*, by Jay W. Forrester. *Journal of the American Institute of Planners* 36 (May 1970): 206-18.

Kain, John F. "Coping with Ghetto Unemployment." *Journal of the American Institute of Planners* 35 (March 1969): 80-83.

———. "Housing Segregation, Negro Employment and Metropolitan Decentralization." *Quarterly Journal of Economics* 82 (May 1968): 175-97.

Kain, John F., ed. *Race and Poverty: The Economics of Discrimination*. Englewood Cliffs, N.J.: Prentice-Hall, Inc., 1969.

Kain, John F., and Quigley, John M. "Housing Market Discrimination, Homeownership, and Savings Behavior." *American Economic Review* 62 (June 1972): 263-77.

———. "Measuring the Value of Housing Quality." *Journal of the American Statistical Society* 65 (June 1970): 532-48.

Kristoff, Frank. "Housing Policy Goals and the Turnover of Housing." *Journal of the American Institute of Planners* 31 (August 1965): 232-45.

Lansing, John B., and Barth, Nancy. *Residential Location and Urban Mobility: A Multivariate Analysis*. Ann Arbor: Survey Research Center of Institute for Social Research at the University of Michigan, 1964.

Lansing, John B., and Marans, Robert W. "Evaluation of Neighborhood Quality." *Journal of the American Institute of Planners* 35 (May 1969): 195-99.

Laurenti, Luigi. *Property Values and Race*. Berkeley: University of California Press, 1960.

Lee, Tong Hun. "Housing and Permanent Income: Tests Based on a Three-Year Reinterview Survey." *Review of Economics and Statistics* 50 (November 1968): 480-90.

Lowry, Ira S. "Filtering and Housing Standards: A Conceptual Analysis." *Land Economics* 36 (November 1960): 362-70.

Maisel, Sherman. "Rates of Ownership, Mobility, and Purchase." In *Essays in Urban Land Economics*. Los Angeles: University of California Press, 1966.

Maisel, Sherman, and Winnick, Louis. "Family Housing Expenditures: Elusive Laws and Intrusive Variances." In *Urban Housing*, edited by William L. C. Wheaton et al. New York: The Free Press, 1966.

Mayo, Stephen K. "An Econometric Model of Residential Location." Ph.D. dissertation, Harvard University, 1971.

Meyer, John; Kain, John F.; and Wohl, Martin. *The Urban Transportation Problem*. Cambridge, Mass.: Harvard University Press, 1965.

Mills, Edwin S. "The Value of Urban Land." In *The Quality of the Urban Environment*, edited by Harvey S. Perloff. Baltimore: Johns Hopkins Press, 1969.

———. "Welfare Aspects of National Policy Toward City Sizes." *Urban Studies* 9 (February 1972): 117-24.

Mooney, Joseph D. "Housing Segregation, Negro Employment and Metropolitan Decentralization: An Alternative Perspective." *Quarterly Journal of Economics* 83 (May 1969): 299-311.

Morgan, James N. "Housing and the Ability to Pay." *Econometrica* 33 (April 1965): 289-306.

Muth, Richard F. *Cities and Housing*. Chicago: University of Chicago Press, 1969.

———. "The Demand for Non-Farm Housing." In *The Demand for Durable Goods*, edited by Arnold C. Harberger. Chicago: University of Chicago Press, 1960.

———. "The Spatial Structure of the Housing Market." *Papers and Proceedings of the Regional Science Association* 7 (1961): 207-20.

National Committee Against Discrimination in Housing. *The Impact of Housing Patterns on Job Opportunities*. New York, 1968.

Needleman, Lionel. *The Economics of Housing*. London: Staples Press, 1965.

Netzer, Dick. *Economics and Urban Problems*. New York: Basic Books, 1970.

Neutze, Max. *The Suburban Apartment Boom*. Baltimore: John Hopkins Press, 1968.

Nevitt, A. A., ed. *The Economic Problems of Housing*. New York: Macmillan, 1967.

Offner, Paul, and Saks, Daniel H. "A Note on John Kain's 'Housing Segregation, Negro Employment and Metropolitan Decentralization.'" *Quarterly Journal of Economics* 85 (February 1971): 147-60.

Page, A. N., and Seyfried, W. R., eds. *Urban Analysis: Readings in Housing and Urban Development*. Glenview, Ill.: Scott, Foresman & Co., 1970.

Palmore, Erdman, and Howe, John. "Residential Integration and Property Values." *Social Problems* 10 (Summer 1962): 52-55.

Pascal, Anthony H. *The Economics of Housing Segregation*. RM-5510-RC. Santa Monica, Calif.: The Rand Corp., 1967.

———. "The Analysis of Residential Segregation." In *Financing the Metropolis*, edited by John P. Crecine. Beverly Hills, Calif.: Sage Publications Inc., 1970.

Perloff, Harvey S., and Wingo, Lowdon, Jr., eds. *Issues in Urban Economics*. Baltimore: Johns Hopkins Press, 1968.

Phares, Donald. "Racial Change and Housing Values: Transition in an Inner Suburb."

Social Science Quarterly 52 (December 1971): 560-73.

Pinkerton, James. "City-Suburban Residential Patterns by Social Class: A Review of the Literature." *Urban Affairs Quarterly* 4 (June 1969): 499-519.

Potvin, D. Joseph. "Suburban Zoning Ordinances and Building Codes: Their Effect on Low and Moderate Income Housing." *Notre Dame Lawyer* 45 (Fall 1969): 123-34.

Rapkin, Chester, and Grigsby, William G. *The Demand for Housing in Racially Mixed Areas*. Berkeley: University of California Press, 1960.

Reid, Margaret G. *Housing and Income*. Chicago: University of Chicago Press, 1962.

Reno, Lee P. *Pieces and Scraps: Farm Labor Housing in the United States*. Washington, D.C.: Rural Housing Alliance, 1970.

Ridker, Ronald G., and Henning, John A. "The Determinants of Residential Property Values With Special Reference to Air Pollution." *Review of Economics and Statistics* 49 (May 1967): 246-57.

Rodwin, Lloyd. *Housing and Economic Progress*. Cambridge, Mass.: Harvard University Press and Technology Press, 1961.

Rucker, George W. *Rural Housing: Need and Non-Response*. Washington, D.C.: Rural Housing Alliance, June, 1969.

Sager, Lawrence Gene. "Tight Little Islands: Exclusionary Zoning, Equal Protection and the Indigent." *Stanford Law Review* 21 (1969): 767-800.

Schafer, Robert. "Slum Formation, Race and an Income Strategy." Review of *Cities and Housing* by Richard F. Muth. *Journal of the American Institute of Planners* 37 (September 1971): 347-54.

Schafer, Robert, and Pynoos, Jon. "An Introduction to Urban Theory." *Journal of Urban Law* 48 (1971): 361-408.

Silver, Irving R. "A Study of the Demand for Housing in a Metropolitan Area." Ph.D. dissertation, Massachusetts Institute of Technology, 1969.

Smart, Walter; Rybeck, Walter; and Shuman, Howard E. *The Large Poor Family–A Housing Gap*, Research Report no. 4. Washington, D.C.: National Commission on Urban Problems, 1968.

Smith, Wallace F. *Filtering and Neighborhood Change*. Research Report no. 24. Berkeley: Center for Real Estate and Urban Economics, University of California, 1964.

————. *Housing: The Social and Economic Elements*. Berkeley: University of California Press, 1970.

Sporn, Arthur D. "Empirical Studies of the Economics of Slum Ownership." *Land Economics* 36 (November 1960): 333-40.

Stegman, Michael A., ed. *Housing and Economics: The American Dilemma*. Cambridge, Mass.: M.I.T. Press, 1971.

Sternlieb, George. *The Tenement Landlord*. New Brunswick, N.J.: Rutgers, The State University, 1966.

Sternlieb, George, and Indik, Bernard. "Housing Vacancy Analysis." *Land Economics* 45 (February 1969): 117-21.

Stokes, Charles J. "A Theory of Slums." *Land Economics* 38 (August 1962): 187-97.

Sutermeister, Oscar. "Inadequacies and Inconsistencies in the Definition of Substandard Housing." *Housing Code Standards: Three Critical Studies*. Research Report no. 19. Washington, D.C.: National Commission on Urban Problems.

Taeuber, Karl E. "The Effect of Income Redistribution on Racial Residential Segregation." *Urban Affairs Quarterly* 4 (September 1968): 5-14.

Turvey, Ralph. *The Economics of Real Property: An Analysis of Property Values and Patterns of Use*. London: George Allen and Unwin, Ltd., 1957.

U.S. Bureau of the Census. *Measuring the Quality of Housing: An Appraisal of Census Statistics and Methods*. Washington, D.C.: Government Printing Office, 1967.

U.S. Department of Agriculture. Economic Research Service. *Rural Housing: Trends and Prospects*. Agricultural Economics Report no. 193. Washington, D.C.: Government Printing Office, 1970.

U.S. Department of Housing and Urban Development. *F.H.A. Techniques of Housing Market Analysis*. Washington, D.C.: Government Printing Office, 1970.

U.S. National Advisory Commission of Rural Poverty. *The People Left Behind*. Washington, D.C.: Government Printing Office, 1967.

U.S. National Capital Planning Commission. *Problems of Housing People in Washington*. Washington, D.C.: Government Printing Office, 1966.

U.S. President's Committee on Urban Housing. *A Decent Home*. The Report of the Committee. Washington, D.C.: Government Printing Office, 1969.

U.S. President's Committee on Urban Housing. *Technical Studies*. Vols. I and II. Washington, D.C.: Government Printing Office, 1969.

Wheeler, James O. "Work-trip Length and the Ghetto." *Land Economics* 44 (February 1968): 107-12.

Williams, Norman, Jr., and Wacks, Edward. "Segregation of Residential Areas along Economic Lines: Lionshead Lake Revisited." *Wisconsin Law Review* (1969), 827-47.

Wilson, James Q., ed. *The Metropolitan Enigma*. New York: Doubleday, 1970.

Winger, Alan R. "An Approach to Measuring Potential Upgrading Demand in the Housing Market." *Review of Economics and Statistics* 45 (August 1963): 239-44.

Wingo, Lowdon, Jr. *Transportation and Urban Land*. Baltimore: Johns Hopkins Press, 1961.

IV. PRODUCTION

Aaron, Henry. "Income Taxes and Housing." *American Economic Review* 60 (December 1970): 789-806.

Aaron, Henry; Russke, Frank S., Jr.; and Singer, Neil M. "Tax Reform and the Composition of Investment." *National Tax Journal* 25 (March 1972): 1-13.

Altschuler, Karen B., and Betts, Robert S. *Mobile Homes: Evolution of the Market, Consumer Costs, Taxation Controversy, Comparative Costs*. Working paper 123. Berkeley: Center for Planning and Development Research, University of California, January 1970.

Bartke, Richard W. "Fannie Mae and the Secondary Mortgage Market." *Northwestern University Law Review* 66 (1971), 1-78.

Cassimatis, Peter J. *Economics of the Construction Industry*. New York: National Industrial Conference Board, Studies in Business and Economics, no. 111, 1969.

Colean, Miles L., and Newcomb, R. *Stabilizing Construction: The Record and Potential*. New York: McGraw-Hill, 1952.

Drury, Margaret. *Mobile Homes: The Unrecognized Revolution in American Housing*. Ithaca, N.Y.: Department of Housing and Design, Cornell University, 1967.

Franklin, Herbert M. "Operation Breakthrough: A First Appraisal." *Journal of Housing* 26 (September 5, 1969): 409-11.

French, Robert Mills, and Hadden, Jeffrey K. "An Analysis of the Distribution and Characteristics of Mobile Homes in America." *Land Economics* 41 (May 1965): 131-39.

Gillies, James M., and Mittlebach, Frank. *Management in the Light Construction Industry*. Los Angeles, 1962.

Givens, Richard A. "Job Security in the Building Industry—And High Quality Low-Rent Housing." *Labor Law Journal* 18 (August 1967): 468-77.

Goldfinger, Nathaniel. "The Myth of Housing Costs." *AFL-CIO American Federationist*, December 1969, pp. 1-6.

Grebler, Leo; Blank, David; and Winnick, Louis. *Capital Formation in Residential Real Estate*. Princeton, N.J.: Princeton University Press, 1956.

Haar, Charles. *Federal Credit and Private Housing: The Mass Financing Dilemma*. New York: McGraw-Hill, 1960.

Hayes, Samuel L., III, and Harlan, Leonard M. "Real Estate as a Corporate Investment: Equity Participation in Real Estate Developments Affords Unrecognized Potential." *Harvard Business Review* 45 (July-August 1967): 144-60.

Heimann, John C. *The Necessary Revolution in Housing Finance*. Washington, D.C.: Urban America, Inc., 1967.

Herzog, John P. *The Dynamics of Large-Scale Housebuilding*. Berkeley: Institute of Business and Economic Research, University of California, 1963.

————. "Structural Change in the Housebuilding Industry." *Land Economics* 39 (May 1963): 133-41.

Jones, Oliver, and Grebler, Leo. *The Secondary Mortgage Market: Its Purposes, Performance and Potential*. Los Angeles: Real Estate Research Program, Graduate School of Business Administration, University of California, 1961.

Kelly, Burnham. *The Prefabrication of Housing*. Cambridge, Mass.: Technology Press and Wiley Press, 1951.

Kelly, Burham and associates. *Design and Production of Houses*. New York: McGraw-Hill, 1959.

Keyserling, Leon H. "Discussion of Tax Incentives for Real Estate." In *Tax Incentives*, edited by Stanley Surrey et al. Lexington, Massachusetts: Heath-Lexington Books, 1971.

Klaman, Saul B. "Public/Private Approaches to Urban Mortgage and Housing Problems." *Law and Contemporary Problems* 32 (Spring 1967): 250-65.

Laidler, David. "Income Tax Incentives for Owner-Occupied Housing." In *The Taxation of Income from Capital*, edited by A. C. Harberger and M. J. Bailey. Washington, D.C.: The Brookings Institution, 1969.

Maisel, Sherman J. *Financing Real Estate: Principles and Practices*. New York: McGraw-Hill, 1965.

————. *Housebuilding in Transition*. Berkeley: University of California Press, 1953.

————. "A Theory of Fluctuations in Residential Construction Starts." *American Economic Review* 53 (June 1963): 359-83.

Mills, Daniel Quinn. *Industrial Relations and Manpower in Construction*. Cambridge, Mass.: M.I.T. Press, 1972.

Muth, Richard F. "Interest Rates, Contract Terms, and the Allocations of Mortgage Funds." *Journal of Finance* 17 (March 1962): 63-80.

Myrdal, Gunnar. "Realizing the Promise of Industrialized Housing." *Journal of Housing* 24 (September 1967): 428-30.

Ott, David J., and Ott, Attiat. "The Tax Subsidy Through Exemption of State and Local Bond Interest." *The Economics of Federal Subsidy Programs*. U.S. Congress, Joint Economic Committee, 92d Cong., 1st sess., 1972, pt. 3, pp. 305-16.

Rose, Sanford. "The Future Largest Landlords in America." *Fortune*, 82 (July 1970): 90-93, 133-34.

Shelton, John P. "The Cost of Renting Versus Owning a Home." *Land Economics* 44 (February 1968): 59-72.

Sporn, Arthur D. "Some Contributions of the Income Tax Law to the Growth and Prevalence of Slums." *Columbia Law Review* 59 (November 1959): 1026-63.

Surrey, Stanley. "Federal Income Tax Reform: The Varied Approaches Necessary to Replace Tax Expenditures with Direct Governmental Assistance." *Harvard Law Review* 84 (December 1970): 352-408.

Taubman, Paul, and Rasche, Robert. "The Income Tax and Real Estate Investment." In *Tax Incentives*, edited by Stanley Surrey et al. Lexington, Mass.: Heath Lexington Books, 1971.

U.S. Advisory Commission on Intergovernmental Relations. *Building Codes; A Program for Intergovernmental Reform*. Washington, D.C.: Government Printing Office, 1966.

U.S. Congress. Senate. Subcommittee on Housing and Urban Affairs. Committee on Banking and Currency. *A Study of Mortgage Credit*. Washington, D.C.: Government Printing Office, May, 1967.

U.S. Congress. Subcommittee on Urban Affairs. *Industrialized Housing*. Hearings before the Subcommittee on Urban Affairs of the Joint Economic Committee, 91st Cong., 1st sess., 1969.

Winger, Alan R., and Madden, John. "The Application of the Theory of Joint Products: The Case of Residential Construction." *Quarterly Review of Economics and Business* 10 (Summer 1970): 61-69.

Winnick, Louis. *Rental Housing: Opportunities for Private Investment*. New York: McGraw-Hill, 1958.

V. POLICIES AND PROGRAMS

Aaron, Henry J. *Shelter and Subsidies: Who Benefits From Federal Housing Policies?* Washington, D.C.: The Brookings Institution, 1972.

Aaron, Henry J., and von Furstenberg, George M. "The Inefficiency of Transfers in Kind: The Case of Housing Assistance." *Western Economic Journal* 9 (June 1971): 184-91.

Abrams, Charles. *The City Is the Frontier*. New York: Harper & Row, 1965.

Ackerman, Bruce. "Regulating Slum Housing Markets on Behalf of the Poor: Of Housing Codes, Housing Subsidies and Income Distribution Policy." *Yale Law Journal* 80 (May 1971): 1093-1197.

Advisory Committee to the Department of Housing and Urban Development. *Freedom of Choice in Housing: Opportunities and Constraints*. Washington, D.C.: National Academy of Sciences, 1972.

Allen, Muriel I. *New Communities: Challenge for Today*. Background paper no. 2. Washington, D.C.: American Institute of Planners, Task Force on New Communities, 1968.

Alonso, William. "What Are New Towns For?" *Urban Studies* 7 (February 1970): 37-56.

Anderson, Martin. *The Federal Bulldozer: A Critical Analysis of Urban Renewal, 1949-1962*. Cambridge, Mass.: M.I.T. Press, 1964.

Beagle, Danny; Haber, Al; and Weilman, David. "Urban Renewal, Regionalization, and the Limits of Community Control." *Leviathan*, 1969.

Bellin, Seymour S., and Kriesberg, Louis. "Relationship between Attitudes, Circumstances and Behavior: The Case of Applying for Public Housing." *Sociology and Social Research* 51 (July 1967): 453-70.

Bellush, Jewel, and Hausknecht, Murray, eds. *Urban Renewal: People, Politics and Planning*. Garden City, N.Y.: Doubleday, 1967.

Berger, Curtis; Goldston, Eli; and Rothrauff, Guido A., Jr. "Slum Area Rehabilitation by Private Enterprise." *Columbia Law Review* 69 (1969): 739-69.

Bish, Robert L. "Public Housing: The Magnitude and Direction of Direct Benefits and Effects on Housing Competition." *Journal of Regional Science* 9 (December 1969): 425-38.

Brown, William H., Jr. "Access to Housing—The Role of the Real Estate Industry." *Economic Geography* 48 (January 1972).

Burstein, Joseph. "New Techniques in Public Housing." *Law and Contemporary Problems* 32 (Summer 1967): 528-49.

Case, F. E. "Code Enforcement in Urban Renewal." *Urban Studies* 5 (November 1968): 277-89.

Dasso, Jerome. "An Evaluation of Rent Supplements." *Land Economics* 44 (November 1968): 441-49.

Davies, J. Clarence. *Neighborhood Groups and Urban Renewal*. New York: Columbia University, 1966.

de Leeuw, Frank. *Operating Costs in Public Housing—a Financial Crisis*. Washington, D.C.: Urban Institute, n.d. (1970).

DeSalvo, Joseph S. "Effects of the Property Tax on Operating and Investment Decisions of Rental Property Owners." *National Tax Journal* 24 (March 1971): 45-50.

————. "Reforming Rent Control in New York City: Analysis of Housing Expenditures and Market Rentals." *Papers and Proceedings of the Regional Science Association* 27 (November 1970): 195-227.

————. "A Methodology for Evaluating Housing Programs." *Journal of Regional Science*, 11 (August 1971): 173-85.

Downs, Anthony. "Moving Toward Realistic Housing Goals." In *Agenda for the Nation*, edited by Kermit Gordon. Garden City, N.Y.: Doubleday-Anchor, 1968.

————. "Housing the Urban Poor: The Economics of Various Strategies." *American Economic Review* 59 (September 1969): 646-51.

Edson, Charles. *Homeownership for Low-Income Families*. 3 monograph series. Chicago: National Legal Aid and Defender Association, 1969.

Eichler, Edward P., and Kaplan, Marshall. *The Community Builders*. Berkeley: University of California Press, 1967.

Ellickson, Robert. "Government Housing Assistance to the Poor." *Yale Law Journal* 76 (January 1967): 508-44.

"Enforcement of Municipal Housing Codes." *Harvard Law Review* 78 (February 1965): 801-60.

Fisher, R. *Twenty Years of Public Housing*. New York: Harper, 1959.

Fossum, John C. "Rent Withholding and the Improvement of Substandard Housing." *California Law Review* 53 (March 1965): 304-36.

Frieden, Bernard J. *The Future of Old Neighborhoods: Rebuilding for a Changing Population*. Cambridge, Mass.: M.I.T. Press, 1964.

Frieden, Bernard, and Newman, JoAnn. "Home Ownership for the Poor?" *Trans-action* 7 (October 1970): 47-53.

Friedman, Gilbert B. "Uninsurables in the Ghetto." *The New Republic*, September 14, 1968, pp. 19-21.

Friedman, Lawrence M. *Government and Slum Housing*. Chicago: Rand McNally & Co., 1968.

Friedman, Lawrence M., and Krier, James E. "A New Lease on Life: Section 23 Housing and the Poor." *University of Pennsylvania Law Review* 116 (February 1968): 611-47.

"Government Programs to Encourage Private Investment in Low-Income Housing." *Harvard Law Review* 81 (April 1968): 1295-1324.

Greer, Scott. *Urban Renewal and American Cities: The Dilemma of Democratic Intervention*. Indianapolis: The Bobbs-Merrill Co., 1965.

Gribetz, Judah, and Grad, Frank P. "Housing Code Enforcement: Sanctions and Remedies." *Columbia Law Review* 66 (November 1966): 1254-90.

Groberg, Robert P. *Centralized Relocation: A New Municipal Service*. Washington, D.C.: National Association of Housing and Redevelopment Officials, 1969.

Gruen, Claude. "Urban Renewal's Role in the Genesis of Tomorrow's Slums." *Land Economics* 39 (August 1963): 285-91.

Hartman, Chester. *Housing and Social Policy*. Englewood Cliffs: Prentice-Hall, Forthcoming.

———. "Relocation: Illusory Promises and No Relief." *Virginia Law Review* 57 (June 1971).

———. "The Limitations of Public Housing: Relocation Choices in a Working Class Community." *Journal of the American Institute of Planners* 29 (November 1963): 283-96.

Hartman, Chester, and Carr, Gregg. "Housing Authorities Reconsidered." *Journal of the American Institute of Planners* 35 (January 1969): 10-21.

Heilbrun, James. *Real Estate Taxes and Urban Housing*. New York: Columbia University Press, 1966.

Heinberg, J. D., and Oates, W. E. "The Incidence of Differential Property Taxes on Urban Housing: A Comment and Some Further Evidence." *National Tax Journal* 23 (March 1970), 92-98.

Hipshman, May B. *Public Housing at the Crossroads: The Boston Housing Authority*. Boston: Citizens' Housing and Planning Association of Metropolitan Boston, 1967.

Hollingshead, A. B., and Rogler, L. H. "Attitudes Towards Slums and Private Housing In Puerto Rico." In *The Urban Condition*, edited by Leonard Duhl. New York: Basic Books, 1963.

Hood, Edwin T., and Kushner, James A. "Real Estate Finance: The Discount Point System and Its Effects on Federally Insured Home Loans." *University of Missouri-Kansas City Law Review* 40 (Autumn 1971): 1-23.

Isler, Morton. *Thinking About Housing*. Report no. 10-112-6. Washington, D.C.: Urban Institute, 1970.

Keyes, Langley C. *The Rehabilitation Planning Game: A Study in the Diversity of Neighborhood.* Cambridge, Mass.: M.I.T. Press, 1969.

Krier, James E. "The Rent Supplement Program of 1965: Out of the Ghetto, Into the . . . ?" *Stanford Law Review* 19 (1967): 555-78.

Kriesberg, Louis. "Neighborhood Setting and the Isolation of Public Housing Tenants." *Journal of the American Institute of Planners* 34 (January 1968): 43-49.

Ledbetter, William H., Jr. "Public Housing—A Social Experiment Seeks Acceptance." *Law and Contemporary Problems* 32 (Summer 1967): 490-527.

Lempert, Richard, and Ikeda, Kiyoshi. "Evictions from Public Housing: Effects of Independent Review." *American Sociological Review* 35 (October 1970): 852-60.

Liblit, Jerome, 3d. *Housing–The Cooperative Way.* New York: Twayne, 1964.

Lozano, Eduardo E. "Housing Costs and Alternative Cost Reducing Policies." *Journal of the American Institute of Planners* 38 (May 1972): 176-81.

Lubove, Roy. *The Progressives and the Slums: Tenement House Reform in New York City 1890-1917.* Pittsburgh: University of Pittsburgh Press, 1962.

Luttrel, Jordan D. "The Public Housing Administration and Discrimination in Federally Assisted Low-Rent Housing." *Michigan Law Review* 64 (March 1966): 871-90.

Lym, Glenn R. "Effect of a Public Housing Project on a Neighborhood: Case Study of Oakland, California." *Land Economics* 43 (November 1967): 461-66.

Maass, Arthur. "Benefit-Cost Analysis: Its Relevance to Public Investment." *Quarterly Journal of Economics* 80 (May 1966): 208-26.

Mace, Ruth L., and Wicker, Warren J. *Do Single-Family Homes Pay Their Way? A Comparative Analysis of Costs and Revenues for Public Services.* Research monograph 15. Washington, D.C.: Urban Land Institute, 1968.

McFarland, M. Carter, and Vivrett, Walter K., eds. *Residential Rehabilitation.* Minneapolis: University of Minnesota School of Architecture, 1965.

McPherson, James Alan. " 'In My Father's House There Are Many Mansions and I'm Going to Get Me Some of Them, Too!' The Story of the Contract Buyers League." *The Atlantic* 219 (April 1972): 51-83.

Manvel, Allen D. *Local Land and Building Regulation.* Research report no. 6. Prepared for the National Commission on Urban Problems. Washington, D.C.: Government Printing Office, 1968.

Marcuse, Peter. "Comparative Analysis of Federally-Aided Low- and Moderate-Income Housing Programs." *Journal of Housing* 26 (November 1969): 536-54.

———. "Homeownership for Low Income Families: Financial Implications." *Land Economics* 48 (May 1972): 134-143.

Marmor, Theodore. "On Comparing Income Maintenance Alternatives." *American Political Science Review* 65 (March 1971): 83-96.

Mayer, Albert. *The Urgent Future.* New York: McGraw-Hill, 1967.

Mulvihill, Roger. "Problems in the Management of Public Housing." *Temple Law Quarterly* 35 (1962): 163-94.

"Municipal Housing Codes." *Harvard Law Review* 69 (April 1956): 1115-26.

National Committee Against Discrimination in Housing. *How the Federal Government Builds Ghettos.* New York, 1967.

National Housing and Economic Development Law Project. *Handbook on Housing Law.* 2 vols. Englewood Cliffs, N.J.: Prentice-Hall, Inc., 1970.

Netzer, Dick. *Economics of the Property Tax.* Washington, D.C.: The Brookings Institution, 1966.

"No Room for Singles: A Gap in the Housing Law." *The Yale Law Journal* 80 (December 1970): 395-432.

Nourse, Hugh O. "The Effect of Air Pollution on House Values." *Land Economics* 43 (May 1967): 181-89.

———. "The Effect of Public Housing on Property Values in St. Louis." *Land Economics* 39 (November 1963): 433-41.

"The Oakland Leased Housing Program." *Stanford Law Review* 20 (February 1968): 538-50.

Oates, Wallace E. "The Effects of Property Taxes and Local Public Spending on Property Values: An Empirical Study of Tax Capitalization and the Tiebout Hypothesis." *Journal of Political Economy* 77 (November/December 1969): 957-71.

Oldman, Oliver, and Aaron, Henry. "Assessment-Sales Ratios Under the Boston Property Tax." *National Tax Journal* 18 (March 1965): 36-49.

Organization for Social and Technical Innovation. *Self-Help in Housing: Final Report on Self- or Mutual-Help Techniques in Management of Housing for Low-Income Persons.* Report no. 10. Cambridge, Mass.: OSTI Press, 1970.

Orr, Larry L. "The Incidence of Differential Property Taxes on Urban Housing." *National Tax Journal* 21 (September 1968): 253-62.

———. "The Incidence of Differential Property Taxes: A Response." *National Tax Journal* 23 (March 1970): 99-101.

Peattie, Lisa Redfield. "Public Housing: Urban Slums Under Public Management." In *Race, Change, and Urban Society*, edited by Peter Orleans and William Russell Ellis, Jr. Beverly Hills, Calif.: Sage Publications, 1971.

Perloff, Harvey. "New Towns Intown." *Journal of the American Institute of Planners* 32 (May 1966): 155-59.

Philadelphia Housing Association. *Housing Grants for the Very Poor.* 1966.

Prescott, James R. "Rental Formation in Federally Supported Public Housing." *Land Economics* 43 (August 1967): 341-45.

Rapid Rehabilitation of Old-Law Tenements, An Evaluation. New York: Institute of Public Administration, 1968.

Rapkin, Chester. "New Towns for America: From Picture to Process." *Journal of Finance* 22 (May 1967): 208-19.

"Residential Rent Control in New York City." *Columbia Journal of Law and Social Problems* 3 (June 1967): 30-65.

Ross, William B. "A Proposed Methodology for Comparing Federally Assisted Housing Programs." *American Economic Review* 57 (May 1967): 91-100.

Rothenberg, Jerome. *Economic Evaluation of Urban Renewal.* Washington, D.C.: The Brookings Institution, 1967.

Rydell, C. Peter. "Review of Factors Affecting Maintenance and Operating Costs in Public Housing." *Papers and Proceedings of the Regional Science Association* 27 (November 1970): 229-45.

Sanderson, Richard L. *Codes and Code Administration.* Chicago: Building Officials Conference of America, 1969.

Schafer, Robert. "The Effect of BMIR Housing on Property Values." *Land Economics* 48 (August 1972): 282-86.

Schermer, George, Associates, and Jones, Kenneth C. *Changing Concepts of the Tenant-Management Relationship.* Washington, D.C.: National Association of Housing and Redevelopment Officials, 1967.

Schorr, Alvin. "Housing the Poor." In *Power, Poverty and Urban Policy*, edited by Warner Bloomberg and Henry Schmandt. Beverly Hills, Calif.: Sage Publications, 1968.

Schoshinski, Robert S. "Public Landlords and Tenants: A Survey of the Developing Law." *Duke Law Journal* June 1969, pp. 399-474.

Sengstock, Frank S., and Sengstock, Mary C. "Home-Ownership: A Goal for All Americans." *Journal of Urban Law* 46 (1969): 317-602.

Slitor, Richard E. *The Federal Income Tax in Relation to Housing.* Research report no. 5. National Commission on Urban Problems. Washington, D.C.: Government Printing Office, 1968.

Smolensky, Eugene. "Public Housing or Income Supplements—the Economics of Housing the Poor." *Journal of the American Institute of Planners* 34 (March 1968): 94-101.

Solomon, Arthur Paul. "Housing the Urban Poor: A Critical Analysis of Federal Housing Policy." Ph.D. dissertation, Harvard University, 1971.

Steiner, Gilbert. *The State of Welfare.* Washington, D.C.: The Brookings Institution, 1971.

Sternlieb, George. "New York's Housing: A Study in *Immobilisme.*" *The Public Interest,* no. 16 (Summer, 1969), pp. 123-41.

Taggart, Robert, III. *Low-Income Housing: A Critique of Federal Aid.* Baltimore: Johns Hopkins Press, 1970.

Tilly, Charles et al. *Rent Supplements in Boston.* Cambridge, Mass.: M.I.T.-Harvard Joint Center for Urban Studies, 1968.

Tobin, James. "Raising the Incomes of the Poor." In *Agenda for the Nation,* edited by Kermit Gordon. Garden City, N.Y.: Doubleday-Anchor, 1968.

Turnkey III: A Casestudy of the Pilot Program of Home-Ownership Under Public Housing in North Gulfport Mississippi. Washington, D.C.: Nonprofit Housing Center, Urban America, 1969.

U.S. Advisory Commission on Intergovernmental Relations. *Relocation: Unequal Treatment of People and Businesses Displaced by Governments.* Washington, D.C., 1965.

U.S. Congress. House. Committee on Banking and Currency. *Basic Laws and Authorities on Housing and Urban Development.* Revised annually. Washington, D.C.: Government Printing Office, 1971.

U.S. Congress. House. Committee on Banking and Currency. *Papers on Housing Production, Housing Demand, and Developing a Suitable Living Environment.* Submitted to the Subcommittee on Housing Panels of the Committee on Banking and Currency, House of Representatives, 92d Cong., 1st sess., June, 1971.

U.S. Congress. Senate. Committee on Banking and Currency. *Report on Federal Housing Programs.* May 9, 1967.

U.S. Department of Health, Education and Welfare. *The Role of Public Welfare in Housing.* Washington, D.C., 1969.

"Urban Planning and Urban Revolt: A Case Study." *Progressive Architecture,* January 1968, pp. 134-56.

von Furstenberg, George M. "Distribution of Federally Assisted Rental Housing." *Journal of the American Institute of Planners* 37 (September 1971): 326-30.

Weaver, Robert. "Goals of the Department of Housing and Urban Development." *Urban Affairs Quarterly* 11 (December 1966): 3-23.

Welfeld, Irving H. "Rent Supplements and the Subsidy Dilemma." *Law and Contemporary Problems* 32 (Summer 1967): 465-81.

————. "A New Framework for Federal Housing Aids." *Columbia Law Review* 69 (December 1969): 1355-91.

Wendt, Paul F. *Housing Policy–The Search for Solutions.* Berkeley: University of California Press, 1962.

————. "Large-Scale Community Development." *Journal of Finance* 22 (May 1967): 220-39.

Wendt, Paul F., and Cerf, Alan R. *Real Estate Investment Analysis and Taxation.* New York: McGraw-Hill, 1969.

Whittlesey, Robert B. *The South End Row House and Its Rehabilitation for Low-Income Residents.* Boston: South End Community Development, Inc., 1969.

Wilson, James Q., ed. *Urban Renewal: The Record and the Controversy.* Cambridge, Mass.: M.I.T. Press, 1966.

Winchester, Walter, and Baskin, Sheldon. "FHA Middle Income Housing and Some Tax Aspects." *Massachusetts CPA Review* 40 (October/November 1966): 74-86.

Index

Abandonment, 206-7
Attitudes (preferences), 27, 97, 99, 104, 115-16,
    120-23, 132, 144-45, 147-57, 183-89, 191-99,
    254, 255, 259, 406-22, 453-54, 526, 550
    see also, Consumer sovereignty

Banks. *See* Financial institutions
Building codes, 249, 250, 303, 343-58

Central city, 87-90, 92, 95, 194, 241, 247, 252,
    263-65, 349-51, 474-83, 512-15, 532, 534, 557
Childrearing, 133, 137-38, 153-54, 550-52
    see also, Family life cycle
Civil disorders, 49, 51, 88, 91
Civil Rights, 98, 108-13, 379-80, 390, 417-18
    see also, Discrimination
Class (socio-economic), 106, 117-18, 121-22,
    132-33, 137-45, 218-22, 452-55, 546-47, 550-55
    see also, Lower class, Middle class, Upper
    class, Working class
Community control, 17, 19, 21-22, 26, 55-73,
    104-6, 127, 133, 472, 484-86, 489-91
    see also, Local government, Rent strikes,
    Tenants' unions
Construction
    building technology (materials), 329, 330-42,
        343-49, 351-55, 359-69, 372-75
    construction industry, 300, 321-28, 329-42,
        343-58, 359-71, 372-401, 428
    costs, 40, 304, 330-42, 347-48, 352, 372-75, 421,
        426-27, 439, 443, 445-47, 463-68, 493-96,
        510-22, 566-68
    efficiency, 303, 321-28, 329-42
    labor (supply and wages), 42, 321-28, 330-42,
        359-71, 372-75, 376-91, 427
    new construction, 10, 38, 236, 257, 301, 303,
        307, 315, 355, 372-75, 410, 424, 443-44, 477
    racial discrimination, 5, 19, 111-12, 376-91,
        480-81, 488
    statistics, 119, 321-28, 332-42, 345-51, 369-70,
        377-80, 384-85
    see also, Rehabilitation
Consumer sovereignty, 123, 134, 208, 471, 538,
    559, 560, 564-66, 577
    see also, Attitudes
Cost/Benefit analysis, 55-73, 236, 439, 441, 574-77

Crime, 185-88, 454, 505, 549-50
    see also, Security
Demand, 5, 66, 203, 277-338, 239-44, 244-50, 261,
    263-64, 269-71, 303, 311-15, 316-20, 334, 337,
    392-93, 424-26, 434-47, 556-59, 561-62
Density (exterior), 272-73, 279, 283, 528
    see also, Housing conditions, overcrowding
Depression (1929-1938), 27, 403, 407, 429, 448, 450
Design, 122, 132, 135, 145-46, 166-70, 171-80, 184,
    186, 189-90, 416, 476-77, 527-29
Developers, 63, 403, 435, 478-80, 484-85, 488, 529,
    538-39
Discrimination (by race, class, income), 21, 22,
    87-91, 93-94, 97-106, 108-13, 120-23, 151-57,
    208-9, 225, 251-66, 267-73, 274-78, 282-89,
    290-97, 376-91, 409-10, 417-21, 453-54, 481,
    489, 527, 530, 538, 540

Education, 2, 93-95, 100, 102-3, 142, 154-55
Effects of poor housing, 131-32, 158-65, 166-70,
    548-55
Elderly (housing for), 9, 66, 67, 440, 454
Employment (job training), 91, 93-95, 100,
    211-27, 369-70, 378-79, 382-91, 488, 555
Equity participation, 43, 532-33
Ethnic communities, 104-6, 192-98, 420, 453
    see also, Neighborhood
Expenditures, 5, 65-67, 203, 230, 233, 237, 239-50,
    257-59, 261-62, 265, 267-73, 285, 288, 290-97,
    299, 302, 311-12, 350, 392-95, 424, 428,
    436-47, 460-68, 511, 514

Family income(s), 119, 253-54, 290, 409, 460-61
Family life cycle, 136-39, 217-21, 419-21
Family size (household size), 167-70, 220-22, 409,
    461
Fannie Mae. *See* Federal National Mortgage
    Association
Federal Home Loan Bank Board, 38, 300, 319,
    407, 430, 432
Federal Housing Administration, 40, 127, 288,
    308, 353, 407, 430-31, 473-83, 484-92
Federal National Mortgage Association
    (FNMA), 32, 36, 38, 300, 307, 309, 432
Federal Reserve Board, 36, 307, 319
Filtering, 66-67, 205-6, 231-38, 262, 443

Financial institutions, 59-74, 275-77, 307-17, 423, 425-26, 429-30

Fiscal policy, 32, 300, 308, 316-20

Foreign housing experiences, 337, 342, 406, 410, 414, 436, 518-19, 524, 540

Ghetto, 21-22, 55, 87-89, 91, 93, 98, 100, 103, 106, 111, 251-66, 454, 532, 548-55
see also, Slum

Ginnie Mae. See Government National Mortgage Association

Governmental Housing Programs
housing allowances (rent certificates), 124, 236-38, 546
rent supplements, 9, 36, 99, 114, 117-18, 123-24, 236, 414, 563-66, 570
Section 221 (d) (3) (BMIR), 9, 124, 410, 460, 486, 534
Section 235, 9, 37-38, 460-71
Section 236, 9, 37-38, 462
subsidies, 9, 15-16, 30-31, 37, 44, 99, 100-102, 119, 121, 124, 208, 236-38, 304, 400, 422, 431, 440, 447, 452-53, 495, 539, 544, 545, 557, 560, 566-77
see also, Public housing

Government National Mortgage Association, 32, 300, 319, 431-33

Health, 128, 130-32, 162, 166, 186, 364, 458, 491, 498, 549

Heterogeneity, 21-22, 121-23, 135, 146, 205, 261, 419-20, 526, 540-41
see also, Homogeneity

Homeownership, 57, 63, 115-16, 184, 300, 393-99, 406-14, 460-71
see also, Single family houses

Homogeneity, 21-22, 121-23, 135-46, 175-76, 527
see also, Heterogeneity

Housing Act of 1934, 25, 407, 430

Housing Act of 1937, 17, 25, 233, 407, 433

Housing Act of 1949, 7, 101, 114

Housing Act of 1968, 7, 37, 301, 460

Housing bundle, 1, 2, 131, 203-5, 232-33, 279-81, 506, 524, 529, 544

Housing codes, 4, 77-80, 82, 470, 497-509

Housing conditions (general), 2, 23, 82, 117, 132, 158-65, 229, 242-50, 502
deterioration, 2-4, 244, 273, 445, 501
dilapidation, 2, 160, 234, 501
overcrowding, 4, 6-7, 161-63, 166-70, 247, 276, 442, 498
plumbing, 2, 161, 343, 345-50, 353, 358, 362
sound, 544
substandard, 3, 77-78, 117, 159, 161, 206, 292-97, 343, 444-45, 484, 497-98, 501-2, 548-55

Housing goals, 5, 7, 8, 11, 37, 44, 88, 97-102, 108-14, 119-24, 135-46, 165, 189-90, 236, 265-66, 316-20, 336-42, 355-58, 369-71, 389-91, 395, 406-22, 543-47, 556-57, 560

Housing and Home Finance Agency (HHFA), 523

Housing need, 5, 7

Housing stock, 57, 206, 211-27, 229-31, 239-50, 256-57, 261, 424, 484

HUD. See U.S. Department of Housing and Urban Development

Income maintenance (income supplements), 422, 555-59

Income tax, 243, 317, 320, 392-401, 518
capital gains, 396, 398, 437, 496, 533
depreciation, 206, 307-15, 396, 495, 533-34, 569
Tax Reform Act of 1969, 38, 305, 320, 568
tax shelter, 437, 496, 574

Inflation, 299, 310-11, 316-17, 319

Interest rates, 277, 299, 307-15, 316-20, 334, 335, 338, 425-26, 431-32, 438, 495, 533

Journey to work, 197, 204, 208-27, 255-56, 523

Labor unions, 321-28, 359-71, 376-91
see also, Construction, labor

Landlords, 19, 53, 56-59, 75-79, 233-34, 439, 444

Landlord-Tenant Law, 19, 70-71, 75-86
eviction, 56, 77-78, 81-82, 85-86, 453-55, 486-87 490, 539

Land prices, 67, 212-13, 427-28, 453, 480, 518-20, 530

Lifestyles, 136-40, 191-99, 408, 413, 416, 419, 549-52

Lobbying, 17, 21, 25, 30-47, 54

Local government, 18, 55-74, 90, 105, 280-89, 343, 345, 351-52, 356-57, 451, 480, 499-501, 504, 516, 517, 522

Low-income tenants, 25, 28, 66, 75-80, 82, 84-85, 236, 395, 409-10, 411-13, 418-19, 438, 440, 443, 446-47, 460-71, 486, 503, 514, 539, 546, 558-77
see also, Lower class

Location. See Residential Location Theory

Lower class, 27-28, 182, 184-87, 251-66, 526, 550-55
see also, Class

Maintenance, 20, 78, 232, 240, 243, 397, 399, 437, 444-45, 514-15

Management, 456-59

Middle class, 27-28, 92, 99, 139, 165, 251-61, 273, 296, 448, 450-55, 453, 526, 546
see also, Class

Migration, 87, 92, 95, 199, 263

Mobile homes, 288-89, 300, 344

Model cities, 72, 91, 112, 121, 127, 463-64

Monetary policy, 300, 301, 307-15, 316-20, 341

Mortgage credit, 31, 32, 38, 236, 277, 299, 300, 301, 307-15, 425-29

Mortgage, insurance or guarantees of (VA), 8, 25, 308, 309-15, 409-10, 428, 430-32, 452-53, 460-71, 472-83, 533

Multi-family housing, 111, 223-25, 287-88, 300, 301, 371, 406, 410

National Association of Homebuilders, 17, 30-48, 372, 428
National Association of Housing and Redevelopment Officials, 17
National Association of Real Estate Boards, 17, 32
National Tenants' Organization, 21, 49-54
Neighborhood, 5, 171, 174, 176, 193, 195-97, 267-73, 274-78, 413
see also, Social interaction
Neighbors, 151-52, 173, 175, 177-80
New towns (communities), 197, 523-35

Open housing/fair housing, 19, 95, 255, 266, 283
Open space (yards), 184, 279, 406, 408, 528

Physical determinism, 131, 144, 159-62, 171-80, 412
Planners, 141-43
Poverty, 27-29, 100, 207, 220, 262-65, 450, 452-53, 456-58, 503, 512, 547, 554-57
Prefabricated housing, 330, 333, 344, 347, 362
"Problem families," 119, 121, 452, 454-55, 458
Profits, 73, 126, 233, 237, 245-50, 431, 435-39, 446, 472, 504, 537
Property ownership, 55-73
Property tax (real estate tax), 393, 396, 439, 510-22
Public assistance, 8, 9, 11, 25, 28, 87, 90, 99, 100-101, 114-15, 121, 237-38, 400, 409, 436, 450, 484-92, 509, 529, 530, 536-42
Public housing, 9, 16-20, 26, 28, 51-54, 64, 83, 99, 108-18, 120-22, 125-26, 132, 151-52, 159-61, 178, 179, 184-85, 239, 287, 407, 410-15, 415-20, 432, 434-48, 448-59, 472-98, 543-46, 560, 563-65, 571-72
  leased housing, 16, 111, 122-23, 433, 560-63, 566, 568, 571-72
  turnkey housing, 16, 122, 433, 573
Public services, 3, 20, 52, 140, 195-97, 205, 225, 506, 516-18, 554
see also, Housing bundle

Racial discrimination. *See* Discrimination
Real estate brokers, 209, 259, 274-78
Rehabilitation, 122, 398, 399, 472-83, 484-92, 493-96
Relative deprivation, 1, 8, 132, 164-65
Relocation (displacement), 57, 101, 472, 482, 486-88, 505
Rent control, 69-73, 249-50, 434-47
Rent, income ratio, 5, 7, 53, 66, 126, 291, 292, 424-25, 436, 462-68, 514

Rent strikes (withholding, receivership), 19-20, 49-51, 69, 79
Residential Location Theory, 87, 89-91, 203-4, 211-27, 231, 250, 255-66, 284-88

Schools. *See* Education
Secondary mortgage market. *See* FNMA, GNMA
Security, 132, 150, 181-90, 549, 550
Single family houses, 30, 198, 288, 301, 308, 371, 406-9, 419, 460-71
see also, Homeownership
Sites (site selection), 18, 108-13, 122, 479, 545-55
Slums, 117, 186, 230, 234-36, 237-50, 453, 532, 548-55
see also, Ghetto
Social integration, 135-46, 147-57, 171-80, 420, 548-52
Social mobility, 100, 140, 193, 208, 291-97
Starts. *See* Construction, new
State government, 11, 357, 507, 516
Status (equal), 133, 150-57
Substandard housing, causes of, 3, 78, 117, 159-60, 232, 239-50, 343, 444-45, 548-55
Suburbs, 9, 90, 135-40, 142-46, 181, 194, 198, 203-4, 251-54, 262-64, 284-89, 351, 515, 524
Supply, 66-67, 203, 228-38, 239-50, 256-66, 269-71, 399, 406, 426, 435-37, 443, 447, 452, 514, 556-59, 561-62

Tenants (leases), 51, 76, 82-83, 85, 112
Tenant selection, 18, 108, 111-13, 120, 123, 436, 455, 487, 538-39, 549
Tenants' unions (councils), 19, 20, 21, 49-54, 69-72, 457, 489-92
see also, Community control
"Tipping" point, 120-21, 133-34, 274

Upper class, 15, 265, 273
see also, Class
U.S. Bureau of the Census, 2, 3, 4, 246, 344
U.S. Congress, 7, 17, 33, 39, 90, 114, 410-11, 414, 462
U.S. Department of Housing and Urban Development (HUD), 7, 37, 121, 460, 472-75
U.S. Saving and Loan League (USSLL), 17
Urban renewal, 16, 25-27, 63-64, 101, 112, 234-35, 243, 245, 421, 473, 548

Welfare. *See* Public assistance
Working class, 28, 68-69, 139, 165, 182-84
see also, Class

Zoning, 16, 98, 209, 242, 279-89, 406

DATE DUE